Michael S. Forstadt

goren's new bridge complete

BY Charles H. Goren

GOREN'S BRIDGE COMPLETE

GOREN'S NEW CONTRACT BRIDGE COMPLETE

CONTRACT BRIDGE COMPLETE

CONTRACT BRIDGE MADE EASY: A SELF-TEACHER

CONTRACT BRIDGE IN A NUTSHELL

THE STANDARD BOOK OF BIDDING

BETTER BRIDGE FOR BETTER PLAYERS

THE PRECISION SYSTEM OF CONTRACT BRIDGE BIDDING

GOREN'S PLAY AND DEFENSE

GOREN'S 100 CHALLENGING BRIDGE HANDS

PRECISION BRIDGE FOR EVERYONE

PLAY AS YOU LEARN BRIDGE

INTRODUCTION TO COMPETITIVE BIDDING

(with Ronald P. Von der Porten)

Chas H Goren

goren's new bridge complete

DOUBLEDAY
NEW YORK LONDON TORONTO SYDNEY AUCKLAND

The Goren Editorial Board

RICHARD L. FREY

Chairman

AUGUST BOEHM   TANNAH HIRSCH

ALBERT DORMER   AMALYA KEARSE

LEE HAZEN   OMAR SHARIF

ALAN TRUSCOTT

PUBLISHED BY DOUBLEDAY
A division of Bantam Doubleday Dell Publishing Group, Inc.
666 Fifth Avenue, New York, New York 10103

DOUBLEDAY and the portrayal of an anchor with a dolphin
are trademarks of Doubleday, a division of Bantam Doubleday
Dell Publishing Group, Inc.

Library of Congress Cataloging-in-Publication Data
Goren, Charles Henry, 1901–
  Goren's New bridge complete.
  Rev. ed. of: Goren's Bridge complete. 1980.
  Includes index.
  ISBN 0-385-23324-8
  1. Contract bridge. 2. Contract bridge—Bidding.
I. Goren, Charles Henry, 1901–. Bridge complete.
II. Title. III. Title: New bridge complete.
GV1282.3.G6532 1985   795.41'5   85-10344

Foreword

Almost fifty years ago, a young interloper named Goren introduced point count bidding in an assault on Ely Culbertson's bridge empire. Ely, uncharacteristically, misjudged the bridge-playing public's ability to change from honor tricks to points. (Uncharacteristically, because he was seldom slow to adopt the ideas of other experts and present them as part of the Culbertson System. His comment was, "People aren't going to take their shoes off to count higher than ten.")

As the beneficiary of this mistake, I vowed not to repeat it. Therefore, each new edition of Contract Bridge Complete has included new ideas that had been successfully introduced. But until now the Goren standard has been a method recommending opening bids on four-card majors, with only a brief word explaining the five-card-major methods.

Comes the revolution

As of the publication of this book, the preferred Goren method becomes a five-card-major system. Of course, you may continue to open four-card majors if you prefer; even the most devout five-card-majorite occasionally finds it desirable to do so; later, I will explain when and why.

Advocates of five-card-major methods have always claimed that they make the bidding easier, and in many respects they do. It's nice to know at once that, if you hold three cards in the major suit your partner has opened, you are sure that your side had at least an eight-card trump fit. This doesn't mean that your search for the best combined strain is ended. But it is comforting to know that you can safely give an immediate raise with only three trumps.

It is on the hands when you don't have three trumps, or when your partner doesn't have a five-carder, that you have to learn your way around. And this book will make it much easier for you to do so.

Of course other good ideas are included

As always, from shuffle, cut, deal and play, you'll find this book complete. For example, artificial forcing 1 Club openings are explained and recommended or not, as I see them. But don't expect such modern (should I say "futuristic"?) treatments as the initial pass to show a good hand, or the artificial opening bid to show a poor one. These and similar methods are designed primarily to confuse the opponents. The main object of my methods remains to communicate useful information between partners, so as to arrive at the best declaration for your side.

"Complete" in my title still means that here you will find the keys to situations you are likely to encounter frequently; the "Unusual No Trump," for example (of which I warn: the more unusual the better).

The "convenient Club"—a bid of 1 Club on a three-card suit, and the same requirement for 1 Diamond—has become not only convenient but absolutely necessary using five-card-major principles. These are *not* artificial bids—although they are frequently so called. They promise at least three cards in the suit, preferably headed by a queen or better honor.

However, many 1 Club openings are artificial. They promise nothing about the holding in clubs, but indicate a strong hand and are forcing. The best of these, in my opinion, are fully covered, for those who like to have a bid that shows a hand of a certain strength and assures a second chance: strong, but not strong enough to open with 2 Clubs, which I recommend you adopt as the strongest of all the opening bids. You'll find the reasons for this recommendation fully discussed in the appropriate chapter.

No trumps—weak or strong—come in for full treatment, as indeed they merit. They are so-called "limit" bids that immediately describe the nature of opener's hand and, with the aid of simple conventional responses, such as Stayman, they add the virtue of accuracy to the power of preempting all other bids at the 1-level. Even the Stayman Convention has variations: using a 2 Club response to 1 No Trump merely as an inquiry to locate a possible four-card major in opener's hand, or 2 Diamonds, making the same inquiry but showing enough strength to insist that the bidding continue to at least game. Called "Two-Way Stayman," this has advantages but also has the disadvantage of telling the opponents when they may compete with safety and when it will be dangerous to do so. My preference? It's the simple 2 club response, which may be strong or weak as the later bidding will indicate.

Transfer bids in response to opening No Trumps—2 Diamonds to force opener to bid 2 Hearts; 2 Hearts to force a 2 Spade rebid, etc.— claim, among other advantages, that the strong hand is led up to rather than through. Useful no doubt, but costly if, as often happens, one or the other of the partners forgets.

They are all here, along with many others, for those who wish to learn and perhaps to try.

But the method I prefer is what some wag named "KISS"—an acronym for "Keep it simple, stupid." Of course, that last word doesn't apply to us; it is aimed primarily at our partners. Nevertheless, the advice is something I heartily endorse. The simple game is the way to play bridge for fun and relaxation. And it is often the way to win.

Charles H. Goren

Contents

Contents

Contents

Contents

goren's new bridge complete

Goren's New Bridge Complete **1**

the bidding

1.   Opening bids in a suit

EVERY BUILDING needs a sound foundation. In terms of contract bridge, the building is the auction, and its cornerstone is the opening bid. Careful selection of the opening bid can ease the whole construction of the auction.

Before determining *what* to bid, it is critical to decide whether to bid at all! To solve this problem, we use the point count method of evaluation. The Milton Work point count has remained the standard for more than half a century. In descending order from the Ace, the court cards count:

4–3–2–1

The primary reason this author championed the point count method is its simplicity. Each suit contains 10 points, and counting by tens is natural to most of us. The bothersome fractions of other methods were eliminated. But simplicity alone is not why this method became dominant. It has stood the test of time, and experts all over the world have employed it, and continue to employ it, with great success.

The basics of the point count method have remained unchanged through the years. However, there have been some slight refinements to achieve greater accuracy.

THE POINT COUNT TABLE
(Table of High Cards)

Ace	4 points
King	3 points
Queen	2 points
Jack	1 point

The pack contains **40 points.**   An average hand contains **10 points.**

DISTRIBUTIONAL POINTS*

Void	3 points
Singleton	2 points
Doubleton	1 point

* A void means you hold no cards in a suit; a singleton is a holding of one card; a doubleton, two cards.

5

Unguarded Honors: Except for the Ace, an unguarded honor loses some of its value. Accordingly, holding a singleton King, Queen or Jack, count either its high-card value or its distributional worth, whichever is higher, but not both. Treat Q x or J x* in similar fashion.

Some additional refinements:

1. Deduct 1 point for an aceless hand, except for No Trump opening bids.
2. Add 1 point if you hold all four Aces.

For the purpose of opening the bidding, you determine the value of your hand by adding the high-card points (HCP) to the distributional points (DP).

When you expect to play the hand in No Trump, count only your HCP. Shortness is not an asset at No Trump, only at a suit contract.

Each player values and revalues his hand every time it is his turn to bid. The combined point count of the partnership usually determines how high you should bid. The following table is a guide to how many points you and your partner need to undertake various contracts:

3 NT.	26 points
4 H or 4 S	26 points
5 C or 5 D	28 points
Small Slam (12 tricks)	33 points
Grand Slam (13 tricks)	37 points

Bear in mind that these point totals are only guidelines, not Holy Writ. When your hands contain extreme distributional features, or where there is a fit in more than one suit, you can make game, or slam, with far fewer points in the combined holding than indicated in the table.

Quick Tricks: These are honor-card combinations, also known as defensive tricks, that rate to win tricks if the opponents play the hand. To qualify as Quick Tricks, these honor cards must be likely to win a trick on the first or second round that the suit is led. A table of Quick Tricks follows:

2 QUICK TRICKS	1½ QUICK TRICKS	1 QUICK TRICK	½ QUICK TRICK
A K	A Q	A	K x
		K Q	

* The symbol "x" denotes a card lower than a 10.

Quick Tricks are the determining factor when your hand evaluates to exactly 13 points. You *must* open the bidding if your hand is worth 14 points. If it counts to only 13, open the bidding if you have 2 quick tricks. If you have fewer than 2 quick tricks, you should not open the bidding unless you have a good major suit.

Choosing the suit to open

Bidding methods have taken enormous strides in the past two decades. Some of the new ideas have fallen by the wayside; others have stood the test of time. All the ideas that we are now incorporating in our methods, and which are to be found in this and succeeding chapters, have one thing in common: They work!

Now that you have learned when to open, let's explore what to bid. For the purposes of this chapter, we'll confine ourselves to opening bids in a suit at the 1- or 2-level.

What constitutes a biddable suit has undergone significant change as bridge has developed. This applies most particularly to the major suits. Where it was once commonplace to open a four-card major suit of reasonable quality, the great majority of players and teachers have swung to the belief that a major suit must contain at least five cards before it is deemed biddable.

Whether this is wise is moot. The method has become so prevalent these days that most bridge instructors teach their students to play five-card majors. To enable our readers to adapt to the current trend and thereby broaden their choice of partners, a not inconsiderable practical benefit, we will integrate five-card majors into the Goren system.

It is not a question of whether five-card-major methods are superior to four-card majors. It is a fact of life that many aspiring players *believe* that it is easier to bid using a five-card-major style. That psychological argument is persuasive enough to make five-card majors worth adopting.

Major-suit opening bids

To open in first or second position with a bid of 1 Heart or 1 Spade, you guarantee at least five cards in the bid suit. Any five-card suit is considered biddable. If you hold two five-card suits, bid the Spades first, regardless of the respective strengths of the two suits.

♠ 10 x x x x   ♡ A Q J 10 x   ◊ x   ♣ A x

Bid 1 Spade. If you open 1 Heart, you will never convince partner that your Spades are as long as your Hearts.

♠ x x   ♡ K Q x x   ◇ A J x x   ♣ A x x

Bid 1 Diamond. Since you have only four Hearts, that suit is not biddable. Note that you don't need to remember principles about touching suits. Ignore the Heart suit for the moment. This is just one example of why many find it easier to play five-card majors.

♠ K J x x x   ♡ K Q x   ◇ x x   ♣ K x x

Pass. Your hand does not contain 2 Quick Tricks and, since it is aceless, it is worth only 12 points.

♠ A K x x   ♡ K Q x x   ◇ Q x x x   ♣ x

Bid 1 Diamond. Again, playing five-card majors simplifies your choice of opening bid. If the hand belongs in a major suit, the subsequent auction will reveal it.

Five-card majors feature one other advantage worth noting—that of comfort. You feel much better about raising partner's suit with three low cards if you *know* that he has at least five cards in the suit. This is most important in competitive bidding, especially these days when opponents are apt to get the auction to a high level quickly. For instance, suppose that your partner opens the bidding with 1 Spade and the next hand interferes with 3 Diamonds. You hold:

♠ J x x   ♡ Q x x   ◇ x x   ♣ A Q 10 x x

You would like to compete with 3 Spades, but that would be risky if partner could hold only four Spades. Playing five-card majors, however, you can rely upon a secure eight-card fit, so you are able to bid 3 Spades with confidence.

Minor-suit opening bids

Hands that do not contain a five-card or longer major suit and that do not meet the requirements of a 1 No Trump opening bid (see Chapter 3) must be opened with 1 of a minor suit. If you have two four-card minors, open 1 Diamond. If you have no four-card minor and only one three-card minor, bid it. With two three-card minor suits, open 1 Club unless your Diamond holding is 4 points stronger than the Clubs.

♠ A x   ♡ Q J x x   ◇ x x x x   ♣ A K x

Bid 1 Diamond. It is your longer minor suit.

♠ x   ♡ A Q x x   ◇ Q x x x   ♣ A J x x

Bid 1 Diamond. With two four-card minors, bid the Diamonds regardless of the respective strength of the two suits. That prepares a 2 Club rebid to a 1 Spade response.

♠ K J x x   ♡ A J x   ◇ K Q x   ♣ x x x

Bid 1 Diamond. With the Diamond suit so much stronger than the Clubs, depart from the principle of opening 1 Club with two three-card minors.

♠ K Q x x   ♡ J x x x   ◇ A K   ♣ x x x

Bid 1 Club. With only one three-card minor, bid it. You never open a two-card suit, no matter how strong.

Simple, isn't it?

Exceptions

Occasionally, you will run across a hand where it is prudent to modify the rule barring an opening bid on a four-card major.

♠ A K J x   ♡ K Q J x   ◇ x x x   ♣ x x

Bid 1 Spade. Even at gunpoint we wouldn't consider a 1 Diamond opening bid. With all your strength concentrated in the major suits, treat the Spades as a five-card suit.

♠ K J x x x   ♡ x   ◇ K x   ♣ A Q x x x

Bid 1 Club. Only when the suits are Spades and Clubs do you open the lower-ranking of two five-card suits. That eases rebid problems. You do so on all minimum or powerful hands. On good hands you can open 1 Spade and then show your Clubs. (See Reversing, below.)

Third- and fourth-seat opening bids

In third or fourth seat, you may relax the five-card requirement to open 1 Heart or 1 Spade. Since partner has already passed, you will often know that game is out of reach. Therefore, it may be desirable to open a good four-card major, not only for its preemptive value but to indicate a lead to partner should the opponents buy the contract. In the third seat you might open an 11- or 12-point hand. Naturally, in fourth seat you would throw in such a hand.

♠ K Q 10 x ♡ K x ◇ x x x x ♣ A x x

Bid 1 Spade in third position. You plan to pass any response partner makes, and you would like a Spade lead should the opponents end up declaring the hand.

♠ J x x ♡ A Q J x ◇ x x x ♣ A x x

Bid 1 Heart in third seat, for the same reasons as above.

♠ J x x x ♡ A x x ◇ A x x ♣ K x x

Pass. There is no good reason why you should want to open this featureless 12-point hand.

♠ K Q x x ♡ A J x x ◇ x x ♣ A x x

Bid 1 Club. You have a full opening bid, so there is no need to depart from your agreed-upon methods.

Reversing

To many players, a "reverse bid" is a mysterious concept. Perhaps the term itself causes much of this confusion, for the principle itself is simple enough. *Whenever you choose for your rebid a new suit at a level higher than two of your original suit, you show a very good hand.* That's all there is to it!

♠ A K x x ♡ A J x x x ◇ x x ♣ x x

You open the bidding with 1 Heart and partner responds 2 Clubs. You must not bid 2 Spades. That is bidding past two of your original suit and shows extra values which you do not possess. Content yourself with a rebid of 2 Hearts.

♠ A Q 10 x ·   ♡ A K J x x   ◇ K x   ♣ x x

This is a much stronger hand. If the bidding starts the same way, you should rebid 2 Spades. Although this forces partner to give you preference to the 3-level if he prefers your first suit, your hand is good enough for that contract to be playable. This so-called "reverse bid" shows the equivalent of at least 17 points.

♠ x x   ♡ x x   ◇ A K Q x   ♣ A 10 x x x

You would like to bid both minor suits, but to open 1 Club leaves you unprepared. Should partner respond with 1 of a major suit, you are not strong enough to reverse with 2 Diamonds. The best strategy is to open 1 Diamond and rebid 2 Clubs. This gets both your suits into the picture without distorting your strength.

♠ x x x   ♡ A K x x   ◇ A J x x   ♣ Q x

You open the bidding with 1 Diamond and partner responds 2 Clubs. This is the only sequence where bidding past two of your own suit *does not* promise extra strength. You don't have a Spade stopper, so you can't rebid 2 No Trump, and you should never rebid a four-card suit. Instead, bid a comfortable 2 Hearts.

To summarize: If you have a minimum opening bid, you might on occasion have to bid irregularly to avoid showing extra strength. But with a strong hand you need have no fear of scaling the heights, and such hand should be bid naturally, i.e., bid long suits ahead of shorter suits.

The forcing 2 Club opening bid

It is becoming increasingly obvious that an ever-growing number of players are adopting weak 2 bids. Indeed, in tournament play weak 2 bids are the norm. Does this mean that you have to give up the forcing 2 bid? Not at all—the good news is that you can have your cake and eat it! By using an opening bid of 2 Clubs to show the traditional strong 2 bid, we reserve 2 Diamonds, 2 Hearts and 2 Spades for a specific type of weak bid in the suit named. In other words, we can play both the strong 2 bid and the weak 2 bid at the same time. What could be more efficient?

The opening 2 Club bid is employed when you want to make a strong 2 bid of any type. It is *artificial;* that is, it says nothing about the Club suit. It is *forcing* on responder, who must give the opening 2 Club bidder another chance to speak. At his second turn the opening bidder will describe what sort of forcing 2 bid he holds. For example:

♠ A K Q x x x   ♡ A x   ◇ A K J x   ♣ x

Open 2 Clubs and bid Spades next. That is the equivalent of a forcing 2 bid in Spades had you been playing strong 2 bids. Don't worry about the singleton Club—the bid has nothing to do with the Club suit.

♠ A   ♡ A Q J x x x   ◇ A K 10 x x   ♣ A

Open 2 Clubs. Your plan is to show Hearts and then Diamonds to describe a powerful two-suiter.

♠ A Q x   ♡ K Q x x   ◇ A J x   ♣ A Q J

Open 2 Clubs and rebid 2 No Trump. That is the equivalent of a traditional 2 No Trump opening bid of 23–24 HCP.

♠ A K x   ♡ x   ◇ K Q x   ♣ A K Q x x x

Open 2 Clubs. Since that bid doesn't necessarily have anything to do with Clubs, you will have to rebid 3 Clubs at your next turn to tell partner that your suit is Clubs.

As you can see, the forcing 2 Club bid conforms to the normal requirements for a strong 2 bid. These are:

> With a good five-card suit—25 points
> With a good six-card suit—23 points
> With a good seven-card suit—21 points

Holding a second five-card suit, you can shade these requirements by 1 point. Note that you count high-card and distributional values.

When you value your hand for the purpose of making a forcing 2 Club opening bid, assume that partner's hand is worthless. Therefore, discount insufficiently guarded honors—ignore holdings like a single-ton King, Q x or J x.

Let's look at some of our earlier examples and see how they conform:

♠ A K Q x x x   ♡ A x   ◇ A K J x   ♣ x

This hand is worth 24 points—21 HCP and 3 DP (2 for the singleton and 1 for the doubleton, even though it includes the Ace).

♠ A   ♡ A Q J x x x   ◇ A K 10 x x   ♣ A

This hand evaluates to 26 points—22 HCP and 4 DP.

Both these hands easily fall within our requirements of a forcing 2 Club opening bid. But consider this example:

♠ A K x x   ♡ A K x x   ◇ x   ♣ A K x x

This is a 23-point hand—21 HCP and 2 DP. Therefore, it is quite a bit short of a forcing 2 Club opening. The correct opening bid is 1 Club. The hand contains too many losers to force to game unconditionally. Unless partner has the values for a response to a 1 Club opening, it is doubtful whether you can make game.

Responses to the forcing 2 Club opening bid

The 2 Club opening bid demands a response. Even with nothing in your hand, you must give opener another chance to bid. The negative response with 0–7 points is 2 Diamonds. This is an artificial response, and has nothing to do with the Diamond suit—it simply denies the values for a positive response.

Any response other than 2 Diamonds is *positive* and natural. A response in a suit shows a minimum of 8 points and at least a five-card suit headed by the Q J or better. After a positive response to a 2 Club opening, the partnership cannot stop short of game.

There are two cases where, after a forcing 2 Club opening bid, the auction can stop short of game. One is if, after a negative response, the opening bidder simply rebids his own suit. Responder is then permitted to pass if he has no trick to contribute to his side's cause. The other is where, after a negative response, opener rebids 2 No Trump. Responder may pass if he has fewer than 3 points.

Let's take some examples of responding to a 2 Club opening bid:

♠ x x x x   ♡ J x x x   ◇ x   ♣ 10 x x x

Respond 2 Diamonds. All this says is that you have 0–7 points; it says nothing about Diamond length or shortness. Don't panic and pass. Partner's bid forces you to keep the bidding open.

♠ x x x   ♡ K J x x x x   ◇ x x   ♣ x x

Respond 2 Diamonds. With only 6 points you are not strong enough for a positive response. First show your point count, then plan to bid your Hearts. That shows a biddable suit within a weak hand.

♠ K J x x x   ♡ K J x   ◇ x x x   ♣ x x

Respond 2 Spades. Your 9 points qualify for a positive response, and the quality of your five-card suit is sufficient. Now the partnership cannot drop the bidding before game has been reached.

♠ x x x   ♡ x x   ◇ A Q x x x   ♣ K x x

Respond 3 Diamonds. Since 2 Diamonds would be an artificial bid showing weakness, you must jump to make a positive response in Diamonds. This is the only positive response that requires you to jump the bidding one level.

♠ Q J x x   ♡ K x   ◇ J 10 9 x   ♣ Q 10 x

Respond 2 No Trump. When you were playing strong 2 bids, this was the negative response. Here, however, it is a natural, positive response showing 8 or more points and a balanced* hand.

There are a few cases where responder must improvise a response to handle an unusual problem. Suppose that partner opens 2 Clubs and you hold:

♠ A J x x   ♡ K Q x x   ◇ x   ♣ J x x x

With 13 points, you have more than enough for a positive response, but your hand is unbalanced and you do not have a biddable suit. Our recommendation is to bid 2 Diamonds as a waiting move. You intend to drive to at least a small slam, but at this stage of the auction you have no idea where to head. After opener begins to describe his hand with his next bid, you will be able to compensate for your initial underbid.

♠ x x x x x   ♡ A x x   ◇ K J x x   ♣ x

Here you have a similar problem. Your 10 points are ample for a positive response, but your five-card suit is too weak to bid. The wisest course is to respond 2 Diamonds and await developments.

To see our methods in action, let's follow the bidding of some sample hands.

* No void, singleton or six-card or longer suit

OPENER	RESPONDER
♠ A Q J	♠ K 10 x x x
♡ A K Q J x x	♡ 10 x x
◇ x	◇ A x
♣ A x x	♣ x x x

The bidding:

OPENER	RESPONDER
2 Clubs (1)	2 Spades (2)
3 Hearts (3)	4 Hearts (4)
4 No Trump (5)	5 Diamonds (6)
7 No Trump (7)	Pass

1. I have 23 points and a six-card suit, enough for a forcing 2 Club opening bid.

2. I have at least 8 points and a biddable Spade suit for my positive response.

3. I have at least a five-card Heart suit.

4. I have support for your suit (at least three cards).

5. How many Aces do you have? (See Chapter 7)

6. One Ace.

7. Since you must have the King of Spades for your suit to be biddable, I can count 13 tricks.

OPENER	RESPONDER
♠ A K Q x x x	♠ J x x
♡ K x	♡ A x x x
◇ A K Q 10	◇ J x x
♣ x	♣ x x x

The bidding:

OPENER	RESPONDER
2 Clubs (1)	2 Diamonds (2)
2 Spades (3)	3 Spades (4)
4 Diamonds (5)	4 Hearts (6)
6 Spades (7)	Pass

1. I have 24 points and a six-card suit, sufficient to start the ball rolling with a forcing 2 Club opening bid.

2. I have 6 points; not enough for a positive response.
3. My suit is Spades.
4. I have support for you.
5. I have Diamond control.
6. Well, I have the Ace of Hearts.
7. A small slam seems safe.

OPENER	RESPONDER
♠ A K J x x x	♠ Q x x
♡ A x x	♡ x x x
◊ A K J	◊ 10 x x
♣ x	♣ x x x x

The bidding:

OPENER	RESPONDER
2 Clubs	2 Diamonds
2 Spades	2 No Trump
3 Spades (2)	4 Spades (3)
Pass	

1. I have nothing of any value.
2. I can only reckon on nine tricks—not quite enough to bid game.
3. My Queen of your suit is worth a trick, so I'll raise to game. (Had responder held a low Spade instead of the Queen, he would have passed.)

The double raise

In most bidding sequences we encounter in this book, the double raise of partner's suit is strong. One of the few exceptions occurs in an auction such as:

OPENER	RESPONDER
2 Clubs	2 Diamonds
2 Hearts	4 Hearts

When responder starts with a negative 2 Diamonds and then jump raises opener's major suit, it does not promise a strong hand. It shows good trump support, no worse than Q x x x or five low cards, but denies an Ace, King or singleton in a side suit. It warns partner not to look for slam unless all he needs is excellent trump support. For example, in the auction shown responder might hold:

♠ x x   ♡ J x x x x   ◇ x x x   ♣ Q x x

The weak 2 bid

Now that we use the forcing 2 Club opening bid, we no longer need opening bids of 2 Diamonds, 2 Hearts and 2 Spades to describe very powerful hands. We put them to good use by converting them into bids which simultaneously rob the opponents of bidding room while giving an accurate description of our holding to partner. Should the opponents end up buying the hand, we have also provided partner with a good lead.

The requirements for a weak 2 bid are:

a) 6–12 points and a six-card suit headed by at least two of the three top honors vulnerable, or any two honors when not vulnerable.
b) No four-card suit outside the long suit.
c) 1½–2 defensive tricks
d) No void.

Although useful and easy to learn, this bid can be dangerous if misused. Let's study a few examples.

♠ A Q 10 x x x   ♡ K x   ◇ x x x   ♣ x x

Open 2 Spades. A classic weak 2 bid at any vulnerability.

♠ x x   ♡ Q J 9 x x x   ◇ x x   ♣ A J x

Open 2 Hearts if you are not vulnerable. Vulnerable, your suit quality is not good enough—you need either A K, A Q or K Q in the bid suit.

♠ 10 x x   ♡ x x   ◇ A K Q x x x   ♣ x x

Open 2 Diamonds at any vulnerability.

♠ A x   ♡ x x   ◇ x x x   ♣ K Q 10 x x x

Pass. Any opening bid of 2 Clubs is artificial and strong, and the hand is not good enough for a 1 Club opening bid.

♠ Q x x x   ♡ K Q 10 x x x   ◇ x x   ♣ x

Pass. A weak 2 bid should not contain a side four-card suit, especially a major. A bid of 2 Hearts suggests that the hand can be played only with Hearts as trumps; in this case, Spades could easily present a viable alternative—depending on partner's holding, you could go down at 2 Hearts when you could make game in Spades.

♠ A K x   ♡ K Q x   ◇ K x x x x   ♣ Q x

Open 1 Diamond. This hand is worth 13 points and contains 3 quick tricks. It is much too strong for a weak 2 bid.

Responding to weak 2 bids

Since opener holds fewer than 13 points, responder can always pass if he, too, holds a hand weaker than an opening bid. However, that might not be the correct action tactically. If you have trump support for partner's suit, it is often correct to raise the level of the auction, especially if your hand is poor defensively. Opener is barred from bidding after a raise—the idea is simply to add to the barrage.

If responder has a hand of opening-bid strength or better, he can either bid a new suit or bid 2 No Trump. Both these actions are forcing for one round. They are aimed at getting opener to define his weak 2 bid.

If responder bids a new suit, opener should raise with three-card support or a doubleton honor. If the response was 2 No Trump, there are two popular methods of replying to the force.

The most popular of the two is for opener to show a feature. A feature is defined as a stopper for No Trump purposes, i.e., Q J x or better. Should opener have no feature and a minimum weak 2 bid, he rebids his own suit.

To demonstrate these principles, assume partner has opened 2 Hearts. Your side is not vulnerable and you hold:

♠ A x x x   ♡ J   ◇ K Q x x   ♣ J 10 x x

Pass. With neither support for hearts nor an opening bid, wait to see what develops.

♠ 10 x x   ♡ 10 x x   ◇ A K x x x   ♣ Q x

Bid 3 Hearts. The combined strength of the opponents is at least equal to that of your side, so you want to raise the level to make it more difficult for them to enter the auction. Partner is not permitted to act over your raise.

♠ K Q 10 x x x   ♡ A x   ◇ A Q x x   ♣ x

Bid 2 Spades. A change of suit is *forcing for one round*. If opener has three-card support for your suit, or A x, he should raise Spades and you will bid game in your suit. If he doesn't have support he should rebid his suit and you can raise to game. This permits you to find your best (longest) trump suit.

♠ A K x   ♡ K Q x   ◇ K x x x   ♣ Q x

Bid 2 No Trump. Game is possible if partner has a suitable hand. If he shows a feature in a side suit, you can bid game in No Trump if his feature is in Clubs, or in Hearts if his feature is in Spades or Diamonds. Should partner deny a feature by bidding 3 Hearts, the prudent course is to pass.

Showing features and the Ogust Convention

Since an opening weak 2 bid can have a fairly wide range, 6–12 points, we need some means for opener to define his strength within those limits. We mentioned earlier that there were two methods in common use—showing a feature or the Ogust Convention. Since feature-showing is more widely adopted, we will deal with that first.

On the following hands, assume in each case that you have opened with a weak 2 bid in your long suit and partner has made a forcing response of 2 No Trump, asking for a feature.

♠ A Q 10 9 x x   ♡ K x   ◇ x x x   ♣ x x

Rebid 3 Hearts. This confirms a sound weak 2 bid and a protected honor in hearts. Partner will now be in an informed position to decide on the final contract,

♠ x x   ♡ Q J 9 x x x   ◇ x x   ♣ A x x

Rebid 3 Hearts. Although you possess a feature in Clubs, the quality of your trump suit relegates your hand to a minimum weak 2 bid. Limiting the strength of your hand is more important than describing your feature.

♠ x x x   ♡ x x   ◇ A K Q x x x   ♣ x x

Rebid 3 No Trump. This specialized rebid shows that your trump suit is headed by the three top honors. It might enable partner to count nine fast tricks for No Trump purposes, especially since his hand will be protected by having the lead come up to it.

The Ogust Convention was developed by our longtime friend and business associate, Harold A. Ogust. If you employ this method, you respond to the 2 No Trump force as follows:

> 3 Clubs—weak hand, weak suit
> 3 Diamonds—weak hand, good suit
> 3 Hearts—good hand, weak suit
> 3 Spades—good hand, good suit
> 3 No Trump—solid suit

Notice that you respond in steps—the better your hand, the more you bid. A "solid" suit is headed by at least the three top honors. Let's consider our previous examples if we were to use the Ogust Convention instead of showing features:

♠ A Q 10 9 x x   ♡ K x   ◇ x x x   ♣ x x

Rebid 3 Spades—good hand, good suit.

♠ x x   ♡ Q J 9 x x x x   ◇ x x   ♣ A x x

Rebid 3 Clubs—weak hand, weak suit.

♠ x x x   ♡ x x   ◇ A K Q x x x   ♣ x x

Rebid 3 No Trump to show your solid suit. Note that this is the same bid you would make if you were showing features.

We have no strong feelings about which method of rebids you adopt. As we stated previously, showing features is the more prevalent way to describe your hand. What is important is that you and your partner *agree in advance* which method to employ. Prior partnership agreement applies to all understandings in bridge.

OPENING BID QUIZ

You are the dealer. What do you bid with each of the following hands?

1. ♠ A J 10 x
   ♡ K J 10 x
   ◇ A x x
   ♣ x x

2. ♠ K x x x
   ♡ x x x
   ◇ A K 10
   ♣ K Q x

3. ♠ K x x x x
   ♡ A K 10 9 x
   ◇ x
   ♣ A x

4. ♠ K J x x
   ♡ A 10 9 x
   ◇ A x
   ♣ J x x

5. ♠ x
   ♡ K J 9 x
   ◇ Q J 9 x
   ♣ A K 10 x

6. ♠ x
   ♡ K J x x x x
   ◇ x x
   ♣ K J x x

7. ♠ x
   ♡ A K J 10 x
   ◇ A K Q J x
   ♣ A x

8. ♠ A K J
   ♡ A Q x
   ◇ A Q J x
   ♣ K 10 x

9. ♠ A J x
   ♡ x x
   ◇ K Q J 10 x x
   ♣ x x

10. ♠ A K 10 9 x
    ♡ A x
    ◇ x
    ♣ A K J 10 x

11. ♠ J x x x
    ♡ J x x x x
    ◇ A x
    ♣ K Q

12. ♠ A x x x
    ♡ K x x x x
    ◇ K x
    ♣ K x

13. ♠ A Q x x
    ♡ K Q J x
    ◇ Q x x x
    ♣ x

14. ♠ A x
    ♡ J x x x x
    ◇ x x
    ♣ A K J x

15. ♠ Q x x x
    ♡ A K Q x
    ◇ x x
    ♣ A K J

Your partner opens the bidding with 2 Clubs. What do you respond with each of the following hands?

16. ♠ Q J 10 9 x x
    ♡ x x
    ◇ x x x
    ♣ x x

17. ♠ Q x x
    ♡ Q x x
    ◇ K 10 9
    ♣ Q 10 x x

18. ♠ A K 10 x x x
    ♡ J x
    ◇ 10 x x
    ♣ K x

Your partner opens the bidding with 2 Diamonds. What do you respond with each of the following hands?

19. ♠ K x x x
    ♡ Q J 10 x x x
    ◇ x
    ♣ Q x

20. ♠ A x x
    ♡ A x
    ◇ K J x
    ♣ A x x x x

21. ♠ J x
    ♡ x
    ◇ K x x x x
    ♣ A K x x x

ANSWERS TO OPENING BID QUIZ

1. One Diamond.

Playing five-card majors, neither the Spades nor the Hearts are considered biddable. With just one three-card minor suit, you must bid it.

2. One Club.

When you hold two three-card minors, bid the Clubs unless there is a disparity equivalent to an Ace between the suits. That is not the case here.

3. One Spade.

With two biddable major suits of equal length, start with the higher-ranking regardless of the quality of the suits. When you bid Hearts next, you give partner the option of choosing between the two suits without increasing the level of the auction.

4. One Club.

Although the Clubs are not much of a suit, you have no choice. Under no circumstance can you open a two-card minor, and the quality of your major suits is not such that you want to depart from your system and open a four-card major—if the hand should be played in a major suit, you have all the bidding room you need to find that out. The virtue of the 1 Club bid is that it keeps the bidding as low as possible.

5. One Diamond.

When your choice of opening bid lies between two four-card minor suits, bid the Diamonds. That prepares a comfortable rebid of 2 Clubs should partner respond 1 Spade or 1 No Trump. Partner can then choose between your two suits without raising the level of the auction.

6. Pass.

This hand is worth 11 points, 8 in high cards and 3 in distribution. Therefore, it does not qualify as an opening bid. You could consider a weak 2 bid in Hearts were it not for the fact that the hand is flawed because of a side four-card suit. To avoid distorting the value of your hand, pass.

7. Two Clubs.

This hand counts to 25 points and so constitutes a forcing opening bid. The only game force in your methods is 2 Clubs—partner must respond. Your plan is to bid the Hearts first and then the Diamonds, following our policy of bidding the higher-ranking suit first with suits of equal length.

8. Two Clubs.

When you have 23–24 points, a balanced hand and a guard in every suit, open 2 Clubs and plan to rebid No Trump as cheaply as possible.

9. One Diamond.

You hold 13 points and two defensive tricks, so you should open. In addition, you have an easy rebid with 2 Diamonds. Don't open 2 Diamonds—your hand is too strong. Always choose to open with a one-bid rather than a weak 2 bid if your hand qualifies.

10. One Club.

You have a very powerful hand, but it doesn't quite measure up to a forcing 2 Club bid. When your touching suits are Clubs and Spades, bid the clubs first if your hand is very strong.

11. Pass.

Although you have 13 points and two defensive tricks, you should not open this hand. Your long suits are weak and your points are concentrated in your short suits. Experience shows that high cards do not work very effectively when they are in short suits, so your point count flatters the value of your hand.

12. One Heart.

Bid your five-card major suit. Any other opening bid is a distortion.

13. One Diamond.

This leaves you prepared for any response partner may make. If he bids a major suit, you can raise in comfort.

14. One Heart.

It is almost always preferable to bid your longer suit before the shorter. It gives you the best chance to find your longest combined suit, which should prove to be the best trump suit.

15. One Club.

Even though you have an excellent four-card Heart suit, don't depart from your five-card-major principle. The opening bid of 1 Club keeps the bidding low and gives you time to uncover a possible major-suit fit.

16. Two Diamonds.

With fewer than 8 points, you cannot make a positive response. Your first duty is to show your weakness. Thereafter, you can bid Spades. That will tell partner that you have a biddable Spade suit and no more than 7 points.

17. Two No Trump.

This is a natural, positive response. You have created a forcing-to-game situation and now await partner's description of his hand.

18. Two Spades.

Your 13 points should produce at least a small slam opposite the powerful hand that partner has announced. However, there is no need for you to jump the bidding—that robs you of bidding room that you might need. Since your positive response means that the bidding cannot be dropped short of game, the partnership can proceed slowly to explore the hand's possibilities.

19. Pass.

Although 2 Diamonds might not be the contract of your dreams, any attempt to find a better spot to play the hand could lead you into deeper trouble. Any bid by you would be forcing and drive the auction to higher levels. Besides, partner's Diamond suit is likely to be as good as, or better than, your Hearts.

20. Three No Trump.

From your hand you can tell that the missing Diamond honors must be held by your partner. That means that your side should be able to win at least nine fast tricks—six in Diamonds and your three Aces. Bid what you know you can make.

21. Five Diamonds.

This might strike you as a rather risky venture, but it is the wisest tactical action. You have a chance to make your contract but, even more important, you have no burning desire to defend if the opponents were to buy the contract at either 4 Hearts or 4 Spades. When you know that your side has great offensive potential and questionable defense, make the bid that puts the most pressure on your opponents. Here, they will have to guess what to do at the 5-level.

2. Responses to suit opening bids

EXPERIENCE has led us to believe that responder's task in the auction could be simplified considerably were he only to ask himself two questions constantly: (1) *Where* are we going to play this contract? (2) What *level* should we reach?

In searching for the answers to these two questions, responder enlists opener's assistance. In reality, both members of the partnership should keep these two questions before them, but it is responder who first gives the auction its direction. If he supports opener's suit, he continues down the established trail; if he introduces a new suit, he opens a different path for investigation.

The answers to "where" and "level" are determined by counting; in the first case you count *fit* and in the latter *points*. When we confirm a "fit" we mean that we have uncovered a trump suit with at least eight cards in the combined partnership holding. In other words, if opener announces a five-card suit and responder has three, responder knows that his side has located a fit—opener won't know that until responder supports him. If the opener starts with a weak 2 bid and responder has a doubleton in the suit, he knows he can rely on a fit, since opener has promised a six-card suit with his bid.

Once you have found a fit, you probably know where you want to play the contract because an *eight-card fit makes an adequate trump suit*. The absence of a fit is almost as important as locating one. In some instances it suggests a final contract in No Trump; in others it warns of a possible misfit, in which case you must proceed with care. On the other hand, a fit increases the value of a hand and allows you to bid aggressively.

To what level should you bid? You can usually determine that by counting the combined partnership assets. You need 26 points to undertake game in a major suit or No Trump; for a minor-suit game the total is 28. This consideration can help the partnership decide between a minor-suit fit and No Trump. If it appears that the hands contain enough strength to venture a game contract, it might be easier to make nine tricks at No Trump than eleven in the minor suit. However, if it seems that game is beyond your resources, the haven of a trump fit could provide added safety over No Trump.

These general considerations will, in the final analysis, make your bidding simpler and more effective. But bear in mind that point count should always be your servant, not your master. Never let it substitute for common sense.

Responses to a major-suit opening

When opener starts the auction with 1 Heart or 1 Spade, responder can rely on him to have at least five cards in his suit. On many hands this will resolve the question of fit there and then—if responder has as many as three cards in opener's suit, a fit has been found! This is the one key reason why five-card-major methods have become so popular. After only a single bid, half the partnership's problems have been cleared up.

The single raise

As soon as you strike a fit for partner's major, you should convey to him the glad tidings. As this chapter progresses, you will discover that there are a number of ways to advise partner of this, depending on the strength of responder's hand and the quality of the fit. The single raise of opener's major (1 Heart—2 Hearts) guarantees at least three-card support and 8–9 points.

We mentioned earlier that finding a fit increases the value of your hand. When either player has four-card support for a suit in which he knows his partner has at least four cards, he revalues his distributional points (DP) as follows:

> Void . . . . 5 DP
> Singleton . . . . 3 DP
> Doubleton . . . . 1 DP

In addition, if responder's high cards in opener's suit evaluate to less than 4, add 1 point.

If responder has four-card support for opener's major suit, he upgrades his hand's value according to this table. If he has only three-card support, his valuation remains unchanged.

Should opener start the auction with a bid of 1 Heart, the following hands would all qualify for a single raise:

A. ♠ A x   ♡ Q x x x   ◇ x x   ♣ 10 x x x x
B. ♠ K x x   ♡ 10 9 x   ◇ K J x x x   ♣ x x
C. ♠ Q x x x x   ♡ Q x x   ◇ x x   ♣ A x x

Note that, in example C, we recommend you raise partner's suit despite the fact that you have a five-card spade suit. By so doing you help partner answer the question where to play, while accurately describing your hand in one bid.

The invitational jump raise

Formerly, hands containing four-card or better support for opener's major and 10–12 points presented an awkward problem for responder. In effect, they are worth a raise to 2½ of his suit; unfortunately, the lawmakers of bridge forgot to make such an option legal. As a result, responder had to improvise by first bidding a new suit at the 2-level, then raising partner.

Now a jump raise of opener's suit (1 Heart—3 Hearts) does the work that two bids used to do. In the trade, it is known as a *limit raise*. It sets the trump suit and *invites* opener to bid game with a better-than-minimum opening bid. After an opening bid of 1 Heart, the following hands are typical examples of a limit raise:

A.	♠ Q J x	♡ A x x x	◇ x x	♣ A x x x
B.	♠ K x	♡ 10 x x x	◇ Q J x x	♣ A x x
C.	♠ x	♡ K Q x x	◇ K x x x	♣ J 10 x x

The one essential ingredient of all limit raises is four-card trump support. That is because opener, in assessing game possibilities, will consider ruffs in responder's hand. If responder made his limit raise with only three trumps and the defenders lead trumps at every opportunity, those ruffs might not materialize.

The forcing raise

Now that we have eliminated the jump raise as a way to show the equivalent of an opening bid with good support for opener's major, we need a means to show that type of hand. The bid that can best be spared for this purpose is a jump to 3 No Trump.

Formerly, that showed a hand of 16–18 points with specifically a 4-3-3-3 hand pattern. Because of these severe restrictions, it seldom came up; and when responder does get such a hand, there are other ways to bid it.

Our new definition of a jump to 3 No Trump after an opening bid of one of a major (1 Heart—3 No Trump) is a hand of 13–16 points with four-card or better trump support. This bid is forcing to at least four of opener's major—he may not pass.

With a minimum opening bid, opener simply corrects to four of his suit. With a better hand, he can make a move toward slam. In any case, the question of where to play the hand has been resolved; it is simply a matter of deciding at what level.

Assuming partner opened the bidding with 1 Spade, these are examples of a forcing jump raise of 3 No Trump:

D.	♠ Q x x x	♡ A x	◇ K J x x	♣ K x x
E.	♠ 10 x x x	♡ A K x	◇ A K x	♣ x x x
F.	♠ A K x x	♡ x x	◇ J 10 x	♣ A Q x x

As with a limit raise of opener's major, responder must have four-card support for his jump.

If the opponents intervene in the auction after partner opens the bidding with one of a major suit, the single raise of 8–9 points and the limit raise of 10–12 points retain their meanings. Now, however, a jump to 3 No Trump becomes useful in its natural sense. So if responder wants to make a forcing jump raise after an enemy overcall, he employs a cue-bid of the opposing suit. To illustrate:

OPENER	OPPONENT	RESPONDER	
1 Spade	2 Clubs	3 No Trump	(natural, balanced)
1 Spade	2 Clubs	3 Clubs	(four-card spade support, 13–16 points)

Note that the 3 Club cue-bid does not promise anything about the Club suit; indeed, it might even be made with three low cards in Clubs. It is simply a *substitute* for the important forcing jump raise.

The two-over-one response

In keeping with modern trends and as an adjunct to five-card major opening bids, we now advocate that the requirements for a two-over-one response be bolstered. *If responder makes a simple response in a new suit at the 2-level, he creates a game-forcing situation.* The only exception occurs when *responder rebids his own suit.* In other words:

OPENER	RESPONDER
1 Heart	2 Clubs
2 Diamonds	2 Hearts (the auction is forcing to game)

But:

OPENER	RESPONDER
1 Heart	2 Clubs
2 Diamonds	3 Clubs (opener may pass)

This approach has several advantages. However, to make it viable, responder needs to have the equivalent of an opening bid or a compensating fit for opener's suit before the ventures to the two-level in his own suit. As noted, this requirement is waived if responder plans to rebid his own suit immediately. Thus, after a 1 Spade opening bid, responder may bid 2 Diamonds, providing he follows with 3 Diamonds, holding:

♠ x   ♡ Q J x   ◇ A Q J x x x   ♣ x x x

Responder should have a minimum of 9 HCP and a strong six-card suit for this action. Obviously, all or most of responder's strength should be concentrated in his long suit.

By adopting this method, we actually save bidding space. Since a two-over-one response creates a game-forcing situation, responder need not jump and consume valuable bidding room just to prevent opener from passing below game—both partners can probe for the best contract in a leisurely manner, secure in the knowledge that the bidding won't suddenly die. if responder does jump at his second turn, he shows extra values—either in suit length or quality, or high cards. Let's look at some examples:

♠ K x   ♡ A J x   ◇ K J x   ♣ K J 10 x x

Partner opens 1 Spade, we respond 2 Clubs and opener rebids 2 Diamonds. Naturally, we don't intend to stop below game. Should we now choose to rebid 2 No Trump, the auction would still be forcing because our initial response was a game force. Here, however, we are 4 HCP better than a minimum two-over-one response and we have a double stopper in the unbid suit. We can show our extra strength by jumping to 3 No Trump.

♠ x x   ♡ A K x   ◇ K x x   ♣ A 10 x x x

Partner opens 1 Heart. We have the values for a forcing raise in Hearts, but we have only three-card support. We can make sure that the auction doesn't die short of game by responding 2 Clubs, setting up a game force. Partner rebids 2 Diamonds. Although a simple rebid of 2 Hearts would maintain the force, we would like to convey to partner the quality of our trump support. Therefore, we make an unnecessary but highly descriptive jump to 3 Hearts. Opener, who is looking at a weakish Heart suit, might need no more to move toward slam. Suppose our hand was:

♠ x x   ♡ K x x   ◇ A K x   ♣ A 10 x x x

We have exactly the same hand as before, except that we switched the red suits. Now a rebid of 2 Hearts would be in order. Opener can conclude that we have a good hand with normal trump support. Inferences such as this can be important later in the auction.

The forcing 1 No Trump response

The observant reader might have noticed that we have not yet discussed how to respond with certain categories of hands. Suppose partner opens 1 Spade and we hold

G.	♠ 10 x	♡ A Q x	◇ J 10 9 x	♣ J x x x
H.	♠ x	♡ Q 10 x x x x	◇ x x x	♣ A x x
I.	♠ J 10 x	♡ x x x x	◇ x x x	♣ K Q 10
J.	♠ Q x x	♡ x x x	◇ Q J x x	♣ A K x

The systemic response in our modern methods is 1 No Trump. On all four hands! We will detail why this is the case below. If, for the moment, you can accept that it is correct to make the same response on such a wide variety of hands, we can classify that response as a *catchall bid*. It covers all the types of hands for which we have no ready systemic treatment.

Look and see how widely our four example hands differ. They range from a good fit for opener's suit (J) to a complete misfit (H); from a bare minimum response on 6 HCP (H) to a near opening bid (J). Yet the description of each starts with the same initial response: 1 No Trump. That is what we mean by a catchall bid.

Obviously, a 1 No Trump response does not necessarily tell partner that we have a balanced hand. Only (G) looks suitable for No Trump; (H) should play better in Hearts and (I) and (J) are suitable for Spades.

We use the 1 No Trump response as a waiting bid to give us the opportunity to further define our response with our second bid. Since we need another round of bidding to achieve this objective, the 1 No Trump response is *forcing for one round,* i.e., opener may not pass.

Can we afford to give up the natural meaning of a 1 No Trump response? Experience has shown that seldom if ever after a major suit opening does 1 No Trump become the final contract. Either opener has an unbalanced hand and shows another suit or the opponents enter the auction. Thus, 1 No Trump is the bid that can best be spared to help round out our system.

To show how useful this response will be, let us see how the auction will develop with each of our example hands. With hand (H) we intend to rebid 2 Hearts to show a long suit within a hand of limited strength. On (I) we plan to rebid 2 Spades, thereby showing trump support and 6–7 points; note that this delayed raise of partner's suit is weaker than an immediate raise, which would show 8–9 points. We are going to jump to 3 Spades with hand (J) to show 10–12 points and specifically three-card support for opener's suit; the immediate jump raise shows the same strength but requires a fourth trump.

You can see a pattern emerging that will make your system of responses easier to remember: Immediate raises are more emphatic than delayed raises. They show either more points or better support.

We deliberately bypassed our planned rebid for hand (G). No matter what suit opener shows at the two level in response to 1 No Trump, we intend to rebid 2 Spades. Since opener has guaranteed at least a five-card suit with his opening bid, we know that spades will be a playable contract. Thus, our delayed raise to 2 Spades shows either a 6–7 point hand with three-card support or better, or 8–9 points and only two-card support. If opener is interested in game, he can probe to find out about the quality of our support; if he is content with a part-score contract, 2 Spades should be as good a contract, or perhaps even better, than 1 No Trump.

How to respond to a forcing No Trump

By and large, opener makes his normal rebid. With a six-card major, he rebids it; with a second suit of four cards or longer, he can bid that; with a strong, balanced hand, he can raise No Trump. However, there is one type of hand on which opener must improvise his rebid:

♠ A K x x x   ♥ K J x   ♦ A x x   ♣ x x

Suppose that after an opening bid of 1 Spade, partner has responded with 1 No Trump. Opener's hand does not fit into any of the categories mentioned above. He does not have a six-card suit, so he can't rebid his Spades; he has no second suit; his hand is too weak to raise to 2 No Trump. But since the response was forcing, opener must bid something. The solution is to rebid 2 Diamonds.

While the idea of making a rebid in a three-card suit might come as something of a surprise, it is not much of a distortion. As part of our five-card major methods, we already freely open a three-card minor suit. Responder must allow for this possibility in the rest of the auction. Because opener might have rebid with a three-card minor suit, opener tends to return to the anchor major with a doubleton unless he has five-card support for opener's minor.

If opener has to choose between two three-card minor suits for his rebid, he should select clubs unless the difference in strength between the suits is 3 points or more. This is similar to our practice for opening the bidding with a three-card minor suit.

$$\spadesuit K J x x x \qquad \heartsuit A x \qquad \diamond K x x \qquad \clubsuit Q x x$$

Rebid 2 Clubs if the response to your 1 Spade opening bid was 1 No Trump. But

$$\spadesuit Q J x x x \qquad \heartsuit A x \qquad \diamond K Q x \qquad \clubsuit J x x$$

Rebid 2 Diamonds—the disparity in strength between the two suits is too great.

There is a sound reason for this. Since responder might be acting with a very weak hand, you can't be sure that the hand belongs to you. Should the opponents buy the contract, it might prove costly on defense should partner during the play of the hand elect to lead a club rather than a diamond.

Before we proceed to a new section, it might be helpful to summarize the different types of major-suit raises that responder can offer:

POINTS	SUPPORT	BID
6–7	3 or more	Forcing 1 NT, then support at the 2-level
8–9	3 or more	Direct raise to 2 of opener's major
10–12	Exactly 3	Forcing NT, followed by a jump raise of opener's suit
10–12	4 or more	Jump raise of opener's suit to the 3-level
13–16	4 or more	3 NT (Forcing jump raise)

Other responses to a major-suit opening

There is nothing radical in the methods we propose here—if you are already playing bridge, you probably use these same responses now. With 0–5 points, pass. A new suit by responder at the one-level (1 H—1 S) shows at least a four-card suit and is forcing for one round—opener may not pass. The subsequent bidding will reveal responder's ambitions.

The jump to 2 No Trump

When responder jumps to 2 No Trump, he shows 13–15 points, a balanced distribution and protection in all the unbid suits. The jump is forcing to game. Respond 2 No Trump to your partner's 1 Spade opening bid on both of the following hands:

♠ x x	♡ K J x x	◇ K J 10	♣ A J x x
♠ Q x	♡ A Q x	◇ K Q x	♣ J x x x x

Do *not* jump to 2 No Trump on a balanced 13–15 HCP if you have an unprotected suit. Instead, make use of the two-over-one response. Partner opens 1 Spade:

♠ K x   ♡ x x x   ◇ K J x x   ♣ A Q 10 x

Respond 2 Clubs. Your opening bid facing partner's opening should produce a game somewhere, but at this stage of the auction you have no clear sense of the best contract. You begin your probe with 2 Clubs—that establishes a game force and gives you the time and room to explore for your best contract.

The double jump raise

The jump raise from 1 to 4 of a major suit is a specialized bid. It describes a hand rich in trump support and distribution—it must contain a singleton or a void—but with no more than 9 HCP. The intent of the bid is twofold: You hope to make your contract while at the same time you deprive the opponents of a convenient chance to enter the auction. Below are sound examples of a double jump raise from 1 Heart to 4 Hearts:

♠ x	♡ K J x x x	◇ Q J 10 x x	♣ x x
♠ x x	♡ K x x x	◇ x	♣ K J x x x x

This double jump is often referred to as a "shut-out"—nomenclature of which we strongly disapprove. It has led to the belief that, when responder jumps to the 4-level, opener is obliged to pass no matter what his holding. Nothing could be further from the truth. Indeed, if opener has a hand rich in controls of the side suits but with weakish trumps, he should realize that his chances for slam are excellent. So shun the phrase "shut-out" bid—a double jump raise is a far more accurate description.

By a passed hand, however, the double jump raise has a different connotation. Now it is stronger than a jump to three of opener's suit. There is a valid reason for this. Suppose that you passed a hand that just did not qualify for an opening bid—perhaps it was a point too weak or did not have quite enough defensive strength. However, when you have a fit for partner's suit, you revalue your hand and now it is upgraded to a full opening bid. If you make the limit raise to 3 of opener's suit, he might pass and so you miss a game. Even a two-over-one response by a passed hand is not 100 percent forcing. Suppose you hold:

♠ Q J x x   ♡ x   ◇ A J x x   ♣ Q J x

You hand is worth 13 points but, because you have only 1 quick trick, you could not open the bidding. However, when partner opens 1 Spade your hand revalues to 15 points (your singleton becomes worth 3 points and you must add 1 point for your Spade honors). To bid anything less than 4 Spades puts tremendous pressure on partner to bid again with minimum values.

While on the subject of bidding by a passed hand, let us note here that the only forcing response available to a player who passed at his first turn is a jump in a new suit. This bid is reserved for two-suited hands with a fit for opener's suit. Suppose that, as dealer, you pass with:

♠ 10 9 x x   ♡ x   ◇ A K J 10 x x   ♣ x x

Partner opens 1 Spade. A jump to 3 Spades does not do this hand justice and 4 Spades, while better, does not give partner a good picture of your holding. The best way to describe your hand is to start with a jump shift of 3 Diamonds, then raise Spades at your next turn. Partner may have the key controls in the unbid suits to go on to slam.

The jump shift

When a two-over-one response showed a hand of 10–11 points, we needed a way to insure that the bidding was kept open to game and to show interest in slam. Thus, a jump shift by responder simply showed a hand of 19 points or better.

Now, many of the hands in this category can be handled quite adequately by starting with a forcing response at the 2-level and then jumping at your next turn, if necessary. That frees the jump shift for a more descriptive purpose:

A jump shift by responder shows a strong hand either with a self-sustaining suit of its own or with a good fit for opener's suit.

Even if you hold 19 points or more, avoid making a jump shift if you do not know *where you want to play the hand!* However, you can jump shift on somewhat weaker hands if you know where you want to go. To illustrate, assume that partner opens the bidding with 1 Spade in each of the cases below:

♠ x   ♡ A K J 10 x x x   ◇ K x x   ♣ A x

Respond 3 Hearts. Even though you do not have a fit for Spades, you are strong enough to jump shift. You intend bidding 4 Hearts at your next turn to show a self-sustaining Heart suit.

♠ K Q x x   ♡ A K x x x   ◇ A x   ♣ x x

Bid 3 Hearts. When you raise Spades next, you will have shown a powerful hand with a good Heart suit and excellent Spade support.

♠ A x   ♡ K Q x x   ◇ A K x x x   ♣ K x

Bid 2 Diamonds. Although in terms of high cards this is the strongest of the three hands, it does not qualify for a jump shift. The final contract could be in Spades, Hearts, Diamonds or No Trump, and you will need room to find the best spot. Since you create a game-forcing auction with your 2 Diamond response, you can afford to conduct a leisurely auction to probe for your best spot. Put your methods to good use!

Responses to minor-suit openings

Since we do not open four-card major suits, when partner opens one of a minor suit he will frequently hold one, or even two, four-card majors. If responder holds a four-card major, there is a chance that the all-important 4–4 fit exists, and our bidding must be designed to uncover it.

The quality of responder's four-card major suit is not of prime consequence—the weaker his suit is, the stronger opener's fit is likely to be. The important principle in discovering a fit is for responder to bid his suits *up the line*. That simply means that, with two four-card suits, responder should make his cheapest bid, regardless of suit quality. With only one four-card suit, responder's priority, if it is a major suit, is to bid it. With two suits of unequal length, responder bids his longer suit first. Let's see how this works in practice. Suppose that partner opens the bidding with 1 Club:

♠ Q J x x   ♡ K 10 x x   ◇ Q x x x   ♣ x

Respond 1 Diamond. Even though that is your weakest suit, don't depart from the up-the-line principle. By responding 1 Diamond you do not *deny* a four-card major. If opener does have a four-card major, he will bid it and you have located your fit. If he bypasses the major suits, it means that no 4–4 fit exists.

♠ A K x x   ♡ J x x x   ◇ x x x   ♣ x x

Respond 1 Heart. With two four-card majors, bid the lower-ranking first, conforming to our principle. If opener holds four Spades but not four Hearts, he will introduce the Spade suit; if he holds four Hearts, he will raise to advertise the fit; if he bids anything else, abandon your search for a major-suit fit. Note that, if you choose to respond 1 Spade and opener doesn't raise, you might lose a possible 4–4 Heart fit.

♠ x x   ♡ A x x x   ◇ K J x x x   ♣ x x

Respond 1 Diamond. With two suits of unequal length, bid the longer first. Again, that does not deny a four-card major, and you will still locate the 4–4 fit if partner has a Heart suit.

♠ Q x x x   ♡ J x x x   ◇ x x x   ♣ x x

Pass. Don't take leave of your senses in your eagerness to locate a 4–4 major fit. You need 6 points to respond to an opening bid. Don't panic because you are afraid that partner might have opened the bidding with a "short Club"—more often than not, he will have a real club suit. This is a case where the cure is worse than the disease. If you make a habit of "rescuing" partner at the 1-level on subminimum hands, you will be fattening the wallets of a wide circle of your bridge acquaintances. Partner will start driving to high levels in the expectation of finding something of value in your hand, and carnage could ensue. When you have nothing, bid nothing!

Suppose that partner opens the bidding with 1 Diamond:

♠ x x   ♡ Q x x x   ◇ x x   ♣ A 10 x x x

Respond 1 Heart. You do not have the strength for a two-over-one response of 2 Clubs, so bid your major.

♠ K J x x   ♡ K x   ◇ x x   ♣ A Q x x x

Respond 2 Clubs. If you can bid your long suit before showing your shorter suit, do so. You are not denying a four-card major. When you show your Spades on the next round of bidding, opener will know that you have at least five Clubs and probably only four Spades. If you bid your Spades first and then your Clubs, partner will never know which is your long suit.

♠ K J x   ♡ Q x x   ◇ x x x x   ♣ 10 9 x

Respond 1 No Trump. This *denies* a four-card major and shows 6–10 points. Don't raise partner's minor-suit opening with only four-card support if you have any other bid available. In response to a minor suit, 1 No Trump is *not forcing*.

♠ Q x x x x   ♡ K Q 10 x x   ◇ x   ♣ K x

Respond 1 Spade. With two five-card suits, bid the higher-ranking suit first, regardless of the relative quality.

Minor-suit raises

We have already warned about the danger of the "Short Club" syndrome. When partner opens one of a minor, especially 1 Diamond, presume that he has a genuine suit—that will be the case most of the time. And when he has opened on a three-card suit (and he will *never* have fewer than three cards) he probably has planned a rebid should you raise. The moral of this is: Don't be afraid to raise opener's minor suit with only four-card support, either on the first or on subsequent rounds of the bidding. He knows what sort of suit he opened, and he can take appropriate action. True, you would prefer to have five-card support, but sometimes you aren't dealt that.

A single raise (1 Diamond—2 Diamonds) shows 6–10 points, at least four-card support and denies a four-card major. With both a four-card major and a support for opener's suit, show the major first.

A jump raise (1 Club—3 Clubs) shows 11–12 points, at least five-card support and denies a four-card major.

With 13–16 points and a hand unsuitable for No Trump, responder must make a temporizing bid in a new suit before either jump-raising opener's minor suit if the initial response was at the 1-level, or raising Diamonds if responder started with a forcing two-over-one response. Again, five-card support for the secondary jump is a *sine qua non*. (See *Secondary Jumps by Responder*.)

Assume that partner opens the bidding with 1 Diamond:

♠ x x ♡ x x x ◇ A J x x ♣ K x x x

Respond 2 Diamonds. That describes your point count and support while denying a four-card major. What if opener has only three diamonds? If he has a minimum opener, two diamonds is probably as good a spot as any to play the hand—you have no eight-card fit anywhere. And if he is better than minimum, he will know how to continue.

♠ 10 x x x ♡ x ◇ K J x x ♣ A x x x

Respond 1 Spade. Your priority is to show a four-card major, regardless of its quality.

♠ A Q x ♡ x x ◇ Q J x x x ♣ Q x x

Respond 3 Diamonds. With one bid you show both your strength and your five-card support.

♠ A Q x ♡ x x ◇ Q J x x x ♣ A J x

Respond 2 Clubs. Once you have created a game-force situation, you can thereafter continue to give preference to Diamonds to convince opener of your length in his suit. Change a low club to a low heart and you have a tougher choice. It lies between a jump to 2 No Trump without a Heart stopper, or 1 Spade and run the risk of partner continually putting you back to Spades. We prefer 1 Spade—we are not terrified of playing 4–3 major-suit contracts, even at the game level.

♠ A x x ♡ x x ◇ A Q x x ♣ A x x x

Bid 2 Clubs. You cannot jump raise partner's minor without five-card support, so you must temporize with 2 Clubs and support Diamonds at your next turn.

♠ x x   ♡ K Q x x   ◇ K J x x x   ♣ x x

Respond 1 Heart. An immediate jump to three Diamonds would deny a four-card major suit, and as a result you could miss a 4–4 heart fit. Therefore, you first show the major and support diamonds later. Remember 4 Hearts scores more points than 5 Diamonds, and needs only ten tricks as against 11 in the minor suit game.

Other responses to a minor-suit opening

Responder's jump to 2 No Trump over a minor suit opening bid shows a balanced hand and 13–15 points. *It denies a four-card major suit.* If you have a four-card major, you must first bid the suit and then jump in No Trump at your next turn if no major-suit fit is revealed.

The jump shift is the same as over a major-suit opening. It shows either a self-sustaining suit or a two-suited hand with at least a good four-card fit for opener's minor.

Since you don't need 3 No Trump as a forcing jump raise of a minor suit, that bid retains its natural meaning—a balanced hand of 16–18 points with all unbid suits stopped. Since the bid consumes so much bidding space, and since a short suit in responder's hand can be valuable to opener at a suit contract, it is best to confine this bid to hands with specifically 4-3-3-3 distribution. Here is a typical hand for the bid:

♠ A J x   ♡ K J x   ◇ A x x   ♣ K 10 x x

Free bids

There has been much discussion, sometimes heated, about free bids. This department suggests a commonsense approach to the subject.

When an opponent intervenes over an opening bid, responder is relieved of the obligation to bid. If, therefore, responder does choose to act, he must have a definite reason for doing so. Consider these illustrations after partner's 1 Spade opening has been overcalled with 2 Hearts:

♠ J 10 x x   ♡ x   ◇ Q 10 x x   ♣ x x x x

Pass. You have 7 points and, had the opponent not interposed, you would have raised partner to 2 Spades. Now you have been released from your obligation and you should take advantage of it since you have no defensive values.

♠ J 10 x x   ♡ x   ◇ A 10 x x   ♣ x x x x

Respond 2 Spades. Now you have 9 points and a defensive trick—enough to give partner some encouragement.

Now let's assume that partner opens 1 Club and the next player overcalls with 1 Heart.

♠ K x x x x   ♡ x x x   ◇ Q J x   ♣ x x

Pass. With 6 points and a five-card major suit, you would have responded had there been no interference. Now it is best to pass. Remember, partner still has another chance to bid, and he will exercise that option if he has a good hand.

♠ A Q x x x   ♡ x x x   ◇ Q J x   ♣ x x

Respond 1 Spade. Your 9 points and five-card suit fully entitle you to have your say in the auction.

We feel these methods won't impose too much of a strain on your memory, but will allow you to bid with new accuracy. However, should you prefer a simpler method, see the scheme of responses incorporated in Chapter 6: Four-Card-Major Opening Bids.

RESPONSES QUIZ

Partner opens the bidding with 1 Heart. What is your response with each of the following hands?

1. ♠ Q x x x x ♡ x ◇ Q x x x ♣ x x x	2. ♠ A K x x x x ♡ x x ◇ A Q x ♣ K x	3. ♠ Q x x x ♡ K x x ◇ A x x ♣ x x x
4. ♠ K x x ♡ 10 x x x ◇ Q x ♣ J x x x	5. ♠ K x x x ♡ 10 x x x ◇ A Q x x ♣ x	6. ♠ K x ♡ A x x ◇ 10 9 x x x ♣ K x x
7. ♠ Q x ♡ A Q x x ◇ A K x x ♣ x x x	8. ♠ K Q x ♡ K x x ◇ K J x x ♣ A x x	9. ♠ A x ♡ x x ◇ Q 10 x x x x ♣ x x x
10. ♠ A J ♡ x ◇ A K x x x ♣ A K J x x	11. ♠ K Q J 9 x x ♡ x ◇ A K x ♣ K J x	12. ♠ x ♡ K J x x x ◇ x x ♣ K J 10 x x

Partner opens the bidding with 1 Club. What is your response with each of the following hands?

13. ♠ K 10 x ♡ Q J x ◇ K J x x ♣ A x x	14. ♠ 10 x x x ♡ K x x x ◇ x x x ♣ x x	15. ♠ A Q x x ♡ K 10 x x ◇ x ♣ A J x x
16. ♠ x x ♡ x x x ◇ Q 10 x x ♣ K Q x x	17. ♠ A Q x ♡ A x x ◇ x x ♣ K x x x x	18. ♠ K x x ♡ A x x ◇ Q x x x ♣ J x x

Partner opens the bidding with 1 Diamond. What is your response with each of the following hands?

19. ♠ x x ♡ J 10 x ◇ K x ♣ Q 10 8 x x x	20. ♠ Q x ♡ A Q x x ◇ A x ♣ Q 10 x x x	21. ♠ K J x ♡ A K x ◇ Q x x x ♣ K J x

ANSWERS TO RESPONSES QUIZ

1. Pass.
Your singleton is in partner's suit. This drawback coupled with the fact that you have only 4 HCP does not warrant a response. Save your valor for another time.

2. One Spade.

You are strong enough for a jump shift, but your spade suit isn't self-sustaining. Therefore, it is better to make a simple one-over-one response, which is forcing for one round, and then jump on the next round.

3. Two Hearts.

The immediate raise describes your point count and support in one bid. Leave the Spade suit on the shelf; your Heart support is of more consequence to partner.

4. One No Trump.

An immediate Heart raise overstates your values. This 7-point hand is best shown by first using the Forcing No Trump, then supporting Hearts.

5. Three Hearts.

With 12 points—9 in high cards and 3 in distribution—you can express your values in one fell swoop with a limit raise. When you can describe your hand precisely with one bid, it is invariably right to do so. Your bid invites partner to go to game with anything better than a dead-minimum opening bid.

6. One No Trump.

You have the strength for a limit raise but only three-card support for opener's suit. You handle that by first employing the Forcing No Trump, then raising to 3 Hearts. Again, this invites partner to bid game, but he needs slightly better values because he knows that you have only three-card trump support.

7. Three No Trump.

When you have four-card support for opener's major and enough strength to guarantee a game, use the artificial jump raise of 3 No Trump. If partner is interested in slam, he will make some bid other than converting to 4 Hearts.

8. Two Diamonds.

There are several possible contracts, so it is best to begin the investigation

with a quiet two-over-one game-forcing bid. Any subsequent bid by us below the level of game, except a diamond rebid immediately, will continue the force. We should learn a great deal about opener's hand before our investigation is complete. Don't jump to 3 No Trump—that's a forcing raise in Hearts and you are a trump short for that action.

9. One No Trump.

To bid diamonds at the 2-level would be a drastic overbid. It is better to use the Forcing No Trump and then bid Diamonds later. As a matter of fact, on a good day partner's rebid will be 2 Diamonds, leaving us with an easy raise to describe our hand.

10. Two Diamonds.

Despite our powerful 20 points, this hand is not suitable for a jump shift—it requires a slower investigative approach. We suspect that we might belong in a slam, but we don't know where to play the hand. Thus, a jump shift would hamper our probe because it consumes too much bidding space. We start by bidding the higher-ranking of our two five-card suits.

11. Two Spades.

In contrast to the previous problem, although this hand is weaker in strength it contains *direction*—we know where we want to play the hand. By jump shifting we convey to partner that we intend placing the final contract either in his suit or in our own.

12. Four Hearts.

This hand meets all the requirements for a double jump raise: long trumps, a singleton or void, fewer than 9 HCP. This bid does not prevent partner from bidding on, and it makes it very difficult for the opponents to enter the auction even though they own the spade suit.

13. Two No Trump.

The perfect hand: 13–15 HCP, balanced distribution and stoppers in all the unbid suits.

14. Pass.

Partner's 1 Club opening bid is not forcing, so there is no need for us to keep the bidding open with fewer than 6 points. At the risk of repeating ourselves on this important and frequently misunderstood issue: Don't bid if you don't have the values for it.

15. One Heart.

When we have more than one four-card suit, we bid our suits up the line to conserve space. Partner's rebid will locate an eight-card fit if one exists.

16. Two Clubs.

If you can limit your hand with one bid, do so. That is why the Club raise is more attractive than introducing the Diamond suit. We not only tell partner of our support, but we place an upper limit of 10 points on our holding. A response of 1 Diamond, on the other hand, would be unlimited.

17. One Heart.

We have no attractive bid, so we must temporize by bidding a three-card suit. A jump to 3 Clubs would be a limit raise showing 11–12 points, and we can't bid 2 No Trump without a Diamond stopper. Our intention is to jump in Clubs at our next turn, and harp on Clubs thereafter.

18. One No Trump.

Again, we seize the opportunity to describe our hand with one bid. Not only do we limit our strength to 10 points, but we deny a four-card major.

19. One No Trump.

Not an ideal hand for this bid, but what can we do? We have 6 HCP, so we must respond, and we do not have a four-card major to bid. If you even considered 2 Clubs, read this chapter again.

20. Two Clubs.

The governing principle is to bid our suits in order of length, if possible. The forcing two-over-one response does not deny a four-card major. If there is a 4–4 fit, the later rounds of bidding will uncover it.

21. Three No Trump.

The classic holding for this action. A balanced 16–18 points and stoppers in all suits. This is not a "shut-out" bid, if you will excuse the term. It shows a strong hand and partner is free to bid on if he thinks your values will stretch to slam.

3.   Opening No Trump bids

LOOKING AROUND US we are forced to recognize that we live in a world where even the most well-established institutions are subjected to an increasingly critical scrutiny. It therefore affords considerable reassurance to note that the strong 1 No Trump opening, indicating a balanced hand with 16 to 18 points in high cards,* continues to enjoy the respect of the community. In the same way, the opening bids of 2 No Trump and 3 No Trump are still regarded as the most satisfactory means of describing balanced hands of exceptional power.

In my previously published works the virtues of a strong 1 No Trump opening were commended with some warmth: it was pointed out that the bid is highly descriptive and tells responder at once the nature and strength of opener's hand. In consequence the responder is frequently able to select the most suitable final contract without the necessity for a further exchange of bids. At the same time, should the responder feel the need for more information concerning the details of the opener's hand, modern methods of investigation enable it to be obtained in such measure as may be required.

In view of the general efficiency of auctions that begin with a bid of 1 No Trump, it was suggested that the No Trump opening merited a more intensive use. Events have shown that this view was not at variance with public taste. Opening bids in No Trump have never stood higher in popular esteem and, partly as a result, the exploratory sequences that can follow the opening have been developed in more detail than previously. The subject of No Trump bidding, therefore, is now deserving of a separate chapter.

In No Trump bidding, only the high cards are assigned numerical values: the opening bidder may not allow any points for distribution.

---

* Exceptionally a hand that includes a strong five-card suit may be opened with 1 No Trump, but players who allow this exception should recall that for purposes of slam bidding their No Trump range is 15 + to 18 points.

Opening No Trump bids

Ace . . . . 4 points
King . . . . 3 points
Queen . . . . 2 points
Jack . . . . 1 point

The pack contains **40 points.**

Add 1 point for any hand containing all the Aces.

Although no points are allowed for distribution, it is conceded that a long suit is a decided asset and that game may be made with a point of two less when a good suit is held. The reason why a point may not officially be added to the value of the opener's hand if he holds a five-card suit is that in No Trump bidding it is highly desirable to keep the figure 40 as a constant, so that when the responder reaches the conclusion that his side has 37 points, he knows that it is mathematically impossible for the opposition to hold an Ace, inasmuch as their combined assets cannot amount to more than 3 points.

All the same, the value of a five-card suit held by the opener or the responder is to be brought into the reckoning whenever a game bid is under contemplation. Thus the requirements for a raise to either 2 No Trump or 3 No Trump are lowered by one point where the responder has a good five-card suit. Moreover, if the opener's bid of 1 No Trump brings forth a raise to 2 No Trump from the responder, the opener may feel himself entitled to press on to 3 No Trump if his assets include a five-card suit and his hand is not below par in other respects. Note that there is no embargo against either opening No Trump or raising to No Trump with a biddable five-card major suit in a hand that appears better adapted for playing at a No Trump contract than at a trump contract.

In a similar way the value of the ten-spot is not to be overlooked. When I originally presented the point-count method of valuation to the public I assigned the value of ½ to a 10, but I soon reached the conclusion that it is better practice to avoid these fractions and permit the ten-spots to sway you one way or the other on close hands. This method of allowing for the presence of these useful cards has proved highly acceptable to the public, to whom fractions are a mental hazard.

The 1 No Trump opening bid

Requirements for an opening bid of 1 No Trump are:

1. The hand must contain a point count of 16, 17, or 18.

2. The hand must be of balanced distribution, that is:

$$4\text{--}3\text{--}3\text{--}3$$
$$4\text{--}4\text{--}3\text{--}2$$
$$5\text{--}3\text{--}3\text{--}2$$

The fact that the five-card suit happens to be a major is no bar to the No Trump bid.

3. At least three suits must be protected. The following holdings constitute protection in this sense:

A x   K x   Q x x   J x x x

Hands counting 19 or 20 are too strong for an opening 1 No Trump, and since they are not quite big enough for a 2 No Trump bid, they should be opened with one of a suit with the intention to jump in No Trump if partner responds.

It will be found that some hands, especially those containing a five-card suit or two biddable four-card suits, present a choice between opening at 1 No Trump or opening at a suit. In such case the possession of tenace combinations, such as the A Q of a suit or the K J x of a suit, is a factor that argues strongly in favor of opening at No Trump, for it will be found that such holdings are liable to be especially effective when held in the hand of the declarer at a No Trump contract. Therefore, when faced with a close decision, you may well allow yourself to be influenced by the presence or absence of tenace combinations. Suppose you hold this hand as dealer:

♠ K x   ♡ K J x   ◇ A Q 10 x x   ♣ K 10 x

The fact that you have a rebiddable five-card suit should not deter you from opening at 1 No Trump. Your hand is very well endowed with tenace combinations and there is a strong possibility that one of these holdings may provide an additional winning trick in consequence of the opening lead being made from the hand on your left.

Now suppose you have this hand:

♠ A x   ♡ x x x   ◇ A K x x   ♣ A J 10 x

It cannot be denied that your hand is relatively balanced and contains 16 points in high cards, but all the same an opening bid of 1 No Trump is not to be recommended. The hand contains no tenace combinations and it is not by any means clear that an advantage is to be gained by arranging matters so that the opening lead comes up to your hand. Moreover, your two biddable suits are deserving of mention and therefore you should open the hand at 1 Diamond with the intention to rebid at 2 Clubs. By so doing you indicate that your hand is geared to playing at a trump contract should a suitable fit come to light. You also increase the likelihood that, should the subsequent bidding suggest the wisdom of playing the hand at No Trump, your partner will be enabled to become the declarer and in that way extract a possible advantage from the opening lead. On all counts, therefore, the preferred course of action is to open with 1 Diamond.

Responses to opening bids of 1 No Trump

When partner opens with 1 No Trump you need not strain a point to keep the bidding open. There is no real danger of missing anything if you are able to perform the simple function of counting, for partner's hand is limited to 18 points. (Even an extra 10 or a fifth card in some suit might render an 18-point hand too big for 1 No Trump, so that if you have fewer than 8 points, don't concern yourself too deeply with the hand.)

Responder must not lose sight of the fact that it takes approximately 26 points to produce game at No Trump. When a five-card suit is held, the chances for game are reasonable with 25 points.

When the partnership assets amount to 33 or 34 points, you have enough to warrant the undertaking of a slam contract. (In these cases, unless responder is counting some points for distribution, no checking for Aces is necessary, since the enemy cannot have two Aces inasmuch as their high-card holding is limited to 6 or 7 points.)

A combined holding of 37 or 38 should yield a grand slam (the opposition cannot have an Ace inasmuch as they hold at most 2 or 3 points).

The principal consideration in selecting the response to a 1 No Trump opening is whether your hand is balanced or unbalanced.

Responses with balanced hands

Where responder holds a hand which is distributed 5-3-3-2, there is no advantage in showing the five-card suit if it is a minor. (With a major suit, responder has some options.) It is better to raise the No Trump if the required count is held. Here are the requirements.

With a balanced hand and fewer than 8 points, pass.

Raise to 2 No Trump with 8 or 9 points. (You may raise with 7 points if you have a good five-card suit.)

Raise to 3 No Trump with 10 to 14 points.

Raise to 4 No Trump with 15 or 16 points.

Raise to 6 No Trump with 17 or 18 points.

If you hold 19 or 20 points, a bid of 6 No Trump is not quite adequate. First make a jump shift to 3 of some suit and then follow up with 6 No Trump. Showing a suit and jumping to 6 No Trump is a little stronger action than just jumping to 6 No Trump.

Raise to 7 No Trump with 21 or more, for then your partnership is assured of at least 37 points.

The 2 Club Convention (Stayman Convention)

There is a certain class of responding hand that presents a problem: the responder has a marked shortage in a particular suit or suits, but does not have a good enough five-card suit for exploring the suit possibilities of the hand. Hands of this type are not uncommon and old-timers will remember that the prevalence of this type of hand gave rise to a somewhat distressing situation in the early days of contract, when players found that by opening at No Trump they were passing up the opportunity to play at a sound major-suit contract when each player had four trumps.

In their first attempt to remedy this state of affairs, the leading authorities of the day did not hit upon the best solution. They laid it down as a law of the Medes and the Persians—who obviously never played bridge—that the suit possibilities of a hand should be explored before bidding No Trump. In advocating this practice they were somewhat reminiscent of the ascetic who chose to recline on a bed of nails, for they lost many of the advantages to be derived from an opening bid of 1 No Trump. Not until late in the day did it dawn on some explorers that with proper management one could have the penny and the cake as well. Today it is generally recognized that the best strategy is to open No Trump on all suitable hands and yet hold the door open to investigation of the major-suit possibilities should it prove desirable.

This is accomplished by the use of a 2 Club response as an asking bid. Conventions of this type have put in appearances under assorted names and with many variations, but we are convinced that only when such a convention is distilled down to its basic elements does it serve an overall useful purpose. So here it is in basic English.

You open with 1 No Trump and partner responds 2 Clubs. This is an artificial bid and has no relationship to the Club suit itself. If partner happens to have Clubs, it is a mere coincidence. But the bid is forcing, and the opening No Trump bidder, if he has a four-card major suit, shows it at once. However, the four-card suit must be headed by at least the Queen. If the opening No Trumper has no four-card major, he makes the routine rebid of 2 Diamonds. This bid is artificial and has no relationship to the suit itself. If the opening bidder happens to have two four-card majors, he first shows the Spades, and if it is expedient to do so, he shows the Hearts later. Consequently if the opener's first rebid is 2 Hearts, he denies possession of a biddable Spade holding. But if his rebid is 2 Spades, it does not rule out a biddable Heart suit. *

Therefore the use of this convention (also known as the "Stayman Convention") changes the nature of the responses, so that when the No Trump bidder's partner calls 2 Spades, 2 Hearts or 2 Diamonds, it is a sign of relative weakness (responder definitely holds fewer than 8 points in high cards) and requests the No Trump bidder to withdraw from the auction. There is an exception to be noted, when opener holds 18 points plus strong support for his partner's take-out, in which case he may offer a single raise. But in no circumstances may he take any other form of action.

This convention should have no effect upon the normal jump-shift responses to the opening bid. Holding:

♠ A Q 10 x x   ♡ x   ◇ A Q 10 x   ♣ x x x

it is still proper to bid 3 Spades, forcing to game. With this hand there is nothing to be gained by use of the convention. However, where responder has a hand of moderate strength which contains a reasonably good five-card major suit, he may be faced with a choice of trying for game in a major suit or at No Trump. Since a response of 2 Hearts or 2 Spades would announce weakness, he must first bid 2 Clubs, and, assuming opener's response to be 2 Diamonds, he then shows his five-card major. For example responder holds:

♠ K J x x x   ♡ A x x   ◇ x x x   ♣ 10 x

After partner opens 1 No Trump, responder cannot be sure of the best final contract. It may be in No Trump or it could be in Spades.

---

* Obviously the order of responses can be reversed with opposite negative conclusions and some prefer to play in this fashion, but *de gustibus non est disputandum.*

Responder therefore bids 2 Clubs, which forces partner to speak. If partner rebids 2 Diamonds (denying a four-card major), responder now bids 2 Spades. Note that this bid is not forcing. If opener has a bare 16 points with no special support for Spades, a pass is in order.* However, the opening No Trump bidder should strive to make a further call with even the slightest excess value; leaning perhaps somewhat in favor of a raise. However, where a raise is not available and opener has anything above the minimum requirements, he may try 2 No Trump. Observe that where the 2 Club responder's hand is strong enough to insist upon a game, he should jump to 3 of his major suit if opener's rebid is 2 Diamonds; raise to game with a fit in opener's major suit rebid; or jump to 3 No Trump.

Where responder's 2 Club inquiry has been met by a 2 Diamond rebid, responder must not bid a four-card major of his own. In this sequence such a bid unconditionally promises a five-card suit. Holding four-card suits, he must, therefore, return to No Trump.

Let us examine a few illustrative cases. In each of the following you are South and the bidding has proceeded as indicated.

1.	♠ K x x x	♡ A J 10	◇ A Q 10	♣ Q J x
	SOUTH	WEST	NORTH	EAST
	1 No Trump	Pass	2 Clubs	Pass
	?			

Bid 2 Spades. You are required by the 2 Club Convention to show a biddable four-card major if you have one and it is not open to you to take any other course of action.

2.	♠ A Q x x	♡ Q J x	◇ A x x	♣ K x x
	SOUTH	WEST	NORTH	EAST
	1 No Trump	Pass	2 Clubs	Pass
	2 Spades	Pass	3 Spades	Pass
	?			

Pass. You have a bare minimum and partner's raise is not forcing. With 10 points or more, he would have jumped to game himself.

---

* However, some play *forcing* 2 Club responses, requiring that opener makes one further bid if the sequence goes: 1 No Trump—2 Clubs; 2 Diamonds—2 Hearts or 2 Spades. Others use 2 Clubs as a one-round force; 2 Diamonds as forcing to game. (See Chapter 12.)

3. ♠ A J x x   ♡ K x   ◇ K Q 10 x   ♣ K J x

SOUTH	WEST	NORTH	EAST
1 No Trump	Pass	2 Clubs	Pass
2 Spades	Pass	2 No Trump	Pass
?			

Bid 3 No Trump. Partner has indicated possession of 8 or 9 points. Your 17 points insures a minimum of 25 for the partnership. In situations of this type it is advisable to speculate on the other point.

4. ♠ K Q x x   ♡ A x x   ◇ x x x   ♣ J x x

NORTH	EAST	SOUTH
1 No Trump	Pass	?

Bid 3 No Trump. The 2 Club Convention should not be employed on 4-3-3-3 hands. Such holdings will usually produce as many tricks in No Trump as in a suit.

5. ♠ 10 x x x   ♡ A Q J x   ◇ A Q   ♣ K 10 x

SOUTH	WEST	NORTH	EAST
1 No Trump	Pass	2 Clubs	Pass
?			

Bid 2 Hearts. With both majors, normal procedure is to show Spades first. However, in the present instance, the Spade holding is not biddable. The opener, therefore, must bid 2 Hearts. To be biddable according to the provisions of this convention, the texture of the suit should be at least Q x x x. In rare instances—for example, if opener's hand includes a doubleton—J x x x may be shown.

6. ♠ x x x x x   ♡ x x x x   ◇ J x x   ♣ J

NORTH	EAST	SOUTH
1 No Trump	Pass	?

Pass. On hands this weak it is better to leave well enough alone. No situation is desperate if partner has not been doubled.

7. ♠ x x   ♡ J 10 x x   ◇ x x   ♣ A K 10 x x

NORTH	EAST	SOUTH
1 No Trump	2 Diamonds	?

Bid 2 No Trump. East's overcall prevents you from employing the 2 Club Convention. You have no recourse, therefore, but to offer the No Trump raise. When partner has opened with 1 No Trump you may raise without a stopper in the adverse suit, and should strain to do so in the circumstances. Partner is still in position to show a biddable Heart suit if he has one.

8. ♠ A Q x x   ♡ K x x x   ◇ x   ♣ Q x x x
    NORTH   EAST   SOUTH
    1 No Trump   2 Diamonds   ?

Bid 3 Diamonds. On hands of game-going potential where the opponents have deprived you of the 2 Club bid, it is still possible to check back for a major-suit fit by means of a cue bid in the opponent's suit. If partner bids either 3 Hearts or 3 Spades you will raise to 4. If he bids 3 No Trump, you will accept that contract.

With unbalanced hands

Although the 2 Club convention may at times be used with unbalanced hands, in most cases it should not affect normal jump responses in a suit.

    A. ♠ Q J 10 x x x   ♡ J x x x   ◇ x   ♣ K x

Bid 4 Spades. The jump to game in a major shows a good six-card or longer suit with fewer than 10 points in high cards. You have no wish to locate a possible 4-4 fit in Hearts with such a weak holding in that suit. There may be an excellent chance to shed Heart losers on partner's minor suit winners.

    B. ♠ x   ♡ Q 10 x x x x   ◇ Q x x   ♣ A x
    C. ♠ x   ♡ J 10 x x x x x   ◇ Q x x   ♣ A x

Bid 4 Hearts. Facing a No Trump opening, you should have no fear about losing too many trump tricks. Yet if partner has something like K x, he may have difficulty in establishing your suit in a No Trump contract.

When responder holds 10 points or more, a jump takeout will usually suggest an unbalanced hand, although it may sometimes be made on a balanced hand with slam ambitions.

    ♠ K x x   ♡ A Q 10 x x x   ◇ x   ♣ K J x

Bid 3 Hearts. You are certain of game and very much interested in slam if partner has control cards and better than a minimum.

♠ K x x   ♡ A x x   ◇ x   ♣ K J 10 x x x

Bid 3 Clubs. You have an excellent Club suit and ample high card values to insist upon a game.

After a jump takeout, the No Trump opener should not rebid in another suit *except as a cue bid*. Such a bid confirms partner's suit and expresses willingness to explore slam prospects, if such was partner's intention. With a minimum No Trump, opener should rebid 3 No Trump or raise responder's suit, as his hand may suggest. With better than a minimum *and trump support,* opener should cue-bid his cheapest ace. Consider the following hands opposite either of the examples shown above:

♠ Q J 10 x   ♡ K J x   ◇ A x x   ♣ A Q x

Opener should rebid 3 Diamonds over 3 Clubs; he should rebid 4 Clubs over 3 Hearts, confirming trump support and showing his cheapest ace. In no event should he show his aceless four-card Spade suit. (If partner were interested in locating a fit in spades, he would precede his jump bid with a Stayman 2 Club inquiry.)

♠ A x x   ♡ K J x   ◇ K Q x   ♣ A x x x

Opener should rebid Spades over either 3 Clubs or 3 Hearts.

♠ Q J 10 x   ♡ K J x   ◇ Q J x   ♣ A Q x

Opener should rebid 3 No Trump over either 3 Clubs or 3 Hearts. Although he has support for both suits, he has a minimum and no slam interest.

♠ A Q J x   ♡ K J x   ◇ K x x   ♣ Q x x

Opener should bid 3 No Trump over 3 Clubs, but should raise 3 Hearts to 4 because his weakness in both minors makes 3 No Trump possibly dangerous. Note that a simple raise of responder's skip bid is not a slam invitation, nor does it show more than minimum values.

Rebids by opening No Trump bidder

The opening No Trump bidder should bear in mind that his opening call almost fully describes his hand. Responder therefore knows within 2 points what opener has when he bids 1, 2, or 3 No Trump. Therefore a No Trump bidder should not subsequently take drastic action unless invited to do so by responder.

In fact, there are several situations in which it is incumbent upon the opener to pass:

1. When responder bids 3 No Trump.
2. When responder bids 4 Hearts or 4 Spades.
3. When responder raises to 2 No Trump and opener has just 16 points.
4. When responder bids 2 Diamonds, 2 Hearts or 2 Spades and opener has 16 or 17 points. However, with 18 points and a good fit, opener may raise.

The 2 No Trump opening bid

An opening bid of 2 No Trump must not be confused with an opening bid of 2 Clubs. The 2 No Trump bid is *not* forcing. If responder has next to nothing, he is allowed to pass.

The requirements are:

1. The point count must be 21 or 22 in high cards.
2. The hand must be of balanced distribution.
3. All four suits must be protected.

Responses to 2 No Trump opening bids

With balanced hands

With fewer than 5 points, pass.

With 6 to 10 points, raise to 3 No Trump. You know there is no slam, since the most partner can have is 22 points (22 + 10 = 32).

With 11 points, raise to 4 No Trump. This is a quantitative raise in No Trump. Opener passes with 21 points, but bids a slam with 22 points (22 + 11 = 33).

With 12 to 14 points, bid 6 No Trump. You have at least 33 points if opener is minimum (21 + 12 = 33), and at most 36 if opener is maximum (22 + 14 = 36).

With 15 points, bid 5 No Trump. This is forcing to 6 No Trump and asks partner to bid 7 if he has a maximum.

With 16 points or more, you may bid 7 No Trump. No checking for Aces is necessary, since the opponents cannot have an ace if partner has bid correctly (21 + 16 = 37; the opponents have at most 3 points).

Why isn't a 2 No Trump opening bid forcing? Since the opening bid defines partner's hand within very narrow limits (a balanced hand of 21 to 22 points), responder knows that his side does not have game on those hands where he is very weak. An opening bid of 2 Clubs, however, is unlimited, and opener must be given the chance to describe his hand.

With unbalanced hands

Bid any good six-card major suit regardless of the high-card content of your hand. (See page 245 for a special method of responding to 2 No Trump with a weak six-card major suit: The Texas Transfer Convention. Also, see page 250: The Flint Convention).

If you are interested in locating a 4-4 major-suit fit, use the Stayman Convention (bid 3 Clubs).

The 2 No Trump rebid after a 2 Club opening

The requirements are:
1. The point count must be 23 or 24.
2. The hand must be of balanced distribution.
3. All four suits must be protected.

In this case, too, the 2 No Trump bid is not forcing. Should partner have responded to the 2 Club opening with 2 Diamonds, he can pass.

Responses to the "strong" 2 No Trump opening follow the same pattern as responding to the "junior" 2 No Trump opening bid. Since opener is 2 points stronger, simply deduct 2 points from the balanced hand requirements.

With unbalanced hands, too, the same principles apply. The Stayman Convention is still available to probe for a 4-4 major-suit fit. For example:

OPENER	RESPONDER
2 Clubs (a)	2 Diamonds (b)
2 No Trump (c)	3 Clubs (d)

(a) Artificial and forcing
(b) Negative response—fewer than 8 points
(c) 23 to 24 points, balanced distribution
(d) The Stayman Convention, asking opener to bid a four-card major if he has one. (Responder may use Stayman *only* if his initial response was 2 Diamonds.)

The 3 No Trump opening bid

The requirements are:
1. The point count must be 25, 26, or 27.

2. The hand must be of balanced distribution.

3. All four suits must be protected.

What should you bid with these hands?

1. ♠ Q J 10	♡ K x x	◇ A x x	♣ A K J x
2. ♠ K x x	♡ K Q x	◇ A x x	♣ A K J x
3. ♠ K x x	♡ A K x	◇ 10 9 x x	♣ A x x
4. ♠ A K J	♡ K Q x	◇ A J x	♣ K Q x x
5. ♠ A Q J x x	♡ A Q 10	◇ A J	♣ K J x
6. ♠ A K J	♡ K Q x	◇ A K J	♣ K Q J x

HAND 1. This is a maximum 1 No Trump bid. A balanced hand, containing 18 points.

HAND 2. This hand is too big for 1 No Trump. It contains 20 points and should be opened with 1 Club with the intention of jumping to 2 No Trump if partner responds with a one-over-one.

HAND 3. This hand should be opened with 1 Club. Though it has the proper distribution and has three suits protected, it contains only 14 points.

HAND 4. This balanced hand, with all suits protected and 23 points, should be opened with 2 Clubs, planning to rebid 2 No Trump.

HAND 5. Open 2 No Trump. The hand contains 22 points in high cards with four suits well protected. Possession of a five-card major suit does not bar an opening No Trump bid.

HAND 6. Open 3 No Trump. This is a maximum, containing 27 points. Hands that are any stronger than this should be opened either with a 2 bid or with an opening bid of 4 No Trump, which announces a holding of 28 or 29 points and has no relationship to the Blackwood Convention.

Responses to 3 No Trump opening bids

Bear in mind that opener has 25, 26, or 27 points. Try to ascertain whether your partnership has enough assets to reach 33 for a small slam or 37 for a grand slam.

With 7 points and no five-card suit bid 4 No Trump.

With 8 or 9 points bid 6 No Trump. Your team will have at least 33 and at most 36.

With 10 or 11 points bid 5 No Trump. Partner should bid 7 with a maximum opening. Bidding 5 No Trump is stronger than a direct leap to 6 No Trump.

With 12 points bid 7 No Trump. No checking for Aces is necessary. The opposition cannot have one, since partner has at least 25 points and your total of 37 is assured.

NO TRUMP BIDDING QUIZ

You are the dealer. What would you open with each of the following hands?

1. ♠ A Q x x x
   ♡ Q x
   ◇ Q 10 x
   ♣ A K x

2. ♠ K J x
   ♡ A Q
   ◇ K Q 10 x x
   ♣ Q x x

3. ♠ A J x
   ♡ A 10 x
   ◇ A J 10 x
   ♣ A 10 x

4. ♠ K J x x
   ♡ A Q 10 x
   ◇ A 10
   ♣ Q 10 x

5. ♠ Q x x
   ♡ Q x x
   ◇ Q x
   ♣ A K Q J x

6. ♠ x x
   ♡ A K x x
   ◇ A J 10 x
   ♣ A 10 x

Your partner opens with a bid of 1 No Trump and you hold each of the following hands. What is your call?

7. ♠ J x
   ♡ A Q x x x
   ◇ x x x
   ♣ 10 9 x

8. ♠ J 10 x
   ♡ A K 10 9 x
   ◇ J 10 x x
   ♣ x

9. ♠ x x
   ♡ x x x
   ◇ J x x
   ♣ K J x x x

10. ♠ J x x x
    ♡ Q x x x
    ◇ x
    ♣ A J x x

11. ♠ 10 8 x x x x
    ♡ x
    ◇ 10 x x
    ♣ x x x

12. ♠ A K Q x x
    ♡ x x x
    ◇ J 10 x
    ♣ J 9

On the following hands you open 1 No Trump and your partner responds 2 Clubs (conventional). What is your rebid?

13. ♠ Q x x x
    ♡ K 10 x
    ◇ A K x
    ♣ A x x

14. ♠ Q J x
    ♡ A x x
    ◇ A x
    ♣ A Q 10 x x

15. ♠ K Q 10 x
    ♡ A J x x
    ◇ K x
    ♣ Q J x

16. ♠ Q 10 x x x
    ♡ K Q x
    ◇ A x
    ♣ A Q x

On the following hands your partner opens with 1 No Trump and the next player overcalls with 2 Hearts. What is your action?

17. ♠ A J x x x
    ♡ x x x
    ◇ x x x
    ♣ K 10

18. ♠ Q J
    ♡ 10 x x x
    ◇ 10 8 x x
    ♣ K J x

19. ♠ A J x
    ♡ Q 10 x
    ◇ K J 9 x
    ♣ A 10 9

ANSWERS TO NO TRUMP BIDDING QUIZ

1. One Spade.

The writer is entirely willing, on occasion, to open No Trump with a rebiddable major suit, or with a holding as weak as Q x in a suit. The combination of the circumstances, however, prejudices him in favor of a suit opening with this hand.

2. One No Trump.

In view of the plentiful tenace holdings, and in particular the A Q of Hearts, it is desirable to protect them by opening 1 No Trump despite the presence of a rebiddable suit.

3. One Diamond.

This hand is distinctly too strong for 1 No Trump. It should be opened 1 Diamond, with the intention to treat it as a 19-point hand by jumping in No Trump on the next round.

4. One No Trump.

With two biddable major suits it is sometimes desirable to open with one of them instead of opening at No Trump. In this instance, 1 No Trump is preferred because the hand contains several tenace combinations.

5. One No Trump.

The presence of several unsupported Queens is a factor that always predisposes this writer in favor of bidding No Trump. Over the years, this has proved a satisfactory policy.

6. One Diamond.

With a small doubleton and a plethora of quick tricks, this hand appears generally more suitable for a trump contract than for No Trump.

7. Two No Trump.

Your partner's maximum is 18 points, and when a five-card suit is held the chances for game are reasonable with 25 points. It would be inexpedient to bid Hearts, since it is probable that you can win no more tricks at a Heart contract than you partner can win at a No Trump contract.

8. Three Hearts.

When the responding hand includes a singleton, it is advisable to explore for game at a major-suit contract rather than to raise No Trump. Note that the jump to 3 Hearts is better than a conventional bid of 2 Clubs, since it indicates the strong five-card suit.

9. Pass.

The hand might play better at a Club contract than at 1 No Trump, but a bid of 2 Clubs would be conventional and you would have to rebid 3 Clubs in order to play the hand at your suit. Such a contract would be too high for comfort and therefore it is better to allow your partner to take his chances at 1 No Trump.

10. Two Clubs.

This is a conventional inquiry for a four-card major suit. If partner obliges by bidding 2 Hearts or 2 Spades, you raise to game. If partner can only say 2 Diamonds, you indicate your point count by bidding 2 No Trump.

11. Two Spades.

Your hand would probably be quite useless at No Trump, and yet it figures to take several tricks at a Spade contract. Your partner is expected to pass 2 Spades unless he has strong support and a maximum hand.

12. Three No Trump.

Game at No Trump, with the opener's hand protected against the opening lead, is likely to be safer than game at Spades. A response of 3 in a major suit is actually more to be recommended when the suit is lacking in one or two of the top cards than when it is solid.

13. Two Spades.

Partner has asked for a biddable major suit and you are happy to oblige. The fact that your hand contains no semblance of a ruffing value does not enter into the matter, because your partner is the captain.

14. Two Diamonds.

You must rebid 2 Diamonds at this point since you have no biddable four-card major. It is not open to you to depart from the rails by rebidding 2 No Trump or 3 Clubs. Should your partner bid 2 Hearts or 2 Spades over 2 Diamonds, you intend to raise the suit.

15. Two Spades.

With two four-card majors, it is our practice to show the Spades first, with the intention to bid Hearts on the next round if Spades are not supported.

16. Two Spades.

There is no immediate method of showing a five-card major suit in response to the 2 Club convention: you simply show your suit as though it were a four-card suit. You may rebid it later in the auction if granted the opportunity, but to bid 3 Spades at this point could perplex partner sorely.

17. Two No Trump.

Your partner's 1 No Trump opening indicates 16 or 18 points, and there is therefore a chance for game if he is in the upper range. Accordingly, the idea of simply bidding 2 Spades is not altogether attractive, since such a bid might be construed as merely indicating a desire to contest the partial. The most accurate way of indicating your values is by bidding 2 No Trump, which also has the advantage of protecting your partner's Heart holding. If you were to become declarer at a Spade contract, a Heart opening through dummy could prove most unwelcome.

18. Double.

On this occasion the 2 Heart overcall is to be welcomed with the same enthusiasm as manna from heaven. Without it you would have had to be content with a part-score of 1 No Trump. In the actual case there is every expectation of gaining a sizable penalty. Because your partner is known to hold some cards in the heart suit, most likely including at least one honor, you have an excellent chance to score a trick with your 10-spot.

19. Four No Trump.

This time your hand is so strong that it is clear the opponent's 2 Heart overcall is based on a very long Heart suit and little or nothing else. You could, of course, double, but the ensuing penalty might not compensate you for missing a possible slam. The best course is to ignore the overcall and make a natural raise to 4 No Trump. Partner is expected either to pass—if he has a minimum hand—or to raise to 6 No Trump if he has a maximum.

4.

Rebids by opener

PROGRESS is seldom uniform and as the frontiers of knowledge are pushed rapidly back in one sector, it will be found that a process of consolidation takes place elsewhere. The subject of the opener's rebid was examined in considerable depth in the previous version of this work and the methods put forward have proved satisfactory in practice. In view of the general competitiveness of modern bidding the writer has judged it expedient to add a new section (The Rebid in Competition) devoted to the situations that arise when opponents have entered the auction, but in other respects it has not been found necessary to change the established order of things.

My views concerning the significance of the opener's rebid are, perhaps, already known to the reader. It is on record that, if coerced into taking a position, I would nominate this as the most important of the bids that go to make up a normal constructive sequence. Opener does not pretend to give a clear picture of the strength of his hand, or its type, with an opening bid of 1 in a suit. Such a bid may be made on as few as 13 points or as many as 22 or 23 in some cases. It is at his second turn that the opener is given the opportunity to bring the picture more sharply into focus.

The second bid will usually announce to which class of openings the particular hand belongs. Roughly speaking, the opener's hand will fall within four classifications:

A. *The Minimum Range.*

B. *The Good Hand.* This is just above minimum range.

C. *The Very Good Hand.* This is the type of hand on which opener makes a jump rebid. He wishes to reach game unless partner has made a shaded response.

D. *The Rock Crusher.* This hand is just below a 2 bid in strength, and now that partner has responded, you will insist upon reaching game willy-nilly.

Let us examine his appropriate form of action in each case.

A. *The Minimum Range.* This covers hands of the value of 13, 14, and 15 points, but may sometimes include 16 point hands.

With hands of this strength, if opener does not have the urge to bid again, he should not do so, unless his partner's response was forcing. If partner offers a single raise, naturally he should pass. If partner responds 1 No Trump to a minor-suit opening opener should not bid again, unless his hand is unsuitable for No Trump play.

Where responder names a new suit, of course, opener must speak again, but he should do so at the lowest convenient level. How does opener indicate that his hand is in the minimum range? He may do so in several ways:

1. By a rebid of 1 No Trump (not 2 No Trump).

2. By a simple rebid of his own suit.

3. Where he has support for partner's major-suit take-out, he may give a single raise with hands in this class, if it is the most convenient bid.

B. *The Good Hand.* This includes hands of the value of 16, 17, and 18 points, but may sometimes include 19-point hands. On this type of holding, opener should make a constructive rebid of some kind. He should avoid making any rebid which will induce partner to believe that the hand is in the minimum range. In other words, he should not make a simple rebid of his own suit, he should not rebid 1 No Trump, he should not offer his partner a mere single raise.

C. *The Very Good Hand.* This covers hands of the value of 19, 20, and 21 points. Game will be there unless something is wrong with partner's response. A jump rebid of some kind is therefore indicated.

D. *The Rock Crusher.* This describes hands of the value of 22 points or more. On this type of hand, opener makes a jump-shift rebid in an effort to describe the strength of his hand.

Rebid by opener when partner has given a single raise

When you open with 1 of a suit, next hand passes, and partner raises to 2 of the same suit, you are not expected to feel greatly encouraged. Responder may have kept the bidding open on moderate values, ranging from 8 to 9 "dummy points." Unless you have considerably more than an opening bid, there will be no chance for game, and you should pass even though your hand contains another suit.

But if you have definite excess values, there is a chance for game. In such cases you test the nature of your partner's response. This you may do in one of several ways. The usual method is to bid 3 of your suit, which states, in effect, "Partner, I cannot tell how good your raise was. If you had a sketchy raise and were just keeping the bidding open for me, I'll expect you to pass, but if your raise was good, please go on to game. In other words, if your raise was based on 8 points, I wish you to pass, but if you had 9 I would like you to go on to 4." The quality of your trump support should decide close cases.

It is important for the opener to assess his values accurately when partner gives a single raise, before he decides whether to pass, to bid again, or to contract for game. When the responder raises the opening bid from 1 to 2, opener must revalue his hand if it contains a long trump suit. In addition to all the points he counted for high cards and distribution when he opened the hand, he must make the following adjustment:

Add 1 additional point for the fifth trump
Add 2 additional points for the sixth and each subsequent trump

After making this calculation, try to determine whether it is possible that the partnership has 26 points. If you find that the combined assets cannot reach this figure, by all means pass. In other words, if you had only 15 points, you know that the partnership cannot possibly have 26 when partner offers a single raise.

If you find that your hand upon revaluation is worth 18 points or more, then you may take a chance and contract for game, because partner has promised at least 7. But if you have less—let us say, 16 or 17 points—there may or may not be a game, depending upon how good partner's raise happened to be. In such a case you proceed to 3, asking him to go on if he had a representative raise.

Let us examine a few cases, in each of which you have opened with 1 Spade and partner has responded 2 Spades, both opponents passing.

♠ A K x x x   ♡ A x x   ◊ Q x x   ♣ x x

Pass. Your hand was originally worth 14 points, 13 in high cards and 1 for distribution. Now that Spades have been supported, you may add 1 point for the fifth Spade, giving your hand an adjusted value of 15 points. Even if partner has a maximum raise, you will not have the necessary 26 and should pass.

♠ A K 10 x x   ♡ A 10 x   ◊ K J x   ♣ x x

This hand had an original valuation of 16 points. Now that Spades have been supported, you add 1 point for the fifth Spade, bringing it up to 17 points. If partner had only 8, you do not wish to reach game, but if he had as many as 9, you would like to go on. Your proper procedure is to bid 3 Spades, and if partner has 9 points, he should carry on to 4.

♠ A J 9 x x x   ♡ A K   ◇ Q J 10   ♣ x x

This hand had an original valuation of 17 points, and now that Spades have been supported, you add 1 point for the fifth Spade and 2 points for the sixth Spade, bringing it up to an adjusted value of 20 points. Therefore, even if partner has only 8 points, you will have sufficient and should contract for 4 Spades.

Your rebid need not be in the same suit. You may test out partner's raise by showing another suit or by bidding 2 No Trump, depending on the type of your hand.

♠ x   ♡ A Q 10 9 x   ◇ A 10 x   ♣ A 10 9 x

You open with 1 Heart and your partner raises to 2. Your hand contains 15 high-card points and is valued at 17 for purposes of suit play. You cannot promise a game, but you should make a mild try to get there. You may bid 3 Clubs or Diamonds, hoping that partner will now be able to contract for game in Hearts on your display of additional strength. If he merely returns to 3 Hearts, you had better pass. That would mean that he had only a minimum raise of about 8 points, which would not be enough for game.

♠ A K Q 10 x   ♡ A J 10   ◇ Q 10 x   ♣ Q x

This time your hand contains 19 points in high cards. You open with 1 Spade and your partner raises to 2. Partner's hand contains at least 8 points. The suggested call is, therefore, 3 No Trump, asking partner to choose game in the denomination he considers best.

Opener can also make a "game try" in a suit in which he needs help. For example, suppose he holds:

♠ A K 10 x x   ♡ K x x   ◇ A 10 x x   ♣ x

This hand had an original valuation of 16 points. Responder's spade raise has improved its worth to 17 points. Whether or not the combined holding will make game is less likely to depend on whether responder holds 8 or 9 points than on where those points are. Therefore, opener bids the suit in which he needs help—in this case, 3 Diamonds. That asks responder to focus on his holding in Diamonds to determine his side's potential for making game.

Rebids by opener after a 1 No Trump response to a minor

When partner responds to your minor-suit opening bid by calling 1 No Trump, you must remember that he has a maximum of 10 high-card points and may have as little as 6. If it is not altogether likely that the partnership has 26 points, abandon hope of a No Trump game. To put it another way, if your hand was within the minimum range, game should not be contemplated after this response. If you have a balanced hand, do not rebid a five-card suit in this situation.

There are, generally speaking, three types of hands that belong to the No Trump family. They are distributed 4-3-3-3, 4-4-3-2, or 5-3-3-2. If your hand contains a singleton or two doubletons, you may look for an excuse to play in a suit, but even then it is not obligatory to do so. However, if your hand is unbalanced and not suited for No Trump, you may either rebid your suit or name some other suit. If your hand is within the qualification of what we have referred to as a good hand—in other words, above the minimum range—there may be a chance for game, depending upon the quality of partner's No Trump take-out. If you have 17 or 18 points, for example, you will be able to visualize the total of 26 if partner has a maximum No Trump response (in the vicinity of 9 points).* If you have 20 points yourself, then surely you proceed to 3 No Trump, for you know that partner has at least 6 points.

For example:

♠ K J x   ♡ x x   ◇ A K J x x   ♣ J x x

You open with 1 Diamond, partner responds with 1 No Trump. Pass, despite the fact that you have an excellent Diamond suit and a worthless doubleton in Hearts. You have a balanced hand which is suitable for play at 1 No Trump. You have only 13 high-card points, and even if partner has a near maximum, you will be far short of the number necessary for game.

♠ A K x x   ♡ 10 x x   ◇ A Q x x   ♣ x x

On the same sequence of bids you should pass. There is no hope for game and you have a balanced hand. *The best place to play an indifferent hand is 1 No Trump.*

♠ x x x   ♡ x x   ◇ A K x x   ♣ A Q J x

However, on this holding we advise a rebid of 2 Clubs to make allowance for those situations in which partner had a Club suit which

* Hands that count 17 or 18 normally should be opened with 1 No Trump, if the pattern is satisfactory, in preference to 1 of a suit.

he was unable to show at the level of 2. If you pass 1 No Trump and his hand was something like:

♠ x x   ♥ J 10 x   ♦ Q J x   ♣ K 10 x x x

you would be defeated in 1 No Trump, with a 3 Club contract on ice.

♠ x x x   ♥ A J x   ♦ A K x x x x   ♣ x

Bid 2 Diamonds. Although your hand is minimum in high cards, it is unsuitable for play at No Trump and your six-card minor suit should be rebid. Note that a rebid of your suit over partner's response of 1 No Trump invariably suggests a six-card suit, or a very strong five-card suit.

♠ K x   ♥ A Q x   ♦ A x x   ♣ A K 10 x x

Raise to 3 No Trump. You have 20 points in high cards and partner has at least 6. Note that this hand was too big to open with 1 No Trump and had to be opened with 1 of a suit.

Rebid by opener after take-out to 1 of a suit

When you open with 1 of a suit and partner responds with 1 of another suit, it is, of course, your duty to speak once more. It is at this point that you should clarify the nature of your opening bid, both as to type and as to strength. If your opening bid was of approximately minimum strength, this is the time to make the announcement. The message is conveyed to partner either by a rebid of 1 No Trump or by a rebid of 2 of your suit, whichever best describes your hand. Such a rebid sends the following message: "Partner, be on your guard. My opening may be an absolute minimum and in any case I have not much more than an opening bid. My hand ranges from 13 to 16 points."

♠ x x   ♥ A K J x x   ♦ K x x   ♣ K x x

You open with 1 Heart and partner responds with 1 Spade. Your hand contains 14 high-card points, which places it in the minimum range. Your proper rebid is 1 No Trump.

♠ x x   ♥ A K 10 x x x   ♦ A x x   ♣ x x

You open with 1 Heart and partner responds with 1 Spade. Again your hand is within the minimum range. It is worth 13 points, 11 in high cards and 1 for each doubleton, but it is of the suit type and is best described by a rebid of 2 Hearts.

These rebids are frequently referred to as "sign-offs," but the sign-off bid by the opener should not send a cold chill down his partner's back. Responder should not become obsessed by the notion that opener has a bad hand. He must not lose sight of the fact that partner did open the bidding, and the so-called sign-off merely announces that his hand ranges from 13 to 16 points.

♠ x x   ♡ A K J 10 x x   ◊ K x x   ♣ x x

You open with 1 Heart and partner responds 1 Spade. Your rebid is 2 Hearts. Partner now bids 2 No Trump, denoting a desire to go game. The suggested action by you at this time is a 3 Heart bid. This is a warning bid which says, "Partner, be very cautious, I still have my opening bid, but it was based on minimum high-card strength. I have bid my suit three times to show extra length but no additional high-card strength."

♠ A Q 10 x   ♡ x x   ◊ x x x   ♣ A Q x x

You open with 1 Club and partner responds with 1 Diamond. Your proper rebid is 1 Spade. *The naming of a second suit at the level of 1 requires no additional strength.*

♠ K J x x   ♡ x x   ◊ x   ♣ A K x x x x

You open with 1 Club and partner responds 1 Heart. Your proper rebid is 1 Spade. *The naming of a biddable four-card major suit at the level of 1 takes precedence over rebidding even a good six-card minor suit.*

♠ x x   ♡ A Q 10 9 x   ◊ K Q J 10   ♣ x x

You open with 1 Heart and partner responds 1 Spade. You have a minimum hand which is not suitable for No Trump, because of the two worthless doubletons, and apparently you should rebid 2 Hearts. However, since a 2 Diamond rebid is just as cheap and permits partner to return to 2 Hearts, it is the recommended action. This will be particularly helpful when partner is very short in Hearts and has some length in Diamonds. Partner must realize that this is the cheapest possible level at which you could have shown this suit.

When you make it impossible for partner to return to 2 of your first suit, you advertise a very good hand. For example:

♠ x x   ♡ A Q 10 x   ◊ A K J x x   ♣ A x

You open with 1 Diamond and partner responds with 1 Spade. Your rebid should be 2 Hearts. To be sure, this makes it impossible for partner to return to 2 Diamonds, but if he is obliged to return to 3 Diamonds, you are in no danger, for you have a very good hand. Partner should realize that you have great strength when you choose this sequence of bids. In order to justify this sequence of bids, commonly known as a "reverse," your hand should be worth at least 17 points, including high cards and distribution. That is to say, in any bid of this character, which catapults the partnership into a nine-trick contract, the opener should have what we refer to as a very good hand, and a very good hand is described as one whose value is at least 17 points.

Since you are showing a hand worth about 18 points and partner has enough for a response, a "reverse" puts your combined holding in the game zone. Therefore, the sequence is forcing to at least 3 of opener's first-bid suit.

Raising partner's one-over-one response to 2

When your partner responds with 1 of a major suit for which you have some support, you must decide whether or not to offer partner an immediate raise. This raise by you does not require any great excess values, for it is important to announce the ability to play at partner's major suit early in the hand. Wherever your hand contains four of partner's trumps, or where it contains a singleton and normal trump support* for partner, you may raise once even with a minimum hand. This is to make sure that the deal is played at the proper contract if partner has a weak hand and does not carry on. Where you have normal trump support for your partner and even slight additional values, you may give a single raise at once. Such a raise normally describes hands which are worth 14, 15, or 16 points in support of partner.

Even though you are the opener, when partner names a suit which you are about to raise, you start from scratch and value your hand as though you were the dummy for your partner's bid. Let us examine a few cases:

♠ A x x   ♡ x x   ◊ A K J x x   ♣ x x x

You open with 1 Diamond and partner responds with 1 Spade. A

---

* At least three trumps, usually with a high honor.

raise to 2 Spades is not recommended, because you have a minimum hand. Merely rebid to 2 Diamonds. However, if you hold:

♠ A x x   ♡ x   ◊ A K J x x   ♣ x x x x

a raise to 2 Spades is indicated. Observe that you have a singleton, which makes the Spade raise desirable. Furthermore, your hand is now worth 14 points in support of Spades and is therefore regarded as slightly above minimum.

♠ A x x x   ♡ x x   ◊ A K J x   ♣ x x x

In this case you have no additional honor strength, but the possession of four Spades makes it best to give an immediate raise, even though your hand is worth only 13 points in support of Spades.

Raising partner's response from 1 to 3

When the opening bidder raises his partner's take-out from 1 to 3, he describes a hand with substantial values in excess of the opening. Such hands should be worth, in support of partner's suit, 17, 18, or 19 points. To illustrate:

♠ A J 10 x   ♡ A K J x   ◊ x   ♣ Q J x x

You open with 1 Club and partner responds with 1 Spade. You have more than adequate trump support, and 19 points in support of Spades. You are therefore justified in jumping to 3 Spades.

This is not a forcing bid. Partner is permitted to pass if his 1 Spade response was of a shaded nature. If, for example, partner holds

♠ Q x x x x   ♡ x x x   ◊ Q J x   ♣ x x

he need not go on.

Raising partner's response from 1 to 4

A raise from 1 to 4 by the opening bidder is stronger than the raise from 1 to 3. There is a logical reason for this. If opener jumps to 3 and responder has a very weak hand, he may not go on. If, however, the opener is strong enough to insist upon a game contract, he should assume the entire responsibility himself. This requires a little more than is needed to jump from 1 to 3.

In this case opener shows a hand that is worth 20 or 21 points in support of partner's suit:

♠ A J x x   ♡ x x   ◊ A K J x   ♣ A Q x

You open with 1 Diamond and partner responds with 1 Spade. Your hand is worth 20 points in support of Spades. You should therefore assume responsibility for a game contract by going to 4 Spades. Partner might have nothing but five Spades to the King and would still have a play for game, yet he certainly would not bid it if you jumped to only 3 Spades.

The jump rebid to 2 No Trump

This rebid by the opener describes a hand that is well-suited to No Trump play and one that contains 19 or 20 high-card points. This is a very important requirement to bear in mind. There is a tendency on the part of a great many players to jump to 2 No Trump whenever they hold slightly more than an opening bid. "Slightly more" is not sufficient. For example:

♠ J x ♡ K J x ◇ A K J x x ♣ A Q x

You open with 1 Diamond and partner responds with 1 Spade. You have a hand that is well suited to No Trump play and one that contains 19 high-card points. Your proper rebid is 2 No Trump. If partner's Spade response included 6 high-card points, he should go on to 3 No Trump. If, however, part of partner's points were made up of distribution and he has less than 6 high-card points, he may pass the 2 No Trump bid, which, of course, is not forcing.

♠ x x ♡ A x x ◇ A K x x ♣ A x x x

The opening bid has been 1 Diamond and the response 1 Spade. Some players commit the error of bidding 2 No Trump merely because they have more than a minimum opening. This is highly improper. This hand contains 15 high-card points, which places it, for rebid purposes, within the minimum range, and the proper rebid is 1 No Trump. Unless partner has 11 high-card points, there will be no game. And if partner has 11 high-card points, he will bid again even after the 1 No Trump rebid.

The jump rebid to 3 No Trump

It has been seen that when the opener's hand is suited for No Trump and contains 19 or 20 points in high cards, he should jump to 2 No Trump. When his hand contains slightly more than this— 21 or 22 points—he should take the full responsibility upon himself and contract for 3 No Trump after a one-over-one response. For example:

♠ x x   ♥ A Q 10   ♦ A K J x   ♣ A K 10 x

You open with 1 Diamond and partner responds with 1 Spade. Your hand contains 21 high-card points, and you should jump to 3 No Trump, for which you should have a good play even if partner has fewer than 6 high-card points. Remember that if you jump to 2 No Trump and partner has a more or less balanced hand with only 5 high-card points, he will not go on to 3.

The jump rebid in opener's suit

When the opening bidder has a good six-card (or longer) suit and a hand that will produce about seven tricks in the play, he may make a jump rebid to 3 of that suit, provided the hand contains at least some high-card strength in excess of the opening. Expressed in terms of point count, the opening bidder's hand should be worth 19 to 21 points in rebid valuation. Perhaps an explanatory note regarding "rebid valuation" is in order at this point. You will recall that after partner has supported your suit, you add 1 point for the fifth trump and 2 for the sixth and each subsequent trump. These additional points were added because it was presumed that after the raise the trump suit became self-sustaining. Where the opening bidder himself has a self-sustaining suit, he may, for practical purposes, treat it as though partner has supported it, simply because it requires no support. In those cases, therefore, where opener has a long and powerful suit in addition to his original valuation, including high cards and distribution, he may add 1 point for the fifth trump, 2 points for the sixth, and so on, to determine the rebid value of the hand.

Let us see how this works with an example:

♠ x x   ♥ A K 10 9 x x   ♦ K x   ♣ A Q x

You open with 1 Heart and partner responds 1 Spade. The proper rebid is 3 Hearts. Your hand had an original valuation of 18 points, 16 in high cards and 1 for each doubleton. However, for rebid purposes, it is reasonable to consider the Heart suit self-sustaining, for you need no support in Hearts from partner. Therefore, in addition to your original valuation, you add 1 point for the fifth Heart and 2 for the sixth Heart, giving the hand a rebid valuation of 21 points.

Expressed in other terms, this hand is worth about seven playing tricks and justifies the jump rebid.

Note that the jump rebid by opener in his own suit is not forcing where the response has been made at the level of one. If partner has made his Spade response on a hand of minimum values, which may not be helpful at the Heart contract, he is at perfect liberty to pass. A jump rebid in your own suit should not be made if your only excuse for doing so is the length of your suit. Remember that the jump rebid promises something additional in the way of high-card strength. If your hand contains a rebid valuation of 19, you will be within the required limits. Another way to state the requirement for a jump rebid in your own suit is: 16 to 19 original points with a solid five-card suit or a good six-card suit.

The jump rebid to game

Suppose you hold:

♠ x   ♡ A K Q J 10 x   ◇ A x x   ♣ K Q x

You open with 1 Heart and partner responds 1 Spade. No matter how weak a response partner has made, you should be unwilling to play this hand for less than game, and your proper rebid is 4 Hearts—not 3 Hearts, which partner might pass.

There are some players who raise an objection to such a rebid on the grounds that "it sounds too much like a shut-out." Let me hasten to point out that this department takes a dim view of the expression "shut-out." It is almost on the *verboten* list. When any player opens with 1 of a suit, he announces certain high-card values. When he subsequently jumps, he announces additional high-card values, or, what is more to the point, a great amount of playing strength. If the opening bidder jumps from 1 to 4, that is a stronger bid than a jump from 1 to 3. This is in sharp contrast with the technique of the responder. Where the responder jumps from 1 to 3, that shows high cards and distribution. But where the responder jumps from 1 to 4, it shows distribution but not high cards.

IN A NUTSHELL

A jump rebid to 4 of his suit (game) by the opening bidder denotes a very strong hand (about 8½ or 9 winners—22 rebid points). It is stronger than a jump rebid to 3, which is not forcing and shows 7 to 8 winners (19 to 21 rebid points).

There is no such thing as a "shut-out" rebid.

The jump shift by opening bidder

When the opening bidder wishes to insist upon a game he may do so in one of two ways: by jumping to game on the next round, as we have seen above; or by making a jump *in a new suit*. This, incidentally, is the only way the opening bidder can force the responder to speak again. A responder may pass if he hears a new suit mentioned. A responder may pass if he hears a jump in the same suit, or a jump in No Trump. But he has no option if partner jumps in a new suit. For example:

♠ K x x x   ♡ A K J x x   ◇ A K J   ♣ x

You open 1 Heart and partner responds 1 Spade. This hand has great possibilities. A jump bid of 3 Spades would be grossly inadequate. Partner might have nothing more than five Spades to the Queen Jack, in which case he would pass and a game in Spades might be missed.

A jump to 4 Spades might be acceptable, but even that does not do complete justice to your holding. This hand is worth 23 points in support of Spades, and partner will not need very much to produce a slam.

The recommended rebid is 3 Diamonds, a jump shift. *This forces partner to speak again, regardless of the nature of his hand.* It is your intention to contract for game in Spades on the next round. If partner has a good hand, the obligation to carry on (to a slam) will then be his. The jump shift by the opening bidder is made on hands that are worth, at the very least, 21 points.

Another case:

♠ J x   ♡ A K Q 10 x   ◇ x   ♣ A K Q x x

You open with 1 Heart and partner responds with 1 Spade. Surely you are unwilling to play this hand for less than a game, but you are not quite certain as to the exact contract. In order to be sure that partner does not pass and that game will eventually be reached, you must jump in a new suit, and your proper rebid is 3 Clubs.

Rebid by opener after take-out to 2 of a suit

Thanks to our modern five-card-major method and its concomitant hefty two-over-one response, opener's rebid follows completely natural lines.

The principal changes from our former methods are:

A rebid of 2 No Trump no longer promises extra strength. It shows

13 to 16 points, balanced distribution, and protection for all unbid suits. With 17 points you should jump to 3 No Trump.

A raise of partner's suit to the 3-level no longer requires additional strength. It shows 13 to 16 points and at least three trumps headed by an honor.

A new suit at the 3-level still *does* show extra strength, at least 17 points.

Here are some examples:

♠ Q J x   ♡ A J 10 x x   ◇ A x x   ♣ J x

You open 1 Heart and partner responds 2 Clubs. Rebid 2 No Trump. This bid may now be made on a minimum hand.

♠ x x   ♡ A K x x x   ◇ Q x x   ♣ K J x

You open 1 Heart and partner responds 2 Clubs. Raise to 3 Clubs. This raise can be made on a minimum hand as long as your three-card support contains an honor.

♠ A Q x   ♡ A Q J x x   ◇ K J x   ♣ x x

You open 1 Heart and again partner responds 2 Clubs. This hand is stronger than minimum, so you will prefer a rebid of 3 No Trump.

♠ A Q x x x   ♡ x x   ◇ A K 10 x   ♣ x x

You open 1 Spade and partner's response is 2 Hearts. You have no alternative but to rebid 2 Spades; responder should make some allowance for the fact that you may have been forced to rebid a five-card suit.

♠ A Q x x x   ♡ x x   ◇ A K 10 x   ♣ A x

You open 1 Spade and again partner responds 2 Hearts. This time you are strong enough to show your second suit at the 3-level. Rebid 3 Diamonds.

Choice between rebidding your own suit and raising partner's suit

The opener is frequently faced with the question: "Shall I rebid my suit or support my partner?" He may resolve the doubt by answering the following question: "What impression do I wish to make upon my partner: do I wish to appear aggressive or do I prefer to seem mild-mannered?"

If the opener wishes to display additional values, he should raise his partner. If, however, his hand is of the near minimum type, he should prefer to rebid his own suit as a mild warning. To illustrate:

♠ A K 10 x x x   ♡ K x x   ◇ Q x   ♣ x x

♠ A K J x x x   ♡ Q J x   ◇ K x   ♣ x x

You open with 1 Spade and partner responds 2 Hearts. *With No. 1* your proper rebid is 2 Spades. You have an absolute minimum hand, and though you have normal trump support, your hand is not worth 14 points in support of Hearts. The safer procedure is to rebid your Spades to definitely identify your hand as being in the minimum range. But *with No. 2,* even though your Spades are somewhat stronger, they should not be rebid. You have adequate trump support for Hearts and distinctly more than a minimum hand, so that the major suit raise should be given at once.

Another form of this problem is presented when the opener has the choice of rebidding another suit or raising his partner. This is frequently a delicate question. Let us examine a few cases:

♠ K J x x   ♡ K J x x   ◇ x x   ♣ A Q x

You open with 1 Club and partner responds with 1 Heart. You have a choice of bidding 1 Space or supporting your partner with 2 Hearts. Which is preferable? The hand is of moderate strength, and it would be doubtful strategy to bid both your suits and also support Hearts. Your partner would expect more strength. It is better, therefore, to raise to 2 Hearts, after which you may feel that you have done your full duty on the hand, which is worth only 15 points in support of Hearts. However, if you had slightly more strength, as with:

♠ A Q x x   ♡ K Q x   ◇ x x   ♣ A Q x x

a mere raise to 2 Hearts would not do justice to the hand. It is worth 18 points in support of Hearts, but inasmuch as you lack four trumps, the jump to 3 is not acceptable, and you are 1 point short for a jump to 2 No Trump. It is better tactics, therefore, to rebid 1 Spade, with the hope that partner will bid again (which he probably will do), after which you will also support Hearts. By naming two suits and supporting partner's suit, you will have given an adequate description of your hand.

When your partner's suit is a minor suit, it is not nearly so important to support it. For example, you hold:

♠ A J x x   ♡ x   ◇ J x x x   ♣ A K x x

You open with 1 Club; partner responds with 1 Diamond. You may raise the Diamonds, if you choose, or you may show your four-card major. The latter bid is far preferable. If over 1 Spade partner bids 1 No Trump, you intend to bid 2 Diamonds. If over 1 Spade partner bids 2 Diamonds, you intend to raise to 3 Diamonds, and partner will realize that you are short in Hearts.

Raising minor-suit take-outs

When the responder takes out into 2 Clubs or 2 Diamonds, the opener may find himself in possession of such good support for his partner that he is tempted to raise to 4 of that suit. In many cases this impulse should be suppressed in favor of a single raise, to allow partner the opportunity to bid 3 No Trump should he desire to do so. Eleven-trick game contracts should be avoided if there is a reasonable change to bring in nine tricks at No Trump.

Suppose you open with 1 Heart and partner responds with 2 Diamonds.

♠ Q x   ♡ A Q J x x   ◇ A Q J x   ♣ K x

A jump to 4 Diamonds is not recommended. A raise to 3 affords partner the opportunity to try for 3 No Trump.

It is not as desirable to raise a minor suit as to show other important features. For positional reasons you may elect to bid No Trump, concealing your support for partner's minor, as in this case:

♠ K x   ♡ A K x x x   ◇ Q 9 x x   ♣ K x

Assume that you have opened with 1 Heart and partner responds 2 Diamonds. Your rebid should be 2 No Trump rather than 3 Diamonds.

Third-round rebid with a two-suiter

It was observed in the chapter on opening bids that when two five-card suits are held, the normal procedure is to open with the higher-ranking and show the lower-ranking suit on the next round if it is convenient to do so. When both suits have thus been shown and it becomes the opener's third time to bid, assuming that he must insist upon one of his own suits, the proper procedure is to rebid the lower-ranking suit in order to permit the return to his first suit at the same level. For example, as South you hold:

♠ A J x x x   ♡ K Q 9 x x   ◇ K x   ♣ x

The bidding has proceeded:

SOUTH	WEST	NORTH	EAST
1 Spade	Pass	2 Diamonds	Pass
2 Hearts	Pass	2 No Trump	Pass
?			

At this point you wish to elicit from partner a choice between Spades and Hearts, since you are not enthusiastic about No Trump. The rebid of 3 Spades would be improper, because it denies that the Hearts are five cards long. The correct bid is 3 Hearts. This permits partner to return to 3 Spades, to raise to 4 Hearts if he chooses, or to insist upon 3 No Trump if he must.

Rebids after forcing responses

When you have opened the bidding and your partner makes a jump response of any type—a double raise, a 2 No Trump response, or the more powerful jump shift—you can relax as far as game is concerned, but this does not make your choice of a rebid any less important.

Your guiding principle in rebidding over a forcing response should be this: Your rebid should show where, from your hand, you prefer that the hand should be played. For example:

♠ J x   ♡ x x   ◇ A K x x x   ♣ A J x x

You open with 1 Diamond, partner responds 2 No Trump. Bid 3 No Trump. You do not want to play the hand in either Diamonds or Clubs, because your hand is too weak to relish the eleven-trick contract necessary for game in a minor.

The rebid in competition

An overcall by either one of the opponents will sometimes exert a considerable influence on the choice of rebid to be made by the opening bidder. The opener should not necessarily feel that, in face of this challenge by the opponents, it is cowardly not to proceed as originally planned. Instead he should take a new look at his holdings and ask himself how best to portray them to his partner in the light of the latest developments. To be sure, he may frequently conclude that it is proper to make the same rebid as he originally intended, but occasionally some other course of action will suggest itself.

Different problems arise according to whether the opponent who overcalled is situated on the left of the opener or on the right.

1 When the left-hand opponent has overcalled

One other phenomenon that occurs in competitive auctions is that an overcall sometimes has the effect of placing the opener at a disadvantage when he has a strong hand but no guard in the opponents' suit:

♠ J 10 x　　♠ A x　　◇ A K Q　　♣ A J x x x

The bidding has proceeded:

SOUTH	WEST	NORTH	EAST
1 Club	1 Spade	2 Hearts	Pass
?			

In view of North's free bid of 2 Hearts, it may safely be assumed that the partnership assets amount to considerably more than 26 points, and that a game contract is to be reached. With no independent Spade stopper, however, South cannot venture to bid 3 No Trump, and he could not happily bid 3 Clubs, which could indicate a far weaker hand. A raise to either 3 Hearts or 4 Hearts is a possibility, but since South has only two trumps it is conceivable that a Heart contract might turn out to be inferior to 3 No Trump.

In this somewhat testing situation it is recommended that South should gird up his loins and bid 2 Spades, the opponent's suit. This is a forcing cue-bid and its effect is to apprise North that the show must go on until game is reached. Thus a cue-bid indicates that game-going values are present and at the same time ensures that all the possibilities of the hand can be explored.

It is possible that North may temporarily construe 2 Spades as a prelude to announcing big support for Hearts, but all the same his primary obligation at this point is to make a bid that describes the nature of his own hand. Thus, if North has a suitable Spade holding he should bid 2 No Trump over 2 Spades, enabling South to clarify his hand by raising to 3 No Trump. Lacking a Spade stopper, North may rebid his Hearts or show delayed support for Clubs, and in either case it is charitable to suppose that the most satisfactory final contract will eventually be attained.

A final observation concerns the competitive situation where the responding hand bids 1 No Trump over an overcall. The writer has noticed over the years that this particular response, which normally is distinctly limited in strength, is apt to induce a Pavlovian reaction in the opening bidder, who tends to assume that the possibility of reaching a game contract has now become remote. Whilst such a reaction may well be justified when the 1 No Trump bid is made in an uncontested auction, a distinct mental adjustment is called for when the responder has freely bid 1 No Trump in competition. Opener holds:

♠ J x   ♡ K 10 x   ◊ Q J x   ♣ A K J x x

The bidding has proceeded:

SOUTH	WEST	NORTH	EAST
1 Club	1 Spade	1 No Trump	Pass
?			

The opener is to remind himself that the response of 1 No Trump *in competition* indicates a holding of 10, 11, or 12 points. Game is by no means beyond the bounds of possibility, and opener should therefore raise to 2 No Trump.

2   When the right-hand opponent has overcalled

The big thing about an overcall made by the player on the right of the opening bidder is that the opener, as a result, becomes relieved of the solemn obligation to rebid his hand. This is because the responding hand automatically gains another chance to speak. To illustrate:

SOUTH	WEST	NORTH	EAST
1 Heart	Pass	1 Spade	2 Clubs
?			

Inasmuch as North's 1 Spade response could be based on as many as 17 or 18 points, South, unless careless of his personal safety, would not dream of passing up his rebid in an *uncontested* auction. The 2 Club bid by East changes the situation: South is not obligated to bid because the auction will still be open when the bidding reverts to North.

It follows that any bid the opener makes at this point is in the nature of a voluntary effort. Because of this, the myth has arisen that a free rebid by the opener cannot be made on a minimum or near-minimum hand, and that unless considerable extra values are present the opener should pass up his rebid. This appears somewhat akin to the suggestion that a straitjacket offers a suitable form of attire for a person who apprehends the possibility of being engaged in a bout of fisticuffs. It appears to this writer that, when the opponents contest the auction, it becomes necessary to describe one's hand with even more urgency than usual, rather than to pass up the opportunity for a bid. Let us take the bidding sequence above:

SOUTH	WEST	NORTH	EAST
1 Heart	Pass	1 Spade	2 Clubs
?			

South holds the following hands:

1. ♠ x x	♡ A Q 10 x x	◇ A K 10 x	♣ x x
2. ♠ Q 10 x	♡ A K 10 x x	◇ J x x	♣ A x
3. ♠ K x	♡ A J 10 x x x	◇ A x x	♣ x x

It cannot be denied that none of these hands contains appreciably more than the values normally associated with an opening bid, but in each case South has a perfectly sound rebid to make and he should make it. With the first hand it would strike this observer as illogical for South, having opened on the strength of two biddable suits, to conceal the Diamonds. With the second, to withhold the natural raise to 2 Spades would represent a form of denial amounting almost to masochism. With the last hand there is nothing to be gained by failing to stress the rebiddable quality of opener's Hearts. Note that each of these is the bid that would be made had East passed.

Just the same, a distinction is to be drawn between hands where the opener has something useful to say and hands where there is no additional information for him to convey at this point.

♠ A x x x x   ♡ Q x   ◇ K x x x   ♣ K Q

The bidding has proceeded:

SOUTH	WEST	NORTH	EAST
1 Spade	Pass	2 Clubs	2 Hearts

It is of course perfectly normal to open this hand with 1 Spade, the general intention being to bid 2 Diamonds over a response of 2 Clubs and to rebid 2 Spades if partner's initial response is 2 Hearts. At the same time it would be realistic to admit that, for rebid purposes, the Spade suit is not exactly mint specimen, and that in view of the way the bidding has progressed it is not altogether likely that the hand belongs in Diamonds. What you would really like to do with this hand is to say, "Partner, I admit to having an opening hand which includes a Spade suit of sorts, but please do not imagine that I possess the treasures of Araby." The intervening bid of 2 Hearts by East gives opener the chance to round out just that message by the simple expedient of passing.

Another group of situations that can present the opener with a rebid problem occurs when the responder has confessed abject weakness by refusing to keep the bidding open. In this extremity it may be remarked that although courage is an essential ingredient in the composition of a successful player, it is not to be confused with stubbornness.

You may recall the story of the headstrong cow who insisted upon her right of way against an oncoming freight train. After pausing awhile, the engineer at length plowed through and blasted the animal into eternity. An observer commented on the outstanding courage of the animal. "Great courage," came the reply, "but darn poor judgment."

When you open with 1 of a suit and partner fails to keep it alive, assume he has nothing, and do not carry on the fight unless you can virtually fulfill contract in your own hand.

You are South (vulnerable) and hold:

    ♠ A K 10 x x x   ♡ K x   ◇ x x   ♣ J x x

The bidding has proceeded:

SOUTH	WEST	NORTH	EAST
1 Spade	Pass	Pass	2 Hearts
?			

What should you do? It is foolhardy to contest the auction when you know your partner has nothing. You are not even close to fulfilling a 2 Spade contract unassisted. When I saw this hand played, the actual South stubbornly rebid 2 Spades, was doubled and set 800 points.

The complete hand:

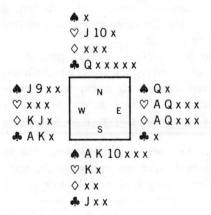

Similarly, as South you hold:

♠ A Q x x x   ♡ A Q x x   ◇ x x   ♣ A Q

The bidding has proceeded:

SOUTH	WEST	NORTH	EAST
1 Spade	Pass	Pass	2 Diamonds
?			

True, you have 18 high-card points, but since your partner has announced a worthless hand, you will have to lead everything out of your own hand and may wind up taking no more than four tricks. You cannot reasonably expect to go places and should give up the fight. Any further action by you will result in a loss of 800 to 1,100 points, depending upon developments. The complete hand:

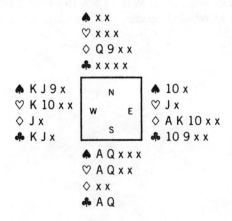

When, however, you hold a hand like this:

♠ A K x x x   ♥ A K J x x   ♦ x   ♣ x x

and the bidding has proceeded:

SOUTH	WEST	NORTH	EAST
1 Spade	Pass	Pass	2 Diamonds
?			

Here you should bid 2 Hearts, because even though partner has no high-card strength, he may have some length in Hearts, in which case even a game in Hearts might not be beyond hope, and a contract of eight tricks should not be risky.

Cue-bids: Finally, there is the situation where partner's response vastly improves your hand and the opponents have come into the auction.

(a) ♠ A Q x x x   ♥ A   ♦ K Q x x x   ♣ x x

The bidding has proceeded:

SOUTH	WEST	NORTH	EAST
1 Spade	Pass	2 Diamonds	2 Hearts

Bid 3 Hearts to tell partner that you have first-round control of Hearts, a fit with his Diamonds, and are interested in slam if he has a Club control and some sort of fit (it may be a singleton) in Spades.

On the same auction, your hand might be:

(b) ♠ A K Q J x x   ♥ A x   ♦ K x x   ♣ x x

Bid 3 Hearts. You plan to rebid Spades to show your solid suit, even if partner rebids his Diamonds. You might also make the same cue-bid with one fewer low Diamond and another low card in either Hearts or Clubs. The significant factors are your control of Hearts and your solidifying holding in partner's Diamond suit, assuring game and suggesting slam possibilities.

But if in the preceding example (a) your partner's response had been 2 Clubs, you would have to content yourself with a bid of 3 Diamonds, while with hand (b) you would jump to 4 Spades, leaving to partner any move toward slam.

In rare cases, you might cue-bid although holding a singleton in the opponent's suit. For example, suppose hand (a) above were:

♠ A K J x x   ♥ x   ♦ A J x x x   ♣ K Q

No other forcing bid is satisfactory with this hand.

The use of a cue-bid in such a situation will generally promise at least 18 points (some of which may be distributional) but will always promise no more probable losers than can be present to assure game.

––––––––––––

A handy summary

I have concluded that the reader should be enabled to find, within the space of a single chapter, all essential data concerning the nature and strength of each bid in the early rounds of a constructive auction. The succeeding pages of this chapter present my endeavor to satisfy that requirement. I can affirm that the task of preparing these pages has caused me to examine afresh the credentials of every Standard opening, rebid and response. The fact that the methods put forward have withstood this scrutiny, and that it has proved possible to present so complete a guide within the space of a few pages, has, I am gratified to say, reinforced my faith in both the essential soundness of the system and in its simplicity.

COMPLETE GUIDE TO BIDS, REBIDS AND RESPONSES

The qualifications for opening the bidding

Opening bid	Qualifications*
1 in a suit	13 to 21 points, biddable suit. An opening hand with no biddable suit may be opened with 1 Club. A 13-point hand with no suitable rebid may be passed.
1 No Trump	16 to 18 high card points, reasonably balanced, at least three suits protected.
2 Clubs (forcing to game, except when opener rebids in same suit after 2 Diamond response or rebids 2 No Trump)	With a good 5-card suit, 25 points. With a good 6-card suit, 23 points. With a good 7-card suit, 21 points. With a good secondary 5-card suit, 1 point less is needed. For game in a minor suit, 2 points more are needed.
2 No Trump	21 to 22 points, reasonably balanced, all four suits protected.
2 Diamonds, 2 Hearts, or 2 Spades 2 Clubs and 2 No Trumps are strong bids. 2 Diamonds, 2 Hearts and 2 Spades are weak.	6 to 12 points, good 6-card suit.
3 in a suit	*Vulnerable:* Opener expects to make seven tricks in his own hand. He has no more than 10 points in high cards. *Not vulnerable:* Opener expects to make six tricks. He has no more than 9 points in high cards.
3 No Trump	25 to 27 points, balanced hand, all four suits protected.
4 in a suit	*Vulnerable:* Opener expects to make eight tricks in his own hand. *Not vulnerable:* Opener expects to make seven tricks. Opener normally has not more than 10 points in high cards, but a bid of 4 Spades or 4 Hearts may be made on a better hand if partner has passed.
4 No Trump	28 or 29 points, balanced hand, all four suits protected.

* Unless high card points are specified, distributional points are counted in requirements.

The qualifications for responding

Opening bid	Response	Qualifications
1 in a suit	Pass	0 to 5 points.
	1-level response in a new suit (forcing)	6 to 18 points. For free response at least 9 points are needed.
	2-level response in a new suit (forcing)	12 to 18 points. (In competition these requirements may be relaxed slightly.)
1 of a major	1 No Trump (forcing)	6 to 12 points, no suit that can be bid at the 1-level. May contain support for opener's major.
1 of a minor	1 No trump	6 to 10 points, reasonably balanced, no suit that can be bid at the 1-level.
1 in a suit	2 No Trump	13 to 15 points, balanced hand, all unbid suits protected, no 4-card major suit that can be bid at the 1-level.
1 of a major	3 No Trump (forcing)	13 to 16 points, at least 4-card support.
1 of a minor	3 No Trump	16 to 18 points, balanced hand, 4-3-3-3 distribution, all unbid suits protected.
1 in a suit	Jump shift in a new suit (forcing)	18 points or more, self-sustaining suit or fit for partner's suit.
	RAISE OF OPENER'S SUIT	
	In raising partner's suit, the value of your hand is determined by "dummy" points. To your high-card count, add 1 point for a doubleton, 3 for a singleton, 5 for a void.	
1 of a major	Single raise	8–9 points, at least 3 trumps.
1 of a minor	Single raise	6 to 10 points, at least 4 trumps, no 4-card major.
1 of a major	Double (limit) raise	10 to 12 points, at least four trumps. Invitational to game.
1 of a minor	Double raise	10 to 12 points, usually five trumps, no 4-card major. Invitational.
	Raise to game	Strong trump support, distributional hand, no more than 9 points in high cards. (But a passed hand may raise to game with 13 or more dummy points.)
		(See refinements to dummy point count on page 63.)

The qualifications for responding *(cont'd)*

Opening bid	Response	Qualifications
1 No Trump	Pass	0 to 7 points.
	2 Diamonds,* 2 Hearts or 2 Spades	0 to 7 points, 6-card suit; or 5-card suit, unbalanced hand.
	2 No Trump	8 to 9 points, balanced hand (but may include long minor suit).
	3 No Trump	10 to 14 points, balanced hand (but may include long minor suit).
	4 No Trump (not forcing)	15 to 16 points, balanced hand.
	2 Clubs* (conventional and forcing)	8 points or more, no upper limit. At least one major of four or more cards.
	3 in a suit (forcing to game)	10 points or more, good 5-card suit.
	4 Spades or 4 Hearts	10 to 14 points, 6-card suit.
	Slam bid or slam exploratory bid	15 points or more.
2 Clubs (forcing)	2 Diamonds (conventional negative response)	0 to 7 points, any distribution. 2 Diamonds is also obligatory on any 8-point hand that does not contain a biddable 5-card suit.
	2 Hearts, 2 Spades, 3 Clubs, or 3 Diamonds	8 points or more, at least a 5-card suit with two honors. Forcing to game.
	2 No Trump	8 to 10 points, balanced hand. Forcing to game.
2 No Trump	Pass	0 to 4 points, balanced hand.
	3 Clubs (conventional and forcing to game)	5 points or more, no upper limit. At least one major suit of four or more cards.
	3 Diamonds, 3 Hearts or 3 Spades (forcing to game)	5 points or more, 5-card suit (but a 6-card major suit may be bid regardless of high-card content of the hand).

* See also 2 Club/2 Diamond Convention, Chapter 11

The qualifications for responding (cont'd)

Opening bid	Response	Qualifications
2 No Trump (cont'd)	3 No Trump	5 to 10 points, balanced hand.
	4 Hearts or 4 Spades	10 points maximum, 6-card suit (sign off; no interest in slam).
	4 No Trump (not forcing)	11 points, balanced hand.
	Slam bid or slam investigation	12 points up.
3 in a suit	3 No Trump or bid in a new suit	Game-going hand. Responder may not rely on opener to hold any points outside his long suit.
	Raise	*Vulnerable:* 3 probable tricks.
		Not vulnerable: 4 probable tricks.
		Responder may also raise with a slightly weaker hand as a tactical and preemptive measure.
4 in a suit	Raise or a new suit	Responses to four in a major are slam tries. Responses to four in a minor are game or slam tries. In either case responder may not rely on opener to hold any points outside his long suit.

Opener's rebid following a suit opening of 1

Responder's bid	Opener's rebid	Qualifications
New suit at 1 level	1 No Trump	13 to 15 points, balanced or nearly balanced hand.
	2 No Trump	19 or 20 points, protection in unbid suits.
	3 No Trump	21 or 22 points, protection in unbid suits.
	Rebid of 2 in original suit	13 to 16 points, 6 card suit, no other suit biddable at lower level.
	Rebid of 3 in original suit	Good 6-card suit, 19 to 21 points, in rebid valuation. (Add 1 point for fifth trump, 2 points for each subsequent trump.)
	Rebid of 4 in original (major) suit	Very good 6-card suit, 22 points up in rebid valuation.
	New suit at 1-level or lower-ranking suit at 2-level	13 to 16 points. (Rarely, as high as 18 points.)
	'Reverse' bid in a higher-ranking suit	Opener's hand must be worth at least 19 points at one of his suits.
	Jump shift in a new suit	21 points up.

RAISE OF RESPONDER'S SUIT
Revalue your hand as though you were dummy for your partner's bid

	Single raise	14 to 16 points, at least 3 trumps, including a high honor.
	Double raise	17 to 19 points, normally 4-card trump support.
	Raise to game	20 points up, at least 4-card trump support.

Opener's rebid following a suit opening of 1 (*cont'd*)

Responder's bid	Opener's rebid	Qualifications
New suit at 2 level (not a jump)	2 No Trump	13 to 16 points, protection in unbid suits.
	3 No Trump	17 points up, protection in unbid suits.
	Minimum bid in a new lower-ranking suit	13 points up, biddable suit.
	"Reverse" bid in a new higher-ranking suit; or a new suit at 3 level, not a jump (forcing)	Opener's hand must be worth at least 17 points at one of his suits.
	Jump shift in a new suit (game forcing)	21 points up.
	RAISE OF RESPONDER'S SUIT *Revalue your hand as though you were dummy for your partner's bid*	
	Single raise	13 to 16 points in support of responder's suit; at least three trumps headed by an honor. (Exception: where responder bids 2 Hearts over 1 Spade, opener may raise with 14 points.)
	Double raise (forcing if responder has bid a minor suit)	At least 19 points in support of responder's suit. (But opener may elect to raise only to 3 of a minor suit with a hand of this strength.)
1 No Trump after a minor suit opening	Pass	13 to 15 points, reasonably balanced.
	2 in a new suit, lower ranking	13 to 16 points, unbalanced.
	Rebid of 2 in original suit	Usually a 6-card suit.
	Raise to 2 No Trump	17 to 18 points, reasonably balanced.
	Jump bid in a new suit (forcing) or raise to 3 No Trump	19 points up.

Opener's rebid following a suit opening of 1 (*cont'd*)

Responder's bid	Opener's rebid	Qualifications
1 No Trump after a major suit opening	Consult Chapter 1.	
2 No Trump	Raise to 3 No Trump or exploratory bid in a suit	Maximum of 17 points.
	Slam bid or slam exploratory bid	18 points up.
3 No Trump after a minor suit opening suit opening	Pass	13 or 14 points, reasonably balanced.
	4 in a suit	13 or 14 points, unbalanced.
	Slam bid or slam exploratory bid	15 points.
Jump shift in a new suit (single jump, forcing to game)	Minimum rebid at No Trump	13 to 14 points, reasonably balanced.
	Jump to 3 No Trump (over a response at 2 level)	15 to 17 points.
	All other bids	13 points up.
Single raise of opener's suit	3 in same suit or exploratory bid in a new suit	16 to 18 points in rebid valuation. (Add 1 point to fifth trump, 2 points for each subsequent trump.)
	4 in same suit (major suit)	18 or more points in rebid valuation.
	2 No Trump	16 to 18 points in high cards.
	3 No Trump	19 or more points in high cards.
Double raise of opener's suit (limit raise)	4 in same suit or (if opening bid is in a minor suit) a mini-mum exploratory bid in a new suit	14 to 20 points.
	3 No Trump	14 to 20 points, protection in unbid suits.
	Slam bid or slam exploratory bid	21 points up.

Opener's rebid following a suit opening of 1 (cont'd)

Responder's bid	Opener's rebid	Qualifications
3 No Trump after a major suit opening	4 in the agreed suit Slam bid or slam exploratory bid	13 to 17 points. 18 points up.
Raise to 4 in opener's major suit	Pass Slam bid or slam exploratory bid	13 to 19 points. 20 points up, good controls. Opener may also try for slam on a slightly weaker hand if he has exceptionally good controls.

REBID QUIZ

You open with 1 Club and your partner bids 1 Heart. The opponents pass. What is your rebid with each of the following hands?

1. ♠ K Q 10
   ♡ x x
   ◇ K J x
   ♣ A 10 9 x x

2. ♠ x
   ♡ A x
   ◇ J x x x
   ♣ A Q 10 x x x

3. ♠ x
   ♡ A Q x
   ◇ K J 10 x
   ♣ A Q J 10 x

4. ♠ A J x
   ♡ A x x
   ◇ x x
   ♣ K Q 10 x x

5. ♠ K J x
   ♡ Q x
   ◇ J x
   ♣ A K Q J x x

6. ♠ A Q x
   ♡ 10 x
   ◇ A Q x
   ♣ A K x x x

You open with 1 Diamond and your partner responds 2 No Trump. What is your rebid with each of the following hands?

7. ♠ A x
   ♡ A x
   ◇ K 10 9 x x x
   ♣ 10 x x

8. ♠ K x
   ♡ K x
   ◇ A Q x x x x
   ♣ A 10 9

9. ♠ A 10 x
   ♡ 10 x
   ◇ A K J x
   ♣ A J 10 x

10. ♠ K x x x
    ♡ A x x
    ◇ A K Q J
    ♣ Q J

11. ♠ x x x
    ♡ A K x
    ◇ A J x x x
    ♣ A Q

12. ♠ 10 8 x x x
    ♡ x
    ◇ A Q J x x
    ♣ A x

You open with 1 Diamond and your partner jump-shifts to 2 Spades. What is your rebid with each of the following hands?

13. ♠ K 10
    ♡ A x
    ◇ A K 10 9 x
    ♣ J x x x

14. ♠ J x x
    ♡ Q J 9
    ◇ A x x x x
    ♣ A Q

15. ♠ Q 10
    ♡ K 10
    ◇ A K Q J 10 x x
    ♣ x x

You open with a Spade and your partner responds a forcing 1 No Trump. What is your rebid with each of the following hands?

16. ♠ J 10 x x x x
    ♡ K x
    ◇ A 10 x
    ♣ A x

17. ♠ Q J 10 x x x
    ♡ A x
    ◇ A Q x
    ♣ K x

18. ♠ A K 10 9 x
    ♡ A Q 10 x
    ◇ x
    ♣ A x x

19. ♠ K J 9 x x
    ♡ x
    ◇ A x x
    ♣ A 10 9 x

20. ♠ A K x x x x
    ♡ none
    ◇ A x x
    ♣ K J 10 x

21. ♠ A Q J x x
    ♡ x x
    ◇ K Q x
    ♣ A J x

You open with 1 Heart and your partner bids 2 Clubs. What is your rebid on each of the following hands?

22. ♠ A x
    ♡ A Q J 10 x x
    ◊ 10 x x
    ♣ K 10

23. ♠ Q 10 x
    ♡ A K Q x x
    ◊ K J x
    ♣ 10 x

24. ♠ A 10 9 x
    ♡ A Q J 10 x
    ◊ x
    ♣ K Q x

25. ♠ 10 9 x
    ♡ A K J x x
    ◊ x x
    ♣ A K x

26. ♠ A x
    ♡ A Q x x x
    ◊ Q 10 x
    ♣ A Q J

27. ♠ 10 x
    ♡ A K x x x
    ◊ A 10 x x
    ♣ Q x

ANSWERS TO REBID QUIZ

1. One No Trump.

This rebid tells partner that your hand is in the minimum range, and that you have a balanced distribution with protection in the unbid suits. 1 No trump is thus a much more suitable rebid than 2 Clubs, which would be the only alternative.

2. Two Clubs.

This rebid also shows a minimum hand, but it suggests an unbalanced distribution with a long Club suit. Partner isn't obligated to pass 2 Clubs, but at the same time he is advised that game is unlikely unless he himself has the equivalent of an opening bid.

3. Two Diamonds.

This is a "reverse" bid and shows considerable strength. It also indicates that your Clubs are longer than your Diamonds. Your hand is much too strong for a raise to 2 Hearts, and it would be inadvisable to jump to 3 Hearts with only three trumps. Naturally, you intend to support Hearts on the next round.

4. Two Hearts.

With no guard in Diamonds, 1 No Trump is ruled out. Thus the choice lies between 2 Clubs and 2 Hearts. Since you have a better than minimum hand, it is preferable to raise partner's suit rather than to rebid your own suit.

5. Three Clubs.

It would be unsound to rebid only 2 Clubs, or to bid some number of No Trump with no guard in Diamonds. A jump rebid in Clubs, which is highly encouraging but not forcing, is therefore the best solution.

6. Two No Trump.

This hand appears exceptionally well-suited to No Trump play and accordingly you jump to 2 No Trump to indicate 19 or 20 points.

7. Three No Trump.

Partner's bid of 2 No Trump is forcing and shows 13 to 15 points in a balanced hand. You may not pass, no matter how unprepossessing your hand may be. The most suitable bid you can make is 3 No Trump, which your partner will pass. There is no point in rebidding Diamonds, as you would not welcome being raised to 4 Diamonds.

8. Three Diamonds.

Your hand is worth 18 points and your partner may have 15. Slam is thus a strong probability if your partner's hand fits well with your own. Therefore you rebid the Diamond suit. If partner next says 3 No Trump, indicating that he is not enthusiastic for you to play at a high level in Diamonds, you should raise to 4 No Trump as a general slam try. But if he supports Diamonds, either by raising the suit or by cue-bidding some other suit, you should venture 6 Diamonds after a Blackwood inquiry for Aces.

9. Three Clubs.

The maximum possible high-card count in the combined hands is 32, which, without a long suit to run, may not be quite enough for slam at No Trump. Slam is likely to be a sound contract only if you can locate a 4–4 trump fit that will produce an extra trick. Therefore you bid 3 Clubs. If partner continues with 3 No Trump, you pass.

10. Six No Trump.

The combined values amount to at least 33 points, which is enough for slam at No Trump. There is no point in bidding Spades, since if partner had a suitable Spade holding he would no doubt have responded with 1 Spade initially.

11. Four No Trump.

This bid is to be interpreted as a natural raise of partner's No Trump call, not a Blackwood request for Aces. Partner is expected either to bid 6 No Trump or to pass, according to the strength of his hand.

12. Three Spades.

This exploratory bid is put forward to test the possibility that 4 Spades may be a safer contract than 3 No Trump. If partner's next bid is 3 No Trump, he should be allowed to play there.

13. Three Diamonds.

When responder makes a jump shift and opener has more than a minimum opening, slam is a near certainty. In the present case, opener should first show where the bulk of his strength lies in rebidding Diamonds. It would be inadvisable to bid 3 Clubs, since the suit is so weak that even if partner supported it you could not bid a Club slam with confidence.

14. Two No Trump.

The Diamond suit is not rebiddable over partner's jump shift. 3 Spades is a possibility to be considered, but 2 No Trump has the advantage of describing a minimum hand with values in the unbid suits.

15. Four Diamonds.

In this situation a jump rebid by opener in his own suit is understood to indicate a solid suit. This enables partner to take control of the bidding and place the declaration at either a small slam or a grand slam depending on his control of the side suits.

16. Two Spades.

Since the Spade suit may take too long to establish at No Trump, you do better to select the trump contract.

17. Three Spades.

With this 18-point hand there is still a chance of game despite partner's weak response of 1 No Trump. As you are lacking the top cards in Spades, it is preferable to jump to 3 Spades (non-forcing) rather than to raise to 2 No Trump, which would be the alternative method apprising partner of your values.

18. Three Hearts.

This is a forcing bid and is based on the hope of finding either a fit in Hearts or a delayed fit in Spades. Admittedly, 3 Hearts has a faint aura of death-or-glory, but you cannot afford to wait for absolute certainties in this game.

19. Two Clubs.

This is the best call because partner could easily hold four, five, or even six Clubs as part of his 1 No Trump response. The 2 Club rebid also indicates that you have five Spades and four Clubs. (With five of each you would have bid Clubs first.)

20. Three Clubs.

Although you have no very urgent desire to play the hand at a Club contract, 3 Clubs is the best move at this point. If partner's next bid is 3 Hearts, you should diagnose that most of his strength is likely to be wasted, and to allow for this possibility you can simply say 3 Spades, which he can pass. If partner does not bid 3 Hearts over 3 Clubs, the chances are that a game can be made in either Spades or Clubs.

21. Two No Trump.

With 17 points in high cards you raise to 2 No Trump, which is not forcing. If partner has an upper bracket 1 No Trump response (8 to 10 points) he either bids 3 No Trump or shows delayed support for Spades; if he has 6 or 7 points, he passes.

22. Three Hearts.

Your hand is worth 19 points in rebid valuation and therefore a jump rebid in your suit is justified. Since partner's response has been made at the level of 2, you are in a game-forcing situation, with slam a distinct possibility.

23. Two No Trump.

Quite clearly the Heart suit is rebiddable, but on balance it is more constructive to advise partner of your all-round strength by bidding 2 No Trump. In this sequence 2 No Trump shows 13 to 16 points in high cards.

24. Two Spades.

Your hand contains just about enough values for this reverse rebid in a higher-ranking suit, which indicates a strong hand. One reason for selecting this strong rebid is that you have an excellent fit in partner's Club suit, which you intend to support at your next turn.

25. Three Clubs.

You have a choice between rebidding 2 Hearts or raising Clubs. The Club raise is recommended on the grounds that your partner already knows you have five Hearts, but doesn't yet know that you have Clubs.

26. Three No Trump.

With 19 points in high cards you jump to game in No Trump to indicate that your hand is too strong for a rebid of 2 No Trump.

27. Two Diamonds.

The practice of rebidding 2 Hearts with this type of hand is not to be recommended. 2 Diamonds shows no greater strength than 2 Hearts and has the advantage of telling partner more about the nature of your hand.

5.　　　　　　　　　Rebids by responder

EARLIER it was pointed out that when the opener makes his rebid he is taking perhaps the most significant step in the auction. The opening bid of 1 in a suit covers a wide range of hands. It is the second bid that narrows down the range and places the hand in a specific category. This applies with equal force to the responder.

It is worthwhile at this point to remind ourselves of the type of thinking that the responder was recommended to employ when selecting his initial bid. The responding hand is to be considered as coming within one of the five categories enumerated below, and the general plan of campaign worked out accordingly. It will be found that there is some slight overlapping and that there are occasions when the responder may assign his hand to either one category or another, depending on his judgment.

6 to 10 points

Your hand is of the minimum class and you should make a mild response. If you have 6 or 7 points, do not bid again unless your partner forces you to. If you have 8 or 9 points, you should bid once more if partner makes a strong bid urging you to proceed.

11 to 13 points

You have a good hand. It is worth two bids. In order to be sure that you have the opportunity to make a second bid, you should make some response which partner is not permitted to pass. In other words, a temporizing bid. You must not give a single raise or bid a non-forcing 1 No Trump, either of which partner may pass.

13 to 16 points

You have a very good hand, the equivalent of an opening bid, facing an opening bid. You must therefore see to it that you reach game if a suitable contract is available. You are assured that the partnership has 26 points. Therefore you should go to game yourself or continue to make forcing responses (new suits) until you reach a satisfactory game contract.

16 to 18 points

You have a strong hand. You must show that you have more than just an opening bid. You may do this (provided your hand is of the right type) by occasionally jumping to 3 No Trump or by bidding a suit and then making a big jump the next round.

19 points and up

This hand will produce a slam unless partner has a minimum. You must therefore give the immediate slam signal by jumping in a new suit. Note that even if partner has only 13 points, your 19 will bring the total to 32, which is 1 point away from a slam.

Let us examine a few examples:

♠ x x   ♡ A K x x x   ◇ J x x   ♣ K J x

You are responder. Your partner opens with 1 Spade. You note that your hand is equal to an opening Heart bid (13 points). You therefore estimate that there is a probable game in the hand, and you start investigating to determine the best contract and temporarily bid 2 Hearts. Partner makes the mild rebid of 2 Spades. Since you estimate a game on this hand, you do not give up. You search for that game by bidding 2 No Trump, even though you do not have complete protection in Diamonds.

♠ J x x   ♡ A K x x x   ◇ x x   ♣ K J x

Your partner bids 1 Spade. As in the pevious case, you estimate there is game because you have the equivalent of an opening bid. Your hand is worth 13 points in support of Spades. However, you cannot properly jump to 3 Spades because you lack the necessary trump support for a jump bid, so you temporize by calling 2 Hearts. Partner now rebids 2 Spades, designating a hand of more or less minimum proportions, but you do know now that he has a good Spade suit for which three to the Jack is normal support. There is no further information which you require. You have found a suitable contract, Spades, and you know that you have the necessary values for game. You therefore bid a forcing 3 Spades on the way to a spade game.

♠ Q x x   ♡ A K x x x   ◇ A x   ♣ K x x

Your partner opens with 1 Spade. You respond 2 Hearts and partner rebids 2 Spades. You are now convinced that the best final contract will be Spades. Now for the question of how far you may go. Game is certain and slam is possible if partner has the top of his minimum-range opening. Yet even the 5-level may be unsafe if partner has an unsuitable hand. The perfect way to suggest slam without jeopardizing game is to jump to 4 Spades. A jump after a two over one response signifies mild slam aspirations.

$$\spadesuit \ Q \ x \ x \qquad \heartsuit \ A \ Q \ x \ x \qquad \diamondsuit \ K \ x \ x \qquad \clubsuit \ Q \ 10 \ x$$

Partner opens with 1 Club. You respond 1 Heart. Partner's rebid is 1 No Trump, which may indicate an absolute minimum. Your hand is the equivalent of an opening bid (13 points), and since you are facing an opening bid, it is your duty to contract for game. You have found a convenient contract, No Trump. Therefore bid 3 No Trump. It would be improper for you to raise to only 2 No Trump, because partner, if he has only 13 points, will not be able to carry on.

$$\spadesuit \ J \ x \ x \qquad \heartsuit \ A \ K \ x \ x \qquad \diamondsuit \ K \ x \ x \qquad \clubsuit \ x \ x \ x$$

Your partner opens with 1 Club. You respond with 1 Heart. Partner's rebid is 1 No Trump. While you are satisfied with No Trump you cannot promise game, because your hand is short of an opening bid in value (11 points). It is possible that the opening bidder has something to spare, in which case there should be game. Your proper procedure is to bid 2 No Trump; if partner has nothing to spare, he should pass. If he has a point or two in excess of his opening bid, he should go on to 3 No Trump.

$$\spadesuit \ x \ x \ x \qquad \heartsuit \ A \ x \ x \ x \ x \qquad \diamondsuit \ x \ x \qquad \clubsuit \ A \ x \ x$$

Partner opens with 1 Diamond. You respond with 1 Heart. Partner's rebid is 2 Diamonds. What should you do? You should be persuaded that there is no hope for game. Therefore you pass. When the opener makes a minimum rebid, responder should not act again with fewer than 11 points, but he may occasionally do so with 10. This hand is worth only 8 points at No Trump and 9 points at Hearts. It does not, therefore, qualify for further action.

$$\spadesuit \ Q \ J \ x \qquad \heartsuit \ A \ x \ x \ x \ x \qquad \diamondsuit \ x \ x \qquad \clubsuit \ A \ x \ x$$

Partner opens with 1 Diamond. You respond 1 Heart. Partner's rebid is 2 Diamonds. This hand is worth 11 points at No Trump. You must therefore make a second bid. There is still a chance that the partnership possesses 26 points. You therefore make one more move toward game by bidding 2 No Trump. If partner does not contract for game, you then retire gracefully.

When your hand is well suited to No Trump, which partner has bid, you must not waste time by giving him the needless information that you have a rebiddable suit. For example, you hold:

♠ x x   ♡ A x x   ◇ A K J x x   ♣ J x x

The bidding has proceeded:

NORTH	EAST	NORTH	WEST
1 Club	Pass	1 Diamond	Pass
1 No Trump	Pass	?	

It is proper for you to go straight to 3 No Trump, undeterred by your worthless doubleton in Spades. You may assume that partner has that suit protected. Your hand has the value of 13 points in high cards alone and is well suited to No Trump play. Remember, a rebid of 2 Diamonds would deny that your hand is suited for No Trump, and partner could be expected to pass.

Responder clarifies his raise

When the responding hand has given his partner a single raise in a *major* suit, he has given a good idea of his values (8 or 9 points). The opening bidder may determine which of these two values was given by inquiring in the form of another bid.

Let us assume that the bidding has proceeded:

OPENER	RESPONDER
1 Spade	2 Spades
3 Spades	?

If the responder has a top raise (9), he should bid again. If he has a bottom raise (8), he should pass.* For example, you are the responder with each of the following hands. The bidding has proceeded as above:

1. ♠ Q x x x   ♡ x x   ◇ A Q x x   ♣ x x x
2. ♠ K x x   ♡ x x x   ◇ A Q x   ♣ x x x x

With NO. 1 you should bid 4 Spades. You have a sound raise

---

* With a capable declarer as partner you may casually go on to game with 8 points if they are of the gilt-edged variety. It may then be that you are playing for game with only 25 points, which should not be looked upon as a shot in the dark.

containing 9 points. With NO. 2, you should contract for game. Your hand is worth 9 points, but inasmuch as it is evenly balanced you may try 3 No Trump. If partner does not find that suitable he may go on to 4 Spades.

When the opening bidder tests out his partner's raise by a rebid of 2 No Trump, the same general principle applies.

OPENER	RESPONDER
1 Spade	2 Spades
2 No Trump	?

Again you are the responder. If your hand is evenly balanced and most of your points consist of high-card values, you should raise to 3 No Trump. If you have four trumps and your raise is worth 9 or more points, you should take your partner to 4 Spades. If you don't have these requirements you should, as a rule, merely return to 3 of partner's suit. This bid does not amount to another raise. It is a preference and, to a certain extent, a sign-off. Its message is, "Partner, I had a raise of merely 7 or 8 points and I prefer Spades to No Trump."

With NO. 1 of the preceding examples, responder should leap from 2 No Trump to 4 Spades, announcing a good raise with 4 Trumps. With NO. 2, he should raise to 3 No Trump because he has 9 points in high cards alone.

When the responder has given a single raise in a *minor* suit and the opener rebids to 3 of the same suit, the responder should try for game at No Trump even with an unstopped suit if he has about 8 or 9 points in high cards. For example, you hold:

♠ K x   ♡ x x x   ◇ A x x x   ♣ Q x x x

Partner opens with 1 Diamond, which you raise to 2. Partner rebids 3 Diamonds. You should try for 3 No Trump.

When a single raise has been given in a major suit and opener names another suit, responder is forced to speak at least once more. For example:

OPENER	RESPONDER
1 Heart	2 Hearts
3 Clubs	?

The 3 Club bid is a one-round force. It says, in effect: "Partner, even though you did not show any particular strength, we might still have

enough for game. I need help in the suit I bid. Naturally, you must not pass 3 Clubs since we have agreed on Hearts as the trump suit. But if you think that your club holding will prove useful to me, bid 4 Hearts. If not, return quietly to 3 Hearts."

The worst holding responder can have in the suit in which opener makes a game try is three low cards. The most favorable holding is a high honor or shortness. For example, as responder you have:

♠ Q x x   ♡ K 10 x x x   ◇ x x x   ♣ J x

This hand is pretty close to a minimum raise of partner's 1 Heart opening bid, yet you should accept partner's game try of 3 Clubs by bidding 4 Hearts. However, let's suppose that opener make a game try of 3 Diamonds. Now your holding in the suit in which he needs help is the worst possible, so you should sign off with 3 Hearts.

The rebid of 2 No Trump by the opener after a single raise is not forcing. In rare cases, with only three trumps and a minimum but balanced hand, the responder should pass it.

Rebid by responder when opener gives a single raise

OPENER	RESPONDER
1 Heart	1 Spade
2 Spades	?

If the responder has a weak hand, he will naturally pass. If he has some slight unexpected strength, he may think in terms of game. He should rely upon the opener to have somewhat more than a minimum opening bid when he raises the response; that is, somewhere between 14 and 16. If responder's hand is worth 10 or more points, he may therefore feel that there is a possible game.

Suppose under the preceding bidding sequence you are the responder and hold:

1. ♠ A K J x x   ♡ x x x   ◇ J x x   ♣ x x
2. ♠ A K J x x   ♡ x x x   ◇ Q J x   ♣ x x
3. ♠ K J 9 x   ♡ x x   ◇ x x x   ♣ A Q 10 x

With NO. 1, you may bid 3 Spades. The hand is worth 11 points, 10 points originally, plus 1 for the fifth Spade after partner supports the suit. Since opener might have 15, you must not abandon hope for game.

With NO. 2, you have enough to go to 4 Spades. Your hand is worth 13 points, and even if partner has an absolute minimum of 13, you will have the necessary count for game.

With NO. 3, your hand is worth 11 points. You must not therefore abandon hope for game, since partner may have 15. You should bid again by calling 3 Clubs. This may induce partner to contract for a game in No Trump if he so chooses, and it may allow him to judge whether or not there is a game in Spades. If he merely returns to 3 Spades you should give up the ghost. However, he may be able to bid 4 Spades when you indicate that you have 11 points.

A somewhat similar case:

RESPONDER	OPENER
1 Spade	2 Hearts
3 Hearts	?

If your hand is worth 12 points, you should contract for game, for partner will surely have at least 14. Suppose you hold:

♠ x x   ♡ A J 9 x x x   ◇ K J x   ♣ x x

With this hand you should bid 4 Hearts. Your hand is worth 13 points, 11 originally and 2 for the extra Hearts.

When a raise is to 3 in a minor suit the same considerations apply, except that the responder must fix his gaze on a No Trump game rather than an eleven-trick game in the minor suit, if his hand is at all suitable for No Trump play. For example:

OPENER	RESPONDER
1 Spade	2 Clubs
3 Clubs	?

Responder should chance a bid of 3 No Trump on:

♠ 10 x   ♡ A x x   ◇ Q x x   ♣ A Q 10 x x

A return to opener's major suit by responder is forcing to game. For example:

OPENER	RESPONDER
1 Spade	2 Clubs
3 Clubs	3 Spades
?	

Responder cannot be trying to improve the contract with a weak hand. If he had that type of hand, he would either have raised to 2 Spades originally, or he would now pass 3 Clubs. Responder is trying for the best game, and might even be interested in slam. He might have:

♠ Q x x   ♡ A Q x   ◊ x   ♣ A J 10 x x x

Rebid by responder after he has responded 1 No Trump

OPENER	RESPONDER
1 Spade	1 No Trump
2 No Trump	?

In this sequence of bids, opener has shown a very good hand. Opener's rebid of 2 No Trump states to partner, "Partner, if your No Trump response was on the lower side (6 or 7), we will not have enough. But if it was on the upper side (8 or 9), I should like you to contract for 3 No Trump."

Occasionally, with a capable declarer as partner, you may choose to go on with 7, but we wish to hear no complaints if you do so and go down a trick. For example, in the above bidding sequence you as responder hold:

♠ x x   ♡ 10 x x   ◊ K Q x x   ♣ K x x x

You should accept partner's invitation and bid 3 No Trump. You have 8, and your 1 No Trump response was therefore on the upper side.

Rebid by responder when opener names another suit

Responder takes his choice

A frequently misunderstood obligation of the responder is the one that involves showing a preference between partner's two suits. The responder should not assume the role of captain of the team. His duties are more akin to those of an assistant, and he should indicate which of the two suits is preferable, according to his holdings.

A preference is sometimes indicated by passing, sometimes by returning to the first suit. In making a choice, length is far more important than high cards in the trump suit. As a rule, it is the duty of the responder to select the trump suit in which the partnership has the greater number.

For example, your partner has bid Spades and Hearts, and you have: ♠ x x x and ♡ A K. It is your solemn duty to take your partner back to Spades. You should never be heard to say, "But, partner, I have the two top Hearts." Those two top Hearts need not be trumps. They will be winners even with Spades as trumps. Spades will make the better trump suit, because if partner has a losing Heart he can use one of the little Spades to dispose of it.

When the same length is held in each of partner's suits, the practice is to prefer the suit he bid first. This has the advantage of giving partner one more chance, if that is your desire, and has the further advantage of returning to the suit in which the partnership will, more often than not, have the more trumps. For example:

♠ J x x   ♡ K x x   ◇ K x x x   ♣ x x x

Partner opens with 1 Spade. You respond 1 No Trump. Partner rebids 2 Hearts. You have no actual preference. The fact that you have a King in Hearts and only a Jack in Spades does not render Hearts any better for trumps. The two suits are exactly equal as far as you are concerned, but it would be a good practice to return to 2 Spades, because you have a very good delayed raise and would like to give your partner another chance. In fact, should the opener make one more move, you will contract for game.

♠ J x   ♡ 10 x x   ◇ x x x x   ♣ A J x x

Your partner opened with 1 Heart. You respond with 1 No Trump. Partner's rebid is 2 Spades. This is a strong bid and shows that partner has five Hearts and four Spades. You naturally prefer Hearts, and it is your duty to return to that suit even though it increases the contract.

The responder must never refuse to show a preference for the partnership's best trump suit just because he is frightened. Where a preference actually exists he must indicate it. Occasionally there will be no actual preference and the responder may use his own judgment. It is my practice not to show an immediate preference for partner's first suit with a worthless doubleton. In those cases it is my policy either to pass or make some other bid. For example:

♠ A J x x x   ♡ x x   ◇ x x   ♣ 10 x x x

Partner opens with 1 Heart and you respond with 1 Spade. Partner bids 2 Diamonds. Since opener has been unable to make a jump bid you may conclude that there is no possible hope for game. I do not recommend a return to 2 Hearts, although it is partner's first suit, for I am not interested in giving partner any further chance. As far as I'm concerned, I have no preference between Hearts and Diamonds. Being too weak to make another bid in spades, I pass. However, holding:

♠ A J x x x   ♡ x x x   ◇ x x x   ♣ x x

I would return to partner's first suit because, holding three trumps, I am at least mildly prepared to play it there.

Some additional cases:

A. ♠ x x x   ♡ K 10 9 x   ◇ A J x   ♣ x x x

Partner opens with 1 Club. You respond with 1 Heart. Partner bids 1 Spade. Note that this bid is not forcing upon you because you are not the opening bidder. If your first response was based on barely 6 points and you like your partner's second suit as much as you do the first, you may pass. Where, however, your partner's second suit is shown at the level of 1, you should make every effort to bid again if your hand is worth more than 6 points. In this case you have 8 points and should therefore respond to his 1 Spade bid in the cheapest possible way, which is 1 No Trump. Note that if the Ace of Diamonds were changed to the Queen, you would still have responded with 1 Heart, but you should pass 1 Spade.

B. ♠ x   ♡ x x x x   ◇ A J x x x   ♣ K Q x

Partner opens with 1 Spade. You respond 1 No Trump. Partner rebids 2 Spades. Proper strategy is to pass. This deal could easily be a misfit, and you should take no further action opposite a partner who has advertised a minimum-type opening.

C. ♠ K x x x   ♡ A x x   ◇ K x x   ♣ 10 x x

Partner opens with 1 Diamond. You respond with 1 Spade. Partner bids 2 Clubs. You could, if you wish, return to 2 Diamonds. This would be a mere preference, and since you have previously bid only at the level of 1, it would still promise no more than 6 points. Your hand has the value of 10 points, and they are gilt-edged points, for the King of Diamonds is a more impressive King than any other. You should exercise your judgment by making a second constructive bid of 2 No Trump.

Rebids that force responder

It is essential for the responder completely to understand the forcing principle. He must know the cases in which he is obliged to bid further, whether he likes it or not, and the cases in which he may pass if he chooses.

The responder is allowed a wider latitude than the opening bidder. In most cases he has made no commitment. His partner is the one with the strong hand, and responder may have been bidding just to give the opener another chance. Consequently, he is at liberty to drop the bidding at almost any time.

The fact that a responder hears his partner name a new suit does not force him to speak again. That obligation rests only on the shoulders of the opening bidder. However, where opener's rebid is a "reverse" bid, responder is required to keep the bidding open at least until the 3-level in opener's first-bid suit has been reached.

When a responder hears a jump in the same suit, that does not compel him to bid again, although such a jump is forcing on the opening bidder.

When a responder hears his partner jump in No Trump, he need not bid again if he does not choose to. Such a jump would be an unconditional obligation to rebid if he had been the opener.

But when a responder hears his partner jump in a new suit, then he has no right to opinions. He is absolutely bound to speak and to keep going until game is reached. A jump shift is a force to game whether it is made by opener or responder.

Let us examine a few cases. Suppose your partner has opened with 1 Diamond and you have responded with 1 Heart, holding:

♠ x x x x   ♥ K Q 10 x   ♦ x x   ♣ x x x

If your partner's rebid has been:

(A) 2 Clubs, you should pass. You prefer Clubs to Diamonds and have no interest in making any further bid. As responder you are not forced to speak again just because your partner named a new suit.

(B) 2 No Trump, you should pass. You did your full duty by this hand when you responded with 1 Heart. A jump in No Trump does not force the responder to bid again. Partner has 19 or 20, which is not quite enough. If he had 21 points he would have gone to 3 No trump himself.

(C) 3 Diamonds. A jump rebid in the same suit does not force the responder. You should therefore pass.

(D) 3 Clubs. Now you have no choice. The jump in a new suit has forced you to bid again and to keep on going until game is reached. You cannot rebid your own suit. You are unable to support Diamonds. Your hand is not suitable for a Club raise. So there is only one call left for you—namely, 3 No Trump.

Partnership language

It is just as important to know what a bid means as to know how much strength it shows. As the bidding develops, the responder assumes the duty of directing the partnership into the proper contract as well as calculating the strength of the combined holdings. Some rebids are more engaging than others. For example, the constant repetition, at minimum stages, of the same suit indicates great length of suit but not very much strength. For instance:

OPENER	RESPONDER
1 Diamond	1 Heart
2 Clubs	2 Hearts
2 No Trump	3 Hearts

What is the meaning of the 3 Heart bid? It is very clear that responder has a weak hand with great length in Hearts, and even the Hearts cannot be very strong, because, if they were, by this time the responder could have been in a position to bid 4 Hearts after opener has shown such strength.

Another case:

OPENER	RESPONDER
1 Diamond	1 Spade
2 Clubs	2 Diamonds

The question arises: Is the 2 Diamond bid to be construed as encouraging? The answer is No. The responder has shown a mere preference for Diamonds over Clubs. He has never increased the contract, and the opener should be very cautious about carrying on.

OPENER	RESPONDER
1 Spade	2 Spades
2 No Trump	3 Spades

What is the meaning of the 3 Spade bid? It is this: "Partner, I did not have a very strong raise. I know you are asking me to go to game, but I am unable to do so. This hand must play at Spades as far as I am concerned, but I have only 8 points in support."

OPENER	RESPONDER
1 Heart	2 Diamonds
2 No Trump	3 Hearts

What is the meaning of the 3 Heart bid? Does it show a dislike of No Trump and a mere preference for Hearts, or is it a strong bid? It is a strong bid. The responder is merely saying, "I am not sure whether we should play this hand at 4 Hearts or at 3 No Trump. I wish to give you a choice, partner. You must know I have a good hand, because I first took the trouble to bid 2 Diamonds, increasing the contract, and then I again increased the contract to 3 Hearts. If my hand were not that good, I would have responded with a mere 2 Heart raise in the first place."

On this sequence of bids the 3 Heart call is forcing. The opener must select a game contract at either No Trump or Hearts. A typical hand justifying such bidding by responder is:

♠ x x   ♡ K x x   ◇ A K J x x   ♣ x x x

OPENER	RESPONDER
1 Heart	1 No Trump
3 Hearts	?

The responder holds:

1. ♠ x x x   ♡ x x   ◇ K J x   ♣ Q 10 x x x
2. ♠ K x x   ♡ x x   ◇ K x x x   ♣ Q x x x

With NO. 1, responder should pass; he has only 6 points, the absolute minimum, which he has already shown. With NO. 2, he should go on to 3 No Trump. He has a good No Trump response consisting of 8 points.

A semi-forcing bid need not be responded to, but if the responder does reply, it becomes a force to game:

OPENER	RESPONDER
1 Heart	1 Spade
3 Hearts	3 Spades

Responder was not forced to rebid 3 Spades. He could have passed. But since he accepted the semi-force, it now becomes a force to game, and neither partner may pass until game is reached.

Where opener has reversed, responder is compelled to bid again. His first duty is to warn opener if he sees no chance for game. He does so by bidding 2 No Trump. Any other bid by responder maintains the forcing situation, for example:

OPENER	RESPONDER
1 Diamond	1 Spade
2 Hearts	2 Spades

Responder is showing a five-card suit and opener must bid again, since his reverse was forcing to 3 Diamonds, his first-bid suit.

OPENER	RESPONDER
1 Diamond	1 Spade
2 Hearts	3 Diamonds

Since responder did not deny interest in game by rebidding 2 No Trump, his preference to 3 Diamonds is game forcing. Remember, opener has shown a hand worth 19 points and responder must have 7 or more. If this bid were not forcing, responder would have to jump to 4 Diamonds to show game-going values, and that would, on many hands, bypass the safest contract of 3 No Trump.

Responder's new-suit rebids are forcing

When the responder names a new suit the opener must bid again, not only on the first round but on subsequent rounds. For example:

♠ A K J x x   ♡ A Q J x   ◇ x   ♣ x x x

Your partner opens with 1 Diamond. You respond with 1 Spade. Partner bids 2 Diamonds. You are quite set on going to game, but it is not essential for you to jump the bid in Hearts at this point. You may force another bid from partner by merely naming a new suit. Remember, the opening bidder must bid again every time he hears a new suit. On the next round you will be in a better position to judge where this hand should play.

This device may be employed by the responder as a temporizing measure when he wishes time to make up his mind about a hand. For example, you hold:

♠ x x   ♡ x x   ◇ A K J x x x   ♣ A J x

Your partner opens with 1 Spade. You respond with 2 Diamonds. Partner rebids 2 Spades. You know that this hand belongs in game, because you have distinctly more than an opening bid, but you are disinclined to assign this hand to an eleven-trick contract. If partner can stop Hearts, you would rather try for 3 No Trump.

You are perfectly safe, therefore, in bidding merely 3 Clubs, a one-round force. This is not intended as Ace-showing. As far as partner is concerned, you really have a Club suit. If he does not bid 3 No Trump, you will then decide whether to play for 4 Spades or 5 Diamonds.

Here is another interesting use of the new-suit force by responder to find the best contract. Responder holds:

♠ K Q J 9 x   ♡ K x   ◇ x x x   ♣ A x x

The bidding has proceeded:

OPENER	RESPONDER
1 Heart	1 Spade
2 Diamonds	?

The best game contract may be in Spades, Hearts, or No Trump, depending upon the texture of opener's hand. If opener has three Spades, that suit should be best. If he has six or five excellent Hearts, that should be the final trump. In the absence of either, 3 No Trump appears to be the most suitable vehicle. How is responder to find out? Merely by bidding 3 Clubs. If opener prefers Spades he will bid 3 Spades and responder's worries are over. If opener rebids Hearts, that's the spot. If opener bids 3 No Trump, responder stops exploring.

When a player takes his partner out of a game contract, to which partner has voluntarily leaped, into a non-game contract, the inference is plain that he is looking for a slam. Otherwise the rescue would be senseless. For example, as responder, you hold:

♠ x x   ♡ x x   ◇ K J 10 x x x   ♣ x x x

The bidding has proceeded:

OPENER	RESPONDER
1 Club	1 Diamond
3 No Trump	?

What should you do? Pass, definitely. Do not make the mistake of bidding 4 Diamonds simply because you do not like No Trump. A player who has jumped to 3 No Trump does not have to be rescued.

Again, as responder, you hold:

♠ x x x   ♡ A Q x   ◇ x   ♣ K Q J x x x

The bidding has proceeded:

OPENER	RESPONDER
1 Spade	2 Clubs
3 No Trump	?

Here you have good reason to suspect that there is slam in the hand and wish to elicit further information from your partner. You may, if you choose, temporize by bidding 4 Clubs, which must be construed not as a rescue bid but as a slam try.

Responder's delayed jumps

When responder jumps in a new suit on the second round of bidding, that jump is forcing to game (unless responder is a passed hand). When responder jumps in his own suit or in support of opener's suit, whether it is forcing or merely invitational depends on whether the delayed jump is in a major or a minor. The rule is:

When responder makes a jump rebid in a *minor* suit, either his own or in support of opener, that minor-suit jump is forcing to game.

When responder makes a delayed jump in a major, either his own or opener's, the major-suit jump is invitational to game. Opener is free to pass with a minimum opening or a misfit.

Let's illustrate with a few sequences:

A) OPENER	RESPONDER	B) OPENER	RESPONDER
1 Diamond	1 Heart	1 Diamond	1 Heart
1 Spade	3 Diamonds	1 Spade	3 Spades

C) OPENER	RESPONDER	D) OPENER	RESPONDER
1 Club	1 Diamond	1 Club	1 Heart
1 Heart	3 Diamonds	1 Spade	3 Hearts

In Cases (A) and (C), responder's second-round jump is forcing. Thus, his hand must be at least of opening-bid strength with, respectively, four-card support for opener or a good six-card suit of his own. A suitable example for (A) would be:

♠ A x   ♡ K J 9 x x   ◇ A J x x   ♣ x x

For (C):

♠ x x   ♡ A x x   ◇ A Q 10 x x x   ♣ K x

In Cases (B) and (D), responder's delayed jump is only inviting game. It describes a point count of 11 or 12 and, similarly, four-card support or a good six-card suit. An example of (B):

♠ Q x x x   ♡ K Q x x   ◇ K J x   ♣ x x

Of (D):

♠ K x   ♡ A K 9 x x x   ◇ x x x   ♣ x x

A curious reader may well ask: "What should responder do with an opening bid plus a good six-card major?" The answer lies in employing the mark-time bid of the fourth (or unbid) suit, as we've seen from previous illustrations. Suppose you hold:

♠ K x x   ♡ Q J 9 8 x x   ◇ A Q   ♣ x x

Partner opens 1 Diamond, you respond 1 Heart, partner rebids 1 Spade. You wish to force to game and show the six-card Heart suit, but a delayed jump to 3 Hearts has been defined as invitational. Here, you must mark time with a bid of 2 Clubs, the fourth suit, which establishes a game-forcing situation so that partner can't pass when you next bid at the 3-level. *Only at responder's second turn and only at the 2-level can a bid of the fourth suit be used as artificial (and forcing).* Responder plans to bid 3 Hearts at his next opportunity to describe a six-card major and an opening bid, giving opener the final choice between 4 Hearts and 3 No Trump.

As an incidental but important note, since the fourth suit bid in this situation may be artificial, opener must hold protection in the fourth suit to insist upon No Trump.

Cases in which a new-suit rebid by responder is not forcing

An exception is to be noted to the rule that the naming of a new suit by responder forces opener to speak once more. When the opener's rebid has been 1 No Trump, responder may show a new suit without forcing opener to bid again. For example, you are responder and hold:

♠ K J x x x   ♡ Q x x x x   ◇ x   ♣ x x

The bidding proceeds:

OPENER	RESPONDER
1 Club	1 Spade
1 No Trump	2 Hearts

The opener may pass; the 2 Heart rebid over 1 No Trump is not forcing. The opener has indicated a minimum hand by rebidding at 1 No Trump and if the responder wishes to insist on game he must jump the bidding.

If the responder rebids in a higher-ranking suit, even over 1 No Trump, it is forcing:

OPENER	RESPONDER
1 Club	1 Diamond
1 No Trump	2 Spades

The 2 Spade bid makes it impossible for opener to return to 2 Diamonds; hence it is a strong bid, made in the expectation of getting to game, and opener must bid again.

A new suit by responder does not force the opener if either of the players has previously passed.

A new suit by responder does not force the opener when it is made directly over an adverse double. Suppose South holds:

♠ J x x   ♡ A Q J x x   ◇ A x x   ♣ x x

The bidding:

SOUTH	WEST	NORTH	EAST
1 Heart	Double	1 Spade	Pass
?			

South may pass. Since North has not redoubled, he cannot visualize game, and Spades should be as safe a spot as any.

REBIDS BY RESPONDER QUIZ

Your partner opens 1 Club, you respond 1 Diamond, and your partner rebids 1 Spade. The opponents pass. What would you do now with each of the following hands?

1. ♠ x x x
   ♡ J x x x
   ◇ K Q x x x
   ♣ x

2. ♠ x x x
   ♡ K J x
   ◇ A Q 10 x
   ♣ x x x

3. ♠ A Q x x
   ♡ x x
   ◇ K J 10 x x x
   ♣ x

4. ♠ K x x
   ♡ x x
   ◇ Q J 10 x x
   ♣ A Q 10

5. ♠ K Q 10 x
   ♡ A 10 x x
   ◇ A J x x x
   ♣ none

6. ♠ x x
   ♡ x x x
   ◇ A K x x x
   ♣ Q 10 x

Your partner opens 1 Club, you respond 1 Heart and your partner rebids 1 No Trump. What would you call with each of the following?

7. ♠ J 10 x
   ♡ A Q J x
   ◇ 10 x x x
   ♣ K x

8. ♠ x
   ♡ Q J 10 9 x
   ◇ A 10 x x x
   ♣ x x

9. ♠ A x
   ♡ Q 10 x x x x x
   ◇ x
   ♣ A 10 x

Your partner opens 1 Heart, you respond 2 Diamonds, and your partner rebids 2 Hearts. What would you say now with each of the following?

10. ♠ x x
    ♡ x x x
    ◇ A 10 9 x x
    ♣ A K x

11. ♠ x x
    ♡ x
    ◇ K J 10 x x x x
    ♣ A J x

12. ♠ A K J
    ♡ x x
    ◇ A Q x x x
    ♣ J x x

Your partner opens 1 Club, you respond 1 Heart, and your partner raises to 2 Hearts. What would you call now with each of the following?

13. ♠ Q J x
    ♡ A J 9 x
    ◇ J 9 x x
    ♣ Q x

14. ♠ x x x
    ♡ A K x x
    ◇ K x x
    ♣ x x x

15. ♠ x x
    ♡ A Q 10 x x
    ◇ K x x
    ♣ A 10 x

16. ♠ 10 x
    ♡ A J x x
    ◇ x x x x
    ♣ A Q J

17. ♠ x
    ♡ A K 10 x
    ◇ 10 x x x
    ♣ A Q J x

18. ♠ A x x x
    ♡ A K x x x
    ◇ x x
    ♣ J x

Your partner opens 1 Spade, you respond 2 Clubs, and your partner rebids 2 Hearts. What would you call now with each of the following?

19. ♠ 10 x	20. ♠ Q J x	21. ♠ K
♡ K x	♡ K J x	♡ J x x
◇ x x x x	◇ x x x	◇ K J 9 x
♣ A K J 10 x	♣ A Q 9 x	♣ A J 9 x x

Your partner opens 1 Spade, you respond 2 Hearts, and your partner rebids 3 Clubs. What would you call now with each of the following?

22. ♠ 10 x	23. ♠ 9	24. ♠ K 10
♡ A Q 10 x x x	♡ K Q 10 x x	♡ A K x x x
◇ A x x	◇ Q J 10 x	◇ x x
♣ K x	♣ Q J x	♣ J x x x

25. ♠ K J 8	26. ♠ K 10 x x	27. ♠ J 10
♡ A J 10 x x	♡ A K J x x	♡ A K J x x
◇ x x x	◇ x	◇ x x x x
♣ K x	♣ J 10 x	♣ K x

Your partner opens 1 Spade, you raise to 2 Spades, and your partner rebids 2 No Trump. What would you call now with each of the following?

28. ♠ A x x x	29. ♠ J x x x	30. ♠ Q x x x
♡ x x	♡ J x x	♡ K x x x
◇ x x x	◇ K J x	◇ x x
♣ K J 10 x	♣ Q x x	♣ Q x x

ANSWERS TO REBIDS BY RESPONDER QUIZ

1. Pass.

Opener's simple change of suit is not forcing, and it seems clear there is no game in the hand. You have a minimum responding hand and have virtually given your all by bidding 1 Diamond. The only problem is to select the safest partial, and since your hand is likely to be very useful at 1 Spade, you simply pass.

2. One No Trump.

The proper final contract is uncertain at this point: your partner could have a minimum opening hand of about 13 points, or he could have as many as 19. The best you can do is show the nature of your own hand by bidding 1 No Trump. Partner then knows that you have no more than 10 points, or 11 at the very most. With 15 or fewer, he will pass.

3. Four Spades.

Your hand is worth 14 dummy points in support of Spades and therefore justifies raising your partner all the way to game. 3 Spades would be unduly timid.

4. Three Clubs.

This hand is highly likely to produce a game—on the principle that an opening bid opposite an opening bid equals a game—but it is not yet possible to be sure of the best spot. Accordingly, you jump to 3 Clubs, which is forcing. Hopefully, partner may now bid 3 No Trump if he has a Heart guard. Alternatively, if he bids 3 Spades, showing a rebiddable suit, you intend to raise to 4 Spades.

5. Three Hearts.

Your partner's Spade bid has improved the value of your hand enormously and you can best indicate this by making a jump shift in Hearts before showing that you really intend the hand to be played at Spades.

6. Two Clubs.

With this type of hand it is far more important to show three-card support for your partner's first suit than to rebid your own five-card suit. You are not strong enough to jump to 3 Clubs, which would be forcing.

7. Two No Trump.

By rebidding 1 No Trump, your partner has shown a relatively balanced hand. His high-card strength is likely to range from 13 to 15 points. (With 16, he could have opened 1 No Trump.) It is possible that the values for game are present and therefore the raise to 2 No Trump is justified with 11 high-card points.

8. Two Diamonds.

It is clear that the combined hands cannot contain the values for a game contract. Your hand is such that it will probably be easier to make 2-odd in either Hearts or Diamonds than it would be for your partner to make 1 No Trump. 2 Diamonds represents a change of suit, but it does not show extra strength; a simple bid in a new suit is not forcing after the opener has rebid 1 No Trump.

9. Four Hearts.

3 Hearts would not be forcing after your partner's 1 No Trump rebid and thus would err on the side of caution. After all, you virtually have opening values—taking your distributional strength into account—and it is reasonable to assume that your partner is not entirely bereft of Hearts, since his rebid showed a balanced hand.

10. Three Hearts.

You promised partner another bid when you made your two-over-one response. Since you have a known eight-card fit and a ruffing value in Spades, you have a clear-cut raise of partner's suit. Partner could have a very good hand and still rebid only 2 Hearts.

11. 3 Diamonds.

Your original intention was to rebid your own suit. Do so. This auction is not forcing on partner, who can and should drop the bidding if he senses a misfit.

12. Two Spades.

To bid a three-card suit is not a strategy to be recommended in every case, but in this instance 2 Spades, which is forcing, is clearly the best way to inspire partner to bid No Trump if he has an appropriate guard in Clubs. You are morally bound to seek a game contract and the makeup of your hand suggests seeking it in No Trump if possible.

13. Two No Trump.

With 11 points in high cards, your hand is worth an effort to reach game and, having already shown your major suit, you should now indicate your scattered values and the balanced nature of your hand by bidding 2 No Trump.

14. Pass.

Your partner's hand is likely to be in the minimum range and a game contract would be speculative, at best. With no distributional features that you could show, it is better to accept a partial than to risk getting too high.

15. Four Hearts.

Here you are clearly worth a game as you have opening values in your own hand. At the same time, there would be very little point in any bid but 4 Hearts: you are assured of having sufficient trumps, and it is highly unlikely that game at No Trump could be safer than game at Hearts.

16. Three Clubs.

The thinking behind this call is that if partner has only three Hearts, game may be safer at No Trump than at 4 Hearts. You can best examine this possibility by indicating that your strength lies in Clubs and Hearts, leaving the next move to partner.

17. Four Clubs.

You could hardly look your partner in the eye again if you were to bid this hand without ever mentioning that you held very strong support for Clubs. The double raise shows a game-going hand and partner may be expected to select either 4 Hearts or 5 Clubs.

18. Two Spades.

It is not entirely beyond the realms of fancy for your partner to have four Spades and only three Hearts. You cater to this possibility by means of the forcing bid of 2 Spades.

19. Two Spades.

Your Clubs do not warrant rebidding at the 3 level and you should resist temptation to bid 2 No Trump without a Diamond guard. The best you can do is select one of your partner's suits and in these circumstances it is your solemn duty—with equal length in each—to return to the suit your partner bid first.

20. Two Spades.

Your hand is strong enough for a game call, since you have opening values. However, it is not necessary to bid game straight off: a preference by responder is forcing after a two-over-one response and you afford partner the chance to further describe his holdings in case he is slam-minded.

21. Two No Trump.

This call shows your values very accurately and indicates also that you are well protected in Diamonds. Partner can either raise to 3 No Trump, or bid a suit.

22. Three Hearts.

By introducing a new suit at the level of 3 odd, partner indicates at least 17 points. He also undertakes to bid once more over any rebid that you make below the level of game. Therefore you make a waiting bid of 3 Hearts, enabling partner to clarify his hand. It is not impossible that a slam contract may be reached.

23. Three No Trump.

Your partner has shown a strong hand and you yourself are reasonably well endowed with high cards. However, you are not in a position to support either one of his suits; and therefore you take the opportunity to state that in your view 3 No Trump is likely to be the appropriate spot.

24. Four Clubs.

By bidding Spades in front of Clubs, partner has indicated at least five Spades. Game is therefore likely to be playable at either one of the black suits, and indeed there is something to be said for supporting Spades at this time. However, partner is not prohibited from bidding 4 Spades over 4 Clubs, and this last bid keeps both options open. It would be unsound to rebid 3 Hearts over 3 Clubs, since a five-card Heart suit has already been indicated.

25. Four Spades.

You have such an excellent holding in each of your partner's suits that a slam is by no means a remote possibility. However, you are not in a position to take a slam initiative, since you are wide open in Diamonds. Accordingly, you jump to 4 Spades. If partner happens to have a singleton Diamond, or the King of Diamonds, he may be able to bid a slam.

26. Four No Trump.

When you responded 2 Hearts, your general intention was to indicate the nature of your hand by jumping to 4 Spades on the next round. Now that your partner has made the strong rebid of 3 Clubs, a bid of 4 Spades by you would be inadequate. You should bid a slam without further ado, provided your partner has at least two Aces.

27. Three Spades.

This is to be preferred to 3 Hearts, which would tend to suggest a very long suit. Partner already knows that you have five Hearts and may be expected to indicate support for the suit if he has it.

28. Four Spades.

If partner had had a minimum opening, he would have passed 2 Spades. By bidding, he has indicated a chance for game even though your maximum is 9 points. Since your hand contains the most you could have for 2 Spades, you should bid game. 3 No Trump might be safe, but 4 Spades is certain to be an excellent contract and therefore you should bid it.

29. Three No Trump.

Partner's minimum holding is about 17 points in high cards and you yourself have 8. The combined holding, therefore, is at least 25, and it is more likely to be 26 or 27. Thus you raise to 3 No Trump. You don't bid 4 Spades, because you have no ruffing values.

30. Three Spades.

In terms of high cards this hand is a complete minimum, and therefore you cannot properly encourage your partner to undertake a game contract. At the same time, the hand is likely to play more safely at Spades than at No Trump, and this message is conveyed by signing off at 3 Spades.

6. Four-card-major opening bids

WHEN YOU come down to the nitty-gritty, there is not a world of difference between playing a five-card-major and a four-card-major system.

The differences between the two methods have been greatly exaggerated. To begin with, on more than a third of the hands where you hold a major suit, it is at least five cards. Then there are those hands where you hold a four-card major and a four-card minor, in suits that do not touch, which in both methods you would open with the minor suit. Toss in those hands where the four-card major is not biddable and you will find that, in the great majority of instances, you make the same opening bid no matter which methods you are using.

Where the two do diverge is in the areas of prepared minor-suit openings and, more particularly, in responder's actions. These were highlighted in our opening chapters.

Should you find yourself partnered by a rigid adherent to four-card major openings, it will be quite simple to accommodate your partner's preference after reading this chapter. Soon you will acquire the reputation of being a versatile player and ideal partner who has mastered the intricacies of both four- and five-card majors. As many years of experience in the world of bridge have proved, an accommodating and understanding partner is a rare and valuable breed.

Biddable suits

A four-card major is considered biddable if it contains at least 4 HCP. Greater latitude is permitted in opening with a minor suit. In all situations, a five-card suit is considered biddable, no matter how weak.

For example, these are all biddable suits:

A x x x   K J x x   Q J 10 x*   x x x x x

Bear in mind that an opening bid is not an isolated event. It is the first step in a campaign, and it is imperative to look one step ahead and consider what partner is most likely to respond. You must then

---

* This is the only exception to the requirement of at least 4 HCP.

have a clear idea of what your second bid will be. If that second bid is going to prove embarrassing, you have made an error in your initial action. Either you should not have opened, or you opened the bidding in the wrong suit! This, in essence, is the Principle of Preparedness.

It has been suggested many times that no opening bid should be made unless the hand contains a rebid. This should certainly be the deciding factor in marginal cases. However, some thought before selecting the opening bid can solve many problems. Study these illustrations:

$$♠ A K J x \qquad ♡ x x x \qquad ◇ A x x \qquad ♣ x x x$$

In the early days of contract bridge, our Founding Fathers would have valued this hand at 3 + quick tricks with a biddable suit. The impulse to open the bidding would have proved irresistible. Only when partner responded to the 1 Spade opening bid with 2 Hearts would the fact that there was a problem begin to dawn on opener. No rebid made a grain of sense: They couldn't rebid a four-card suit; to raise Hearts with three low cards was unthinkable; to bid No Trump on so weak a holding and with an unguarded suit went against basic principles, and to pass would violate a sacred commitment.

This dilemma should have been foreseen, and would have been avoided with an original pass. See how the point count would have done their thinking for them. The hand is worth only 12 points, and such hands should not be opened.

Permit us to change this hand slightly while retaining exactly the same high-card count:

$$♠ A K x x \qquad ♡ A J 10 x \qquad ◇ x x \qquad ♣ x x x$$

Let us assume that you open the bidding with a Spade and partner responds 2 Diamonds. You have a comfortable rebid of 2 Hearts; that permits partner to return to 2 Spades if he so chooses. And should partner respond 2 Hearts, you would be delighted to raise to 3 Hearts. In either case, you have painlessly fulfilled your obligation to bid another time.

Examine this hand in terms of point count. With the slight change in distribution, you have increased the value of the hand to an opening bid—12 HCP and 1 point for the doubleton. That makes your hand an optional opening bid—an option you should be glad to exercise since the hand contains 3 quick tricks and, most important, an easy rebid.

$$♠ K 10 x x x \qquad ♡ A K J x \qquad ◇ x x \qquad ♣ x x$$

This, too, should be opened. The hand is worth 13 points, has 2½ quick tricks and no rebid problems.

Some players make a distinction between the requirements for vulnerable and not vulnerable opening bids. We cannot subscribe to that theory except in the case of preemptive opening bids. We feel that if you deem a hand to be worth an opening bid, then the vulnerability ought not to be a deterrent.

♠ K Q 10 x x x   ♡ A x   ◇ Q x x   ♣ x x

Open this hand. It has 13 points, two defensive tricks and the Spade suit is eminently rebiddable by even the most exacting standards.

The "Convenient Club" opening

This is not a system. It is just what its name implies—a convenience. We make his point because we can't recall the number of times we have heard a player inquire: "Partner, do you play the Short Club?" as if they were referring to some special convention. The point of the "Short Club" opening is simply this: There are some hands that should be opened because they contain more high cards than we would willingly pass. Some of these hands offer no convenient opening because they present a difficult rebid problem. To facilitate a rebid on such hands, you may open 1 Club on a three-card suit if it is headed by at least the queen. For example:

♠ A K J x   ♡ x x x   ◇ J x x   ♣ A J x

This hand has 14 HCP and 3 quick tricks, so it should not be passed. But if you choose to open 1 Spade it is evident that you will find it difficult to rebid should partner respond at the two level in a red suit. For your own personal convenience, you should open this hand with 1 Club. Now if partner responds in a red suit, you can select 1 Spade as your rebid. If the response is 1 No Trump or 2 Clubs, you pass.

You do not open 1 Club *because* your club holding is short; you do so *in spite of it*. It is a practice devised especially to help you out of a predicament and should be of no concern to responder. He should treat all 1 Club opening bids as if they are genuine suits and make his natural response. Of course, he should not raise a 1 Club opening bid without four-card support.

Here is another type of hand with which you have to open 1 Club on a short suit:

♠ Q 10 x x   ♡ K x x x   ◇ x x   ♣ A K x

You have a full opening bid, but neither major suit is biddable. A 1 Club opening bid leaves you well placed. If responder bids a major, you can raise him; if he responds 1 Diamond, you can rebid 1 Heart.

When partner has already passed, you need not concern yourself unduly about your rebid. Unless partner makes a forcing response, you do not intend bidding again with minimum hands:

♠ A K J x   ♡ x x x   ◊ J x x   ♣ A J x

In third position, the proper opening bid with this hand is 1 Spade. You intend passing any response by partner except for a jump shift.

Choosing between two four-card suits

It is a mathematical fact that the opener is more likely to be dealt a hand containing two four-card suits than any other hand pattern. It is a bridge fact that, unless opener chooses the right one of the two for his opening bid, grave repercussions can be felt later in the auction.

When two biddable suits are adjacent in rank, or touching, you open the higher-ranking. With Hearts and Diamonds, for example, you open 1 Heart:

1. ♠ x x x   ♡ A K x x   ◊ A Q J x   ♣ x x

On the next round you can bid 2 Diamonds, offering partner the chance to return to your first-bid suit without increasing the level of the auction. If you were to open 1 Diamond and then bid Hearts, that would not be possible.

When your two four-card suits are Spades and Clubs, you can usually conserve bidding room by opening 1 Club:

2. ♠ K Q 10 x   ♡ x x x   ◊ J x   ♣ A Q J x

After a response of 1 Diamond or 1 Heart, you can now bid your Spade suit at the one level.

We also recommend an opening bid of 1 Club when your suits are Clubs and Hearts.

3. ♠ x x   ♡ A J 9 x   ◊ J x x   ♣ A Q J x

If partner responds 1 Diamond, you have an easy one-level rebid in Hearts; if partner responds 1 Spade, your rebid is 1 No Trump.

Over the years, we have found that it is hands which contain four Spades and four Diamonds that prove to be the most bothersome. We suggest the following simple guide to help you solve the problem:

Look for the shortest suit in your hand, either a singleton or a doubleton. Start the auction with the suit that ranks below your shortage. To illustrate:

4. ♠ K Q x x   ♡ x x   ◇ A K J x   ♣ x x x

Your shortest suit is Hearts, and your long suit that ranks below it is Diamonds. Therefore, open 1 Diamond. Your partner is more likely to respond in Hearts than Clubs (there are more Hearts divided among the three hands you can't see), and you can then rebid 1 Spade. Should you open 1 Spade and were partner to rebid 2 Hearts, you would be stuck for a sound rebid.

Now let's change the location of the short suit:

♠ K Q x x   ♡ x x x   ◇ A K J x   ♣ x x

This time you open 1 Spade, intending to bid 2 Diamonds should partner respond 2 Clubs. If partner inconveniently responds 2 Hearts, you have to raise to 3 Hearts. That is not as terrible as it looks, for partner must have five Hearts to bid the suit at the two-level; therefore, you have a guaranteed eight-card fit.

Sometimes your high-card strength will not be concentrated in your long suits, but will be more widely scattered—an Ace here, a King there, and so on. You can describe this type of hand by choosing a No Trump rebid after responds in a new suit:

♠ A J x x   ♡ 10 x   ◇ K J x x   ♣ A Q 10

With your high cards scattered among three suits, you can describe your hand very accurately by rebidding in No Trump should partner bid Hearts. Therefore, you can afford to open this hand with 1 Spade. If partner responds 2 Clubs, you can either raise to 3 Clubs or bid 2 Diamonds—we prefer disclosing our excellent support; if partner responds 2 Hearts, we can continue with 2 No Trump to show a balanced minimum opening bid.

Here is another hand where the intention to rebid in No Trump affects your choice of opening bid:

♠ Q x x   ♡ K Q 10 x   ◇ A Q   ♣ K Q J x

You can describe this 19-point hand by opening 1 Heart and then jumping in No Trump over any response that partner makes. True, you can also show it by opening 1 Club and then jumping in No Trump, but that runs the risk of missing a 4–4 Heart fit. And if you elect to open 1 Club and rebid 1 Heart should partner respond 1

Diamond, you have lost a chance to show how strong you are with your first two bids.

We cannot stress too highly the advantage of selecting your opening bid with a view to rebidding in No Trump. A No Trump rebid not only describes your shape, it also pinpoints your strength within a relatively narrow range, thereby enabling your partner to place the final contract with considerable accuracy.

Choosing between three four-card suits

The principle followed here is similar to that which applies in selecting your opening bid when you hold two four-card suits—you tend to open the suit that ranks below the singleton.

♠ A K x x ♡ A J 10 x ♢ x ♣ K J x x

The correct opening bid is 1 Club, the suit below the singleton.

♠ A J x x ♡ A Q x x ♢ A J x x ♣ x

The proper opening bid is 1 Spade. (For the purpose of selecting the opening bid, the Spade suit ranks immediately below Clubs.) If partner responds 2 Clubs, your rebid should be 2 Hearts—always bid the major in preference to the minor in this type of auction; you might get a chance to bid your diamonds later.

Every rule has its exceptions. We invite you to turn your attention to the pair of hands below:

OPENER	RESPONDER
♠ A K x x	♠ x x
♡ A Q x x	♡ K J x x x
♢ K Q 10 x	♢ J x x
♣ x	♣ x x x

Above we suggested that you open the suit below your singleton. In this case, that would mean that you should open the bidding with 1 Spade. The trouble is that your hand is so rich in high cards that you might find partner with relatively little, as is the case here. He might be unable to respond to an opening bid of 1 Spade—on the hand shown, he would have no option but to pass, yet you should be able to make 11 tricks at a Heart contract.

On such strong hands, we suggest you break the rule for opening with the suit below the singleton and instead open 1 Diamond. The idea is to keep the bidding as low as possible to offer partner every inducement to respond at the one-level. Here he has just enough to dredge up a 1 Heart response, and you get to your excellent game.

Reverse bids

The same general rules apply to reverse bids as we discussed in Chapter 1. However, here is a case where it is an advantage to play four-card majors. Do you remember this hand?

♠ A K x x   ♡ A J x x x   ◇ x x   ♣ x x

Playing five-card majors, we were faced with a problem. After we opened 1 Heart and received a 1 No Trump or 2 of a minor response, we could not afford to show our Spade suit—that would be a reverse bid and show extra values. Playing four-card majors we avoid that difficulty by opening 1 Spade! No matter what partner responds, we have a convenient rebid of 2 Hearts.

Responses

Responding with 6 to 10 points

When your partner has opened the bidding with 1 of a suit and your hand contains some slight trick-taking power, you should strive to keep the bidding alive. This provides the opener with another chance to bid should he have another suit at which the hand might play better, or should he have a very powerful opening, one that is just short of a demand bid.

If you have little or nothing, of course, you must pass. The bidding may be kept open with a moderate hand in one of three ways:

I. By bidding 1 No Trump (1 Heart by partner, 1 No Trump by you).

II. By raising your partner from 1 to 2 in his suit (1 Heart by partner, 2 Hearts by you).

III. By bidding some other suit *at the level of 1* (1 Heart by partner, 1 Spade by you).

I. KEEPING THE BIDDING OPEN BY A BID OF 1 NO TRUMP

This is regarded as one of the milder responses. When you desire to keep the bidding alive with a moderate hand but are unable to give partner a raise and have no suit that you can show at the level of 1, the practice is to respond with 1 No Trump. Such a response must contain at least 6 points in high cards and may contain as many as 10 points. Note that distributional points are not counted in making No Trump responses. *Playing four-card majors, the 1 No Trump response is not forcing.*

In each of the following cases, partner has opened with 1 Spade and you hold:

♠ x x x   ♡ A x x x   ◊ x x x   ♣ x x x

Pass. You have only 4 points.

♠ x x x   ♡ K 10 x x   ◊ Q 10 x   ♣ J x x

Bid 1 No Trump. You have the required 6 points in high cards.

♠ x x   ♡ Q x x   ◊ K J x x x   ♣ x x x

Bid 1 No Trump. You have 6 points in high cards and are not able to show your suit at the level of 1.

♠ x x x   ♡ A x x   ◊ K x x   ♣ K x x x

Bid 1 No Trump. You have 10 points, which is maximum for such a response.

II. THE RAISE TO 2 IN THE SAME SUIT

This response is, generally speaking, a little more encouraging than the response of 1 No Trump. The first requirement is that you be mildly satisfied with partner's suit, which means that you must have what is considered normal trump support; that is, at least x x x x or Q x x or J 10 x. Until you learn otherwise, you must act on the assumption that your partner holds a four-card suit. If you determine, on subsequent rounds of bidding, that your partner holds a rebiddable (a good five-card) suit, then you may be satisfied with that suit as trump with less than normal support. If the hand is satisfactory in other respects, you may now raise with three small trumps or Q x. And if your partner has bid the suit a third time without support from you in that suit, you may presume that he has six and may raise with two small trumps.

In other words, if partner bids a suit once, assume a four-card suit. If he bids twice, assume a five-card suit. If he bids it a third time, assume a six-card suit. Generally speaking, for the trump suit to be acceptable, the partnership should possess eight cards of the suit.

In addition to trump support, your hand must possess certain trick-taking qualities to justify a raise. These trick-taking qualities can best be represented by assigning certain points. However, for purposes of raising, we must consider "Dummy Points" (see Chapter 2).

The limits of a single raise of partner's suit are 7 to 10 points inclusive. These points naturally include both high cards and distribution. Let us observe a few examples.

Your partner opens with 1 Spade and you hold:

♠ 10 x x x   ♡ x x   ◇ K Q J x   ♣ x x x
(7 points)

You have enough to justify keeping the bidding open by a raise to 2 Spades. The hand is worth 7 points, 6 in high cards and 1 for the doubleton. If the small Diamond were a Heart, the correct response would be 1 No Trump.

♠ Q x x x   ♡ x   ◇ Q 10 x x   ♣ x x x x
(8 points)

With this hand you may raise to 2 Spades. The hand is worth 8 points in support of partner, 3 for the Queen of trumps, which is promoted, 2 for the Queen of Diamonds, and 3 for the singleton Heart.

In some cases you may offer partner a single raise with slightly less trump support if no other suitable bid is available. Suppose partner opens with 1 Spade and you hold:

♠ 10 9 x   ♡ x   ◇ K x x x x   ♣ Q x x x

you should bid 2 Spades. This hand is worth 7 points in support of Spades, 5 in high cards and 3 for the singleton Heart, but a deduction of 1 point is made because the hand possesses the defect of having only three trumps. A No Trump response would be improper; first, because the hand does not contain the necessary 6 points in high cards, and secondly, because the singleton Heart renders such a response highly undesirable.

III. KEEPING THE BIDDING OPEN BY A BID OF 1 IN A SUIT

When your partner opens with 1 of a suit, you may keep the bidding alive on certain mediocre hands by naming a new suit, provided you are able to do so at the level of 1. Such a response does not promise any more strength than does the response of 1 No Trump. This is an important observation. A 1 No Trump response ranges from 6 to 10 points, all in high cards. A one-over-one response may be made with as little as 6 points, which may include as few as 4 points in high cards.

Of course where it becomes necessary to increase the contract to show your suit, more strength is required. In order to respond at the level of 2 with a new suit, your hand must be of at least average strength (an average hand is worth 10 points). With weak hands, the wisest procedure is to make the cheapest response, and 1 of a suit is cheaper than 1 No Trump.

♠ J x x   ♡ K J x x   ◊ x x   ♣ Q 10 x x

Partner opens with 1 Diamond. You have the necessary high-card strength and should keep the bidding open. It is the practice of many players to respond with 1 No Trump. This is unsound. Your proper response is 1 Heart. Remember that a bid of 1 Heart does not promise any more strength than does a bid of 1 No Trump. Furthermore, the one-over-one response makes partner's rebid easier in any case in which his second suit happens to be Spades. By bidding 1 Heart you permit him to rebid by showing his Spade suit at the level of 1, whereas a 1 No Trump response would have forced him to the level of 2 in order to show the suit. This he may fear to do.

Avoid responding 1 No Trump when you can bid 1 of a suit, even if it is necessary to shade the suit to as little as J x x x.

The above principle may be demonstrated with the following example:

♠ x x   ♡ K J x x x   ◊ J x x   ♣ x x x

If partner opens the bidding with 1 Spade, you should pass. Holding 5 points, you have not sufficient high-card strength to respond with 1 No Trump. But if partner opens with 1 Club or 1 Diamond, you may respond with 1 Heart. Valued at Hearts, the hand is worth 6 points, 5 in high cards and 1 for the doubleton. It will be seen, therefore, that this hand was not strong enough for a response of 1 No Trump, yet it was strong enough for a response of 1 Heart.

Responding with 11 to 13 points

When you have a responding hand of this class, the chances of making a game will depend largely upon the values disclosed by your partner's second bid. Accordingly, you should select your first response with the thought in mind that you may bid again if your partner's rebid is encouraging, but that you may pass if it is not. An important element in the responder's strategy is that with a hand of this strength he is able to show a new suit at the level of 2 without forcing the auction to game or even promising another bid.

♠ J x x x   ♡ J x   ◊ x x x   ♣ A K Q x

With a slightly weaker hand, the responder would be constrained to bid 1 Spade over his partner's 1 Heart opening. In the actual case, it is in order to respond with 2 Clubs, intending to raise 2 Hearts to 3 and to go to 2 No Trump over 2 Diamonds.

To respond at the level of 2, your hand must be of at least average strength. An average hand is worth 10 points. Wherever you have a choice between responding with 2 of a suit and 1 No Trump in borderline cases, you should choose the No Trump response, because it does not force partner to speak again with a minimum hand. Wherever you have no more than 9 points in high cards, assuming the hand is of a balanced nature, you are within the limits of a 1 No Trump response. However, with 10 points (including distribution) and a good five-card suit, you may respond 2 Clubs with:

♠ x x x   ♡ x x   ◊ A x x   ♣ K Q 10 x x

While a bid at the level of 2 will tend to show a five-card suit, it is proper to bid a four-carder lacking a suitable alternative, even to the extent of responding 2 Hearts to partner's 1 Spade, holding:

♠ Q x x   ♡ A K x x   ◊ K x x   ♣ x x x

This hand is too strong for 1 No Trump, but it would be incorrect to respond either 2 No Trump or 3 Spades.

♠ 10 x x   ♡ x x   ◊ K x x   ♣ A J x x x

Partner has opened with 1 Heart. It is mandatory to keep the bidding alive with 8 high-card points, but your hand is not strong enough to justify a 2 Club response. Therefore respond with 1 No Trump.

Free responses of 2 in a suit

You may make a free response of 2 in a suit on about the same strength you would require if second hand had passed, provided your suit is lower-ranking than partner's suit.

♠ x x x   ♡ x x   ◊ A Q 10 x x   ♣ K J x

Partner has opened with 1 Heart, second hand overcalls with 1 Spade. Your hand is worth 11 points, 10 in high cards and 1 for distribution. You may therefore bid 2 Diamonds freely. Note that your suit is lower in rank than your partner's and permits him to rebid at the level of 2. But suppose as South you hold:

♠ x x x   ♡ A K x x x   ◇ x x   ♣ K x x

NORTH	EAST	SOUTH
1 Diamond	1 Spade	?

On this sequence of bids you should not make a free bid of 2 Hearts. Your hand has a total value of 11 points, 10 in high cards and 1 for distribution, but is not strong enough to force partner to bid at the level of 3. You should pass and hope for another chance.

Great caution is indicated when a free bid made by responder is in a suit higher in rank than his partner's suit.

♠ x x x   ♡ K Q 10 x x   ◇ Q J x x   ♣ x

Your partner opens with 1 Club and an opponent overcalls with 1 Spade. It would be extremely impolitic for you to bid 2 Hearts. Such action forces partner to speak again, and if his rebid is 3 Clubs, which is not at all unlikely, you will find yourself in a mess brought on by your own conduct. Had your partner's opening bid been 1 Spade and the overcall been 2 Clubs, a 2 Heart bit by you would not be attended by nearly so much danger, since it permits partner to rebid his suit, if necessary, at the level of 2. Similarly:

♠ K Q x x x   ♡ 10 x x   ◇ A x x   ♣ x x

Partner opens with 1 Heart and an opponent overcalls with 2 Clubs. You cannot afford to bid 2 Spades, for your partner may not be prepared to rebid safely at the level of 3, and unless he happens to have strength in Clubs, he cannot safely bid No Trump. In this case, however, you may stretch a point and raise your partner to 2 Hearts even though you have slightly less than normal trump support. Your hand is worth 9 points in support of Hearts and is therefore worth a free raise, which is not forcing. But if you had only two small Hearts, you would not be in a position to raise without any kind of trump support and it would be more discreet for you to pass.

Another illustration: As South you hold:

♠ x x x   ♡ A 10 x x x x   ◇ Q x x x   ♣ x

The bidding has proceeded:

NORTH	EAST	SOUTH
1 Club	1 Spade	?

Despite the six-card suit, you dare not bid 2 Hearts, since this may force your partner to bid 3 Clubs, or possibly 2 No Trump, neither of which you will find very comfortable. You should pass. Actually it should require no great restraint to pass, for this hand is not the least bit impressive. If you value it, you will note that it is worth only 9 points, 6 in high cards and 3 for distribution.

Again as South you hold:

♠ K J x   ♡ A Q x x x   ◇ x x x   ♣ x x

The bidding has proceeded:

NORTH	EAST	SOUTH
1 Club	1 Spade	?

There may be contemplation on your part to bid 2 Hearts, but this is not good strategy, If partner is obliged to bid 3 Clubs, you will hardly know what to do; to try 3 No Trump over 3 Clubs may prove disastrous, because you have not yet learned whether your partner has a good hand. However, some action by you must be taken, and the recommended call is a free bid of 1 No Trump. This will denote a good hand but will give partner the option of passing if he has a minimum. If he rebids 2 Clubs or 2 Diamonds, you will have the opportunity to bid Hearts on the next round.

Choice of responses

On a great many hands there is a choice of response; that is, any of several bids may be technically correct. It is incumbent upon the responder in those cases to make the best of the choices.

Choice between a single raise and a 1 No Trump response

Some players regard this as a choice of rotten apples, inasmuch as these two responses are the less favored children. Where there is a close choice between raising your partner to 2 of his suit and 1 No Trump, the distribution of the hand will frequently determine the choice. Where you have a 4-3-3-3 distribution with normal trump support, our practice is to respond with 1 No Trump if the raise is of a minimum character (7 or 8 points); but we offer the raise in preference to the No Trump bid when the hand is worth 9 or 10 points in support of partner's major suit.

But where the hand contains a short suit, even a doubleton, the raise is preferred to the 1 No Trump response.

For example:

♠ A x x   ♡ 10 x x   ◊ K J x x   ♣ x x x

Partner opens with 1 Spade. You have a choice of responding with 1 No Trump or 2 Spades. Note that the hand is completely balanced, and in support of Spades we have 7 points. There are 8 high-card points, but inasmuch as the dummy contains a flaw, we must subtract a point and the hand is therefore worth only 7. Consequently, the 1 No Trump response is preferred. If one of the Hearts were transferred to the Clubs, we would prefer the raise to 2 Spades. Note that this would increase the "dummy points" by 1, for the hand would then be worth 8 points.

Even with a balanced hand a single raise should occasionally be preferred to a 1 No Trump response.

♠ K x x   ♡ Q x x x   ◊ A x x   ♣ J x x

Partner opens with 1 Spade. This hand contains 10 high-card points and would come within the limits of a 1 No Trump response. However with this hand we prefer the somewhat more favorable-sounding call of 2 Spades.

Choice between raising your partner and bidding your own suit

THE RULE OF FOUR-PLUS

This phase of bidding provides a stumbling block to even the more experienced players. One frequently is presented with a choice between giving partner a single raise in his major suit and naming some other suit. Since it is usually more important to support your partner's major suit than to show your own, the question first to be answered is: "Can I afford to do both?"

If your hand is good enough to justify two bids, you should show your suit first and support partner's suit later. If you feel that your hand is not strong enough to do both, you should confine yourself to a single raise of partner's suit, hoping he can take further action.

Stated in terms of point count, *if responder's hand is above average strength (11 or 12 points), it is worth two bids and is therefore too strong for a single raise.* For example:

♠ A x x   ♡ x x   ◊ A J x x x   ♣ x x x

Your partner opens with 1 Spade. The question is whether to raise to
2 Spades or to bid 2 Diamonds. Is this hand worth two bids? If your
instinct tells you that it is not, you are right. The proper response is
2 Spades and not 2 Diamonds. The hand is worth 9 points in support
of Spades and is well within the limits of a single raise.

Observe the following example:

♠ A x x x   ♡ x   ◇ A 10 x x x   ♣ x x x

Again the question is whether to raise the Spades or to show the
Diamonds. Is this hand worth two bids?

This hand is worth 11 points in support of Spades, and is therefore
too strong for a single raise. In all such cases you make a temporizing
bid first (2 Diamonds in this case), intending to raise partner's suit
on the next round. You are sure to have another chance, because the
2 Diamond bid is a one-round force on the opener.

In applying this principle you will frequently find it necessary to
bid 2 in a very weak suit, as a waiting bid. For example:

♠ Q x x x   ♡ x x   ◇ K 10 x x   ♣ A x x

Your partner opens with 1 Spade. With 11 points, this hand is too
good for a single raise but not good enough for a jump raise. This is
another one of those hands which might best be described by a raise
to 2½ Spades, a bid unfortunately not permitted by the lawmakers.
You must therefore arrange to bid twice by first calling some other
suit. There is no objection to a take-out to 2 Diamonds, since it is
your full intention to raise Spades on the next round. Sometimes, it
may be expedient to make this temporizing bid with a three-card
minor suit. For example: Partner opens with 1 Spade and you hold:

♠ Q x x x x   ♡ x x   ◇ K x x   ♣ A 10 x

This hand is worth 11 points in support of Spades. It is therefore
obviously too good for a single raise, yet it is not strong enough for
a jump to 3 Spades, which would insist upon game and which would
promise a hand equal to an opening bid in strength (at least 13 points).
Responder must arrange to bid twice, and the suggested response is
first 2 Clubs. This should not shock even the most squeamish, for
there is not the remotest danger that the hand will ever play in Clubs.

In cases such as are illustrated by the four previous examples, the
responder's task is simplified if the opponent overcalls the opening
bid. In each of these cases the responder should bid 2 Spades, a free

bid, denoting a good hand. It is not now necessary to make indirect bids in the side suits, since the voluntary action on the part of responder indicates a good hand (about 9 to 12 points).

Rebid by opener after take-out to 2 of a suit

If you choose your opening 1 bid properly, you will already have planned the rebid you will make if partner takes you out into 2 of his suit.

The principal things to remember are:

A rebid in the same suit you bid before, or a suit rebid which permits partner to return to your first suit at the level of 2, does not promise additional strength.

A bid of 2 No Trump, a raise of partner's suit to 3, a bid of 3 in a new suit, or any bid which makes it impossible for partner to return to 2 of your first suit suggests a strong hand.

♠ J x x   ♡ A K x x   ◇ A 10 x x   ♣ J x

Open 1 Heart. If partner responds 1 Spade, your rebid is 1 No Trump. But if partner's response is 2 Clubs, rebid 2 Diamonds, not 2 No Trump. This permits partner to pass or to return to 2 Hearts if his hand so indicates.

♠ x x   ♡ A K x x x   ◇ Q x x   ♣ K J x

You bid 1 Heart, partner responds 2 Clubs. Rebid 2 Hearts. Your trump support is good enough to raise, but your hand as a whole—worth 13 points in support of Clubs—is not good enough for a raise to three in a minor suit. Such a bid would show 15 or more points.

A rebid of 2 No Trump by the opener when partner has taken out to 2 of a suit describes a good hand, one that ranges in high-card values from 15 to 18 points.[*] The 2 No Trump rebid should not be used as a rescue of partner's response.

♠ A Q x   ♡ A Q J x x   ◇ K J x   ♣ x x

Partner responds 2 Clubs to your opening bid of 1 Heart. With this stronger hand, you will prefer a rebid of 2 No Trump. A rebid of 2 Hearts would announce a hand in the minimum range, 13 to 15 points. This hand is worth 17 in high cards alone and must therefore be described in more encouraging fashion, even though this prevents your telling at once about your rebiddable suit. By virtue of the fact that partner responded at the two-level and you have a least 15 points,

---

[*] For the alternative treatment of the 2 No Trump rebid, see Chapter 4.

this bid is forcing to game except where responder makes a simple rebid of his own suit over 2 No Trump.

A raise of responder's takeout from 2 to 3 has been described as indicating a strong hand, worth 15 points or more. Note that this is a slight weakening of the requirement, to conform with modern practice. Two exceptions occur: If partner responds in the minor suit you had planned as your own rebid, it is correct to raise (e.g. 1 Heart, 2 Diamonds, you may bid 3 Diamonds even with a holding such as hand 1 above). And if you open 1 Spade and partner responds 2 Hearts, you may raise to 3 with only slight additional values, provided you are satisfied with Hearts.

When partner's response has precluded a weaker rebid, a similar exception is allowed to the rule that a 2 No Trump rebid shows a strong hand. For example:

♠ A Q x x   ♡ x x x   ◇ A 10 x x   ♣ K J

You open 1 Spade, prepared to bid 2 Diamonds if partner responded 2 Clubs. Instead, partner responds 2 Hearts. You have no alternative but to rebid 2 No Trump; responder should make some allowance for the fact that he may have forced you to do this on a weaker than usual hand.

FOUR-CARD MAJOR OPENING QUIZ

You are the dealer. What do you bid with each of the following hands?

1. ♠ A 10 9 x
   ♡ x x
   ◇ A K x x
   ♣ K 10 x

2. ♠ K x x x
   ♡ x x
   ◇ A K 10 x
   ♣ K Q 10

3. ♠ K J 10 x
   ♡ A K x x
   ◇ Q x
   ♣ x x x

4. ♠ A x x
   ♡ K Q J x
   ◇ A Q J 9 x
   ♣ x

5. ♠ K Q 10 x
   ♡ A 10 9 x x
   ◇ K x
   ♣ x x

6. ♠ J x
   ♡ J x x x
   ◇ A Q 10 x
   ♣ A K x

7. ♠ A Q x x
   ♡ Q x x x
   ◇ K Q J x
   ♣ x

8. ♠ Q x x x
   ♡ A K Q x
   ◇ A K J
   ♣ x x

9. ♠ Q 10 x x
   ♡ J 10 x x
   ◇ A K x
   ♣ A x

Your partner opens the bidding with 1 Heart and the next hand passes. What do you bid with each of the following hands?

10. ♠ K x
    ♡ x x
    ◇ K 10 x x x
    ♣ Q x x x

11. ♠ J x
    ♡ A K x
    ◇ K J x x
    ♣ 9 8 x x

12. ♠ 10 x x
    ♡ x x
    ◇ K Q J x
    ♣ A K J 10

Your partner opens with 1 Spade and the next hand bids 2 Clubs. What is your call?

13. ♠ K x x
    ♡ A Q x x x
    ◇ K 10 x
    ♣ J x

14. ♠ K x x
    ♡ A J x x x
    ◇ x x x
    ♣ 10 x

15. ♠ J x x
    ♡ Q x x x
    ◇ A x x
    ♣ x x x

ANSWERS TO FOUR-CARD MAJOR OPENING QUIZ

1. One Spade.

With your high cards scattered among three suits, you can afford to open 1 Spade. If partner does respond 2 Hearts, you can rebid 2 No Trump. If he bids any other suit, you can raise.

2. One Diamond.

Once again you have your high cards in three suits, but now your spade suit is not biddable. However, you can rebid 1 Spade should partner respond 1 Heart; if he responds 2 Clubs, you can raise.

3. One Spade.

With two touching four-card suits, bid the higher-ranking first.

4. One Diamond.

Including distribution, your hand is worth 19 points. Therefore, you are strong enough to bid your hand naturally—i.e., show the long suit first. You intend reversing with 2 Hearts at your next turn to show your strength.

5. One Spade.

This hand is a mandatory opening bid, but it is not strong enough to reverse by opening 1 Heart and showing your Spades next. To provide a rebid, open 1 Spade even though your Heart suit is longer.

6. One Diamond.

You would normally open the higher-ranking of touching suits or, in this case, Hearts. Unfortunately your Heart suit is not biddable since it does not contain 4 HCP.

7. One Spade.

With three four-card suits, open the suit below the singleton. Spades rank immediately below Clubs for the purpose of this rule.

8. One Heart.

No choice—your Spade suit isn't biddable and your hand is too strong for 1 No Trump.

9. One Diamond

This is a mandatory opening bid, but neither major suit is biddable. And since you have only two Clubs, a convenient 1 Club opening bid is out of the question.

10. One No Trump.

This shows a moderate hand with 6 to 10 points in high cards. 2 Diamonds, although it counts to 10 points, would misrepresent the hand since it would suggest greater high-card strength or a much better suit.

11. Two Diamonds.

There is certainly a very strong probability that your partner will wind up playing this hand at a Heart contract, but it would not be advisable to raise Hearts first crack out of the box. Your hand is too strong for 2 Hearts, and a raise to 3 Hearts would be misleading because such a call is nearly always based on at least 4 trumps. Therefore you bid 2 Diamonds, with the intention of raising Hearts next.

12. Two Diamonds.

With 14 points in high cards you should set your sights on a game. 2 Diamonds is selected because if partner rebids 2 Hearts, you can continue with a forcing bid of 3 Clubs. Partner will then doubtless bid 3 No Trump if he has a guard in Spades.

13. Two Hearts.

If there had been no overcall, you would have bid 2 Hearts over 1 Spade, indicating a five-card suit and at least 10 points. There is no reason why you shouldn't do the same after the overcall. 2 Hearts is forcing and should lead to the right contract.

14. Two Spades.

Your hand is not strong enough to warrant two constructive bids. If you bid 2 Hearts, you will be at a loss how to proceed should partner rebid 2 Spades. Even though you do not have four trumps, give the raise that lets partner decide whether to move toward game. You may get a chance to bid Hearts later.

15. Pass.

If there had been no overcall, you would have been obliged to bid 1 No Trump over 1 Spade to cover the possibility that your partner had a giant hand on which game could be made. In the actual case, you need not enter the bidding with a weak hand, as your partner can bid again if he wants to.

7.   Slam bidding

I HAVE grave doubt as to the propriety of treating slam bidding as a distinct topic rather than as part of bidding tactics in general, but since that seems to be the accepted practice, I shall fall in line.

True enough, there are certain bids which by their very nature carry direct slam inferences. A jump in a new suit, for example, or a cue bid in a suit adversely bid. But the development of the bidding which reaches a slam should not differ widely from the style employed in getting to game. If we have a method for determining that a hand will take ten tricks, with Hearts as trumps, why is that method not equally suitable for determining that we have eleven tricks with Diamonds as trumps or twelve tricks at a Spade contract? The big thing in slam bidding is to determine whether or not the partnership resources amount to twelve tricks, a simple proposition indeed, but surprisingly difficult to sell.

What about Aces? you ask. You may find that your side can win twelve tricks but unfortunately the enemy can cash two tricks first. Naturally this is a condition to be avoided. After it is determined that the partnership has the necessary winning tricks, then comes the check-up. Various conventions have from time to time been devised for the purpose of making this checkup, but bear in mind that the purpose of these conventions is not to find out if you have a slam. Regular bidding methods are employed for that purpose. The conventions are calculated to find out if the opponents can win two tricks in a hurry. In other words, conventions like the Blackwood are not for the purpose of getting to a slam. They are for the purpose of staying out of one that cannot be made.

In other words, first find out that you have a slam. Then employ the slam convention for the purpose of checking up on Aces.

Slam valuation

In slam bidding the big thing is the diagnosis; that is, determination that the partnership has twelve or thirteen trick-winners. We have observed that when the partnership possesses the sum total of two opening bids (26 points), game will usually result. In other words, if both partners are satisfied with Spades as trump and each one has the equivalent of an opening bid, the hand should produce ten tricks. If the partnership has a surplus of a couple of tricks, it has the material for a slam. In other words, 33 or 34 points represents the trick-taking power of twelve tricks.

The following cases will illustrate how we determine that the partnership has the necessary trick-taking powers. You hold:

♠ K J x x x   ♡ A x   ◇ x x   ♣ K Q x x

Your partner opens with 1 Diamond. You respond 1 Spade. Your partner raises to 3 Spades. What is your diagnosis? You should diagnose a slam. Your hand is worth 16 rebid points (15 originally and 1 for the fifth Spade now that the suit has been supported). Partner has advertised a strong hand, probably 17 points or more. You therefore have the necessary 33 points. As a precautionary measure you may barge into a Blackwood bid, to protect against partner's holding some such hand as:

♠ A Q x x   ♡ K Q x   ◇ K Q x x x   ♣ x

Another example:

♠ 10 x x   ♡ A 9 x   ◇ A K J x   ♣ Q J x

Your partner opens with 1 Club, you respond with 1 Diamond. Partner's rebid is 2 No Trump. This is the classic case for simple addition. At No Trump we count only the high cards, so that your hand is worth 15 points. Partner, having made a jump to 2 No Trump, has promised 19 or 20 high-card points. You therefore know that you have at least 34, and you contract for 6 No Trump. What about Aces? you may ask. Should we check? In No Trump bidding it is impossible for the opponents to have two Aces if the partnership possesses 33 points, for there are only 7 points left in the pack.

The partner's hand was:

♠ A J x   ♡ K Q x   ◇ Q x x   ♣ A K x x

This leads us to the following conclusion: If you hold a responding hand which is as good as an opening bid and your partner opens the bidding and jumps, keep your eyes open for a slam. In other words, *an opening bid faced by an opening bid and followed by a jump equals a slam.* All of this, of course, assumes that there is a suitable contract and that the hand is not a misfit. I assume for the purpose of this rule that your partner's jump is in a declaration which you find to your taste.

We have seen that estimating slams on direct No Trump bidding is nothing more complicated than a simple addition of assets. With 37 or 38 points you should be willing to chance a grand slam (the opponents could not have an Ace). With 33 or 34, a small slam (the opponents could not have two Aces). This assumes a balanced hand. With a good five-card suit, you may get by with a point less; and with a six-card suit, with 2 or 3 points less. But in those cases it is wise to satisfy yourself as to the number of Aces held by the partnership.

If partner shows a strong 2 bid, you may assume that he can take nine tricks in his own hand (and that he has at least 25 points with a five-card suit). By adding his assets to the total number of tricks you are confident your hand will produce, you will usually arrive with a fair degree of accuracy at the full trick-taking capacity of the combined holding.

Slam diagnosis by opener when responder jumps

You open, and partner jumps (1 Spade—3 No Trump, 13–16 points and four-card support). If you have no excess values, you merely contract for game. Partner's response is based on a hand that is equivalent to an opening bid.

You have an opening bid. This spells game, and where you have excess values it follows that your hand may produce tricks in excess of game.

If your hand ranges in value from 13 to 16, it is regarded as of the minimum class. With those hands, slam will not be available and you simply contract for game.

If your hand is worth 17 points or more (don't forget to revalue your hand after partner supports it by adding 1 point for your fifth trump and 2 points for your sixth trump), then you may have a slam. If partner has a 3 Spade bid which is worth 16, you will have the necessary 33 points. With hands of this value, try once (by showing some Ace); if partner does not react favorably, quit at game.

If your hand is worth 20 points, you know that you have the necessary 33 and should not settle for less than a slam, provided you have checked for Aces. Hands that are worth 18 or 19 are usually safe enough to be taken to the level of 5, so that if you are concerned only with Aces, a Blackwood bid is permissible on hands of this strength.

Remember, however, that to try Blackwood with holdings worth only 16 or 17 is a dangerous practice, for if the hand breaks badly, you may not be able to take eleven tricks if partner presents an unsuitable dummy.

Let us assume a few cases in each of which you open with 1 Spade and partner jumps to 3 No Trump, the forcing spade raise. You hold:

♠ A K J x x   ♡ x x   ◇ A x x   ♣ K x x

This hand is worth 17 rebid points. It had an original value of 16, but 1 point must be added for the fifth Spade now that partner has supported the suit. Inasmuch as partner's 3 Spade raise will be as much as from 13 to 16, it will be seen that if he has a maximum you will have the necessary 33 points. You should therefore try for a slam, but you must do so in a mild manner. A Blackwood call is not appropriate. First, because it will not provide you with enough information: even if partner has two Aces, you may be a long way from a slam, for you may not have the necessary tricks. Furthermore, a contract of 5 may not be safe if partner has a minimum raise of 13 points. You may make one try by bidding 4 Diamonds, showing the Ace. If partner wishes to proceed toward a slam, he may do so. If he returns to 4 Spades, you will retire gracefully.

You hold:

♠ A K J x x   ♡ x   ◇ A x x x   ♣ K x x

This holding is worth 18 rebid points. Now you may have a slam if partner has 15. You may therefore be slightly more aggressive than was recommended in the preceding example. A contract of 5 odd should now be safe, and you may make two tries for a slam.

♠ A K J x x   ♡ x   ◇ A J x x   ♣ K Q x

This hand is worth 21 rebid points, which, with partner's assured 13, brings the partnership up to 34 points, ample for a slam. You have merely to check for Aces now, and if partner has one, you may undertake to bid a slam.

In the following example you have opened with 1 Diamond, partner responds with 2 No Trump. You hold:

♠ A K x   ♡ K x x   ◇ A K J x   ♣ Q J x

You have 21 points, partner has 13, 14, or 15. You know, therefore, that you have at least 34 points, assuring you of a sound play for slam, and that you have a maximum of 36 points, so that you will not be inclined to contract for a grand slam. No checking for Aces is necessary, because the opponents cannot have two of them, and furthermore, even if your partner has two Aces and a King, you will not contract for a grand slam because you cannot count 13 tricks.

Bids carrying slam implications

Jump shift in a new suit

A jump shift by responder is the accepted method of announcing his early interest in slam. Since the mere naming of a new suit by responder forces opener to speak again, it is not necessary to jump in a new suit when game is responder's only objective. The jump shift is thus reserved especially for those hands where responder has slam aspirations.

If responder sees that the partnership is knocking on the slam door, he should make a jump shift providing that his hand is suitable. As we mentioned earlier, the jump shift says more about responder's hand than simply a desire to play in slam. It also suggests where to play the hand: either in opener's suit or responder's.

A jump from 1 of a minor to 3 No Trump

This bid is far from a signal to partner to subside. It is an exact descriptive bid which announces: "Partner, I have a high-card count of 16, 17 or 18. You can therefore calculate almost exactly our high-card assets. At the same time, I must warn you that my distribution is 4-3-3-3, so don't count on ruffing in my hand. With any other distribution, we might have play for slam in one of our four-card suits."

A two-over-one response, followed by a jump

Since a two-over-one response is a game force unless it is followed by a rebid of the suit, responder does not need to jump to make sure that the bidding does not die before game has been reached. Therefore, if responder follows a two-over-one response with a delayed jump in a suit, he is signifying slam interest.

Cue bid of an opponent's suit

The cue bid of an opponent's suit is another bid that carries strong slam inferences. The cue bid guarantees the ability to win the first or second round in that suit, i.e., the cue-bidder will have either the ace or a void or, at worst, a singleton.

More often than not, the cue bid of an enemy suit is made with the intention of getting to slam. Occasionally, however, its purpose will be to get to 3 No Trump—usually when it is apparent from the early rounds of bidding that slam is out of the question.

You usually have no need to use a cue bid of the enemy suit to reach game—direct methods are generally more effective. There are many slams, however, that cannot be bid intelligently unless one of the partners has control of the overcaller's suit and can convey this information to his cohort.

Note that there are two important exceptions to this rule: A cue bid after an opponent intervenes can be used to show support for opener's major without having control of the bid suit; and if an opponent intervenes after a 1 No Trump opening bid, the cue bid is used as a Stayman inquiry for four-card major suits.

If you have not yet explicitly agreed on a trump suit, a cue bid of the enemy suit implicitly fixes the last suit bid by your side as trumps. To illustrate:

♠ Void ♡ A K x x ◇ K J 10 x x ♣ Q J x x

Your partner opens the bidding with 1 Diamond and your right-hand opponent intervenes with 1 Spade. Certainly, your side can be sure of at least game in Diamonds, and if partner has any strength in the Club suit, a small or grand slam is likely. Cue bid 2 Spades now. That says: "Partner, I can take care of your Spade losers. I have excellent support for your suit. I can guarantee game and am looking for slam. Describe your hand to me!" Not bad for one bid. You can now go about exchanging information at your leisure to find out whether you have the right controls for slam. The cue bid has another advantage—it allows you to uncover duplication of values. If a substantial part of partner's strength happens to be in the suit in which you made a cue bid, he will realize that those values are of doubtful worth to your side's cause. Suppose that after the auction above, opener holds:

♠ A K x ♡ x ◇ A Q x x x ♣ x x x x

He should realize that his two tricks in spades represent a duplication of values and that his hand has decreased in value. Slam should be avoided and he can warn partner of this by rebidding 2 No Trump to show stoppers in the enemy suit.

Choice between a cue bid and a new suit

When you have a choice between showing your own suit and making a cue bid in the overcaller's suit, you should usually prefer the former. It can be very difficult to describe a good suit late in the auction, but it is never too late to show control of the adverse suit with a cue bid. Suppose that partner opens 1 Spade and your right-hand opponent overcalls 2 Clubs. You hold:

♠ K Q x x   ♡ A J x x x   ◇ x   ♣ A Q x

This hand certainly has a slammish look if you can find a fit, but to cue bid clubs now only robs you of the space you might need to probe for the best spot. The recommended bid is 2 Hearts. Since that is forcing, you have conserved your bidding space. You plan to support spades next, then cue bid clubs. This sequence of bids gives partner the clearest picture of your hand, and gives him the all the room he needs to describe his holding.

Again, a belated cue bid of the enemy suit is not always an attempt to reach slam. Where both partners have showed limited holdings and no clear final contract has emerged, a cue bid quite probably is a probe for a possible No Trump contract.

The singleton in slam bidding

Aces and Kings alone do not make a slam. Quite as many slams are dependent upon the possession of a singleton.

Let us take an example. You are South and hold:

♠ A K Q x x   ♡ x x x   ◇ K x x   ♣ J x

The bidding has proceeded:

SOUTH	WEST	NORTH	EAST
1 Spade	Pass	2 Diamonds	Pass
2 Spades	Pass	3 Clubs	Pass
3 Diamonds	Pass	4 Spades	Pass
?			

What should South do?

The unimaginative player would pass, of course, because he would feel that he had already shown the full strength of his hand. The player with vision would stop to picture his partner's holding and would realize that there was only one Heart loser because partner must have a singleton or a void and the King of Diamonds would solidify that suit.

North holds:

♠ J 9 x ♡ x ◇ A Q J x x ♣ A Q 10 x

The recognition of the singleton in Hearts is the interesting feature of the hand. It may be stated as a general principle of bidding that when a player names three suits and incorporates a jump in his sequence of bids he shows a singleton or void in the fourth suit.

If North held a doubleton Heart he might bid three suits, but then he would not be justified in jumping to 4 Spades. Over the 3 Diamond bid it would be sufficient to bid only 3 Spades.

Had South held precisely the same strength in high cards:

♠ A K Q x x ♡ K x x ◇ J x x ♣ x x

he would have passed the 4 Spade bid. He would have then realized that his King of Hearts opposite his partner's singleton or void was of no great consequence and his Diamond holding was not such as to assure the partnership against losing a trick in that suit.

In the next case you are South and hold:

♠ J x ♡ Q x x ◇ K x ♣ A K J x x x

The bidding has proceeded:

SOUTH	NORTH
1 Club	1 Diamond
2 Clubs	3 Spades
3 No Trump	5 Clubs
?	

What do you do?

Despite the fact that you have a minimum bid, you should contract for 6 Clubs. It will be seen that you have the right King. Had it been the King of Hearts, you would have had no reason to be optimistic. Your partner is marked with, at most, a singleton Heart. He has presumably shown five Diamonds, four Spades, and at least three Clubs. This is his hand:

♠ A Q x x ♡ x ◇ A Q J x x ♣ Q 10 x

In this hand the important consideration was not the number of Kings which partner held, but specifically which ones.

Finding the singleton

A belated cue bid beyond game, when nothing has previously been said about a suit the opponents have bid, should be taken as a request to partner to bid a slam if he has no more than one loser in the adverse suit. An illustration from a tournament:

NORTH: ♠ K Q x x x   ♡ 10 x   ◊ x   ♣ K Q 10 x x
SOUTH: ♠ A J 10 9 x   ♡ A K J x x   ◊ x x   ♣ A

The bidding is:

SOUTH	WEST	NORTH	EAST
1 Spade	2 Diamonds	3 Clubs	Pass
3 Hearts	Pass	4 Spades	Pass
5 Clubs	Pass	6 Spades	

The bidding follows routine lines up to South's 5 Club bid. This must not be construed as any desire to play Clubs, since Spades have been so vigorously supported. The bid therefore denotes possession of the Ace of Clubs and implies a desire for partner to bid a slam if he can take care of the adverse Diamonds. Had North's hand contained one Heart and two Diamonds he would have been obliged to return to 5 Spades; no slam could be made. The key to the slam was the singleton Diamond.

It is equally important to know when there is no singleton in the crucial spot:

OPENER: ♠ A K J 10 x x   ♡ Q x   ◊ A Q x x   ♣ x
RESPONDER: ♠ Q x   ♡ J x   ◊ K 10 x x x x   ♣ A Q 10

The bidding:

OPENER	RESPONDER
1 Spade	2 Diamonds
3 Spades	4 Clubs
4 Diamonds	4 Spades
5 Spades	Pass

When the opener jumped to 3 Spades, his partner had good reason to be slam-minded—his own hand was about equal to an opening bid, opposite an opening bid and a jump. The Spade suit is now accepted as trump by inference, and the responder's bid of 4 Clubs must be construed as an Ace-showing bid. This, incidentally, is the proper procedure even if you are playing the Blackwood Convention. There should be no hurry about the 4 No Trump asking bid. Opener's showing of the Diamond support at this point is natural, and responder can do no better than show his Spade support in response. It is the opener's bid of 5 Spades that is the subject of our attention. What is its meaning?

Logically, it means this: "Partner, we have talked about everything else, and the only thing that worries me is the Heart situation. How are you fixed in that department? If you have only one Heart loser, I think we can make a slam." Responder must stop despite the strong bidding of his partner. With a singleton in Hearts he would, of course, have proceeded to a slam. Similarly, with a singleton Heart, opener would have bid 6 himself.

The right singleton—the right Ace

NORTH:	♠ x x	♡ Q	◇ A Q x x	♣ A K J 10 x x
SOUTH:	♠ A x x	♡ x x x	◇ K J 10 x x	♣ Q x

The bidding:

NORTH	EAST	SOUTH	WEST
1 Club	Pass	1 Diamond	1 Spade
3 Diamonds	Pass	3 Spades	Pass
6 Diamonds	Pass	Pass	Pass

South's cue bid, though aggressive, is justifiable. His hand closely approximates the value of an opening bid, and a slam is by no means a fanciful notion. Further, if North manifests no interest in slam, information as to the Ace of Spades may permit him to bid 3 No Trump.

When North learns of the Ace of Spades he can bid a slam in Diamonds, relying on the establishment of the Club suit for discards.

Note that South had the right Ace. Had it been the Ace of Hearts, the partnership would have been subject to the immediate loss of two Spade tricks. Note also that North had the right singleton. A short Spade holding would not have served the purpose.

Slam try below game

It would appear to be good business reasoning that it is better, when convenient, to try for a slam below the game level. You will have explored slam possibilities and have found yourself in position to quit, if necessary, without jeopardizing the game.

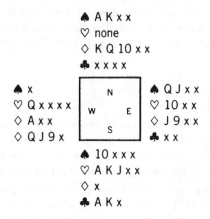

                    ♠ A K x x
                    ♡ none
                    ◇ K Q 10 x x
                    ♣ x x x x

    ♠ x   ♠ Q J x x
    ♡ Q x x x x   N   ♡ 10 x x
    ◇ A x x   W   E   ◇ J 9 x x
    ◇ Q J 9 x   S   ♣ x x

                    ♠ 10 x x x
                    ♡ A K J x x
                    ◇ x
                    ♣ A K x

The bidding is given as it actually took place:

NORTH	EAST	SOUTH	WEST
1 Diamond	Pass	1 Heart	Pass
1 Spade	Pass	3 Spades	Pass
4 Spades	Pass	5 Clubs	Pass
5 Spades	Pass	Pass	Pass

Down 1!

To be set 1 at a contract of 5 in a major suit which you have reached on your own power is equally devastating to the exchequer and the morale. There is nothing ignominious in being down 1 at a contract of 6. At least the victim may take a certain pride in the display of virility that led to the loss. He meets a soldier's death with important issues at stake. But he who climbs to 5 Hearts or Spades with no one in pursuit, and there encamps, is in a most unenviable position; he finds no hope of glory, no pride in having dared. South should have planned his bidding tactics so that he could try for a slam below the game level. South's second bid of 3 Spades is indefensible. Such a bid announces a willingness to contract for game but does not suggest a slam. Once the Spade bid is heard, South should visualize a slam and should at this point make a definite slam signal; that is, a *jump in a new suit*. His call should be 3 Clubs. North, a little nervous about his partner's Heart response, and having already described the values of his hand, may be reluctant to raise the Clubs and may step lightly by bidding 3 Diamonds. South now bids 4 Spades. By this time North will know very well that South has a powerful hand and is interested in big things, but North is still able to check out at a safe level.

Blasting

In many circles there is a lasting stigma attached to bidding a slam and being set one. This induces a tendency toward overcautiousness which deprives these players not only of the increased revenue that is the reward of the daring, but, what is probably more important, the thrill of bringing in a big one. The bridge player, unlike the fisherman, derives no pleasure in telling about the one that got away.

The science of slam bidding is very fascinating. There are many ways in which ingenuity can be exercised in the effort to learn this, that, and the other thing about your partner's hand. There are other features than can be ascertained in a purely mechanical manner, such as by the showing of Aces (either wholesale or retail).

Occasionally a hand comes up in which no amount of science can help you to determine definitely that a slam can be made. Success may depend upon your partner's holding a doubleton of some suit or an odd Jack. In those cases blasting, or taking the bull by the horns, may be the best bet.

Occasionally unscientific treatment of the hand is apt to produce the best results. This is particularly true when everything depends on the luck of the opening lead. If the opposition is not given too many suggestions during the auction, there is at least an even chance that the opening lead will be favorable, as witness the following hand:

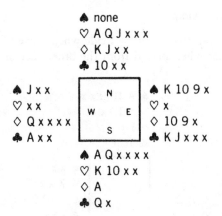

♠ none
♡ A Q J x x x
◇ K J x x
♣ 10 x x

♠ J x x
♡ x x
◇ Q x x x x
♣ A x x

♠ K 10 9 x
♡ x
◇ 10 9 x
♣ K J x x x

♠ A Q x x x x
♡ K 10 x x
◇ A
♣ Q x

The bidding:

NORTH	EAST	SOUTH	WEST
1 Heart	Pass	1 Spade	Pass
2 Hearts	Pass	6 Hearts	

South knew that it might depend on the opening lead, which would be either Diamonds or Clubs. Of course partner might have the Ace of Clubs, in which case South would certainly wish to be in a small slam, although not necessarily in a grand slam. North might have the King of Clubs, which would make the chance of fulfillment very bright. Finally, East might not lead a Club. In the actual case, East elected to lead the 10 of Diamonds and the contract was brought home without any difficulty. A Club lead, of course, would have defeated the contract, but there are many players who would not have led a Club with East's hand.

Positional slams

A slam can frequently be made when played from one side of the table but not when played from the other. Let us examine a case or two:

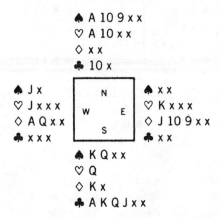

♠ A 10 9 x x
♡ A 10 x x
◇ x x
♣ 10 x

♠ J x   ♠ x x
♡ J x x x   ♡ K x x x
◇ A Q x x   ◇ J 10 9 x x
♣ x x x   ♣ x x

♠ K Q x x
♡ Q
◇ K x
♣ A K Q J x x

South opened with 1 Club, and when North responded with 1 Spade, he properly leaped to 4. Note that a jump bid to 3 Spades by South would not have been forcing, and if North happened to have responded with a shaded bid of 1 Spade, containing perhaps 5 points, he would surely not carry on. South was willing to bid the 4 Spades however weak a response North had made. North, on the other hand, having two Aces and knowing that partner could hardly rely upon him for more than 6 points, tried for a slam by bidding 5 Hearts, designating the Ace. South now elected to bid 6 Clubs. North, it seems to me, should have passed. North actually went on to 6 Spades, which was defeated with a Diamond opening and the unfortunate location of the Ace. South's technique had been faultless. When there was merely game in contemplation he was satisfied to be in 4 Spades, but when it became apparent that a slam was available he realized the importance of becoming declarer himself, in order to protect the King of Diamonds from attack on the opening lead.

South reasoned that if North happened to have five Spades, a discard of a Diamond could be made on North's long Spade. North should have realized that his partner had a specific reason for bidding 6 Clubs rather than 6 Spades, and North's own weakness in Diamonds should have suggested to him that his partner might be trying to protect the King of the suit. True enough, South could have saved the day by bidding 6 No Trump, but such action was hardly indicated.

In the bidding of powerhouses, when a player holds King x of a suit he should make any reasonable effort to become declarer himself; and by way of corollary, when he holds two worthless cards of any unmentioned suit he should try to permit partner to play the hand just in case his partner should happen to have the King or a tenace position.

Showing extra values

A bid which frequently leads up to a slam is the forcing jump raise. If you name any other suit after a double raise, it is a definite slam try and partner is requested to give you any valuable information he may possess. If his forcing raise has been a minimum, he merely returns to 4 of the original suit. If he has additional values, he may take action in various ways. Let us examine a few cases.

♠ A K x x x   ♡ x   ◊ K x x x   ♣ A x x

You open with 1 Spade, partner raises to 3 No Trump, the forcing jump raise. Your hand has the value of 17 rebid points. If partner's bid is maximum (16 points), you will have the necessary 33. This means that while there is a chance for slam it is not a very bright one, and you should make a mild try. This you do by bidding 4 Clubs, which designates the Ace. Remember that Spades have been agreed upon and the naming of a new suit is forcing. If partner merely returns to 4 Spades, you relax in the knowledge that you have done your duty. If he shows the Ace of Hearts, you can do no more than return to 4 Spades, but you will be in position to answer a further invitation should it be extended by partner.

♠ A K x x x   ♡ A J x   ◊ x x   ♣ A x x

You open with 1 Spade, partner jump raises to 3 No Trump. Your hand has a rebid value of 18 points. This gives you a reasonable chance for slam if partner has more than a minimum. If, for example, he has 15 points, the slam should be assured, for your points are all gilt-edged. The proper procedure is to bid 4 Clubs, showing the Ace. This affords partner the chance to bid 4 Diamonds, which in turn will allow you to bid 4 Hearts. In this manner you have succeeded in showing both your Aces below the game level. Notice in this case it was easier to show the Ace of Clubs first. Had you shown the Ace of Hearts over the 3 Spade bid, partner would have had to bid 5 Diamonds if he chose to show the Ace of Diamonds. If he did show it, you would have had considerable qualms about showing the Ace of Clubs at the level of 6. In situations such as this where there is an unnamed suit, holding two Aces, it is usually more convenient to show the lower Ace first.

♠ K Q J x   ♡ K x x x   ◇ A x   ♣ x x x

Your partner opens with 1 Diamond. You respond with 1 Spade. Now opener jumps to 3 Spades. What is your diagnosis? This hand possesses slam possibilities. Your hand is worth 14 points. If partner's jump was based on 19, you will have the necessary ingredients. Since he might have that much, you should make a try by bidding 4 Diamonds. This indicates merely possession of the Ace, not a desire to play Diamonds (since Spades have been agreed upon). The rest you should leave more or less to your partner.

♠ x x   ♡ A K J x x   ◇ K Q x   ♣ x x x

Your partner opens with 1 Spade. You bid 2 Hearts. Partner raises to 4 Hearts. Here again you should recognize slam possibilities. Your hand is worth 15 rebid points, 14 originally and 1 for the fifth Heart now that that suit has been supported. Partner may have as many as 18 or 19 points for his jump. Inasmuch as you have no side Ace to show, you indicate your desire for slam in the only way open to you, by bidding 5 Hearts.

♠ A K J x x   ♡ J x   ◇ x x x   ♣ K Q x

Your partner opens with 1 Heart. You respond with 1 Spade. Partner jumps to 2 No Trump. Inasmuch as the final contract will definitely be in No Trump, you value only your high cards and observe that you have 14. Partner's jump rebid to 2 No Trump shows 19 or 20. Therefore you are assured of the necessary 33 or 34 points and should assume the responsibility. The proper call is 6 No Trump. Don't make an attempt to play this hand at Spades. Your Spades will win tricks at No Trump.

♠ x   ♡ K Q x x x   ◇ K x x x   ♣ K x x

Partner opens with 1 Club. You respond with 1 Heart, which partner raises to 3. You should recognize slam possibilities. Your hand is worth 14 rebid points at Hearts, and partner, for his jump to 3, may have 19 points. You have no Aces to show, but bidding 4 Clubs will serve the same purpose. In view of partner's opening in that suit and subsequent jump, partner probably has the Ace of Clubs and will recognize that you are showing the King. If your partner's next bid is 4 Diamonds, you should gamble it out for a slam. This action is based on the possession of a singleton Spade. Remember partner may be unable to bid the slam because of the possession of two small Spades. This hand is suitable for Blackwood because your prime concern is with the Aces. His complete hand was:

♠ x x   ♡ A J x x   ◇ A x   ♣ A Q J x x

OPENER: ♠ K Q x   ♡ A Q J x x x   ◇ A x   ♣ x x
RESPONDER: ♠ A 10 9 x x x   ♡ K x   ◇ x x x   ♣ A x

The bidding:

OPENER	RESPONDER
1 Heart	1 Spade
3 Hearts	3 Spades
4 Spades	5 Clubs
5 Diamonds	5 Hearts
7 No Trump	

The 3 Heart rebid by opener is not an absolute force, but partner is expected to bid if his hand is not hopeless. Responder's rebid of 3 Spades is just marking time. Opener raises to 4 Spades, showing that his previous jump was influenced by Spade support. Responder now shows the Ace of Clubs, whereupon opener shows the Ace of Diamonds. At this point responder, by his bid of 5 Hearts, is attempting to indicate the King of that suit, Spades having already been agreed upon. The opener is now able to count thirteen tricks, relying on six Hearts, five Spades (as far as he knows), and the two Aces.

OPENER: ♠ A Q J x x   ♡ K x   ◇ K Q   ♣ K 10 x x
RESPONDER: ♠ K 10 x x x   ♡ Q J 10   ◇ x   ♣ A Q J x

The bidding:

OPENER	RESPONDER
1 Spade	3 No Trump
5 Spades	?

In actual play responder accepted the invitation and contracted for a slam in Spades because he had a very good 3 Spade bid. Naturally two Aces were lost and the slam defeated. The question arose as to the place of the guilt. In this hand the Blackwood Convention, to be sure, would have kept the partnership from error, but still the pitfall should have been avoided. Responder contended that opener should have been satisfied merely to contract for game and should not have invited the slam. The opener argued that he had a full trick over and above his bid and was justified in issuing one invitation. With this I concur. Responder should have realized that the opponents had both the red Aces, else South would have bid 4 Diamonds or 4 Hearts and a slam try. South's 5 Spade bid was very clear. It said, "Partner, I have a fine hand but I have no Aces to show you, other than in trumps." The moral: If partner has a reasonable opportunity to show an Ace and fails to do so, you are to assume that he does not have it.

The Blackwood Convention

This is perhaps the most widely used of all the slam conventions and, I venture to say, the most subject to abuse. On the surface it appears to be a very simple device. In actual practice, however, the exercise of very fine judgment is required to attain the ultimate in results by its use. Unfortunately there has been broadcast the notion that the Blackwood Convention is easy to learn and to apply. Nothing can be farther from the truth. In fact, Blackwood is a very difficult convention, though a highly useful one, and students should not be lulled into a sense of complacency by being told of the ease with which it can be applied. It requires a great deal of study, a great deal of practice, and the exercise of very delicate judgment. The difficulty arises in making the decision whether or not to use Blackwood or the other methods. I know one dear little lady, when asked why she did not proceed toward slam, replied, "I couldn't; she didn't ask me for Aces."

This convention should not be employed as a substitute for thinking. The conduct of certain bridge players gives one the impression that they have a desire to insert a nickel in the Blackwood juke box and expect a slam to come bursting forth.

The original sin is in the assumption that the Blackwood Convention may be employed in all slams. This is most emphatically not so. Permit me to quote from the writings of Easley Blackwood, the man who originally introduced this device:

"We do not pretend that the Blackwood Convention will solve all your slam problems, because there are certain types of hands that cannot be covered by Blackwood.

"In some deals both the Blackwood Convention and cue bidding are impossible, because an exchange of information between the partnership is either unnecessary or unobtainable. When that happens a player must use his own initiative and jump directly into a slam.

"The Blackwood Convention is so easy and simple that it can be learned in less than five minutes, and for that reason it is subject to abuse, and players are warned against trying it too often.

"During the preliminary rounds a player must make certain that Blackwood will produce better results than either cue bidding or a direct try for slam."

When the preliminary rounds of bidding have indicated that a slam is probable, and a suit has been agreed upon, either player may institute the convention by calling 4 No Trump. No special holding is required, but the player making the 4 No Trump bid must be quite convinced that the hand will play safely for eleven tricks; in other words, that the partnership assets are approximately 33 points.

The responses are as follows:

> With no Aces bid 5 Clubs.
> With one Ace bid 5 Diamonds.
> With two Aces bid 5 Hearts.
> With three Aces bid 5 Spades.
> With four Aces bid 5 Clubs.

Observe that the answer with four Aces is the same as the one employed to show no Aces. This is for economy of space. An ambiguity could not possibly develop, because the previous bidding will make it clear that the responder (where he has four Aces and bids 5 Clubs) could not possibly be Aceless. The Blackwood bidder may then ask for Kings, which he could not do conveniently if partner responded 5 No Trump.

After Aces have been shown, the 4 No Trump bidder may ask for Kings by bidding 5 No Trump. However, there is the very distinct proviso that the 5 No Trump bid must never be made unless it has been previously determined that the partnership is in possession of all four Aces.

In other words, the opener late in the bidding calls 4 No Trump. Responder bids 5 Diamonds, showing one Ace. The opener now bids 5 No Trump, asking for Kings. Responder knows that the opener has three Aces. Otherwise he could not tell that the partnership has all four Aces and would not be privileged to call for Kings.

The responder to the 5 No Trump bid shows the number of his Kings exactly as he shows the number of his Aces in response to 4 No Trump.

Not every 4 No Trump bid is part of the convention. A suit must have been mentioned on the way up. If an opening No Trump bid is raised to 4 No Trump, that is simply an assist and is not part of the convention.

The player who makes the conventional 4 No Trump bid must be careful to plan so that any response by partner will not embarrass him. Such might be the case when the agreed suit, for example, is Clubs. The 4 No Trump bidder must in that case have at least two Aces, because otherwise the partnership will be in a slam after a 5 Diamond response and the opposition will hold two Aces.

It is essential to determine whether or not information as to how many Aces partner has will solve your problem. After all, many a hand with all the Aces has no chance to produce a slam. A singleton in partner's hand may be the decisive factor.

Another important consideration is which of the two players should start the convention. As a general rule, the stronger of the two hands should be given the opportunity to do so, because he can better judge what the hands will produce. For example:

| NORTH: | ♠ A x x | ♡ K x x | ◇ A x x x | ♣ A J x |
| SOUTH: | ♠ K Q J x x | ♡ A Q x | ◇ K Q J | ♣ K x |

After Spades have been agreed upon, which of these two players should start the 4 No Trump bid? If North does it, he will find out that the partnership has all the Aces and Kings, but he will be worried about a losing Diamond and possibly a losing Heart. If, however, South is the one who starts the convention, he will be able to bid 7 No Trump immediately he learns that partner has three Aces and one King.

Note that hands containing voids do not lend themselves to Blackwood treatment, for partner's Ace may be in your void suit, where it would be useless. Hands containing worthless doubletons or trebletons very frequently do not react favorably to Blackwood treatment. This is another way of saying that when your only concern is how many Aces has my partner, Blackwood is ideal. But when you must know specifically which Aces your partner has, Blackwood should not be employed, but the Ace-showing method resorted to, hoping that partner will voluntarily show you specifically which Aces he holds.

Let us turn back to a hand previously discussed on page 149.

To Blackwood players:
beware of the worthless doubleton

NORTH: ♠ K Q x x x   ♡ 10 x   ◇ x   ♣ K Q 10 x x
SOUTH: ♠ A J 10 9 x   ♡ A K J x x   ◇ x x   ♣ A

You are South. During the bidding partner had bid Clubs and jumped in Spades, while the opponents have bid Diamonds. Would it be proper for you to employ the Blackwood Convention? The answer is a distinct "No." In order for your side to produce a slam, your partner need not have an Ace, but second-round control in Diamonds, which he would have whether he held a singleton or a King and Queen. This slam does not necessarily depend upon an Ace. In the actual holding you will observe that North has the singleton Diamond and the slam is spread. But North, consistent with his previous bidding, might have had two Diamonds and one Heart. Remember that the Blackwood Convention cannot ferret out a singleton.

Observe the hand previously discussed on page 150.

NORTH: ♠ x x   ♡ Q   ◇ A Q x x   ♣ A K J 10 x x
SOUTH: ♠ A x x   ♡ x x x   ◇ K J 10 x x   ♣ Q x

Presume that you are North and that you have bid Clubs and jumped your partner's Diamond response, whereas the adversaries have bid Spades. Is North in a position to employ Blackwood? Here again the answer is "No," for if partner has the Ace of Hearts you will not choose to undertake a slam, because of the two Spade losers. But if partner has the Ace of Spades, you will be glad to commit your team to a slam on the theory that the losing Spade can be discarded on the Club suit. In other words, here your problem is not "Does partner have an Ace?" but "Which Ace is it?"

Let us observe the case of the void:

NORTH: ♠ J 9 x x   ♡ A x x   ◇ K x   ♣ x x x x
SOUTH: ♠ A K Q x x   ♡ K Q J x   ◇ A Q J x   ♣ none

You are South and open with 2 Clubs. Partner bids 2 No Trump, you bid 3 Spades and partner raises to 4 Spades. Would it be proper for you to employ Blackwood? The answer again is a distinct "No," for if partner admits that he has an Ace you will be unable to tell whether it is a Club or a Heart. You should therefore *tell*, rather than *ask*. Since Spades have been agreed upon, you bid 4 Diamonds, showing the Ace. Partner will now bid 4 Hearts, showing the Ace of that suit. You now show the Club control, after which he will show the King of Diamonds and you can safely contract for 7 Spades.

NORTH:	♠ A 10 x x	♡ K J 9 x x x	◇ x x	♣ x
SOUTH:	♠ K Q J x x	♡ A Q x	◇ A J x	♣ x x

South opens with 1 Spade, opponent overcalls with 2 Clubs, North bids 2 Hearts. South gives a jump raise to 4 Hearts, and North bids 4 Spades. South, of course, recognizes slam possibilities. Is a Blackwood call appropriate? No, for if South learns that his partner has only one Ace he will be unable to bid a slam, because of the two losing Clubs. North, too, cannot profitably call 4 No Trump, because when he learns that South has two Aces he cannot bid a slam with assurance, for partner might have the Ace of Hearts and the Ace of Clubs. Instead of "asking" for Aces, South instead chooses to "tell" by bidding 5 Diamonds. This permits North to bid 6 Spades (or 6 Hearts).

NORTH:	♠ A K J 10 x x	♡ x x	◇ A x	♣ Q x x
SOUTH:	♠ Q x x	♡ K x x	◇ x x	♣ A K J x x

South opened with 1 Club, North bid 1 Spade. South raised to 2 Spades. North, in an effort to ferret out a slam, chose to bid 4 No Trump. Was this a sound call? When South acknowledged one Ace, North faced an impossible problem. He chose to risk that South could stop the heart suit and bid 6 Spades. He was defeated when a heart lead netted the defense two tricks. The worthless doubleton in Hearts should have warned North away from Blackwood. Had he chosen instead to temporize by "showing" the Ace of Diamonds and subsequently followed it up with a bid of 5, South, having second-round control of Hearts, could then try 6 Clubs, a contract which could not be defeated.

NORTH:	♠ x x	♡ A J x x x x	◇ K Q J	♣ x x
SOUTH:	♠ A K J x x	♡ K Q 9 x	◇ x	♣ K Q x

South opens 1 Spade, North responds 2 Hearts. South, willing to gamble on the ability to establish the Spade suit without loss, knows that his only concern is with the number of Aces North holds, and it matters not which ones. His proper call is 4 No Trump. This will imply satisfaction with Hearts as the "agreed" suit. If North shows three Aces, South should risk a grand slam; if two Aces, he will be content with a small slam. When North actually comes up with just one Ace, South is forced to sign off at 5 Hearts.

When it may be desirable for partner to start the 4 No Trump bid, the bidding may be steered in that direction by making temporary bids of various types to afford him the opportunity, when the 4 level is reached, to ask for Aces.

Assuming that the bidding has proceeded in a very aggressive manner and that a slam becomes probable, is it desirable for you or your partner to initiate the 4 No Trump bid with these hands?

♠ A x x x ♡ x x x ◇ A 10 x ♣ A K x

With this hand you should permit partner to bid the 4 No Trump, because you can give specific information about your hand which will help partner decide. If you bid the 4 No Trump and find out that your partner has one Ace and three Kings, you will still be worried about small-card losers; in other words, the trick-taking potentialities of the hand.

♠ A Q J x x ♡ A Q x x ◇ x ♣ A x x

With this hand you may initiate the Blackwood Convention, because specific information about Aces and Kings will permit you to judge the possibilities of the hand. This is assuming, of course, you have previously determined that the partnership assets amount to 33 points.

♠ Q J x x ♡ A 9 x x x ◇ x x x ♣ A

With this hand it is much better for your partner to start the convention, because information about Aces and Kings will not solve your problem.

It is an integral part of the Blackwood Convention that the 4 No Trump bidder is the captain of the team. When he hears the response, he, and he alone, decides on the final contract, and the responder must abide by his decision.

There is one exception: When the bidding has shown that the partnership has all four Aces, the responder may exercise his own judgment as to the final contract. Occasionally the responder, instead of telling how many Aces he has, may bid a slam directly when his hand contains a void. This might be done in a case where, let us say, Diamonds are the agreed suit and partner has asked for Aces. The Blackwood response would be 5 Diamonds, showing one Ace, but the responder has a void in an unmentioned suit and he fears that the

Blackwood bidder will be discouraged and pass the 5 Diamond bid. He may exercise his discretion by bidding a slam directly over the 4 No Trump bid. For example:

♠ A K x x x   ♡ Q x x   ◇ Q J 10 x x   ♣ none

Your partner has opened with 1 Heart, has vigorously supported your Diamonds, and then bids 4 No Trump (Blackwood). Your conventional response would be 5 Diamonds, showing one Ace. This may discourage partner from bidding a slam, so you may take control of the situation and bid 6 Diamonds instead of telling about your Ace.

There is an important amendment to the Blackwood Convention employed by many players. When cue bids have been made on preliminary rounds to show Aces or voids, and subsequently the Blackwood 4 No Trump is called, any Ace that has previously been cue-bid or any Ace in a suit that partner has cued must not be shown. For example, you hold:

♠ K Q J   ♡ 10 9 x x x   ◇ A x x x   ♣ x

Your partner has opened with 1 Heart, which, as a passed hand, you have jumped to 3. Your partner now bids 4 Clubs, an obvious cue bid. You bid 4 Diamonds, showing the Ace. Partner now bursts forth into Blackwood. Your normal response would be 5 Diamonds, showing one Ace, but since you have previously made a cue bid indicating this Ace, it does not count and you are obliged to respond with 5 Clubs, showing no Ace other than Diamonds. If instead of the King of Spades you held the Ace, your proper response would be 5 Diamonds, showing one Ace other than the one which you cued.

Blackwood response after interference bid

Occasionally, after a 4 No Trump bid, an adversary will insert an overcall in order to interfere with the normal response. If you do not choose to double for a penalty, the Aces are indicated as follows:

The responder starts to count Aces from the suit in which the overcall has been made. For example: After the Blackwood 4 No Trump bid an opponent bids 5 Diamonds. You have two Aces which you wish to show, so you start counting at 5 Diamonds; a pass would show no Aces, 5 Hearts would show one Ace, 5 Spades would show two Aces, 5 No Trump would show three Aces, and 6 Clubs would show all four.

There is one other exception which permits the responder to set up the final contract. When the 4 No Trump bidder mentions an unbid

suit at the level of 5 after partner's response, the responder is forced
to call 5 No Trump, which becomes the contract. This is done in
cases where it is learned that the adversaries have two Aces but that
No Trump will be the best contract.

The Gerber 4 Club Convention

Sometimes a grand slam can be made with a great many
points less than the normal 37, when responder holds a very long
suit.

In cases of that kind, of course, it will be desirable to check on
Aces—since the opposition may have as many as 10 points. At such
times the Gerber Convention (4 Clubs) will be useful.

Your partner opens 1 No Trump and you hold:

♠ x   ♡ x x   ◇ A K J x x x x x   ♣ A x

You know that you will play for at least 6 Diamonds, but if partner
has the key cards you can make a grand slam. It is possible that
partner has a maximum No Trump but lacks one of the Aces. For
example, he might hold:

♠ K Q J   ♡ A Q J   ◇ x x x   ♣ K Q x x

In order to determine this, you burst into 4 Clubs (the Gerber
Convention). This is a request for Aces. If partner shows two Aces
and two Kings, you may contract for 7 No Trump. Even if he shows
two Aces and only one King, you may, if you choose, take the
reasonable risk that he has a Queen with his King and bid 7 anyhow.

A response of 4 Clubs over an opening bid of 1, 2, or 3 No Trump
is artificial and is treated in the Blackwood manner as a request for
Aces. The responses are:

4 Diamonds	No aces or four*
4 Hearts	One Ace
4 Spades	Two aces
4 No Trump	Three Aces

Where the 4 Club bidder desires information as to partner's Kings,
he employs 5 Clubs as his asking bid. The response is made in the
same fashion as above.

* See Blackwood responses (page 159). The original Gerber Convention specified 5
Clubs to show all four Aces but dual use of the 4 Diamond response, clearing the
way for 5 Clubs as the only rebid asking for Kings, has been widely adopted by
experienced players.

SLAM BIDDING QUIZ

You are South in the following examples and the bidding has proceeded:

SOUTH	NORTH
1 Diamond	2 Spades
3 Diamonds	4 Diamonds
?	

What would you do next with each hand?

1. ♠ K 10	2. ♠ J x x	3. ♠ K x
♡ A J x	♡ 10 x	♡ K 10 x
◊ K Q J 9 x	◊ A Q J x x	◊ A J 9 x x x x
♣ J x x	♣ K J x	♣ x

You are South and the bidding has proceeded:

NORTH	SOUTH
1 Spade	2 Clubs
4 Clubs	?

What would you do with each of the following?

4. ♠ Q x	5. ♠ J 9 x	6. ♠ K J
♡ K 10 x	♡ Q x	♡ A J 10
◊ A x	◊ Q x x	◊ x x x
♣ A J x x x x	♣ A Q J x x	♣ K J 10 x x

You are South and the bidding has proceeded:

SOUTH	NORTH
1 Spade	2 Hearts
3 Hearts	4 Diamonds
?	

What would you call with each of the following?

7. ♠ A Q 10 x x	8. ♠ K Q x x x	9. ♠ K Q J x x
♡ A 10 x x	♡ A Q J x	♡ A Q 10 x
◊ K 10 x	◊ x x	◊ K x
♣ x	♣ x x	♣ x x

You are South. The bidding is indicated by the side of each problem. What is your call?

10. ♠ x x x
    ♡ A J x x x
    ◇ K Q J
    ♣ Q x

NORTH	SOUTH
1 Spade	2 Hearts
4 Hearts	?

11. ♠ K 10
    ♡ A Q 10 x x x
    ◇ x
    ♣ K J x x

NORTH	SOUTH
1 Spade	2 Hearts
4 Hearts	?

12. ♠ J x x
    ♡ Q x x x x x
    ◇ none
    ♣ A K 10 9

NORTH	SOUTH
1 Spade	2 Hearts
4 Hearts	?

13. ♠ Q x
    ♡ K 10
    ◇ A Q J x x x
    ♣ x x x

NORTH	SOUTH
1 Heart	2 Diamonds
2 Spades	3 Hearts
4 Diamonds	?

14. ♠ A x x
    ♡ Q x x
    ◇ A Q J 10 x x
    ♣ x

NORTH	SOUTH
3 Hearts	?

15. ♠ A x
    ♡ A Q 10 x
    ◇ J 10 x
    ♣ K J x x

NORTH	SOUTH
1 Diamond	1 Heart
3 Diamonds	4 No Trump
5 Diamonds	?

16. ♠ K x
    ♡ x
    ◇ A K J 10 x x x
    ♣ A Q J

NORTH	SOUTH
1 Spade	3 Diamonds
4 Diamonds	4 No Trump
5 Hearts	5 No Trump
6 Diamonds	?

17. ♠ A Q x x
    ♡ A Q 10
    ◇ none
    ♣ A J 9 x x x

NORTH	SOUTH
1 Diamond	2 Clubs
3 Diamonds	3 Spades
4 Diamonds	?

18. ♠ K J 8 x x x
    ♡ x x
    ◇ A x
    ♣ Q 10 x

NORTH	SOUTH
1 Club	1 Spade
4 Spades	?

19. ♠ A 10 x x x
    ♡ A Q J 9 x
    ◇ A
    ♣ Q 10

NORTH	SOUTH
Pass	1 Spade
4 Spades	?

20. ♠ none
    ♡ A K J x x
    ◇ A K Q 10
    ♣ A x x x

SOUTH	NORTH
2 Clubs	3 Clubs
?	

21. ♠ K J 10
    ♡ A x
    ◇ A K Q x x x
    ♣ x x

NORTH	SOUTH
1 Spade	3 Diamonds
3 Hearts	3 Spades
4 Spades	?

22. ♠ K x x x x
    ♡ A K Q 10 x
    ◇ A x x
    ♣ none

SOUTH	NORTH
1 Spade	3 Spades
?	

23. ♠ A K Q 10 x
    ♡ K Q J x
    ◇ x x
    ♣ x x

SOUTH	NORTH
1 Spade	2 Hearts
3 Hearts	4 No Trump
5 Diamonds	5 Hearts
?	

ANSWERS TO SLAM BIDDING QUIZ

1. Four Hearts.

Your hand is definitely worth a slam effort but you are not in a position to take control by bidding 4 No Trump. (If an Ace is missing, the critical question is whether there are two quick losers in Clubs.) Therefore the sound move is to cue bid the Ace of Hearts and leave the next step to partner.

2. Four Spades.

You have a minimum hand and, despite partner's strong bidding, you cannot properly initiate a slam venture. By showing delayed support for partner's major suit, you indicate your preference for a ten-trick contract at Spades, rather than an eleven-trick contract at a minor suit.

3. Four No Trump.

This a very promising slam hand, despite only 11 high-card points, since you have an ideal holding to develop partner's Spade suit. The hand is well-suited to the use of the Blackwood Convention, as you have second-round control of both unbid suits. As long as your partner holds two Aces, you can confidently bid 6 Diamonds.

4. Four No Trump.

Your partner's raise to 4 Clubs is forcing and indicates a game even if you have a minimum hand. If you took away the Ace of Diamonds you would still have a very sound 2 Club bid. Therefore, with your actual hand it will be reasonable to bid a slam after first making sure that your partner has at least one Ace.

5. Four Spades.

You have a rock-bottom 2 Club bid and, since you are not permitted to pass 4 Clubs, you are motivated in favor of trying to find the safest game contract. As there could be three losers in the hand, it behooves you to suggest the possibility of playing at 4 Spades rather than 5 Clubs.

6. Four Hearts.

With 13 points in high cards, including an excellent holding in opener's suit, the chances are that 6 Clubs will be a safe contract. However, there is just a possibility that your partner has only one Ace, and in this case a Blackwood bid of 4 No Trump—which would elicit a response of 5 Diamonds—would get you overboard. There is also the possibility that even if your partner has two Aces, there may be two Diamond losers in the hand. The proper procedure is to cue bid the Ace of Hearts, inviting prtner to decide to bid slam.

7. Six Hearts.

Although you have, in terms of high cards, a minimum opening hand, you have an exceptionally favorable distribution and your partner's cue bid of 4 Diamonds—which indicates the Ace—removes any possibility that there might be two quick losers in the hand. It is just conceivable that the slam might depend on a finesse in Spades, but this is an acceptable risk. It is much more likely that

twelve tricks will be there for the taking.

8. Four Hearts.

Your partner's sequence of bidding invites your cooperation in bidding a slam if you hold undisclosed values in high cards or distribution. Unfortunately, you have neither, and therefore it is incumbent to sign off by returning to the agreed trump suit at the minimum level. Admittedly you have an excellent Heart holding, but this forms part of your original opening bid and should not be allowed to go to your head.

9. Five Diamonds.

It is unusual to respond to a cue bid by raising the same suit, but in this instance it is a sound move. 5 Diamonds says that you are willing to cooperate in a slam venture, and that you have the King of Diamonds or a singleton Diamond. It also indicates that you do not wish to take command by bidding 4 No Trump. The objection to this last course of action is that if your partner responded by showing two Aces, you would have no way of knowing whether there were two Club losers in the hand.

10. Pass.

This is a borderline decision and a pass is recommended only because of this writer's predisposition to caution in certain sequences. As you have already shown your 13 points and your partner may be expected to hold 17 or more for his raise to game, and in theory the combined hands could contain just about enough points for slam. But your holding in your partner's Spade suit is unfavorable so far as slam prospects are concerned, and the value of your minor suit holdings is uncertain.

11. Four No Trump.

You have the same number of high-card points as in the previous problem, but they are differently distributed. The hands appear to fit well and as long as your partner holds two

Aces there will surely be a good chance for slam.

12. Five Clubs.

When you are void of a suit, the Blackwood convention tends to be a broken reed, for unless partner holds all the missing Aces, you have no way of knowing whether one of them coincides with your void. Therefore, when the precise identity of Aces is important, it is advisable to proceed by way of a cue bid.

13. Four No Trump.

Your partner has thoughtfully arranged his sequence of bids so as to mark himself with a void or singleton Club. Therefore you can bid slam in Diamonds even if an Ace proves to be missing.

14. Four Hearts.

This is an instance where your partner's preempt makes it easy for you to decide the proper level at which the hand should be played. It is unsafe to rely on a preempting partner to hold any specific honor cards outside the trump suit, and therefore 6 Hearts could hardly be better than the even-money chance of the Diamond finesse succeeding.

15. Six Diamonds.

In view of your partner's strong bidding it is reasonable to assume that twelve tricks are available and the only question is whether the opponents can take two quick tricks in Clubs. Since you hold the K J of the suit, the slam will, in practice, fail only when West holds both the Ace and Queen, which is an acceptable risk. Even then, East may not lead a Club. It would not be advisable to bid 6 No Trump, as your ruffing value in Spades may be needed.

16. Seven Diamonds.

It is reasonable to assume no trump losers. Thirteen tricks will be cold if your partner's indicated King is in Clubs—a 50-50 chance. If it isn't, there will be several extra chances:

your partner may hold a fine Spade suit, or a Club singleton; or the Club finesse may be successful. All these chances add up to an excellent prospect for a grand slam.

17. Six No Trump.

Your partner has bid very strongly, but even if you ascertained, by means of the Blackwood Convention, that your partner had an Ace and four Kings, it would still be unwise to bid a grand slam, since the Club Queen might be missing, or your partner's diamonds might not be solid. But 6 No Trump, with your major-suit tenaces protected against the opening lead, must be safe.

18. Five Diamonds.

This hand contains enough tricks for slam but the Heart suit may be wide open. If you bid 4 No Trump, and your partner responds showing two Aces, you will be no wiser. An Ace-showing cue bid of 5 Hearts enables partner to bid the slam if he has a suitable hand.

19. Six Spades.

This bid is arrived at quite simply. First, even if a Blackwood inquiry revealed that your partner held the Club Ace, you could not safely investigate a grand slam, since success would depend upon your partner having specific cards. Secondly, even if your partner lacked the Club Ace, you would still be prepared to gamble on Six Spades. (Clubs might not be led, or your partner might hold the King.) So why launch a Blackwood sequence that could only serve to inform your opponents?

20. Five No Trump.

Your partner is formally requested to bid 7 Clubs if he holds the K Q of Clubs (see Grand Slam Force, Page 266). To mention Diamonds would muddy the waters, since when you subsequently got around to bidding 5 No Trump, partner might not know which suit was intended to be trump.

21. Five Spades.

This is a call which enlists your partner's capacity for deductive reasoning. It beseeches him to bid slam if he holds second-round control of Clubs. (If you had any other problem on your mind, you would have solved it by a different bid, such as 4 No Trump.) 5 Spades is thus superior to 4 No Trump, which would yield satisfactory results only if your partner held two Aces.

22. Five No Trump.

This is a classic case where the Grand Slam Force solves the problem. Part-ner is requested to bid 7 Spades if he has two of the top three Spade honors. It is reasonable to assume that any Diamond losers in your partner's hand can be discarded on your Heart suit.

23. Pass.

It is a hard and fast principle that the partner who initiates the use of the Blackwood Convention is the captain, and his decision not to bid 6 must be respected, if not exactly welcomed.

8.   Preemptive bidding

IT HAS BEEN CONCEDED during our previous discussions that
bridge is a game for four persons and that the opponents may, on
occasion, be disinclined to absent themselves from the auction. It is
now time to concede that the opponents will sometimes possess
sufficient strength to enable them to make a game contract or a slam.
When such a condition appears to be present, you should examine
your hand to see whether you have the qualifications for a preemptive
bid.

A preemptive bid is an opening of 3, 4, or 5 in a suit. Such bids
denote hands that are relatively weak in high cards. They are made in
fear that the opponents have a better holding and in an effort to
destroy their lines of communication. They are naturally based on a
very long trump suit.

A hand should not be opened with a preemptive bid merely because
it has a long suit. Where adequate defensive strength is held, an
orthodox opening bid of 1 in a suit is preferred. A preemptive bid
should never be made with a hand which contains more than 9 points
in high cards when not vulnerable and 10 points when vulnerable.

To put it in another way: Experienced players never preempt unless
the future of the hand appears to be hopeless.

In making a preemptive bid you must have a reasonable amount of
safety. You should be prepared, if you are doubled, to lose no more
than 500 points. That is to say, if you are not vulnerable, you may
overbid by three tricks. If you are vulnerable, you should restrict the
overbid to only two tricks.

♠ K Q J x x x x x   ♡ x   ◇ x x   ♣ x x

You may reasonably expect to take seven winning tricks with Spades
as trumps, and therefore you may open 3 Spades even if you are
vulnerable. Not vulnerable, you may open 4 Spades.

It is to be frankly admitted that from time to time a preemptive
opening may cost you more than 500 points if an unkind Fate has
stacked the trump suit against you. Occasionally, too, you may
experience the misfortune of conceding a sizable penalty when there

was no game for your opponents to make. You should not be dismayed by such an outcome. There will be many other hands where the opponents cannot profitably double your preemptive bid. On these hands the opponents will be placed at a great disadvantage because they will have to start searching for their best contract at a considerably higher level than usual. They may, as a result, bid an unsuccessful game or slam in one suit when they could have bid it successfully in another suit. In such a case your preempt will have gained very handsomely indeed, even though the actual entry in the 'We' column may be of the order of only 50 or 100 points.

Opening with a 3 bid

In deciding whether to open preemptively, your position at the table is a factor to be brought into the reckoning. In first or second position it is highly advisable to pay strict observance to the rule of 6 or 7 playing tricks (according to vulnerability). Your partner, whose hand is unlimited, will then be in the happy position of knowing the number of tricks that can be made by the combined hands. Notice that the emphasis is on the number of probable tricks you hold rather than high cards. You are not obliged to hold any particular number of high-card points for a preempt opening, but you should most certainly not have more than 9 or 10, most of which should be in your long suit. If you were to elect to open 3 Spades on A K J x x x, with an Ace elsewhere in the hand, and missed an easy game as a result, your partner would in all probability never forgive you.

Also to be avoided is a 3 bid in first or second position when the hand offers the possibility of playing in a secondary major suit. To illustrate:

♠ Q J x x   ♡ x   ◇ x x   ♣ K Q J 9 8 x

The reader is counseled not in any circumstances to open 3 Clubs with this type of hand. Your partner would be most unlikely to introduce a four-card Spade suit over 3 Clubs and you could wind up missing an easy contract of 4 Spades.

In third position the situation is somewhat different, since your partner's hand is limited by his pass and the fourth player's hand is unlimited. A preempt opening can be especially effective under these circumstances and the rule of 6 or 7 playing tricks may therefore be applied with greater flexibility. Not vulnerable against vulnerable opponents, you have these cards:

♠ K J 9 x x x x   ♡ x   ◊ x x x   ♣ x x

With only 4 points in your hand, there are 36 high-card points outstanding. But if you divide the six outstanding spades among the remaining three hands, each player averages to have one distributional point for his spade shortage. Therefore, 39 is the smallest total of points that are missing from your hand. Neither your partner nor your right hand opponent has opened the bidding; hence the odds are that fourth hand has a minimum of 15 points. Give your partner a 13-point pass and the enemy are certain to have a combined total of better than 26 points, which suggests that they can make a game if not a slam. Nobody else knows this as yet, but they soon will; meanwhile, it is up to you to do some inside trading. You should open with 3 Spades even though your hand cannot be relied on to provide the normal quota of tricks for a 3 bid.

Responding to 3 bids

Since preemptive bids are not made with good hands, if your partner preempts, you should not raise unless you have an unusual amount of strength. You can expect your partner to have overbid by three tricks if you are not vulnerable, and by two tricks if you are, so you know how many tricks he can win. You must provide the rest.

It is in this area of bidding that some of the most spectacular miscalculations are to be observed. Players who themselves are apt to open with a 3 bid on the smell of an oil rag are, ironically enough, usually those who are most likely to overbid their hands when their partner has preempted.

Suppose that your partner opens with 3 Spades, not vulnerable, and the next player passes. You have this hand:

♠ x x   ♡ Q J x x   ◊ K Q 10 x   ♣ A Q x

It may be that at this point you will experience a strong urge to bid 3 No Trump. Do not succumb to it. Ask yourself from what source nine tricks are likely to come, bearing in mind that your partner's spade suit is most unlikely to be solid and that you cannot rely on him to hold any specific high cards in the plain suits. Viewed in that light, it is apparent that your prospects for making a game are poor indeed, and therefore you should pass 3 Spades. Your best chance of registering an appreciable score on the hand will occur if the opponents are constrained to enter the auction, in which case they may well get out of their depth.

Another temptation to which the responding hand is heir is that of taking the opener out of his suit when a proper consideration of the matter would indicate that the suit should be raised. The opener bids a non-vulnerable 3 Spades and the responder has these cards:

♠ x   ♡ A J x x   ◇ A Q x x   ♣ A K x x

If the responder bids 3 No Trump on this hand his partner will have every justification for deploring the fact that the practice of immersing miscreants in boiling oil is no longer approved by society. 3 No Trump would doubtless be passed by the opener, who would assume that the responder held a suitable hand for that call, and it would inevitably be defeated. The proper procedure is for the responder to raise to 4 Spades. The hand contains 4½ quick tricks and the opening bid has promised six winning tricks with Spades as trumps.

It will be found that to make game in opener's suit the responder needs about 13 points opposite a vulnerable 3 bid and about 16 points opposite a non-vulnerable 3 bid. Moreover, these should be made up mostly of quick tricks. To make game in No Trump the responder should either have reasonable prospects of making nine tricks in his own hand or he should have grounds for thinking that he will be able to capitalize his partner's long suit.

It will be seen that the qualifications for bidding constructively over your partner's 3 bid are high. At the same time, it may be good tactics to raise a 3 bid as a defensive measure when you have the following type of hand:

♠ x x   ♡ 10 x x   ◇ Q x x   ♣ A K x x x

If your partner opens 3 Hearts you should reinforce his preemptive efforts by raising to 4 Hearts. It is not to be expected that your partner will make his contract, but it is probable that 4 Hearts, even if doubled, will prove a profitable sacrifice. There is a strong possibility that the opponents can make a game, and it will be far more difficult for the fourth-hand player to compete effectively over 4 Hearts than over 3 Hearts.

The reader is cautioned against doubling the opponents too hastily when he holds the responding hand and his partner's 3 bid is overcalled.

♠ K J 8 x x   ♡ x x   ◇ A J x   ♣ J x x

Suppose your partner opens 3 Hearts and the next player bids 3 Spades. It would be most unwise to double with this hand, for you may not rely on your partner to contribute any defensive tricks if the hand is played by the opponents. If you pass there is a chance that the hand will be played at 3 Spades and that you will defeat it, but if you double, the opponents will hie themselves to a more suitable resting place. When your partner has opened with a 3 bid it is a sound policy not to double an overcall unless you can also double any alternative contract that the opponents may retreat to.

In responding to a 3 bid, a player who is void of his partner's suit should pass rather than attempt a rescue, whether the 3 bid is doubled or not. A new-suit response to a 3 opening is forcing for one round and should never be made on a weak or moderate hand.

Rebids by a player who has opened preemptively

Turning to the problems that may confront the opening 3 bidder in the later rounds of the auction, it is to be noted that, once having made a preemptive opening, a player should at all times leave subsequent decisions to his partner. Having shown his suit, he should avoid the temptation of rebidding it. Let us suppose that you open 3 Diamonds and the next player overcalls with 3 No Trump, which is followed by two passes. Your hand is:

♠ x x x   ♡ x   ◇ K Q J x x x x   ♣ J x

You have a very fine Diamond suit but you must not bid it too often—and once more would be too often. It may seem to you that the opponents are likely to make 3 No Trump and that 4 Diamonds would be cheap, but your partner has decided otherwise and you must respect his decision.

Other preemptive bids

While we have seen that it is sometimes permissible to take certain liberties when opening with a 3 bid, especially in third position and when the vulnerability situation is favorable, such is not the case with a 4 bid. It is inadvisable to open with either 4 Hearts or 4 Spades with less than the proper strength, inasmuch as an opponent who holds two or three defensive tricks is more likely to venture a double, on the principle that since you are already in a game contract he has little to lose and much to gain. A typical hand for a non-vulnerable 4 bid would be:

♠ A Q J x x x x   ♡ x   ◇ 10 x   ♣ x x

A preemptive bid of 4 in a major suit may sometimes be made on a good hand for strategic purposes when partner has already passed. For example:

♠ x   ♡ A K Q 10 x x x   ◊ A J 10 x   ♣ x

If partner has previously passed, the chances of reaching a slam are so remote that they may, for practical purposes, be dismissed. A preemptive bid of 4 Hearts may therefore be good strategy. First of all, you expect to make it. Secondly, it minimizes the danger of the disquieting competition in Spades that may be expected from the opposition.

Preemptive bids may also be made after your opponents have opened the bidding. On rare occasions it may also be expedient to preempt when your own partner has opened. After an opening bid of 1 Club or 1 Diamond and a pass by the next player, a preemptive bid of 3 Hearts* is in order with this hand:

♠ x   ♡ K Q J x x x x   ◊ J x x   ♣ x x

The object of jumping to 3 Hearts—one range higher than a jump shift—is partly to describe the nature of your hand and partly to try to prevent the opponents from contesting the auction in Spades.

Finally the reader should be aware—if only so that he may prepare a means of defense against it—that more and more players are adopting the forcing 2 Club bid, and are employing 2 Hearts or 2 Spades as a mild preemptive bid. The maneuvers are described in Chapter 1.

The double of an opposing preempt

While discussing the subject of preemptive bids, it is convenient to consider the best means of defense against them. It is my practice to take the same form of action against a 3 bid as against a 1 bid: that is to say, to double for a takeout and to treat all other bids as natural. A number of alternative methods of entering the auction over a 3 bid have been offered to the public over the years but none of them demonstrate a clear advantage and indeed the use of the double is now recognized as superior to other methods, both in theory and practice.

A somewhat stronger hand is needed before taking action against a 3 bid than against a 1 bid, but at the same time it would be losing policy to be too cautious. A 16-point hand like the following represents the normal minimum for a double of 3 Diamonds at equal vulnerability:

* If the partnership is playing "Splinter Bids" a jump to 3 Hearts would not be preemptive.

♠ A 9 x x   ♡ K J x x   ◊ x   ♣ A Q x x

On hands where you would like to double the 3 bid for penalties, it is usually advisable to pass and hope that your partner will reopen with a takeout double, which you of course can pass for penalties. For example, suppose the player on your right opens 3 Hearts and you have this hand:

♠ x x   ♡ A J 9 x   ◊ A K x   ♣ Q x x x

You are not strong enough to bid 3 No Trump and a double would invite partner to bid Spades. Therefore you had better pass. If your partner reopens with a double you can pass again, this time with considerably greater enthusiasm, while if he bids 3 Spades you will be justified in going to 3 No Trump.

Should your opponents open the bidding with a weak 2 bid, treat it as if they had opened with a 1 bid in that suit:

♠ K J x x   ♡ x x   ◊ A Q x x   ♣ Q 10 x

Double an opening weak 2 bid in Hearts for takeout. Pass if the opening 2 bid is in Spades or Diamonds.

Responding to a double

When responding to a double of a 3 bid you must call the full value of your hand, as the doubler will pass a non-forcing response unless he holds appreciably more than a minimum double. Let us suppose that your partner doubles an opening bid of 3 Clubs and you hold:

1. ♠ x x   ♡ Q J x x x   ◊ K J x   ♣ A x x
2. ♠ A J x x   ♡ Q 10 x x   ◊ x x x   ♣ A x

With the first hand your correct response is a jump bid of 4 Hearts, in the same way that you would jump to 2 Hearts in response to a double of 1 Club. With the second hand the responder may expect to be able to make either 4 Hearts or 4 Spades, but a cue bid of 4 Clubs, the opponents' suit, would display more acumen because the values are sufficient for game and the hand is playable at either of the major suits.

PREEMPTIVE BID QUIZ

You are the dealer and vulnerable. What do you bid with the following hands?

1. ♠ A
   ♡ K Q J 9 x x x x
   ◇ x x
   ♣ x x

2. ♠ Q x
   ♡ K 10 9 x x x x
   ◇ x x
   ♣ J 10

3. ♠ A x x
   ♡ 10
   ◇ A Q J 10 9 x x
   ♣ K x

Your partner opens the bidding with 3 Spades and the next hand passes. What do you do with each of the following hands? Neither side is vulnerable.

4. ♠ x x
   ♡ K Q x
   ◇ A 10 x
   ♣ Q x x x x

5. ♠ x
   ♡ A Q x
   ◇ A K Q J 10 x x
   ♣ K x

6. ♠ J
   ♡ A Q J x x
   ◇ A J x
   ♣ A x x x

7. ♠ 10 9 x
   ♡ x
   ◇ K J 10 x
   ♣ x x x x x

What do you call in each of the following problems? You are South, both sides vulnerable, and the bidding has proceeded:

WEST	NORTH	EAST	SOUTH
Pass	Pass	3 Spades	?

8. ♠ 8
   ♡ A Q 10 x x x
   ◇ A K x
   ♣ Q x x

9. ♠ Q J x x
   ♡ 10 x
   ◇ A 10 x x
   ♣ A K x

10. ♠ x
    ♡ K J 10 x
    ◇ K Q 9 x
    ♣ A K 10 x

11. ♠ K x
    ♡ Q x
    ◇ A J x
    ♣ A K Q J x x

In the following problems you are South, neither side vulnerable, and the bidding has proceeded:

WEST	NORTH	EAST	SOUTH
3 Diamonds	3 Spades	Pass	?

12. ♠ J x
    ♡ A Q 10 x
    ◇ x x x
    ♣ Q J x x

13. ♠ Q J x
    ♡ Q 10 x
    ◇ K J x
    ♣ Q 10 9 x

14. ♠ x x x
    ♡ Q x x
    ◇ Q J x x
    ♣ J x x

15. ♠ K Q J
    ♡ x
    ◇ A 10 x
    ♣ K Q 10 x x x

ANSWERS TO PREEMPTIVE BID QUIZ

1. Four Hearts.

Your high-card count is maximum for this bid: with more you would open 1 Heart. In the actual case 4 Hearts is preferable to opening 1 Heart because it may shut out an opposing Spade contract. In opening 4 Hearts you are overbidding your hand by two tricks, which is permissible.

2. Pass.

Some authorities have been known to advocate a 3 bid on this type of holding and the writer has heard the practice well spoken of by players on the way to the bankruptcy court. At that, we prefer to take the position that a ragged suit is not a suitable vehicle for a vulnerable 3 bid. The hand promises to take no more than five winning tricks.

3. One Diamond.

With 17 points, including distribution, you may not open with a preemptive bid in any circumstances. Such a hand is not to be initiated on the defeatist assumption that the opponents can outbid you.

4. Pass.

Any other form of action would indicate a misunderstanding of the nature of opener's hand. Opener does not figure to provide more than six winning tricks, and by no stretch of the imagination is it likely that the responding hand would provide four more. Therefore you simply pass.

5. Three No Trump.

If the opponents lead a Heart or a Club, you will have nine tricks in your own hand. This is just precisely the number you need to have for the 3 No Trump bid, for it must be anticipated that opener's hand may prove useless if not played at a Spade contract. Note that your partner is bound to respect your decision to play at 3 No Trump—or risk being cast out by decent society.

6. Four Spades.

Partner is likely to have six winners with Spades as trumps and with reasonable luck your hand will supply four more. In addition, the Jack of Spades is sure to prove a valuable card: you would still be justified in pressing on to 4 Spades if you had a low Spade instead of the Jack. Note that a bid of 3 No Trump, with no assurance of being able to gather in your partner's Spade suit, would represent a grave indiscretion.

7. Four Spades.

You do not expect to make this contract, but neither do you expect to lose heavily if doubled. Partner has undertaken to come through with six tricks just as long as Spades are trumps, and your hand may be expected to furnish two or three tricks. At the same time, the opponents surely have the values for a game or slam in Hearts.

8. Four Hearts.

You make this bid with trepidation and in the knowledge that you may wind up being nailed to the floor if partner has an unsuitable hand. At the same time, if your partner has a reasonable share of the outstanding points, there should be a chance for ten tricks. You should not allow the opponents' preempt to achieve its purpose without a fight.

9. Pass.

3 Spades can doubtless be defeated, but your partner would interpret a double as a request for him to bid a suit. Therefore the best you can do is pass. Your partner, in view of the bidding, will credit you with a certain degree of strength and he may be able to reopen with a double which you, of course, would be happy to pass.

10. Double.

This is a typical hand for doubling a 3 bid: you have 16 points in high cards and you can support any suit that your partner may bid. Should your partner's strength lie mainly in Spades, the opponents' suit, he is at liberty to convert your double into a penalty double by passing.

11. Three No Trump.

A certain degree of fortitude is needed when combating a 3 bid. It is obvious that if your partner has nothing you will be set, but you must take that chance.

12. Four Spades.

The hand justifies a raise because your partner, by overcalling at the level of 3, has indicated a fine suit and at least 16 points in high cards and distribution. Since you have 10 points in high cards, there is a reasonable possibility of making a game, yet you cannot bid 4 Hearts since this would suggest a longer suit. Therefore 4 Spades is the only sound call.

13. Three No Trump.

Your Spade holding could certainly be considered very adequate for a raise, but there is reason to suppose that 3 No Trump may provide a safer spot. This is because, in view of the 3 Diamond opening, your Diamond combination is likely to prove more valuable if protected from the adversities of the opening lead than it would be if you became the dummy hand at a Spade contract. Admittedly, 4 Spades could be best, but all you can do is to take a reasoned decision in the light of the available information.

14. Pass.

This hand does not really justify any form of action. Your partner's hand is limited in strength by his simple overcall and the chances are that he will be fully extended to make 3 Spades.

15. Four No Trump.

The quality of your Spade holding is such that your partner's overcall can be assumed to be based on a six-card suit. A slam now becomes a distinct possibility provided your partner holds two or more Aces, and you are therefore justified in using the Blackwood convention.

9.

Overcalls

THE PROPER USE of the overcall may spell the difference between a winning and a losing player. Losses incurred by indiscriminate overcalling may at times be so staggering that a somewhat lengthy dissertation on this topic is in order.

An overcall is a competitive bid made when an opponent has opened the bidding. It must not be confused with a response made when partner opens the bidding and an opposing call is inserted, for example:

NORTH	EAST	SOUTH
1 Spade	2 Clubs	2 Diamonds

South's 2 Diamond bid is not regarded as an overcall. It is simply a free response and is discussed in the chapter on Responses. But in this sequence:

EAST	SOUTH
1 Spade	2 Diamonds

the 2 Diamond bid is an overcall.

Naturally, with a partner who has opened the bidding you are in a position to take a certain amount of liberty, but when an opponent opens the bidding and you may be all alone in the world, the excercise of greater care is indicated. The idea developed some years ago that if the bidding is opened adversely and you hold 1½ honor tricks and a biddable suit, you should make your presence felt by overcalling. That was in the days before the public had familiarized itself with the penalty double.

Every overcall should serve some specific purpose. There are several considerations that might induce you to enter the bidding. One of the most important is to suggest a lead to your partner. For example, you hold:

♠ K Q J 9 x   ♡ A x x   ◇ x x x   ♣ x x

Your right-hand opponent opens with 1 Club. The potentialities of the hand are as yet unknown, but it is not looking too far ahead to visualize a possible adverse 3 No Trump contract, or possibly a game contract in Hearts. As far as you are concerned, the lead most ardently desired is a Spade, a suit which your partner could hardly be expected to select for his opening shot should it become his duty to lead. An overcall of 1 Spade is therefore in order, even though you have no real expectation of playing the hand or a desire to go places. This suggests a danger in overcalling with Jack- or 10-high suits.

On some hands you may be able to outbid the opponent for a part score. You may hold a fairly good hand on which, for some reason or other, you do not choose to make a take-out double. For example:

♠ x   ♡ A K 10 9 x   ◇ A J 9 x x   ♣ J x

Your opponent bids 1 Spade. It is usually not good policy to double with two-suiters, because the bidding might become too involved before you have a chance to show both suits. Your best bet is to overcall with 2 Hearts. The next time it will probably be convenient to show the Diamonds, and partner can exercise his choice without increasing the contract. With hands that are stronger or more flexible, strength-showing bids other than overcalls are made. They will be discussed some pages hence.

You have heard much about nuisance or bother bids. Many times the person most bothered by your bid is your patient partner. Remember this: Unless you are playing against someone who has been attacked by Dracula, you must not expect him to fold up and collapse into his shelter just because you overcall his 1 Club bid with 1 Diamond.

Overcalls can have a certain nuisance value. This is when they deprive the opponents of some bidding space. Suppose, for example, the bidding is opened with 1 Diamond and you overcall with 2 Clubs. You have deprived the opponent of the opportunity to respond at the level of 1 in either Hearts or Spades. This may prove embarrassing to him. If, however, the opening bid is 1 Spade and you overcall with 2 Clubs, you have deprived the responder of nothing, because he would have had to bid at that level anyhow. In such cases a 2 Club overcall gives the enemy all the best of the bargain. They can either double you (even on suspicion, because a fulfilled 2 Club contract will not yield a game) or they can go on.

There is the further disadvantage of providing the declarer with clues that will be of assistance to him in the play of the hand. An overcall, far from being a nuisance to the opponents, will many times be of actual assistance in the bidding. Let us suppose that you are South and hold the following hand:

♠ Q x x   ♡ Q x x   ◇ x x   ♣ A Q x x x

The bidding has proceeded:

NORTH	EAST	SOUTH
1 Spade	2 Diamonds	?

What should you do? For one thing, you should inwardly acknowl-
edge your indebtedness to East for helping to clarify the situation.
You can now be content to bid 2 Spades. In the absence of the overcall
you would have been in some quandary about your response. The
giving of a mere single raise would have been inadequate, and yet a
bid of 2 Clubs, followed by a subsequent Spade raise, would have
been somewhat on the aggressive side. The overcall by East clarified
your response because it made it clear that you had a hand on which
you were willing to make a free raise.

If you have come to the conclusion that you have a sound purpose
in overcalling, you should then inquire into the risk. You must expect
to be doubled every time you overcall and you must be prepared to
find a very anemic dummy. Figure out what the damages are going
to be. If they come to more than 500 points, you cannot afford the
luxury of overcalling. This little guide takes care of such questions as
vulnerability and the level of your bid.

In overcalling, the number of high cards held is of minor importance.
When you go down 700, do not ever be heard to sing the song of a
sucker, "But, partner, I had 14 points." The important consideration
is the type of trump suit you have, not the number of points in your
hand. I should like to repeat that in order to overcall you should have
a good trump suit or plenty of credit with the local bank. A good
rule of thumb *is not to overcall at the level of 2 unless you can promise that
you will not lose more than two trump tricks.*

Suits like these are treacherous:

A Q 9 4 2
K J 7 3 2

Such suits may produce very few tricks against an unfortunate trump
break, whereas the following combinations, no richer in point count,
give you the comfort of a well-heated home.

K Q J 9 7
Q J 10 9 8

With trump suits like these there can be no feeling of impending disaster.

When playing with a partner of the type who constantly wishes to "get into the act," extreme caution should be exercised in making overcalls on hands which contain a singleton in some side suit. To illustrate, you hold:

♠ A x x x   ♡ x   ◇ A Q J x x   ♣ J 10 x

If the opening bid by your right-hand opponent is a Spade and you overcall with 2 Diamonds, there is always the risk that your eager-beaver partner will feel it his duty to show his five-card Heart suit. This will place you in an awkward position, for a rebid of 3 Diamonds would be attended with great danger and the pass of 2 Hearts would place you in anything but a comfortable position.

Note that if the opponent had opened the bidding with 1 Heart, action by you is not attended with nearly the same risk, for even if partner chooses to act on his own initiative, you will have some support for any suit that he chooses to bid.

Reopening the bidding

When an opponent opens the bidding and his partner fails to keep it alive, you may take great liberties in competing for the part score. You have the distinct comfort of knowing that one of your opponents is "broke" and the other was not able to open with a demand bid. It follows, therefore, that your partner probably has a smattering of strength. In this position you may compete on a prayer. For example, you are South with this hand:

♠ Q 10 x x x   ♡ K Q x   ◇ Q x x   ♣ x x

The bidding has proceeded:

WEST	NORTH	EAST	SOUTH
1 Club	Pass	Pass	?

You should contest the auction by bidding 1 Spade. Partner must not expect too much of you in this situation.

Use of the 1 No Trump bid to reopen

When an adverse opening bid of 1 in a suit has not been kept alive and you are in fourth position, it has been pointed out that you can take great liberty in competing for the part score. You may do so in some cases by calling 1 No Trump. Partner must not construe this as a normal 1 No Trump call, but merely as a refusal to sell out cheaply. For example, you are South and hold:

♠ A Q   ♡ Q x x   ◊ K 9 x x   ♣ J x x x

The bidding:

WEST	NORTH	EAST	SOUTH
1 Spade	Pass	Pass	?

You may bid 1 No Trump. If partner has values, he may speak. If he hasn't much, you may as well play it at 1 No Trump. Partner must realize that you cannot have a really good hand, else you would have doubled first and then bid No Trump later. He must not raise the No Trump unless he passed with a very good hand.

The jump overcall

Over a considerable period of time the jump overcall has been used as a strength-showing bid when an adversary has initiated the auction. It described a hand with a strong trump suit, and one that would produce game with only a smattering of strength from partner.

On such occasions as it could profitably be employed, the merits of this call were undeniable, so that the bid survived for a great number of years. However, it eventually became manifest that the frequency with which this weapon could be employed was not great enough to warrant giving up an otherwise useful weapon.

Interference with the enemy, when it appears that they may have the preponderance of strength, is a far more useful purpose to which to put the jump overcall. The bid furthermore has the merit of pointing out to partner that defensive values are lacking, and that an eventual sacrifice bid should be given serious consideration.

It may be in order to outline briefly the specifications for the preemptive jump overcall. (See page 207 for treatment of hands that formerly called for a strong jump overcall.)

(A) The bid should be based on a fairly good suit, at least six cards long.

(B) The hand should contain no more than 9 points in high cards, regardless of vulnerability.

(C) The strength of the hand should be concentrated in the bid suit.

(D) The pre-emptive bidder should have the reasonable expectation of winning within three tricks of his contract when not vulnerable and within two tricks when vulnerable, that is to say the limit of loss ought normally not to exceed 500 points.

Let us examine a few cases in which you are South. The previous bidding has been set forth in each instance.

♠ K Q J 9 8 x x   ♡ x   ◇ x   ♣ J 10 9 x

WEST	NORTH	EAST	SOUTH
1 Heart	Pass	1 No Trump	?

3 Spades. This is an ideal holding for the pre-emptive overcall. Your maneuver may deprive the opponents of space for further exploratory bidding. If they do go on, they may stumble into the wrong contract. If they double you for "a small profit," partner could produce a card or two in Clubs which might enable you to fulfill the contract.

♠ A J 10 x x x   ♡ K x   ◇ x x x   ♣ x x

Neither side vulnerable.

EAST	SOUTH
1 Heart	?

1 Spade. Jump overcalls should be avoided on hands that contain any significant defensive strength. This hand has the equivalent of two quick tricks and will be better described by a simple overcall.

♠ x x   ♡ x   ◇ A J x   ♣ K Q 10 9 8 x x

Both sides are vulnerable.

EAST	SOUTH
1 Heart	?

2 Clubs. You have sufficient playing strength for a jump to 3 Clubs, but here also there is too much defensive strength. The pre-emptive overcall should be based on a hand containing not more than

nine high-card points, most of which should be concentrated in the bid suit.

♠ K Q J x x x   ♡ J 10 9 x x   ◇ x x   ♣ none

East-West are vulnerable.

EAST	SOUTH
1 Diamond	?

1 Spade. The jump overcall should be avoided, if possible, on a two-suited hand. Partner may fit Hearts but not Spades. A pre-emptive bid would greatly reduce the chances of finding a possible Heart fit.

♠ x   ♡ x x   ◇ A x x x x   ♣ K J 9 x x

WEST	NORTH	EAST	SOUTH
1 Heart	3 Clubs	Pass	?

5 Clubs. Since partner has announced a hand containing little defensive strength, the opponents are assuredly spread for at least a game in one or both of the majors. A premature sacrifice bid by you will put them to the guess concerning their proper action. You may be able to "steal" the hand for a relatively modest fee.

♠ J x x x x   ♡ none   ◇ A 10 x x x   ♣ x x x

WEST	NORTH	EAST	SOUTH
1 Heart	3 Diamonds	4 Hearts	?

Pass. It is not at all improbable that the enemy has a slam in this hand. Whatever strength you have is in a suit of which partner has at least six or seven cards, so that defensively your hand may be regarded as nonexistent. We would not be inclined to make any bid that might goad the enemy into aggressive action.

♠ Q J 10 x   ♡ K J 9 x   ◇ A x   ♣ K Q 9

East and West are vulnerable.

WEST	NORTH	EAST	SOUTH
1 Club	2 Diamonds	2 Spades	?

Pass. It would be unwise to act prematurely. You have been warned that partner's hand is of doubtful value, so that your offensive potentialities are distinctly limited. It should be borne in mind that East's response is forcing and proper strategy is to lie in wait for further developments. Your silence combined with partner's announced weakness may induce the enemy to overreach themselves.

Double jump overcalls

The single jump overcall is a bid of exactly one more than necessary and shows five or six tricks according to the conditions of vulnerability. A double jump overcall, e.g. as 3 Spades over 1 Diamond, does not show any greater high-card strength. It is also a pre-emptive bid made on the same type of hand, but containing one additional winner. For example, the opening bid on your right is 1 Heart. You are not vulnerable, and hold:

♠ Q J 10 x x x   ♡ x   ◇ Q J 9 x   ♣ x

You may overcall with a jump to 3 Spades. This bid may have the effect of keeping the opponents out of a 4 Heart contract. However, if you are vulnerable the double jump overcall might prove too costly and a bid of just 2 spades is recommended.

The 1 No Trump overcall

This bid denotes a strong hand. While an opening 1 No Trump bid should never contain more than 18 points, a 1 No Trump overcall may be based on hands ranging between 16 and 19 points inclusive, with the proviso that the adversaries' suit must be safely stopped. It is a bid to use when you are prepared to play at 1 No Trump, if partner is weak, and are willing to go on to game if partner raises. The hand will, as a rule, meet with the technical requirements for a take-out double, but the double has the disadvantage of compelling you to bid No Trump on the next round, when a higher level will have been reached. Suppose you hold:

♠ K Q x   ♡ A K x   ◇ A Q J x   ♣ 10 x x

Your opponent opens the bidding with 1 Spade. If you double and partner responds with 2 Clubs or 2 Diamonds, you will feel obliged to try 2 No Trump, which may not be safe if partner is weak. The best strategy is to overcall the Spade bid with 1 No Trump. If partner is weak, you are prepared to play it there. If he raises, you are willing to try for game.

The unusual No Trump overcall

Among the more recent developments in contract bridge, perhaps one of most colorful is the "Unusual No Trump Convention," which provides that where a player makes a bid of any number of No Trumps which could not possibly mean what it says, then the No Trump bid is to be construed as a take-out double, and partner is expected to respond in his better minor suit. The common sense of the situation is this: if a player makes a take-out double of one major suit, it is reasonable to suppose that he would like to hear his partner respond in the other major. But where the prospective doubler is not prepared for the other major, he obtains the effect of doubling for a minor-suit response by using an unnatural overcall in No Trump.

It is important to emphasize that overcalls in No Trump have not lost their natural significance. For example, the bidding has proceeded:

EAST	SOUTH
1 Spade	1 No Trump

South's bid of 1 No Trump is a good old-fashioned overcall, describing a balanced hand with 16 to 19 points and sound protection in Spades. Similarly:

EAST	SOUTH
1 Spade	2 No Trump

South's bid is not unusual. It describes a balanced hand with about 22 to 24 high-card points and adequate stoppers in Spades.

Let us examine a few other illustrations:

WEST	NORTH	EAST	SOUTH
1 Heart	Pass	Pass	1 No Trump

This is a natural bid and designates a hand of moderate strength on which South does not wish to "sell out" to the opponents. It does not require the same amount of strength as a standard No Trump bid.

WEST	NORTH	EAST	SOUTH
3 Hearts	Pass	Pass	3 No Trump

This overcall is used in its natural sense and indicates a desire to play at that contract. It is by no means a request to partner to show any suit, and he should resist the impulse to show even a six-card suit, unless he has a most extraordinary hand from the standpoint of distribution.

WEST	NORTH	EAST	SOUTH
1 Heart	Pass	2 Hearts	2 No Trump

This is an unusual overcall in No Trump and requests a minor suit take-out. With a good hand and strength in Hearts, South might have chosen either to double or to make a jump bid of 3 No Trump.

WEST	NORTH	EAST	SOUTH
1 Spade	Pass	3 Hearts	3 No Trump

This cannot be a natural bid inasmuch as West has opened the bidding and East has announced slam aspirations. Therefore, South must have a minor two-suiter, and is laying the groundwork for a possible sacrifice.

It is not always easy to determine whether a No Trump overcall is unusual or not. This can best be decided on a logical basis.

Normally, any overcall in No Trump at the level of 2 or higher, made after the opener and his partner have both bid, is unusual and asks for the better minor. To delve into the matter further and to clarify this definition, it is best to deal in terms of specific examples. Let us examine some specimen cases.

In the following examples you are South, and the bidding has proceeded as indicated:

♠ Q 10 x   ♡ x   ◇ A Q J x x   ♣ K Q J x

WEST	NORTH	EAST	SOUTH
1 Spade	Pass	2 Spades	?

Bid 2 No Trump. This is nearly the classic example of an unusual No Trump overcall. You have excellent minor suits and no interest in the other major. The fine texture of your suits is necessary to justify forcing partner to enter the auction at the 3 level.

♠ x x   ♡ none   ◊ A J 10 9 x x   ♣ A Q 10 x x

EAST	SOUTH
1 Heart	?

Bid 2 Diamonds. Do not make the mistake of making an unusual call of 2 No Trump. This bid, when employed immediately over an opening bid, has a natural meaning and shows a relatively balanced hand of about 22 points. In the present instance, you should plan on showing both suits yourself if the opportunity presents itself.

♠ A   ♡ x   ◊ A 10 x x x x   ♣ J x x x

EAST	SOUTH
3 Hearts	?

You should pass. A No Trump overcall in this position is a natural bid, indicating a desire to play the hand in No Trump. Note that if partner reopens the auction with a double or a bid of 3 Spades, you must not bid No Trump, for that would also be a natural bid.

♠ J 9 x x x   ♡ x x   ◊ A K Q x   ♣ Q x

WEST	NORTH	EAST	SOUTH
1 Heart	Pass	2 Hearts	Pass
Pass	2 No Trump	Pass	?

Bid 4 Diamonds. Partner is employing the unusual No Trump overcall requesting your better minor suit. You have a fine hand with a very good fit for partner, and some interest in game should be manifested. A mere 3 Diamond bid would sound forced and might easily be passed out.

♠ 10 9 x x x   ♡ x x x x   ◊ Q   ♣ A x x

WEST	NORTH	EAST	SOUTH
1 Heart	Pass	2 Hearts	Pass
4 Hearts	4 No Trump	Double	?

Bid 5 Clubs. Partner is asking for your best minor and you have a distinct preference for Clubs. A pass would be courting disaster, for

partner would be forced to pick the suit himself, and if he chose Diamonds you would have to enter the 6 level to bid Clubs.

♠ x x x　　♡ 10 9 x x x　　◇ Q x x　　♣ x x

WEST	NORTH	EAST	SOUTH
4 Spades	4 No Trump	Pass	?

Bid 5 Hearts, not 5 Diamonds. The 4 No Trump overcall of a pre-emptive bid of 4 Spades is not treated as an unusual No Trump overcall but rather as a "super" take-out double, and asks for your best suit which is, of course, Hearts. Partner's hand should look something like this:

♠ x　　　♡ A K Q x　　◇ K J 10 x　　♣ A K J x

♠ x x　　♡ K 10 9 x x　　◇ none　　♣ Q J 9 x x x

EAST	SOUTH	WEST	NORTH
Pass	Pass	1 Spade	Pass
2 Diamonds	Pass	2 Spades	Pass
Pass	?		

Bid 2 No Trump. While the unusual No Trump overcall is conventionally employed to ask partner to bid his better minor suit, there are occasional instances where the common sense of the situation makes it apparent that while the No Trump bidder is asking his partner to take the bid out, his choice should be made from the two unbid suits rather than the two minors. This is just such an example. South does not wish to abandon the fight, yet he is too weak to make a take-out double. So he makes an unusual bid in No Trump. East's 2 Diamond call should make it apparent that South is not interested in that suit, so the inference is clear that it is either in Clubs or Hearts that he wishes his partner to make a choice.

Action by partner of overcaller

Partner of an overcaller is many times in a strategic position to judge the entire possibilities of the hand. He knows approximately how much partner has; knows that he has a good trump suit and that he can come within two or three tricks of making his bid. The partner is therefore in a position to add his own assets to those shown by the overcaller, and thus to form a conclusion as to game possibilities.

There is seldom any point in raising an overcall unless there is a chance for game. If the partner believes there is a chance for game, he may raise, assuming, of course, that he is satisfied with the trump named in the overcall.

Normal trump support for an overcall is less than that required to support an opening bid, because, while an opening bid may be based on a four-card suit, an overcall usually is not. The overcaller's partner may presume that the overcaller has a good five-card suit, so three small trumps are sufficient support, or even Queen x, particularly if the overcaller's side is vulnerable. For example, you are South and hold:

♠ x x x   ♡ Q 10   ◇ K J 9 x x   ♣ K Q x

With both sides vulnerable, the bidding has proceeded as follows:

SOUTH	WEST	NORTH	EAST
Pass	1 Spade	2 Hearts	Pass
?			

What should you do? Your partner's vulnerable overcall has shown the ability to take at least six tricks and is based upon a good Heart suit. Your hand should develop at least three tricks for partner, which means that you have some reasonable prospects of going game. What do you bid? Surely not 3 Diamonds. In the first place, partner might pass. He is not the opener. Secondly, if he is placed in a position where he is obliged to rebid Hearts, you will not know whether he had any additional values or whether he just couldn't stand 3 Diamonds, and you will be called upon to bid 4 Hearts blindly, if at all. Your proper procedure is to raise to 3 Hearts. If partner wishes to leave it, he may do so. If partner wishes to go on, you have given him an inducement to do so.

Similarly, you are South and hold:

♠ x x x   ♡ 10 x x   ◇ K Q x   ♣ A K x x

With North and South vulnerable, the bidding has proceeded:

WEST	NORTH	EAST	SOUTH
1 Spade	2 Hearts	Pass	?

What should you do? You have normal trump support for a vulnerable overcall at the level of 2, and your hand has a reasonable chance to develop four playing tricks. Since partner has promised to take six, the total reaches ten, and you should bid 4 Hearts. A bid of 3 Clubs would be little short of an atrocity. Partner might pass. He did not open the bidding and is not obligated to make any further bids.

Another illustration. You are South and hold:

♠ A K x   ♡ x x x x   ◇ x x x x   ♣ K x

North and South are vulnerable. The bidding has proceeded:

WEST	NORTH	EAST	SOUTH
1 Heart	1 Spade	Pass	?

What should you do? Your partner has guaranteed to take five tricks. You can take three. The hand should be safe for eight tricks. You therefore raise to 2 Spades.

Again, as South you hold:

♠ K 9 x x   ♡ x   ◇ A 10 x x   ♣ Q 10 x x

North and South are vulnerable. The bidding has proceeded:

WEST	NORTH	EAST	SOUTH
1 Diamond	1 Spade	Pass	?

What should you do? Partner has promised to take five tricks. You can produce at least four. You should therefore jump to 3 Spades. This is not forcing, since partner was not the opener. He may drop it if he has a questionable overcall, but he should be given a strong inducement to go on to game if he chooses.

If you are satisfied with your partner's overcall but have a suit of your own, you should think twice before showing it. Remember that he has not invited you to bid, that he has not shown a hand of general strength; all his values may be massed in his own suit, and he may not have the slightest interest in yours. It is usually not good policy to show your own suit unless you have such a hand that you would have overcalled independently of your partner. To illustrate, as South you hold:

♠ A K 10 9 5   ♡ x x   ◇ K 10 x   ♣ x x x

The bidding has proceeded:

WEST	NORTH	EAST	SOUTH
1 Club	1 Heart	Pass	?

Prospects for game appear dim unless partner has a fit in Spades with you. Nevertheless, you should bid 1 Spade for a dual purpose. If partner has three-card support and a reasonably sound overcall, he may decide to raise you, in which case game possibilities are lurking on the horizon. On the other hand, should the opposition outbid you on this hand (a prospect which though remote is still possible), your Spade bid has prepared the basis for the defense of the hand.

When partner overcalls and your hand is rather strong though lacking in normal support for his suit, you can test game possibilities by offering a No Trump contract, assuming that you have the adverse suit protected. As South you hold:

♠ K 10 x   ♡ A J 10 x   ◇ J x   ♣ A J 9 x

The bidding has proceeded:

WEST	NORTH	EAST	SOUTH
1 Club	1 Diamond	Pass	?

Since you have an opening bid in your own right, you are quite willing to risk a game contract at No Trump providing partner is willing to carry on. You should therefore bid 2 No Trump.

When you approve of partner's overcall, and your values may be subject to attack on the opening lead, you can offer partner a choice. As South you hold:

♠ K J x   ♡ Q x   ◇ A J x x   ♣ 10 9 x x

The bidding has proceeded:

WEST	NORTH	EAST	SOUTH
1 Spade	2 Hearts	Pass	?

What should you do?

Your values in Spades suggest that you try 2 No Trump. If partner defects to hearts, you will retire also. If, on the other hand, partner carries on to 3 No Trump, there should be reasonable play for that contract.

Where you have a choice between showing your own suit and supporting your partner's overcall, if your partner has bid a major suit, by all means support him. If your partner has bid a minor suit, you may try the major if your hand is sufficiently strong. To illustrate, as South you hold:

♠ Q x x   ♡ x x   ◊ A Q J x x   ♣ x x x

The bidding has proceeded:

WEST	NORTH	EAST	SOUTH
1 Heart	1 Spade	2 Hearts	?

Here your problem is whether to compete by bidding 3 Diamonds or by raising to 2 Spades. The bid of 2 Spades is recommended. But if you held:

♠ A Q J x x   ♡ x x   ◊ Q x x   ♣ x x x

and the bidding proceeded

WEST	NORTH	EAST	SOUTH
1 Heart	2 Diamonds	2 Hearts	?

you should try 2 Spades, inasmuch as you are prepared to raise to 3 Diamonds in any event.

Do not rescue an overcall when it is not doubled

As South you hold:

♠ x x   ♡ x   ◊ 10 x x   ♣ K 10 9 x x x x

The bidding has proceeded:

WEST	NORTH	EAST	SOUTH
1 Spade	2 Hearts	Pass	?

What should you do? This is no hand with which to seek involvements. Offer up a prayer of thanksgiving that you have not been doubled and don't do anything that might put such ideas in the enemy's mind. Pass quickly. If you permit matters to rest, you will probably learn that West, the opener, who rather likes his hand, will rescue your partner and save you the trouble. But if partner is doubled at 2 Hearts, you might give serious consideration to bidding 3 Clubs.

MORAL: *Do not rescue a partner who has not been doubled.*

Rescuing

What if partner's overcall has been doubled for penalties? Should you rescue? That involves the use of good, sound judgment. "Never rescue" would be just as bad advice as "Always rescue."

Suppose you are South and hold:

♠ x   ♡ x x x   ◇ A K 10 9 x   ♣ J x x x

The bidding has proceeded:

WEST	NORTH	EAST	SOUTH
1 Heart	1 Spade	Double	?

Should you rescue to 2 Diamonds? By all means *No*. In the first place, you have no means of knowing that 2 Diamonds will be a better contract than 1 Spade. Secondly, a rescue would increase the commitment to eight tricks. And finally, your hand as dummy will produce two tricks for your partner, which is as many as he had the right to expect. Again, as South you hold:

♠ x x   ♡ x x x   ◇ Q J 10 9 x x   ♣ x x

The bidding has proceeded:

WEST	NORTH	EAST	SOUTH
1 Spade	2 Clubs	Double	?

Should you rescue to 2 Diamonds? As a dummy your hand is completely useless. If you rescue to 2 Diamonds, you are sure of winning four tricks in your own hand plus whatever high cards partner might contribute. Since you will be developing four tricks which would not otherwise exist, a rescue to 2 Diamonds is recommended.

Showing adverse stoppers when partner has overcalled

Bidding No Trump for the sole purpose of showing stoppers in the suit adversely bid is not good policy. Remember, when partner has merely overcalled, you should take no action unless you think there is some chance for game. Do not keep the overcaller's bid open as though he were the opener. For example, as South you hold:

♠ x x x x   ♡ x x   ◇ A Q x   ♣ Q x x x

The bidding has proceeded:

WEST	NORTH	EAST	SOUTH
1 Diamond	1 Heart	Pass	?

What should you do? Nothing. Do not bid 1 No Trump to show that you have Diamonds stopped. That would indicate a desire to go on, a desire which you do not have. At least, you shouldn't.

OVERCALLS QUIZ

Your right-hand opponent opens with 1 Heart. What is your action with each of the following hands?

1. ♠ A x
   ♡ 10 x x
   ◇ J 10 x x
   ♣ A K x x

2. ♠ x x
   ♡ K 10 x
   ◇ A Q J 9 x
   ♣ x x x

3. ♠ K Q J 8 x x x
   ♡ x x x
   ◇ x
   ♣ x x

4. ♠ K x x
   ♡ K J x x
   ◇ A Q x
   ♣ K 10 x

5. ♠ x
   ♡ x x x
   ◇ x x x
   ♣ A K Q 10 x x

6. ♠ A K J 9
   ♡ x x
   ◇ K 10 x
   ♣ A 10 9 x

Your left-hand opponent opens with 1 Club, your partner overcalls with 1 Spade, and the next hand passes. What is your action with each of the following?

7. ♠ J 9 x
   ♡ x x
   ◇ A K 10 x x
   ♣ J x x

8. ♠ x x
   ♡ A J x
   ◇ K x x x
   ♣ 10 x x x

9. ♠ x x
   ♡ 10 8 x x
   ◇ A K J
   ♣ K 10 x x

10. ♠ Q
    ♡ A K 10 8 x x
    ◇ A Q 10 x
    ♣ x x

11. ♠ Q x
    ♡ A Q 10 x
    ◇ A K J x
    ♣ J x x

12. ♠ Q 10 x
    ♡ J 9 x x
    ◇ K 10 x
    ♣ K J x

13. ♠ J x x
    ♡ x x
    ◇ A x x x
    ♣ x x x x

14. ♠ x
    ♡ Q J 10 x x x x
    ◇ x x x
    ♣ K x

15. ♠ Q J x
    ♡ A x
    ◇ x x x
    ♣ A x x x x

Your left-hand opponent opens with 1 Spade, your partner passes, and the next hand passes. What is your call with each of the following?

16. ♠ x x
    ♡ A J 9 8 x x
    ◇ x x
    ♣ K 10 x

17. ♠ Q x x
    ♡ K 10 x
    ◇ J 9 x
    ♣ A Q 10 x

18. ♠ K Q J x x
    ♡ A x
    ◇ Q x
    ♣ x x x x

You are South and the bidding has proceeded:

EAST	SOUTH	WEST	NORTH
1 Spade	Pass	Pass	2 Clubs
Pass	?		

What is your call with each of the following?

19. ♠ A Q x	20. ♠ x x	21. ♠ x x x
♡ A J 9	♡ A x x	♡ K Q J x x x
◊ J x x x	◊ A K x x x	◊ 10 x x
♣ Q 10 x	♣ 10 9 8	♣ x

ANSWERS TO OVERCALLS QUIZ

1. Pass.

To bid 2 Clubs on a four-card suit would be unsound and no other form of competitive action is suitable either. It has been written that the talk of the lips tendeth only to penury and this no doubt applies especially to taking action with this type of hand.

2. Two Diamonds.

One of the first lessons that life teaches is that if partner can lead the wrong suit against a final contract of 3 No Trump, he will; the 2 Diamond bid therefore has some value as a lead-directing maneuver. Additionally, it prevents opener's partner from showing a Spade suit or a Club suit at a low level.

3. Three Spades.

There are some timid souls who prefer to bid 1 Spade with this type of hand, and while it is to be admitted that such an overcall has the merit of safety, it does not pay proper regard to the principle that if a thing is worth doing, it's worth doing well. The hand is ideal for a preemptive overcall because you can expect to make six winning tricks with Spades as trumps and you have almost no defensive values.

4. One No Trump.

This overcall shows 16 to 19 points in high cards, with a sound guard in the opponents' suit. It is a better move than a takeout double as it describes the hand accurately in a single bid.

5. Three Clubs.

This is a weak jump overcall, not to be confused with a preemptive double jump overcall (Problem 3) which usually shows a seven-card or longer suit. The hand is ideal for 3 Clubs because (a) all the strength is concentrated in one suit, (b) you have only 9 points in high cards, and (c) you expect to win within three tricks of your contract.

6. Double.

The Spade suit is eminently biddable, but if you bid a Spade you are putting all your eggs in one basket. By doubling for takeout you suggest strength in the unbid major suit, and at the same time tell partner he can safely bid a minor suit if his hand warrants it. If your opponent had opened 1 Diamond or 1 Club, an overcall of a Spade would have been in order, since you have no support for Hearts.

7. Two Spades.

The partner of the overcaller should not feel it incumbent to bid 2 Diamonds with this type of hand. When partner overcalls, it is to be assumed that he has a one-suited hand and is probably not very anxious to have you bid a new suit, especially a minor suit. Your hand may be expected to be worth several tricks in support of a Spade contract, and therefore you should raise.

8. Pass.

Generally it is not worthwhile to respond to a simple overcall with fewer than 10 points, unless perchance you are able to raise. Partner's hand is known to be of modest dimensions, for if he had as many as 16 points he would probably have doubled for takeout instead of overcalling.

9. One No Trump.

Your hand is not too strong for this bid, which is forward-going and indicates about 10 to 12 points in high cards.

10. Three Hearts.

With such a strong hand as this it is reasonable to hope that a game can be made. Since a bid of 2 Hearts might be passed out, it is advisable to bid 3 Hearts, which is forcing for one round. If partner can do no more than rebid his Spades, you should do him the honor of raising the suit.

11. Two Clubs.

With this 17-point hand you are subjected to some of the emotions of a bird in a gilded cage: game should be there somewhere, but you have no convenient bid to make, inasmuch as either 2 Diamonds or 2 Hearts might be passed by your partner. A forcing cue bid in the opponent's suit provides virtually the only solution.

12. One No Trump.

It is usually proper to raise partner with adequate support. In this instance, however, if partner were to play the hand at a Spade contract, your Club holding would be exposed to the adversities of a Club opening lead, which might greatly curtail its usefulness. Accordingly, 1 No Trump is a better move.

13. Two Spades.

Clearly, in view of the weakness of your hand, you cannot bank on your partner to make eight tricks. Equally clearly, your partner may place you with a somewhat stronger hand than you actually have. Nevertheless, a preemptive raise with this type of hand is a recognized tactical gambit. It is likely that the opener intends to contest the bidding if you remain silent.

14. Two Hearts.

This bid is made in an attempt to improve the shining hour by removing partner from a contract in which

he would almost certainly be set. It is recommended only with a partner who appreciates that 2 Hearts is not forcing in response to an overcall. Partner is expected to pass if he cannot raise.

15. Three Spades.

The normal disinclination to offer a jump raise on three-card support does not apply when partner has made an overcall, which is usually based on a five-card or longer suit. With two Aces and appreciable ruffing values, your hand is highly suitable for a Spade contract.

16. Two Hearts.

To enter the fray at the 2 level with only 8 high-card points may seem risky, but it would be equally unsafe to pass, since your partner could have quite a strong hand in this situation. When the opponents' bidding peters out at a low level, there is always a good chance that the hand belongs to you.

17. One No Trump.

In view of your balanced hand, and the presence of several tenace holdings, the chances are that the best contract is at No Trump. You should not be deterred from bidding 1 No Trump, showing a hand of this strength, by the insubstantial nature of your guard in the opponent's suit: the Queen of Spades is likely to be of more value if you can become the declarer at a No Trump contract than it would be under any other circumstances.

18. Pass.

It is likely that the opponents are in their worst contract, and that any action you took would be to their advantage. You can be reasonably sure of picking up a satisfactory number of points simply by passing.

19. Two No Trump.

If you could be sure that your partner had the values for a genuine bid, your hand would be worth 3 No Trump.

But the fact is that he has reopened in the balancing position and must be allowed considerable leeway. Accordingly, you proceed cautiously until his values are confirmed.

20. Three Clubs.
A bid of 2 Diamonds would not be forcing and could be passed out and defeated. This would be a minor tragedy, since you can be confident of making at least a partial in Clubs, and by raising to 3 of them you indicate that you are prepared for partner either to pass, or continue in Clubs, or bid 3 No Trump if he has a Spade guard.

21. Two Hearts.
Although Two Clubs has not been doubled, you should remove it to 2 Hearts provided that your partner can be relied on not to interpret it as a forward-going bid. 2 Hearts will probably be passed unless your partner has some values in reserve.

10.

Take-out doubles

IT IS STRANGE that the take-out double, one of the most valuable tools in the bridge player's kit, should be so much neglected and yet so frequently abused.

Before delving into the refinements of the take-out double, it may be well to pause for a second for purposes of identification. How is the student to distinguish between a take-out and a penalty double? Here's how!

The double of 2 No Trump is always for penalties.

The double of 1 No Trump is intended primarily for penalties, but partner is permitted the wide exercise of judgment and may refuse to leave the double in if his hand contains a long suit and has little defensive values.

What about the double of an opening 3 bid? In the methods herein recommended, *the double of a 3 bid is treated in the same manner as the double of a 1 bid*. It is intended primarily for take-out, but naturally, at this high level, the partner may exercise a certain amount of discretion and may pass if he thinks it more profitable to play for penalties.

A double, in order to be for a take-out, must be made at the player's first opportunity to double that suit. For example:

SOUTH	WEST	NORTH	EAST
1 Spade	Pass	1 No Trump	Pass
2 Spades	Double		

This is a double for penalties. The logic of the situation is this: If West had been desirous to hear from partner, he would not have passed 1 Spade but would have doubled then and there, requesting partner to bid.

After partner has made any bid, all doubles are for penalties. For example:

SOUTH	WEST	NORTH	EAST
1 Club	1 Diamond	Double	

This is a penalty double, since North's partner has already bid.

Requirements for the take-out double

The take-out doubler announces that his hand is at least as good as an opening bid, or, to put it another way, a take-out double over an opening bid of 1 in a suit should be based on no less than 13 points, including high cards and distribution. If the double is made after a 1 No Trump opening, doubler should have at least 16 points in high cards.

There are other factors to be weighed when contemplating a take-out double. Some hands which contain a great many more than 13 points are not suitable for a take-out double, as will presently be seen.

The take-out doubler should never lose sight of the fact that he is forcing partner to bid, a partner who may be completely devoid of values. If you are contemplating a take-out double, it is rather good practice for you to try to guess in what suit your partner will make his response (let's face it, more likely than not it will be your worst suit). If that response is apt to prove embarrassing to you, something is wrong with your take-out double. You ought not to force your partner into a position which you might find distasteful yourself. For example:

♠ A Q x x   ♡ x   ◇ A J x x   ♣ A x x x

Both sides are vulnerable. Your right-hand opponent opens with 1 Spade. What should you do? The casual player, without pausing to visualize partner's probable response and impressed by his high-card holding, would make a take-out double, a step which we do not recommend. Let's be realistic about it. It is almost a moral certainty that partner will reply with 2 Hearts. What then? The natural inclination will then be to bid 2 No Trump. Attempting to win eight tricks at No Trump with a partner who may have nothing is a highly hazardous undertaking. At the moment there is no safe avenue of escape for you. What is wrong? You should have thought of all this before you doubled. You might then have foreseen this awkward situation and, instead of doubling, might have decided to employ "snake-in-the-grass" tactics, just waiting around for something to turn up.

In other words, it is the doubler's position, in addition to promising certain high-card strength, to offer safety to his partner. He announces, in effect: "You will find my hand to be a satisfactory dummy for you" or "I have a very convenient suit in which I myself can play the hand."

Take the following example:

♠ K 10 x x   ♡ K 10 x x   ◇ A Q x x   ♣ x

Your opponent opens with 1 Club. Though your hand contains only 12 high-card points, it is a highly acceptable double. Regardless of which suit your partner names in response, your dummy will be more than adequate for him because, valued as a supporting hand, it is worth about 15 points.

Possession of a good five-card suit is no bar to the use of the double. For example:

♠ A K J 10 x   ♡ K x x x   ◊ x x   ♣ A x

Your opponent opens the bidding with 1 of a minor suit. To make a mere overcall in Spades would not describe the strength of your hand and would risk partner's passing with a smattering of values sufficient to produce game. This hand has the value of 17 points, and some affirmative action must be taken. The best procedure is to double first and to bid Spades thereafter. This will inform partner that you have better than an opening bid. The double has the added advantage of providing two possible final contracts. Partner might be short in Spades and have some length in Hearts, in which case a game might be available in the latter suit.

The take-out double is a technical bid announcing, "I have a good hand, partner; it is at least as good as an opening bid. I will tell you more about it later. Meanwhile, just answer my questionnaire."

Now that the jump overcall has been relegated to the category of "pre-emptive-type" bids, hands which formerly called for such treatment are now included under the heading of the take-out double. For example, as South you hold:

♠ K x   ♡ A K J 10 x x   ◊ A J 10 x   ♣ x

East opens the bidding with 1 Diamond. You must resist the temptation to bid 2 Hearts, since that call now shows 9 high-card points or less. The proper strategy is to double first, and then bid an appropriate number of Hearts on the following round.

A double to reopen the bidding

There is one instance in which a take-out double may be made with fewer than 13 points. That is to prevent the bidding from dying out when the adversaries have quit at a low level. For example, as South you hold:

♠ A J x x   ♡ K x x x   ◊ K x x   ♣ x x

The bidding has proceeded:

WEST	NORTH	EAST	SOUTH
1 Club	Pass	Pass	?

What should you do? It is not at all uncommon in situations of this type to hear a player give forth some such utterance as this: "They didn't bid a game, so there is no use fighting against 1 Club. That won't get them very far." We do not admire such lack of enterprise. As we view it, it is more becoming for a player in this situation to express himself in some such fashion as this: "Why should we permit them to play a hand so cheaply when it is likely that we can obtain a part score?" South, in this sequence, may deduce that partner has a certain amount of strength. East is woefully weak, since he was unable even to keep open a Club bid. He quite probably has a good deal less than 6 points. North's hand may have been just short of the requirements for a take-out double or an overcall. You should give your partner a chance to compete by making a take-out double. North must make allowances in situations of this kind and should not presume that you have a normal type of double. You should be very careful not to proceed further after doubling, because in that case partner will assume that your double was of the standard variety.

Responses by partner of doubler

When partner makes a take-out double, it is your absolute duty to respond irrespective of the weakness of the hand. *The only excuse for passing is the ability to defeat the opponents in the bid which your partner has doubled.* Do not be afraid to bid with a "bust" hand. Your partner has assumed full responsibility. If you suffer a loss, blame it on him.

If your response can be made at the level of 1, a four-card major should be shown in preference to a five-card minor, provided the four-card major is headed by a high honor. For example:

♠ x x x   ♡ Q x x x   ◇ x   ♣ K x x x x

Your partner has doubled 1 Diamond. You should respond with 1 Heart rather than 2 Clubs.

Consideration of safety may dictate a departure from this rule. Suppose that as South you hold:

♠ J x x x   ♡ x x   ◇ J x x x x   ♣ x x

The bidding has proceeded:

WEST	NORTH	EAST	SOUTH
1 Club	Double	Pass	?

With a hand this weak it is better policy to respond with 1 Diamond rather than 1 Spade.

Some players make an exception to the above rule when they have a fairly good hand and hope to get a chance to show both suits in response. For example:

♠ K 10 x x   ♡ x x   ◇ x x   ♣ A x x x x

Partner doubled an opening bid of 1 Heart. The above rule calls for a response of 1 Spade. Some players, however, prefer to respond with 2 Clubs, hoping to get another chance, at which time they will bid 2 Spades. This will give partner an accurate description of the hand; he will know responder held five Clubs, four Spades, and a good hand, containing about 9 points.

There is one objection to this type of strategy. When you respond in a minor suit, partner may become discouraged and not carry on the bidding; whereas if you respond with a major suit, you are much more likely to get another chance.

When the responder holds two suits and a good hand, the practice is to show the higher-ranking suit first, with the intention of showing the other suit on the next round. For example:

♠ x x x   ♡ x x   ◇ A 10 x x   ♣ K Q x x

Partner has doubled a bid of 1 Heart. You should respond with 2 Diamonds. This hand is worth 10 points and therefore is strong enough to warrant two bids from you. Clubs should be shown on the next round if the opportunity presents itself.

♠ K 10 x x   ♡ A J x x   ◇ x x x   ♣ x x

Partner has doubled a bid of 1 Diamond. Respond with 1 Spade, fully intending to bid Hearts on the next round unless Spades are vigorously supported. Your hand is worth 9 points, 8 in high cards and 1 for distribution, and is therefore worth two bids.

Occasionally you will find that the only four-card suit in your hand has been bid by the opponents. This presents an embarrassing problem. Do not respond with No Trump unless you can very safely stop the adverse suit. Rather than bid No Trump you may be obliged to respond in a three-card suit. In that case you should select the cheapest possible bid you can make. For example:

♠ 10 x x   ♡ J x x   ◇ Q x x x   ♣ x x x

Your partner has doubled a bid of 1 Diamond. Do not respond with 1 No Trump. Your Diamond stopper is too sketchy. Respond with your cheapest three-card suit. In this case, 1 Heart.

The response of 1 No Trump denotes a fairly good hand and should be based on not less than 8 or 9 points in high cards and a stopper in the opposing suit. There was an old school of players who treated the 1 No Trump response to a double as a specialized bid announcing certain high-card strength but making no promises as to a stopper in the adverse suit. This practice has been abandoned by all experienced players. The No Trump response normally shows a stopper in the adverse suit, and the doubler need not have an additional stopper to support the No Trump if his hand is otherwise suitable.

If your hand contains four cards in a major and also a safe stopper in the opponent's suit, a choice of response is presented. As a rule, it is better policy to name a major than to respond in No Trump. For example:

♠ J 10 x x   ♡ K J x   ◇ Q J x   ♣ x x x

Partner has doubled a bid of 1 Heart. Respond with 1 Spade rather than 1 No Trump. If partner displays any enthusiasm, you may bid No Trump later.

But when you have the adversaries' suit well stopped and your hand contains about 8 or 9 points, you may respond in No Trump in preference to showing a four-card minor suit. For example:

♠ K 10 9 x   ♡ x x   ◇ Q x x   ♣ K 10 x x

Partner has doubled 1 Spade. This is a fairly good hand under the circumstances. You have a little better than 8 points, and the adversaries' suit is safely stopped. You could respond with 2 Clubs, but that will probably lead nowhere, and a better response is 1 No Trump. It will be noted that the No Trump response to partner's double denotes a fairly good hand. In some quarters the unsound practice exists of using the No Trump response to partner's double to indicate a bad hand. This should be avoided.

Responding with strong hands

Inexperienced players are prone to underestimate the value of their hands opposite partner's take-out double. The following table should be of assistance:

Fewer than 5 points: Poor hand. Respond as cheaply as possible; if there is an intervening bid, pass except with freak distribution.

6 to 8 points: Fair hand. Endeavor to make a free bid if there is an intervening bid; bid again if partner raises a forced response.

9-10 points: Good hand. Take some action if opener's partner butts in. Plan to bid twice in competition. Jump respond with a good suit. Go to game if partner raises your response.

11-12 points: Probable game. Bid one more than necessary in response even though you may have only a four-card suit. You must encourage partner to go to game, even with a minimum double. However, a jump-response is *not* forcing.

13 points or more: Game hand. Respond with a cue bid in opponent's suit (it is not necessary to have first round control) or jump directly to game. A cue-bid response is the ONLY forcing bid in response to a take-out double. Any other response, though encouraging, may be passed.

Examples: Partner has doubled a bid of 1 Diamond.

♠ Q J x x   ♡ A J x   ◇ x x x   ♣ K x x

The proper response is 2 Spades, one more than necessary. It is not necessary to have a good Spade suit.

♠ Q J 10   ♡ J x x   ◇ K J x   ♣ K J x x

You have 12 points and a jump is indicated. But when you jump in a minor you promise a somewhat better suit. So make your jump in No Trump; respond 2 No Trump.

But suppose you hold:

♠ A 10 x   ♡ Q J 10   ◇ x x   ♣ K Q 10 x x

Your proper response is 3 Clubs.

Strengthen this example to:

♠ A 10 x   ♡ Q J 10 x   ◇ x   ♣ A Q J x x

Now your response is 2 Diamonds, a cue bid of the opponent's suit, the only absolutely forcing bid available.

The penalty pass of partner's take-out double

It has been pointed out above that doubler's partner is under an absolute duty to respond, however weak his hand may be. The double should be passed only when responder is quite sure he can defeat the contract.

This does not refer to doubles of 1 No Trump which are essentially for penalties and should usually be left in. Reference is being made to take-out doubles of suit contracts.

The double of 1 in a suit should never be left in with less than three sure trump tricks. Bear in mind that if you pass the double of 1 in a suit, partner will select a trump for his opening lead. Are you prepared for it? If you are not, then definitely your business pass is improper.

Inexperienced players will sometimes pass a take-out double on the ground that "Partner, I didn't have a thing to bid." This is anathema. Basic in the principles of bridge is this: That one never passes a take-out double out of a sense of fright. The pass of partner's take-out double is an aggressive step and indicates a desire to conquer. The person who passes, therefore, should be well equipped.

Procedure by doubler's partner after an intervening bid

When your partner has doubled the opening bid and opener's partner, who speaks before you, takes action, you are no longer under the duty to respond. You have been relieved of that obligation by the enemy. A bid by you at this point is therefore voluntarily made and denotes some measure of strength. It is not, however, regarded as a free bid in the general meaning of that term. The requirements are not nearly so stringent as they would be if partner had opened the bidding and second hand had overcalled. By doubling, partner is trying to get a message from you, and the opponents are trying to obstruct your communications. You will sometimes find it necessary to stretch a point to get the message through to your partner.

Bear in mind that if your hand is worth about 7 or 8 points, you should regard it as fair to middling and ought to feel justified in making a free bid. For example, you hold:

$$\spadesuit\ A\,Q\,x\,x\qquad \heartsuit\ x\,x\qquad \diamondsuit\ x\,x\,x\qquad \clubsuit\ x\,x\,x$$

Your partner has doubled a bid of 1 Heart. Opener's partner bids 2 Hearts. You may make a free bid of 2 Spades.

$$\spadesuit\ x\,x\,x\qquad \heartsuit\ K\,x\,x\qquad \diamondsuit\ A\,Q\,x\,x\qquad \clubsuit\ x\,x\,x$$

Partner has doubled a bid of 1 Spade. Opener's partner bids 2 Clubs. You should make a free bid of 2 Diamonds. Your hand is worth 9 points.

$$\spadesuit\ x\,x\qquad \heartsuit\ x\,x\,x\qquad \diamondsuit\ Q\,J\,10\qquad \clubsuit\ A\,10\,9\,x\,x$$

Partner has doubled a bid of 1 Heart. Opener's partner bids 1 Spade. You should make a free bid of 2 Clubs. Had the opener's partner bid 2 Hearts, it would have required a bid of 3 to show your suit, which in this case would have been somewhat doubtful wisdom but still a close question. Your hand is worth 8 points.

Where your free bid may be made at the level of 1, the requirements may be shaded if you have a long major suit.

Procedure by doubler's partner when an opponent redoubles

If your partner makes a take-out double and the opener's partner redoubles, you are relieved of the obligation to bid, because the auction reverts to your partner and permits him to take himself out. A pass by you indicates, in most cases, that you have nothing to say at the present time and you would prefer to have your partner take himself out of the redouble. It implies that you are more or less willing to have him select any of the suits, that you have no special choice. However, a bid at this point does not promise strength and should not be regarded as a free bid. Partner has asked you for your best suit. If you can afford to show it, the chances are you should. If you have a five-card suit, it is generally good practice to show it regardless of its texture. Even a four-card suit may be shown if it does not consume any bidding space. For example:

♠ x x x   ♡ K J x x   ◇ x x x   ♣ x x x

Partner has doubled a bid of 1 Diamond. The next hand redoubles. It is proper for you to bid 1 Heart. This does not consume any bidding space. If partner wishes to bid 1 Spade or 2 Clubs, he can do so at the same level as if you had passed. Had the opening bid been 1 Club, doubled by your partner and redoubled, it is doubtful that you should bid the heart with a hand this weak, inasmuch as partner's suit might be Diamonds. A Heart bid would force him to the level of 2 to name his suit, whereas had you passed he could have rescued himself from the redouble by a bid of 1 Diamond.

Action by doubler after partner responds

A great many players are able to visualize partner's possible strength. Few, however, learn to visualize partner's probable weakness. Generally speaking, a doubler who has already advertised his strength should underbid on subsequent rounds, and the responder, who has made no promises, should adopt an aggressive attitude. In actual play, however, for some strange reason, the opposite seems to be true. The doubler keeps rebidding his values, while his partner, who never did care for his hand, rarely seems to work up any enthusiasm.

The advice I hand out for general consumption reads something like the following: "If you are the take-out doubler, I suggest that you bid about half as much as it has been your habit to. If you are the partner of the take-out doubler, it is my recommendation that you bid twice as much as you have been in the habit of doing."

Let us take an illustration. As South you hold:

♠ A K 10   ♡ x x   ◇ K 10 x   ♣ A K J 10 x

The bidding has proceeded:

WEST	NORTH	EAST	SOUTH
1 Heart	Pass	Pass	Double
Pass	2 Clubs	Pass	?

What do you do?

Most players could not resist the impulse to make a jump raise in Clubs. They do not stop to realize that with an opening bid on your left and opposite a partner who may be extremely weak, an eleven-trick contract would not have a very good prospect of success. However, if partner can manage to stop the Heart suit, a game contract at No Trump might be worth risking. The proper procedure, therefore, is to bid only 3 Clubs. A jump to 4 Clubs would be improper on another ground, the simple one that you have no assurance that your partner will not lose four tricks. Let us examine the complete hand:

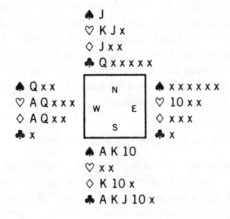

♠ J
♡ K J x
◇ J x x
♣ Q x x x x x

♠ Q x x
♡ A Q x x x
◇ A Q x x
♣ x

N
W E
S

♠ x x x x x x
♡ 10 x x
◇ x x x
♣ x

♠ A K 10
♡ x x
◇ K 10 x
♣ A K J 10 x

It will be observed that a contract of 3 No Trump can be fulfilled, the bid which North should hazard after partner raises to 3 Clubs. The singleton Spade should not act as a bar to such action, inasmuch as partner's strong bidding clearly indicates that he has some strength in that suit.

Sometimes the doubler can tell from partner's response that chances for game are very remote and that the bidding should therefore not be continued. For example, as South you hold:

♠ A Q x x   ♡ x x   ◇ A 10 x   ♣ K J x x

The bidding has proceeded:

EAST	SOUTH	WEST	NORTH
1 Heart	Double	Pass	2 Diamonds
Pass	?		

What should you do?

Your double was on moderate values; partner was unable to jump the bid, so you are to assume that he has less than 11 points. Inasmuch as partner failed to respond with 1 Spade, it is not to be expected that he will have four of that suit. It would therefore be risky, if not altogether pointless, for you to try 2 Spades. If you did so, partner would be justified in looking for a five-card Spade suit in your hand and might base his subsequent action on that assumption. Furthermore, partner was unable to bid 1 No Trump, so that you know he either has insufficient high-card values or lacks a Heart stopper. Since game in Diamonds is out of the question, there is nothing for you to do but pass.

Major-suit raises by the doubler

When you have forced your partner to bid by doubling, you should be extremely cautious in giving raises. Remember that partner may have nothing at all. Therefore, when you offer a raise you represent that he will have a fair chance to fulfill whatever contract you impose upon him, even though he has a very weak hand. For example, as South you hold:

♠ A K Q x x   ♡ K x x   ◇ A J x   ♣ x x

East opens the bidding with 1 Club and you properly double. Your partner responds with 1 Spade. What should you do?

Many players would leap impulsively to 4 Spades. A little analysis will show such action to be unsound. Partner was forced to speak and may be trickless. In that case even a contract of 3 Spades will not be safe. This hand in support of partner's Spade bid is worth 18 points. Let us examine the complete hand:

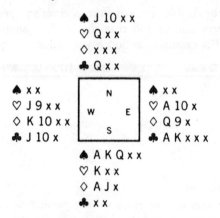

            ♠ J 10 x x
            ♡ Q x x
            ◇ x x x
            ♣ Q x x

  ♠ x x   ♠ x x
  ♡ J 9 x x   ♡ A 10 x
  ◇ K 10 x x   ◇ Q 9 x
  ♣ J 10 x   ♣ A K x x x

            ♠ A K Q x x
            ♡ K x x
            ◇ A J x
            ♣ x x

It will be noted that declarer, against proper defense, will be obliged to lose two tricks in each of the side suits and could barely fulfill a contract of 1 odd.

No sounder advice can be given the doubler than this: *When partner's response has been forced, never jump to any contract which you cannot reasonably expect to fulfill in your own hand.*

When a doubler follows up his original double with a free raise (after his right-hand opponent has bid again), he confirms a fine double and a hand that possesses game-going possibilities. For example, as South you hold:

   ♠ x   ♡ A 9 x x x   ◇ A Q x   ♣ K Q x x

The bidding has proceeded:

EAST	SOUTH	WEST	NORTH
1 Spade	Double	Pass	2 Diamonds
2 Spades	?		

What should you do? Nothing. No action would be safe. A raise to 3 Diamonds, when partner may have nothing, may prove disastrous, as may likewise a bid of 3 Hearts. You have done justice to your holding by making an immediate double. You can afford to pass the bid around to partner, who, if he has anything at all, will not forget that you made a double and surely will not permit the opponents to run off with the contract at this bargain price.

When contemplating a raise after having forced partner to bid, it is well to examine the following table:

> Don't raise to the 2 level unless you have at least 16 points.
> Don't raise to the 3 level unless you have at least 19 points.
> Don't raise to the 4 level unless you have at least 22 points.

Action by doubler's partner when doubler raises

With an indifferent hand the doubler's partner will have no problem when the doubler raises his response, but if he holds a good hand, it will be his duty to take further action.

It should be borne in mind that if responder to the doubler has about 9 points, he must consider that he has a good hand. For example:

♠ J x x x   ♡ A x x   ◇ x x x   ♣ K J x

Your partner has doubled an opening bid of 1 Diamond. You have responded with a Spade, which partner raises to 2. Holding 9 points, you have a good hand. A player holding a good hand should make one more bid if the doubler gives him a raise. Your proper procedure is to bid 3 Spades. Remember that partner has offered to fulfill an eight-trick contract, though he knows you may have little or nothing, and you should surely be safe for nine tricks.

Remember that since partner raised to the 2 level, he has promised at least 16 points. You therefore have almost enough to see a game. If he has an extra point somewhere, you should have a good gamble for the game contract.

♠ J x x x   ♡ K Q x   ◇ x x   ♣ Q J x x

The bidding has proceeded as in the previous example. Your hand is worth 10 points valued at Spades, and partner, by raising, has shown that his hand is worth 16. The necessary 26 are in sight, and you should be willing to contract for 4 Spades. Remember that a probable game becomes a biddable game when your partner raises. Do not be concerned about the complexion of your trump suit. Remember, as far as partner can tell, you have nothing more than four small Spades, and it is not good practice for him to raise your suit unless he, too, has four trumps.

Action by opener's partner

The redouble

When your partner's opening bid has been doubled by your right-hand opponent, your proper procedure is not always clearly indicated. What you do at this point may determine the success or failure of the hand.

A superstition that seems to have gained popularity is the one to the effect that "a bid over a double shows weakness." This is an unsound doctrine, but it is easy to see how the confusion has arisen. It has for many years been a definitely accepted convention that when partner opens the bidding and the next hand doubles, a redouble by the third player denotes a good hand. It may or may not denote support for partner, but the paramount consideration is the desire to get across this information, "Partner, do not be intimidated by the double. I think we have the best hands. I'll tell you more about mine later."

If, therefore, the partner of the opening bidder fails to redouble, the implication is quite plain that he does not have a very strong hand. However, if the opener's partner chooses to bid rather than redouble, it does not imply that he has a weak hand. It may be that he has certain values which he finds it expedient to show at this time. It may be that he cannot afford to wait, for fear that the bidding will mount too high before his next chance to call.

In a condensed form the principle may be stated as follows: When your partner opens the bidding and the next hand doubles:

WITH A GOOD HAND, YOU REDOUBLE

The question arises as to what constitutes a good hand in this sense. A hand is considered to be good enough for a redouble if it is above average in strength. An average hand is worth 10 points. If the hand is worth less than 10 points and you have anything to say, say it at once. If it is worth more than 10 points, then you should redouble first to advise partner that you have the balance of power.

WITH A BAD HAND, YOU PASS

To bid for the sole purpose of announcing you are broke does not seem to make good sense. Yet there is one situation in which the partner of the opening bidder may speak with a bad hand, and that is when he has trump support for partner and is able to give a raise. This merely serves as an obstructive measure and intends to interfere with the opposition without incurring any risk.

WITH AN IN-BETWEEN HAND, YOU USUALLY BID AT ONCE

(Sometimes, with a hand that is not quite good enough to redouble, you may decide to await developments and enter the auction later, but in such cases you ought to be very sure that you can afford to bid later.)

Let us take a few practical examples:

♠ x   ♡ K Q 10 x   ◇ A Q x x   ♣ A 10 x x

Your partner's opening bid of 1 Spade has been doubled by your right-hand opponent. Although you do not like Spades, you have a very good hand. The proper procedure is to redouble to announce your strong holding. If you contend, "What if this hand should be played at 1 Spade redoubled?" the answer is that with all your high cards your partner will surely be able to take seven tricks and the redouble of 1 Spade will produce a game. If, however, as is more probable, the opponents elect to bid, they will fall into your trap and you will be in position to make a devastating penalty double of any suit which they choose to play.

Here it is essential to point out a very important convention which applies to this case: A player who redoubles becomes the temporary captain of the team. The opening bidder is requested to pass the next bid around to the redoubler, who promises to double or bid.

♠ 10 x x   ♡ A K J x x   ◇ K x x   ♣ x x

Again your partner's opening bid of 1 Spade has been doubled. You have a good hand and your proper procedure is clearly defined. You should redouble. There will be plenty of time to show the Hearts later, if expediency so dictates.

♠ J x x x   ♡ x   ◇ x x x   ♣ Q x x x x

Again your partner's opening bid of 1 Spade has been doubled. With this hand you should bid 2 Spades, not for the purpose of showing weakness but with the intention of taking this opportunity to show some Spade support. This may make it possible for partner eventually to sacrifice at 4 Spades, if he believes such procedure will be profitable. The bid has the further advantage of making it somewhat more difficult for the doubler's partner to respond. He must now bid 3 of some suit and may fear to do so. If in a similar bidding situation you hold:

♠ Q J x x x   ♡ x   ◇ x x x   ♣ J x x

you might be justified in bidding 3 Spades. You will note that while this is a jump it cannot be interpreted as showing strength, because over a double the accepted way to indicate strength is by a redouble. Since you fail to redouble, your partner must realize that you do not have a good hand. The 3 Spade bid is made merely as a barricade. In most cases it will make it more embarrassing for the partner of the doubler to enter the auction, under circumstances in which you do not welcome competition from the enemy. It is hardly necessary to point out that the jump in this situation is not forcing.

♠ x x ♡ x x x ◇ x x x ♣ A K J x x

Your partner's opening bid of 1 Spade has been doubled by your right-hand opponent. Your hand is neither good nor bad. It might be called an in-between hand. If you do not bid now, you will find no convenient opportunity to show your values at a later stage. The proper procedure, therefore, is to bid 2 Clubs. Note that your hand valued at Clubs is worth only 9 points, 8 in high cards and 1 for distribution. It is therefore considered of mediocre strength, and immediate action must be taken if ever you intend to let your voice be heard.

♠ A K x x x ♡ x x ◇ x x x ♣ A Q x

As South you open the bidding with 1 Spade. West doubles. Your partner bids 3 Spades and East passes. What should you do?

You should pass. Your hand is worth only 14 points, and you know to a certainty that your partner cannot have more than 10 points, else he would have redoubled. Partner's jump to 3 Spades was intended as a barricade against East. The complete hand:

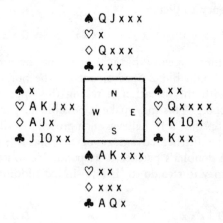

It will be seen that even a 3 Spade contract is down one. But the opponents can make 4 Hearts if they are permitted to get together in the bidding.

As previously stated, with a poor hand the opener's partner should pass the take-out double. For example:

♠ x x   ♡ x x x   ◇ Q x x   ♣ K x x x x

Your partner opened with 1 Spade. The next hand doubles. It is poor strategy for you to bid 2 Clubs. Nothing is to be gained by taking action. Your hand is worth only 6 points at Clubs, and a pass is clearly indicated.

Occasionally, when partner's opening bid is doubled, you will have just a smattering of strength and your course of action will not be clear. For example:

♠ x x   ♡ A x x   ◇ K x x x   ♣ J x x x

Your partner's opening bid of 1 Spade has been doubled by the next hand. What should you do? Your high-card holding, in conjunction with your partner's bid (you have 8 points in high cards), is such that you are quite persuaded that you can prevent the opponents from going game. In other words, this hand may develop into a dogfight for a part score. If you advise partner that you have a little something, he may be able to carry on the fight for a round or two. This bit of information you may convey by an immediate bid of 1 No Trump. If you do not act immediately, it may not be very practical for you to bid on a later round, and the opponents may steal a part score from you.

There is one case in which opener's partner would do well to take out with a very weak hand containing a long suit. That is when the opener's 1 No Trump bid has been doubled. For example:

♠ x   ♡ x x   ◇ J x x x   ♣ Q 10 x x x x

Partner opened with 1 No Trump. Next hand doubles. There is a very distinct danger that the double will be left in and may prove costly. In this case a rescue to 2 Clubs is recommended.

Jump in a new suit

Certain hands are not well adapted to any of the previously cited actions: i.e., hands which include a good suit, little or no support for the suit partner has opened, and no wish to take penalty action against the more likely responses of doubler's partner.

Suppose that the auction is:

NORTH	EAST	SOUTH	WEST
1 ◊	Double	?	

Your hand may be:

a) ♠ 4 3   ♡ K Q J 10 8 6   ◊ 2   ♣ K 9 5 4

A redouble is unsatisfactory because you have no wish to play for penalties against an opposing spade bid, especially if you are vulnerable and the opponents are not. A bid of only 1 Heart neither shuts out the opponents nor conveys a picture of your long, near-solid suit. A pass, followed by a minimum bid in Hearts later in the auction, is equally unsatisfactory, while a pass followed by a skip bid in Hearts would be forcing in what might be a misfit situation.

The solution is a bid of 2 Hearts immediately over the double. Although this is a skip bid in a new suit, it is not forcing, as it would be if your right hand opponent had passed. It is encouraging, often shows an independent suit, and allows partner to bid or pass as his hand may suggest. This bid may also be used with a two-suiter, such as:

b) ♠ 3 2   ♡ A Q J 9 6   ◊ 4   ♣ Q J 8 6 2

You will be awkwardly placed if you pass in the situation cited above and the bidding continues:

NORTH	EAST	SOUTH	WEST
1 ◊	Double	Pass	1 ♠
Pass	2 ♠	?	

Your high card strength was sufficient for a redouble at your first turn, but now you have a problem that could have been avoided by a bid of 2 Hearts immediately over the double.

Finally, suppose after partner's 1 Diamond bid has been doubled for takeout you hold:

c) ♠ 3 2   ♡ 7 6 5   ◊ J 4   ♣ A K Q J 10 3

An immediate bid of 3 Clubs, to show a solid minor suit, may enable partner to bid 3 No Trump. But here again, the bid is merely encouraging, not forcing. This same meaning would apply if the bidding had been:

NORTH	EAST	SOUTH	WEST
1 ♡	Double	?	

South might hold:

	d)	♠ 3 2	♡ 4 2	◇ A K Q J 8 6	♣ 7 3 2
or,	**e)**	♠ 3 2	♡ 4 2	◇ 7 3 2	♣ A K Q J 8 6

A jump in either minor would express a solid suit.

The alternative—use of a skip bid in another suit to show a weak hand when partner's opening bid has been doubled—seems unwise for two reasons: First, when partner has opened the bidding he may be strong enough to prevent the opponents from making anything. Second: The jump bid can better be used to describe one of the hands cited in the foregoing examples. (The reader is reminded, however, that a jump raise of partner's suit is preemptive.)

Use of the take-out double by opening bidder

The take-out double may also be used by the opening bidder to force a partner who has previously declined the opportunity to make a bid. For example, as South you hold:

♠ K J x x   ♡ A K 9 x   ◇ x   ♣ K Q x x

The bidding has proceeded:

SOUTH	WEST	NORTH	EAST
1 Club	1 Diamond	Pass	Pass
?			

What should you do?

Naturally you are going to carry on the fight, and it would be pointless for you to guess whether to rebid in Spades or in Hearts. There is no necessity for you to do so. Inasmuch as partner has not yet spoken, a double by you is for a take-out. There is a tendency in some quarters to confuse this with a business double because the *doubler* has previously bid. That is not the test. The test is whether the partner or the doubler has previously bid. If he has, the double is for penalties; if he has not, it is to be construed as a take-out double.

In this case, since North has not bid, South's double insists that he do so. Here the double will provide for every contingency. If partner has either Hearts or Spades, he will name the suit. If he has neither, he may return to 2 Clubs, or if he has great length in Diamonds, he may elect to pass and play the hand at 1 Diamond doubled. Such practice almost entirely eliminates guesswork.

A few specialized situations

Exposing the psychic bid

As South you hold:

♠ x x x   ♡ K 10 9 x x   ◇ A x x x   ♣ x

The bidding has proceeded:

WEST	NORTH	EAST	SOUTH
1 Club	Double	1 Heart	?

What should you do?

Had East not bid, your response would have been 1 Heart—a response, incidentally, which you would have made with good cheer, inasmuch as your hand is worth 9 points when valued at Hearts. If partner has a sound double, East will be unable to fulfill the contract of 1 Heart. You should therefore double for penalties. It is not unlikely that East is playing "horse" and is attempting to rob you of your bid. Remember that a double by you at this point is for penalties, inasmuch as your partner has already bid. Remember, too, that a take-out double is classified as a bid for this purpose. In this situation North will realize that you have a sound Heart response yourself and will act accordingly.

To put it another way: *Whenever your partner has shown strength by either an opening bid or a double, and your right-hand opponent makes the bid which you had the desire to make, double for penalty.*

Cue bidding as a response

As South you hold:

♠ A   ♡ 10 9 x x   ◇ Q 10 9 x   ♣ K J x x

What should you do if the bidding has proceeded:

WEST	NORTH	EAST	SOUTH
1 Spade	Double	2 Spades	?

Valued as a dummy, your hand is worth 13 points, 10 in high cards and 3 for distribution. Consequently there is no doubt in your mind that you should reach game in one of your three suits. At a quick glance it would seem that a bid of 3 Hearts is in order, but this call meets with several objections. The weakness of the Heart suit renders the bid at this level somewhat awkward. There is always the danger that partner will expect a somewhat better trump suit. Furthermore, there is the objection that partner may not carry on. True enough, a free bid at this level, while it portrays a really good hand, does not necessarily promise a game. It seems that the best procedure is to force partner to select the suit himself. This may be done by a cue bid in the adverse suit. The recommended call is 3 Spades, asking partner to select the suit in which the game contract will be played.

Occasionally a cue bid may be made even with one or two losers in the adverse suit when the hand is strong enough to warrant insistence on game. For example, as South you hold:

♠ Q J x x   ♡ K 10 x x   ◇ A x x   ♣ x x

EAST	SOUTH	WEST	NORTH
1 Club	Pass	2 Clubs	Double
Pass	?		

We recommend a bid of 3 Clubs, since you are prepared to carry on to game in either major suit.

The immediate cue bid

This is the strongest of all defensive bids. It is absolutely forcing and announces practically the equivalent of an opening 2 bid. It usually promises the ability to win the first trick in the suit adversely bid, either with the Ace or by ruffing. (See Exception below.)

For example, an opponent opens with 1 Diamond. You hold:

♠ A K Q x   ♡ A J 10 x x   ◇ none   ♣ K Q J x

You are unwilling to play for less than game (and conceivably a slam) in one of your three suits. You prefer not to make a take-out double: first, because of the slight risk that partner might have sufficient strength in Diamonds to make a penalty pass, and you have no special desire to play against 1 Diamond doubled; secondly, because if you double and partner responds with a weak hand, he may lose his nerve somewhere along the line and drop the bidding short of game. The proper procedure, therefore, is an immediate cue bid of 2 Diamonds. This forces partner to keep bidding until game is reached, and you may then proceed to display your wares in leisurely fashion without the necessity for resorting to jump bids on the way up.

Partner is expected to respond to the cue bid exactly as he would to a take-out double.

Exceptions: Since no other absolutely forcing defensive bid is available, there are times when a cue bid must be chosen even though the hand does *not* include first round control of the suit. To cite an extreme example:

♠ A K x x x x   ♡ A K x x x x   ◇ x   ♣ none

Right hand opponents opens the bidding with 1 Diamond. A cue bid of 2 Diamonds is the only available force that will allow you to show both suits and play as the one partner prefers. The alternative—a blind leap to six in one of the suits—risks finding partner with a singleton or void in that suit and ample support for the other.

As stated, a cue bid is practically the equivalent of an opening 2 bid. Therefore, it may be dropped short of game only in the same circumstances as the opening 2 bid: If the cue bidder merely repeats his suit and responder has a hopeless hand. For example:

♠ x   ♡ J x x   ◇ x x x x x   ♣ x x x x

Partner bids 2 Clubs over dealer's opening bid of 1 Club. You respond 2 Diamonds. Partner bids 2 Spades, you rebid 2 No Trump. If partner merely rebids 3 Spades you may pass. But if he rebids 3 Hearts, you should raise to game.

TAKE-OUT DOUBLE QUIZ

The opponent on your right opens with 1 Spade. What would you do with each of the following?

1. ♠ A 10 x
   ♡ A K J x x
   ◇ x x
   ♣ K Q x

2. ♠ A K x
   ♡ A 10 x x
   ◇ K J x
   ♣ K J x

3. ♠ x x
   ♡ A K x
   ◇ K x
   ♣ A K J 10 x x

The opponent on your left opens with 1 Club, your partner passes, and next hand bids 1 Spade. What is your action with each of the following?

4. ♠ K x
   ♡ A K x x
   ◇ A K x x
   ♣ x x x

5. ♠ A K 10 x
   ♡ K x x
   ◇ A x
   ♣ Q 10 9 x

6. ♠ x x
   ♡ A x x x
   ◇ K Q J 10 x
   ♣ A x

The opponent on your left opens with 1 Heart, your partner doubles, and the next hand passes. What would you bid with each of the following hands?

7. ♠ Q 9 8 x
   ♡ 10 x
   ◇ J 10 x x x
   ♣ x x

8. ♠ x
   ♡ K J x x x
   ◇ A 10 x x
   ♣ x x x

9. ♠ Q J 10 x x
   ♡ A x x
   ◇ J x
   ♣ K 10 x

10. ♠ J 10 8 x
    ♡ A x x
    ◇ A K J x
    ♣ J x

11. ♠ x
    ♡ Q J 10 9 x x
    ◇ K x x
    ♣ x x x

12. ♠ Q x
    ♡ Q x x
    ◇ K 10 x x x
    ♣ A x x

Suppose you are South and the bidding goes as follows:

EAST	SOUTH	WEST	NORTH
1 Spade	Double	Pass	2 Hearts
Pass	?		

What would you call with each of the following?

13. ♠ Q x
    ♡ A Q J x
    ◇ Q J x
    ♣ K J 9 8

14. ♠ K 10 x
    ♡ Q x x
    ◇ A K
    ♣ A K Q 10 x

15. ♠ A x
    ♡ K 10 9 x
    ◇ A Q 10 x
    ♣ A J x

Suppose you are South and the bidding has proceeded:

WEST	NORTH	EAST	SOUTH
1 Diamond	Double	Pass	2 Clubs
Pass	2 Hearts	Pass	?

What would you do with each of the following?

16. ♠ K x
♡ 10 8 x
◇ x x x
♣ A x x x x

17. ♠ J x
♡ x
◇ x x x x
♣ K J 10 9 x x

18. ♠ 10 x x x
♡ x
◇ x x x
♣ K Q 9 8 x

Suppose you are South and the bidding has proceeded:

WEST	NORTH	EAST	SOUTH
1 Diamond	Double	3 Diamonds	?

What is your action with each of the following hands?

19. ♠ Q 10 8 x x
♡ K 10
◇ x x x
♣ J 10 x

20. ♠ 10 x x
♡ 10 9 x
◇ A K x
♣ J 10 8 x

21. ♠ x x x
♡ x x x x
◇ A J x x
♣ x x

22. ♠ Q x x x
♡ Q 9 x x
◇ A x x
♣ A 10

23. ♠ A J 9 8 x x
♡ Q J x
◇ x x
♣ x x

24. ♠ J x
♡ Q 9 8 x
◇ A x x
♣ Q x x x

Suppose your partner opens with 1 Heart and the next player doubles. What would you call with each of the following?

25. ♠ J x x
♡ x
◇ Q J 9 x x
♣ J 9 x x

26. ♠ A 10 9 x
♡ x
◇ Q J x x
♣ A J 10 x

27. ♠ x x
♡ J x
◇ x x x
♣ A J 10 9 8 x

28. ♠ x
♡ Q 10 x x x
◇ Q J x x x
♣ x x

29. ♠ A x
♡ A 10 9 x
◇ J 10 x x
♣ K 10 9

30. ♠ Q J x
♡ Q x
◇ A x x x
♣ 10 9 x x

ANSWERS TO TAKE-OUT DOUBLE QUIZ

1. Double.
It is well to bear in mind that simple overcalls are reserved for hands of limited strength. This hand contains too much in high cards for a bid of 2 Hearts, and the double is therefore preferred despite the weakness in Diamonds. Over a response of 2 Diamonds, you are strong enough to bid 2 Hearts, showing extra values.

2. One No Trump.

We are not among those who take the position that a 19-point hand is too strong for a 1 No Trump overcall (although it would exceed the limits for a 1 No Trump opening). The disadvantage of doubling with this type of hand is that you are somewhat stymied if partner responds with a minimum bid in a suit: if you then continue with 2 No Trump, you are overbidding the hand.

3. Double.

With a hand as strong as this you must double even though you do not have general support for the unbid suits. Over a response of 2 Diamonds or 2 Hearts, 3 Clubs will show the nature and strength of your hand.

4. Double.

This is a hand on which you must double straight away to contest the partial. With 17 points in high cards and strong support for the unbid suits, you have no reason at this stage to suppose that the hand belongs to the opponents.

5. Pass.

It would be unwise to double, inviting partner to bid a red suit. A bid of 1 No Trump is a possibility, but on the whole it seems safer to pass. The situation is forcing on your left-hand opponent, and you are therefore assured of another chance to take action.

6. Double.

Despite the fact that your Diamonds are appreciably stronger than your Hearts, you should double rather than bid 2 Diamonds. Partner will always take a double in this situation as strongly suggesting at least four cards in the unbid major, and therefore the double may help you to a Heart contract if partner has four of them.

7. One Spade.

Although you have only 3 high-card points, you may not pass. When partner doubles you have to gird up your loins and respond no matter how

weak your hand. Usually you bid your longest and strongest suit, but with a weak hand it is better to show a four-card major suit than a five-card minor.

8. One No Trump.

In response to a double, 1 No Trump shows about 7 to 10 points in high cards and is thus more constructive than 2 Diamonds, which would not show any particular level of strength. Notice that in this instance it is proper to bid No Trump with a singleton. Your partner, on his takeout double, is expected to hold strength in the unbid suits, so you need not fear the opponents scampering off with the Spade suit.

9. Two Spades.

A jump response to a double is a different animal from a jump response to an opening bid. It shows a hand that offers reasonable prospects for game opposite a sound double. With a hand of this strength, you have to make a suitable jump response in order to tell partner that you have genuine values and are not responding merely because you are forced to bid. Partner is not absolutely obliged to continue over your jump response, but he is unlikely to pass unless he has a sub-minimum double.

10. Two Hearts.

If your partner doubles and your hand, by happy chance, is so strong that you can guarantee a game, it is sometimes expedient to respond by cue bidding the opponents' suit. In this instance the best contract may be 4 Spades, 5 Diamonds or 3 No Trump. To keep all options open, you force to game with 2 Hearts.

11. Pass.

With a strong solid sequence in the opponents' trump suit, you may elect to convert your partner's takeout double into a penalty double by passing. In this instance you are likely to get your biggest score this way. The pass requests partner to lead a trump against 1 Heart doubled.

Take-out doubles

12. Two No Trump.

This is admittedly a somewhat enterprising bid, but it has two potent features in its favor. First, it may be assumed that your righthand opponent is busted, and that your Queen of Hearts will therefore provide a guaranteed stopper. Secondly, your partner, in view of his takeout double, is likely to have some strength in Diamonds and this will solidify your five-card suit.

13. Pass.

This hand represents no more than a sound double and therefore, although you may experience an urge to support your partner's Heart call, you must take the position that you've already shown your hand. Partner has not made a jump response to the double and, accordingly, he does not figure to have many points. Indeed, his 2 Heart bid could possibly have been made on a very weak hand, and you cannot really guarantee that he will make even 2 Hearts.

14. Three No Trump.

It could well be maintained that 3 No Trump will probably fail if partner's hand happens to be worthless. This writer, however, is more impressed by the argument that if you were to bid only 2 No Trump, you could hardly expect your partner to raise to 3 with the Queen of Diamonds and the Jack of Clubs, which are all you need to make game.

15. Three Hearts.

If you removed one of the Aces, you would still have a sound takeout double. Therefore, with the actual hand, you can raise by one trick. Admittedly, if your partner is busted, he may not make 3 Hearts. It is more pertinent, however, to observe that even though your partner has failed to make a jump response to the double, he could easily have a few scattered points with which a game would be a reasonable contract.

16. Three Hearts.

By bidding a new suit over your response to the double, partner has indicated a powerful hand. It is unlikely that he has less than 17 points, including distribution, and he could have appreciably more. He is also likely to have a strong five-card Heart suit. Therefore it is proper to raise to 3 Hearts. So far you have shown no strength at all.

17. Three Clubs.

This is a sign-off, indicating that your hand is likely to be of very little value to anyone unless played at a Club contract. Rebidding the Clubs suggests length but not strength, for with a good hand you have bid 3 Clubs on the previous round. Partner takes further action at his peril.

18. Two spades.

With this hand you are entitled to assume that, since your partner is evidently not particularly interested in your Clubs, he is likely to have length in Spades. It would, after all, be highly ignominious to pass partner out at 2 Hearts if he held length in the other major suits, as is suggested by his double.

19. Three Spades.

Admittedly, you would like to have a little more strength for this bid, but partner has shown a good hand by doubling and East is trying to shut you out by making a preemptive raise. You should not bow the knee to East's tactics: if you pass 3 Diamonds, your partner would need to have an exceptionally strong hand to reopen in face of your silence, and a game could well be missed.

20. Three No Trump.

Here again you are constrained to accept the challenge and make a slight overbid. One is frequently forced into taking a position when an opponent makes a preemptive raise—which explains why opponents keep on making them—and the best guess you can make is to bid 3 No Trump.

21. Pass.

The temptation to double 3 Diamonds should be firmly resisted. The declarer would certainly play us for all the missing trumps, and we would probably make only one trick in the suit. Admittedly, partner has shown a strong hand, but his interest is primarily in playing the hand in one of the unbid suits.

22. Four Diamonds.

This time East's preemptive raise to 3 Diamonds bothers you not at all—your hand is strong enough for a forcing cue bid. Partner will assume that you have support for the major suits and he will respond accordingly.

23. Four Spades.

You can more or less guarantee making 4 Spades as long as partner has a double, and therefore you should bid it. If you were to bid only 3 Spades, partner would be unable to tell that you held such a strong hand.

24. Three Hearts.

This would not be considered a biddable Heart suit in normal circumstances but you cannot afford to allow yourself to be shut out when your side clearly has the balance of strength. Your partner's take-out double suggests strength in the major suits.

25. Pass.

This writer has long since become convinced that it pays to pass with this type of hand despite having a grave distaste for opener's suit. More often than not, the fourth player will respond to the double and your pair will be off the hook. In the relatively unlikely event that fourth hand passes the double, opener does not have to pass unless it suits him.

26. Redouble.

When your partner's opening is doubled, and you yourself have the equivalent of an opening bid, or nearly so, you should usually redouble despite a shortage in your partner's suit. If the opponents decide to allow opener to play the hand redoubled, your high cards will enable partner to make the contract for a big score. If the opponents take the double out, you can either double anything they call or you can bid No Trump.

27. Two Clubs.

A simple take-out over an opponent's double shows a strong suit with a very limited point count: you have to have fewer than 10 points, for otherwise you would either pass to await developments or you would redouble. The take-out is used when your suit is likely to provide a safer trump suit than your partner's.

28. Four Hearts.

The reader will observe that 4 Hearts appears to be a distinct overbid in terms of high-card values. The principle is that in this situation you should raise preemptively to the limit of your hand. Partner will not expect you to have much in high cards.

29. Redouble.

This hand is strong enough for 4 Hearts, but such a bid would suggest a distributional type of hand. By redoubling, and then raising to game, you indicate that you are strong in high cards as well as in playing strength.

30. One No Trump.

This bid is natural over a double, although of course there would be no point in bidding it with a minimuim hand of 6 or 7 points. With your actual hand you can reasonably hope to make 1 No Trump.

11.   The penalty double

AN OUTSTANDING SOURCE of unrealized wealth is the penalty double, made when an opponent overcalls at the level of 1 or 2. The average player never contemplates penalizing the opponents until they reach the upper levels, and appears to be completely oblivious of the fact that by far the most profitable penalties are gathered at the very low levels. The reason for this seems clear. When your opponents eventually reach a contract of 4, 5, or 6, it is usually as the result of some exploration. While they may have misjudged their strength, they have, more often than not, succeeded in finding a reasonable place to play the hand. But when your partner has opened with 1 Spade and next hand bids 2 Clubs, he has many times just tested his luck with what has come to be known as a "nuisance bid." The question of who more frequently finds him to be a nuisance has not been definitely cleared up. Penalties at this point can be devastating.

First of all, it is important to differentiate between a penalty double and one intended for a take-out. This problem we discussed in the chapter on take-out doubles. Here is a restatement:

Doubles of all No Trump contracts are intended for penalties. All doubles, even at the level of 1, are intended for penalties if made after partner has bid. There is no such thing as a take-out double after partner has made a bid.

The question arises: How is the inexperienced player to tell when to double an adverse bid for penalties? Generally speaking, this is done on a simple arithmetic basis. You count those tricks which you may reasonably expect to win, add them to those partner is expected to deliver, and if the total is sufficient to defeat the contract, let the ax descend. In the higher brackets this calculation is not very difficult, but it is not quite so easy to judge in doubling contracts of 1 and 2.

Perhaps the following suggestion may serve as an effective guide. At least it possesses the merit of simplicity:

When your partner opens the bidding (or in any other way shows strength, as by a take-out double) and your right-hand opponent overcalls in the suit which you wanted to bid, you should double for business. For example, you hold:

233

♠ K J 9 x   ♡ J 10   ◇ A J 10 x   ♣ x x x

Partner opens with 1 Heart. Opponent overcalls with 1 Spade. You should double, and your adversary isn't going to enjoy it. You are doubling not merely to show that you have the Spades. Had second hand passed, you would cheerfully have responded with 1 Spade. That is the test. It is not whether you might have responded with 1 Spade. It is whether you *wanted* to. For example, in the same situation, you hold:

♠ K J x x   ♡ x x x   ◇ K x x   ♣ x x x

In this case you would have responded to partner's opening bid of 1 Heart with 1 Spade, only because you felt it was your duty; for with 7 points, it was incumbent upon you to keep the bidding open. If second hand overcalls with 1 Spade, a double on this hand is not recommended.

Another simple guide: Partner opens with 1 of a suit and the next hand overcalls with 2 of some other suit. On hands which tempt you to call 2 No Trump, pause for five seconds and maybe you will change your mind. Double instead and watch your savings grow. For example, your partner opens with 1 Spade, the next hand overcalls with 2 Diamonds, and you hold:

♠ J x   ♡ A x x   ◇ Q 10 x x   ♣ K x x x

While you are seized with the temptation to bid 2 No Trump, my suggestion is that you resist it. That your hand will produce at least four tricks in defense is a reasonable assumption. These, coupled with your partner's expected three tricks, will account for a two-trick penalty. Assuming the opponents are not vulnerable, this will yield 300 points.

What, you will contend, about the situation in which you will be abandoning game, for which 300 points would not be adequate compensation? The answer is really very simple. If your partner has a minimum hand, you will have no game. Suppose the second hand had not overcalled. Would you have been willing to suggest that you have a good chance for game? I think not, for you have only 10 points facing the opening bid. But if your partner has more than a minimum and a game is probable, it follows that the penalty will be correspondingly greater. In other words, the more your partner has, the more the opponents are going to suffer.

There is this consideration of paramount importance: When the contract which you double will yield a game if fulfilled, you must exercise greater caution and allow yourself a trick leeway for margin of error or for the arrows of outrageous fortune. In other words, don't double a contract of 2 or 3 Spades or 3 or 4 Diamonds unless you expect to defeat it two tricks. But when your partner opens the bidding, and next hand overcalls with 2 Clubs or 2 Diamonds, great latitude is allowed in the exercise of the double "on suspicion." The risk is not great. The doubled contract, though fulfilled, does not yield the enemy a game. An illustration from real life:

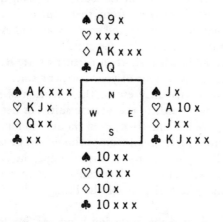

```
                    ♠ Q 9 x
                    ♡ x x x
                    ◇ A K x x x
                    ♣ A Q
   ♠ A K x x x    ┌──────────┐   ♠ J x
   ♡ K J x        │    N     │   ♡ A 10 x
   ◇ Q x x        │ W     E  │   ◇ J x x
   ♣ x x          │    S     │   ♣ K J x x x
                  └──────────┘
                    ♠ 10 x x
                    ♡ Q x x x
                    ◇ 10 x
                    ♣ 10 x x x
```

West opened the bidding with 1 Spade. North was vulnerable and overcalled with 2 Diamonds. East was presented with a problem. He had what he regarded as a little too much to pass, but after the 2 Diamond overcall the thought of a 3 Club bid could not be entertained for even a moment, and there was no other available bid for him. Reasoning that his hand would probably develop at least three tricks in defense, and counting on his partner for the usual minimum of three, he elected to double, relaxing in the knowledge that even if the opponents fulfilled the contract they could not score game. The result was an 800-point penalty, and what is more remarkable about it is that East and West could not have scored game.

Tricks for a penalty double

In counting your expected tricks for the purpose of making a penalty double, too much reliance must not be placed on the Point Count Table. Common-sense methods of deduction should be resorted to.

Sometimes you may allow a greater value than that suggested by the table. Ace Queen is regarded as 1½ quick tricks, but if that suit has been strongly bid on your right, you may be justified in counting on two winners. Similarly, a guarded King is regarded as ½ quick trick, but if your right-hand opponent may reasonably be expected to hold the Ace, you may rely upon the King as a winner. However, when the suit has been bid on your left, the Ace Queen should not be valued at much more than a trick and a King should be discounted almost entirely.

It is rarely sound to count more than two tricks in any one suit, and if you have great length in the suit, it is dangerous to rely on more than one defensive trick from that source. Occasionally none should be counted, as might be the case if you held A K Q x x x and partner had vigorously supported the suit.

Be quick to double when short in partner's suit. Be more cautious when holding as many as four of your partner's suit.

An item of value that may escape the attention of some players is the possession of four cards of the adverse suit. For defensive purposes this may be regarded as one trick, even though no honor card is held. The nuisance value of four small trumps should not be underestimated. It means that if declarer is to exhaust trumps, he must make four pulls, which he will rarely find it convenient to do. If declarer is forced to ruff once, he will probably be brought down to your size in trumps.

On this basis observe the following hand. As South you hold:

♠ A K J 9   ♡ x x x x   ◇ x x   ♣ A K J

The bidding has proceeded:

SOUTH	WEST	NORTH	EAST
1 Spade	2 Diamonds	Double	2 Hearts
?			

What should you do? The recommendation is to double. The defensive tricks may be estimated as follows: Since partner doubled 2 Diamonds, it is unlikely that he has any length in Spades, which makes it probable that two tricks will be cashed in that suit. At least two tricks may be counted in Clubs, and one trick should be counted for the possession of four Hearts. This brings the tally up to five tricks, or book. Anything partner produces will be velvet. You may contend, what if partner has nothing but Diamonds and produces no tricks against a Heart contract? The answer is, in that case your partner has made a very unsound business double.

In doubling the opponents one must always be conscious of the question, "Is there apt to be a rescue, and if so, can I do any damage to that rescue bid?"

When counting on partner's expected tricks to defeat the contract, one must have regard for the type of action that partner has previously taken. If he has opened the bidding with 1 of a suit, it is reasonable to expect him to produce about three tricks in the play of the hand. If he has opened with 1 No Trump, he may be depended on for four tricks. If he has made a take-out double, he may be relied upon to take at least three tricks. When partner has merely overcalled, it may be somewhat incautious to count on him for more than one defensive trick. Similarly, when partner has raised your suit, his raise may be based to a certain extent on distribution and he should not be counted on for more than one trick. And when partner has opened with a pre-emptive bid, you must base no business double on his action. Do not count on him for much of anything. In that case, any business double must be based entirely on your own hand.

Taking partner out of a business double

One of the most popular cartoons by H. T. Webster holds up to ridicule the player who takes his partner out of a business double. This has come to be regarded in many circles as contract's outstanding crime. I fear that this is somewhat in the nature of subversive crime. Since ignorance of the law is no excuse, it is of course a crime, and sometimes of major proportions, to take partner out of a business double from ignorance that it was intended for penalties. But the refusal to stand for partner's penalty doubles in the interest of the partnership is a matter involving the exercise of good judgment, without which no player can succeed at the card table.

Even though you make a business double, your partner may still be entitled to his opinion, though little toleration is to be held out for his whims. If a player's hand is completely unsuitable for defensive purposes, he is at perfect liberty to decline to stand for the double. However, the burden of proof is on the person who overrides his partner's judgment. Let us observe an illustration or two. As South you hold:

$$\spadesuit \ x \ x \qquad \heartsuit \ K \ Q \ J \ 10 \ x \ x \qquad \diamondsuit \ A \ x \ x \ x \qquad \clubsuit \ x$$

The bidding has proceeded:

SOUTH	WEST	NORTH	EAST
1 Heart	2 Clubs	Double	Pass

What should you do? Of course partner has made a business double, but your hand is bound to be a disappointment to him in defense against 2 Clubs. Actually your hand may develop only one trick. You should therefore issue a warning by bidding 2 Hearts, at which contract you should be in no serious danger. However, on the same sequence of bidding, If you hold:

♠ x   ♡ K Q J x x   ◇ A K x x   ♣ J x x

you would naturally pass the double and start clipping coupons. Your hand is very well suited for defensive play. You should not be concerned about the possible loss of a game, because your penalty double will be adequate to repay you.

If your hand is unsuited to defense at a contract which partner has doubled, but is a very fine hand from the offensive standpoint, you should, in refusing to stand for the double, jump the bid to make this point clear to partner. For example, as South you hold:

♠ x   ♡ A Q J 10 x x   ◇ A K J x x   ♣ x

The bidding has proceeded:

SOUTH	WEST	NORTH	EAST
1 Heart	2 Clubs	Double	Pass

What should you do? In this hand you have good defensive values despite your shortage in Clubs, and you do not fear the fulfillment of the adversaries' contract, but there is a question in your mind whether it will be adequate compensation, inasmuch as your prospects for scoring a game are very bright. It is not recommended that you stand for the double, but in taking out the double you should make a jump—you should bid 3 Diamonds—to indicate to your partner that you are bidding aggressively and not merely because your hand is not suitable for defensive play.

It will be seen, therefore, that the mere circumstance that the enemy can be defeated is not always sufficient justification for doubling. You must always inquire, Will it be worthwhile? If you can score more points by going on with the bidding, naturally the double should be eschewed; but in doubtful cases lean toward the double on the theory that you will never go broke by taking sure profits.

Close doubles

Occasionally we must desist from doubling the adversaries in a close situation where it is feared that our double will locate certain strength for the declarer and permit him to play the hand in a somewhat unnatural manner. It is a good principle not to double a close contract if your double is apt to cost you a trick. When your trump holding is something like Q 10 x x, for example, a double may warn the declarer of the adverse trump distribution and may permit him to play that suit unnaturally on the basis of your warning.

On the same line of reasoning, close doubles of slams should never be made. There is not enough profit in them compared to the risk of affording declarer an occasional clue to the successful fulfillment of the contract.

Sometimes a doubtful double must be made in the competitive situation when it is definitely wise for your side to discontinue bidding. in such cases, if you pass the bid to your partner, there is a mild suggestion that you are willing to have him go on.

Doubles of slam contracts

It has been pointed out that few points are gained above the line by doubling slam contracts. As a result of this experience, a convention has been developed in modern times relating to the double of a slam contract by a player who does not have the opening lead. The purpose of the convention is to guide the opening leader in the selection of his attack.

When partner doubles a slam, you must not make your normal opening lead. If you and your partner have bid any suit or suits, these suits should not be led, and obviously a trump lead is out of the question where a suit slam has been reached. The convention makes the following provisions:

1. If dummy has bid any suit or suits (other than trump), the double demands the lead of the first suit bid by dummy.

2. If dummy has bid no side suit, but declarer has bid another suit, the double demands the lead of the first side suit bid by declarer.

3. If neither dummy nor declarer has bid any side suit, but the defensive side has, the double demands the lead of one of the unbid suits.

In other words, the opening leader must not lead his own or his partner's suit. It follows, therefore, that you must not double a slam contract if you are anxious to have your partner make his normal lead. Of course, if the opponents have stepped so far out of line that the opening lead will not matter very much, you might as well strike and collect a bonus. But where it is a question of just another 50 or 100 points, you must forgo the luxury.

For example, as South you hold:

1. ♠ A x x   ♡ K Q J 10 x x   ◇ x x x x   ♣ none
2. ♠ Q J 10   ♡ A Q J x x x   ◇ x x   ♣ x x

The bidding has proceeded:

WEST	NORTH	EAST	SOUTH
1 Spade	Pass	3 Clubs	3 Hearts
3 Spades	Pass	4 Spades	Pass
6 spades	Pass	Pass	?

What should you do?

With NO. 1 you should double. This demands the lead of dummy's first suit, Clubs, which you ruff and defeat the contract.

With NO. 2 you must not double. If you do, partner has instructions not to lead a Heart, which is the lead you want to get.

Doubles of 3 No Trump contracts

The double of a 3 No Trump contract by a player not on lead carries with it certain implications.

1. If the doubler has bid a suit, his partner must unconditionally lead that suit, even though he may have but a singleton in it and a very fine suit of his own.

2. If the opening leader has bid a suit, partner's double requests him to lead that suit.

3. When neither the leader nor the doubler has bid, the double is a suggestion to partner to lead the dummy's first bid suit, unless he has a very fine opening lead of his own.

PENALTY DOUBLE QUIZ

In the following problems, you are South. The bidding has proceeded
as indicated. What is your action?

		NORTH	EAST	SOUTH	WEST
1.	♠ K Q 9 ♡ x x x ◇ x x x ♣ A J x x	1 Spade	2 Clubs	?	
2.	♠ 10 ♡ K x x x ◇ A 10 8 x ♣ A x x x	1 Spade	2 Hearts	?	
3.	♠ x x ♡ x x x ◇ K J 9 x x x ♣ K x	1 Spade	2 Diamonds	?	
4.	♠ Q x x ♡ A x ◇ x x ♣ K Q J 8 x x	1 Heart 4 Hearts	1 Spade 4 Spades	2 Clubs ?	3 Spades
5.	♠ Q x x ♡ x x x x ◇ A K x ♣ 9 8 x	1 Spade 3 Spades	2 Diamonds 4 Diamonds	2 Spades ?	3 Diamonds
6.	♠ A x ♡ J x x ◇ K J x ♣ 10 9 x x x	3 Hearts Pass	Pass 3 No Trump	Pass ?	3 Spades
7.	♠ K x ♡ x x ◇ A J x x ♣ K x x x x	1 Heart 3 Hearts Pass	1 Spade Pass 4 Spades	2 Clubs 3 No Trump ?	2 Spades Pass
8.	♠ K Q J ♡ Q x x ◇ x x ♣ K Q x x x	1 Spade Double	Pass Pass	2 Clubs ?	2 Diamonds
9.	♠ Q J x x x x x ♡ x x ◇ none ♣ K J x x	1 Heart Double 2 No Trump Double	Pass Pass 3 Diamonds Pass	1 Spade 2 Spades Pass ?	2 Diamonds Pass Pass
10.	♠ A J 10 x ♡ K J 10 x x ◇ 8 x x ♣ x	1 Heart Pass	1 Spade Pass	4 Hearts ?	Double

11. ♠ A Q J x
     ♡ K x
     ◇ x x x
     ♣ K Q J x

EAST	SOUTH	WEST	NORTH
1 Diamond	Double	1 Heart	1 Spade
2 Hearts	2 Spades	3 Hearts	Double
Pass	?		

12. ♠ none
     ♡ J 10 x x x x
     ◇ K Q x x
     ♣ J x x

EAST	SOUTH	WEST	NORTH
Pass	Pass	4 Spades	Double
Pass	?		

13. ♠ A J x x
     ♡ K 10 x
     ◇ J x x
     ♣ K J x

EAST	SOUTH	WEST	NORTH
1 Club	1 Spade	Double	Pass
Pass	?		

14. ♠ x
     ♡ x x
     ◇ x x
     ♣ K Q 10 9 8 x x x

SOUTH	WEST	NORTH	EAST
3 Clubs	3 Hearts	Pass	3 Spades
Pass	4 Spades	Double	Pass
?			

15. ♠ none
     ♡ x x
     ◇ K Q 10 x x
     ♣ A 10 9 x x x

SOUTH	WEST	NORTH	EAST
Pass	1 Spade	Pass	2 Hearts
2 No Trump	Pass	3 Diamonds	3 Spades
4 Diamonds	4 Spades	Double	Pass
?			

16. ♠ A K Q 9 x x
     ♡ Q x
     ◇ A x x
     ♣ K x

SOUTH	WEST	NORTH	EAST
1 Spade	Pass	2 Spades	3 Clubs
3 No Trump	4 Clubs	Double	Pass
?			

17. ♠ K Q x x x
     ♡ K J 10 x x
     ◇ K x
     ♣ x

SOUTH	WEST	NORTH	EAST
1 Spade	2 Clubs	Double	Pass
?			

18. ♠ A x x
     ♡ x x x
     ◇ A Q J x x x
     ♣ x

SOUTH	WEST	NORTH	EAST
1 Diamond	Pass	2 Clubs	2 Hearts
Pass	Pass	Double	Pass
?			

19. ♠ A x
     ♡ A x x
     ◇ A K J x x
     ♣ 10 x x

WEST	NORTH	EAST	SOUTH
1 Heart	3 Spades	4 Hearts	?

20. ♠ K 10
     ♡ A K J 10 x
     ◇ 10 8 x x x
     ♣ x

WEST	NORTH	EAST	SOUTH
3 Clubs	3 Spades	Pass	4 Spades
Pass	Pass	5 Clubs	?

21. ♠ K J
     ♡ x x
     ◇ Q J x x x x
     ♣ J 10 9

WEST	NORTH	EAST	SOUTH
3 Hearts	Double	4 Hearts	5 Diamonds
Pass	6 Diamonds	6 Hearts	?

22. ♠ x x
     ♡ x x
     ◇ K Q J 9 x
     ♣ A Q x x

WEST	NORTH	EAST	SOUTH
1 Heart	Pass	2 Clubs	Pass
2 No Trump	Pass	3 No Trump	?

23.	♠ K Q J x x x x	WEST	NORTH	EAST	SOUTH
	♡ none	1 Club	Pass	1 Heart	3 spades
	◇ Q J x x	4 Clubs	Pass	4 No Trump	Pass
	♣ x x	5 Diamonds	Pass	6 Clubs	?

24.	♠ x x x	WEST	NORTH	EAST	SOUTH
	♡ K Q 10 x x	Pass	Pass	1 Club	1 Heart
	◇ x x	3 Clubs	Pass	3 Hearts	Pass
	♣ A x x	3 No Trump	Pass	6 No Trump	?

ANSWERS TO PENALTY DOUBLE QUIZ

1. Two Spades.
Despite having a strong Club holding, this is not an attractive hand on which to make a low-level double, as you have too much strength in your partner's Spade suit. The normal raise is therefore better.

2. Double.
Your trump holding is less than magnificent, but you have good defensive values and are very short on partner's suit. Either your partner will win several tricks in Spades, or you will be able to win an early round of trump and obtain one or more Spade ruffs.

3. Pass.
The temptation to double is strong, but when you hold this type of hand partner is often unable to stand the double. Therefore it is better to defend, undoubled, with the outside chance that partner may reopen with a takeout double, which you of course will be happy to pass.

4. Five Hearts.
When experienced opponents bid strongly, although clearly short on points, they invariably have a freak distribution and a double proves disappointing. Therefore in this type of bidding sequence it is usually better to support partner's suit than to double.

5. Pass.
The fact that you have the A K of the opponents' trump suit is no guarantee that a double would be successful. Competent opponents will be aware that the Ace and King of trumps are missing and will not be out of their depth. You should leave the decision to your partner.

6. Pass —
and hope that West does the same. It is not conceivable that East has more than one stopper in Hearts: he probably has K x or A x. As you can stop the opponents from scampering off with any one of the side suits, you are practically certain to beat 3 No Trump, but if you double West will almost certainly take out to 4 Spades.

7. Double.
This deal has the appearance of being one on which your side might not make a game. Therefore you should double, for even if you collect only a small penalty, you will have reason to be highly satisfied.

8. Three Spades.
On balance it will be a sound policy to remove the double, since a great deal of your strength is in your partner's Spade suit. This may cause the hand to yield a disappointing number of defensive tricks when compared with the score that could have been obtained by playing the hand at your own best declaration.

9. Pass.
On your partner's head be it. He has been warned in unmistakable terms that your hand is unsuitable for de-

fense, and if he still elects to double you must respect his decision.

10. Redouble.

A redouble is usually a sound speculation on hands where you can be reasonably certain of not being set more than one trick, and where you can deal effectively with any contract that the opponents may retreat into. In this deal both conditions are fulfilled.

11. Three Spades.

This is an example where your partner's double should be removed eftsoons or right speedily. Your takeout double of 1 Diamond implied that you held support for the other three suits, and your partner may therefore have doubled 3 Hearts in the expectation of finding you with a degree of Heart strength. Since you haven't got it, you cannot stand the double.

12. Five Hearts.

In this situation your partner's double of 4 Spades will more frequently be based on a strong all-round hand than on considerable strength in the opponent's suit. Therefore the odds favor removing to 5 Hearts, which you expect to make. The danger in passing 4 Spades is that if some of your partner's strength is in Hearts, as may be expected, the double will prove disappointing.

13. One No Trump.

The case of the boy who stood on the burning deck is to be respected but not emulated. The 1 Spade overcall was a dubious tactical maneuver, and now that the opponents have got your number you have no intention of standing fast with a four-card suit.

14. Pass.

This is strictly your partner's party. He has been advised to expect that your hand will be useless defensively, and it is to be presumed that he has the goods to beat the contract in his own hand.

15. Pass.

The use of the Unusual No Trump convention (see Page 191) requires considerable discrimination. Remember that once you have indicated a freakish minor-suit hand by bidding 2 No Trump, subsequent decisions should usually be left to partner. Remember, too, that partner was bulldozed into the bidding and may not even have a genuine Diamond suit. He may have only three Diamonds, in which case your hand will not by any means be a dead duck on defense.

16. Four Spades.

There are some grounds for suspecting here that the bid of 3 No Trump, although perfectly proper, may have caused partner to place us with a more balanced type of defensive hand. We cannot be quite sure of making 4 Spades but the chances of so doing are considerably better than those of securing a sizeable penalty against the opponents' sacrifice contract of 4 Clubs.

17. Two hearts.

When you open the bidding and your partner doubles a butt-in, he is counting on you to hold three defensive tricks. If you do not hold those tricks, and have no compensation in the form of strength in the opponents' trump suit, you should tend to remove the double if a convenient bid is available. This principle applies with extra force when you have an undisclosed five-card suit.

18. Pass.

Your partner's double is indeed welcome, even though you do not hold three blown-in-the-glass defensive tricks, for usually in this situation, partners have a habit of droning on in Clubs. You have compensation for your limited high-card values in the form of three trumps and a shortage in your partner's suit—a considerable asset on defense to a trump contract.

19. Four Spades.

A double would be unsound. Partner has advised you not to count on him for any defensive values, and it is unlikely that experienced opponents will be set more than one trick. The odds therefore favor taking a shot at game.

20. Five Hearts.

One reason for rejecting a double here is that you have a chance to indicate, without ambiguity, a Heart suit that otherwise would have been lost. Showing the Heart suit may conceivably enable your partner to bid slam at Spades.

21. Double.

A pass would imply that you were willing to have your partner bid 7 Diamonds under certain circumstances. Your hand lacks too many controls to enable you to take such a position, and therefore it is better to apply the brakes with a double.

22. Double.

Here the double is designed to promote a Club opening lead. (You would prefer a Diamond, of course, but that would be asking too much.) When your side has not bid, a double of 3 No Trump asks your partner to lead dummy's suit—in this case, Clubs. You hope, of course, to win the Club opening and shift to Diamonds. If you don't double, partner will almost surely lead a Spade, which could hardly do your cause much good.

23. Double.

This is a lead-directing double, asking partner to abstain from the lead he would normally have made (which would doubtless have been a Spade) and to look around for something more startling. In this sequence partner is expected to lead a Heart, which will certainly get the defense off to a good start.

24. Pass.

The opponents' bidding appears to have gone somewhat awry and it is clear that the expected Heart lead will defeat the slam. At that, it would be a grievous error to double, since the double would require partner to make an unusual lead, which would of course mean not leading the suit you have bid.

12.

Conventions and advanced bidding situations

Advanced bidding situations

RIFTS in friendships of long years' standing, as well as sizable financial disasters, are frequently brought about on hands in which each partner is short of the other's suit. One denies the other for round after round, until one of the opponents finds it high time to enter the auction with a resounding double.

Success at the bridge table involves not only making the most of your good cards but holding your losses to a minimum on hands that were not destined to show a profit. A willingness to take a short loss on hopeless hands is one of the distinguishing features of the experienced player.

In cases of misfits, which one of the partners should quit? You have all listened at one time or another to bidding like this:

OPENER	RESPONDER
1 Spade	2 Hearts
2 Spades	3 Hearts
3 Spades	4 Hearts

and so on ad infinitum.

Now who should quit in this case? I have sought for some time to hit upon a practical solution. At one time I recommended that it be done on a priority basis. The younger of the two partners, it was suggested, should be the first to resign. This practice was not endorsed by the Bureau of Vital Statistics, which was burdened by too heavy a demand for birth certificates. So that possible solution had to be abandoned.

In any such case the exercise of good judgment is called for. A few general principles, however, may be laid down.

1. The player who can buy the hand at the cheapest price should, as a rule, be given the courtesy of the road. It is not always wise in these cases to look for the best possible contract. In case of a storm, an inferior contract, undoubled, is better than a superior one that is doubled and down. When it is probable that a loss must be taken, a player with Spades should have priority over a player with Hearts, for the one holding Hearts must bid to a new level to buy the hand.

2. The player with high cards should be willing to become dummy, permitting the player with the long suit to be declarer. Let us see how this applies to a case from real life.

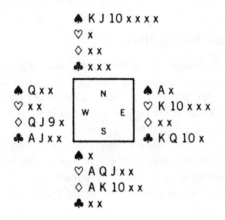

```
                    ♠ K J 10 x x x x
                    ♡ x
                    ◊ x x
                    ♣ x x x
       ♠ Q x x       ┌─────────┐      ♠ A x
       ♡ x x         │    N    │      ♡ K 10 x x x
       ◊ Q J 9 x     │  W   E  │      ◊ x x
       ♣ A J x x     │    S    │      ♣ K Q 10 x
                     └─────────┘
                    ♠ x
                    ♡ A Q J x x
                    ◊ A K 10 x x
                    ♣ x x
```

The bidding:

SOUTH	WEST	NORTH	EAST
1 Heart	Pass	1 Spade	Pass
2 Diamonds	Pass	2 Spades	Pass

What should South do? When I saw this hand played, South went on. In fact, he went on indefinitely, as is the tendency of most players who hold two five-card suits. That holding seems to instill in them some pride of possession.

South should have realized that game was hopeless when North failed to support one of his red suits and also was unable to bid No Trump. Despite his shortage in Spades, South should have passed the 2 Spade bid, realizing that game was hopeless. South's hand makes a good dummy because of its high-card content. North must have length in Spades to repeat them in the face of an announced two-suiter. North's hand will probably be a useless dummy, so South should be inclined to permit North to be declarer.

A splendid opportunity for the thoughtful handling of a misfit was presented to the holder of the following hand:

♠ K Q 10 x   ♡ A Q x x x   ◇ none   ♣ A J x x

He opened with 1 Heart and partner responded with 2 Diamonds. His rebid was 2 Spades and partner bid 3 Diamonds. What should he do? He knows that his partner has a maximum of two Hearts, since with three it would have been his duty to return to the opener's first suit, the opener having shown a five-four. The responder is known to have a maximum of three Spades, since with four he would not have gone out of that suit into another Diamond bid. Responder cannot have anything very good in Clubs, else he would have tried No Trump on opener's display of great strength. It is evident that responder has a long string of Diamonds and nothing else and that it is a hopeless hand. Opener, therefore, made a very fine pass. His mate held:

♠ x x   ♡ x x   ◇ A Q 10 x x x x   ♣ Q x

The forcing pass

A pass is not always a confession of weakness. It may be a definite sign of strength. When in a competitive auction you and your partner have shown great strength and have bid up to 4 Hearts, and your right-hand opponent now makes an obvious sacrifice bid of 4 Spades, a pass by you does not indicate fear, because it is quite apparent that you could double a 4 Spade bid if you chose. If you double, you are in effect saying to your partner that you do not care to go on to 5 Hearts. If, however, you feel that the penalty may not be adequate compensation, and you believe that you may have a fair chance to make 5 Hearts, you pass and permit partner to make the decision.

In such a sequence of bids, of course, partner is obliged to act. If he does not choose to bid 5 Hearts, he must, without reference to the merits of his own hand, automatically double, which you would have done yourself had you been quite sure there was no chance for 5 Hearts. A pass by you at this point is known as a forcing pass. It forces partner either to double the opponents or to go on with the bidding.

It is not always easy to identify a forcing pass. Not every pass in a competitive auction is forcing. A pass becomes a force when it is quite evident from the common sense of the situation that your side has the better holding and that the opponents are trying to wrest it from you.

Let us take an illustration or two.

You are South and vulnerable. The opponents are not. You hold:

♠ A x x x   ♡ x x   ◇ K Q x x   ♣ x x x

The bidding has proceeded:

NORTH	EAST	SOUTH	WEST
1 Spade	2 Hearts	2 Spades	3 Hearts
4 Spades	5 Hearts	?	

What should you do?

You are quite convinced that the opponents cannot make 5 Hearts. Should you double? Since you have a very fine raise, should you try 5 Spades? You are not sure. In that case, why not let partner decide? You should pass. This is not a confession of weakness; you made a free raise early in the auction, and thus showed strength. On the contrary, it is an announcement of strength. Your pass says, "Partner, I think we have a fair chance to fulfill a contract of 5 Spades. What do you think?" If partner does not think so, he will double the 5 Heart bid.

Another case. The opponents are vulnerable. You are not. As South you hold:

♠ x x   ♡ A K Q x   ◇ 10 x x x   ♣ A Q 10

The bidding has proceeded:

SOUTH	WEST	NORTH	EAST
1 Heart	Pass	3 Hearts	3 Spades

What do you do?

Had East passed, you would have bid 4 Hearts in routine manner. It is true that East's 3 Spade bid does not prevent you from bidding 4 Hearts if you choose to. Should you so choose? The answer is No. Your partner has made a bid that invites game. The hand belongs to you and you could go on to game (unless the opponents pay an adequate price for taking it from you). Your proper procedure is to pass it around to your partner. He will do one of three things, whichever is most suitable to his hand. He may go on to 4 Hearts, which he announced the partnership could make. He may decide to play for 3 No Trump, to which you will have no objection. Or—and this is the important consideration—he may be able to double a 3 Spade bid, and if wishes to do so, you would find it quite delectable.

In the actual case, the 3 Spade bid was doubled by North and defeated 1,100 points.

In the next case it is you who have made a forcing bid. You are South; you are vulnerable; you hold:

♠ x   ♡ A K Q 10 x x   ◇ A K x   ♣ A Q x

The bidding has proceeded:

SOUTH	WEST	NORTH	EAST
2 Hearts	Pass	2 No Trump	3 Spades

The only proper call at this point is a pass. Your forcing 2 bid was a minimum, made with the intention of rebidding 3 Hearts over partner's 2 No Trump response. This would allow partner to pass with a completely worthless hand. You convey that message by passing East's 3 Spade bid. You would like partner to take some action. He may be able to bid one of the minor suits, muster up a raise to 4 Hearts, bid 3 No Trump with a good spade stopper, or make a penalty double with spade length and a hand with which you could not make game. Finally, he may be absolutely broke and powerless to do anything but pass. You have already told your story; now it is up to him. Note that a double in this position must be reserved as a penalty-seeking action; otherwise non-vulnerable opponents will be able to come in on nothing and escape punishment.

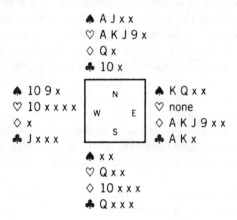

♠ A J x x
♡ A K J 9 x
◇ Q x
♣ 10 x

♠ 10 9 x
♡ 10 x x x x
◇ x
♣ J x x x

♠ K Q x x
♡ none
◇ A K J 9 x x
♣ A K x

♠ x x
♡ Q x x
◇ 10 x x x
♣ Q x x x

With North and South vulnerable, the bidding has proceeded:

NORTH	EAST	SOUTH	WEST
1 Heart	2 Hearts	Pass	3 Clubs
3 Hearts	?		

What should East do at this point? Only one call may be regarded as correct, and that is a pass. A bid of 4 Diamonds or a raise of the Clubs would be little short of an atrocity. There is no need for East to act when his previous cue bid committed the partnership to game, and West in his next turn is duty bound to take some action, either by doubling the enemy or by going on with the bidding as best he can.

In the actual case, West doubled and East passed. As the cards lay, it may be seen, East and West could not have made a game. We pass lightly over North's bid of 3 Hearts. Those things will happen, and no one will ever completely stamp out such practices.

Part-score bidding

A number of the bidding principles which we have discussed in the preceding pages must be modified to a certain extent when the bidding side has the benefit of a part score. Similarly, defensive bidding tactics must be adjusted somewhat when it is the opposition that has possession of the part score. Note the use of the expression "modified" and "adjusted," and those in a mild sense. I do not recommend a complete upheaval of normal bidding methods in part-score situations, as is the unsound practice in certain quarters.

The new-suit (by responder)-forcing principle does not apply where the responder's bid is sufficient to complete the game. For example, with 60 on score, opener bids 1 Spade and responder bids 2 Clubs. Opener need not bid again. If responder has mild slam aspirations, he must jump to 3 Clubs. The jump shift in these conditions is forcing for only one round.

An opening demand bid is still a demand, despite the part score, and responder must reply once. He need not bid again unless opener jumps in a new suit, in which case the obligation to speak once more arises.

When an advanced score of 60 is held, responder should be willing to stretch a point to keep the bidding alive, since a contract of 1 No Trump will complete the game.

The possession of a part score by either side will frequently influence decisions as to opening bids. Part scores of 20 and 30 should, for practical reasons, be disregarded, and the bidding should proceed, except for the final call, as though such a score did not exist. But when an advanced score is held, such a consideration as preparing for a rebid disappears entirely. For example, you hold:

♠ A K x x   ♡ A J x   ◇ J x x   ♣ x x x

With a clear score a pass is recommended on this hand. It is worth only 13 points and is almost sure to present a difficult rebidding problem on the next round. However, with a part score of 60, this hand should be opened with 1 Spade, since any response of 2 by partner may be dropped.

Similarly, holding:

♠ A K 10 x   ♡ x x x   ◇ x x x   ♣ A Q x

With a clear score it is recommended that this hand be opened with 1 Club, but with a part score such action is impractical. The proper procedure is to open with 1 Spade.

When the opponents have a part score and it is to be presumed that they will try to "sneak out," doubtful hands must be opened against them. Holding:

♠ A Q x x   ♡ x x   ◇ x x x   ♣ K Q 10 x

you should open against a part score with 1 Club, because otherwise you may expect the opponents to open and it will be difficult for you to compete at a later stage.

Since slams are available even to players with part scores, our tactics must be adjusted to this condition. An opening demand bid is permissible with slightly less playing strength than is normally required. For example, either of the following hands should be opened with a demand bid when you have a part score of 40 or 60:

♠ A x x   ♡ A K Q J x x   ◇ A x x   ♣ x
♠ A x   ♡ K Q J 10 x x   ◇ A x x x   ♣ x

When you have an advanced score of 70 or 80 and partner opens with 1 of a suit, you should not pass simply because the bid completes game. You should give partner a mild chance if you have a good hand. For example, with a 70 part score, partner opens with 1 Spade and you hold:

♠ A 10 x   ♡ K x   ◇ A Q x x   ♣ x x x x

If partner has a very fine hand, you may have a chance for big things. Your proper procedure is to bid 2 Spades. This is overbidding the game and suggests that you might be interested in going places if partner chooses to act aggressively. If he does not, 2 Spades will surely be safe. You must not make the mistake of responding with 2 Diamonds, which partner, in view of the part-score situation, may pass.

Observe that the range of the 2 Spade bid with the advanced part score is much larger than normal, for although we might, with a clear score, offer a single raise on a mediocre holding, we would not in this situation shade the raise. For example, you hold:

♠ A Q x   ♡ x x   ♢ J 10 x x   ♣ x x x x

With a clear score you would "eke out" a single raise with this hand if partner opened 1 Spade. However, with a 70 part score, the recommended procedure is to pass.

Similarly, under the same conditions you hold:

♠ A x x x   ♡ Q x x   ♢ A K Q x x   ♣ x

With a clear score you would have responded with 2 Diamonds, intending to jump in Spades on the next round, but in this case you dare not bid 2 Diamonds, and it is suggested that you do one of two things—either overbid the game with 3 Spades or, preferably, make a jump shift to 3 Diamonds. This forces partner for one more round. You will show Spade support subsequently.

Protection bidding

A further modification of standard practices takes place in certain so-called "protective" situations. When the bidding is about to die out at a low level and the opponents have clearly indicated that they do not have the balance of strength between them, great liberties may sometimes be exercised to reopen the bidding. The requirements for both the take-out double and the overcall are considerably reduced in a reopening situation. Let us examine a few typical cases. You are South. West opens the bidding with 1 Heart and the next two hands pass. What action do you take on each of the following hands:

1. ♠ Q x x x	♡ x x	♢ A J x x	♣ K x x
2. ♠ K J x x	♡ x x	♢ A x x x x	♣ x x
3. ♠ x x	♡ K x	♢ A Q J 9 x x x	♣ K x
4. ♠ Q x x x	♡ K Q x x	♢ Q J 9 x	♣ x

1. Double. The requirements for a take-out double may be reduced to 11 points for purposes of reopening the bidding.

2. Bid 1 Spade. Competition should be offered and the safest course of action is to bid 1 Spade rather than 2 Diamonds. It is cheaper, and affords competition in a higher-ranking suit.

3. Bid 3 Diamonds. A 2 Diamond call would merely sound competitive. This is an excellent hand for offensive purposes and a display of strength is indicated. Note that when used in a protective position, the jump overcall is not considered preemptive.

4. Pass. Partner does not figure to have much strength, since he clearly has nothing in hearts and yet was unable to overcall the opening bid. To reopen the bidding would run the risk of permitting the opponents to find a better contract.

You are South and the bidding has proceeded:

EAST	SOUTH	WEST	NORTH
1 Heart	Pass	1 No Trump	Pass
Pass	?		

	♠ x	♡ A J x x	◇ K Q 10 x	♣ Q J x x
1.	♠ x	♡ A J x x	◇ K Q 10 x	♣ Q J x x
2.	♠ K 10 x	♡ K x	◇ J 10 x x	♣ A J 10 x

With HAND 1 we would advise a pass, for while you have the necessary values to double, your partner is too likely to bid Spades.

With HAND 2 a double is recommended. You had nearly enough for a double originally, and the slight distributional feature is in your favor.

Again you are South and the bidding has proceeded:

EAST	SOUTH	WEST	NORTH
1 Heart	Pass	2 Hearts	Pass
Pass	?		

1.	♠ A J 10 x x	♡ x x x	◇ K 10 x	♣ J x
2.	♠ A 9 x x	♡ A x x x	◇ A x x	♣ Q 10

With HAND 1 we would bid 2 Spades. Partner is marked with a few high cards and is probably short in Hearts. Competition is therefore reasonably safe.

With HAND 2 we would double. Partner can have no more than 1 Heart. Game is a distinct possibility if he has any length in Spades. If partner should bid Clubs, he is very apt to have at least five, but in any event, the risk is reasonably well calculated.

Four opposite four

The advantages of a four-four fit in trumps are not lost on the experienced player, but the average declarer prefers the feeling of security that a five-card suit gives him. The following is an illustration to point up the principle of the "four-four."

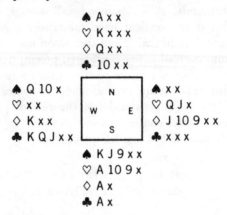

♠ A x x
♡ K x x x
◇ Q x x
♣ 10 x x

♠ Q 10 x
♡ x x
◇ K x x
♣ K Q J x x

♠ x x
♡ Q J x
◇ J 10 9 x x
♣ x x x

♠ K J 9 x x
♡ A 10 9 x
◇ A x
♣ A x

The bidding actually proceeded:

EAST	SOUTH	WEST	NORTH
Pass	1 Spade	Pass	2 Spades
Pass	3 Spades	Pass	4 Spades
Pass	Pass	Pass	

In the play of the 4 Spade contract, declarer lost a trick in each suit and was defeated a trick. The players consoled each other with the observation that it all depended on the Spade finesse. However, a little resourcefulness on the part of South would have landed the game despite the unfavorable Spade distribution.

Instead of rebidding 3 Spades, South could have seized an additional chance by trying 3 Hearts, a one-round force. Partner is offered the opportunity of choosing between two possible suit contracts. There is always the chance that partner has raised with only three Spades on a hand containing four Hearts.

At Hearts the game could not be lost, because the fourth and fifth Spades would provide discards for the two losing Diamonds out of dummy after trumps were extracted.

It is apparent, therefore, that provided each of the partners has four trumps, the five-card suit is much more desirable as a side suit than as trump, because the long suit will provide discards for losers in the other hand.

This principle does not apply, however, to a choice between eight trumps divided five-three and eight trumps divided six-two. *The six-two division is better,* because declarer, with six trumps, can stand repeated forces in any adverse long suit. This he could not do with only five trumps in his hand.

Observe this unusual hand:

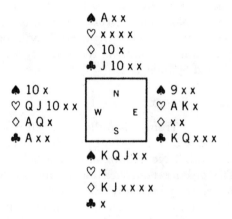

```
              ♠ A x x
              ♡ x x x x
              ◊ 10 x
              ♣ J 10 x x
  ♠ 10 x                      ♠ 9 x x
  ♡ Q J 10 x x     N          ♡ A K x
  ◊ A Q x       W     E       ◊ x x
  ♣ A x x          S          ♣ K Q x x
              ♠ K Q J x x
              ♡ x
              ◊ K J x x x x
              ♣ x
```

East opened with 1 Club and South overcalled with 1 Diamond. South thereafter bid Spades twice, showing that he had six-five distribution (see on page 9). When East and West got to 4 Hearts, South chose to sacrifice, bidding 4 Spades and thus giving North a choice between Spades and Diamonds.

Though he had three Spades as against two Diamonds, *and though Diamonds required a contract one trick higher,* North should have preferred Diamonds, the six-two suit, as a safety measure. At Spades, South would be forced on the second trick by a Heart opening and continuation. He could play safe for down four, but would probably go over to the trump Ace and try a finesse for the Diamond Queen, after which he would be forced in Hearts again. Now he could not both draw trumps and establish his Diamonds, and he would probably win only five tricks, going down 900. At Diamonds, however, South would have plenty of trumps for Heart ruffs and would lose only his two singletons and two trump tricks, going down 300 points even at a higher contract. (Even the double-dummy defense of a Spade opening and continuation by West, without touching Hearts, could beat South only 500 points.)

In this case, therefore, the five-three Spade suit produced only five tricks as against nine tricks for the six-two Diamond suit, a difference of four tricks; and it will be noted that neither suit broke badly.

CONVENTIONS

In an effort to approach completeness it is our purpose to present some of the bidding "gadgets" which have made their appearance in recent years. Among the more popular with a limited group of tournament players are the "weak No Trump," Texas Convention (Transfer bids), the Michaels Cue Bid, the 2 Club-2 Diamond Convention, the "Grand Slam Force," the Flint Convention, the Flannery Convention, the Negative Double and Splinter Bids.

The weak No Trump

The "weak No Trump" is really not at all new. In the early days of contract bridge it was standard procedure in various circles to open the bidding with 1 No Trump on modest holdings of balanced distribution. The practice flourished for a time, faded out and in isolated spots has recently been revived.

The "weak No Trump" has certain advantages. It covers hands ranging in high-card strength from 12 to 14, and has a tendency to crowd the opposition out of a certain amount of bidding space without unduly exciting partner. It achieves its best results when the outstanding strength is evenly divided and the opponents can be goaded into entering the auction. It is subject to the risk, however, of incurring severe losses when opener's partner has a bad hand, and should not be used with minimum hands when vulnerable.

In discussing defense to the "weak No Trump," let us examine a few specimen cases: You are South on each of the following hands and East has opened with 1 No Trump. What action do you take?

1.	♠ x	♡ A J 10 x x x	◇ K Q J x	♣ x x
2.	♠ K Q x x x	♡ A Q x x x	◇ x x	♣ 10
3.	♠ K x x	♡ A x x	◇ A J x x	♣ J 10 9
4.	♠ A J 9 x x	♡ A 10 x x	◇ J	♣ A x x

1. Bid 2 Hearts. In order to overcall, you should have the requirements for a normal overcall at the 2 level.

2. Pass. Your suits do not have a good enough texture to make any offensive action a reasonable risk. Even a 2-level contract could prove very costly. If, however, your partnership is employing the

Landy Convention, an artificial 2 Club overcall is recommended, for it asks partner to bid one of the major suits. The hand is reasonably safe so long as you do not have to guess which one of your suits to bid.

3. Pass. In order to make an immediate take-out double you should have at least 14 high-card points. Remember that the take-out doubler's hand should normally be at least as strong as the hand of the player whose bid he is doubling. Where the hand is completely balanced an additional point should be required for safety's sake.

4. Double. While it is true that you wouldn't like to contend with a Diamond response from partner, your side has a fair prospect to score either a game or a substantial set, so some risk must be assumed. If partner does bid Diamonds, you may fall back on the Spade suit.

Drury Convention

It has been our practice through the years to employ a light opening bid in third position after two passes. Properly managed, this works very well, but there are certain disadvantages to the practice. They stem principally from the circumstances that a player who has passed originally is subjected to the urge to explode in an effort to compensate for his prior pass. The Drury Convention was designed to curb such unwarranted enthusiasm and it works in the following manner.

Let us assume that, having previously passed, you have the desire to offer a double raise when your partner opens in third position with, let us say 1 Spade. Under the Drury Convention you refrain from giving a jump raise and resort instead to an artificial response of 2 Clubs. This is the conventional manner of asking the opener about the quality of his third-hand bid (in this case 1 Spade). If the third-hand bid was shaded the opener is expected to rebid 2 Diamonds, which allows the responder to sign off at 2 Spades. If the third-hand bid happens to have been sound then the opener must rebid anything other than 2 Diamonds. For example, you are third hand after two passes and open the bidding with 1 Spade holding:

♠ A K J x x   ♡ A J x   ◇ x x   ♣ x x x

Partner employing the Drury Convention responds 2 Clubs. This is an inquiry as to the quality of your Spade bid. Inasmuch as you have a sound opening bid of 1 Spade, you rebid 2 Spades and partner proceeds in accordance with his values.

Let us assume that you had made a shaded opening bid of 1 Spade on:

♠ K J x x x   ♡ K J x   ◇ K x x   ♣ x x

surely reasonable in third position; partner responds 2 Clubs. Having a shaded opening your rebid should be 2 Diamonds and partner takes it up from here.

Partner opens in third position with 1 Heart. Next hand passes. What is your action with the following hands?

1.	♠ A K J x	♡ x x x	◇ Q 10 x x	♣ Q x
2.	♠ x x	♡ K x x x	◇ A J x	♣ K x x x
3.	♠ Q J x	♡ x x	◇ x x	♣ A Q J 10 x x

1. 1 Spade. While you have the point count to justify a double raise after passing, you lack the normal trump support. If partner rebids 1 No Trump or 2 Hearts, you intend to raise him.

2. 2 Clubs. If partner rebids 2 Diamonds, denoting a subminimum opening, there is no reason to venture higher than the 2 level. If partner rebids 2 Hearts, announcing a sound opening, you will, of course, raise to 3.

3. 2 Clubs. While this response will be interpreted as the Drury Convention, your subsequent rebid of 3 Clubs will announce a Club suit with the values required for a 2-level response.

Bearing in mind that the initiation of this conventional call announces a fit in partner's major suit, certain by-products are effected.

You have passed originally, and partner opens 1 Spade. Next hand passes.

♠ Q x x   ♡ A K x x x   ◇ x x   ♣ Q 10 x

You respond 2 Clubs. Partner calls 2 Diamonds, indicating a subminimum hand. Since you have shown your Spade support by responding with 2 Clubs, you should bid 2 Hearts allowing for the possibility that partner may have opened a hand with four Spades and three Hearts.

Partner opens third hand with 1 Heart and next hand passes. You hold:

♠ x   ♡ K Q 10 x   ◇ A 10 9 x x   ♣ Q x x

What is your bid?

3 Hearts. This call promises a minimum of four trumps and the equivalent of an opening bid. Had your trump holding been less

formidable, you would have employed the Drury Convention. Observe that the jump to 3 Hearts has afforded you a certain advantage; it may have barricaded the opposition from entering the auction with a competitive bid of 2 Spades.

Landy Convention

The Landy Convention was originally designed as a defensive measure against the weak No Trump opening and was subsequently enlarged in scope. Its primary purpose is to locate a suitable major suit contract after an enemy 1 No Trump opening.

The convention calls for the use of an artificial 2 Club overcall against adverse 1 No Trump opening bids to elicit a bid from partner. The reason for the convention is to avoid complications which may develop from the casual use of the take-out double. Observe that the double of a 1 No Trump opening has always been something of a two-way bid. The player making the double somehow wishes his partner will have a hand which justifies leaving in the double for penalties, so that when a player has a holding not suited to this type of action, he should be wary of employing the double. When he wishes to insist upon a take-out, he therefore employs the artificial bid of 2 Clubs, a bid which suggests a length in the major suits with not enough high card strength to warrant a double for penalties.* To illustrate, against a vulnerable 1 No trump opening made by your right-hand opponent, you would overcall 2 Clubs with the following hands:

1.	♠ A 10 9 x x	♡ Q J 9 x x	◊ x x	♣ x
2.	♠ K Q 10 x	♡ J 10 9 x x	◊ A x x	♣ x
3.	♠ A J 9 x	♡ K Q 10 x x	◊ K 9 x	♣ x

Naturally, the vulnerability has everything to do with your daring, and whereas you might taunt the opposition with the vulnerability in your favor, you keep something in reserve when you are susceptible to a vulnerable penalty. Vulnerable, against a strong No Trump opening, what is your call with the following?

1.	♠ A Q 10 x x	♡ A Q 10 9 x	◊ x	♣ x x
2.	♠ K Q 10 x	♡ A K Q x	◊ J 10 9 x	♣ x
3.	♠ K 9 x x	♡ A J 9 x x	◊ K x	♣ x x
4.	♠ Q 9 x x	♡ A K J 10 x x	◊ A x	♣ x

* A variant, invented by J. G. Ripstra, uses either 2 Clubs or 2 Diamonds, whichever suit is longer.

1. 2 Clubs. Should partner respond with 2 Diamonds, it is your intention to bid 2 Hearts. Partner, holding 3 Spades and 2 Hearts, will know enough to prefer your Spades. Even though you are vulnerable, the take-out figures to be safe call since partner will normally have a fit in one of your suits. To overcall in either Spades or Hearts is placing all your eggs in one basket.

2. Double. You are quite willing to defend with a hand this strong, and have no reason to insist that partner pick his better major.

3. Pass. This is not a propitious time for you to get into the act. If your left-hand opponent has a reasonably good hand, you will be in danger of sustaining a serious injury should you choose to compete. If the enemy permits the bidding to die, your partner will be in a position to protect the fort.

4. 2 Hearts. The purpose of the Landy Convention is to offer partner a choice of suits. You are quite willing to play your contract opposite a singleton in preference to forcing partner to bid an inferior three-card suit.

In the pass-out position, Landy is often used to reopen the auction with mediocre unbalanced hands, thereby preserving the sanctity of the penalty double, which actually is lowered in requirement to 11 to 12 points to pick up partner who may have had to pass with 12 to 14 points and a balanced hand. The 2 Club call in this "dead" position is still an urgent request for one of the major suits.

With neither side vulnerable, your left-hand opponent opens 1 No Trump, which is passed around to you. What action do you take with the following hands?

1. ♠ 6 2   ♡ K 9 8 5   ◇ A J 8 4   ♣ J 9 3
2. ♠ J 10 9 6 2   ♡ A J 7 4   ◇ A 7 4   ♣ 5
3. ♠ 4   ♡ K Q 10 9 4 2   ◇ A 6 2   ♣ J 10 9
4. ♠ K 9 3   ♡ A K 6 2   ◇ Q J 4 2   ♣ 10 7

1. Pass. You do not have the requirements for a reopening double, and to institute the Landy Convention would prove to be embarrassing if partner elects to respond in Spades.

2. 2 Clubs. You are quite content to contract for a part score in any other suit. Since your hand is worth approximately 12 or 13 points, it is quite possible that your assets combined with partner's will be enough to achieve a plus result.

3. 2 Hearts. You do not have the values for a penalty double, and are only interested in the Heart suit. While there is a slight degree of risk involved, the knowledge transmitted to partner by virtue of

your bid might lead to the defeat of an adverse contract should the opposition choose to compete further.

4. Double. If partner leaves it in, you can start clipping coupons. If, instead, he takes out in a suit, his call will not meet with your displeasure.

Texas Convention (Transfer bids)

The object of this convention is to transfer the play of the hand to the opening bidder when his original opening was either 1 or 2 No Trump so that any tenaces contained in his hand would not be subject to an attack on the opening lead.

If partner opens with 1 or 2 No Trump and it is your intention to contract for game immediately in one of the majors, you jump to the 4 level in the suit which ranks immediately below your true suit. Thus, if you wish to play 4 Hearts, you bid 4 Diamonds, if you wish to play 4 Spades, you bid 4 Hearts. Partner must oblige and bid the next ranking suit regardless of his holding and becomes declarer.

Partner opens 1 No Trump. You hold:

1. ♠ Q J 10 9 x x   ♡ A x x   ◇ Q 10 x   ♣ x
2. ♠ x x   ♡ A Q J 10 x x   ◇ K x   ♣ x x x

1. 4 Hearts. Partner must call 4 Spades.
2. 4 Diamonds. Partner is forced to bid 4 Hearts.

Other transfer bids: Transfer bids at lower levels are also employed by some players in responding to 1 No Trump. For example, a response of 2 Diamonds calls for partner to bid 2 Hearts; a response of 2 Hearts calls for partner to bid 2 Spades. (This method is sometimes extended so that 2 Spades calls for 3 Clubs; 3 Clubs calls for 3 Diamonds.) The use of such bids not only transfers play so that the lead comes up to the stronger hand, it also permits the responder to indicate a second suit when he has a two-suiter, or to give partner a choice—between 3 No Trump of the suit responder has shown by his transfer demand— should the responder then rebid 3 No Trump after opener has complied.

The main drawback to the use of the transfer principle is that one member of the partnership usually forgets and makes a natural call over the No Trump opening or the opener is caught napping and forgets to make the transfer to the true suit.

Michaels Cue Bid

There are certain hands of mediocre proportions on which there appears to be a desire on the part of the holder to take some action. The hand may not measure up to the specifications for a takeout double, yet the urge to act is definite. To answer the need suggested by these hands, my late friend and associate, Mike Michaels, devised a procedure known as the Michaels Cue Bid. Here are its provisions.

A direct cue bid of a minor suit opening shows a hand that is primarily distributional with the majority of its strength (usually from 8–14 points) concentrated in the major suits. It is employed only when a take-out double or an overcall will not furnish an accurate description of your holding. Thus, with the following hands, you would cue bid 2 Clubs over an initial 1 Club opening made by your right-hand opponent.

1.	♠ K 9 x x x	♡ Q J x x x	◇ x x	♣ x
2.	♠ A K 10 x	♡ A 10 x x x	◇ x x	♣ x x
3.	♠ x x x x x x	♡ A J x x x	◇ x	♣ x

If the opening bid is in a major suit, a subsequent cue bid denotes a two-suited hand with at least a five-five distribution. One of the suits is the opposing major, and the other, one of the minors. If responder does not have three-card support for the implied major suit, he calls 2 No Trump, which conventionally asks the cue bidder to name his minor suit.

Partner has cue bid 2 Spades over the initial 1 Spade opening, and next hand passes. What action do you take with the following hands?

1.	♠ x x x x x	♡ Q x	◇ A x x	♣ 10 x x
2.	♠ x x x x	♡ A x x x	◇ K x	♣ Q x x
3.	♠ x x x	♡ x x	◇ A K J 10 x x	♣ x x

1. 2 No Trump. Since you do not have three-card support for partner's Hearts, your 2 No Trump command call will uncover a convenient trump suit when partner obliges you by naming his five-card minor.

2. 4 Hearts. Partner has forced you to take a preference at the level of three and has shown a five-card Heart suit and a five-card minor. Your supporting cards in his suits should make a game bid odds-on to make regardless of the relative weakness of his hand.

3. 3 Diamonds. There is no point in inquiring for partner's minor

suit when your own suit can stand on its own merits. Partner will realize your suit is quite good, for otherwise you would have made the conventional 2 No Trump response asking him to name his minor.

The conditions of vulnerability are of paramount importance when employing the Michaels Cue Bid. The length and strength of suits tend to be stronger when vulnerable and are relaxed as the vulnerability conditions vary.

2 Club–2 Diamond Convention

A method of inquiring for the possibility of a major suit fit when partner opens the bidding with 1 No Trump is the 2 Club-2 Diamond convention. Both of the possible responses of 2 Diamonds or 2 Clubs request the opening no trumper to show a four-card major if he has one. The 2 Diamond response establishes a game forcing situation while the response of 2 Clubs is considered forcing for one round only.

This procedure was devised by David Carter of St. Louis and developed by my friend John Gerber, of Houston, Texas, both a player and a non-playing captain of several American International Teams.

Since the 2 Diamond response is unconditionally forcing to game, the minimum requirements for this bid are 10 points which will assure the partnership's assets amounting to at least 26 points. There is no special requirement for the 2 Club call, which ranges from about 2 up to 9 points.

Partner has opened the bidding with 1 No Trump. What is your response with the following hands?

1. ♠ x x x x   ♡ A K J x   ◇ K x   ♣ x x x
2. ♠ A Q J x x x   ♡ A x   ◇ x x   ♣ Q x x
3. ♠ J x x x   ♡ A x x x x   ◇ x x   ♣ x x
4. ♠ x x x x   ♡ Q x x x   ◇ K x x   ♣ x x

1. 2 Diamonds. If partner rebids in either major, it is your intention to raise him. Note that it is not necessary for you to jump to game, since your original response of 2 Diamonds demands that the partnership arrive at some game contract. If partner chooses to bid 3 No Trump when you raise his major suit, the balanced nature of your hand should render that contract agreeable.

2. 3 Spades. There is no point in using the 2 Diamond call when you have a self-sufficient suit and you know where you are headed. Use the direct approach. If partner displays an interest in slam by

cue bidding an Ace, you will be quite willing to continue the probe for a slam.

3. 2 Clubs. If partner rebids in a major suit, you will content yourself with that part score contract. If, instead, his rebid is 2 Diamonds, you will then mention your hearts. Partner will raise you only if he has a maximum No Trump and a good fit, for you have forewarned him of the limited nature of your hand when you responded with 2 Clubs rather than 2 Diamonds.

4. Pass. There is no point in searching for a possible major suit fit when you have a balanced hand and game is quite out of the question. The best place to play an indifferent hand is 1 No Trump.

Grand slam force

When trumps have been agreed upon, either by inference or directly by a raise or a jump raise, a leap to 5 No Trump, by-passing a 4 No Trump Ace-asking bid, is a direct request that partner bid a grand slam in the agreed trump suit if he holds two of the three top honors (Ace, King or Queen). For example, holding:

♠ A J 10 x x   ♡ A K Q x x   ◇ none   ♣ A x x

You open with 1 Spade, and partner jumps to 3 No Trump, the forcing Spade raise. Your one and only concern is the texture of his trump holding, for surely his outside values will take care of your two little Clubs. You therefore bid 5 No Trump, the grand slam force. Partner will dutifully bid 7 Spades if he holds the King and Queen of that suit, or settle for a small slam if he has but one or none.

Variations

The Romans use an interesting variation of this convention. When the grand slam force is introduced, responder jumps to 7 if he has two of the top three honors, bids 6 in the agreed suit with one of the top three honors, and bids 6 Clubs if he has none. This variation clarifies what may be a rather difficult situation if you have opened the bidding with one Heart, and partner jump-raises the Hearts to 3 No Trump. Your hand is:

♠ A K Q x   ♡ K Q J 10 x x   ◇ A x x   ♣ none

If you call 5 No Trump and partner bids 6 Hearts, you will not be certain whether he has the Ace of trumps or not. Playing the Roman variation, you know you are off the Ace of trumps when partner bids 6 Clubs, and you do not have to suffer the humiliation of being in a grand slam off the trump Ace. Naturally, if Clubs are the agreed suit, this information is not available.

Another interesting version of the grand slam force arises when partner has shown some sign of strength, but you are concerned about Aces. Modifying the first example to

♠ A J 10 x x   ♡ A K Q x x   ♢ x   ♣ A x

After partner jump-raises your Spades, you call 4 No Trump (Blackwood). Suppose partner responds with 5 Diamonds. Since you are in possession of all the Aces, you are ready to introduce the grand slam force. You do so by bidding 6 in the unbid minor, which in this instance is 6 Clubs. Partner then leaps to the grand slam if he holds both the King and Queen of trumps, or contracts for the small slam if he does not.

Variants: Additional and somewhat complex variations may be employed when the agreed trump suit is high enough to provide otherwise idle bids between 5 No Trump and the sign-off of 6 in the agreed suit. One such treatment uses these intervening bids somewhat as follows when the agreed suit is Spades:

A return to the agreed suit, 6 Spades, indicates the minimum trump holding consistent with previous bidding; e.g. J x x or x x x x if responder has given a single raise, Q x x x or x x x x x if responder has given a double raise.

A response of 6 Clubs would show at least Q J x x or Q x x x x if responder has given a double raise, at least Q x x x or x x x x x after having given a single raise.

A bid of 6 Diamonds would show either the Ace or King of trumps, four cards long.

A bid of 6 Hearts also indicates the Ace or King, but with additional length—five or six cards in the suit, enough to let partner bid the grand slam with A x x x x or K x x x x in Spades.

If the agreed suit is Hearts, a sign-off at 6 Hearts would be made with either of the first two holdings, with 6 Clubs and 6 Diamonds used to show one of the top *two* honors with appropriate length.

When the agreed suit is a minor: Sometimes a player will wish to bid a grand slam if his partner holds either the Ace or the King of a minor suit but not if his raise did not include one of these two higher honors. In some partnerships, an unusual jump to 5 Spades (assuming Spades have not previously been bid: e.g., opener bids 1 Heart, partner responds 2 Clubs and opener jumps to 4 Clubs) permits the Club bidder to inquire whether his partner has one of the two top honors, Ace or King; in which case he responds 5 No Trump, where, without this conventional variation, he would have to sign off at 6 in the agreed suit since he did not hold two of the three top honors.

Warning: Since all variations in an otherwise simple convention introduce further chance for misunderstanding, it is wise to use them only after a full discussion has made the agreed method clear to both members of an experienced partnership.

Flint Convention (3 Diamonds over 2 No Trump)

Players who consider themselves notably poor holders have been heard to mourn the lack of machinery to allow a partnership to stop in a major suit at the 3 level after an opening bid of 2 No Trump. Suppose your partner opens 2 No Trump and you hold this hand:

1. ♠ x x x   ♡ J 10 x x x x   ◊ x   ♣ x x x

It is reasonable to conjecture that you have a better chance of making 3 Hearts than your partner has of making 2 No Trump; yet under normal conditions you cannot play there, since a response of 3 Hearts would be forcing. It would, of course, be possible to arrange that, after a 2 No Trump opening, 3 of a major suit is a sign-off, but then you would be in difficulties when you held this very common type of hand:

2. ♠ x x   ♡ A J x x x   ◊ K 10 x x   ♣ J x

With this hand you want to bid 3 Hearts, showing a five-card suit and genuine values. Slam is not impossible and 3 Hearts is the time-honored way of exploring the prospects.

The solution, where you hold Hand 1, lies in the use of the "transfer" principle. In response to 2 No Trump, 3 Diamonds is artificial, asking opener to bid 3 Hearts *irrespective of his Heart holding.* If the responder, holding a string of Hearts and little else, wishes to play 3 Hearts, he passes. Alternatively he can bid a long weak suit of Spades, which the opener is expected to pass.

3. ♠ x   ♡ 10 x x x x x x   ◊ J x x x   ♣ x
4. ♠ x x x x x x ♡ x   ◊ 10 x x   ♣ x x x
5. ♠ K x x   ♡ x x   ◊ K J x x x   ♣ Q x x

With each of these hands you bid 3 Diamonds in response to your partner's 2 No Trump opening. Over your partner's enforced rebid of 3 Hearts, you proceed as follows:

3. Pass. 3 Hearts is clearly the proper resting place and the purpose of the convention has been achieved.

4. 3 Spades. The object of this sequence of bidding is to enable you to stop at 3 Spades.

5. 3 No Trump. With this hand you would have bid 3 Diamonds as a mild exploratory bid if you were not playing the Flint convention. You still do so. Partner will at first place you with a weak hand containing a long major suit. But when you bid 3 No Trump on the second round he will place you with this type of hand, and is then at liberty to proceed further over 3 No Trump if he wishes.

Occasionally the opener will have a hand with which he would find it irksome to play at only 3 Hearts.

♠ A x   ♡ K Q J x   ◇ A Q J x   ♣ A K x

Suppose you open 2 No Trump and your partner bids a conventional 3 Diamonds. If your partner's suit is Hearts, your hand becomes so overpoweringly strong that you are willing to underwrite 4 Hearts provided partner has thirteen cards; but you cannot bid 4 Hearts over 3 Diamonds in case his suit is Spades. The ingenious answer is to bid 3 Spades over 3 Diamonds! Then, if partner's suit is Hearts, he is obliged to bid 4 of them, which is what you want. If his suit is Spades, he passes 3 Spades.

The principle may be pushed still further. If opener has strong support for Spades rather than Hearts, he bids 3 Hearts over 3 Diamonds. Then, if responder converts to 3 Spades, opener raises to 4 Spades. Finally, holding a good fit for *both* major suits and good controls, opener rebids 3 No Trump over 3 Diamonds. This tells the responder that opener is ready to play at the 4 level in either major.

The Flannery 2 Diamond opening

An ingenious convention has been devised by William Flannery of Pittsburgh. Holding a hand of moderate strength—11 to 15 points—including four spades and five hearts, he opens with a bid of 2 Diamonds, announcing with a single bid what it would ordinarily take two bids to show and doing so with greater accuracy. Partner knows at once that opener holds four spades and five hearts and his responses select the trump suit:

2 Hearts or 2 Spades are signoffs.
3 Hearts or 3 Spades are invitational.
4 Hearts or 4 Spades = 15 or more "dummy points."

Whether or not you wish to burden yourself with learning all of the additional features of the Flannery Convention, the above responses permit you to bid those hands with 4-5 in the majors with little chance either of playing in the wrong suit or of playing too high. However, the Convention also includes the following:

A response of 2 No Trump is forcing and asks opener to clarify his distribution which he does as follows:

3 Clubs or 3 Diamonds = three cards in the suit named.

4 Clubs or 4 Diamonds = 4 cards in the suit named.

3 Hearts shows 4-5-2-2 with minimum strength.

3 Spades shows 4-5-2-2 with maximum strength.

If responder is interested in a possible notrump contract, he can ask partner with an immediate response of 3 Clubs or 3 Diamonds whether he has a stopper in the suit bid (A x, K x, or Q x x). If opener doesn't hold the requested stopper he rebids 3 Hearts to show a minimum and 3 Spades to show a maximum.

Transfer bids may also be used in response: 4 Clubs and 4 Diamonds are transfers to 4 Hearts and 4 Spades respectively.

Negative double of overcall

It will be found that opponents are apt to make a nuisance of themselves by employing frequent overcalls, more particularly when their suit is Spades. The opener's partner may find this practice somewhat vexing in such a situation as the following:

NORTH	EAST	SOUTH	WEST
1 Club	1 Spade	?	

South holds:

♠ x x x   ♡ A 9 8 x   ◇ J x x x   ♣ K x

A free bid of 2 Hearts, in this situation, would show greater values than South possesses, and therefore under normal conditions he has no very good riposte: it is likely that the hand belongs to the opening side, and it is possible that a game might be undertaken if opener has a Heart suit, but South's safest course of action at this time is to pass and hope opener can take further action on his own.

However, it has been found in actual experience that the opener does not always take the correct action, and accordingly responders have tended to become frustrated. The practice, initiated by Alvin Roth, has therefore grown up among some players of treating a double by responder as a take-out request, enabling him to avoid being silenced.

The principle is that when an opening bid has been overcalled, a double by opener's partner shows a hand on which any normal bid would be unsatisfactory: it can be made at the level of 1-odd with as little as 7 points. A double of this kind is termed a negative double to distinguish it from the more normal penalty double, which of course ceases to be available.

The opening bidder responds to the double on the basis that the responder has shown scattered values. Thus the opener's rebid should in principle reflect the combined values of the two hands. For example, as South you hold:

1. ♠ A Q x   ♡ 10 x x   ◇ A K Q x x   ♣ Q x

2. ♠ x x   ♡ Q x x x   ◇ A K J x x   ♣ A x

The bidding has proceeded:

SOUTH	WEST	NORTH	EAST
1 Diamond	1 Spade	Double	Pass
?			

With Hand 1, playing the negative double, South bids 2 No Trump. His partner has shown at least 7 points and it is reasonable to suppose that these values are present mainly in Hearts and Clubs. With Hand 2, South bids 2 Hearts. The doubler may be expected to pass 2 Hearts unless he has more values than he has already indicated.

The reader will perhaps be more interested in methods of coping with an opponent's negative double than in brandishing the weapon himself. This presents no problem if it is borne in mind that when the right-hand opponent has made a negative double, a redouble shows high-card strength. A jump raise of the overcaller's suit tends therefore to be preemptive. As South you hold:

♠ Q x   ♡ K Q 10 x   ◇ x x x   ♣ A 10 9 x

The bidding has proceeded:

WEST	NORTH	EAST	SOUTH
1 Club	1 Spade	Double	?

You should redouble to show that, regardless of what antics the opposition may be up to, you at any rate are adhering to the old standards and your partner may count on you for genuine high-card values.

Overcalls may be used more freely against opponents who are using the negative double, for the use of the double in this conventional sense makes it more difficult for them to wield the ax when they wish to double for penalties. When opener's partner would like to double the overcall for penalties, he must pass and hope that his partner will reopen with a take-out double which may then be passed for penalties. This opens up a whole area of strategic maneuvers and penalty possibilities against the player who reopens by doubling, only to find that his partner has a bust hand.

Splinter Bids

Slam possibilities often depend on one partner being short in the "right" suit. To pinpoint such shortages, a special meaning is attached to a bid which would otherwise rarely be used.

A splinter bid is an unusual jump in a new suit—usually one that skips two levels of bidding. It announces a singleton or void in that suit and good support for partner's last bid suit. For example:

A		B		C	
OPENER	RESPONDER	OPENER	RESPONDER	OPENER	RESPONDER
1 Heart	4 Clubs	1 Heart	1 Spade	1 Diamond	1 Heart
			4 Clubs	1 Spade	4 Clubs

In each of these auctions, the bid of Four Clubs announces a singleton or void in that suit and good (at least four-card) support for partner's last bid. Note that in Example C the support is for Spades, not Diamonds.

The partner of the splinter bidder can show slam interest by cue bidding another suit, or deny slam interest by bidding game.

The repeat of a splinter bid announces a void or the singleton Ace.

QUIZ ON CONVENTIONS
AND ADVANCED BIDDING SITUATIONS

You are South in each of the following cases. The previous bidding is indicated. What is your action?

1. ♠ K x	SOUTH	WEST	NORTH	EAST
♡ J 10 x	1 Diamond	Pass	2 Hearts	3 Clubs
◇ A K x x x	?			
♣ A x x				

2. ♠ x x x	NORTH	EAST	SOUTH	WEST
♡ Q 10 x	1 Heart	2 Clubs	2 Diamonds	Pass
◇ A K J x x	2 Spades	3 Clubs	?	
♣ Q x				

3. ♠ Q J 10 9 x	SOUTH	WEST	NORTH	EAST
♡ A K x	1 Spade	Pass	3 Spades	5 Clubs
◇ A Q 10 x	6 Spades	Pass	Pass	7 Clubs
♣ A	?			

You are the dealer and your side has a 60 part-score. What do you call with each of the following hands?

4. ♠ K Q 9 x	5. ♠ J x x	6. ♠ J
♡ x x	♡ Q x x	♡ A Q J x x x
◇ A K 10	◇ A Q x x	◇ A K J x x
♣ Q x x x	♣ A Q 9	♣ x

You have a 60 part-score. Your partner opens 1 Heart and next hand passes. What is your call with each of the following?

7. ♠ A K 9 8 x x	8. ♠ x x	9. ♠ Q x x
♡ K x	♡ J x x	♡ x x x
◇ A J 10	◇ A J x x	◇ J x x
♣ x x	♣ A Q 9 x	♣ Q x x x

Both sides have a part-score of 60. You are the dealer. What would you call with each of the following?

10. ♠ 10 x	11. ♠ Q J	12. ♠ A Q
♡ 9	♡ K Q	♡ A Q
◇ A K J 10 x x	◇ J x x x x	◇ 10 8 x x
♣ A x x x	♣ K x x x	♣ K J x x x

The Landy Convention. The player on your right opens 1 No Trump. What would you call with each of the following hands?

13. ♠ K Q 10 x	14. ♠ Q x x x	15. ♠ A J x x
♡ A K J x	♡ K x x	♡ K Q J x x
◇ J x x x	◇ A J x	◇ K x
♣ x	♣ K Q x	♣ K x

The Landy Convention. The player on your left opens 1 No Trump and your partner bids 2 Clubs. The player on your right passes. What would you respond with each of the following?

16. ♠ 9 x x x
♡ 10 x
◇ K J x x x
♣ x x

17. ♠ K x
♡ A J x x x x
◇ x
♣ x x x x

18. ♠ 10 x
♡ x x
◇ Q x x
♣ J 10 9 x x x

The opponent on your right deals and opens 2 Hearts (Weak 2 bid). What would you call with each of the following hands?

19. ♠ A J 10 x x
♡ x x
◇ A K x x
♣ x x

20. ♠ A x
♡ A Q x x
◇ x x x x
♣ A x x

21. ♠ K x x x x
♡ x
◇ A J 10 x
♣ A K x

The Texas Convention. Your partner opens at 1 No Trump and you hold the following hands. What is your call?

22. ♠ K 10 8 x x x
♡ A
◇ x x x
♣ 10 9 x

23. ♠ A 10 9 x
♡ K x x x x x
◇ x
♣ Q x

24. ♠ K Q x x x x
♡ x x
◇ x x
♣ A Q 10

Flint Convention. You open at 2 No Trump and your partner responds with 3 Diamonds. What is your bid?

25. ♠ A Q J
♡ K x
◇ A K Q 10 x
♣ K J x

26. ♠ K Q
♡ A x x x
◇ A K J x
♣ A K x

27. ♠ K x x x
♡ A Q J x
◇ A K x
♣ A Q

Negative Double. You are South. The bidding has proceeded as indicated. What is your call?

28. ♠ J x x
♡ A x x
◇ Q x x
♣ A Q 10 x

NORTH	EAST	SOUTH	WEST
1 Diamond	1 Spade	?	

29. ♠ A Q x
♡ A K J x x
◇ Q x
♣ J x x

SOUTH	WEST	NORTH	EAST
1 Heart	1 Spade	Double	Pass
?			

30. ♠ K x x x
♡ x x
◇ A x x x
♣ x x x

WEST	NORTH	EAST	SOUTH
1 Club	1 Spade	Double	?

ANSWERS TO QUIZ ON CONVENTIONS
AND ADVANCED BIDDING SITUATIONS

1. Pass.

Although you have a very sound hand, there would be no particular virtue in bidding at this point. The situation is made to order for a forcing pass, which simply says that you prefer to allow your partner to make the next call than to make it yourself.

2. Three Hearts.

A pass would be forcing, as partner has shown reversing values and you have responded at the 2 level. But a pass would also suggest that you had no clear-cut line of action to take at this point. This would be incorrect, as it is your bounden duty to indicate that you have excellent support for your partner's (five-card) Heart suit.

3. Pass.

This is a classic situation for a forcing pass because it tells partner that you have control of the opponents' suit and are prepared under certain conditions to undertake a grand slam in Spades rather than to accept a sure but limited penalty by doubling 7 Clubs. If partner has the A K of trumps and his hand is up to par in other respects, he should bid 7 Spades.

4. One Spade.

With no part-score, 1 Club would be the proper opening because 1 Spade would leave no sound rebid after a 2 Heart response from partner. With 60 below the line, you intend to pass partner's response and therefore you open with the better and higher-valued suit.

5. One No Trump.

When you have a part-score, it is permissible to take certain liberties with the normal range of points required for a 1 No Trump opening, provided your hand is of a No Trump type.

6. Two Hearts (or two Clubs).

This hand would not normally qualify for an opening demand bid, but when a part-score is held it is advisable to lower the requirements slightly. 2 Hearts is forcing for one round only.

7. Two Spades.

In a part-score situation, the jump shift, forcing for one round only, should be employed more freely. If you bid only 1 Spade, and partner bids 2 Hearts with a good hand, slam may be missed.

8. Two Hearts.

Normally you would bid 2 Clubs, but as you have an advanced score partner may pass any call you make, and if he does you would rather be in Hearts.

9. One No Trump.

Normally you would pass 1 Heart with an easy conscience, but in the actual circumstances it is worthwhile to strain to convert the partial.

10. Three Diamonds.

With no part-score, the automatic opening would be 1 Diamond. But because the hand is weak in the major suits, a preemptive bid may work out better.

11. Pass.

This is the type of deal that may be thrown in if you pass, but bought by the opposition if you open. You have 12 points in high cards, admittedly, but your major-suit holdings must be devalued because of their shortness.

12. One No Trump.

Ordinarily a bid of 1 No Trump would not be countenanced on such an eccentric hand pattern, but with this type of holding in the major suits it is wise to make every effort to become declarer at No Trump. This opening also greatly reduces the possibility of unwelcome competition in Spades or Hearts.

13. Two Clubs.

With 14 points in high cards, and two four-card major suits, you have just enough for a Landy overcall except under the most unfavorable vulnerability conditions. If your hand were longer in the major suits, you could afford to be slightly shorter in points.

14. Pass.

This hand is not long enough in the major suits to qualify for a bid of 2 Clubs. Nor is it strong enough for a double.

15. Double.

The Landy Convention is best reserved for suitable hands that do not qualify for any other form of action. This hand is strong enough for a double, which is to be understood as primarily for penalties.

16. Two Spades.

A bid of 2 Diamonds would be anti-systemic, for partner's 2 Club call guarantees four cards in both major suits. It is not unknown to respond to a Landy overcall by bidding even a three-card holding in Spades or Hearts.

17. Three Hearts.

The jump response to a Landy overcall is invitational, not forcing. The bidding has shown that your pair has at least ten hearts, and the King of Spades is to be regarded as an extremely valuable card because of partner's expected length in the suit.

18. Pass.

With this hand you are justified in crossing partner's intentions and leaving him to play in what will clearly be the best contract.

19. Two Spades.

Your opponent's mild preempt is of little effect here except to advise you

that he has less than a normal opening, with a six-card Heart suit. Your hand warrants normal overcall action.

20. Pass.

Again you are activated by the same motives as over a 1 bid. Your hand does not warrant a No Trump overcall and you therefore pass for the time being.

21. Double.

Because you have strength in three suits, the double is preferred to 2 Spades. Your hand revalues to 18 points as a dummy and you therefore have values to spare.

22. Four Hearts.

After your partner's 1 No Trump opening, you are willing to contract for game at Spades, and in view of your weakness in the minor suits you are happy for partner to be the declarer.

23. Two Clubs.

A Texas response of 4 Diamonds, asking partner to bid 4 Hearts, would not be wise. You have no special reason for wanting partner to be the declarer, and you also wish to allow partner the opportunity to show a Spade suit if he has one.

24. Four Hearts.

The Texas Convention greatly facilitates a slam exploration in hand like this. Over your partner's automatic response of 4 Spades, you intend to bid 5 Clubs, indicating that you are interested in a slam if partner can look after the red suits.

25. Three Hearts.

It may well be that your partner has chosen a singularly unpropitious moment to deploy the convention, but nevertheless you are obliged to rebid at 3 Hearts.

26. Three Spades.

If partner has a long suit of Hearts, your 3 Spade bid will force him to bid 4 Hearts, which he will surely make. If partner's suit is Spades, he may pass 3 Spades.

27. Three No Trump.

With this hand you are in the happy position of being willing to under-write a game in either of the major suits if partner has a string of one of them.

28. Two Clubs.

In this type of hand we are not in sympathy with the use of the Negative Double, which should be reserved for hands that offer no other suitable form of action. Without the overcall

we should have bid 2 Clubs, and therefore we bid it just the same.

29. Two No Trump.

Partner has shown modest values and, in view of his inability to raise Hearts or bid No Trump, it is clear that his holdings are likely to be in the minor suits. We accordingly rebid our hand on that basis.

30. Three Spades.

After East's Negative Double, our raise is to be understood as a strictly preemptive effort. Normally this hand would qualify for only 2 Spades.

13.

Opening Club bids: artificial and forcing

BIG HANDS present their own special problems. Unless we are to use a primitive method whereby the opener bids whatever he thinks he can make, it is obviously essential for a player to be able to tell his partner that Dame Fortune has seen fit to bestow an extremely good hand and that he wishes to have ample opportunity to describe it. Lacking such a mechanism, the opener's partner would need to find some response on every occasion. This, in turn, would require that a player never open anything but a strong hand, and the entire bidding structure would be reared upon a treacherous quicksand instead of upon a firm foundation, from which it is either safe to proceed or on which it is reasonably safe to rest.

The simplest solution of this problem is the opening bid of 2 in a suit. (See Chapter 1.) This bid tells partner in one brief and instant message what the opener's suit is; or, depending on the later development of the bidding, it suggests one or two or more alternative trump suits. It also demands a final contract of at least a game, unless the opponents are kind enough to enter the fray with a bid that provides an opportunity for a profitable penalty double. Safeguarded by point count's restrictions upon the opening bidder, so that partner cannot be subject to the sadistic whims of the incurable optimist, this method provides a satisfactory "yours not to reason why" basis of taking care of powerhouse hands.

However, time does not stand still and several ideas have been advanced in an endeavor to patch up any possible flaw. Two such methods involve the mechanisms of the natural 2 bid itself.

In one version, the 2 bidder or his partner may stop short of game: following a negative 2 No Trump response, if opener merely makes a minimum rebid of the same suit he bid initially, responder is not forced to bid again with a worthless hand. This remedy is not in itself entirely satisfactory; there are some hands when responder is not able to tell that the meager assets he holds are indeed worthless.

Another and perhaps more vulnerable flaw in the natural 2-bid is that the negative response of 2 No Trump may throw the play into the "wrong" hand should No Trump become the final contract. The declarer loses the potential advantage of having the opening lead come up to the strong hand; the defenders gain because they are able to make the opening lead "through strength" and because they are able to see most of declarer's working assets and better judge his side's weaknesses when the strong hand is put down as dummy.

To meet this disadvantage, some players use a "next suit negative" instead of a 2 No Trump response. If opener bids, for example, 2 Hearts, responder bids 2 Spades as a conventional denial of strength, with no reference to his holding in the spade suit itself. Should opener's bid be 2 Spades, the negative response is 3 Clubs—next *suit* negative— so that any No Trump response is positive and No Trump is never bid by the weak hand when it is truly weak.

1 Club forcing

As I have earlier warned my readers, the various systems employing 1 Club as a forcing opening are not to be confused with the so-called "Short Club." In all of these systems, beginning with the earliest of them all, the Vanderbilt Club introduced by the father of contract bridge himself, Harold S. Vanderbilt, the bid has no relation to a holding in the Club suit itself but it does promise a definite minimum of high-card strength.

The Italian Blue Team followed this idea to record-setting world championship success with three different versions: Roman Club, Little Roman, and Neapolitan Club. Of these, none has achieved a wide following in the United States; perhaps the most widely known is now called The Blue Team Club, combining some of the features of Neapolitan and Roman.

Two systems using the strong artificial opening 1 Club bid have acquired some following in America: Howard Schenken's "Big Club" and, more recently and with considerable success in both international and national tournament play, C. C. Wei's "Precision Club," about which I have written a book.* The entire Blue Team switched to "Precision" in 1972, when Italy won the World Bridge Olympiad.

There are dozens of other 1 Club systems, among them, Bangkok played by the Thailand team; Canary, getting its name from the fact that it features *CAN*apé and *RelaY* principles; French Club; Lea System, which suggests an opening 1 Club bid with virtually all hands of 12 points or more, answered by step responses based on point

---

* *Charles H. Goren Presents the Precision System of Contract Bridge Bidding* (Doubleday & Company).

count—a concept so ancient that it may even have preceded the old Vienna System, using 1 Club on medium strength hands, first played by the World Champion Austrian team back in the '30s and more recently revived, in modernized form, by Australia's use of it in 1971 Bermuda Bowl competition. Doubtless, I have neglected to mention many other variations of this much-tinkered-with and sometimes effective idea. Who knows, some day it may become a bridge law that every hand must be opened with 1 Club. Until then, if you like the idea of an artificial opening 1 Club bid, I recommend that you first try a system that can be grafted upon Standard American with the least need to alter the method you already play. Two of these, Blue Team Club and Precision, are among the four whose principal features are presented in condensed form in the remainder of this chapter.

The Blue Team Club

The opening bid of 1 Club shows a hand of 17 or more high card points, with any distribution. *Exception:* In rare cases, extremely unbalanced hands may be opened 1 Club with slightly less. For example: 6-1-1-5 distribution with 16 HCP; 0-6-1-6 with 15 HCP concentrated in the long suits.

The 1 Club bid is forcing and artificial, and the first response is also artificial with a few exceptions. Responses are:

1 ◊—0–5 points.
1 ♡—6 or more points; not more than two controls. (Ace = 2 controls; King = 1 control.)
1 ♠—3 controls.
1 No Trump—4 controls.
2 ♣— 5 controls.
2 ◊—6 controls.
2 No Trump—7 or more controls.
2 Hearts or 2 Spades shows a six-card suit including two honors in a hand totaling less than 6 points.

Opening bids other than 1 Club: Opening bids of 1 in a suit other than Clubs show at least a four-card suit (exceptionally three cards in Diamonds) and from 12 to 16 points. For the most part, such hands are bid in natural fashion, noting however that a limit of strength has been placed by failure to open the bidding with 1 Club. Four-card suits are bid, so that five-card majors *must* be rebid, with rare exceptions, such as when partner's response at the 1 level permits opener to give a better picture of his general strength by a rebid of 1

No Trump. Over a 1 No Trump response, however, even a weakish five-card suit, ♡ K J x x x, must be rebid. jump rebids by opener are lighter than in Standard methods; a six-card or longer suit containing three honors, ♠ A Q J x x x, is worth a jump rebid on anything but the weakest opening.

Opening hands with eleven or twelve cards in two suits are usually considered strong, even if their high-card point count is in the low range. Hands with nine or ten cards in two suits are strong if the hand counts to 15 or 16 points, largely concentrated in the long suits. With such hands the Canapé principle is usually followed; the shorter suit, or the lower ranking of five-card suits, is bid first.

Responses to 1 Diamond, 1 Heart, 1 Spade: The only negative response to these 1 bids is a pass. A jump to 2 No Trump shows 11–12 points in a balanced hand; a double raise shows four-card support and 11–12 points. Neither of these responses is forcing. New suit responses at the 1 or 2 level are forcing for one round, as in Standard methods.

Bids that are game-forcing include: An immediate jump shift, which announces a solid or semi-solid six-card suit; a reverse rebid by responder; a jump second response in a new suit, and a reverse in one of partner's suits, sometimes shown by a jump to 4 in a minor.

1 No Trump opening: The opening No Trump bid may show either a 16-17 point balanced hand or a 13-15 point hand with Clubs as the only long suit, especially in hands that include only a doubleton Diamond.

Opening bids of 2 and 3 Clubs: Because the opening bid of 1 Club is artificial and forcing, you must use another opening bid for a hand worth less than 17 points. The five-card Club suit is usually taken care of by an opening bid of 1 Diamond, with three cards in that suit, or by an opening bid in any other biddable suit, or by a bid of 1 No Trump. Longer Club suits are shown as follows:

2 Clubs: Either a one-suited hand with at least six Clubs, a good suit, and less than seven winners; or a two-suited hand with at least five Clubs when Clubs are the stronger suit.

3 Clubs: A one-suited hand with at least six Clubs in a suit that includes no more than one loser. The hand must include at least seven winners, one of which must be outside the Club suit.

Responses: A 2 Diamond response to an opening 2 Club bid is conventional and requests partner to show other features of his hand. All other responses are non-forcing and follow standard lines. A 3 Diamond response to an opening 3 Club bid shows a Diamond stopper and asks opener to show his stoppers in other suits. Other responses below 3 No Trump merely show stoppers in the suit bid and deny stoppers in suits that have been skipped; thus, a 3 Spade response would deny stoppers in both Diamonds and Hearts, 3 No Trump shows stoppers in all unbid suits. Jumps to 4 Diamonds, 4 Hearts or 4 Spades show solid suits and are slam invitations.

Opening bid of 3 No Trump is gambling, based on a solid 7-card minor suit, with *no outside strength*.

The opening bid of 3 Diamonds, 3 Hearts or 3 Spades usually shows a good seven-card suit; an opening bid of 4 in these suits shows a solid suit, seven or eight playing tricks and not more than one defensive trick.

Once suits have been established, the Blue Team Club uses asking bids and other devices in its moves toward slam.

The Neapolitan Club

This is the system upon which the Blue Team Club is based, and most of the methods just described are used in the Neapolitan System. Overcalls are made very freely, especially at the 1 level; jump overcalls are intermediate in strength; takeout doubles are made on high-card point values rather than distribution—they do not, for example, suggest that the doubler has four cards in the "other major," as is usually the case in standard methods.

Roman Club

The 1 Club bid is artificial and forcing, but may show any one of four different hands:

Most often, the bid is made with 12-16 points in a balanced suit pattern, 4-3-3-3 or 4-4-3-2 distribution. After a 1 Diamond response (negative, denying 9 or more points) opener bids a major or 1 No Trump. After a positive response in a suit (8-11 points minimum) opener shows a minimum by a single raise, a bid of a new suit at the same level as the response, or a rebid of 1 No Trump.

Responses of 1 No Trump show 12-16 points; 2 No Trump, more than 16. Opener rebids conventionally to show his exact point count.

1 Club may also be bid with: A hand with 21-22 points and balanced distribution, shown by a jump rebid in No Trump after partner's response; or a two-suited hand with 17-20 points, at least four cards in Clubs and five cards in another suit; or an unbalanced

hand worth a game bid, with which opener's rebid is a jump in his suit and responder shows his exact holding in that suit by a rebid in one of six prescribed steps.

If opponent overcalls an opening bid of 1 Club, responder shows 12-16 points without a stopper by cue-bidding opponent's suit.

Other opening 1-bids: Natural, usually a four-card suit but guaranteeing at least one suit of more than four cards. With two suits, the Canapé principle, shorter suit first, is followed except when the shorter suit is Clubs. All opening suit bids are forcing. Responder must rebid and with fewer than 9 points does so by a raise or the cheapest possible response, both of which are negative.

1 No Trump Opening: Balanced hands, 17-20 points. A response of 2 Clubs demands a rebid of 2 Diamonds, following which any minimum rebid is weak, intended to be passed. A response of 2 Diamonds is an inquiry for four-card majors and is forcing to game. Also forcing to game are responses of 2 in a major or 3 in a minor, with opener showing exact strength by step rebids.

2 No Trump opening: Balanced hand with 23-24 points. Responses as above.

Opening bid of 2 Clubs or 2 Diamonds: Each of these bids announces 4-4-4-1 or 5-4-4-0 distribution, with respectively 12-16 or 17-24 points. A response of 2 No Trump is positive and demands that partner show his *short* suit. Other responses are negative and if the response strikes opener's short suit he makes the cheapest possible suit rebid.

Opening bid of 2 in a major: These openings show at least a five-card suit in a hand that also includes a four-card or five-card Club suit.

Defensive bidding: Overcalls in a suit show a maximum of 12 points but are usually made only on a good suit. Takeout doubles show 12-16 points. Unless there is an intervening bid (in which event responses are normal) responder bids his *shortest* suit if he can do so at the 1- or 2-level. Should intervening player bid, responder's double is for takeout, not penalty. A 1 No Trump overcall is the equivalent of an opening No Trump bid, but a 2 No Trump jump overcall shows a strong two-suiter, neither of which is opener's suit. Overcalls in opponents' suit are natural, but a *jump* cue-bid shows a very strong three-suiter, singleton or void in enemy suit, in a hand that includes only four losers.

Asking bids: Once a suit has been agreed, the Roman System includes a complex series of asking bids, usually initiated by a jump at the level of 4 or higher in an unbid suit. Responses are by steps.

Schenken 1 Club ("Big Club")

Opening 1 Club: 17 or more high card points, artificial and forcing. A strong Spade suit or major two-suiter may be shaded to 14 HCP plus 5 distributional points. With a No Trump type hand, 19-22 HCP Distributional points are counted as in Goren Point Count except that for the opener distributional points are awarded for length: 1 for each four-card suit (Q x x x or J 10 x x or better); 1 extra for fifth card of any suit; 2 points for each card more than five. After 1 Diamond negative response (less than 9 HCP and 1½ honor tricks) opener's non-jump suit rebid may be passed; a jump suit rebid is forcing for one more round; 1 No Trump shows 19-20 HCP; 2 No Trump = 21-22.

Responses to 1 Club: 1 Heart, 1 Spade or 2 Diamonds show at least 9 HCP and 1½ honor tricks; at least a strong four-card suit or a suit of five cards or longer. 1 No Trump = 9-11 HCP; 2 No Trump = 12-14 HCP, balanced hand. All positive responses forcing to game. 2 Clubs (artificial, semi-positive, one-round force) = 6-8 HCP.

Single jump response shows solid suit; double jump shows semi-solid suit.

If oponents overcall, a double up to the level of 3 Diamonds shows positive response and requests takeout by opener. A bid shows less than 9 HCP.

Opening bid of No Trump: Same point count requirements as Standard American. 1 No Trump = 16-18; 2 No Trump = 23-24; 3 No Trump = 25-26. 1 point may be added to HCP count for a good five-card suit.

Responses to No Trump: 2 Clubs asks for four-card major but when followed by a rebid of three in a minor it shows 6 or 7 points in a five or six-card suit. Opener may pass or, with a strong opening, go to 3 No Trump.

2 Diamonds is forcing to game and shows 11 HCP or more, nine or ten cards in two suits (usually the minors), a singleton or void. After 2 Diamonds, opener rebids 2 Spades to show Spade stopper; 2 Hearts to show Heart stopper; 2 No Trump to show both majors stopped.

Opening bids of 1 Diamond, 1 Heart, 1 Spade: Usually the same as Standard American, but limited to 12-16 points. With good six-card or seven-card suit, point count may be shaded to 10-11.

Responses: Pass with less than 7 HCP. Single raise is constructive; 8-11 points. Jump raise, invitation, 12-13 points. 1 No Trump, 8-

11 HCP, balanced hand. 2 No Trump (not forcing), 12-13 HCP. 3 No Trump = 14-16 HCP.

Opening bid of 2 Clubs: Six-card or longer Club suit 11-16 HCP. (May be bid with strong five-card suit.) New suit response is not forcing except if jump shift. 2 No Trump is also forcing.

Opening bid of 3 Clubs: Solid (usually at least six-card) Club suit, 10-15 HCP.

Opening bid of 2 Diamonds: Strong, artificial and forcing, calling for Ace-showing responses. With balanced hands, the 2 Diamond bid shows 23 HCP or more; with freak hands, shows a long solid or semi-solid suit (not more than one loser and strong slam possibilities).

Opening 2 Spade and 2 Heart bids are "weak"—8-12 points, 1½-2 honor tricks, lacking support for the "other major." 2 No Trump is the only forcing response. Opener then rebids suit as a signoff, shows a "feature" if his hand warrants, or bids 3 No Trump with a solid suit.

Ace-showing responses: 2 Hearts = none; 2 No Trump = Ace of Hearts; 2 Spades, 3 Clubs or 3 Diamonds = Ace of suit bid. A bid of 3 in Spades, Hearts, Diamonds or of 4 in Clubs shows that Ace and the Ace of the suit next lower ranking. 3 No Trump = Aces of Spades and Diamonds or of Hearts and Clubs. 4 No Trump = any three Aces.

King-asking: After Aces have been shown, opener can ask for Kings by making the cheapest suit rebid over partner's response. The same process, if repeated, asks for Queens. Responder shows holdings as he does for Aces.

New response to opening bid of 2 Clubs: Optionally, a response of 2 Diamonds may be forcing and artificial, showing a good Diamond suit or support for one or both majors. Opener may bid a four-card major, rebid his Club suit, or bid 2 No Trump.

Asking bids, special optional step responses to 1 Club and other features are part of the system.

Special conventions to use with Standard American: To adopt his system for use with Standard American, Schenken recommends a limited 17-22 HCP opening 1 Club bid. Stronger hands are shown by opening suit bids of 2 Diamonds, 2 Hearts or 2 Spades, but the 2 Club bid is played as the long Club suit previously described.

The Precision 1 Club

The Precision System was designed by C. C. Wei, a Chinese engineer and shipping magnate, to provide a method of using an artificial 1 Club opening that would be more often used, that could be most easily grafted onto or used with Standard American methods, and that would cover—at least in the early stages of the bidding—the entire gamut of opening bids from 11 points up and of responses from zero to hands of unlimited strength. To accomplish the first objective, he reduced the requirement for the artificial 1 Club opening to 16 points—a mere 1 point differential that vastly increased the number of hands on which the 1 Club machinery could be brought into operation. He also combined two features of other well-known systems so as to make it practical to bid only five-card or longer major suits on the first round and still provide a bid—a weak (13-15 point) No Trump—to handle balanced hands of less than the 16 points required for an opening bid of 1 Club or for a Standard American 1 No Trump opening.

OPENING BID OF 1 ♣:
   16 or more high card points; conventional and forcing.

RESPONSE OF 1 ◊:
   7 or fewer HCP; conventional; negative.

OTHER RESPONSES:
   Natural; positive, constructive.

OPENING BID OF 1 NT:
   13-15 HCP; balanced distribution.

OPENING MAJOR SUIT:
   11-15 HCP; five-card or longer suit.

Except for 1 Club opening, which is conventional, similar to 2 Clubs opening in standard methods, *almost all other Precision bids are also played as part of Standard American.* Therefore, it is easy to learn. But the player who adopts the Precision System enjoys the enormous advantage of knowing, often from the very first bid, whether the partnership is in part score, game or slam territory.

Only two situations are not covered precisely by these principal features: First, what to do with the hand distributed 4-4-1-4, with the singleton in Diamonds, with fewer than 16 points, so that none of the precepts of the system would be violated; the majors could not be bid because they were only of four-card length; the hand was short in the one suit in which four-card length is permitted, Diamonds; and finally, it did not qualify for an opening 1 Club bid because it lacked the required high-card strength.

Second: What to do with the responding hand that was similarly distributed but that was too strong for the artificial 1 Diamond response showing 8 or more HCP, but that did not qualify for a response of 1 in each major (no 5-card suit) or 2 Clubs, also needing five-card length, or of 1 No Trump which in good logic promised a balanced hand; i.e., no singleton.

The ingenious solutions to these two problems are among the things that have helped to make the Precision System popular, including, as they do, a variation of the Roman 2 Club or 2 Diamond bid to show 4-4-4-1, and a bid romantically entitled "The Impossible Negative."

Having outlined the major principles upon which the Precision System is based, perhaps the simplest presentation is to reproduce with his permission the major portion of Wei's summary of the system.

The Goren point count is used for high cards; distribution points are counted for the responding hand only, and only when raising partner's suit: Void = 5; Singleton = 3; Doubleton = 1.

OPENING BIDS WITH HANDS OF 16 *or more*
HIGH CARD POINTS (HCP)

HCP		BID
22-23	Balanced hand, no 5-card major	2 NT
16 up	All other hands of any distribution (forcing)	1♣*

Responses to 1♣ Opening

0–7	Negative	1◇*
8 up	With at least 5-card suit: forcing to game unless both hands are min. and no fit is found. With 4-4-4-1 first bid "the impossible negative." Then, in rebid, responder either jumps in No Trump if opener bids his short suit; or jumps in his short suit if opener bids anything else (e.g. 1♣—1 ◇; 1♡—2♠; responder has a singleton ♠).	1♡/1♠/2♣/2◇* 1◇*
8-10	Balanced hand, no 5-card suit	1 NT*
11-13	Balanced hand, no 5-card suit	2 NT*
14-15	Balanced hand, no 5-card suit	3 NT
16 up	Balanced hand, no 5-card suit (later rebid will distinguish from 11-13 point hand)	2 NT*
4-7	6-card suit; little strength outside	2♡/2♠
4-7	7-card suit; little strength outside	3♣/◇/♡/♠

If opponents intervene over 1♣

If opponent doubles 1♣:

0-7	At least four card in ♣ suit	Pass
0-7	Fewer than four cards in ♣ suit	1◇*
8 up	With four cards in both majors	Redbl.*
8-10	Bal. hand; 1 or no 4-card major	1 NT*
11 up	Ignore intervening double	

If opponent overcalls 1♣:

0-4		Pass
5-8	No five-card suit; (for takeout)	Dbl.*
5-8	With 5-card suit; bid at convenience	Show suit
5-8	With 6-card suit	Jump in suit
9 up	Unbal. hand; no-stopper; (Responder shows suit next round)	min. NT*

*Forcing bid.

HCP		BID
9-11	Balanced; at least 1 stopper	2 NT (jump)*
12-14	Balanced; at least 2 stoppers	3 NT (jump)
9 up	With at least 2nd-round control	Cue-bid*

ALL BIDS MARKED * ARE FORCING

Rebids by Opener after 1 ◇ Response

16-18	Bal. hand (May incl. wk. 5-card minor)	1 NT
19-21	Bal. hand (May incl. wk. 5-card minor)	2 NT
24-26	Bal. hand (May incl. wk. 5-card minor)	3 NT
16-21	Unbal.; show 5-card or longer suit;	1♡/♠/2♣/◇
	(Or 4-card major with 4-4-4-1 dist.)	1♡/1♠
22 up	(or with 9 playing tricks) jump in suit	2♡/2♠/3♣/3◇*

Rebids by Opener after Positive Response

16-18	Balanced hand; simple rebid in	NT*
19-21	Balanced hand; jump rebid in	NT*
16 up	Unbal.; 5-card or longer suit; bid suit	Suit*
	(Responder is required to raise with J-x-x or	
	better support)	
19 up	With strong 4-card support in partner's re-	
	sponse suit, opener makes a trump-asking	
	bid by a	Single raise*
19 up	Solid or semi-solid 6-card or longer suit	Jump shift*

After a positive response in a suit, opener's and responder's rebids are usually natural; both partners should keep in mind that the auction must continue to game, unless both hands are minimum and an adequate trump fit cannot be established. Opener's first rebid should always describe the nature of his hand.

OPENING BIDS WITH LESS THAN 16 HCP

11-15	At least a four-card diamond suit	1◇
11-15	At least a five-card major	1♡/1♠
13-15	Bal'd hand; may have 5-card minor	1 NT
11-15	6-card or longer ♣ or 5 ♣s and another 4-	2♣
	card major suit	
8-10	6-card or rarely 5-card major suit (weak)	2♡/2♠
	(New suit response is forcing; 2 NT response	
	asks opener to show singleton or void)	

HCP		**BID**
11-15	4-4-1-4, or 4-4-0-5 (singleton or void in diamonds; opener cannot have 5-card major) (NOTE: The somewhat lower range for opening bids is because only high cards are counted by the opening bidder.)	2◇*

PREEMPTIVE OPENING BIDS

	Semi-solid 7-card minor; outside entry; (invitational to 3 NT)	3♣/3◇
	Normal preempts; 6 winners not-vul; 7 vul;	3♡/3♠
	Solid 7-card minor; little outside strength	3 NT (Gambling)
	Solid 7-card major; usually with outside A or K (Transfer to 4♡/4♠. If responder is interested in slam he makes cheapest response; opener bids outside control or four of his suit without side control.)	4♣/4◇*

RESPONSES TO 1◇ OPENING BID

11-15	At least 4-card support, forcing, responder denies a 4-card major. Opener rebids in major to show stopper; his 2 NT rebid shows stopper in both majors.	2◇*
Up to 10	5-card or longer support for diamonds; preemptive; jump	3◇
8-10	Balanced hand; no 4-card major, non-forcing	1 NT
16 up	Balanced hand [Opener rebids 3♣ to show min. (11-13) and 2 NT responder then rebids 3◇ (conventional) requesting opener to show distribution; any other rebid by opener shows maximum (14-15 HCP)]	2 NT*
14-15	Balanced hand; no 4-card major	3 NT
8-15	4-card suit or longer; forcing	1♡/1♠*
11-15	4-card suit or longer; no 4-card major	2♣*
16 up	Good 5-card or longer suit; shows a trump fit or a long semi-solid suit. (By agreement, a jump-shift may be Ace-asking; see Optional Treatment)	Jump shift*

HCP		BID

RESPONSES TO 1♡/1♠ OPENING BID

HCP		BID
8-10	Limited raise; dist. points included; at least 3-card support. With longer support, point count may be reduced.	2♡/2♠
11-13	Limited jump raise (no more than 11 HCP) 4-card or good 3-card support, e.g., Q-x-x	3♡/3♠
14 up	4-card or longer support (dist. hand; no more than 11 HCP)	4♡/4♠ Jump raise to game
8-15	Balanced hand with mild support for opener's suit or unbalanced hand with insufficient HCP to justify a 2-over-1 resp. With min. (11-13 HCP) opener rebids 6-card suit; bids lower ranking 4-card suit; bids his better 3-card minor. With max. (14-15 HCP) opener jump-rebids 6-card suit; reverses in a higher ranking suit; jumps in second 5-card suit; raises to 2 NT with 5-3-3-2 dis. Should responder then rebid a new suit, opener should pass but may raise with max. and good 3-card support. All jump rebids by opener are non-forcing.	1 NT*
16 up	Same as over 1◇ opening (forcing)	2 NT*
14-15	Usually 4-card support for opener's major; responder lacks a void or singleton in side unit.	3 NT*
11-15	5-card major or 4-card minor (Exception: 1♠ over 1♡ may be only 8 HCP)	New suit*
16 up	Good 5-card suit, etc.; same as over 1◇	Jump shift*
11 up	Singleton or void in suit to be bid; 4-card or better support for opener. Slam invitation	Dbl. jump shift*

RESPONSES TO 2♣ OPENING BID

HCP		BID
11 up	Conventional and forcing (with ♣ fit, may be made with only 8 HCP)	2◇*
	Opener's rebids:	
	4-card second suit	2♡/2♠
	Stoppers in two other suits	2 NT*

HCP			BID
	6-card suit; 1 other suit stopped		3♣
	5-card ◇ suit (6♣; 5◇)		3◇*
	6-card solid ♣ suit		3 NT
	After 2 NT or 3♣ rebid by opener, to request		
	opener to clarify stoppers, responder rebids		3◇*
	Opener's rebids show:		
	After 2 NT	After 3 ♣	
	♡ and ◇ suit	♡ suit	3♡*
	♠ and ◇ suit	♠ suit	3♠*
	♠ and ♡ suit	◇ suit	3 NT*
8-10	5-card suit; invitat'l; opener may pass with		2♡/2♠
	min. and mild support		
10-11	Invitation to 3 NT		2 NT
14 up	Good 5-card suit; natural		Jump shift*

RESPONSES TO 1 NT OPENING BID

HCP			BID
8-11	Non-forcing Stayman. With both majors,		2♣*
	opener shows ♡ suit first. Any rebid by		
	responder is invitational to game		
12 up	Game-forcing Stayman		2◇*
	Opener's rebids are:		
	4-card major (♡ before ♠ with both)		2♡/2♠*
	5-card minor (5-3-3-2)		3♣/3◇*
	No 4-card major or 5-card minor		2 NT*
	After 2 NT rebid by opener, to request opener		
	to further clarify distribution responder rebids		3♣*
	Then Opener's next rebid is:		
	4-card ◇ suit (3-3-4-3)		3 ♡*
	Two 4-card minors, 3 cards in ♡ (2-3-4-4)		3 ♡*
	Two 4-card minors, 3 cards in ♠ (3-2-4-4)		3 ♠*
	4-card ♣ suit (3-3-3-4)		3NT
0-7	5-card suit (opener should pass)		2♡/2♠
5-7	6-card suit, little strength outside		3♣/3◇
10-11	No 4-card major; invitation to 3 NT		2 NT
11 up	One suited hand; forcing to game; jump to		3♡/3♠*
	(Opener raise with 3-card support)		
	Gerber convention asking for aces		4♣*
	Texas transfers to 4♡/4♠ respectively		4◇/4♡*
18	Quantitative NT raise		4 NT

HCP		BID
	RESPONSES TO 2◇ OPENING BID	
	Very weak hand; sign-off	2♡/2♠/3♣
8 up	Conventional and forcing	2 NT*
	Openers rebids are:	
	4-4-1-4, 11-13 HCP	3♡
	4-4-1-4, 14-15 HCP	3♠
	4-4-1-4, 14-15 includes A or K in ◇	3 NT
	4-4-0-5, 11-13 HCP	4♣
	4-4-0-5, 14-15 HCP	4◇*
5-7	Invitation to game	3♡/3♠/4♣
	Sign-off; considerable strength in ◇ suit	3 NT

OPTIONAL TREATMENTS:

TRUMP SUIT ASKING BIDS*   BID

After a 1♣ opening and positive response in a suit, opener's direct single raise of partner's suit requests responder to define his trump holding:
Responder rebids conventionally by steps:

5-card suit or longer, lacking A, K or Q	1 step
5-card suit headed by A, K, or Q	2 steps
5-card suit headed by 2 of 3 top honors	3 steps
6-card suit headed by 1 top honor	4 steps
6-card suit headed by 2 top honors	5 steps
5-card or longer suit headed by 3 top honors	6 steps

(e.g.: 1♣—1♡; 2♡—2 NT (2 steps)
responder holds 5-card ♡ suit headed by A, K or Q.)

CONTROL ASKING BIDS*

After a trump suit asking bid, or after a trump suit has been agreed, a new suit by opener is a control-asking bid. Responder shows holding in asked suit by step rebids.

No control (3 low cards)	1 step
Third round control (doubleton or Q)	2 steps
Second-round control (singleton or K)	3 steps
First-round control (void or Ace)	4 steps
First and second round control (A-K, A-Q)	5 steps

(e.g.: 1♣—1♡; 2♡—2 NT; 3◇—4♣ (4 steps)
responder has Ace or a void in ◇ suit)

HCP   **BID**

ACE-ASKING BIDS*

A jump shift (except over 2♣, 2◇ or 1 NT opening)
is Ace-asking. Responses are:

No side Ace; no top honor in asked suit	NT (min)
Top honor in asked suit; no side Ace	Raise
Ace in *bid* suit; no top honor in asked suit	New suit
Ace in bid suit + top honor in asked suit	Jump suit
2 Aces; no top honor in asked suit	Jump NT
2 Aces + top honor in asked suit	Jump raise

(e.g.: 1♣—1 NT; 3◇—4◇. Responder has
A, K, or Q, in ◇ but no side Ace.)

Optional treatments: In place of the Precision 2 Diamond bid, Roman
2 Diamonds may be used with two four-card major suits and a
singleton or void in Diamonds or a singleton Club. With Diamond
shortage, the range is 11-15 HCP. With Club singleton and 11-13
HCP the range is 11-13. All other three-suited hands of fewer than
16 points are opened 1 Diamond. Responses to this form of Roman
2 Diamonds are as follows:

Instead of the "Impossible Negative," there are two possible
alternatives. A) Responder bids 1 No Trump; then jumps in the suit
immediately under his singleton to show his 4-4-4-1 distribution. Or,
B): Splinter bid, otherwise indicated as "Unusual jump shows singleton." After opening bid of 1 Club, responder jumps to 2 Hearts,
2 Spades or 3 Clubs/3 Diamonds to show a singleton or void in that
suit, and a hand of 8 or more points. With fewer than 9 points, he
responds 1 Diamonds in any case. Since 1 Heart, 1 Spade, 2 Clubs
and 2 Diamonds are positive and forcing, the jump to any higher
level is "unusual." When this alternative is played, the customary
meaning of the jump—good six-card suit and 4 to 7 points. The
double-jump may be used by agreement to show either a six-card or
seven-card suit.

The bids listed as "Optional Treatments" need not be adopted if
you wish to use the Precision methods in their simplest form, combining
them with Standard American.

Practice plan for quicker learning: C. C. Wei has suggested a practice
plan for learning his system which can readily be adapted to practice
of other systems using an artificial 1 Club opening.

SESSION 1: The two players go over the summary and establish firm partnership understanding by marking item by item each sequence of the bidding.

SESSION 2: Partners (one pair only) practice bidding without interference by dealing out two thirteen-card hands:
  a) 1♣ OPENING: Remove three small cards from each suit. Bid as partners.
  b) LIMITED OPENING: Remove three small cards each from ♣ and ◇ suits; deal two hands; bid them as partners.
  c) 2◇ OPENINGS: Remove eight cards (all except A, K, Q, J) from Diamond suit; deal and bid two hands.
  d) DISTRIBUTIONAL HANDS: Deal two hands 5-5-3 at a time from unshuffled pack.
  After bidding, analyze resulting contracts; correct misunderstandings; make notes to supplement the summary. One such practice bidding session is equal to ten tournament sessions.

SESSION 3: Invite two friends to help give you bidding practice. Deal yourselves the hands as above; the remaining cards to your friends. Bid as usual in four-hand game, but do not play. Analyze your bidding results; note and correct bidding misunderstandings.

SESSION 4: Deal as in regular bridge and bid competitively. After bidding, examine hands (do not play) and correct misunderstandings or errors.

Because uninteresting hands which will not cause bidding misunderstandings are excluded and because playing time is saved, bidding experience gained will be equal to 40 tournament sessions.

DEFENSE AGAINST ARTIFICIAL 1 CLUB SYSTEMS

When the opponents use a strong opening bid of 1 Club and an artificial weak response of 1 Diamond, your defensive tactics should be altered. You can take advantage of the fact that these bids do not show where their strength lies; also, you must overcome some of the features of these methods which would otherwise put you at a disadvantage. The principal problems of the defender are: What to do when holding the suit in which an artificial bid has been made; what to do with balanced hands that would be the equivalent of an opening No Trump bid and therefore a sound 1 No Trump overcall in standard methods; what to do with hands presenting an opportunity for preemptive action.

First, a brief review is in order. A 1 Club opening, though unlimited as to top strength, need not immediately conjure up the specter of a sure game or slam for the opponents. It does tell you that an opponent has at least 16 or 17 points in high cards; therefore, it will be difficult for you to score a game without distributional values that will nullify some of this high card strength. Since the opponents have not yet mentioned their real suits (except by coincidence), you will rarely have need for the usual takeout double or cue bid asking partner to bid some "other" suit. Therefore, the cue bid and the takeout double may be used for purposes other than the customary ones. Meanwhile, their failure to name a natural suit leaves the opponents somewhat vulnerable to preemptive tactics that will rob them of room to exchange information about their distribution.

The following methods of defensive bidding against artificial 1 Club systems have proved effective:

Overcalls in Clubs and Diamonds are natural, not cue bids. Because the opening 1 Club bid and the weakness 1 Diamond response are both artificial bids, overcalls in these suits are not cue bids, but show length in the suits. Sometimes your holding will warrant a simple overcall in opener's bid. Sometimes you will want to bid preemptively by jumping to 3 Clubs or 3 Diamonds—or perhaps even higher. Examples:

SOUTH	WEST	NORTH	EAST
1 Club	2 Clubs		

SOUTH	WEST	NORTH	EAST
1 Club	Pass	1 Diamond	2 Clubs/
			2 Diamonds

In both examples, defender's bids show a genuine suit and do not request partner to bid. Generally, the simple overcall shows a hand with some defensive potential. A jump to 3 Clubs or 3 Diamonds is preemptive; it is not a forcing bid and does not show a strong hand. On the contrary, it usually indicates a hand of little defensive strength.

Other overcalls are normal, usually based on a one-suit hand.

Jump overcalls are preemptive. Sound preemptive bidding is always a useful weapon. Against opponents who have not yet really named a suit, it may be particularly effective because they have made no efforts to locate strength or define shape. A preempt that steals bidding space might make it difficult for the opponents to reach their best contract; might force them to accept a comparatively small penalty. But let me re-emphasize the word "sound" when you are considering preemptive action. Against artificial 1 Club openings, a weak jump overcall on a ragged suit invites disaster. A light penalty double by the partner of the 1 Club opener, or negative double converted into a penalty double by opener's pass, may result in a heavy penalty. What's more, it may do so on a hand where the opponents have no game. Therefore, do not allow the opening 1 Club bid to panic you into unsound preemptive action.

However, when you have a good suit that will produce a number of tricks even without support from partner, preempt as much as you can afford within the limits of the Rule of 2 and 3: that is, risk no more than a two trick set when vulnerable; a three trick set when not vulnerable. Exceptionally, it may be worthwhile to risk a slightly higher penalty when the vulnerability favors your side and when your partner has already passed: in other words, in a situation where one partner's pass, opener's 1 Club bid and your own weakness combine to make it virtually certain the opponents have a game and possibly a slam.

When you have a strong balanced hand: Stay out of the auction, at least for the time being. When an opponent has announced a hand with at least 16 high card points it will always be difficult for you to make game, and usually you will be able to do so only if partner has strong distributional values opposite your high-card strength. Assuming that your opponent has at least the equivalent of a strong No Trump opening,* you will learn this by the 1 No Trump rebid of the 1 Club opener. You will also know, by that time, whether opener's partner has fewer than 8 points. If responder has made a positive response, he announces at least 8, and you will have done well to keep silent. Perhaps your silence will mislead your opponents as to the location of missing key cards, especially after you have shown up with considerable strength without having bid. However, suppose the bidding goes:

SOUTH	WEST	NORTH	EAST
1 Club	Pass	1 Diamond	Pass
1 No Trump			

If you have the equivalent of a top-range double of an opening bid of 1 No Trump, a double at this time will show it—and with less risk that North is holding the balance of power and can redouble.

---

*In some systems a 1 Club opening followed by a 1 No Trump rebid shows as many as 20 points.

Minor and major two-suiters: Distributional values are the key factor to successful bidding against strong 1 Club bids. Singletons or voids may go far to offset the opener's announced high card strength. As previously mentioned, you will seldom have occasion to use a No Trump overcall or a takeout double in its natural sense against a 1 Club opening or 1 Diamond response because neither of these bids shows a suit. Therefore you can use these actions to show two-suited hands. In the simplest method a take-out double shows the majors and a 1 No Trump overcall shows the minors. It is possible to adopt just the opposite meaning, but the suggested method is easier to remember because an Unusual No trump usually calls for a minor suit response.

A more complete but more complex method of showing all types of two-suiters with a single bid was originated by Alan Truscott and improved, in my opinion, by a suggestion from his wife, the former Dorothy Hayden. The scheme is based rather logically on the theory that distributional hands offer the most likely possibility of successful competition against the top card strength announced by the opening bid of 1 Club.

Jump overcall (2 ◊, 2 ♡, 2 ♠, 3 ♣): Shows suit bid and next higher suit.

Double: (of 1 ♣) shows Clubs and Hearts

(of 1 ◊) shows Diamonds and Spades

1 No Trump: Shows Spades and Diamonds.

Simple overcalls are normal, showing the suit bid. (In the original Truscott version the simple overcall was used to show a two-suiter instead of the jump overcall as in the table shown above. Obviously this sacrificed the possibility of making a simple overcall with a one-suited hand. The jump overcall has the additional advantage that, because it is a jump, it helps to call partner's attention to the conventional meaning of the bid.)

Three-suited hands: With three-suiters it is usually best to stay out of the auction, at least until the opponents have settled into your short suit or void. There is at least a fair chance that they may land in one of your suits. If the opponents stop short and your values seem sufficient, you can re-open the bidding with a cue bid or a takeout double. Remember that if you do not become declarer, and sometimes even if you do, it cannot help your opponents to be tipped off to your distribution.

QUIZ ON OPENING CLUB BIDS

You are playing a 1-Club system in which an opening bid of 1 Club would be artificial and forcing, indicating at least 16 points in high cards, with any distribution. Your partner's actual opening bid is 1 Heart. What would you respond with each of the following hands?

1. ♠ 9 x x	**2.** ♠ Q x x	**3.** ♠ A x
♡ Q x x	♡ 10 x x	♡ K x x x
◇ A x x x	◇ Q x x	◇ x x
♣ J x x	♣ A Q x x	♣ Q J 10 x x

You and your partner are playing Precision Club.
What would you open as dealer with each of the following hands?

4. ♠ A Q J x x	**5.** ♠ K J x	**6.** ♠ A Q J
♡ A K J x x	♡ A K Q	♡ K Q 10
◇ 10 x	◇ Q x x x	◇ A K x
♣ x	♣ A Q x	♣ K J x x
7. ♠ Q 9 8 x x	**8.** ♠ A K J 10 x x	**9.** ♠ K Q
♡ Q 10 x x x	♡ A Q 10 x	♡ x x
◇ A	◇ x	◇ A J x
♣ A K	♣ x x	♣ K J 9 8 x x

Your partner opens 1 Club (Precision Club). After a pass by next hand, what would you respond with each of the following?

10. ♠ A Q x x	**11.** ♠ x	**12.** ♠ x x
♡ J x x	♡ 9 x x	♡ A J 10 x x x x
◇ Q x x	◇ 9 x x x	◇ x x
♣ x x x	♣ 10 x x x x	♣ x x
13. ♠ Q x x	**14.** ♠ K Q J 10 x x	**15.** ♠ A J x x
♡ Q J x	♡ x x	♡ K J x x
◇ K x x	◇ x x x	◇ Q x x x
♣ K x x x	♣ x x	♣ J

You are South in each of the following bidding sequences. You are playing Precision Club. What would you call in the circumstances indicated?

16. ♠ J 10 x x	NORTH	SOUTH
♡ Q J x x	1 ♣	1 ◇
◇ K x x	1 No Trump	?
♣ x x		
17. ♠ Q J 9 x	NORTH	SOUTH
♡ J x	1 ♣	1 ◇
◇ x x x x	2 ♡	?
♣ 10 x x		

18.	♠ J x x x ♡ x x ◇ J x x x ♣ x x x	NORTH 1 ♣ 2 ♡	SOUTH 1 ◇ ?
19.	♠ x x x ♡ A x x ◇ x x x ♣ x x x x	north 1 ♣ 1 ♠	SOUTH 1 ◇ ?
20.	♠ x ♡ A J x ◇ A K x x x ♣ A x x x	SOUTH 1 ♣ ?	NORTH 2 ♠
21.	♠ A K Q 10 x x ♡ K J x ◇ A x x ♣ x	SOUTH 1 ♣ ?	NORTH 3 ♡
22.	♠ Q 10 x x ♡ K x ◇ A x x ♣ x x x x	NORTH 1 ♣ 2 ♡	SOUTH 1 NT ?
23.	♠ A J 9 x x ♡ x x ◇ A 10 ♣ Q 10 9 x	NORTH 1 ♣ 3 ♡	SOUTH 1 ♠ ?
24.	♠ K J 9 8 x ♡ x x x x ◇ A J 10 ♣ x	NORTH 1 ♣ 2 ♣	SOUTH 1 ♠ ?

ANSWERS TO QUIZ ON OPENING CLUB BIDS

1. Pass.
Since you are playing an artificial Club system, your partner's failure to open 1 Club indicates a limited hand. You cannot expect to have more than about 22 points in high cards, and in view of the balanced nature of your hand, game is out of the question.

2. One No Trump.
There would be no point in committing this hand to the 2 level by responding 2 Clubs, since your partner has not opened 1 Club and you cannot therefore expect to make a game.

3. Four Hearts.
Hands which are strong on support for opener's suit are frequently dealt

with in a different way when playing an artificial Club system than when playing Standard. The principle is that, when your partner opens 1 Heart or 1 Spade, showing a limited hand, you should usually make a limit raise when there is clearly no slam in the hand. In this instance it is clear that 4 Hearts is the correct contract, so you simply bid it.

4. One Club.
Although this hand contains only 15 points, you may open the Precision Club with it because you have two strong five-card suits.

5. One Club.
Precision calls for a 1 Club opening with a balanced hand in the 19 to 21

point range. The intention is to disclose the nature and strength of your hand by rebidding 2 No Trump.

6. Two No Trump.

This is the exception to the principle that strong hands are opened with 1 Club. To preserve the unity of the Precision scheme for No Trump type hands, those containing 22 or 23 points are opened with 2 No Trump.

7. One Spade.

This hand does not rate a 1 Club opening because it contains only 15 points. The fact that it also has two five-card major suits does not represent adequate compensation, since those two suits do not contain the majority of the high-card values.

8. One Club.

With longer suits, the point-count requirements for a 1 Club opening can be relaxed a little. 14 points represents the minimum level when a strong six-card suit and a biddable four-card suit are held.

9. Two Clubs.

Although this hand contains a useful six-card suit, it does not rate a 1 Club opening on 14 points, since no biddable secondary suit is held. Therefore the correct opening bid is 2 Clubs, which shows 11 to 15 points and a good five-card or longer Club suit.

10. One No Trump.

Although this hand rates a positive response, you may not bid 1 Spade with a suit of only four cards. The proper response is 1 No Trump, indicating 8 to 10 points in a balanced hand.

11. One Diamond.

You may not pass a Precision opening bid of 1 Club. The fact that your hand appears hopeless, and that your longest suit is Clubs, is quite irrelevant, for your partner's hand is a completely unknown quantity.

12. Three Hearts.

A 3-level response to the Precision Club (including 3 Clubs) is termed a constructive response and indicates a seven-card suit and 4–7 points, most of which are in the bid suit.

13. Two No Trump.

This response indicates 11–13 points in a No Trump type of hand. It is of course forcing to game.

14. Two Spades.

This is another form of constructive response. A bid of 2 Hearts or 2 Spades over 1 Club indicates a six-card major and 4–7 points, most of which are in the bid suit.

15. One Diamond.

The reader may perhaps have scratched his head in an endeavor to find a suitable method of expressing this hand in response to 1 Club, and concluded that there isn't one. The conclusion is justified, inasmuch as the hand contains positive values but is unsuitable for a bid in No Trump and has no five-card holding that could serve as a vehicle for a suit response. The solution is the Impossible Negative: Respond 1 Diamond, but jump in a new suit or in No Trump on the next round.

16. Two Clubs.

Your partner's bidding indicates the equivalent of a strong No Trump opening. Game is possible if opener is maximum, and accordingly you bid a Stayman 2 Clubs, intending to raise a major-suit response and to bid 2 No Trump over 2 Diamonds.

17. Two Spades.

Your hand just qualifies for bidding a new suit over your partner's one-round force of 2 Hearts. Your bid indicates 4–7 points and also suggests that you do not have three-card support for opener's suit.

18. Two No Trump.

You have to bid something over 2 Hearts, and by bidding 2 No Trump you indicate 0–3 points and less than three cards in your partner's suit.

19. Two Spades.

Your partner's bid of 1 Spade is not forcing, but you should offer a single raise whenever you have three-card support together with 2–4 points.

20. Pass.

Since your partner is known to have a six-card Spade suit, with several points in it, 2 Spades should prove to be a safe partial. At the same time, you cannot really expect partner to make 4 Spades, and therefore you simply pass.

21. Four No Trump.

Your partner's 3 Heart bid shows a seven-card suit, and therefore there would be very little point in your mentioning that you too have a powerful suit. 6 Hearts should surely prove a fine contract if partner has an Ace, so you proceed straight to a Blackwood inquiry.

22. Two Spades.

The possibility of locating a four-four fit in Spades should not be neglected. Although you have an extremely valuable card in your partner's Heart suit, you should not raise at this time as the raise would suggest three-card support.

23. Four Diamonds.

You have extra strength above the values required for a minimum positive response; you also have adequate support for your partner's very powerful Heart suit, together with a possible ruffing value in Diamonds. Therefore, instead of simply raising to 4 Hearts, you should cue bid the Ace of Diamonds. Opener will understand that you have accepted his suit as trump and are indicating a Diamond feature.

24. Three Clubs.

Opener's raise to 2 Spades is an asking bid. Opener has agreed to your suit as trump and wants to know the length of your suit and the number of honors held. By rebidding at two steps above your partner's bid, you indicate a five-card trump suit with one of the top three honors (Ace, King or Queen).

Goren's New Bridge Complete **2**

the play of the hand

14. Elementary card combinations

Declarer

IT IS an elementary principle of card playing that the best results can be obtained by forcing an opponent to play ahead of you. This is especially true when you are attempting to capture one or more of his high cards. A simple illustration is the following.

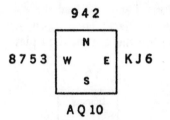

942

8753 W E KJ6

AQ10

Your object is to win tricks with the Queen and the 10. This you will succeed in doing only if the King and Jack are held by East, and also if you compel East to play before you are obliged to do so. Therefore the proper procedure is to enter the North hand and lead a small card, covering whatever East plays. By repeating this procedure you will win tricks with both the 10 and the Queen. Note if you play first from the South hand you would win only the Ace and lose the other two.

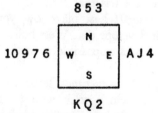

853

10976 W E AJ4

KQ2

Similarly, here you are trying to win tricks with both the King and the Queen. This can be done only if East holds the Ace, and provided he is compelled to play before you. The proper procedure is to lead a small card from the North hand. If East plays the Ace, your troubles are over. If he plays small, you win with the Queen and enter the North hand again to repeat the process. Note that if

you had led the King out of your hand you could have taken only
one trick, with the Queen.

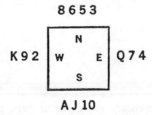

8 6 5 3

K 9 2

Q 7 4

A J 10

Your object is to win two tricks in the suit. If you lead from the
South hand, this is impossible, but if you lead from the North hand
and play the 10, West will win a trick with the King. You subsequently enter the North hand and lead the suit again. If East plays
small, you win with the Jack. Here again you have obtained the
maximum by compelling the opponent to play before you use your
high card.

A 6 4

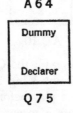

Q 7 5

Your object is to win two tricks in the suit. Assuming that the
outstanding cards are normally divided against you, the Ace will
naturally win one of them, but to win a trick with the Queen you
must force the opponent who holds the King to play ahead of you.
Your only hope is that East has that card, so that after cashing the
Ace you lead a small one. If East plays low, you play the Queen,
hoping it will win. If it develops that West holds the King, you will
not succeed, but then it was impossible to make two tricks in any
event.

The inexperienced player sometimes leads the Queen from the
South hand, expecting to win a trick with it. This is impossible,
because if West plays properly he will place his King on your Queen,
and now you can win only one trick in the suit.

*It is important to bear in mind that it is almost impossible to win
a trick with a card that you lead.* You must try to compel the opponent who has the missing card to make his play before you make
yours.

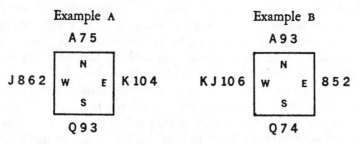

Example A   Example B
A 7 5   A 9 3
J 8 6 2 [N W E S] K 10 4   K J 10 6 [N W E S] 8 5 2
Q 9 3   Q 7 4

Notice that in EXAMPLE B you are helpless to take more than one trick no matter how you play, but in EXAMPLE A, if you lead a small card from the North hand toward your Queen, you will win two tricks in the suit. Note how different it would be if South improperly played the Queen first.

If we add a Jack to the South holding, producing the following combination:

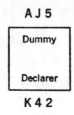

A 9 3

Dummy

Declarer

Q J 4

and two tricks are needed *in a hurry,* it now becomes proper to lead the Queen, because if West has the King and covers, your Jack will immediately become good. If he fails to cover, the Queen will win a trick. The difference in this case is that you retain the equivalent of the card that you lead.

It is important to bear in mind that a finesse is not so much an effort to get an opponent's high cards out of the way as it is an attempt to win tricks with your own high cards. It is rarely possible to win a trick with a card that you lead unless you have the card next below it. Whenever you take a finesse you must make a wish and say, "I wish the outstanding card to be in such and such a position. If it is, I will win the trick with such and such a card."

A J 5

Dummy

Declarer

K 4 2

Your problem is to win all three tricks with this combination. What is the proper procedure? First, you must make a wish. Which one of the opponents do you wish to have the Queen? If East has it, luck is not with you, because when you lead the Jack, East will play the Queen and you will be forced to win with the King. Now you can win only two tricks. You have made the mistake of trying to win a trick with a card that you led; second, you have not compelled the opponent with the high card to play before you did. The proper procedure is to wish for West to have the Queen and to make him play ahead of you. A small card, therefore, should be led from the South hand, and if West plays low, insert the Jack, hoping it will win a trick. In other words, the card played third hand to a trick has a fair chance to win. The card played first hand to a trick has practically none. By the addition of one more card, the 10, we have the following position:

A J 10

K 4 2

With this holding you can win all three tricks, provided you can guess which one of the opponents holds the Queen. This is a mere guess, and if you believe that West has it you should lead a small card from the South hand, making West play before North. The 10 will then win the trick. If, however, you think that East has the Queen, you should first play the Ace and then lead the Jack. If the Queen covers, the 10 will be good. If East plays low, the Jack is permitted to ride and will win the trick. In this case the lead of the honor card to the first trick will succeed because you have the next card.

K J 10

4 3 2

Your problem is to win two tricks with this holding. Obviously one must be lost to the Ace, so that it does not much matter which

opponent has it. The important question is, "Who has the Queen?"
If East has it, you will be obliged to lose two tricks, but if West holds
it, you may win two tricks by compelling West to play before you.
The proper procedure, therefore, is to lead a low card from the South
hand and, if West plays low, to follow with the 10. This will succeed
in forcing out the Ace. The South hand is subsequently re-entered
and another small card led, with the assumption that the Jack will
win the trick. Here again you are leading toward your high cards,
compelling the opponent who may have the missing honor to play
before you use your high cards.

Q 10 9

5 4 2

Your object is to win one trick in the suit. If West holds both the
Ace and the King, you will be successful if you lead from the South
hand. If West plays the King, North will play the 9 and subsequently
re-enter the South hand in order to lead again toward the Queen.
However, inasmuch as it is improbable that West has both the Ace
and the King, the better procedure is to wish that he holds the Jack.
A small card is led from the South hand, and when West plays low
North follows with the 9, hoping that this will drive out the King or
the Ace. The South hand is entered and another small card is led,
and since West is known to hold the Jack one trick must be built up.

A K 9 4

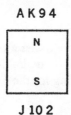

J 10 2

Your object is to win all four tricks. This can be done if West
holds the Queen. The Jack, therefore, is led from the South hand.
If West covers, all your cards are high. If West plays low, the small
card is played from the North hand and the process repeated. If East
has the Queen, this play will not succeed. It is true that if East has the

Queen and one other, the finesse will have been a losing play, but you have no way of telling this, and in the long run the finesse is the better play with this combination, as will be seen in the chapter on probabilities.

If, however, the 10 is not held, so that your holding is the following:

A K 4 2

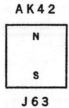

J 6 3

it would now be improper to play the Jack, because if West has the Queen he will presumably cover, and now one of the opponents must win a trick with the 10. Your best chance is that the Queen has only one small card with it and will drop when you play the Ace and the King. In any event, it is impossible to win all four tricks no matter how you play the cards, because if the Queen drops, it will mean that one of the opponents has the 10 9 x x and must win the fourth round of the suit. This is apparent from the following example:

A K 4 2

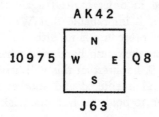

10 9 7 5   Q 8

J 6 3

Finesses

In taking finesses, there comes a time when there are very few entries in the dummy and it is desirable to retain the lead in the hand from which you are leading for the finesse.

J 9 2

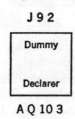

A Q 10 3

The lead is in the dummy and there are no other entries. What is the proper card to lead? The 9. This is the same in value as the Queen, but if the finesse succeeds, the lead is still retained in the North hand, where it is desired. At the next trick the Jack should be led, so that if the finesse wins, the third lead can come from the dummy hand. Notice that if the Jack were led and it held, South playing small, the next lead would have to be won by declarer and you would be unable to come through again. This would be disastrous if the actual holdings were as follows:

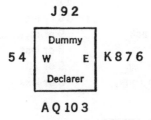

J 9 2

	Dummy	
5 4	W E	K 8 7 6
	Declarer	

A Q 10 3

Notice, too, that if you led the Jack you could not afford to unblock with the 10, because East, as above, might have the K 8 7 6 and, by covering the 9, subsequently would succeed in taking a trick with the 8.

Finesses to capture an honor

Where declarer holds A K J and others, and the dummy several others, the object is to capture the opponent's Queen. This may be done by leading out the Ace and the King, with the hope that the Queen will drop, or by finessing the Jack, hoping that the Queen is located under the King. Which is the better play? That depends on the number of cards that are out against you. If there are only four cards out, for the purpose of finessing you assume that they are equally divided. (In point of actual fact the chances are they will not be so divided. (See chapter on Percentages.) However, for the purpose of finessing only, we work on the theory that the suit will break.) Therefore, with four out, the better play in the long run is to try to drop the Queen. If there are five cards out against you, you assume that they will be divided three–two and that the Queen is probably in the hand that holds three cards. Therefore the lead of the Ace and the King will probably not drop the Queen, and the finesse becomes the better play.

The same principle applies in attempting to capture the King.

There is a common conception that holding ten trumps, without the King, the proper play is to lead the Ace. This is not sound. Since there are three cards out against you, they will probably be divided two–one, and the King is more apt to be in the hand that holds two. Therefore the Ace will probably not drop the King and the finesse would be the better play.

| | TOTAL CARDS OF SUIT | |
HOLDING	IN DECLARER'S TWO HANDS	PLAY
Ace Queen	11	Ace
Ace Queen	10 or less	Queen
Ace King Jack	9 or more	King
Ace King Jack	8 or less	Jack
Ace Queen Ten	9 or 10	Queen
Ace Queen Ten	8 or less	Ten

The double finesse

A Q 10 9 2

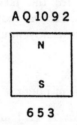

6 5 3

What is the proper play to realize the maximum number of tricks with this holding? The correct procedure is for South to play a low card, intending to finesse the 9 in the North hand. If this succeeds in driving out the King, your troubles are over. If the 9 loses to the Jack, the South hand is re-entered and the finesse is repeated, hoping that West now holds the King. The complete holding may be as follows:

A Q 10 9 2

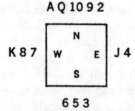

6 5 3

At first appearances it might seem that the finesse of the 9 was a losing play, as it allowed East to win with the Jack, but it is apparent that no matter how you play this holding you must lose one trick. If you had played the Queen first, it would have held the trick, but then the Ace would succeed in dropping the Jack and the opponent's King would still be good. In other words, the opponents have five cards of the suit, so that one of them must have at least three. The play of the Queen and the Ace to the first two tricks cannot possibly clear the suit, so that unless West has both the King and the Jack, the opponents must take one trick. However, if West had held both, you would have won all the tricks by playing the 9 first. A certain number of players dislike giving up tricks during the play of the hand. When there is no emergency, do not have any objection to giving the opponents a trick early in the play if it is not possible to prevent them from winning it in any event.

Make it a point always to give away cheerfully that which the opponents are going to take from you anyway.

If you had held nine of the suit instead of eight, the reasoning would be somewhat different. Now the opponents would have only four cards, and it is possible that each might have two, in which case, if the Queen wins the trick, the Ace will drop both the King and the Jack and you need not lose any tricks.

Perhaps an easy way to remember when to take the single finesse with the Ace, Queen, and 10 and when to take the double finesse is as follows:

Divide the outstanding cards as equally as possible. If one of the opponents must have at least three cards, you finesse them three deep; that is, the 10. If one of the opponents may have only two cards, finesse two deep; that is, the Queen.

Elementary card combinations when the opponent has led a suit

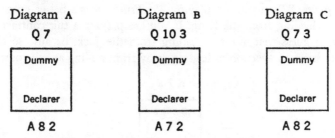

Diagram A	Diagram B	Diagram C
Q 7	Q 10 3	Q 7 3
Dummy	Dummy	Dummy
Declarer	Declarer	Declarer
A 8 2	A 7 2	A 8 2

You are South, the declarer at No Trump. West leads the 5 of Hearts. What card do you play from dummy?

In DIAGRAM A obviously the Queen must be played. Your only hope is that West is leading from the King and that the Queen will hold. If it does not win this trick, it can never win a later one, as it will now be alone. If you make the mistake of playing the 7 from the North hand, East will not play the King even if he has it, so that either a 9, 10, or Jack will force your Ace, and the Queen will then be lost to the King.

In DIAGRAM B the 10 is the proper play, in the hope that it will force the King from East. You will win with your Ace, and the Queen will be high. If the 10 is covered by the Jack, you will win with the Ace and, hoping that West has the King, you will subsequently lead toward the Queen, expecting to win a trick with it.

In DIAGRAM C the proper play from dummy is small. There is no hurry about playing the Queen, because if West has the King, the Queen will still be protected and can be developed into a winning trick later on. The reason for playing low is that there is a bare possibility that East will play the King, relieving you of any further anxiety.

Q 10

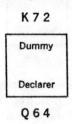

A 8 2

You are South, the declarer. West leads the 5 of Hearts. Here the proper play from dummy is very difficult to determine and is really a guess. If you think West is leading from the King, you should play the Queen, hoping it will win the trick. If you think West is leading from the Jack and that East has the King, the play of the 10 will force East's King and give you two tricks. But to repeat—this is a mere guess. When you are playing No Trump it is a better guess that West is leading from the King. If you are playing a suit contract it is better to guess that West is leading from the Jack, because so many players have an aversion to leading away from a King at suit contracts.

K 7 2

<table>
<tr><td>Dummy</td></tr>
<tr><td>Declarer</td></tr>
</table>

Q 6 4

West leads the 5 of Hearts. In this case obviously the correct play from dummy is a low card. The play of the King could not gain, but if East should happen to play the Ace, both your King and Queen will be good. If West led from the Ace, you will win with the Queen, and the King will subsequently be good for another trick.

K 7

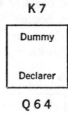

Q 6 4

In this case the proper play is the King, hoping it will hold the trick. The play of the 7 will hardly be successful, because even if East has the Ace he should not put it on the 7 but should wait to capture the King. East, therefore, will play some intermediate card on dummy's 7 that will force the Queen and will leave the King alone in dummy.

If the lead happens to be from the Ace, the King will hold the trick, and now West will be unable to lead that suit again, if he gets in, without permitting you to win a trick with the Queen.

Ducking

♠ A K 7 6 3

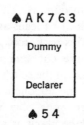

♠ 5 4

Assume that you are playing a No Trump contract and that the North hand has no other high cards. You are anxious to take four tricks in Spades. How is this to be done? Since your opponents have six Spades, your only hope is that each of them will have three. If you play the Ace, King, and another, the two remaining Spades will be good, but you will have no means of getting over to the dummy to use them. The proper procedure, therefore, is to give the opponents their trick at the beginning, rather than at the end. If you play a small Spade from your hand and a small one from the dummy, one of the opponents will be obliged to win. You now hope that each will have two cards left in the suit, so that when you play the Ace and the King it will clear all the Spades and the two small ones will be good.

This play of conceding the first trick is known as "ducking." Notice that had there been an Ace on the side in the North hand, it would not be necessary to duck. You could, if you choose, play the Ace and the King and another Spade, hoping that the opponents each had three, and then you could subsequently enter the North hand with the Ace to cash the two good Spades.

♠ A 9 7 6 3

```
┌──────┐
│  N   │
│      │
│  S   │
└──────┘
```

♠ 5 4 2

Sometimes it is necessary to duck twice in order to establish a suit. In the above example, no matter how the cards are distributed, the opponents must win at least two Spade tricks. Assuming that the North hand has no entry, it will be futile to play the Ace of Spades first and then two more, because if the remaining two become established, there is no way to cash them. In order that the opponents be given their two tricks early in the play, a small Spade is led by South and a small one played from dummy. This is won by the opponents. When declarer regains the lead he leads another low Spade and again plays small from dummy. This trick, too, goes to the opponents. Now there is only one more Spade out, and it must fall upon the Ace, giving the declarer three tricks in the suit.

If it should develop that the opponents' five cards are four in one hand and one in the other, your play will not succeed, but then nothing could have been done about it and you are the victim of a "bad break."

♠ A Q 2

```
┌──────────┐
│  Dummy   │
│          │
│ Declarer │
└──────────┘
```

♠ 10 6 3

West leads the 4 of Spades. What is the proper play from dummy? The correct play is the deuce. This is the one way to make all three

tricks in case West has both the King and the Jack. If West is leading
from the King and East has the Jack, nothing is lost, because the
finesse of the Queen can be taken next time. If West is leading from
the Jack and East has the King, the gain is obvious.

♡ K J

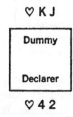

♡ 4 2

The contract is Spades. West leads the 5 of Hearts. What card do
you play from dummy? That depends on who you think has the Ace.
If you believe that East has it, the Jack is the correct play, hoping
that it will force out the Ace. Since it is a suit contract, the chances
are that West would not lead away from the Ace, so that the best
play is the Jack. In a majority of cases the opening leader will not
underlead an Ace against a suit contract. If, however, the contract is
No Trump, then West might very well lead from the Ace, and since
most persons select their best suit for the opening lead, possibly the
chances favor the play of the King instead of the Jack.

In DIAGRAM A West leads the 6. With this particular holding you
might just as well play the King, because if it does not win the trick
now, it never will.

In DIAGRAM B West leads the 5. The contract is No Trump. Play
the Queen. If it does not win the trick on the opening lead, it has
no hope. It will do no good for dummy to play low, because no
matter what East has to play, you can take no tricks.

Diagram A	Diagram B	Diagram C
K 2	Q 4	J 2
Dummy	Dummy	Dummy
Declarer	Declarer	Declarer
7 4 3	10 9 6	A 9 4

In DIAGRAM C Contract: No Trump. West leads the 5. The proper
play from dummy is the Jack. Your only hope is that the lead was
from the King Queen. Otherwise it will be impossible to take two
tricks.

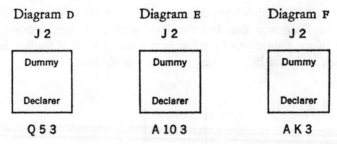

Diagram D   Diagram E   Diagram F
   J 2   J 2   J 2

   Q 5 3   A 10 3   A K 3

In DIAGRAM D West leads the 4. The proper play from dummy is the small one. This guarantees that you will win a trick, because East must play either the King or the Ace, and the Jack will drive out the other honor. Many players thoughtlessly play the Jack from the dummy, which cannot possibly gain and which now lays the Queen open to capture.

In DIAGRAM E West leads the 4. Do not make the mistake of playing the Jack from dummy. If you do, it will probably be covered by the King or the Queen, forcing you to win with the Ace. Now if East obtains the lead he will come through your 10 and you will be held to one trick in the suit. The play of the deuce from dummy guarantees that you will win two tricks, because East will be forced to play either the King or the Queen, in which case the Jack will drive out the other honor and the 10 will be good.

In DIAGRAM F West leads the 5. Dummy must play the Jack. If it does not win a trick now, it never can.

10 7 3

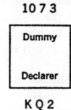

K Q 2

West leads the 8. The proper play from dummy is the 10. If East has the Ace, the play is immaterial, but if West has both the Ace and the Jack, the 10 will win the trick and will guarantee two tricks for the declarer. If West is leading his fourth best, the 10 will definitely win the trick. (See Rule of 11, pages 447–48.)

QUIZ ON ELEMENTARY CARD COMBINATIONS

In each of the following cases you are South, the declarer, at No Trump. You have entries in each hand. What is the proper way to develop these combinations?

1. DUMMY   K Q 6
    DECLARER   8 4 2
       You need two tricks.

2. DUMMY   Q J 2
    DECLARER   7 5 3
       You need one trick.

3. DUMMY   K Q J 2
    DECLARER   7 6 4 3
       You need three tricks.

4. DUMMY   K Q 5 4
    DECLARER   J 3 2
       You need three tricks.

5. DUMMY   Q 10 5 4
    DECLARER   J 7 2
       You need two tricks.

6. DUMMY   K J 4
    DECLARER   6 5
    You need as many tricks as possible.

In the following cases you are South, the declarer at a No Trump contract. The opening lead by West is indicated. What is the proper play from dummy?

7. DUMMY   Q 5 2
    DECLARER   A 10 4
       West leads the 3.

8. DUMMY   K 6 4
    DECLARER   J 7 2
       West leads the 8.

In each of the following hands you are South, the declarer.

9. DUMMY   ♠ 8 6 4 2
          ♡ A 9 6
          ◇ A K
          ♣ 9 8 6 5

   DECLARER   ♠ A K 7
          ♡ K 8 4
          ◇ J 9 3
          ♣ 10 7 4 3

You are playing a contract of 1 No Trump and West leads the 3 of Spades. East plays the Jack and you take it with the King. What card do you lead to the next trick?

10. DUMMY   ♠ 8 7 4 2
          ♡ Q J 10
          ◇ K Q 7
          ♣ A 8 6

   DECLARER   ♠ A K 5
          ♡ 8 6 3
          ◇ A 4 2
          ♣ K 7 4 3

You are playing a contract of 2 No Trump. West leads a low Diamond which you win in dummy with the King. What card do you play to the second trick?

ANSWERS TO QUIZ ON ELEMENTARY CARD COMBINATIONS

1.

Lead low from your hand towards the dummy hand. If you succeed in winning the first trick with the King or Queen, you reenter your hand in another suit and lead low again. Thus you ensure two tricks if West has the Ace. If you were to lead a high card from the dummy on either the first round or the second of the suit, a defender would win it with the Ace and you would take only one trick even if the Ace is in front of the King-Queen.

2.

Lead towards the Queen. If it loses, reenter your hand and lead towards the Jack. In this way you ensure making a trick unless both Ace and King are in East's hand, in which case there is nothing you can do.

3.

Lead towards one of dummy's honors. You must plan to repeat this process twice more if necessary. If the opponents cards in the suit were divided 3–2, you could win three tricks by simply leading honors from dummy, for after the K Q J had been played both opponents would be exhausted and the long card would be a winner. But that form of play would hold you to two tricks if West held either the singleton Ace or the A 10 x x. Leading towards the high cards takes care of those possibilities.

4.

Lead the 2 towards the King. If it holds, reenter your hand and lead the 3 towards the Queen. The principle here is to lead low cards towards the hand that contains the *majority of honors.* In the present case this play prevents West from capturing one of your honor cards if he has the doubleton Ace.

5.

Lead low towards one of dummy's honors. Whether it wins or loses, you repeat the same process on the next round. The principle of this form of play is the same as in the previous problem, and the object is to guard against West's having the A x or K x.

6.

Lead from your hand and finesse the Jack. With a combination of honors that are not in sequence, you usually stand to win more tricks by finessing the lowest honor first. In this instance if West has both Ace and Queen, you win two tricks.

7.

Play low from dummy. You are certain of two tricks provided you play low. (If East plays the King or Jack, you win and subsequently take a trick with either the Queen or the 10.) If you play the Queen on opening lead you may make only one trick if East has the King and West has the Jack.

8.

Play low from dummy. You are certain of one trick provided you don't put up the King. If West has led away from the A Q, you may make two tricks.

9.

A Club. You have six certain winners and need one more for your contract. The correct play is to attack the suit in which you and dummy, between you, hold the most cards. Opponents have only five Clubs and if they are divided 3–2, your fourth Club will be a winner after three rounds of the suit have been played.

10.

A Heart. You can see seven winners and need, therefore, one more. Two rounds of Hearts will drive out the Ace and King, establishing a Heart trick in dummy.

15.   Advanced card combinations

NOW WE COME to the question of more difficult combinations
of the cards.

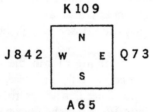

K 10 9

J 8 4 2   W   E   Q 7 3

A 6 5

With the above holding, if you are South and must lead the suit
yourself, you can win only with the Ace and the King; but if one
of the opponents can be induced to lead that suit, you can win three
tricks by developing a finessing situation. For example: If West
should lead the 2, dummy's 9 is played, and East will have to cover
with the Queen. This is won by South's Ace. Now the 5 of Spades
is returned, and when West plays low North's 10 wins the trick.

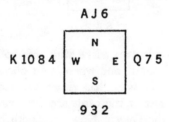

A J 6

K 10 8 4   W   E   Q 7 5

9 3 2

If you are South and are obliged to lead this suit, you can win
only one trick if the opponents play properly. If you led the 9, West
would cover with the 10 and the Jack would lose to the Queen. The
only trick available is the Ace. If, however, West should lead the 4,
your best play is not to play the Jack, because it is improbable that
West has both the King and the Queen, but you can hope that West
has the 10 and one of the other picture cards. In that case, if you play
small from the dummy, East will be obliged to win with the Queen.
The South hand is subsequently re-entered, and now the finesse can
be taken against West's King.

AJ9

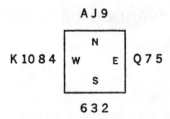

K 10 8 4   Q 7 5

6 3 2

You are South and wish to win two tricks with this holding. What is the proper play? You should lead a small one from the South hand and when West plays low insert the 9, hoping that this will force an honor.

This is a better play than trying to win the trick with the Jack. The Jack play will be proper in only one case, that is where West has both the King and the Queen, whereas the play of the 9 will succeed in two cases, where West has the Queen and 10 or the King 10. The 9 forces a high honor from the East hand, and then the Jack can be successfully finessed on the next round.

K 10 9 8

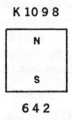

6 4 2

You are anxious to win two tricks with this holding. The proper play is a small card by South, and when West plays low insert the 8. This play will succeed if West has either the Jack or the Queen, regardless of how the rest of the cards are distributed, because the 8 will force, let us say, the Queen. Now the South hand is re-entered and another small card led, inserting the 9 from dummy. Since West has the Jack, this will force the Ace, and the North hand now has the tenace of King 10 over West's Jack.

NORTH: K 6 4 2   SOUTH: Q 7 5 3

Is it possible for you to win three tricks with this combination? The answer is yes, provided the player who has the Ace has only one guard with it and that his partner has three cards of the suit. If you believe that West holds the Ace you should lead a small one from the South hand and, when West plays low, go up with the

King. Now a small one is returned from North and ducked completely, hoping that the Ace will fall. If it does not, there is nothing you can do about it. If you believe that East has the Ace of the suit, the first lead should come from the North hand. When East plays low, the trick is won with the Queen and the return is ducked. In the first case the holding will have been as in DIAGRAM A, in the second case as in DIAGRAM B.

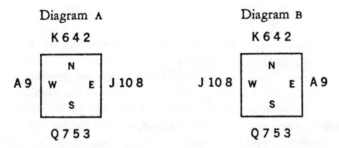

With DIAGRAM A, following, your object is to win three tricks in the suit. This may be done in two ways, depending on who you believe has the King. If you think East has it, you should play the Ace and then lead a small one toward the Queen. If you think West has it, then your only hope is that it will fall on the second round. In that case you should play the Ace and a small one and duck the second round. The holding will then have been as in DIAGRAM B, following.

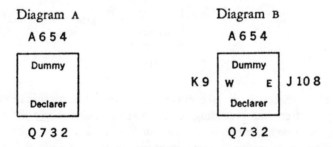

With DIAGRAM A below you are trying to win three tricks. If you think that East has the King, you should play as in the previous example. If you think that West has the King, then it may be that East has the Jack, in which case you should lead low from the North hand and finesse the 10 after the play of the Ace, hoping that this will drive out the King.

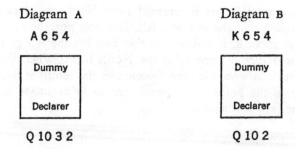

Diagram A   Diagram B

The normal play with DIAGRAM B, above, assuming plenty of entries, is the finesse of the 10 by declarer, hoping that East has the Jack. Suppose, however, from the bidding you are morally certain that East holds the Ace but are not quite sure as to the location of the Jack. A somewhat abnormal play will frequently be effective if you are able to determine the exact number of cards in the suit held by the adversaries. Suppose, for example, during the play of the hand you are able to determine that West holds four cards of this suit. That would leave East with only two cards, one of which you are morally certain is the Ace. The proper play is to lead the 4 from dummy and win with the Queen. At the next trick the 2 is led and ducked in dummy, hoping the Ace will fall. The complete holding will be as follows:

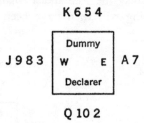

Your object is to take three tricks, but this combination differs slightly from the preceding one. If you can guess where the cards are you can make the proper finesse, but if you guess wrong you will lose two tricks. In order to avoid guessing, in the long run it is better to play upon the theory that two high cards adversely held will usually be found in different hands. You should therefore lead first from the South hand, intending to lose the finesse to East if West does not cover, and subsequently enter the South hand and finesse again. It does not matter who has the King or the Jack. Just so long as they are in different hands, you will succeed. (See chapter on Percentages.)

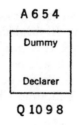

A 6 5 4

Dummy

Declarer

Q 10 9 8

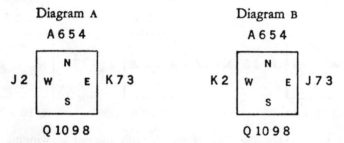

Diagram A

A 6 5 4

J 2   N W E S   K 7 3

Q 10 9 8

Diagram B

A 6 5 4

K 2   N W E S   J 7 3

Q 10 9 8

In either of these cases, if the Ace is played first and then a small one, when East plays low declarer must guess whether to play the 10 or the Queen, and the wrong guess will be fatal. Where two finesses are taken, only one trick will be lost in both these cases.

In DIAGRAM C, when an honor is led through, the automatic cover will hold the defenders to one trick, whereas in DIAGRAM D the recommended play will lose two tricks. On the other hand, the play of the Ace first will succeed in DIAGRAM D but will lose in DIAGRAM C. These cases cancel each other in frequency. The advantage to be gained is that the declarer is saved the hazard of misguessing which card to play on the second round when the Ace is led first.

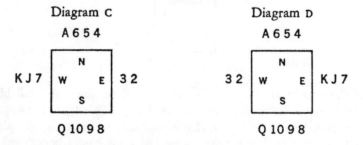

Diagram C

A 6 5 4

K J 7   N W E S   3 2

Q 10 9 8

Diagram D

A 6 5 4

3 2   N W E S   K J 7

Q 10 9 8

The question arises which card to lead first—the Queen or the 10. This is a mere guess and will matter only where there is a singleton Jack or singleton King outstanding. If East has a singleton Jack, the lead of the Queen will win all four tricks. Without any information, these two chances are equal. If the bidding tells you that East is probably short, you must hope that it is the singleton Jack. If East has the lone King, West's Jack will be protected and win a trick in any event. If it is West who is short, you should lead a lower honor from the South hand. This is illustrated by the following diagrams:

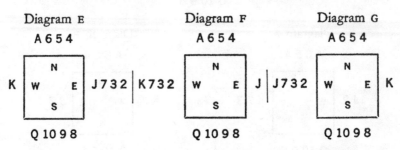

Diagram E	Diagram F	Diagram G
A 6 5 4	A 6 5 4	A 6 5 4
Q 10 9 8	Q 10 9 8	Q 10 9 8

In DIAGRAM E the play of the 10 will succeed in winning four tricks.

In DIAGRAM F, if the Queen is led, the King and the Jack will drop together and all four tricks will be taken in that manner.

In DIAGRAM G there is no way to take all the tricks.

Generally speaking, the play of the 10 is slightly superior to the lead of the Queen because it takes care of the remote contingency that West is void, in which case the Ace will be played from dummy and three tricks won in that manner.

Another frequently occurring combination follows:

A J 3 2

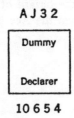

10 6 5 4

If three tricks are required by declarer and no clues are available, the best play is for declarer to lead the 4 and, if West plays low, put up the Jack from the dummy. If this should lose, declarer's next play would be the Ace, hoping that West had a doubleton honor which would now fall or that East had King Queen alone. The Jack play will, of course, also succeed where West has K Q x.

If you have reason to believe that East has only two cards of the

suit and West has three, it is better to lead the 2 from dummy, for
if one of East's two cards happens to be the King, he will almost
surely come up and you will now have a finesse of the Jack on the
next round.

Here is another illustration:

A 4 2

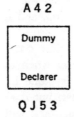

Q J 5 3

Your object is to win three tricks in the suit. The popular lead of
the Queen in this case is not correct, because if West has the King
he will cover and you must lose a trick to the 10 in any event. You
will now win three tricks only if the opponents' cards are divided
three–three. Your best chance is for East to have the King. Then the
distribution will not matter, because you will lose only one trick by
leading the Ace, then a small one toward the Queen. If it wins; the
North hand is re-entered and the process repeated.

Suppose the adverse holdings were as follows:

A 4 2

10 8 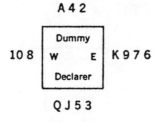 K 9 7 6

Q J 5 3

It will be noticed that in this case the lead of the Queen will limit
the declarer to only two tricks. The proper play will yield three.

J 9 2

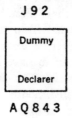

A Q 8 4 3

The correct play is to lead first the small card from the North hand, intending to finesse the Queen. If this succeeds, you must now guess how the remaining cards are distributed. If you think that the King is now alone, you should play the Ace. If you think that the King is still guarded in the East hand, you have a hope that West's 10 will now fall, so that you enter the North hand and lead the Jack. This will be covered by the King, and if the 10 drops, all the tricks are yours.

In the long run the better play on the second lead of the suit is the Jack, because while it loses when the King is alone in the East hand, it gains when the 10 is alone in the West hand. These two combinations cancel each other, but if all the remaining cards are in the East hand, the play of the Jack will gain a trick, while playing the Ace will permit East to win both the King and the 10. The complete holding will be as follows:

J 9 2

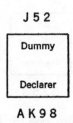

5 | Dummy |
W | | E   K 10 7 6
     | Declarer |

A Q 8 4 3

Here is another example:

J 5 2

| Dummy |
| |
| Declarer |

A K 9 8

Your object is to win all four tricks in the suit. It should be noted that this is very unlikely. There are two ways in which to accomplish this result. One is to hope that West has the singleton Queen, in which case the high card is led from the South hand and the rest becomes routine. This, however, is extremely unlikely, so that your best chance is to hope for East to have both the Queen and the 10, and the distribution is immaterial. The Jack, therefore, is led through and will presumably be covered. South will win with the King, and the North hand is re-entered in order to lead a small card for the purpose of finessing the 9. This will succeed if the original holdings are as follows:

J 5 2

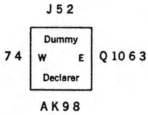

7 4 | Dummy | Q 10 6 3
W   E
Declarer

A K 9 8

Your object is to win all the tricks.

J 5 2

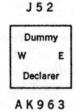

A K 9 6 3

If you believe that East has the Queen and 10, you may play as in the previous example, but this is not the best play. Since there are five cards out, your most reasonable hope is that the Queen will fall on the second round from either hand, which gives you two chances. The best play, therefore, is to lead out the Ace and the King.

Declarer has the lead and has now only one more entry: What is the proper card to lead in the combination below?

A J 10 8

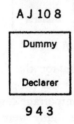

9 4 3

The 3, not the 9. Declarer plans to take two finesses, the first of which must lose. If the 9 is led at the first trick, the second finesse will have to be won in dummy, and declarer has no further entries to repeat the finesse. When the 3 is led and the 10 loses to the Queen, on the second finesse the 9 is led and, if it is not covered, will hold the trick, since dummy can underplay the 8. A hand illustrating this principle is as follows:

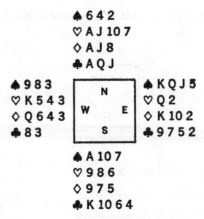

♠ 6 4 2
♡ A J 10 7
◇ A J 8
♣ A Q J

♠ 9 8 3   ♠ K Q J 5
♡ K 5 4 3   ♡ Q 2
◇ Q 6 4 3   ◇ K 10 2
♣ 8 3   ♣ 9 7 5 2

♠ A 10 7
♡ 9 8 6
◇ 9 7 5
♣ K 10 6 4

Declarer is playing 3 No Trump. West leads the 9 of Spades, and
the Ace wins the third round of the suit. If the 9 of Hearts is led and
ducked in dummy, East will win with the Queen. Declarer can subsequently regain the lead with the King of Clubs to take the Heart
finesse, but now the 10 will win and South's hand cannot be re-
entered to repeat the Heart finesse. Declarer could have saved the day
if after leading the 9 he had played the 10 from dummy at the first
trick. This would leave the 7 for the subsequent underplay of the 8.

Assuming plenty of entries, what is the correct way to play this
suit?

J 10 9

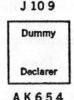

AK654

While normally the finesse for the Queen is postponed for the
second round, in this case it is not proper to do so, because the play
of the Ace first sacrifices an important card from dummy, and a trick
will be lost if the complete holding were as follows:

J 10 9

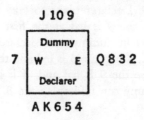

AK654

With this holding, therefore, a first-round finesse should be taken. In other words, the chances of East holding four to the Queen are greater than West holding the singleton Queen.

Your object is to win two tricks.

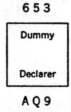

653

Dummy

Declarer

A Q 9

The casual play is to lead from the North hand and finesse the Queen, hoping that East has the King. This is not correct. If East has the King, he will have it a trick or two later just as well, and you can avail yourself of an additional chance by first finessing the 9. This might possibly drive out the King, but if it fails to do so, the North hand can be re-entered and the finesse of the Queen tried at the next lead of that suit. The principle illustrated here is that a finesse is never taken early in the play when it is just as convenient to take it somewhat later. The complete holding may be as follows:

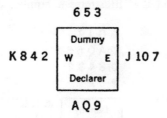

653

Dummy

K 8 4 2   W   E   J 10 7

Declarer

A Q 9

Assuming that you need all four tricks with this combination, what is the proper procedure?

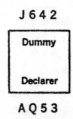

J 6 4 2

Dummy

Declarer

A Q 5 3

The lead obviously must come from the North hand, but you must not make the mistake of leading the Jack, because no matter where the rest of the cards are located you will have to lose at least one trick, since if East has the King he will cover and the 10 or 9 must become good. If West has the King, naturally your finesse will lose. The proper play is to lead a low card from North, and when East follows the Queen should be played. When this wins there is no further finesse. Either the King will drop or it won't. If it drops when you play the Ace, the rest are yours. If it does not, then there was no possible way to attain your end. The holdings might have been as follows:

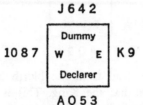

J 6 4 2

10 8 7   K 9

A Q 5 3

Notice that the lead of the Jack would have compelled declarer to lose one trick when East covered. The presence of the 9 in either the North or South hand would have modified this advice somewhat. Now you would have a choice of plays on the second round, because West might be left with the lone 10, in which case the lead of the Jack will pick up another trick.

An interesting hand that illustrates a number of finesse positions is the following:

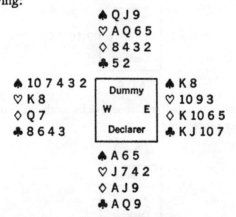

♠ Q J 9
♡ A Q 6 5
◇ 8 4 3 2
♣ 5 2

♠ 10 7 4 3 2   ♠ K 8
♡ K 8   ♡ 10 9 3
◇ Q 7   ◇ K 10 6 5
♣ 8 6 4 3   ♣ K J 10 7

♠ A 6 5
♡ J 7 4 2
◇ A J 9
♣ A Q 9

Declarer is playing 3 No Trump, and West leads the 3 of Spades. Dummy plays the Queen, East the King, and declarer the Ace. The 2 of Hearts is led and the Queen finessed in dummy. The Ace of Hearts drops West's King. The Diamond suit is now attacked. Dummy leads the 2, and declarer finesses the 9, which drives out West's Queen. West continues with a Spade, and dummy's 9 is finessed. The Diamond finesse is now taken and the Ace led, in the hope that the suit will break three–three, but West fails to follow. Now dummy's high cards are run and East must reduce his hand to three cards. Since one of them must be the King of Diamonds, he is obliged to come down to the King and Jack of Clubs. When declarer takes the Club finesse the balance of the tricks are his.

Leading toward high cards

It has previously been shown that in order to obtain full advantage of your high cards you must lead toward them and compel your opponent to play first.

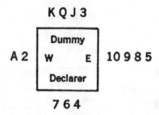

K Q J 3

A 2   10 9 8 5

7 6 4

Your object is to win three tricks in the suit. Do not make the mistake of leading the King from the North hand. If you do so, you will win three tricks only if the opponents' cards are divided three–three. The proper procedure is to lead a low card from the South hand, playing an honor from the North. If this wins, the South hand is re-entered and the process repeated. This forces West to play ahead of you, and if he is obliged to follow with the Ace, North's small card will be used instead of an honor.

Another illustration of repeated leads toward high cards is the following:

♠ K Q 8 6
♡ Q 10 4
◇ A K Q 5
♣ 8 4

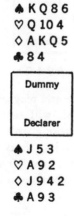

♠ J 5 3
♡ A 9 2
◇ J 9 4 2
♣ A 9 3

You are South, the declarer at a contract of 3 No Trump. West, having opened the bidding with 1 Heart, leads the 2 of Clubs. East plays the 10 and you win with the Ace. You must lead a low Spade toward the Queen, which holds the trick. What is your next play?

You must not lead the Spade back to your Jack, because if the Spades do not break even, you will not have nine tricks. The proper play is to return to the South hand with the Jack of Diamonds and lead a small Spade toward the King. This may compel West to play his Ace, and three Spade tricks are assured. If West does not play the Ace, you will win with the King, and then you must hope that the Spades will break three–three.

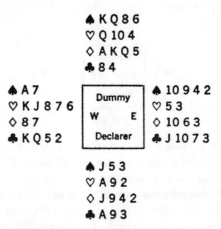

♠ K Q 8 6
♡ Q 10 4
◇ A K Q 5
♣ 8 4

♠ A 7   Dummy   ♠ 10 9 4 2
♡ K J 8 7 6   W E   ♡ 5 3
◇ 8 7   Declarer   ◇ 10 6 3
♣ K Q 5 2   ♣ J 10 7 3

♠ J 5 3
♡ A 9 2
◇ J 9 4 2
♣ A 9 3

Your object is to win three tricks. What is the proper play?

K 10

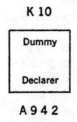

A 9 4 2

South must lead a small one and play the 10 from the North hand. No other play is correct. This will succeed if West has both the missing honors or the Queen twice guarded or the Jack twice guarded. Against almost any other holding it is impossible to make three tricks. The only time the play of the 10 will not work is if East has a singleton honor, which is too remote to be considered.

♠ A

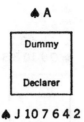

♠ J 10 7 6 4 2

This is your trump holding. You have plenty of entries in both hands, and your object is to lose only two trump tricks. Naturally the Ace of Spades is cashed first and the South hand re-entered. What card should South play? The answer is a low one and not the Jack. In order to succeed, declarer hopes that the six adversely held trumps will be divided three–three. In that case the card that he plays to the second trick is immaterial, because on the third trick the trumps will fall together; but if the adverse trumps are four–two, the play of a low card will succeed if the doubleton contains an honor, whereas the play of the Jack will lose under those conditions. The complete hand is as follows:

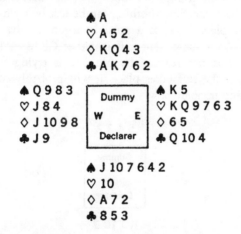

♠ A
♡ A 5 2
◇ K Q 4 3
♣ A K 7 6 2

♠ Q 9 8 3   ♠ K 5
♡ J 8 4   ♡ K Q 9 7 6 3
◇ J 10 9 8   ◇ 6 5
♣ J 9   ♣ Q 10 4

♠ J 10 7 6 4 2
♡ 10
◇ A 7 2
♣ 8 5 3

Another case to illustrate the principle of economy in the play of honor cards is the following: (see over)

South is the declarer at a contract of 4 Spades. West leads the King of Hearts. Declarer wins. What should his first play be? The answer is a low Spade, not the King. This seems to be somewhat unorthodox and may require an explanation. Declarer must lose one Heart trick and pins his hope on the chance that he will lose only two Spade tricks, which will be the case if the adverse trumps are

♠ 3
♡ 5 2
♢ 7 5 4 3 2
♣ Q J 10 8 3

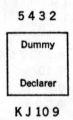

♠ K Q 8 7 6 5 2
♡ A 3
♢ A K
♣ A K

divided three – two. Then declarer's play will be immaterial, since the hand can't be lost, but if the trumps are four – one, the play of the King will lose the hand, since the opponents cannot be kept from cashing three Spade tricks. There is, however, one chance for the declarer even if the trumps are four – one, and that is that the Ace of trumps may be alone. Since nothing can be lost by trying, a low trump is the correct play. There is a possible argument that the play of a low trump risks a subsequent ruff in either Clubs or Diamonds, but this argument is not reasonable. No one is trying for a ruff, and furthermore, if the ruff takes place, it will probably cost the defense a natural trump trick anyhow.

5 4 3 2

```
┌──────────┐
│ Dummy    │
│          │
│ Declarer │
└──────────┘
```

K J 10 9

Assuming that dummy has no entries, what is the proper card for declarer to play? The answer is the King. It is almost certain that declarer will have to lose two tricks, but there is one remote chance that he can hold his losses to one trick, and that is if the Queen is alone. The argument that the Ace might just as well be alone carries no weight, because even if the 9 succeeds in forcing out the Ace, there is no way to capture the Queen without any entry in dummy.

J 10 8 6 4 2

```
┌─────────────┐
│ Dummy       │
│             │
│ Declarer    │
└─────────────┘
```

K 9 7 5

Declarer has the lead and there are no entries in dummy. Declarer is trying to hold his losses to one trick. What is the best play? This is an absolute guess. In order to lose only one trick, declarer must find either the Ace or Queen alone and must make the proper guess. If the Ace is alone, obviously declarer should play a low card. If the Queen is alone, of course the King should be led. In the next case there is no guess.

J 10 8 6 4

```
┌─────────────┐
│ Dummy       │
│             │
│ Declarer    │
└─────────────┘
```

K 9 7 5

There are no entries in dummy and declarer can afford to lose only one trick. The proper play is the King, because unless the Queen is alone, there is no way to win four tricks. If the Ace is alone, it is true that a small card will drive it out, but the Queen would still be good and could not be captured.

J 6

```
┌─────────────┐
│ Dummy       │
│             │
│ Declarer    │
└─────────────┘
```

A 9 7 4 3 2

With plenty of entries in both hands, the declarer's object is to lose only one trump trick with this holding. What is the correct play? Declarer's chances are not very good. He will succeed only where West holds specifically the King 10 doubleton or the Queen 10 doubleton. On no other holding is it possible for declarer to win against proper defense. Therefore he should lead the 2 toward dummy. If West wins, dummy is entered and the Jack led through, hoping that West's 10 will drop on the trick. The complete holding is as follows:

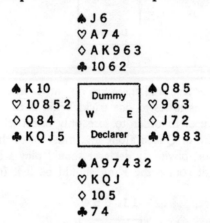

```
              ♠ J 6
              ♡ A 7 4
              ◇ A K 9 6 3
              ♣ 10 6 2

  ♠ K 10      Dummy        ♠ Q 8 5
  ♡ 10 8 5 2               ♡ 9 6 3
  ◇ Q 8 4    W       E     ◇ J 7 2
  ♣ K Q J 5   Declarer     ♣ A 9 8 3

              ♠ A 9 7 4 3 2
              ♡ K Q J
              ◇ 10 5
              ♣ 7 4
```

Declarer is playing a somewhat unsound contract of 6 Hearts, and West cashes the Ace of Spades and continues the suit. Declarer's object is to lose no trump tricks. What is the proper play?

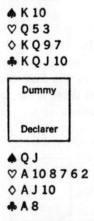

```
              ♠ K 10
              ♡ Q 5 3
              ◇ K Q 9 7
              ♣ K Q J 10

              ┌──────────┐
              │  Dummy   │
              │          │
              │ Declarer │
              └──────────┘

              ♠ Q J
              ♡ A 10 8 7 6 2
              ◇ A J 10
              ♣ A 8
```

I do not like declarer's chances very much. He has one faint ray of hope, and that is that West holds the singleton Jack of Hearts. On no other holding is it possible for declarer to fulfill his contract against proper defense. The Queen of Hearts, therefore, should be led. If East covers, the Jack will drop, and dummy is entered for the finesse of the 8 of trumps. The play of the Queen of Hearts also has the merit that occasionally East, holding the King and one Heart, will make the error of refusing to cover the Queen, in which case all the tricks will be won. The complete holding is as follows:

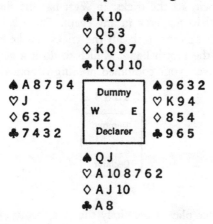

```
                    ♠ K 10
                    ♡ Q 5 3
                    ◇ K Q 9 7
                    ♣ K Q J 10
  ♠ A 8 7 5 4    ┌──────────┐   ♠ 9 6 3 2
  ♡ J            │  Dummy   │   ♡ K 9 4
  ◇ 6 3 2        │ W      E │   ◇ 8 5 4
  ♣ 7 4 3 2      │ Declarer │   ♣ 9 6 5
                 └──────────┘
                    ♠ Q J
                    ♡ A 10 8 7 6 2
                    ◇ A J 10
                    ♣ A 8
```

Ducking

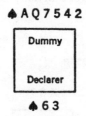

```
        ♠ A Q 7 5 4 2
      ┌──────────┐
      │  Dummy   │
      │          │
      │ Declarer │
      └──────────┘
           ♠ 6 3
```

      The North hand has no entries other than Spades, and your object is to win five tricks. It can be seen that regardless of how the adverse cards are distributed one trick must be lost in any event. Therefore a trick should be conceded to the opponents at once. Now our only hope is for West to have the King. The finesse is taken the next time, and if the King is in the West hand, dummy's Spades will all be good. It is true that if the finesse loses you will succeed in taking no Spade tricks instead of one, but it was your only hope and it was worth spending an extra trick to try it.

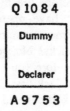

```
        Q 10 8 4
      ┌──────────┐
      │  Dummy   │
      │          │
      │ Declarer │
      └──────────┘
        A 9 7 5 3
```

Assuming that you need all the tricks, is there any hope? There is, but not a very likely one. If East has the singleton King, the play of the Ace will win all the tricks. If West has the singleton King, a trick must be lost to the Jack in any event. There is one other hope. If West has the singleton Jack, all the tricks can be won by leading the Queen from the North hand. Which to do is a guess.

Suppose, however, your combined holding contains ten cards:

Q 10 8 4 2

Dummy
Declarer

A 9 7 5 3

Now the correct play is definitely the Ace, because it will succeed if either of the opponents has a singleton King, whereas if the Queen is led through, it will succeed in only one case, and that is where West has the singleton Jack.

The backward finesse

K 8 7

Dummy
Declarer

A J 9

It has been demonstrated that in order to take three tricks in the suit you should wish for East to hold the Queen. The play, therefore, is first to the King and to return by finessing the Jack. Suppose, however, that you are quite certain that West holds the Queen of the suit and therefore the finesse will fail. How are you certain? Well, West might have opened the bidding with 1 No Trump, which marks him almost certainly with that card. Is it hopeless for you to make three tricks? No, you have one chance, and that is that East has the 10. Therefore you execute what is known as the backward finesse, leading the Jack first. Notice that you must not lead the Ace first. When the Jack is covered by the Queen, you win with the King and return a low card, finessing the 9, with the hope that East holds the 10. If West holds both, there is nothing you can do about it.

The complete holding:

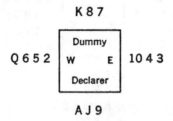

K 8 7

Q 6 5 2   10 4 3

A J 9

The backward finesse may sometimes be employed to keep the dangerous hand out of the lead.

For example:

♠ K 7 5 2
♡ 7 6
◇ A 8 3
♣ J 7 6 5

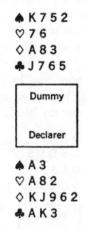

♠ A 3
♡ A 8 2
◇ K J 9 6 2
♣ A K 3

You are South, the declarer at 3 No Trump. The King of Hearts is led, and you win the third round of the suit. The normal Diamond finesse may permit West to obtain the lead, and he is the one you fear. Your proper play, therefore, is to lead the Jack of Diamonds, intending to let it ride to the East hand, which has no more Hearts. This would normally be an improper play except that you must do anything to keep West out of the lead. If West covers, you win with the Ace and then come back to the King, hoping that the 10 will fall or that East has the 10.

The complete holding is as follows:

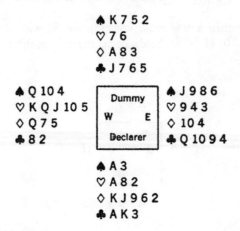

Blocking the opponents' suit

Preventing the run of opponents' suit by blocking it is a play which does not come up very often, but when it does it operates in a very neat fashion. The diagnosis is usually made on the opening lead. The leader has led a fourth best, therefore you conclude that he did not have a sequence of honors. That being the case, his partner must have one of the missing honors, and by refusing to duck you may compel the third hand either to discard his high card, which gives you a trick, or to retain it, thereby blocking the suit. For example:

♠ A 8
♡ K Q 9 5
◇ A J 7
♣ Q 9 5 2

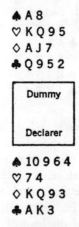

♠ 10 9 6 4
♡ 7 4
◇ K Q 9 3
♣ A K 3

You are playing a contract of 3 No Trump. West leads the 3 of Spades. You will notice that you have eight immediate tricks and the ninth is available in Hearts, but the only danger is that the opponents might run four Spades and the Ace of Hearts. This can be done only if West has a five-card suit. If he has only a four-card suit, there is no danger. If West has five, East can have only two, but the important point is that East must have either the King, Queen, or the Jack, because if West had all three, the proper lead would not have been the low card but the King, so that by playing the Ace to the first trick you will compel East to unblock, which gives you an additional Spade stopper. If East retains his honor card, the suit will be blocked. The complete hand is as follows:

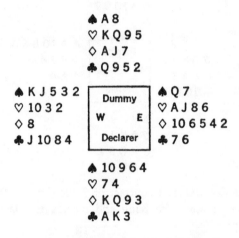

♠ A 8
♥ K Q 9 5
♦ A J 7
♣ Q 9 5 2

♠ K J 5 3 2
♥ 10 3 2
♦ 8
♣ J 10 8 4

Dummy
W E
Declarer

♠ Q 7
♥ A J 8 6
♦ 10 6 5 4 2
♣ 7 6

♠ 10 9 6 4
♥ 7 4
♦ K Q 9 3
♣ A K 3

Declarer is playing a contract of 3 No Trump. East having bid 1 Spade, West leads the 2 of Spades. East plays the Ace and returns the 6. What should declarer play?

♠ 5 3
♥ Q 10 9
♦ J 10 9 7
♣ 8 7 5 2

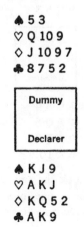

Dummy

Declarer

♠ K J 9
♥ A K J
♦ K Q 5 2
♣ A K 9

He must first determine the meaning of the deuce of Spades lead. It is quite evident that West has led from either four small cards or three headed by an honor, since if he had a singleton deuce he would probably lead some other suit. If East has only four Spades, there is nothing to fear, but if he has five, West will have three to the Queen and declarer can block the suit by going up with the King and driving out the Ace of Diamonds. The complete holding is as follows:

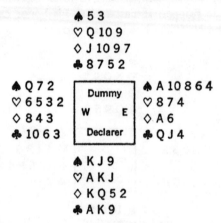

```
              ♠ 5 3
              ♡ Q 10 9
              ◊ J 10 9 7
              ♣ 8 7 5 2

♠ Q 7 2                        ♠ A 10 8 6 4
♡ 6 5 3 2      Dummy           ♡ 8 7 4
◊ 8 4 3     W        E         ◊ A 6
♣ 10 6 3       Declarer        ♣ Q J 4

              ♠ K J 9
              ♡ A K J
              ◊ K Q 5 2
              ♣ A K 9
```

South is the declarer at a contract of 3 No Trump. West leads the 5 of Spades.. East plays the King and returns the Jack. What card should South play?

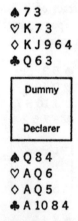

```
              ♠ 7 3
              ♡ K 7 3
              ◊ K J 9 6 4
              ♣ Q 6 3

              ┌──────────┐
              │  Dummy   │
              │          │
              │ Declarer │
              └──────────┘

              ♠ Q 8 4
              ♡ A Q 6
              ◊ A Q 5
              ♣ A 10 8 4
```

South's only hope is to block the opponents' suit. Under the Rule of 11, East is known to have one more card higher than the 5. (Eleven minus 5 equals 6.) Dummy has one, declarer has two, which leaves East with three cards better than the one led, two of which have already been shown. If East's remaining Spade happens to be the 10, the suit will be blocked and declarer can run enough tricks for contract. The proper play, therefore, is to cover the Jack. The complete hand is as follows:

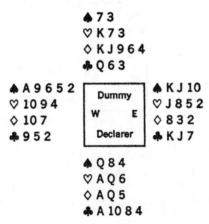

♠ 7 3
♡ K 7 3
◊ K J 9 6 4
♣ Q 6 3

♠ A 9 6 5 2
♡ 10 9 4
◊ 10 7
♣ 9 5 2

♠ K J 10
♡ J 8 5 2
◊ 8 3 2
♣ K J 7

♠ Q 8 4
♡ A Q 6
◊ A Q 5
♣ A 10 8 4

South is playing a contract of 3 No Trump. West leads the 9 of Hearts. What card should declarer play from dummy?

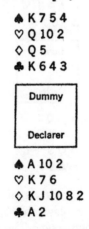

♠ K 7 5 4
♡ Q 10 2
◊ Q 5
♣ K 6 4 3

♠ A 10 2
♡ K 7 6
◊ K J 10 8 2
♣ A 2

This is an obviously short-suit lead, and East is marked with the Ace and the Jack. If declarer plays low from dummy, East will duck and the King will be forced. If West gains the lead with the Ace of Diamonds, he will be able to continue through the Queen of Hearts. Declarer has a certain way to prevent any such attack, and that is by the simple expedient of playing the Queen from dummy. This will force East to win with the Ace and he will be unable to continue the suit with the 10 in dummy. This gives declarer plenty of time to drive out the Ace of Diamonds. The complete holding is as follows:

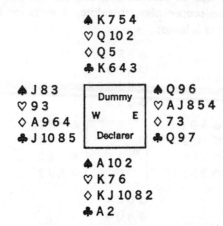

```
                  ♠ K 7 5 4
                  ♡ Q 10 2
                  ◇ Q 5
                  ♣ K 6 4 3
  ♠ J 8 3      ┌─────────┐    ♠ Q 9 6
  ♡ 9 3        │  Dummy  │    ♡ A J 8 5 4
  ◇ A 9 6 4    │ W     E │    ◇ 7 3
  ♣ J 10 8 5   │ Declarer│    ♣ Q 9 7
               └─────────┘
                  ♠ A 10 2
                  ♡ K 7 6
                  ◇ K J 10 8 2
                  ♣ A 2
```

A type of unblocking play frequently available to the declarer is the following:

```
                  ♠ 10 7 5
                  ♡ 9 7 4 2
                  ◇ A 9 5
                  ♣ 10 7 6

               ┌─────────┐
               │  Dummy  │
               │         │
               │ Declarer│
               └─────────┘
                  ♠ K Q J
                  ♡ A K Q J 10
                  ◇ Q 3
                  ♣ A 9 5
```

South is the declarer at a contract of 4 Hearts. West leads the Jack of Diamonds. Dummy plays the 5, and East wins with the King. What card should South play? The answer is the Queen. This play would not be necessary if dummy had a quick entry, but since dummy cannot be entered and since West is morally certain to hold the 10 of Diamonds, the unblocking play will permit the subsequent finesse of the 9 and discard of the losing Club on the Ace of Diamonds.

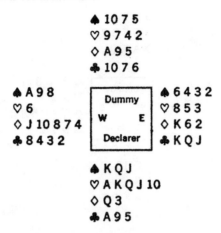

♠ 10 7 5
♡ 9 7 4 2
◇ A 9 5
♣ 10 7 6

♠ A 9 8   ♠ 6 4 3 2
♡ 6   ♡ 8 5 3
◇ J 10 8 7 4   ◇ K 6 2
♣ 8 4 3 2   ♣ K Q J

♠ K Q J
♡ A K Q J 10
◇ Q 3
♣ A 9 5

Occasionally the normal method of play should be departed from because of information gleaned from the auction.

♠ 7 5 4
♡ 6 5 3 2
◇ A K Q
♣ J 6 2

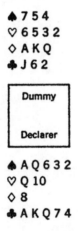

♠ A Q 6 3 2
♡ Q 10
◇ 8
♣ A K Q 7 4

South is declarer at a contract of 4 Spades, West having opened the bidding with 1 Heart, and East, his partner, having failed to keep the bidding open. West leads the King and Ace, then the Jack of Hearts, which declarer ruffs. What is the proper way to play the trumps? It is a moral certainty that West holds the King of Spades as part of his opening bid. Therefore the finesse is bound to fail. Declarer has one chance, and that is that West holds exactly two Spades. If he holds more or less, there is no hope for declarer. Therefore the proper play is the Ace, followed by a small trump, with the hope that the King will fall. The complete hand is as follows:

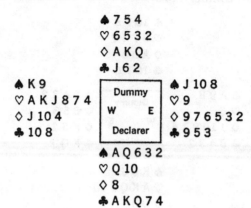

♠ 7 5 4
♡ 6 5 3 2
◇ A K Q
♣ J 6 2

♠ K 9
♡ A K J 8 7 4
◇ J 10 4
♣ 10 8

Dummy
W   E
Declarer

♠ J 10 8
♡ 9
◇ 9 7 6 5 3 2
♣ 9 5 3

♠ A Q 6 3 2
♡ Q 10
◇ 8
♣ A K Q 7 4

QUIZ ON ADVANCED CARD COMBINATIONS

In the following cases you are South, the declarer, at No Trump. The opening lead by West is indicated. What is the proper play from dummy.

1. DUMMY   K J 2
   DECLARER   A 9 5
       West leads the 3.

2. DUMMY   A Q 5
   DECLARER   J 7 6
       West leads the 2.

3. DUMMY   J 8
   DECLARER   K 3 2
       West leads the 6.

4. DUMMY   J 4
   DECLARER   A Q 7
       West leads the 5.

5. DUMMY   J 2
   DECLARER   A 10 7
       West leads the 4.

6. DUMMY   J 10 5
   DECLARER   A 6 2
       West leads the 4.

7. DUMMY   J 4 2
   DECLARER   A 9 3
       West leads the 5.

8. DUMMY   K 10 3
   DECLARER   A 8 6
       West leads the 4.

9. DUMMY   K 10 2
   DECLARER   Q 5 3
       West leads the 4.

10. DUMMY   K 4
    DECLARER   J 6
        West leads the 5.

In the following problems you are South, the declarer, and this is your trump suit. You have entries in both hands. How do you play these combinations to lose as few tricks as possible?

11. DUMMY   8 7 4 2
    DECLARER   A K 10 9

12. DUMMY   A 10 4 2
    DECLARER   Q 9 5 3

13. DUMMY   7 6 5 4
    DECLARER   K J 9 8

14. DUMMY   7 5 3 2
    DECLARER   A 10 9 8

15. DUMMY   A K 9 2
    DECLARER   Q 6 5 4 3

16. DUMMY   A J 7 2
    DECLARER   K 9 6 5

You are South, the declarer, at No Trump. You have entries in each hand. How do you play the following combinations to make as many tricks as possible?

17.	DUMMY	K Q 7 4 3		**18.**	DUMMY	A K 9 8
	DECLARER	A 10			DECLARER	J 4

19.	DUMMY	A K J 10 6 2		**20.**	DUMMY	A Q 6 4 2
	DECLARER	8 3			DECLARER	J 5

21.	DUMMY	Q J 9 4 3		**22.**	DUMMY	A Q 9 3 2
	DECLARER	A 6			DECLARER	J 7 6

23.	DUMMY	A 10 4 3 2		**24.**	DUMMY	A K Q 5 2
	DECLARER	K 9 6			DECLARER	10 9

25.	DUMMY	K Q 6 5 4		**26.**	DUMMY	K Q 10 9 4
	DECLARER	J 9			DECLARER	6 2

27.	DUMMY	A J 5 4 3 2		**28.**	DUMMY	A Q 9 6 5 4
	DECLARER	Q 6			DECLARER	J 7 3 2

In each of the following hands you are South, the declarer.

29.	DUMMY	♠ K 8 7 6 2	**30.**	DUMMY	♠ A 4 3 2

29. DUMMY ♠ K 8 7 6 2
♡ A 3 2
◇ A Q 2
♣ J 3
◇ 3
DECLARER ♠ A Q J 10 3
♡ 9
◇ 8 5 4
♣ A K 4 2

30. DUMMY ♠ A 4 3 2
♡ 8 7 4
◇ K 10 2
♣ 8 3 2
♡ Q
DECLARER ♠ none
♡ A K Q 6
◇ A Q J
♣ Q 10 7 6 5 4

You are playing a contract of 6 Spades and West leads the Queen of Hearts. Plan your play.

You are playing a contract of 5 Clubs and West leads the 3 of Diamonds. Plan your play.

ANSWERS TO QUIZ ON ADVANCED CARD COMBINATIONS

1.

The 2. Although you have what is known as a 'free finesse' of the Jack, you should play low from dummy. If East has the Queen and not the 10, you make three tricks. If East has the 10 and not the Queen, you take the 10 with the Ace, finesse the Jack later on, and again make three tricks.

2.

The 5. If East has the King, you make two tricks whether you play the 5 or the Queen from dummy. If West has the King, you make an extra trick provided you allow the first lead to ride to the Jack, then finesse the Queen.

3.

The Jack. If West has led from the A Q, and you can keep East out of the lead, you have a double stop. The Jack will be of no value unless you play it now.

4.

The Jack. If it holds, and you lose the lead to West rather than to East, he will be unable to continue the suit without giving you three tricks.

5.

The 2. You are certain of two tricks if you play low. If you play the Jack, you may be held to one trick.

6.

An honor. By this means you ensure eventually making two tricks unless East has the K Q. You would also play an honor from dummy if you had the K x x in your hand.

7.

Play low from dummy. West is more likely to have led from either the K 10 or Q 10 than from the K Q specifically. In the first two cases, you ensure two tricks by playing low from dummy.

8.

The 3. The problem to be solved is whether West has led from either the Q 9 or J 9, or from the Q J specifically. The first two cases together are more common than the third case alone, and in those cases you prepare the ground for three tricks by playing low.

9.

The 10. If the 10 is covered by the Jack, you win with the Queen and still have the chance of finding West with the Ace. If you play low from dummy, East will not be so obliging as to play an honor, and on the next round you will have to guess.

10.

You have to guess. The author confesses he is unable to offer guidance on the play of this combination at a No Trump contract, except to observe that you should have arranged the bidding so as to make your partner the declarer. At a suit contract, of course, you would assume that West had not underled the Ace and you would play low from dummy.

11.

Finesse the 10. If it loses, cash the Ace next. You have a very strong chance to make three tricks and a 1 in 4 chance to make four tricks.

12.

Play the Ace and lead low to the 9. This is considerably better than finessing the 10 on the first round.

13.

Finesse the 8. This is better than finessing the Jack, since it provides more extensive protection against a 4–1 break.

14.

Finesse the 10 and then finesse the 9. It is inadvisable to lay down the

Ace on either the first or second round of the suit.

15.

Cash the Queen first. With this consideration, players tend to cash a high card in dummy first, but this costs a trick when East is void. By cashing the Queen, declarer leaves himself with a finesse position against West's J 10.

16.

Finesse the Jack on the first round. If it loses, play the Ace next. The first-round finesse costs a trick when East holds the singleton Queen, which could have been caught by playing the King, but it gains much more frequently when West holds the singleton Queen or East holds the Q 10 x x.

17.

Finesse the 10. This is appreciably better than cashing the A K Q.

18.

Lead the Jack and let it ride. If it holds, or if it loses to the Queen, you play the Ace next. If the Jack is covered by the Queen, you should finesse the 9 on the next round.

19.

Finesse the Jack on the first round. It is wrong to lay down the Ace as a safety play against a singleton Queen. If East has a singleton, it is likely to be a low card, and in this case you will need to take two finesses against West's Q x x x.

20.

Lead low towards the Jack. This ensures four tricks if East has the K x or if the suit is divided 3–3.

21.

Cash the Ace, then lead low to an honor. Playing an honor on the second round is better than finessing the 9, though this last play would be correct if you needed only three tricks.

22.

Finesse the Queen. If it holds, you reenter your hand and lead low to the 9. If the Queen loses, you cash the Jack next.

23.

Play the Ace and finesse the 9. Or, if you prefer it, play the King and finesse the 10. The odds do not favor cashing both top cards unless you desperately need five tricks.

24.

Lead the 10 and let it ride if not covered. This form of play costs a trick when fourth hand has the J x x precisely. But it gains a trick much more frequently when the same player has the x x or x x x x.

25.

Lead low from dummy and finesse the 9. This play has a definite edge over the alternative plan of banking on a 3–3 break.

26.

Finesse the 10. There is a temptation to lead up to the King and see what happens. This is wrong because thereafter it may be impossible to pick up West's J x x x or A J x x.

27.

Cash the Ace. No matter how the cards lie, you have to lose at least one trick, so you should play the Ace first. If you start by leading up to the Queen or finessing the Jack, you lose a trick unnecessarily if there is a singleton King around.

28.

Lead the Jack and let it ride. If you lead low and finesse the Queen, and East shows out, you will be unable to prevent West making a trick with the K 10.

29.

Declarer should win the Heart opening, draw the opponents' trumps, and lead a low Club towards the Jack. If West has the Queen and plays it, declarer discards two Diamonds from dummy on the A K of Clubs and loses no other trick. If East has the Queen of Clubs, declarer still makes the contract if West holds the King of Diamonds.

30.

Declarer's only losers are in trumps, but he has only one entry to dummy (the King of Diamonds) and must plan to employ it at exactly the right moment. If trumps are 2–2, the contract is safe, but if they are 3–1, the best chance will be to play West for a singleton King or Ace. Declarer wins the Diamond in his own hand and leads a low trump! If the Ace or King falls from West, dummy is entered with the King of Diamonds, a Heart is deposited on the Ace of Spades, and a trump is led through East's tenace holding.

16.

Ruffs, crossruffs and dummy reversal

THE READER will be familiar with the idea of a trump suit: it means that any card of that suit ranks above any card of any other suit. If you hold a good suit, you will often make more tricks if that suit is named as trump than you could have made at No Trump. This is especially so if your partner has a fit in the same suit, inasmuch as you may be able to use your partner's trumps for the purpose of ruffing some of your losing cards.

Advantages of trump contract

Not only may you make more tricks by playing at a trump declaration, but you also are better protected against long suits in your opponents' hands. The advantages of playing at a suitable trump contract are clearly seen in the following deal:

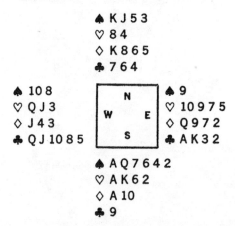

```
                    ♠ K J 5 3
                    ♡ 8 4
                    ◇ K 8 6 5
                    ♣ 7 6 4
    ♠ 10 8            N         ♠ 9
    ♡ Q J 3                     ♡ 10 9 7 5
    ◇ J 4 3      W       E      ◇ Q 9 7 2
    ♣ Q J 10 8 5     S         ♣ A K 3 2
                    ♠ A Q 7 6 4 2
                    ♡ A K 6 2
                    ◇ A 10
                    ♣ 9
```

It is plain that the declarer could not get very rich by playing this hand at No Trump. Clubs would be led and the defenders would snap up the first five tricks. The scenario is quite different if South plays the hand at a Spade contract. If Clubs are led, he is able to ruff the second round. He is also able to ruff his two losing Hearts with dummy's trumps and in that way land a small slam.

The task of deciding whether to play the hand at a suit contract or at No Trump may perhaps seem somewhat complicated, but in actual practice it is seldom very difficult. The normal processes of constructive bidding will lead you to a trump declaration when that is the best contract. All you have to do is make it.

Ruffing losers

It is perhaps more difficult to plan the play of a suit contract than to plan a No Trump contract, if only because there are more ways of winning tricks. Some types of strategy conflict with others, and it is therefore highly desirable to form an overall plan at the very commencement of the proceedings. In planning a No Trump contract it is advisable to first count your winners. The same is true at a suit contract, but now it is equally important to count losers too. The declarer should make this a regular practice. To illustrate:

♠ K 9 7
♡ K Q 7 2
◇ 8 5 3 2
♣ A 4

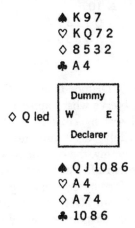

◇ Q led

♠ Q J 10 8 6
♡ A 4
◇ A 7 4
♣ 10 8 6

South is the declarer at a contract of 4 Spades, and the Queen of Diamonds is led. Declarer observes that he has nine winners in the shape of four trump tricks, three Hearts, and two Aces, and that a Club can be ruffed in dummy to round out ten tricks. A Club must be conceded before one can be ruffed, and this must be done before trumps are played, for otherwise the defenders may draw dummy's trumps and leave South a trick short.

Thus the declarer's count of winners is eminently satisfying, but before proceeding he should also count losers. If he wins with the Diamond opening and plays the Ace and another Club, the defenders will cash two Diamond tricks and he will wind up with four losers. To prevent this, declarer's first move is to cash the A K Q of Hearts, divesting himself of a losing Diamond.

The reader is cautioned, having appreciated the importance of counting losers, not to neglect to count his winners also. Consider this hand:

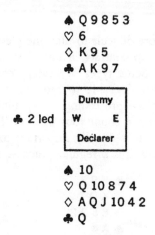

```
              ♠ Q 9 8 5 3
              ♡ 6
              ◇ K 9 5
              ♣ A K 9 7

                  ┌──────────────┐
                  │   Dummy      │
          ♣ 2 led │ W         E  │
                  │              │
                  │   Declarer   │
                  └──────────────┘

              ♠ 10
              ♡ Q 10 8 7 4
              ◇ A Q J 10 4 2
              ♣ Q
```

South is the declarer at 5 Diamonds and a Club is led, declarer winning with the Queen. Observe what happens if declarer endeavors to reduce his immediate losers by crossing to the King of trumps and cashing the AK of Clubs, discarding his losing spade. Now, when a Heart is led from dummy, the opponents will return a trump, holding dummy to one Heart ruff, which is not enough for game.

Declarer avoids this misfortune by counting his winners at the outset. Noting that he needs two Heart ruffs in order to produce the required number of winners, and that he can afford to lose a Spade, he leads a Heart at the second trick, so making sure of the contract.

It has been remarked that there are more ways of winning tricks at a trump contract than at No Trump, but there are also more ways of losing them, in that it is legal for the defenders to ruff too. You may have heard about those poor fellows who sleep on park benches, exposed to the cold winter winds. Their plight is ascribed to the fact that they did not draw trumps at the first opportunity. There is some substance in this cautionary tale, inasmuch as, when you see that you can draw trumps and still have enough tricks for the contract, you should draw them at once. Don't let the defenders ruff your winners. To illustrate.

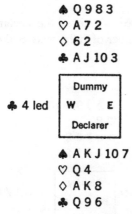

♠ Q 9 8 3
♥ A 7 2
♦ 6 2
♣ A J 10 3

♣ 4 led

Dummy
W   E
Declarer

♠ A K J 10 7
♥ Q 4
♦ A K 8
♣ Q 9 6

The 4 of Clubs is led against 6 Spades. Declarer can count on five Spade tricks, one Heart, two Diamonds and at least three Clubs, amounting to eleven tricks, and he can ruff a Diamond for his twelfth trick. If West has the King of Clubs, it will be possible to make all thirteen tricks, but as South is only in 6 Spades he should go up with the Ace of Clubs and draw all the opponents' trumps (unless they are 4-0, in which case he must ruff a Diamond first). Then he surrenders a trick to the King of Clubs and later discards his small Spade on the established fourth Club.

To finesse the Club on opening lead, losing it to the King, and suffering a Club ruff, would be an act of extreme recklessness.

The crossruff

As a general principle it is not profitable for declarer to use up his own trumps for the purpose of ruffing losing cards. The theory of the ruff is to make a trick with a trump which would otherwise be useless. If declarer has five solid trumps in his own hand, they are naturally good tricks, and he need not ruff anything to convert any one of those five trumps into a winner. Where, however, the dummy has three trumps, let us say, and if one or more of the dummy's three trumps can be used *separately* before trumps are drawn, they will be tricks in addition to the five already counted in the declarer's hand.

However, there are cases in which the declarer may find it expedient to make all the trumps in declarer's hand and dummy's hand separately. That type of play is known as the Crossruff.

Declarer frequently is called upon to decide whether to establish a side suit and draw trumps or whether to try to make his trumps separately.

The crossruff is indicated whenever the declarer, by counting up his high cards and the number of ruffs, reaches the sum total of tricks required.

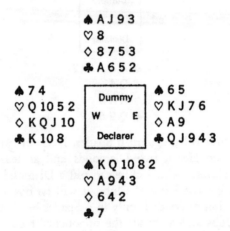

♠ A J 9 3
♡ 8
◇ 8 7 5 3
♣ A 6 5 2

♠ 7 4
♡ Q 10 5 2
◇ K Q J 10
♣ K 10 8

Dummy
W E
Declarer

♠ 6 5
♡ K J 7 6
◇ A 9
♣ Q J 9 4 3

♠ K Q 10 8 2
♡ A 9 4 3
◇ 6 4 2
♣ 7

South is the declarer at a contract of 4 Spades. The defense cashes the first three Diamond tricks and shifts to the trumps. Since declarer has three losing Hearts he must use every one of dummy's trumps for the purpose of ruffing these losers. Even one more lead of trumps will ruin the hand, so declarer's play is to ruff Clubs and Hearts back and forth, since ten tricks can be counted.

The bookkeeping process is one Club trick, one Heart trick, five trumps in the South hand, and three ruffs in dummy—a total of ten tricks.

The danger in the crossruff is that sooner or later one of the opponents will be able to overruff either you or the dummy. In this hand that danger virtually disappears, since after the dummy ruffs one Heart and the declarer ruffs one Club the rest of the trumps are high.

There is this important principle to bear in mind in the playing of the crossruff. Where two suits are being ruffed back and forth and a third suit contains high cards such as the Ace and King, it is usually desirable to cash them early in the play. The reason is that as you

continue your crossruff one of the opponents may run out of the suit
that is being ruffed and discard one of his cards of the suit in which
you have the Ace and King.

For example:

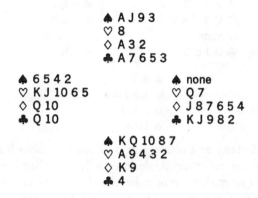

♠ A J 9 3
♥ 8
♦ A 3 2
♣ A 7 6 5 3

♠ 6 5 4 2
♥ K J 10 6 5
♦ Q 10
♣ Q 10

♠ none
♥ Q 7
♦ J 8 7 6 5 4
♣ K J 9 8 2

♠ K Q 10 8 7
♥ A 9 4 3 2
♦ K 9
♣ 4

South is declarer at a contract of 6 Spades and might make all the
tricks if allowed to cash his side suit winners and then crossruff in
Clubs and Hearts so as to score all nine tricks separately. But West
unkindly opens a trump and now declarer must play with care. There
is no danger of an overruff, for after winning the trump lead with
the 7 of Spades all the North-South trumps are high. Dummy still
has three trumps with which to ruff Hearts and it appears that declarer
will score the Ace of Clubs, the Ace and King of Diamonds, three
Heart ruffs in dummy and five trumps in his hand.

Before starting the crossruff, however, it is vital for declarer to cash
both top Diamonds. Note that if he fails to do so and begins to crossruff Hearts and Clubs at once, on the third Club lead West will discard one of his Diamonds. Now declarer will be unable to cash his
Ace and King and he will make no more than eleven tricks.

In playing the crossruff, the drawing of even one round of trumps
will frequently be fatal where a lead must be subsequently relin-
quished, because at that time the defense may lead another trump.

For example:

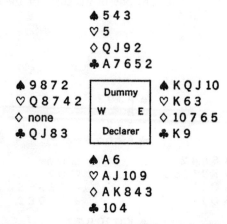

```
              ♠ 5 4 3
              ♡ 5
              ◊ Q J 9 2
              ♣ A 7 6 5 2
♠ 9 8 7 2     ┌──────────┐     ♠ K Q J 10
♡ Q 8 7 4 2   │  Dummy   │     ♡ K 6 3
◊ none        │ W      E │     ◊ 10 7 6 5
♣ Q J 8 3     │ Declarer │     ♣ K 9
              └──────────┘
              ♠ A 6
              ♡ A J 10 9
              ◊ A K 8 4 3
              ♣ 10 4
```

South is declarer at a contract of 5 Diamonds. West leads the 2 of Spades. In order to crossruff, declarer will be obliged to give up a Club trick. If he makes the mistake of pulling even one trump, when East is in with the King of Clubs, he will lead another trump, and now eleven tricks cannot be counted. Immediately on winning the Ace of Spades declarer should play the Ace and another Club. East will lead a trump, but declarer can still cash five Diamonds in his own hand, three Heart ruffs in dummy, the Ace of Spades, the Ace of Hearts, and the Ace of Clubs, for a total of eleven tricks.

Dummy reversal

One of the cardinal principles of declarer's play is not to force the strong trump hand to ruff. While ruffs in dummy are to be sought, ruffs in the closed hand are usually to be avoided. Yet even so fundamental a doctrine as this has its exceptions. The most common exception is where the hand is played at a crossruff, when all of declarer's and dummy's trumps are to be made separately. Another exception is in the type of play known as Dummy Reversal. Let us illustrate the meaning of dummy reversal with the hand on the following page.

South is declarer at a contract of 4 Hearts, and West leads the King of Spades. If trumps are drawn, declarer will lose the three Diamonds and one Club unless the Clubs break three–three. Since they do not, declarer will be down. There is a better way to play this hand, and that is to make the dummy the master hand. When the Spade is

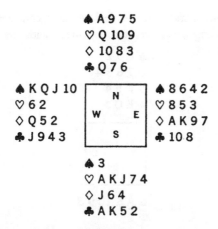

```
                    ♠ A 9 7 5
                    ♡ Q 10 9
                    ◊ 10 8 3
                    ♣ Q 7 6
    ♠ K Q J 10      ┌─────────┐     ♠ 8 6 4 2
    ♡ 6 2           │    N    │     ♡ 8 5 3
    ◊ Q 5 2         │ W     E │     ◊ A K 9 7
    ♣ J 9 4 3       │    S    │     ♣ 10 8
                    └─────────┘
                    ♠ 3
                    ♡ A K J 7 4
                    ◊ J 6 4
                    ♣ A K 5 2
```

won, the 5 is returned and trumped with an honor. Dummy is entered
with the 9 of trumps and the 7 of Spades is ruffed with an honor.
Dummy is entered with the 10 of Hearts and the 9 of Spades ruffed
with South's remaining trump. Dummy is entered with the Queen of
Clubs and the last trump pulled, on which South discards a Diamond.
At the end declarer will lose two Diamonds and a Club, fulfilling the
contract for ten tricks. The execution of the play is relatively simple.
It is the diagnosis to play this hand as a dummy reversal that is
important.

How does one diagnose that the situation is present for such a play?
The answer is, first: dummy's trumps must be good enough to draw
the adverse trumps.

In the above example there are five trumps out. The probability
is that they will be divided three–two. Therefore the outstanding
trumps can be drawn with the Q 10 9. That fulfills the first condition.

The second condition is that the declarer's hand should have the
short suit, as in this case South has a singleton Spade.

In the following hand you are declarer at a contract of 6 Spades. West leads the King of Hearts and continues with the Ace. How do you plan the play?

♠ Q J 2
♡ 7 6 5 4
◇ K 5 4
♣ K Q J

```
      N
  W       E
      S
```

♠ A K 10 9 3
♡ 2
◇ A 3 2
♣ A 10 9 3

Apparently there is no way to get rid of the losing Diamond, and the declarer appears to be doomed to a one-trick set until he notices that the hand meets with the requirements for dummy reversal, or making the dummy the master hand. Notice the two prevailing symptoms. Dummy's trumps are strong enough to pull the opponents' trumps, assuming that they do not break badly. The short suit is in the long trump hand. The proper procedure for the declarer upon trumping the second Heart is to play first the Ace of Spades, then a small Club to the Jack. A Heart is ruffed with the King of Spades. A Spade is led to dummy's Jack, and the last remaining Heart is trumped with the 10 of Spades. Dummy is entered with the King of Diamonds to pull the last trump, on which declarer discards his losing Diamond. The complete holding follows:

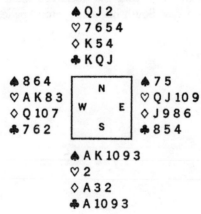

♠ Q J 2
♡ 7 6 5 4
◇ K 5 4
♣ K Q J

♠ 8 6 4   ♠ 7 5
♡ A K 8 3   ♡ Q J 10 9
◇ Q 10 7   ◇ J 9 8 6
♣ 7 6 2   ♣ 8 5 4

♠ A K 10 9 3
♡ 2
◇ A 3 2
♣ A 10 9 3

You are South, the declarer at a contract of 7 Spades. West leads the King of Hearts. What is your plan of play?

♠ A Q 6
♡ A 9 5 2
◇ A J 7
♣ K 8 3

```
        ┌─────────┐
        │    N    │
        │         │
        │    S    │
        └─────────┘
```

♠ K J 10 9 8
♡ 6
◇ K 5 3
♣ A Q J 10

Seemingly everything depends upon the successful finesse of the Jack of Diamonds, which, to be sure, offers a fifty-fifty chance of success. There is, however, a play for the hand which offers a better chance than the mere even-money bet of the Diamond finesse. If the Spades are divided three–two, which is probable, the hand can be made without the Diamond finesse by resorting to dummy reversal, or making the dummy the master hand. Let us examine the symptoms. Dummy's trumps are good enough to draw the opponents' trumps, and the short suit is in declarer's hand. The Heart is returned at once and ruffed. The King of Spades is cashed and another Spade led to the Ace. If the trumps do not break at this point, declarer will be obliged to try the Diamond finesse, but when they do break, another Heart is led and trumped with the 10 of Spades. Dummy is entered with the King of Clubs and the last Heart ruffed with the Jack of Spades. Dummy is then entered with the Ace of Diamonds, in order to play the last trump, on which declarer discards his only losing Diamond. The complete holding follows:

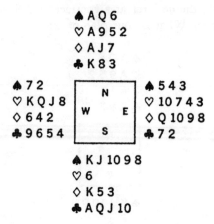

The uppercut

Colorful expressions from all walks of life ultimately find their way into the picturesque lingo of the cardplayer. One of the most descriptive of these expressions is the term "uppercut," which is borrowed from the prize-fight ring and used to describe the trumping of one of your partner's cards, even though it may be high, in order to force out a high trump from declarer. This is done with the hope of building up a trump trick for partner.

For example:

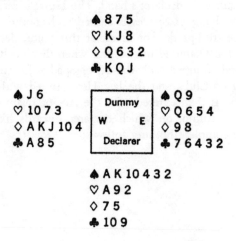

South is the declarer at a contract of 4 Spades, West having over-called with 2 Diamonds. West cashes the King and Ace of Diamonds, East completing the signal. West then plays the Ace of Clubs and follows with the Jack of Diamonds, declarer playing low from dummy. East should realize that declarer is going to ruff, both from the 2 Diamond bid and from the fact that West cashed his Ace of Clubs first. Therefore he should trump his partner's good trick with the Queen of Spades, since it is of no value to him and may force a high trump from declarer. In this way West's Jack becomes promoted to a winner and the contract is set.

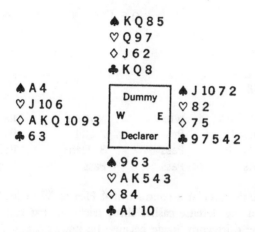

```
              ♠ K Q 8 5
              ♡ Q 9 7
              ◊ J 6 2
              ♣ K Q 8
♠ A 4                          ♠ J 10 7 2
♡ J 10 6        Dummy          ♡ 8 2
◊ A K Q 10 9 3  W        E     ◊ 7 5
♣ 6 3           Declarer       ♣ 9 7 5 4 2
              ♠ 9 6 3
              ♡ A K 5 4 3
              ◊ 8 4
              ♣ A J 10
```

South opened the bidding with 1 Heart and became declarer at a game contract in that suit. West leads the King and Queen of Diamonds, upon which East plays high-low. What should he play next?

It is quite evident that declarer has the Ace of Clubs for the open-ing bid, so that the only hope to defeat the contract is for the defense to gain a trump trick. This does not seem very likely, unless East holds the 8 of Hearts and can be made to trump a Diamond with that card. This will force declarer's King and promote West's holding to a win-ner. West, therefore, should cash the Ace of Spades and lead a small Diamond. If he leads the Ace of Diamonds, East will probably not know that he should ruff. When a low Diamond is led, East will naturally wake up to the necessity of ruffing with his high Heart and the contract will be defeated.

A variation of this play occurs in the following hand:

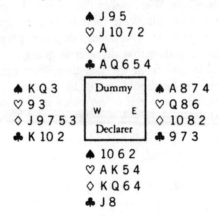

```
                    ♠ J 9 5
                    ♡ J 10 7 2
                    ◇ A
                    ♣ A Q 6 5 4
    ♠ K Q 3      ┌──────────┐    ♠ A 8 7 4
    ♡ 9 3        │  Dummy   │    ♡ Q 8 6
    ◇ J 9 7 5 3  │ W     E  │    ◇ 10 8 2
    ♣ K 10 2     │ Declarer │    ♣ 9 7 3
                 └──────────┘
                    ♠ 10 6 2
                    ♡ A K 5 4
                    ◇ K Q 6 4
                    ♣ J 8
```

The bidding:

SOUTH	WEST	NORTH	EAST
1 Diamond	Pass	2 Clubs	Pass
2 Hearts	Pass	3 Hearts	Pass
4 Hearts	Pass	Pass	Pass

South is the declarer at a contract of 4 Hearts. West leads the Ace of Spades, and the defense cashes three tricks in that suit. East continues with the thirteenth Spade because he knows that a discard can do the declarer no good. (Declarer has bid Hearts and Diamonds and therefore can have no more than two Clubs after he follows to three rounds of Spades.) Declarer discards a Club, and West ruffs with the 9 of Hearts, forcing dummy's 10. It matters not how declarer plays; East's 8 of Hearts must now become a winner.

An extreme case of the repeated use of the uppercut to defeat the contract is shown in the hand on the following page.

South was declarer at a contract of 4 Hearts on strong bidding which included showing the Diamond suit, and apparently must lose only two Spades and the Ace of Hearts. However, inspired defense was able to defeat the contract. After two Spades were cashed, West led the 6 of Spades, East ruffed with the 7 of Hearts, and South overruffed with the 10. The King of Hearts was led, taken with the Ace, and another Spade, although high, was trumped by East with

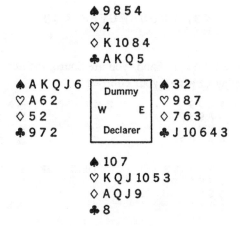

♠ 9 8 5 4
♡ 4
◇ K 10 8 4
♣ A K Q 5

♠ A K Q J 6   Dummy   ♠ 3 2
♡ A 6 2   W   E   ♡ 9 8 7
◇ 5 2   ◇ 7 6 3
♣ 9 7 2   Declarer   ♣ J 10 6 4 3

♠ 10 7
♡ K Q J 10 5 3
◇ A Q J 9
♣ 8

the 9 of Hearts. This forced declarer's Jack, and the 6 of trumps was developed into the setting trick.

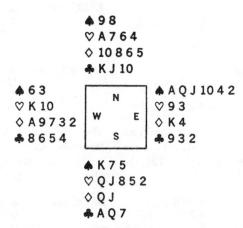

♠ 9 8
♡ A 7 6 4
◇ 10 8 6 5
♣ K J 10

♠ 6 3   N   ♠ A Q J 10 4 2
♡ K 10   ♡ 9 3
◇ A 9 7 3 2   W   E   ◇ K 4
♣ 8 6 5 4   S   ♣ 9 3 2

♠ K 7 5
♡ Q J 8 5 2
◇ Q J
♣ A Q 7

Declarer is playing a contract of 4 Hearts, doubled by West, East having overcalled with Spades. The 6 of Spades was led; East won with the Ace and, hoping that partner had the Ace of Diamonds, led his King at trick two. The Diamond was continued and won by West's Ace. Now on the surface it appears that the defenders can take no more tricks, because West's King of Hearts can be finessed and the suit picked up. However, the third lead of Diamonds can be trumped by East with the 9 of Hearts, forcing out the Jack, and now West is assured of a trump trick by merely covering anything that declarer leads.

QUIZ ON RUFFS, CROSSRUFFS AND DUMMY REVERSAL

In each of the following hands you are South, the declarer. Plan the safest line of play to assure your contract.

1. DUMMY   ♠ Q J 9
            ♡ A 9 3 2
            ◇ K 4
            ♣ A 6 5 3

    DECLARER   ♠ A K 10 8 3
                   ♡ 7 6 5
                   ◇ 9 5 2
                   ♣ 10 2

The contract is 2 Spades and West leads the 4 of Clubs.

2. DUMMY   ♠ K 9 8 6 5 3
            ♡ 6 4 3
            ◇ 7
            ♣ A 8 2

    DECLARER   ♠ A 2
                   ♡ A K Q J 10
                   ◇ K Q
                   ♣ K 9 7 4

The contract is 6 Hearts and West leads a low Diamond. East wins with the Ace and returns a Club.

3. DUMMY   ♠ J 9 7 5 3
            ♡ A J 9 8
            ◇ Q
            ♣ 7 5 3

    DECLARER   ♠ none
                   ♡ K Q 10 6 5 2
                   ◇ A K J 9 2
                   ♣ A J

The contract is 7 Hearts and West leads the Ace of Spades. Plan the play on the assumption that the trumps are 3–0.

4. DUMMY   ♠ 10 8 4
            ♡ 10 3
            ◇ K Q 6 3
            ♣ A J 9 3

    DECLARER   ♠ 5
                   ♡ A K J 8 6
                   ◇ 9 7 4 2
                   ♣ K Q 10

The contract is 4 Hearts. West leads the King of Spades, which holds, and continues with the Queen.

5. DUMMY   ♠ K 10 8 6
            ♡ A J 6
            ◇ 8
            ♣ J 9 6 3 2

    DECLARER   ♠ A Q J 7
                   ♡ K Q 4
                   ◇ 7 5 4 3 2
                   ♣ 7

The contract is 4 Spades. West leads the Queen of Diamonds, followed by the Jack, which you ruff in dummy.

6. DUMMY   ♠ 7 4 3 2
            ♡ A J 8
            ◇ Q 8 6 3 2
            ♣ 5

    DECLARER   ♠ 6
                   ♡ K Q 10 9 6 4
                   ◇ K 4
                   ♣ A J 9 2

The contract is 5 Hearts, the opponents having bid up to the level of 4 Spades. West leads the King of Spades and continues with a low Spade to East's ace, which you ruff.

7. DUMMY	♠ K 6 5	8. DUMMY	♠ 7 6 2
	♡ 7 6 4 3		♡ J 6 2
	◇ A 7 6		◇ A K Q
	♣ A K 6		♣ K Q 8 7
DECLARER	♠ Q J 8 7 3	DECLARER	♠ A 5 4
	♡ A 2		♡ Q 10 7 5 3
	◇ Q J 10 4		◇ 10 4 2
	♣ 10 2		♣ A 4

The contract is 4 Spades, East having opened with a bid of 1 Heart. West leads the 9 of Hearts and East overtakes with the 10.

The contract is 4 Hearts and West leads the Queen of Spades, on which East plays the 9. You win with the Ace and successfully take three rounds of Clubs, discarding a Spade.

ANSWERS TO QUIZ ON RUFFS, CROSSRUFFS AND DUMMY REVERSAL

1.
Win with the Ace of Clubs, and lead a Diamond from dummy. You have to do this to make sure of scoring a Diamond ruff in dummy, which will give you eight tricks. If you try to enter your hand in order to lead towards the King of Diamonds, and the King loses to the Ace, the defenders will be able to lead trumps enough times to prevent a Diamond ruff. For the same reason it would be wrong to duck the Club opening lead, since West could shift to a trump.

2.
You must try to establish dummy's Spade suit. This is a better plan than discarding a Club from dummy on the King of Diamonds and trying to ruff a Club in dummy, since you could easily be overruffed. At trick two you win with the King of Clubs (to preserve dummy's entry). You draw two rounds of trumps and take the A K of Spades. If all follow, you have no problem: you simply ruff a Spade and draw the last trump. If the Spades are 4–1, you have to hope that the second Spade isn't ruffed;

in this case you ruff a Spade and enter dummy by ruffing your winning Diamond! Another Spade is ruffed, the last trump is drawn, and dummy is reentered with the Ace of Clubs to cash the established Spades. The key play is to draw only two rounds of trumps before tackling Spades, since dummy's third trump may be needed to furnish a ruffing entry.

3.
You should aim to treat dummy as the master hand (dummy reversal). Play a low trump to dummy at trick two, ruff another Spade, cross to the Queen of Diamonds and ruff a third Spade. Dummy is entered once again in Hearts and a fourth Spade is ruffed with your last trump. Then the 9 of Diamonds is ruffed, dummy's trumps are played, and the last four tricks are taken with the A K J of Diamonds and Ace of Clubs.

If you make the mistake of drawing three rounds of trumps, you will be able to discard dummy's Club losers and ruff a Club, but you will be left with a losing Diamond if the Diamonds are 5–2.

4.

You must plan to overcome a 4–2 trump break. You need to make a Diamond trick, and therefore you should ruff the second Spade and play a Diamond to the King. If East takes it and continues Spades, you refuse to ruff, discarding a Diamond instead. Then, if the defenders elect to play another Spade, you can ruff it in dummy and make the contract. If you were to draw trumps before playing a Diamond, and the adverse trumps were 4–2, your own trump holding would be exhausted. Then, when the opponents came in with the Ace of Diamonds, they would be able to cash several Spade tricks.

5.

You must play to make seven tricks by a crossruff, plus three Heart tricks. To prepare for the crossruff you must give up a Club. The defenders will probably return a trump, but you will still have enough trumps left. The important point to appreciate is that it is essential to cash three rounds of Hearts before crossruffing. (If one is ruffed, you go down.) If you fail to cash the Hearts, the defenders will throw Hearts while you are ruffing the minor suits, and you will then go down even if the opponents' Hearts were favorably divided initially.

6.

Lead a low Diamond at trick three. If West holds the Ace and ducks, you make the contract by shifting to a crossruff game after winning with dummy's Queen of Diamonds. If East has the Ace of Diamonds and takes it, his best return is a trump. You then abandon the crossruff and play to establish dummy's Diamond suit: if the Diamonds are 3–3, and the trumps 2–2, you succeed.

It would be wrong to play for a crossruff without first leading a Dia-.

mond, for while you were ruffing three losing Clubs, the defenders would be able to discard Diamonds. The chances are that you would never make a Diamond trick, which you need for your contract.

7.

You must expect the King of Diamonds to be badly placed. Therefore you must aim to restrict your trump losses to one trick. Win the Heart opening, cross to dummy with a Club and lead a low trump. If the Queen wins, you again get to dummy with a Club and lead another low trump. Provided the trumps are 3–2, if East goes in with the Ace of trumps at any stage and continues Hearts you can afford to ruff high with the Queen or Jack. This method of handling the trumps is essential. If you were to allow dummy's King of trumps to be captured by the Ace, you would not be able to afford to ruff the third round of Hearts with a high trump. Thus the defenders would gain a trump promotion if West started life with a doubleton or singleton Heart, as is to be expected.

8.

Lead the fourth Club from dummy, discarding your last Spade. Provided the trumps are 3–2, you can then drive out the A K of trumps and make the contract. The object of playing the fourth Club and discarding the last Spade is to avoid an adverse trump promotion. If you were to simply lead a trump from dummy after cashing the A K Q of Clubs, East would play low and your Queen would lose to West's King or Ace. West would then return a Spade to East's King, and if East were to produce the outstanding Club at this point you would be in deep trouble: whether you ruffed it with a high trump or a low one, you could expect to lose two more trump tricks.

17.

Safety plays, entries and holdups

LIKE THE FELLOW who resolved to take a bath once a week whether he needed it or not, the author holds that you just can't be too careful in this world. Considerable attention is therefore paid to the precautionary measures that form such an important aspect of the play of the hand at bridge. It will be found that these are concerned partly with the methods which may be needed to overcome an adverse distribution of the opponents' cards. Of equal importance are the careful handling of entries needed to ensure that established tricks can be cashed at the most suitable time, and the use of such maneuvers as the holdup to deny the defenders the ability to do the same.

Safety plays

The safety play is very much what the name indicates, a means of protection against a bad break. It is a method of play which is calculated to hold your losses in a particular suit within certain limits, in the event of unforeseen distribution.

One line of play, for example, may have the prospect of winning five tricks, but if you attempted to win these five tricks and the cards broke badly, you might find yourself taking only three tricks.

Let us presume that to fulfill your contract you need four tricks. In that case it would be extremely unwise for you to attempt to win the maximum if there were a safer way to guarantee that you will win four tricks. This is the theory of the safety play.

In other words, safety plays many times deliberately sacrifice one trick in order to run the least possible risk of losing two tricks.

Failure by declarer to exercise caution in what are considered normal situations has resulted in staggering losses at the bridge table. "Partner, I was helpless against such a bad break in trumps" is frequently another way of saying, "Partner, I took too much for granted. I should have exercised more caution."

Certain combinations in the safety field have become standardized. Others you may be called upon to figure out for yourself as the situation develops. Mastering safety plays requires steady practice to fix in mind all the outstanding cards in the suit. An hour of private practice with one suit will help more than weeks of actual play. One or two combinations will at first appear to go against your natural instincts, but upon study you will observe their soundness.

Let us take first one of the simplest cases of all:

A Q 10 8 2

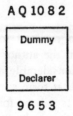

9 6 5 3

If you need five tricks, you play for West to hold King and another Spade and lead from South to finesse the Queen. But if you need only four tricks and play in the same manner, you may come a cropper. If the Queen loses to the King, what do you do next time? If you play the Ace, it may turn out that East is now void and you will lose to West's Jack, which would be the case if the original holdings were as follows:

A Q 10 8 2

J 7 4 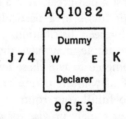 K

9 6 5 3

If, however, you decide to finesse again the next time, it is barely possible that you will lose to the Jack, in which case the original holdings can be as follows:

A Q 10 8 2

7 4 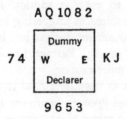 K J

9 6 5 3

In other words, if you misguess you will be lost. To guard against such a misguess the absolute insurance play is the Ace first. Notice in the first case you would drop the singleton King, and your play would win all the tricks. In the second case you would drop the Jack, and your troubles would be over. Assume, however, that on the play of the Ace two small cards fell. Now the South hand would be re-entered and a small one led toward the Queen. If West follows, it must be with either the Jack or the King, and your troubles are over. If West shows out, you will lose two tricks, but then nothing could ever have been done about it. You would have had to lose two tricks in any event. If it is possible for the contract to be fulfilled, the play of the Ace guarantees that you will do so and protects you against a possible misguess which would result from finessing. Bear in mind that this method applies where you can afford to lose one trick but cannot afford to lose two.

A variation of this play is seen in the following situation:

AQ643

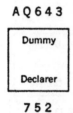

752

With this combination, no matter how favorable the distribution of the opponents' cards, one trick will have to be lost in any event.

Assume that the King is in the West hand. East will then have the J 10 9, and the Jack must eventually win one trick.

Now this holding may prove very treacherous. Assume, for example, that East has the singleton King. The first-round finesse will lose, and the opponents will take three tricks against you. If East has the King and one other Spade, and the finesse is taken, the opponents will win two tricks against you.

Assume that you have plenty of time and plenty of entries. The play of the Ace first will in the long run be profitable. If West holds the King, he will hold it a trick or two later, and the Queen will still be a winner, because the South hand will be re-entered and a small card led toward the Queen. Occasionally when you play the Ace the Jack will fall from the East hand, which may lead you to suspect that the King will fall on the next lead.

Suppose, for example, the adverse holdings were:

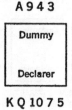

```
                    Dummy

      1098     W         E    K J

                   Declarer
```

When you play the Ace and follow up with a small card you will lose only one trick in the suit. Whereas if you take the finesse immediately you will be obliged to lose two tricks.

It must be understood that these discussions assume that there is no anxiety to prevent the opponents from obtaining the lead in a hurry. If, for example, you need two tricks at once without letting the opponents in, you would naturally have to take the finesse.

There are certain safety plays that cost nothing. They are merely precaution plays. One of them we learned when the elements were being taught to us. For example:

```
                A 9 4 3

                ┌──────────┐
                │  Dummy   │
                │          │
                │          │
                │ Declarer │
                └──────────┘

                K Q 10 7 5
```

Having nine cards, the only way you could lose a trick in the suit is for one opponent to have all four, including the Jack. If, however, you find out which one has the four, you can finesse against the Jack either way. Therefore the safety play is to lead first the King from the South hand. If West shows out, the 10 can subsequently be finessed against East. If East shows out, then the 9 can be finessed in the North hand. This is the first safety play which beginners are taught.

A slight variation of the above is the following:

```
                K 9 6 5

                ┌──────────┐
                │  Dummy   │
                │          │
                │          │
                │ Declarer │
                └──────────┘

                A Q 8 7 4
```

With this combination of cards can you lose a trick? The answer is yes, if one of the opponents has all four outstanding cards. The next question is, can you do anything about it? The answer is, it all depends on which one of them has all four. If West has them, nothing can be done about it with any line of play. Look at *Diagram A*. But if East has them (*Diagram B*), you need not lose a trick. You first play the King and then find that West is void. Then play the 5 from the North hand, and East will be obliged to play the 10. This is won by South's Queen. The North hand is re-entered, and now the 9 is led in order to pick up East's Jack.

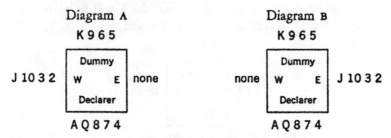

The important thing, however, is to find out early whether East has all four. The instinctive play, to lead the high card from the hand that has the two honors, is not correct in this case, because if you find out that West has them all, it does you no good. There is no use finding out something when you can't do anything about it.

When a hand seems to be a cinch, that is the time to stop and say, what misfortune can befall me? And if that misfortune occurs, can I do anything about it? If there is nothing to be done about the holdings, give it no further thought, as in the case where West holds all four. Do not bother to find out, because you cannot do anything about it. Therefore the proper play is the King from the North hand, to find out if East has all four, because something can be done about that.

```
        A Q 9 5
     ┌───────────┐
     │  Dummy    │
     │           │
     │  Declarer │
     └───────────┘
        J 8 7 6 3 2
```

If you are attempting to win all the tricks in this suit, which card do you lead from the South hand?

First of all, the proper play with ten cards is to finesse. (For discussion of this principle see Chapter 25 "Percentages.") The question is, should the Jack be led or a small one? If the adverse three cards are divided two–one, it will make no difference which card you lead. If East has all three, it will be immaterial, but if West has all three, you will be able to find it out by leading the Jack. West presumably will cover, and North will win with the Ace. When East shows out, the rest is easy. Notice if you had played a small one first, West would have followed with the 4, dummy would have played the Queen, and East would show out, and now West would hold the K 10 over your Jack and cannot be prevented from taking a trick. Needless to say, if on the lead of the Jack, West shows out, the 5 will be played from dummy and East permitted to take his one and only trick. The complete holding:

A Q 9 5

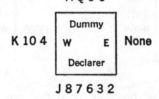

K 10 4

Dummy

W   E

Declarer

None

J 8 7 6 3 2

The above is the type of safety play which cannot possibly lose a trick but might gain a trick. It might be described as a precaution play.

In this holding you are willing to lose one trick but not two. What is the correct play?

J 7 5 2

Dummy

Declarer

A Q 8 4 3

Since the opponents have four cards, you intend to take the finesse. The normal play would be to lead the 2 from the North hand and finesse the Queen. If West should show out, East could not be prevented from winning two tricks. The original holding would have been:

J 7 5 2

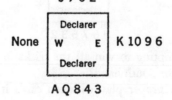

None

Declarer

W   E

Declarer

K 10 9 6

A Q 8 4 3

If West originally had all four of the suit, nothing could ever have been done about it. He would naturally be entitled to two tricks in the suit.

Notice in the first case, however, that had North led the Jack, East could have been limited to one trick in the suit. He would be obliged to cover with the King, South would win with the Ace, and West would show out. Now the 3 is led toward the 7, and East wins the trick with the 9, but the North hand is entered with some other suit, and the finesse is taken against East's guarded 10.

It is true that the play of the Jack might cost an extra trick. That is where East holds a singleton King. The lead of the small one would permit you to take all five tricks, whereas the lead of the Jack permits West to win a trick with the 10. However, in the case where you are willing to lose one trick because you want to be quite sure not to lose two, the Jack is the proper play.

K 10 7 4

```
+-------------+
|   Dummy     |
|             |
|             |
|  Declarer   |
+-------------+
```

A 9 6 5 3

Assume that you are playing a slam contract in Hearts and this is your trump suit. You have no other losers in the side suits. You will, therefore, succeed in your contract if you lose only one Heart trick. If you play properly, you will be successful no matter how the cards are distributed. What is the correct play? If you should first play the King from the North hand, you will meet with defeat if East shows out. If you lead the Ace from the South hand, it will be disastrous if West shows out. When a hand seems as easy as this you must stop and say, what disaster can possibly overtake me? The answer is, of course, all four trumps in one hand. You must, therefore, play in such a manner as to find out which one is void. The proper play is a low card from either hand. Let us assume that the lead is in the North hand. The 4 should be played first. If East shows out, the Ace will win, and a small one led toward the King 10 will hold West to only one trick. If East should play the 2 on the 4, then South would play the 9. This will take care of the situation if West shows out. If West wins the trick, your troubles are over, because the rest of the trumps must fall.

Remember the only thing you feared was all four in one hand. It must also be remembered that you were not trying to make all the tricks. You wanted to be quite certain not to lose two. If, indeed, it turned out that each of the opponents had two Hearts, you will have spent a trick needlessly, but that is a small premium to pay for an insurance policy.

K 9 5

Dummy
Declarer

A J 8 7 3

With this holding, if you can afford to lose one trick but cannot afford to lose two, what is the proper play? If you lead the King from the North hand, you will lose two tricks if it turns out that West had originally Q 10 6 2. The proper play is first the Ace, then the 3, and when West plays low follow with the 9 from the North hand. If East wins the trick with the 10, your troubles are over, because the Queen must fall next time. If West plays the 10, of course that is the end of the problem. If on the second lead West shows out, North wins with the King and now leads the 9 toward the Jack. East will then have held the Q 10 6 2 and will win only with the Queen. The complete hands follow:

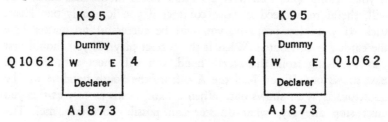

K 9 5

Q 10 6 2 | W   E | 4

A J 8 7 3

K 9 5

4 | W   E | Q 10 6 2

A J 8 7 3

Assuming that you can afford to lose one trump trick but not two, what is the correct play?

K J 3 2

Dummy
Declarer

A 9 6 5 4

The answer is the King first. If you play the Ace first and West shows out, East cannot be prevented from taking two tricks with the Queen and the 10. On the play of the King, if West shows out, the 2 will now be led. This forces East to put up his 10 and he can take only one trick. If it is East who shows out instead of West, nothing is lost by the play of the King, because then the 2 is led toward the Ace and the 5 is led toward the Jack, holding West to only one trick, the Queen.

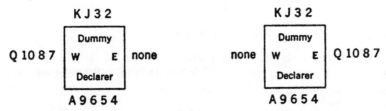

The following diagram contains an interesting combination of cards, but the proper play depends upon just how many tricks you are after. If you need three tricks, there are two different ways of handling it, which have already been discussed on page 328.

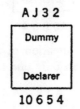

If, however, you are satisfied with only two tricks in the suit but wish to be quite sure not to lose three, another line of play is necessary. The 100 per cent play to guarantee the taking of two tricks is the Ace first, followed by a small one toward the 10. This will guarantee two tricks against any possible distribution of the remaining cards.

If the King, Queen, and a number of others are under the Ace, a low one to the 10 will draw out the Queen. The South hand is then re-entered and a low one is led toward the Jack.

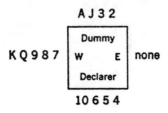

If the five cards are behind the Ace, the Queen will have to come up on the second trick, and the Jack and 10 between them will produce one more trick for the declarer.

AJ32

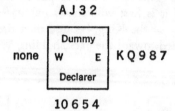

none   KQ987

10654

This play avoids misguessing where a single honor is held by the adversary. If, for example, the 10 is led, declarer will lose three tricks if West happens to have the singleton honor.

AJ32

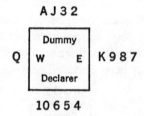

Q   K987

10654

If the 4 is led, with the intention of playing the Jack from the North hand, declarer will win only one trick if East has a singleton honor.

AJ32

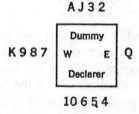

K987   Q

10654

Of course if the adverse cards are divided three–two, any line of play will succeed in winning two tricks.

AJ42

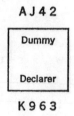

K963

The problem is to insure the taking of three tricks. The common way of playing this holding is to lead the King first and then toward the Jack. This play will lose two tricks whenever East has four or more headed by the Queen 10. The proper play will guarantee the taking of three tricks regardless of the adverse distribution. The correct method is to play the Ace first and then the 2. If East follows, the 9 is played by declarer. If it loses to the 10, the Queen must fall next time. If, on the 2, East shows out, declarer wins with the King and leads toward the Jack. If on the very first play of the Ace, West shows out, the 2 is led to the King 9 and East will be forced to play an honor.

If you need all four tricks, the finesse is the proper play. Very little is to be gained by playing the King first, since if you drop a singleton Queen from the East hand, it is impossible to take four tricks in any event. Whereas if the 3 is led and West holds a singleton Queen, the 10 in the East hand can now be captured.

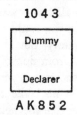

10 4 3

AK852

In playing this hand South leads the King and West drops the Jack. What is the next proper play? Assume that you can afford to lose one trick but not two. It is true if the Queen is now alone in the West hand you can win all the tricks by playing the Ace, but if West should show out, it would mean that East's Queen 9 would both be winners. What is the sure play? The answer is, a small one toward the 10. If West has the Queen alone, the rest of the suit must now fall. If West shows out, the 10 will force East to play the Queen, and while he still has the 9 protected, you can enter the North hand with some other suit and finesse the 8 against him. The holding will have been:

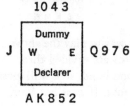

10 4 3

J

Q976

AK852

Would you play any differently if on the lead of the King it was East who played the Jack? The answer is no. The same play is indicated. If East's Jack is accompanied by the Queen, he is welcome to one trick, because the rest will now be good; but if East's Jack was a singleton, then West would now hold the Q 9 7, and a low card toward the 10 will either force him to play the Queen or permit the 10 to win.

A combination of very frequent occurrence is the following:

A 10 6 5 2

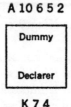

K 7 4

Your object is to lose no more than one trick in the suit. The King should be led first, then a small one toward the Ace 10. If West does not follow, there was nothing you could ever have done about it. The loss of two tricks was obligatory, but if West follows with a small card, you should play the 10 from dummy. If it loses, the rest of the tricks are now good. If East shows out, your precaution will have been rewarded. In other words, do not take for granted that a suit will break three–two and play the Ace the next time on the theory that it makes no difference. It is true that if they break three–two it will not matter, but just in case West has the Queen Jack and two others, it costs you nothing to play the 10. This is another way of stating that when the opponents must take a trick in any event, it frequently pays to be cheerful about it and give it to them early.

Q 8 4 3

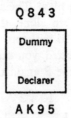

A K 9 5

What is the proper way to play the above combination if you need all four tricks? If the cards are divided three–two, the play is immaterial. If they are four in one hand, it is still possible to make the hand if the singleton is an honor. If East has four, including the Jack 10, it is true that we could make all the tricks if we knew it, but unfortunately there is no way to find out. The best play, therefore, is the King from the South hand. If West should drop the 10, the correct continuation would be the 5 toward the Queen, and if West shows out, the 9 can be finessed against East's Jack. If both opponents follow, of course there is no further problem. If, however, on the play of the King, East drops the 10, the proper continuation is the Ace, and if East shows out, the 8 can be finessed in the North hand.

9 7 6

A K 10 3 2

Assuming that you are willing to give up one trick in the suit, what is the proper way to play this combination? If the cards are divided three–two, there will be no problem. You must, therefore, guard merely against four important cards in the East hand. The proper play is the Ace first. If an honor drops, there is no further problem. If only small ones appear, you must not lead out the King. You should either enter the North hand to lead through for a finesse of the 10 or lead a small one toward the 9. If West shows out, the 9 forces the Jack, and the North hand is entered later on for a finesse against East's Queen.

♠ A 5 3

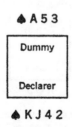

♠ K J 4 2

With this holding the declarer wishes to take three tricks but cannot afford to lose two. The proper play is the King first. Then the 2 is led to the Ace and the 5 returned toward the Jack. If the Queen was located with East, where the finesse would have succeeded, the Jack will still be good for the third trick. If the Spades were three–three, regardless of the location of the Queen, a third trick will become established. If West had four, including the Queen, there was never any way to take more than two tricks. When three tricks are needed, the finesse of the Jack is not the proper play, because West might have a doubleton Queen.

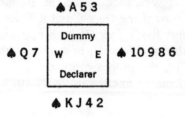

♠ A 5 3

Dummy

♠ Q 7   W   E   ♠ 10 9 8 6

Declarer

♠ K J 4 2

Entries—their care and nurture

We have previously observed that in order to take full advantage of our high cards the lead must come toward them. In order to accomplish this result we must be able to enter the other hand in order to make the lead. Cards which enable a player to reach at will into the hand from which he wishes to lead are called entries. The most obvious entry is an Ace, or King of the suit in which the other hand holds the Ace. There are less obvious ones which we shall discuss presently.

There are certain combinations of cards which require repeated leads from the dummy, in which case more entries will be needed. For example:

4 3 2

Dummy

Declarer

A Q J

In this case it will be necessary to lead twice from the dummy in order to finesse successfully against the King. Two entries must be found for the purpose. Though we are sometimes carelessly inclined to look at this combination as just one finesse, it actually involves two finesses.

At the start of a hand it is wise for the declarer to determine how many such leads he requires. This will lead him naturally to the number of entries he requires. That number of entries may be obvious.

If not, there may be certain later entries which we might call "hidden." A "hidden entry" is one which does not appear on the surface. The simplest development of a hidden entry is the establishment of a low card in a suit when the opposition can no longer follow.

Some entries are certain and some are problematical, as in the following examples:

Diagram A	Diagram B	Diagram C
A K J	K 3	A Q
Dummy	Dummy	Dummy
Declarer	Declarer	Declarer
4 3 2	4 2	3 2

In DIAGRAM A the dummy has two certain entries in the Ace and King and one problematical entry in the Jack. This will prove to be an entry only if the finesse succeeds.

In DIAGRAM B the King is a problematical entry. If the Ace is on the left, the King will be an entry, but if it is on the right, it will not be.

In DIAGRAM C dummy has one certain entry in the Ace and one possible entry in the Queen, which will prove to be such if the finesse succeeds.

Declarer wishes to finesse Clubs. How many times must he lead the suit?

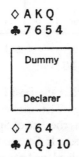

◇ A K Q
♣ 7 6 5 4

Dummy

Declarer

◇ 7 6 4
♣ A Q J 10

It is impossible to tell. Maybe once, if the King shows up at the first trick. Perhaps twice and possibly three times, which would be the case if East held the King and at least three other Clubs. However, the declarer is prepared for such a contingency, because he can enter the dummy just three times in order to make the required three Club leads.

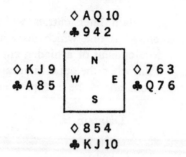

◇ A Q 10
♣ 9 4 2

◇ K J 9   N   ◇ 7 6 3
♣ A 8 5   W   E   ♣ Q 7 6
                 S

◇ 8 5 4
♣ K J 10

Assuming that the lead is in the South hand, Diamonds should be led first. North has one sure entry and two problematical ones. If the King and Jack of Diamonds are both with West, dummy will have three entries. The 10, therefore, is played from dummy. This holds the trick, and now the dummy leads a Club, finessing the 10 from the closed hand. This is won by West's Ace. Assuming that West returns a Diamond, you win with the Queen in dummy, and now, having determined the location of the Queen of Clubs, you lead a Club and play the Jack.

Diagram D	Diagram E	Diagram F	Diagram G
♠ K Q 6	♠ A J 10		
◇ 5 4 3	◇ 5 4 3	♠ A K Q 3	♠ A 6 4 2
Dummy	Dummy	Dummy	Dummy
Declarer	Declarer	Declarer	Declarer
♠ 5 4 3	♠ 5 4 3	♠ J 10 9 2	♠ K Q 7 3
◇ K Q 6	◇ A J 10		

In DIAGRAM D assuming that the lead is in the declarer's hand, how many entries has the dummy? The answer is, one certain one and one problematical one. If West has the Ace of Spades, dummy can be entered with both the King and Queen. If East has it, the dummy will possess only one entry. A low Spade is played toward dummy. If it should win, a low Diamond is led toward the closed hand for the same process.

In DIAGRAM E how many entries has the dummy? One certain one and one problematical one. The Ace, of course, is certain, and if West has at least one of the honors, a second trick can be won in the dummy. A low Spade, therefore, is led and the 10 played from dummy. This loses to the Queen, and a Diamond is returned. The 10 is played by declarer and loses to the Queen. Now a Spade comes back, and the Jack is finessed in the dummy. If it wins the trick, this process is repeated in Diamonds.

In DIAGRAM F the declarer wishes to make four leads from the dummy. The three obvious entries are the Ace, King, and Queen. However, if both opponents follow to the first two leads, there will be no more of the suit left at the fourth lead, and if declarer has been careful to retain the deuce, he can enter the dummy at that time with the 3. This is known as a hidden entry because it does not appear on the surface. If declarer should carelessly use the deuce of Spades early in the play, he will lose his hidden entry.

If, as the declarer overtakes the Spades, he learns at the second trick that one of the opponents has four of the suit, he will not be able to continue the overtaking process and will, therefore, find that the 3 in dummy will not become an entry.

The most frequent occurrence of a hidden entry is where each of the hands has four cards of the suit. The result is that in the vast majority of cases at the end of the third lead of the suit neither of the opponents will have any, so that the fourth one is a winner in either hand.

In DIAGRAM G the declarer will no doubt very likely win all four Spade tricks. Let us assume that he desires to enter the dummy twice. He can obviously do so once with the Ace, but if the suit breaks reasonably, he can subsequently make an entry out of the 6. This can be done by playing first the King, then the Queen, and to the third trick the 7 instead of the 3. Notice if the 3 is not retained, the 7 will be too large a card with which to enter dummy, inasmuch as it is higher than the 6.

In the next illustration it will be obligatory to give up one trick to the opponents, regardless of the distribution:

♠ A 5 3 2

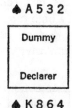

♠ K 8 6 4

Assuming that two entries are desired in the dummy, declarer can retain the 4 of Spades so that the 5 will be a late entry. The King naturally wins a trick. The 6 is led to the Ace, which provides one entry. Subsequently the 8 of Spades is given up to the opposition. This clears the suit, and the 4 may be used to enter the dummy with the 5.

Many times the declarer can win the opening lead very cheaply, but should refuse to do so in order to retain a low card to enter dummy subsequently. Let us take a few simple illustrations:

◇ K 2
♣ K Q 10 9 8

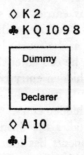

◇ A 10
♣ J

West leads the 6 of Diamonds. East plays the 9. South should win with the Ace. The purpose is to retain the King of Diamonds as an entry to dummy to cash the Clubs after they become established. The Jack of Clubs is overtaken and the suit continued until the Ace falls.

A case that is not quite so obvious is as follows:

◇ J 6 4 3

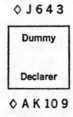

◇ A K 10 9

West leads the 5 of Diamonds. Dummy plays the 3 and East the 2. South can win the trick with the 9, but if it is important to enter dummy for some other purpose, declarer should win the trick with the King, because it is apparent that West has led from four Diamonds (Q 8 7 5) and that the Jack can be converted into an entry after the first trick is won with a high card.

Notice that this play costs declarer nothing, because he will still make three tricks in the suit. Similarly:

◇ Q 7 6

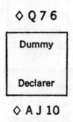

◇ A J 10

West leads the 4 of Diamonds, dummy plays low, and East plays the 8. If a subsequent entry is required into the dummy, declarer should win the first trick with the Ace, retaining the Queen for such time as dummy must be entered. In the above illustrations we have been assuming that the contract was No Trump.

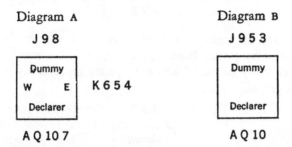

Diagram A

J 9 8

Dummy
W   E   K 6 5 4
Declarer

A Q 10 7

Diagram B

J 9 5 3

Dummy

Declarer

A Q 10

Assume that dummy has no further entries:

In DIAGRAM A the 8 should be played from the dummy and (if East does not cover) the 7 from the closed hand. This permits the trick to be held in the dummy, where the lead is desired. The next play would be the Jack, not the 9, because if the 9 is led, the trick would be won in the closed hand, whereas it is desirable to retain the lead in the dummy.

In DIAGRAM B the Jack should be led from the dummy, so that if it is not covered, the lead will be retained there for the next finesse.

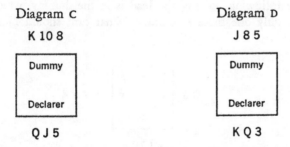

Diagram C

K 10 8

Dummy

Declarer

Q J 5

Diagram D

J 8 5

Dummy

Declarer

K Q 3

In DIAGRAM C, West leads the deuce, East wins with the Ace. If South needs entries in the dummy, the Jack should be played from the closed hand. This will subsequently make both the King and 10 winners.

In DIAGRAM D, West leads the 10, East plays the Ace. If an entry is required in the dummy, declarer would play the Queen, permitting the Jack to become the commanding card.

QJ6

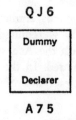

A 7 5

West leads the deuce. If a later entry is desired into the dummy, the 6 should be played from dummy and the Ace used to win the trick. If an entry is desired into the dummy immediately, the Queen should be played.

4 3 2

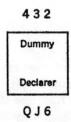

Q J 6

In order to build up a trick with this holding, the declarer must lead twice from the dummy. If he should lead from his own hand, it would be impossible for him to win a trick. Two entries, therefore, are required for this purpose, unless when the first lead comes from dummy East comes up with the Ace or King.

In the following holding the lead is in the dummy, which at this time has only one more side entry. What card should North play?

9 6 2

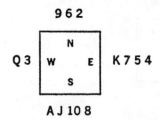

Q 3   K 7 5 4

A J 10 8

He should not make the mistake of leading the 9. Since the 9 will serve a useful purpose later on, it should be retained. The proper play is a small one, inasmuch as declarer intends to lose this trick. He should play the 10 in his own hand, and when it loses to the Queen, dummy should be subsequently entered and the 9 led. If East covers, there is no further problem. If East ducks, South underplays with the 8 and repeats the finesse. To put it briefly, since a trick must be lost, it is idle to waste the 9 on that trick.

By the proper handling of certain card combinations an additional entry may be created when none appears to exist:

♠ 6 4
♣ Q 10 9

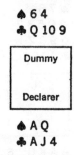

♠ A Q
♣ A J 4

In this case dummy has the lead with no other entry cards. Declarer wishes to take a finesse in both Spades and Clubs. The proper procedure is to lead the Queen. If it is covered, the 10 is an entry to permit the Spade finesse. If East plays low, the Jack should be dropped under the Queen. Now the 10 is continued, and if East still refuses to cover, the lead remains in dummy and the Spade finesse can be tried.

Occasionally entries can be created by ruffing good tricks in order to cross to the other hand.

♠ J 4 3
♡ 7
◊ A K Q 8 4
♣ 10 9 4 3

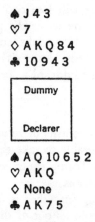

♠ A Q 10 6 5 2
♡ A K Q
◊ None
♣ A K 7 5

Declarer is playing a Spade contract. West leads the Queen of Clubs, which declarer wins with the King. He desires to enter the dummy, first to discard his two Clubs on the good Diamonds and, second, to take the Spade finesse. The simplest way to do it is to trump the Queen of Hearts even though it is good.

In order to preserve entries in a hand which is short of them, the proper management of certain finesse combinations will be helpful.

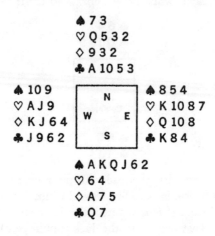

♠ 7 3
♡ Q 5 3 2
◇ 9 3 2
♣ A 10 5 3

♠ 10 9   ♠ 8 5 4
♡ A J 9   ♡ K 10 8 7
◇ K J 6 4   ◇ Q 10 8
♣ J 9 6 2   ♣ K 8 4

♠ A K Q J 6 2
♡ 6 4
◇ A 7 5
♣ Q 7

South is declarer at a contract of 3 Spades. West leads the deuce of Clubs, dummy plays low, and East wins with the King. Since there is no entry in the dummy to take a discard on the Ace of Clubs, it is apparent that the declarer will lose two Hearts, two Diamonds, and a Club, and be defeated one trick. His proper procedure is to hope that West led from the Jack of Clubs, and he should play the Queen under the King. This permits dummy's 10 of Clubs to be finessed, and the Ace can be used to discard a losing Diamond.

The holdup

The holdup play consists of refusing to take a trick early in the hand where it is desirable to take the trick later. It is most frequently employed in No Trump contracts, but it is occasionally used with profit at a suit declaration.

The purpose in holding up (that is, not taking a trick at once) is to run one of the opponents out of that suit. In other words, you plan to take the trick at such time that the partner of the opening leader will have no more of that suit to return to the leader. A suit may have been led against you at No Trump which you feel will eventually become established. If, however, the person with the established suit is unable to regain the lead later on in the play, he will not be a menace. You plan, therefore, to exhaust his partner of that suit and then hope that only the partner of the opening leader can obtain future leads.

Whether or not to hold up is the question which the declarer is frequently called upon to answer early in the play. Perhaps the best way to learn when to hold up is to learn the converse, that is—when not to hold up.

1. When it is apparent that the partner of the opening leader cannot be exhausted of that suit. In other words, when something in the hand tells you that the partner of the opening leader has more of that suit than you do.

2. When the hand is so managed that the leader's partner can never obtain the lead.

3. Frequently declarer must refuse to hold up, because there might be a greater menace in the hand in the form of a shift to some other suit by the leader's partner. For example:

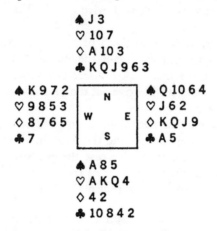

```
                ♠ J 3
                ♡ 10 7
                ◇ A 10 3
                ♣ K Q J 9 6 3

  ♠ K 9 7 2         N          ♠ Q 10 6 4
  ♡ 9 8 5 3                    ♡ J 6 2
  ◇ 8 7 6 5    W        E      ◇ K Q J 9
  ♣ 7              S           ♣ A 5

                ♠ A 8 5
                ♡ A K Q 4
                ◇ 4 2
                ♣ 10 8 4 2
```

South is the declarer at a contract of 3 No Trump. West leads the 2 of Spades, the Jack is played from the dummy, and East plays the Queen. Unless West is false-carding, he has only four Spades and there is no danger in the hand. If East is permitted to win the trick, he may shift to Diamonds, which would defeat the contract. The first trick, therefore, should be taken, since there is a greater danger in another suit.

4. When declarer can see that he is able to insure the contract by taking the trick, he should postpone the attempt for extra tricks until the contract is "in the bag."

5. When by not holding up you can develop an additional trick by lower cards in the suit which would lose if you hold up. For example:

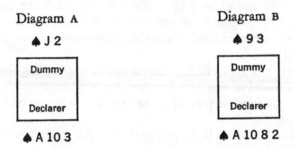

Diagram A   Diagram B

In DIAGRAM A, West leads the 5 of Spades. Dummy plays the 2, and East plays the Queen. It would be absurd for South to hold up, because he would then be able to take only one trick in the suit, whereas if he takes the Queen with the Ace he is assured of an additional trick, because the Jack will drive out the King and thus establish the 10.

In DIAGRAM B, West leads the 5 of Spades. Dummy plays the 3, East plays the Queen. Here again the holdup would be unsound, because by taking the first trick declarer is assured of another trick, inasmuch as the 8 and 9 will drive out the Jack and King, establishing the 10 as a winner.

The play known as the Bath Coup is simply a holdup when declarer has the Ace, Jack, and another and the King has been led by his left-hand opponent. In this particular case the purpose of the holdup is not so much to exhaust the partner of the opening leader as to force the opening leader to make a return that will be favorable to declarer.

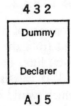

In this case, if West leads the King, assuming that there is no other suit that South is worried about, he should permit West to hold the trick, for if that suit is continued, declarer will win with both the Jack and the Ace.

If, however, the 10 is in either hand, it would be pointless to use the Bath Coup.

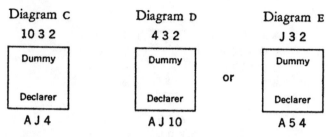

Diagram C	Diagram D	Diagram E
10 3 2	4 3 2	J 3 2
Dummy	Dummy	Dummy
Declarer	Declarer	Declarer
A J 4	A J 10	A 5 4

(with "or" between Diagrams D and E)

In DIAGRAMS C AND D, West leads the King. There is no sense to a holdup here, because if he takes the King, declarer is sure of two tricks.

In DIAGRAM E, the King should be taken, and a subsequent lead toward the Jack will produce another trick.

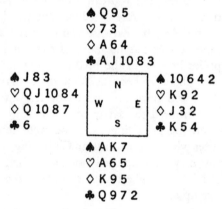

```
                    ♠ Q 9 5
                    ♡ 7 3
                    ◊ A 6 4
                    ♣ A J 10 8 3
    ♠ J 8 3                          ♠ 10 6 4 2
    ♡ Q J 10 8 4        N            ♡ K 9 2
    ◊ Q 10 8 7      W       E        ◊ J 3 2
    ♣ 6                S             ♣ K 5 4
                    ♠ A K 7
                    ♡ A 6 5
                    ◊ K 9 5
                    ♣ Q 9 7 2
```

You are South, the declarer; the contract is 3 No Trump. West leads the Queen of Hearts. East signals encouragingly with the 9. This is the suit which you fear may defeat your contract. If you should take the first trick and subsequently lose the lead, the opponents will cash four Heart tricks and the King of Clubs. You refuse, therefore, to take the Heart trick until the third round, hoping by this time that East will have no more Hearts. Now if the Club finesse loses to East, he will be unable to return his partner's suit. You are able, therefore, to take the rest of the tricks yourself. Notice if you had taken the first or second Heart, East would have had one left to return to his partner when he won with the King of Clubs.

Changing the holdings slightly, we have:

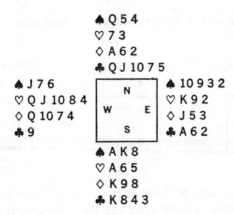

♠ Q 5 4
♡ 7 3
◇ A 6 2
♣ Q J 10 7 5

♠ J 7 6   ♠ 10 9 3 2
♡ Q J 10 8 4   ♡ K 9 2
◇ Q 10 7 4   ◇ J 5 3
♣ 9   ♣ A 6 2

♠ A K 8
♡ A 6 5
◇ K 9 8
♣ K 8 4 3

Here again the Queen of Hearts is opened, and the question is whether to win with the Ace immediately. You know that you will have to surrender the lead to the Ace of Clubs. If West happens to have that card, there is nothing you can do about it. He is bound to win four Heart tricks and the Ace of Clubs, but you have the hope that East may have the Ace. In that case you must not win the Heart trick until such time as East has no more of the suit to return. The same principle applies here as in the preceding example, except that there is no certainty about it, because West might have the Ace of Clubs, in which case you have not gained or lost anything. But if East has it, you have insured the safety of the hand.

In the example on the preceding page you were certain to fulfill the contract no matter who held the missing Club King.

The holdup play may be employed not only when you hold the Ace. It can be used in cases where your stopper is the King, Queen, and another. For example:

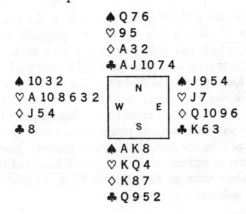

♠ Q 7 6
♡ 9 5
◇ A 3 2
♣ A J 10 7 4

♠ 10 3 2   ♠ J 9 5 4
♡ A 10 8 6 3 2   ♡ J 7
◇ J 5 4   ◇ Q 10 9 6
♣ 8   ♣ K 6 3

♠ A K 8
♡ K Q 4
◇ K 8 7
♣ Q 9 5 2

You are South, declarer at a contract of 3 No Trump. West leads the 6 of Hearts, East plays the Jack. Do you win the first trick?

In order to fulfill the contract, you must bring in the Club suit. If the Club finesse succeeds, there is nothing to worry about, but if it loses, there is danger that the Hearts will be run against you. However, West may have six Hearts, in which case East will have only two. If you refuse to take the first trick, East will return the suit, but that will exhaust his supply of Hearts. Now when he wins the Club finesse he cannot return the suit. If it turns out that West has the King of Clubs, you will still make eleven tricks.

For purposes of holding up, when there is a future lead that you fear by your right-hand opponent, the K Q 4 should be regarded in the same manner as the A 3 2. Changing the holdings slightly:

```
        ♠ Q 9 5
        ♡ 8 7
        ◇ A 7 6
        ♣ Q J 10 4 3

        ┌──────────┐
        │  Dummy   │
        │          │
        │ Declarer │
        └──────────┘

        ♠ A K 7
        ♡ K Q 5
        ◇ K 9 8
        ♣ K 8 7 2
```

Here again the 6 of Hearts is led, and East plays the Jack. Should you win the trick or should you hold up? This is more or less of a guess and depends upon who you believe holds the Ace of Clubs. If East holds that card, it is wise to hold up, so that when he obtains the lead he may not have any more Hearts. If, however, West has the Ace of Clubs, it would be suicide to hold up. By merely giving him the Ace of Clubs your contract is assured, if you take the first Heart trick, because West will be unable to continue with Hearts. Which procedure to adopt will depend on clues derived from the bidding.

It has been poinetd out that if the declarer holds the K J 4, and East in third hand plays the Queen to the opening lead, the same principle applies as though the declarer had the K Q 4 or the A 3 2. In other words, if the holdup would have been proper with the Ace, it is proper with the holding just described.

The fact that your stoppers (King Queen), instead of being both

in your hand, are divided between your hand and the dummy does not
alter the principle of play.

```
                    Q 5
              ┌──────────────┐
              │   Dummy      │
              │              │
              │   Declarer   │
              └──────────────┘
                    K 8 6
```

With this holding, if the holdup is indicated, then you should play
low from both hands in order to be sure not to win the first trick.
For example:

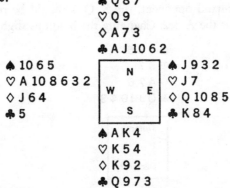

```
                    ♠ Q 8 7
                    ♡ Q 9
                    ◊ A 7 3
                    ♣ A J 10 6 2
♠ 10 6 5         ┌──────────┐    ♠ J 9 3 2
♡ A 10 8 6 3 2   │    N     │    ♡ J 7
◊ J 6 4          │  W     E │    ◊ Q 10 8 5
♣ 5              │    S     │    ♣ K 8 4
                 └──────────┘
                    ♠ A K 4
                    ♡ K 5 4
                    ◊ K 9 2
                    ♣ Q 9 7 3
```

West leads the 6 of Hearts. Since the Club finesse must be taken
into East, we desire to exhaust him of Hearts. The proper play, therefore, is to refuse the first trick. If the Queen is played from dummy,
you cannot help winning the trick. (East should take the precaution
to unblock with the Jack.) Therefore you should play low from both
hands.

A somewhat unusual type of holdup is demonstrated here:

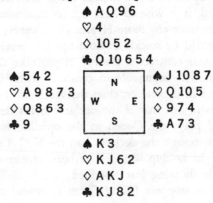

```
                    ♠ A Q 9 6
                    ♡ 4
                    ◊ 10 5 2
                    ♣ Q 10 6 5 4
♠ 5 4 2          ┌──────────┐    ♠ J 10 8 7
♡ A 9 8 7 3      │    N     │    ♡ Q 10 5
◊ Q 8 6 3        │  W     E │    ◊ 9 7 4
♣ 9              │    S     │    ♣ A 7 3
                 └──────────┘
                    ♠ K 3
                    ♡ K J 6 2
                    ◊ A K J
                    ♣ K J 8 2
```

South was the declarer at 3 No Trump, with no adverse bidding. West opened with the 7 of Hearts. East played the Queen. South ducked, and when the 10 of Hearts was continued he ducked again. (If South had played the Jack, West would have ducked, permitting partner to retain the Heart for a "come-through.") A third Heart was led, and this one West took and cleared the suit. When East won with the Ace of Clubs, he was unable to return a Heart. The question might occur to you, what if West held the Ace of Clubs? Then declarer's strategy would have been wrong. But South reasoned that if West had the Ace of Clubs in addition to the Heart suit headed by the Ace, he would have overcalled the opening bid of 1 Club.

Holdup with double stopper

Thus far we have been considering holdups on the opening lead at No Trump when you have only one stopper in the suit led. Occasionally you will have two stoppers, such as the Ace and King, and still the proper procedure will be not to take the first trick. How can you recognize when you hold up with two stoppers in the adversaries' suit? The answer is very simple. When in order to build up your nine tricks you must relinquish the lead twice, it is generally good strategy not to take the first trick, even though you have two stoppers in the suit. This is also with the proviso that there is not some other suit that you fear will be attacked in the meantime.

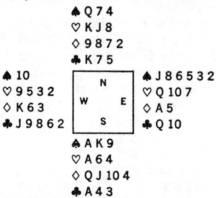

```
                    ♠ Q 7 4
                    ♡ K J 8
                    ◊ 9 8 7 2
                    ♣ K 7 5
    ♠ 10                              ♠ J 8 6 5 3 2
    ♡ 9 5 3 2         N              ♡ Q 10 7
    ◊ K 6 3       W       E          ◊ A 5
    ♣ J 9 8 6 2      S              ♣ Q 10
                    ♠ A K 9
                    ♡ A 6 4
                    ◊ Q J 10 4
                    ♣ A 4 3
```

You are South, at a contract of 3 No Trump. West leads the 6 of Clubs, East plays the Queen. You should allow the Queen to hold. The suit will be continued. Then the Ace of Diamonds is driven out and East has no Clubs to return. If West wins the first Diamond trick, his Clubs will become harmless, because he will have no entry to use them. Observe that if you hold up on the second lead of Clubs instead of the first, you cannot make the hand. You lead a Diamond, which East wins with the Ace and returns the 10 of Clubs. West overtakes with the Jack and continues the suit. Now when he obtains the lead with the King of Diamonds his Clubs are established. Notice here you have a double stopper in the suit led and two important cards to drive out. In such cases a holdup on the first round with two stoppers is indicated.

Another example of holding up with a double stopper which at first blush would appear to contradict some advice previously given is the following:

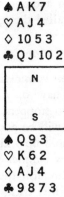

♠ A K 7
♡ A J 4
◇ 10 5 3
♣ Q J 10 2

♠ Q 9 3
♡ K 6 2
◇ A J 4
♣ 9 8 7 3

South is playing 3 No Trump, after East overcalled in Diamonds. West leads the 9 of Diamonds, and East plays the Queen. What should South do?

Since East is marked with both the King and Queen he will have two Diamond tricks even if he refuses this trick. Notice that two important cards must be driven out, the Ace and King of Clubs. If East has them both, the hand cannot be made, but if West has one of them, it is important to hold up even with a double stopper.

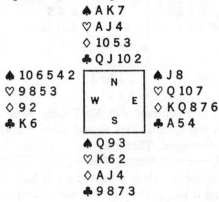

♠ A K 7
♡ A J 4
◇ 10 5 3
♣ Q J 10 2

♠ 10 6 5 4 2
♡ 9 8 5 3
◇ 9 2
♣ K 6

♠ J 8
♡ Q 10 7
◇ K Q 8 7 6
♣ A 5 4

♠ Q 9 3
♡ K 6 2
◇ A J 4
♣ 9 8 7 3

Note if declarer takes the first trick and leads a Club, West will win with the King and return a Diamond. East will clear the suit while he still retains the Ace of Clubs. If declarer refuses the first Diamond trick, the suit will be continued and won with the Jack. Now when West wins with the King of Clubs he has no Diamond to return. It is interesting to note that East could have defeated the contract if he had played the 8 of Diamonds instead of the Queen to the first trick.

Holdup at suit play

Thus far we have been discussing the holdup as it applies to No Trump play. It is applicable as well with a suit as trumps.

South has been pushed to a contract of 5 Spades by his nonvulnerable opponents, West having overcalled with 2 Clubs and East having bid Diamonds. The King of Clubs is led. What should declarer do?

♠ A J 6 5
♡ A Q 9 2
◊ A 8
♣ 7 4 3

```
┌─────────┐
│    N    │
│         │
│    S    │
└─────────┘
```

♠ K Q 10 9 8 2
♡ J 10 4
◊ 3
♣ A 6 2

He should refuse to take it, for if East happens to have the King of Hearts he will then have no Clubs to return to partner, assuming that West has five Clubs. (If West has six Clubs, the play will not succeed unless the Heart finesse wins.) The complete hand:

♠ A J 6 5
♡ A Q 9 2
◊ A 8
♣ 7 4 3

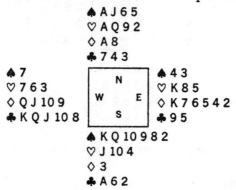

♠ 7   ♠ 4 3
♡ 7 6 3   ♡ K 8 5
◊ Q J 10 9   ◊ K 7 6 5 4 2
♣ K Q J 10 8   ♣ 9 5

♠ K Q 10 9 8 2
♡ J 10 4
◊ 3
♣ A 6 2

South is the declarer at a contract of 4 Hearts. West leads the 6 of Spades, and East plays the King. What should declarer do?

♠ 10 9 2
♡ Q 10 2
◇ K 5
♣ A Q 10 9 4

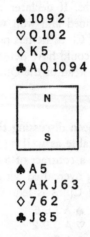

♠ A 5
♡ A K J 6 3
◇ 7 6 2
♣ J 8 5

The trick should be refused. The danger in the hand lies in West subsequently obtaining the lead and coming through the King of Diamonds. The only card that West could possibly use as an entry is the Queen of Spades, and if the first trick is refused, the Queen of Spades is killed as an entry.

The complete holding is as follows:

♠ 10 9 2
♡ Q 10 2
◇ K 5
♣ A Q 10 9 4

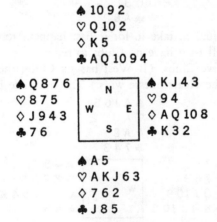

♠ Q 8 7 6   ♠ K J 4 3
♡ 8 7 5   ♡ 9 4
◇ J 9 4 3   ◇ A Q 10 8
♣ 7 6   ♣ K 3 2

♠ A 5
♡ A K J 6 3
◇ 7 6 2
♣ J 8 5

The holdup at suit play is sometimes employed to avoid an adverse ruff.

An interesting illustration is the following:

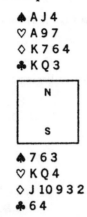

```
                        ♠ A J 4
                        ♡ A 9 7
                        ◇ K 7 6 4
                        ♣ K Q 3

                        ┌─────────┐
                        │    N    │
                        │         │
                        │    S    │
                        └─────────┘

                        ♠ 7 6 3
                        ♡ K Q 4
                        ◇ J 10 9 3 2
                        ♣ 6 4
```

The bidding has been as follows:

EAST	SOUTH	WEST	NORTH
1 Club	Pass	1 Spade	Double
Pass	2 Diamonds	2 Hearts	3 Diamonds
Pass	Pass	Pass	

West leads the 8 of Clubs, and the Queen goes to the Ace. The 10 of Spades is returned by East, and West plays the Queen. What should dummy play? The answer is, the dummy should duck. West probably has five Spades, and East, therefore, has a doubleton. East surely has the Ace of trumps, and he must be exhausted of Spades if a ruff is to be avoided. When the Queen of Spades holds, a Spade will be returned and the Jack will win. Now the South hand is entered and the Diamond finesse taken to East. He will win with the Queen but will be unable to put partner back to obtain a ruff. The complete hand is as follows:

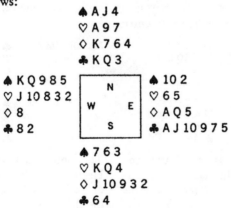

```
                        ♠ A J 4
                        ♡ A 9 7
                        ◇ K 7 6 4
                        ♣ K Q 3

    ♠ K Q 9 8 5      ┌─────────┐      ♠ 10 2
    ♡ J 10 8 3 2     │    N    │      ♡ 6 5
    ◇ 8              │  W   E  │      ◇ A Q 5
    ♣ 8 2            │    S    │      ♣ A J 10 9 7 5
                     └─────────┘
                        ♠ 7 6 3
                        ♡ K Q 4
                        ◇ J 10 9 3 2
                        ♣ 6 4
```

QUIZ ON SAFETY PLAYS, ENTRIES AND HOLDUPS

You are South, the declarer, at No Trump. You have entries in both hands. What is the safest play to limit yourself to one loser with the following combinations?

1. DUMMY	Q 7 6 4	2. DUMMY	K 4 3
DECLARER	A 10 9 5 3 2	DECLARER	A J 6 5

3. DUMMY	A J 5	4. DUMMY	A 9
DECLARER	K 9 4 3 2	DECLARER	K 10 5 4 3

5. DUMMY	A 10 5 2	6. DUMMY	J 10 5
DECLARER	Q 9 3	DECLARER	A K 8 4 2

7. DUMMY	A J 9 6 4 2	8. DUMMY	Q 7 5 2
DECLARER	7 5 3	DECLARER	K J 8 4 3

In the following hands you are South, the declarer. Plan the safest line of play to assure your contract.

9. DUMMY	♠ 7 4 2	10. DUMMY	♠ 8 6
	♡ A K 5		♡ A
	◇ J 7 5 4		◇ A K Q 10 9 5
	♣ 7 5 3		♣ 9 7 5 4
DECLARER	♠ A K Q J	DECLARER	♠ A Q 5 4 3
	♡ 10 6		♡ K 8 7 3
	◇ A K 8 3 2		◇ 6 3
	♣ A K		♣ A Q

The contract is 6 No Trump and West leads the Queen of Hearts.

The contract is 3 No Trump and West leads the 2 of Hearts.

In the following hands you are South, the declarer. Plan the play with particular reference to entries.

11. DUMMY	♠ A 8 5 4 3	12. DUMMY	♠ Q 5
	♡ K 10 2		♡ Q 4
	◇ A 7		◇ Q 4 2
	♣ 7 4 2		♣ A K Q 6 3 2
DECLARER	♠ 7 2	DECLARER	♠ A J 7 3 2
	♡ A Q J 6 4 3		♡ A K
	◇ 6 3		◇ A 10 7 6 5
	♣ A 8 3		♣ 4

The contract is 4 Hearts and West leads the Queen of Diamonds, which you take with the Ace.

The contract is 3 No Trump and a Heart is led. You cash the A K Q of Clubs and West shows out on the third round.

13. DUMMY   ♠ K Q 10
                 ♡ 7 4
                 ◇ 7 6 3
                 ♣ K J 9 8 7

DECLARER ♠ A
                 ♡ A K 5 2
                 ◇ Q J 10 9 4 2
                 ♣ Q 10

The contract is 3 No Trump and a low Spade is led.

14. DUMMY   ♠ A K 4 3
                 ♡ 10 3
                 ◇ 9 8 6 5
                 ♣ A 6 5

DECLARER ♠ 8 6
                 ♡ K 7 5
                 ◇ A K Q 4 3
                 ♣ J 9 7

The contract is 3 No Trump and West leads the 6 of Hearts. East wins with the Ace and returns the 9.

ANSWERS TO QUIZ ON SAFETY PLAYS, ENTRIES AND HOLDUPS

1.
Lead low from the dummy hand. This safety play is certain to work. If second hand plays low, you finesse the 10 in order to guard against K J x. If second hand is void, you go up with the Ace.

2.
Cash the A K, then lead towards the Jack. This safety play is not certain to succeed, but it is the best you can do. It is better than finessing the Jack, because it saves a trick whenever the doubleton Queen lies over the Jack.

3.
Cash the ace, enter your hand in another suit, and lead towards the Jack. By this means you ensure losing only one trick against any 4–1 division of the outstanding cards. If East, for example, holds Q 10 x x, you hold him to one trick, because after the Jack has lost to the Queen you will be able to enter dummy and finesse the 9.

4.
Lead low from your hand and finesse the 9. This saves a trick whenever West holds Q x or J x, for his honor card will be caught when the Ace is played in the second round.

5.
Lead low from the dummy hand, intending to finesse the 9. If East puts up the King, you lead again from the dummy hand on the next round and finesse the 9. You have better than a 50% chance of achieving your object of losing only one trick.

6.
Lead low towards the Jack. This is the only sure way to make four tricks. Even if one defender has all five outstanding cards, he makes only the Queen. You cannot afford to play the Ace first.

7.
Finesse the 9. There is an urge to lay down the Ace, but it is sounder to take the finesse. If it loses to the King or Queen, you finesse the Jack on the next round.

8.
Play the Queen first. If West holds all the missing cards, there is no way you can hold him to one trick, but if East has them, you expose him to repeated finesses against the 10 9 by this method of play.

9.
You need four tricks in Diamonds. The sure line is to win the Heart

lead in dummy and play a low Diamond. If East follows with the 6, you finesse the 8! If West wins this trick, the remaining Diamonds are good. If West shows out, the safety play will have prevented East from winning two Diamond tricks.

10.

You need only five tricks in Diamonds, but the Heart opening lead has removed an entry. If you cash the A K Q of Diamonds, you risk defeat when a defender holds four to the Jack. The safety play is to lead the 10 of Diamonds at trick two. If this loses to the Jack, the remaining Diamond in your hand will be an entry to dummy.

11.

Declarer has only nine tricks and must aim to make good the deficit by establishing a long Spade in dummy. As dummy is short on entries, it is vital to start with a low Spade from each hand. If the defenders cash a Diamond and return a trump, declarer wins in his own hands, leads a Spade to the Ace, and ruffs a Spade with a high trump. If the Spades are 4–2, declarer crosses to dummy with a trump, ruffs another Spade, and returns to dummy with a third trump to cash the established Spade.

12.

Declarer should not be constrained to abandon the Clubs merely because East has a stopper in the suit. The cast-iron play is to lead a fourth round of Clubs, discarding the remaining Heart from the closed hand! Any return from East will then provide an entry to dummy's long Clubs.

13.

This hand is laydown only if played with exact timing. A high Diamond must be led initially. If it loses and the defenders shift to Hearts, declarer next plays the Queen of Clubs, overtaking with the King. If the Ace of Clubs is released, declarer has four Clubs, three Spades, and two Hearts. If the Ace of Clubs is held up, declarer takes one of dummy's Spade tricks and reverts to Diamonds. Declarer can be defeated if he does not follow this precise sequence of play.

14.

Careless play costs the contract if Diamonds are 3–1. Suppose declarer wins the second Heart and plays the A K Q of Diamonds: if the Diamonds are 3–1, he is blocked in dummy on the fourth round, and has no reentry to his hand. To prevent this, declarer holds up on the second round of Hearts. He wins any continuation, discards a Diamond from dummy on the King of Hearts, thus clearing the blockage, and has nine tricks unless the Diamonds are 4–0.

Goren's New Bridge Complete **3**

defensive play

18.

Opening leads

THE TERM "LEAD" refers to the first card played at each trick, whether by defense or declarer. In this chapter, however, we shall be concerned only with the defensive lead to trick one. In other words, the opening lead.

There are a number of bromides current advocating such ideas as "Never lead away from a King," or "Never lead away from an Ace," "Always lead the highest of your partner's suit," et cetera. Some of these have a sound basis. Others have none. However, this general truth should be borne in mind by the reader: that the selection of the opening lead is not an exact science. There is great room for the exercise of the imagination, and on a given hand a number of experts might disagree in the choice of an opening lead.

Only general advice can be given, though indeed there are certain principles which are fundamental and from which deviation should not be made.

In selecting opening leads, it is advisable to get into the habit of classifying various hands. A lead may be proper against a No Trump contract which, with the same hand, would be improper against a suit contract. You must ask yourself, "Am I leading against a part score, a game, or a slam contract? Has my partner bid? Has my partner suggested a lead to me? Will the opponents probably make this hand or will they go down?"

It is improper, as so many players are in the habit of doing, to submit a hand to an expert and ask what is the correct opening lead. That question cannot be answered unless you also provide Mr. Expert with the complete bidding. Incidentally, a knowledge of the personal habits of the players will frequently influence the choice of the lead. Where your right-hand opponent is notorious for opening the bidding with suits that he does not have, many times serious consideration should be given to the lead of that suit, even though it might not otherwise be the first choice.

The choice of the lead should frequently depend upon the manner in which the opponents have reached their contract. If the bidding has progressed smoothly and the chances of defeating the contract appear to be remote, desperate measures are in order. If the opponents appear to have staggered in the bidding and you feel that the prospects of defeating the contract are good, then conservatism is the best policy, and you ought to play safe.

Leads at No Trump

We shall take up those hands where no specific information has been obtained from the bidding. For example: 1 No Trump, 2 No Trump, 3 No Trump.

Against No Trump contracts it is essential to develop tricks out of small cards.

Against a suit contract, if you hold A Q 7 4 3, you would hardly expect to take more than the Ace and the Queen. But at No Trump there is a very good chance that you will take tricks with the small cards. Therefore your longest suit should usually be selected as the opening lead.

It is not always a privilege to have the opening lead. Sometimes it is a hardship. If you hold an honor which is not in sequence with another honor, it is usually a disadvantage to lead, because in the majority of cases it will enable the declarer to make an additional trick. For example:

```
                    A 10 7
                  ┌───────┐
                  │   N   │
        J 84      │ W   E │   Q 5 3
                  │   S   │
                  └───────┘
                    K 9 6 2
```

Notice that if you are either East or West, and lead this suit, North and South will take all the tricks. If, however, either North or South leads the suit, East and West cannot be prevented from taking a trick, which illustrates the point that unless you hold a sequence it is disadvantageous to start a suit.

One of the outstanding weaknesses of the ordinary player is a tendency to lead new suits each time he obtains the lead. It has been estimated that every time the defense leads a new suit they average to lose a half trick, so that it is generally a good policy to stick to the suit you open unless you have a good reason for shifting. For it is better, with Hamlet, to "bear those ills we have than fly to others that we know not of."

The most desirable lead is from the top of a complete sequence.

♠ 9 6 4   ♡ 7 3   ♢ J 10 9 8   ♣ K J 5 2

In this hand the Jack of Diamonds is a much more desirable lead than the 2 of Clubs, because it is certain not to lose a trick regardless of the adverse holding; whereas the Club lead might permit declarer to win a trick with the Queen, which he might not otherwise have been able to do. Where you have a choice between two suits of exactly the same texture, the bidding having given you no information, it is the general practice to lead the major suit rather than the minor, the theory being that the opponents will sometimes conceal a long minor suit but they are less likely to conceal a long major suit.

If, however, the choice lies between a major and minor and the texture of the minor suit holding is better, it should be given preference. For example:

♠ Q 6 3 2   ♡ 9 6 3   ♢ 8 2   ♣ Q 10 8 3

I would recommend a Club lead rather than a Spade, because the Club holding is more nearly a sequence. Notice that if your partner holds only the Jack of Clubs, you have not lost a trick. In fact, you are well on your way to develop two tricks in the suit. If, however, you lead a Spade and again find your partner with the Jack, you are still not certain to build up a trick unless your partner also has the 10.

♠ Q 9 6 5   ♡ 10 9 8 5   ♢ 7 3   ♣ 8 5 3

If I were forced to choose my opening lead between the Spade and the Heart, I would select the Heart, because it is less likely to cost a trick. Sometimes you have a choice between two suits. One is longer, the other is more solid. It is sometimes difficult to select the proper lead. Usually, however, quality should take precedence over quantity. For example:

♠ Q J 10 9   ♡ 8 3   ♢ Q 7 4 3 2   ♣ 6 3

The Queen of Spades is the proper lead. The Spade lead cannot lose a trick, whereas the Diamond lead may permit declarer to win with the Jack, which he might not otherwise have been able to do.

The statement "leads from a tenace should be avoided" is frequently heard. This is an unsound generalization. Leads from four-card suits containing a tenace are not attractive, but when your suit contains five or more cards the objection does not exist.

The lead from A Q 6 2 is very undesirable, but the lead from

A Q 6 4 2 is extremely desirable, for this reason: in the first case you are almost sure to give up a trick to declarer, and yet you will gain only one additional trick if you succeed in making good your small card. Whereas in the second case you are giving up the same trick with the very good expectancy of gaining two tricks with the small cards. After you have given up a trick, if your partner can gain the lead and come through, the contract of 3 No Trump will almost certainly be defeated, because you will probably win four tricks in your suit in addition to your partner's entry trick. Notice how well this principle operates on the following hand:

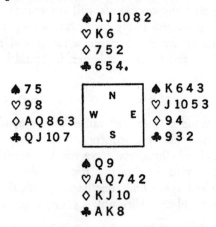

```
                    ♠ A J 10 8 2
                    ♡ K 6
                    ◇ 7 5 2
                    ♣ 6 5 4.

    ♠ 7 5           ┌─────────┐         ♠ K 6 4 3
    ♡ 9 8           │    N    │         ♡ J 10 5 3
    ◇ A Q 8 6 3     │ W     E │         ◇ 9 4
    ♣ Q J 10 7      │    S    │         ♣ 9 3 2
                    └─────────┘
                    ♠ Q 9
                    ♡ A Q 7 4 2
                    ◇ K J 10
                    ♣ A K 8
```

If West should open the Queen of Clubs, declarer will win and take the Spade finesse, which loses to East. Now a Diamond shift comes too late, and the defense can take only two Diamonds and the King of Spades. But if the 6 of Diamonds is opened, declarer is forced to win with the 10. Now when he takes the Spade finesse and East gets in, a Diamond return defeats the contract.

Similarly, holding K J 4 3, the suit does not provide a desirable lead, but the holding of K J 4 3 2 is considerably more attractive. The following combinations are all regarded as undesirable holdings from which to lead. Lest the reader forget, he should be reminded as he goes along that these leads are against No Trump contracts.

J 8 6 4   K 7 4 3   Q 9 4 2   K Q 7 3   K J 6 3   A Q 8 2

Where you have several high cards for entries your longest suit invariably should be selected. For example:

♠ A 8 4 3   ♡ 7 5   ◇ Q 7 6 4 2   ♣ A 5

The proper lead is the 4 of Diamonds, because even though you lose a trick at the opening, you hope to build up several tricks in that suit while you still have two Aces as entry cards.

♠ Q 8   ♡ K J 5 3   ◊ 10 4   ♣ J 8 5 3 2

You have a choice between a weak five-card minor and a strong four-card major. The choice should be in favor of the Club, because there is a chance to develop more tricks with this suit if the suit breaks well for your side. Furthermore, a four-card suit headed by a tenace is not an attractive lead even though it be a major suit. When you have a choice between two suits of the same length, it is not always easy to select the proper lead. For example:

♠ 7 4   ♡ 8   ◊ A 9 6 4 3   ♣ Q 7 5 3 2

Many players prefer to lead a Club from this holding rather than a Diamond, on the theory that the Ace of Diamonds may prove to be an entry after the Clubs are established.

Leading from bad hands

It is a sound policy not to waste efforts on a hopeless hand. That does not mean that you should not pay attention to the defense because you have no values. It simply means that if you have no trick-taking possibilities don't bother to lead your long suit. For example:

♠ 10 9 4   ♡ 10 8 5 4 2   ◊ 7 3   ♣ 5 3 2

Your hand, to all intents and purposes, is dead. It is poor policy to lead the fourth best Heart. Your side's only trick-taking possibilities are in your partner's hand. The only thing you can do, therefore, is to give him a fairly decent start in the race to take tricks. Your best bet is the 10 of Spades, hoping (somewhat against hope) that you may strike your partner's best suit. This is frequently called the short-suit lead. Some players would lead a Diamond because that is the shortest suit. This is definitely unsound. You select the suit not because it is short but almost in spite of the fact that it is. In choosing beween a two- and a three-card suit you should generally select the three-card suit, particularly when, as in this case, you hold the 10 and the 9, which may be helpful cards to promote partner's holding.

Objection to the lead of the fourth best Heart is that such a lead suggests to your partner that you are trying to build up that suit and obviously invites him to continue it. You do not wish to induce your partner to exert any effort in building up the Heart suit. If, by chance, the Hearts do become established, you will have no means of getting in to cash them. It surely does not pay to deposit money with a bank whose doors are closed.

The short-suit lead

We have just observed the use of the short-suit lead on hopeless hands. That type of lead is also made on hands where you fear to lead anything else because you have great hopes of taking tricks. For example:

♠ K 10 8   ♡ J 4 3 2   ◊ A Q 10 4   ♣ 10 9

This presents no desirable opening lead. I regard the Diamond as the most undesirable. If you adopt waiting tactics, the declarer will probably never be able to win a trick in that suit. If you lead the Diamond, he will almost surely take at least one trick. The next in order of undesirability is the Spade. In the first place, your partner will probably misread the lead of the 8; second, you may very easily sacrifice a trick by that lead. The Heart lead, therefore, appears to be the logical one. However, experience has shown that a lead from the Jack and three small cards is, in the long run, not very profitable. From holdings such as those in Spades, Hearts, and Diamonds, the best results are obtained by waiting. By the process of elimination, therefore, we arrive at the Club lead, and the 10 of Clubs should be selected. This is not a case, as in the previous example, where you hope to do anything for partner, but it is the one lead which will probably not lose a trick, and your prospects of defeating the contract are so good that you do not choose to give the declarer even the slightest advantage. If the Heart holding included the 10 of Hearts as well as the Jack, I would recommend the lead of that suit, because if partner has even so much as the 9 of Hearts, not to mention the Queen, the lead will not cost a trick. Obviously, if an additional Diamond were held, making five in all, a Diamond would be the best lead in the hand.

The card to lead

When you have determined the proper suit to lead, the selection of the proper card becomes important. Where you have a complete sequence (a complete sequence is considered three cards next to each other, such as the K Q J, Q J 10, J 10 9), you always lead the top card. A two-card sequence is not treated as such for our purposes. In other words, K Q 3 2, Q J 3 2, J 10 3 2 are not considered complete sequences, and the proper card is the fourth from the top.

There are certain combinations which, though not a complete sequence, are treated as such for the purpose of the opening lead. For example: K Q 10 2, Q J 9 2, J 10 8 2. You will notice that these are within a card of being a complete sequence. The proper leads are the King, the Queen, and the Jack, respectively. The rule is that where the third card is only one removed from the perfect sequence it may be promoted, so that the K Q 10 equals K Q J; Q J 9 equals Q J 10; and J 10 8 equals J 10 9. See Table of Leads for proper card to lead, page 440.

When your partner has made a bid against No Trump declaration

Naturally you do not always lead the suit your partner has bid, though in the long run it is best to do so.

Assuming that you are about to lead your partner's suit, it is important to select the proper card. There is a false impression that you are obliged to lead the highest card of the suit your partner has bid. This is a very unsound and illogical bromide. As a matter of fact, experienced players very rarely lead the highest of partner's suit. In fact, the only time it is correct to do so is when you have only two cards of that suit, or three unimportant cards, or where you have a holding containing two honors in sequence. In all other cases the low card is the correct lead.[1]

Assuming that you are about to lead your partner's suit from any of the following combinations, the underlined card is the proper lead at No Trump:

A 2	K 2	Q 2	9 2	9 8 2
6̲ 5 4	A̅ 6 2	K̅ 6 2	Q̅ 6 2	1̅0 6 2
K̅ 6 3 2	Q 6 3̲ 2	J 6 3̲ 2	9 6 3̲ 2	J 6 2̅
9 6 4 3̲ 2	Q J 6̲ 2̅	K Q 6̲ 2̅	J 10 6̲ 2	5 4 3̅ 2

In other words, where you have four or more of your partner's suit, you lead the fourth from the top. Where you have three of

---

[1] When leading partner's suit, many players prefer to lead low from three small. This is purely a partnership matter.

your partner's suit headed by an honor, you lead the lowest. This lead has two purposes. First, to show the number of cards you hold in the suit, so that your partner can read the number of cards that are out against him; second, the more important, when you have a high card it is better not to waste it on the opening lead, but to keep it behind the declarer in order to kill one of his important cards. In other words, an Ace will capture declarer's King, a King will capture his Queen, a Queen will capture his Jack, and the Jack will take his 10. Note also that when you have a sequence of high honors in your partner's suit, you lead the top of the sequence, regardless of the number of cards held.

Observe the following very usual holding:

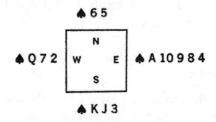

♠ 6 5

♠ Q 7 2   N   ♠ A 10 9 8 4
          W   E
            S

♠ K J 3

East has bid Spades and South No Trump, expecting to take two Spade tricks. If West leads the Queen, South will win two tricks. The lead of the 2 of Spades enables the defense to capture South's Jack.

Whether to lead partner's suit or your own

When you are in doubt whether to lead your partner's suit or your own, resolve all doubts in favor of your partner's suit for two reasons:

1. The best results are usually obtained by having a suit led up to rather than having a suit led away from.

2. The psychology is all in favor of leading partner's suit. If it should develop that your failure to lead his suit permitted the opponents to fulfill their contract, you are bound to have a disgruntled partner on your hands. Whereas if the lead of your partner's suit turns out to be less successful than your own, you will rarely hear your partner complain.

In this department of the game many close questions will arise, and a number of factors must be taken into consideration. Did your partner open the bidding with that suit, or did he overcall? Strangely enough, there is a greater inducement to lead partner's suit when he overcalled, for the reason that the opening bid shows a generally strong hand though the suit itself may be very weak. Whereas the overcall, while it may not denote a generally strong hand, almost always should be based upon a strong suit. Furthermore, more often than not, the purpose of the overcall is to induce partner to lead that suit. Therefore your partner's suggestion should not lightly be disregarded. In order to do so, you should have a very good excuse.

You should be guided, too, by the number of tricks for which your partner contracted when he mentioned his suit. If he named it at a high level, you can be certain that he has a very fine suit. If he bid the suit more than once, you can depend upon its being very strong, and you may reason that the opponents have contracted for game with only one stopper in his suit.

We come to the consideration of what constitutes a good excuse for not leading partner's suit. Holding a singleton is usually a good excuse, provided you have some hope of establishing tricks in your own hand. Even a singleton of partner's suit should be led if your hand is entirely hopeless. For example:

♠ 10   ♡ 8 6 4 3   ◇ 9 6 4 2   ♣ 7 4 3 2

Your partner has bid Spades. Do not lead one of your three worthless suits. Lead the 10 of Spades. For example:

♠ 8   ♡ Q J 10 7 3   ◇ 9 5 3 2   ♣ 7 6 2

Partner has bid Spades. Lead the Queen of Hearts, a perfectly safe lead which has some remote hope if partner has strength in Hearts.

Holding two small cards of your partner's suit, you have a slight excuse for not leading the suit. However, any five-card suit does not constitute that slight excuse; for example:

♠ 6 2   ♡ 9 7 3   ◇ J 8 6 4 2   ♣ 7 5 2

Partner has bid Spades. The Diamond lead is not to be considered. Lead the 6 of Spades.

Another consideration is, did the opponents bid No Trump immediately over your partner's bid, or did they contract for No Trump later and rather reluctantly?

Suppose you held the following hand:

♠ Q 6 2   ♡ Q J 7 4 3   ◇ 9 3 2   ♣ 8 6

Partner has bid Spades. Your supporting cards in Spades makes the lead of that suit obligatory. Do not experiment with the Hearts,

However, suppose you held this hand:

♠ Q 6 2   ♡ K Q J 7 3   ◇ 9 4 2   ♣ 7 5

Partner has bid Spades. The Heart suit, being probably within one trick of establishment, offers a good excuse for not leading partner's suit. You will very likely be permitted to hold the trick, and you may then decide whether to continue the Heart suit or now shift to partner's suit.

Leading the opponent's suit

Where your best suit contains a complete sequence it should be led though the opponents have bid it. For example:

♠ Q J 10 9 4   ♡ Q 10 7 3   ◇ 8 4   ♣ 4 3

You should lead the Queen of Spades even though that suit has been bid by your right-hand opponent. If, however, your holding is:

♠ K J 8 3 2   ♡ Q J 9 3   ◇ 6 4   ♣ 7 5

you have an entirely different situation. The lead of a Spade will probably be into declarer's Ace Queen, thus presenting him with a trick. In this case the Queen of Hearts is the proper lead.

Here knowledge of declarer's habits is important. Some players have a flair for bidding suits which they do not really have, hoping to deter their opponents from leading that suit in a subsequent No Trump contract. Against such players it frequently pays to take a chance and lead that suit if it appears to be your best. Particularly is this true if your holding is Clubs or sometimes Diamonds. Modern bidders very frequently open the bidding with a Club when they do not really have that suit. Therefore, when a Club lead is normal from your hand, as a general rule, you should not refrain from leading it simply because the suit has been bid by your right-hand opponent. For example:

♠ K 9 2   ♡ 8 6   ◇ A 4 3   ♣ K J 9 4 3

If the bidding is opened on my right with a Club and declarer subsequently plays No Trump, I would open the 4 of Clubs. If partner has the Queen of the suit, it will be established at once. If he has the 10, there is a good chance to build up the suit while I still have two likely entries.

Leads against No Trump when partner has doubled the final contract*

A double of a No Trump contract made by a player who does not have the opening lead carries certain inferences.

A. If the doubler has bid a suit, the leader must absolutely lead that suit even if he has but a singleton and has a good suit of his own. For example:

♠ 7   ♡ K Q J 8 5   ◊ 7 3 2   ♣ 8 6 4 3

Your partner has bid Spades and subsequently doubled 3 No Trump. You must lead the 7 of Spades, not the King of Hearts. Partner has stated, "If you lead Spades, I will defeat contract."

B. If the opening leader has bid a suit, partner's double requests him to lead that suit. For example:

♠ K J 8 6 3   ♡ K Q J 3   ◊ A 5   ♣ 6 5

You have bid Spades. Partner, who has not bid, doubles the final contract of 3 No Trump. Without the double your best lead would be the King of Hearts, but partner's double is based on the belief that you will lead Spades. Don't disappoint him.

Here is an illustration from "real life":

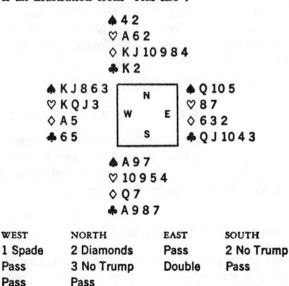

♠ 4 2
♡ A 6 2
◊ K J 10 9 8 4
♣ K 2

♠ K J 8 6 3	♠ Q 10 5
♡ K Q J 3	♡ 8 7
◊ A 5	◊ 6 3 2
♣ 6 5	♣ Q J 10 4 3

♠ A 9 7
♡ 10 9 5 4
◊ Q 7
♣ A 9 8 7

WEST	NORTH	EAST	SOUTH
1 Spade	2 Diamonds	Pass	2 No Trump
Pass	3 No Trump	Double	Pass
Pass	Pass		

* Exclusive of slam contracts. See page 437: Leads against doubled slams.

I am not arguing in favor of East's double. It is extremely risky and lays his side open to the sting of a devastating redouble, but East was willing to run the risk because he felt that if partner did not lead a Spade all hope was gone. Notice that a Heart lead would have permitted the fulfillment of the contract.

C. If both partners have bid, it is not easy to determine which suit to lead when partner doubles. Use your own judgment.

D. When neither the leader nor the doubler has bid, the doubler is suggesting to partner to lead the dummy's first-bid suit unless the leader has a very good opening of his own. But bear in mind that this is only a suggestion—*not a command.* There is current among many players the belief that when the 3 No Trump is doubled in these circumstances the opening leader must lead dummy's suit. There is no *must* about it. You should use your own judgment, and if the dummy's suit has been rebid, it is extremely doubtful that you should lead it. Your partner's double simply states he expects to defeat the contract. He hopes you have a good lead to make. But, if not, probably the safe one would be to lead the dummy's suit. The thing to bear in mind in these circumstances is that it is essential not to waste time trying to establish some indifferent suit of your own.

Presume the bidding to have progressed as follows:

SOUTH	WEST	NORTH	EAST
1 Heart	Pass	1 Spade	Pass
2 No Trump	Pass	3 No Trump	Double
Pass	Pass	Pass	

You are West, holding the following hand:

♠ 9 2   ♡ J 10 4 3   ◇ 10 7 5 4   ♣ K 8 4

Hearts have been bid by the declarer. You do not select that suit. It would not be good policy to lead the fourth best Diamond, hoping to establish that suit. Inasmuch as your partner doubled and you have no indicated lead, the 9 of Spades should be selected.

Leads against suit contracts

Many of the principles applicable to leads against No Trump will not apply if the opposition is playing a suit contract. Against No Trump contracts considerable attention must be devoted to building up tricks from small cards. The length, therefore, of the suit selected is frequently the most important consideration. Against suit contracts, however, your attention is principally concentrated on the first two or three rounds of the suit. The holding of A K Q J against No Trump must produce four tricks, while at a suit contract you are usually safe in assuming that you will take but two. You might take three, but almost certainly you will be unable to take four. It will be observed that against suit contracts the defense must exercise greater haste in building up tricks, because sooner or later good tricks get ruffed.

Holding K Q 6 4 2 against No Trump, the correct lead is the 4. Against a suit contract you lead the King, to be sure that you build up at least one trick. Holding A K 6 4 2 against No Trump, the correct lead is the 4, hoping you will take tricks with the remaining cards. Against a suit contract that lead would be absurd. You do not hope to take more than two tricks.

You have heard a great deal about never leading away from a King against a suit contract. Forget it. The same principle applies here as in No Trump. It is unattractive to lead away from any honor, King, Queen, or Jack, when that honor is not part of a sequence. However, in one respect there is a difference. At No Trump we quite properly lead away from an Ace. At a suit contract, to lead away from an Ace is unorthodox and should be avoided. If that suit must be led, lead the Ace, not the small one. The reason is, at No Trump you cannot lose your Ace. At a suit contract, if you lead away from it, it may be trumped the next time.

Leading partner's suit

In leading partner's suit against trump declarations there is a popular belief that you always lead the highest. This is not true. If you have two cards of a suit, you lead the higher. If you have three worthless cards, you lead the highest. If you have a sequence in your partner's suit, you lead the top of the sequence, but if you hold four small cards of your partner's suit, you lead the lowest in order that your partner will have a count on how many cards are against him. If, however, the Ace is held, regardless of how many cards are with it, the Ace should be led.

Holding three cards headed by an honor, the choice is optional. Some players lead the honor, some lead low, others vary their tactics, depending upon the bidding. As a general rule, I find it more profitable to lead low from the honor of partner's suit because I believe that leading high cards is less productive than waiting with high cards.

The importance of retaining a high card in the suit bid by partner instead of tossing it thoughtlessly out on the table is illustrated in the following hand:

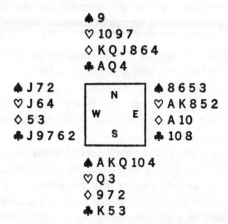

```
              ♠ 9
              ♡ 10 9 7
              ◇ K Q J 8 6 4
              ♣ A Q 4
♠ J 7 2                        ♠ 8 6 5 3
♡ J 6 4          N             ♡ A K 8 5 2
◇ 5 3        W       E         ◇ A 10
♣ J 9 7 6 2      S             ♣ 10 8
              ♠ A K Q 10 4
              ♡ Q 3
              ◇ 9 7 2
              ♣ K 5 3
```

South became declarer at a contract of 4 Spades on bidding which does not have my endorsement. East had opened the bidding with 1 Heart, so West led the Jack. East was obliged to win with the King and Ace and continued the suit. Since the 10 was high in dummy, declarer took a discard. Trumps were drawn, and the Ace of Diamonds conceded. How different had West led a low Heart! Now declarer would have to ruff the third round of Hearts and would be unable to draw trumps, so that West would be enabled to make his Jack of trumps on an overruff of the fourth Heart.

When you have great length in partner's suit it is sometimes advisable not to lead it, because of the likelihood that you will not realize any tricks in that suit. Whereas you might utilize the time in developing some other suit. For example:

♠ 6 2   ♡ K 9 5 4 3   ◇ Q J 10 4   ♣ 7 5

The opponents are playing a Spade contract, your partner having bid Hearts. The proper lead is the Queen of Diamonds. One of the opponents surely has a singleton Heart. If your partner has the Ace, he can win with it later. If the opponents have the Ace, no Heart trick is available to your side. Inasmuch as this may be your only chance to lead, you should use the opening to attempt to build up

Diamond tricks. You might be lucky enough to capture the King of that suit in dummy.

Be very cautious about leading an important card in a suit you have forced partner to bid by doubling.

♠ A Q 2   ♡ 7 3   ◇ Q J 9 5   ♣ A Q 8 4

You have doubled the opening bid of 1 Heart and partner has responded with a Spade. Do not lead Spades against the final contract. It is very likely that the opening bidder, who sits under you, holds the King. Wait for that suit to come through. Remember your partner was forced to bid and may have a 10-high suit. Lead the Queen of Diamonds.

The singleton lead

The question is frequently asked, "Is the singleton a good lead?" In some cases it is the perfect lead. In others it is the worst. The mere lead of a singleton just because it is a singleton is not good. You should have some reason for doing so. It is objectionable because, more often than not, you are helping to develop a long suit in the declarer's hand and at the same time giving him a clear picture of the whole suit.

There are times when the singleton lead is ideal. The conditions are as follows:

A sure trump trick

The reason is this. The singleton lead, being a shot in the dark, may not have worked out well; in which case the declarer can usually draw the trumps and discard his losers on the suit which you have led into. If, however, you have a sure trump trick, you can regain the lead early in the play and proceed to lead into your partner's hand to obtain the ruff, or at least to cash whatever tricks you can. In other words, when you hold a sure trump trick the declarer cannot "run away with the hand."

Surplus trumps

When holding A 8 4, K 9 7, A 6 of trumps, the small trumps accompanying an Ace are otherwise useless, as well as the 7 with the K 9 7, because only one small card is necessary to guard the King. When holding the K 5 or Q 9 3, the small trumps are necessary to guard your honor. Therefore, with this holding, the singleton lead is undesirable. Similarly, holding Q J 4 of trumps, you do not desire to ruff because you have a natural trump trick.

Partner has bid

The lead of a singleton is not apt to be productive unless you are able to reach partner's hand to obtain the ruff. If partner has not bid, you cannot rely on being able to put him into the lead. But where he has entered the auction, the chances that you can do so are good. You hold:

♠ A 5 3   ♡ K 9 7 5   ◊ 4   ♣ 9 7 4 3 2

Your partner has bid Hearts and the opponents have reached the contract of 4 Spades. This is an ideal hand on which to lead a singleton. All three conditions exist. You have a quick trump trick. You have two otherwise useless trumps. You have a reasonable certainty you can put your partner into the lead because he has bid. Therefore you should lead the singleton Diamond rather than Hearts which your partner bid, intending, when you win with the Ace of Spades, to lead the Heart to your partner so that he will return a Diamond.

When the lead of a singleton is unattractive

Whenever you have at least four trumps it is generally undesirable to lead a singleton. You should not be anxious to ruff. Rather lead your longest suit, hoping to force declarer to ruff. When he does so, your four trumps will be a serious menace.

Suppose you hold:

♠ A 10 7 5   ♡ 9   ◊ Q J 10 8 5   ♣ A K 3

The contract is Spades. Do not lead the single Heart. Your trumps are so strong that you wish to weaken the declarer's trumps, and the best procedure is to lead Diamonds. The declarer will eventually have to trump, and when he does so your trumps will become stronger than his. The same reasoning applies to the lead of a doubleton with the idea of obtaining ruffs. For example:

♠ K Q 8 5   ♡ 8 5   ◊ Q J 9 3 2   ♣ A K

Against a Spade contract you might be tempted to lead out the Ace and King of Clubs, hoping to get a third-round ruff. The temptation should be resisted. Try to force declarer by leading the Queen of Diamonds, your longest suit.

You have been warned that leads away from tenaces are unattractive against a suit contract. That rule is subject to the exception that when you have four trumps you should lead your long suit. For example, if you hold:

♠ K J 8 5   ♡ A Q J 5 4   ◊ 7 3   ♣ 9 4

Against a contract of 4 Spades, I would make a lead which most players would shrink violently from: namely, the Ace of Hearts, under other circumstances the worst lead possible, but my trumps are so strong that I desire to force the declarer to use one of his early in the game.

The blind lead of a singleton is, generally speaking, unattractive. However, remember that the lead of a singleton of the suit that partner has bid does not come under the same objection. It is usually an attractive lead.

A singleton lead becomes somewhat more attractive in a hand that would seem otherwise hopeless. If the opponents have arrived smoothly at a 4 Spade contract, your partner not having bid, and you hold very little in the way of high cards, your cause is more or less hopeless. You must therefore make a desperate effort of some sort, and the singleton in this case answers the description. For example:

♠ 9 6 4   ♡ 7 4 3   ◊ 8   ♣ K 9 6 4 3 2

The opponents have reached a 4 Spade contract, which appears hopeless from your standpoint. Only a miracle will defeat it, and the nearest contribution that you have to a miracle is the singleton Diamond. It should be led, with a prayer. A singleton lead against a small slam contract is sometimes effective. It succeeds whenever partner has the Ace of the suit led or the Ace of trumps.

The lead of a singleton Ace can be recommended only in cases where you are convinced that your partner can obtain the lead early. If you have no reason to be sure, the lead of a singleton Ace is very undesirable.

The lead of a singleton King comes under the head of my "Never lead." Too many singleton Kings make on finesses for that card to be given up without a fight. The same reasoning applies, though not quite so strongly, to the singleton Queen. When I think that the lead of a singleton is attractive I will lead it, even though it be a Jack, though I would not if it were a Queen.

The preceding paragraph refers to the singleton honors in unbid suits. It has no application if your partner has bid that suit, in which case the lead is entirely proper.

It does not apply to the situation where a trump lead is mandatory. Where it is indicated that a trump must be opened, that should be done even though your trump happens to be a singleton. This will be further discussed in a succeeding paragraph on the trump lead.

Taking a look at the dummy

Laying down an Ace rates as one of the most unattractive leads. Aces were meant to capture Kings and Queens; when led, they pick up deuces and treys. Many players lead an Ace just to look at the dummy. Remember, they must show you the dummy even if you lead a deuce. This look is an exaggerated advantage. The lead of an Ace will frequently give declarer two tricks in a suit in which he would otherwise have taken only one.

The lead of a King from an Ace King has for a long time ranked at the top of the list. Note, however, that if the Ace King is at the head of a short suit, it is not nearly so attractive as many players believe. Many times it will aid declarer in the establishment of one of his cards, such as a Queen. It is much more important to retain the Ace and King of such a suit as entries to build up tricks in your own hand. For example:

♠ 9 7   ♡ A K 4   ◇ Q 4 3 2   ♣ Q J 10 3

Against a Spade contract the lead of the King of Hearts is not desirable. You must build up a trick in Clubs in a hurry and retain the Ace and King of Hearts as entries to cash the Club trick eventually.

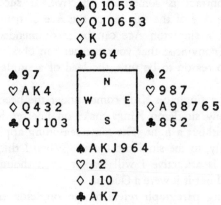

♠ Q 10 5 3
♡ Q 10 6 5 3
◇ K
♣ 9 6 4

♠ 9 7   ♠ 2
♡ A K 4   ♡ 9 8 7
◇ Q 4 3 2 ◇ A 9 8 7 6 5
♣ Q J 10 3 ♣ 8 5 2

♠ A K J 9 6 4
♡ J 2
◇ J 10
♣ A K 7

Another lead that is classified high in the table by other writers is the lead of the Queen, holding Q J 9 5. This is a somewhat dangerous lead, especially if partner has not bid, because many times the dummy comes down with A 10 2, or K 10 2, and the declarer has the other honor. This permits your Jack to be finessed later. One of the most attractive leads is the Queen from the Q J 10 9. If two leads are necessary to establish your trick, you have gotten the start, and you cannot lose a trick by the lead in any event.

The trump lead

There is another maxim, "When in doubt lead trumps." This is not sound advice. Trumps should very frequently be led, but not when you are in doubt. You should do so because you are sure that it is the proper lead. The trump lead is proper when you think that the dummy has a short suit. If, therefore, you start removing dummy's trumps you will be destroying the principal value of that hand.

How can you tell that the dummy will have a short suit? Only by the bidding. If the declarer has bid two suits, Spades and Hearts, and the dummy has taken him back to Spades, it is probable that the dummy will be short in Hearts. Declarer will plan to trump small Hearts in dummy. That being the case, a trump lead will spoil his plans. It becomes, therefore, more or less an axiom that against two-suiters a trump opening is indicated.

Another case in which a short suit in dummy can be visualized is where the bidding has proceeded as follows:

DECLARER	DUMMY
1 Spade	2 Spades
4 Spades	

If you hold some strength in high cards, you may deduce on simple reasoning that the dummy will have a short suit.

Declarer obviously has a good hand because he jumped to 4 Spades as soon as he received a raise. You have a good hand yourself, and there is not much left in high cards for the dummy to have. You have further corroboration by the fact that dummy made a somewhat weak bid. The raise must have been based on a short suit rather than on high cards.

There is a situation of somewhat frequent occurrence which indicates that the dummy will have a very short suit and therefore the ability to ruff. It is the case where there has been competitive bidding and during the auction the declarer has doubled for penalties a bid made by you or your partner, but the dummy has refused to stand for the double and has gone on in declarer's suit.

In this situation a trump lead is almost mandatory. The reason is plain. The dummy will probably have a singleton or void of the suit which his partner has doubled. (If it were otherwise, he would not have taken his partner out of the business double.) The declarer will obviously have a number of cards in the suit you and your partner have bid, which he could dispose of by trumping in the dummy. Repeated trump leads, therefore, are calculated to leave declarer with a number of your suit that he will be unable to ruff out. For example:

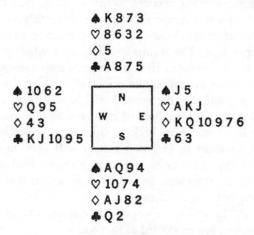

♠ K 8 7 3
♡ 8 6 3 2
◊ 5
♣ A 8 7 5

♠ 10 6 2
♡ Q 9 5
◊ 4 3
♣ K J 10 9 5

♠ J 5
♡ A K J
◊ K Q 10 9 7 6
♣ 6 3

♠ A Q 9 4
♡ 10 7 4
◊ A J 8 2
♣ Q 2

North and South—60 Part Score. (Four-card major opening is a sound tactic.)

SOUTH	WEST	NORTH	EAST
1 Spade	Pass	2 Spades	3 Diamonds
Double	Pass	3 Spades	Pass
Pass	Pass		

Trump leads are usually very effective when your partner has opened with 1 No Trump and the opponents subsequently play the hand. The reason is evident. Your partner has a majority of the high cards. If the opponents are to make the hand, they must take advantage of favorable distribution, which means a short suit in the dummy, and the use of those trumps for ruffing purposes. Therefore, in order to kill this asset of the dummy and to protect your partner's high cards, lead a trump and keep doing so unless the appearance of the dummy makes you change your mind.

Another case of somewhat frequent occurrence in which a short suit may be diagnosed in the dummy is when the opening bid has been on your right, you have doubled for a take-out, and the dummy has given a raise. For example:

SOUTH	WEST	NORTH	EAST
1 Spade	Double	2 Spades	Pass
4 Spades			

It is evident from North's bid that he has no particular strength in high cards but that his raise must have been based on trumps and a short suit. In this situation a trump lead will probably be effective.

Timing

There is one case in which trump openings should be avoided and that is when you suspect from the bidding that the dummy will have a good suit which you are unable to stop. A trump lead is dangerous because with the trumps extracted declarer will obtain discards upon dummy's good suit. In such cases attacking leads are in order. In other words, you must try to establish your tricks in a hurry.

A trump opening is advisable, even though you have only one, in cases where you have made a take-out double of a suit bid and your partner has left it in. In fact, this advice is close to being an always rule and trumps should be led blindly.

As a corollary to this principle, if I may be permitted a diversion, it is virtually a rule that when your partner doubles a suit bid of 1 for a take-out, you should not leave it in unless you are anxious to have your partner open a trump. The reason is this: When you leave in a double of 1 you are predicting that you will make more tricks than the declarer. In other words, you have converted your side into the declarer's with that trump. Now, if you were playing the hand, what would you do? You would pull trumps to protect your high cards, so that the opponents would not make any of their small trumps. Similarly, in this one, you should attempt to keep the declarer from making any of his small trumps by starting to pull them early.

Doubleton leads

The question is frequently asked, "Is the doubleton a bad lead?" As in the case of the singleton, it depends on the circumstances.

A doubleton lead in the blind, and only because it is a doubleton, is even worse than a pointless singleton lead. But under certain circumstances the doubleton lead may not only be very satisfactory but can actually be the one and only lead in a hand.

The doubleton lead is made for one of two purposes:

A. With the hope of obtaining a third-round ruff.

B. For the purpose of avoiding other embarrassing leads. In other words, as an exit.

All the requirements regarding the singleton lead should apply in the case of the doubleton: namely, a quick trump trick, some otherwise useless trumps, and the ability to enter partner's hand.

The doubleton lead is more frequently employed as a protective lead; that is, to protect your holdings in other suits that you do not desire to lead.

For example:

♠ K Q 5   ♡ 9 4   ◇ A Q 8 2   ♣ Q 9 7 3

Against a Spade contract we immediately rule out Spades and Diamonds as opening leads, which leaves the choice between Hearts and Clubs. The Club lead from an unsupported honor is not attractive. I therefore recommend the lead of the Heart. Here the lead is made, not because you desire a ruff, because you actually do not want it, but as a graceful exit in order to wait for the other suits to be led to you. The doubleton lead in this respect bears a close resemblance to the trump opening made when all other leads are unattractive. In the same hand, if Hearts were trump, I would still open that suit, as I consider the lead of the other three suits unattractive.

Under this heading comes also the lead of a worthless three-card suit. The top of a worthless three-card suit is frequently led for the same purpose.

For example:

♠ K Q 6   ♡ 9 8 4   ◇ A Q 3 2   ♣ Q 9 5

In this case, if Spades were trumps, no other lead having been indicated, I would recommend the lead of the 9 of Hearts.

The lead of a doubleton containing the J x, or Q x, is too frequently resorted to. I consider it one of the worst of all leads. Queens and Jacks are much too important to give up without a fight. Too many tricks are won with Queens and Jacks for them to be tossed idly upon the table. I even dislike to lead the 10 from the doubleton, because that card frequently becomes a winner. However, my objection to it is not nearly so strong as in the case of the Jack or Queen.

A popular opening lead is the Ace from A x, hoping to find your partner with the King and to obtain an immediate ruff. Unless the situation is desperate, I dislike this lead. It might be called a "prayer lead." I repeat: Aces were meant to capture Kings and Queens and not to be led out indiscriminately. You will find many times that even though you have obtained an immediate ruff, you will achieve better results by giving up the ruff and retaining the killing power of the Ace.

Another doubleton lead sometimes resorted to is the King from the K x. Only if the situation is very desperate should such a lead be attempted, for the reasons indicated above. However, when the defeat of the contract seems hopeless, the lead of the King from K x may sometimes save a desperate situation.

Another case in which the King might profitably be led from the K x is where your partner has shown distributed strength, such as by making an informatory double or by bidding No Trump, so that you are persuaded that he must have one honor in that suit.

If you lead the Ace and follow it with the King, it is an abnormal opening, because the conventional lead is the King and you therefore give partner the specific information that you have only two of the suit and desire to ruff the third round.

Against suit contracts where you have a choice between leading a worthless doubleton or a worthless tripleton, by all means select the doubleton, because in addition to all other features that they have in common, the doubleton does have the outside chance of bringing home the third-round ruff.

Note here the difference between suit and No Trump contracts. In No Trump you should select the three-card suit rather than the two-card.

When the doubleton is opened for the purpose of obtaining a third-round ruff, the co-operation of partner is frequently required. Naturally it will be difficult sometimes for the partner of the opening leader to determine whether the lead is a singleton or a doubleton. It will involve a certain amount of guessing. Clues can often be obtained from the bidding.

Where the partner of doubleton leader has the Ace and no other quick-entry card, he should be careful not to win the first trick but should wait for the second trick. Observe how this works in the following hand.

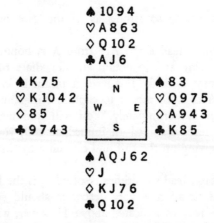

♠ 10 9 4
♡ A 8 6 3
◇ Q 10 2
♣ A J 6

♠ K 7 5   ♠ 8 3
♡ K 10 4 2   ♡ Q 9 7 5
◇ 8 5   ◇ A 9 4 3
♣ 9 7 4 3   ♣ K 8 5

♠ A Q J 6 2
♡ J
◇ K J 7 6
♣ Q 10 2

South is declarer at a contract of 4 Spades, and West leads the 8 of Diamonds. If East wins this trick with the Ace and returns the suit, the dummy will win and take the Spade finesse, which loses to the King. Now West will shift to a Club. Declarer will climb up with the Ace and pull trumps, fulfilling the contract. Note the difference if East refuses to take the first Diamond trick. (East should, however, signal with the 9, suggesting to his partner to continue the suit.) Declarer wins and takes the Spade finesse. Now when West is in he has another Diamond to lead and so obtains the ruff. Note that if East had held the Ace of Clubs instead of the King, it would not have been necessary for him to hold up. He could have taken the first trick with the Ace and returned the suit, hoping to get in with the Ace of Clubs to give partner a ruff.

Whether to lead partner's suit or your own

Against a trump contract it is much easier to decide whether to lead your own or partner's suit.

When you have a great many of your partner's suit it will not be a very good weapon on the defense, because declarer will no doubt be short, and unless you are playing the forcing game (when you have four or more trumps) it is better to look about for a sequence lead in some other suit.

♠ 4 3   ♡ K 7 3 2   ◇ Q 6 4   ♣ Q J 10 9

You are on lead against a contract of 4 Spades, your partner having bid Hearts. It is doubtful whether you will take more than one Heart trick, and that only if partner has the Ace, because one of the opponents almost surely has a singleton. Since you probably will not be on lead again, the best opening is the Queen of Clubs. This will be particularly effective if the King is in dummy and partner holds the Ace.

Holding A K J, with or without others in a side suit, a good idea is to lead the King of that suit first and then shift to partner's suit so that if the Queen is in the closed hand, your partner can lead through and capture it.

Some writers recommend the lead of the King from the A K x, just to have a look at the dummy. I am decidedly against this. It is usually not that important to have a look at the dummy.

Leading from a three-card suit

Sometimes you will be obliged to lead from a three-card suit. If my choice is between K 6 2 and Q 6 2, I always lead from the King rather than the Queen. Because if I lead into an A Q, my King may still live to take a trick, but if the lead from the Queen has lost to a lower honor, I have no hope for the future. In other words, a King is strong enough to survive a bad lead, a Queen probably not. Even if declarer learns where the King is located, he may be able to do nothing about it. But if he finds out where the Queen is, he can very frequently pick it up by finessing in either direction. If you are obliged to lead from a three-card suit which contains an honor, it is important to select the proper card to lead. Holding Q 9 2, if that suit is to be led, the proper card is the 2. It may be argued that partner will be deceived into thinking you have four cards of the suit. That is true, but unfortunately cannot be avoided. Some players have formed the practice of leading the middle card from a holding such as this. That practice has been found to be unprofitable for various reasons. In the first place, the middle card may be too important; as, for example, the 9 in this case, which may develop into a winning card and therefore cannot be spared. In the second place, the lead of the 9 may place partner under the impression that you are leading the "top of nothing" and he will not read you for an honor in that suit. All in all, it is better to deceive your partner as to the exact number of your cards in the suit, in order not to confuse him as to the type of holding you have. How important a card the 9 may be is illustrated by the following diagram:

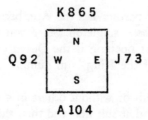

K 8 6 5

Q 9 2   J 7 3

A 10 4

Notice that the lead of the 9 permits declarer to win all the tricks in the suit. The lead of the deuce will not produce the same result.

Leads against slams

Against slam bids a very popular lead is an Ace. This practice, however, does not have the approval of the experts. It takes two tricks to defeat a slam, and cashing an Ace will not attain your end unless, of course, partner appears to have the King. Leading an Ace makes the declarer's work so much easier. It is my policy not to lead an Ace unless I have somewhere a probability of a second trick or infer the probability of a second trick in my partner's hand. For example:

♠ Q 6 5   ♡ A 9 7 4   ◊ 5 3 2   ♣ 8 6 2

The opponents have reached a contract of 6 Spades. I feel that I have a fair chance to make my Queen. Therefore I would cash the Ace of Hearts.

♠ 7   ♡ A 9 6 4   ◊ 8 6 4 2   ♣ 7 6 4 2

If Spades were not vigorously supported by dummy, I would reason there is a fair chance that my partner has a trump trick and I would cash my Ace in that case. But where no immediate trick is in sight it is important to try to build one up before the Ace is released. For example:

♠ 8 5 4   ♡ A 9 5   ◊ 10 9 8 4   ♣ 5 3 2

The only prospect of a trick against a 6 Spade contract is if partner can take one in Clubs or Diamonds. Therefore I would lead the 10 of Diamonds, hoping that my partner might have something like the King behind dummy's Ace, so that I can build up a trick for him before my Ace is released. The lead of the Ace might establish some Heart tricks in dummy upon which declarer can discard a losing Diamond or Club.

♠ 8 6 5   ♡ A 7 4 2   ◊ 9 7 3   ♣ Q 3 2

If the dummy has bid Hearts, the proper opening on this hand is a Club, with the hope that the partner holds at least the King of that suit. It is urgent to build up a trick before your Ace is driven out, so that declarer cannot obtain discards on dummy's Heart suit.

Trump leads against slams are not recommended, although occasionally they turn out well. For example, if declarer has bid two suits and you have the other one well under control, a trump lead may cut down dummy's ruffing power.

The singleton lead against a slam contract from a completely worthless hand is very attractive. Partner probably holds a trick. If it happens to be the Ace of that suit, the hand is immediately defeated. Also, if partner happens to hold a quick trump trick, he will return the suit in time to defeat the slam.

Aggressive leads as a rule are not desirable against No Trump slams. In other words, unless you have a complete sequence do not take a chance to build up tricks. It is better to wait. For example:

♠ 9 8 6   ♡ J 6 4 2   ◊ Q 6 5 3   ♣ J 4

Against 6 No Trump, I would lead the 9 of Spades even though the suit had been bid.

Leads against doubled slams (in a suit)

Where partner has doubled the slam contract and you have the opening lead, the accepted modern convention is that you are not entitled to your own opinion. The double calls for a certain specific lead. The convention is based upon the theory that when the opponents have reached a slam contract they will rarely go down more than a trick, and a double should not be made merely for the purpose of scoring an additional 50 or 100 points but should be made strictly for the purpose of directing your partner's opening lead. The doubler of a slam contract says: "Partner, please do not make the normal opening lead." The leads required by partner's double are as follows:

A. If dummy has bid any suit other than trumps, the doubler demands the lead of that suit. If the dummy has bid more than one suit, it demands the lead of the first suit bid by dummy.

B. If dummy has bid no side suit, but the declarer has, the doubler demands the lead of the first side suit bid by declarer.

C. If declarer and his partner have bid no side suit, the doubler demands the lead of an unbid suit. (In other words, you absolutely must not lead trumps.)

D. If the doubler or his partner has bid a suit, the doubler announces, "Partner, please do not lead that suit." For example: you are North and hold:

♠ 6 5 2   ♡ A 9 7   ◇ 7 4 3   ♣ 10 9 4 2

The bidding has proceeded:

WEST	NORTH	EAST	SOUTH
1 Spade	Pass	3 Clubs	3 Hearts
3 Spades	Pass	4 Spades	Pass
6 Spades	Pass	Pass	Double

A Club is demanded of you.

Underleading Aces

From auction days we have the rule, "Never lead away from an Ace." This refers, of course, to the opening lead. As a general principle it is almost as true today. But even to this rule there are certain exceptions which the experienced player may sometimes recognize. The underleading of an Ace may produce very good results on certain type hands. The conditions are these: You suspect that the King of the suit will be in the dummy. And your suspicions can be obtained, of course, only from the bidding. You may suspect that the King may be in the dummy when the dummy has constructively bid No Trump or when the dummy has made a take-out double showing distributed strength. Now if the declarer has the Jack, possibly he will expect that you are leading from the Queen instead of the Ace and may very likely misguess the situation.

However, the underleading of an Ace is usually done from the Ace and two cards and sometimes from the Ace and three cards, but never when holding more, because the danger of the declarer having a singleton becomes too great, so that the Ace may subsequently be trumped. Suppose you hold:

♠ Q 9 4   ♡ Q 10 5   ◇ K 10 8 4   ♣ A 6 2

The dummy has opened with a No Trump, and the declarer subsequently plays a Spade contract. The dummy will almost surely have the King of Clubs. If the Jack of Clubs is either in the closed hand or in the dummy, the declarer will undoubtedly misguess it. Furthermore, the lead of either Spades or Hearts or Diamonds is unattractive. Therefore the low Club would appear to be the best lead.

What about leading from Kings?

Some years ago an authority broadcast to a very gullible public that one must never lead away from a King. I know how he is going to spend eternity. It is going to be in the hot nether regions, the declarer is always going to be at his right, and our victim will eternally hold four Kings. It will serve him right! I don't contend that you should go out of your way to lead from a King, but when the bidding indicates that the particular suit should be attacked, don't refuse to lead it only because it contains a King.

Deceptive leads

Opportunities to practice deception successfully on the opening lead are not very frequent in occurrence.

Deceptive tactics at this point are likely to become boomerangs, inasmuch as partner is more apt to be deceived than declarer.

Declarer knows his own twenty-six cards. Your partner is looking at only thirteen and requires your assistance to suggest the other thirteen.

In certain cases, however, it may become apparent to you that partner's hand is probably hopeless and that information concerning the exact structure of your own will not be of great interest to him. It is at such times that the opportunity for a deceptive lead may present itself.

One of the oldest chestnuts, which still occasionally proves effective, is the lead of the Jack from the Q J doubleton, particularly in trumps. This is to induce declarer to believe that your partner has the Queen, and sometimes results in your making that card on a finesse. It is somewhat more risky to make this play in a side suit, because there is a chance your partner may have strength in that suit and misread your holding, whereas in trumps it is extremely unlikely that your partner can have any holding where the unorthodox lead will upset him.

A more subtle type of false carding is the lead of the fifth best instead of the fourth best against a No Trump contract. For example: Holding A K 6 4 2, some players will frequently lead the 2 for the purpose of inducing declarer to believe that the lead was from a four-card suit. This may cause declarer to plan the play of the hand in some manner other than that which he might have done had he suspected the possibility of a five-card suit against him. This type of false lead, however, may occasionally prove unfortunate, because partner might reason that you have only four of the suit and may abandon it when he obtains the lead. Probably the best case for that type of false lead is when your partner is not a particularly alert player, whereas the declarer is a keen card reader. In that case your partner will probably not be conscious of whether you have led from a four- or five-card suit, whereas the declarer might be impressed.

Another popular type of deceptive opening lead which is successful many times is the lead of a high card through the suit that the dummy has bid when the opening leader holds the King and is trying to discourage declarer from taking the finesse. For example: The dummy having bid Spades and you hold the K 8 6 2. The lead of the 8 may intimidate declarer into believing that your lead is a singleton. He may, therefore, decline the finesse and try another line of play which is somewhat inferior.

Opening lead table

HOLDING IN SUIT	AGAINST NO TRUMP	AGAINST TRUMP BIDS
A K Q J	A	K
A K Q x x x	A	K
A K Q x x	K	K
A K Q x	K	K
A K x	K	K
A K J 10	A	K
A K J x	K	K
A K J x x	x	K
A K J x x x x	A	K
A K x x x x	x	K
A K 10 9 x	10	K
A K 10 9 x x	10	K
A K x x x	x	K
A Q J x x	Q	A
K Q J x x	K	K
K Q 10 x x	K	K
K Q 7 4 2	4	K
Q J 10 x x	Q	Q
Q J 9 x x	Q	Q
Q J 7 4 2	4	4
J 10 9 x x	J	J
J 10 8 x x	J	J
J 10 7 4 2	4	4
10 9 8	10	10
10 9 7 4	4	10

Opening lead table (continued)

HOLDING IN SUIT	AGAINST NO TRUMP	AGAINST TRUMP BIDS
A Q 10 9 x	10[1]	A
A Q 8 7 4 2	7	A
A J 10 8 2	J	A
A 10 9 7 2	10	A
K J 10 7 2	J	J
K 10 9 7 2	10	10
Q 10 9 7 2	10	10
A 7 4	4	A
K J 4	4[2]	4
K 7 4	4	4
Q 10 4	4	4
J 7 4	4	4
10 7 4	4	4
K 9 8 7	7[3]	7

[1] The Queen is led when you suspect the King is in dummy.

[2] Unattractive lead; may be necessary from the bidding.

[3] Do not treat a lead of the 9 as the top of an interior sequence; partner may conclude incorrectly that it is the top of nothing.

OPENING LEAD QUIZ

The player on your right opens 1 No Trump and the player on your left raises to 3 No Trump. What is your opening lead from each of the following hands?

1. ♠ Q 9 3 2
   ♡ K 9 5 3
   ◇ Q 10 5
   ♣ A 6

2. ♠ 8
   ♡ J 9 6 4 3
   ◇ A 7
   ♣ J 8 7 5 2

3. ♠ J 10 8
   ♡ J 5 4 2
   ◇ Q 2
   ♣ A J 4 3

4. ♠ 10 6 5 3 2
   ♡ A 4
   ◇ 7 5 2
   ♣ K Q 10

5. ♠ Q 2
   ♡ 9 7
   ◇ K Q 10 9
   ♣ Q 7 5 3 2

6. ♠ A Q 5 3 2
   ♡ Q J 8
   ◇ 10 9 7
   ♣ 8 2

The bidding has proceeded:

NORTH	SOUTH
1 Diamond	1 Heart
2 Diamonds	2 No Trump
3 No Trump	Pass

You are West, holding each of the following hands. What is your lead?

7. ♠ A 7 5 3
   ♡ Q 10 8 2
   ◇ 6
   ♣ 10 9 8 4

8. ♠ 10 5 4
   ♡ J 7 5 2
   ◇ 8 6 5
   ♣ 10 9 6

9. ♠ 9 2
   ♡ K J 10 9 5
   ◇ A 5
   ♣ Q 4 3 2

The bidding has proceeded:

SOUTH	NORTH
1 Heart	2 Hearts
4 Hearts	

You are West and hold each of the following hands. What is your opening lead?

10. ♠ J 2
    ♡ K 5 3 2
    ◇ K Q 9 6 4
    ♣ 9 3

11. ♠ Q 10 4 2
    ♡ 8 7
    ◇ K J 10 3
    ♣ K J 4

12. ♠ 10 7 6 5 4 2
    ♡ K 4 3
    ◇ J 10
    ♣ A 7

You are West. The bidding is indicated by the side of each problem. What is your opening lead?

13. ♠ 8 7 5
♡ 4
♢ Q 9 8 3
♣ Q 7 5 4 2

NORTH	SOUTH
1 No Trump	3 Spades
3 No Trump	4 Hearts
4 Spades	6 Spades
Pass	

14. ♠ 7 5 2
♡ A J 3
♢ K 4
♣ J 9 7 5 2

SOUTH	NORTH
3 Clubs	Pass

15. ♠ 8 4 3
♡ K 10 9 2
♢ K 2
♣ K J 9 7

SOUTH	NORTH
1 Diamond	1 Heart
1 Spade	3 Spades
4 Spades	Pass

16. ♠ Q 4
♡ J 5 2
♢ Q 10 2
♣ Q 10 7 5 2

SOUTH	NORTH
1 Spade	3 Spades
4 No Trump	5 Hearts
6 Spades	Pass

17. ♠ A J 8 3
♡ Q 2
♢ J 8 6 4
♣ 10 9 8

SOUTH	NORTH
1 Spade	1 No Trump
2 Hearts	3 Hearts
4 Hearts	Pass

18. ♠ J 10 8
♡ K 9 7
♢ J 9 4 2
♣ K 8 3

SOUTH	NORTH
1 Spade	2 Spades
2 No Trump	4 Spades
Pass	

19. ♠ A K Q 5 4
♡ J 10 7 2
♢ 10 6
♣ J 3

EAST	SOUTH	WEST	NORTH
Pass	Pass	1 Spade	Double
Pass	1 No Trump	Pass	2 No Trump
Pass	3 No Trump	Pass	Pass

20. ♠ J 9 6 2
♡ 7
♢ J 5 4
♣ 10 8 5 3 2

EAST	SOUTH	WEST	NORTH
1 No Trump	2 Hearts	Pass	3 Hearts
Pass	Pass	Pass	

21. ♠ K 10 8 7 2
♡ J 4
♢ Q 10 6 2
♣ J 3

SOUTH	WEST	NORTH	EAST
2 No Trump	Pass	3 Hearts	Pass
3 No Trump	Pass	6 No Trump	Pass
Pass	Pass		

22. ♠ 10
♡ A K 10 6
♢ K Q 10 5
♣ K J 8 3

SOUTH	WEST	NORTH	EAST
1 Spade	Double	Pass	Pass
Pass			

23. ♠ Q J 10
♡ Q 10 6 5 3
♢ A K 9 5
♣ 2

WEST	NORTH	EAST	SOUTH
1 Heart	Pass	Pass	1 No Trump
Pass	2 No Trump	Pass	3 No Trump
Pass	Pass	Double	Pass
Pass	Pass		

24.	♠ 8 5	SOUTH	WEST	NORTH	EAST
	♡ 9 6 5 2	1 Club	1 Diamond	1 Heart	1 Spade
	◇ K J 9 7 6	1 No Trump	Pass	2 No Trump	Pass
	♣ A Q	3 No Trump	Pass	Pass	Double
		Pass	Pass		

25.	♠ Q 7 2	SOUTH	WEST	NORTH	EAST
	♡ J 9 4	1 Spade	Pass	2 Diamonds	Pass
	◇ 10 7	2 Spades	Pass	3 Clubs	Pass
	♣ Q 8 5 4 3	3 No Trump	Pass	Pass	Double
		Pass			

26.	♠ K 10 3	WEST	NORTH	EAST	SOUTH
	♡ 9 7 6 3	Pass	1 Diamond	Pass	1 Spade
	◇ 8 5	Pass	2 Diamonds	Pass	2 Hearts
	♣ A J 6 4	Pass	2 Spades	Pass	3 Spades
		Pass	3 No Trump	Pass	4 Spades
		Pass	Pass	Double	Pass
		Pass	Pass		

27.	♠ 8 4 2	SOUTH	WEST	NORTH	EAST
	♡ 8 6	1 Diamond	Pass	2 Hearts	Pass
	◇ 10 8 5	2 Spades	Pass	4 Diamonds	Pass
	♣ Q 10 7 4 2	4 No Trump	Pass	5 Diamonds	Pass
		6 Diamonds	Pass	Pass	Double
		Pass	Pass	Pass	

ANSWERS TO OPENING LEAD QUIZ

1. 3 of Hearts.

The choice lies between a Spade and a Heart. Against No Trump it is frequently better to lead away from a King than from a Queen, for if declarer has all the outstanding honors your King may still take a trick later, but your Queen probably would not once you had led away from it.

2. 4 of Hearts.

On general principles a major-suit opening is preferred to a minor suit when the opponents have reached a No Trump contract without investigating suit possibilities. This is because they are less likely to have concealed a major suit than a minor.

3. Jack of Spades.

A lead away from a four-card suit headed by the Jack frequently costs a trick, and therefore a Heart lead is not attractive. A Club is a possibility, but on balance a Spade is the lead most likely to prove beneficial.

4. 3 of Spades.

With at least two entries, an effort should be made to establish the five-card suit. A lead of the King of Clubs would be more appropriate against a suit contract than against No Trump.

5. King of Diamonds.

Preference should be given to the strong four-card Diamond holding because of the danger of giving a trick away if a Club is led.

6. 3 of Spades.

The fact that the declarer may have the unsupported King of Spades should not deter you from attacking with this very attractive holding. The chances of being able to run four tricks in the suit when your partner gains the lead are very high.

7. 10 of Clubs.

Your holdings in Hearts and Diamonds suggest the possibility that the hand will develop unfavorably for declarer. You therefore play with the object of giving nothing away, and the Club opening serves this purpose best.

8. 10 of Clubs.

In view of the nature of your hand, it is difficult to see how you can play a starring role in defeating this contract. If the opponents are to be smitten, your partner will have to have at least the equivalent of a sound opening, together with a good suit. If partner had a good Spade suit, he might have bid it, and therefore he is more likely to have the Club suit (which he could not have shown without ascending to the 2 level).

9. King of Hearts.

The best chance is to try to establish the Heart suit, even though South has bid Hearts. If you lead the Jack and either dummy or your partner has the singleton Queen, declarer will duck and you will need to get in twice before you can take any Heart tricks. Leading the King takes care of that possibility.

10. King of Diamonds.

You have a very good chance to shorten the declarer's trump holding by forcing him to ruff Diamonds. If that happens, your four-card trump holding may cause him to lose control of the hand.

11. 8 of Hearts.

Your opening salvo should be a trump because you have all-round strength in the side suits. The trump lead caters for both the desirability of cutting down the number of ruffs and the danger of losing a trick if you lead from a tenace holding.

12. Jack of Diamonds.

You have a quick entry in the trump suit and there are therefore some prospects of being able to gain a ruff in either one of the minor suits. If the Diamond lead proves in-

auspicious, it will be open to you to shift to Clubs later.

13. 4 of Hearts.

The Heart lead is best, even though declarer has bid the suit. You must hope to find partner with either the Ace of Hearts or a quick trump trick, so that you can get a Heart ruff.

14. Ace of Hearts.

It is unusual to lead from the A J x, but in view of your trump holding you should assume that the contract can be beaten by simply cashing your available tricks. To lead a Spade or a Heart might enable declarer to take discards. In any case, it is highly unlikely that declarer has the King of Hearts.

15. 3 of Spades.

The trump opening is recommended because of the likelihood that declarer is planning to ruff Diamonds in dummy. In this case your partner, who is marked with several Diamonds, would be unable to overruff and declarer would have things all his own way.

16. 2 of Diamonds.

The question is which plain suit you should attack, and there are one or two slender clues. Firstly, partner might perhaps have doubled North's Blackwood response had he wanted a Heart opening. Secondly, Diamonds are more promising than Clubs, since we have fewer cards in Diamonds and the opponents are less likely to have a shortage in the suit.

17. 10 of Clubs.

Despite your strength in declarer's side suit, a trump opening would represent an unnecessary hazard. Bear in mind that your partner, as well as the dummy hand, will be short in Spades, and will be able to overruff.

18. 8 of Spades.

In view of the declarer's No Trump rebid, a lead of a plain suit could be expected to cost a trick. In leading a trump from this combination, the correct card, strange as it may seem, is the 8, since partner may have a singleton Queen or King.

19. 5 of Spades.
You should do declarer the honor of assuming he has a Spade stopper. If you open with a high Spade you will probably never succeed in winning more than three tricks in the suit. By leading a low Spade you beat the contract when East holds (a) two low Spades, with a card of entry, or (b) J x of Spades, declarer having bid No Trump with 10 9 x x.

20. 7 of Hearts.
The lead of a singleton trump is not always to be recommended, but a special case arises when partner has opened with a strong No Trump. It is then to be presumed that the opponents are bidding on distributional values, and you therefore try to curtail their ruffing potential.

21. Jack of Hearts.
This presents an awkward problem. You have some hopes of beating this contract and the main consideration is to avoid giving a trick away on opening lead. Both Spades and Diamonds are out. As between Hearts and Clubs, there is some indication that declarer is short on Hearts, in which case the lead of the Jack is unlikely to cost.

22. 10 of Spades.
The trump opening is mandatory in this sequence. In view of your partner's penalty pass, which indicates considerable length in Spades, you should imagine that your side is playing the hand at a Spade contract. In this case, to protect your considerable high-card values, you would want to draw your opponents' trumps, and therefore you lead one.

23. 5 of Hearts.
When either defender has bid a suit, a double asks for that suit to be led against a No Trump contract.

24. 7 of Diamonds.
This is a tough one, inasmuch as the defenders have bid different suits. The opponents presumably have a reasonable quota of points, and therefore it is unlikely that East has doubled on a Spade suit and an entry card. He is much more likely to hold a high card in Diamonds.

25. 10 of Diamonds.
A double when neither defender has bid asks for a lead of dummy's first suit. The diagnosis is confirmed by the fact that you have five cards in dummy's second suit, which means that East can hardly want that suit led.

26. 8 of Diamonds.
East's double is not a mandatory lead-directing double, but it is unlikely that he has many trump tricks, so he must have doubled partly on suspicion and partly on a strong holding in dummy's suit.

27. 8 of Hearts.
A double of slam asks for an unusual lead, which rules out either a Club (the unbid suit) or a trump. As between Spades and Hearts, it is much more likely that East wants a lead of dummy's suit than declarer's.

19. Defensive play by third hand

FOR THE PURPOSE of this discussion the partner of the opening leader will be referred to as the third hand. The play of the third hand to the first trick is the turning point of the hand many times. Partner's opening lead has been more or less in the blind, and it may be the duty of the third hand to guide the opener as to the subsequent play. This will be discussed at greater length in the chapter on signals and discards. For the present we are concerned with the handling of various card combinations by third hand.

There is an old bromide to the effect that third hand must play high. This is only partially true, and in this chapter we will consider various deviations from this principle. The object of third hand's playing high is to force out a still higher card from the declarer's hand, so that the opening leader's cards will be promoted in rank.

Rule of 11

The first thing to observe is that the Rule of 11 is not a rule at all. It is a sugar-coated method of rapid calculation when your partner has opened the fourth best of a suit. This merely enables you to calculate rapidly how many cards (higher than the one led) are held by second, third, and fourth hands combined. This is how it is done. Take the size of the card led, subtract it from 11. The balance represents the number of cards (higher than the one led) that are held by second, third, and fourth hands. For example:

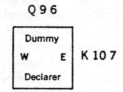

Q 9 6

Dummy
W   E   K 10 7
Declarer

West leads the 5.

Assuming that you are East and you recognize partner's lead of the 5 as his fourth best, your problem is to determine how many cards South (the declarer) holds that are better than the 5. The process is as follows: 11 minus 5 equals 6. That means that the second, third, and fourth hands together hold six cards better than the 5. North and East each have three. South therefore has none, and your 7 will win the trick. West has obviously led from A J 8 5.

This device is also available to the declarer. To illustrate:

A Q 2

```
┌─────────────┐
│             │
│   Dummy     │
│             │
│             │
│  Declarer   │
│             │
└─────────────┘
```

10 8 3

West leads the 7. You are South and declarer. Assuming that West's lead is his fourth best, your problem is to determine how many higher cards East holds. Take the card led and subtract it from 11; 11 minus 7 equals 4. North, East, and South together, therefore, have four cards higher than the 7. Since North and South each have two, East can have none, so you play low from dummy, knowing that the 8 will win the trick. West's lead has been from K J 9 7.

How does this Rule of 11 come about? It is really very simple. There are thirteen cards in a suit, whose numbers range from 2 to 14, the Jack being 11, the Queen 12, the King 13, and the Ace 14. This represents their rank. Since the opening leader automatically has three cards higher than the one led (remember we are presuming he has led his fourth highest), those three do not enter into the calculation, which reduces the top number from 14 to 11.

Another way to state the rule is as follows: When a particular card is led, such as the 7, you ask yourself how many cards higher than the 7 are in the deck. The answer, obviously, is seven. This includes all the cards from the 8 to the Ace. Since three of them are known to be in the opening leader's hand, that leaves four of them out around the table; 11 minus 7 equals 4.

Another way to state the case is to subtract the card led from 14 and you will have the number of cards in the deck that are higher than the one led. Now subtract the three which the opening leader is always known to possess and you have the total in the hands of the other three players.

This rule will sometimes help third hand to determine whether to play his highest card.

Here is an important principle. If the dummy has no vital card that you are interested in capturing, you, as third hand, should always play high, but if there is an important card in the dummy that you would like to trap, it frequently pays for third hand to wait for that card to be played before playing his highest. In other words, third hand acts as a guard over dummy. For example:

K 6 3

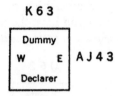

A J 4 3

West leads the 5. Dummy plays low. What should you (East) play? If you play third hand high and win with the Ace, dummy's King becomes established. Proper play is the Jack, in the hope that partner has led from the Queen. If it proves that declarer holds the Queen, you will not have lost anything by your play, because had you played the Ace, declarer would have won with both the King and the Queen. As it is, your Ace stands guard to capture the King.

This play is sometimes erroneously referred to as a finesse against partner. You are not finessing against partner at all. You are finessing against the dummy, which is quite proper. In other words, the dummy contains a high card which you are anxious to capture and you keep the Ace to stand guard over the King.

In cases where third hand is to play high there is a slight variation where his two highest cards are in sequence. In that case the second best card is just as high as the best card, and when following suit it is proper to follow with the bottom of the sequence. This is the reverse of the rule that applies to the leader who must lead the top of a sequence. For example:

6 5 4

K 10 7 3   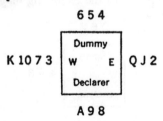   Q J 2

A 9 8

West leads the 3. As East you properly play the Jack, not the Queen. This will prove informative to partner, for when the Jack forces the Ace, partner will realize you have the Queen. But if, thinking it makes no difference, you play the Queen, your partner will have no way of knowing you have the Jack and may fear to continue his suit.

If partner leads a low card of a suit in which you hold the J 10 9 8, you must follow suit with the 8. It is the equal of the Jack, but when the 8 forces out the other high card your partner will then be in a position to know that you have the 9 10 J.

Lead from top of a sequence; follow suit from bottom of a sequence.

Q 6 2

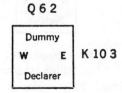

K 10 3

You are East. Your partner West leads the 5, and North, the dummy, plays low. What card do you play? The answer is the 10, not the King. If you play the King, the Queen must eventually be established. If you play the 10, it may possibly drive out the Ace. If the 10 loses to the Jack, you have lost nothing, because the play of the King would permit the declarer subsequently to take a trick with either the Jack or the Queen or possibly both.

If the contract is No Trump, it is barely possible that your partner is leading from the Ace and Jack, in which case your 10 will actually win the trick. If your partner is leading from the J 9 7 5 and you play the King, declarer will win two tricks. If, however, you play the 10, declarer's Ace will be forced out and he will be able to take no further tricks in the suit because you will wait for partner to lead through the Queen.

The same principle applies in the following diagram:

Q 6 2

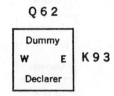

K 9 3

If West leads the 5 and dummy plays low, East should play the 9, retaining the King to capture the Queen.

A case calling for exceptional treatment by third hand is the following:

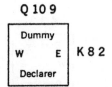

Q 10 9

Against a 4 Heart contract your partner West leads the 4 of Spades. Dummy plays the 9. What card should you play?

Declarer definitely holds the Ace, since it is very remote that partner would have underled the Ace against a 4 Heart contract. If you play the King, the declarer will win and subsequently finesse the 10 against your partner, making three tricks in the suit. If you duck the 9, declarer will win the trick and will still have the Ace. This will give him two tricks instead of three. The complete holding is as follows:

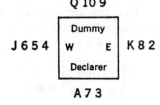

Q 10 9

A 7 3

Unblocking by third hand

When your partner has opened a long suit and you have high cards in that suit, you must be careful not to retain them too long lest they interfere with your partner running that suit. For example:

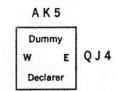

A K 5

It is No Trump and West leads the 6. Declarer plays the King. East's proper play is the Jack, because if he plays low he will be certain to win one trick and the remaining cards of partner's will be blocked out. East should hope that partner is leading from the 10, and when the Ace is subsequently played he should follow with the Queen in order to get out of partner's way. The same principle also applies when third hand holds an honor and one other card of partner's suit.

4 3 2

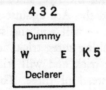

Q 5

It is No Trump. Partner leads the Jack. East should play the Queen in order to get out of partner's way.

4 3 2

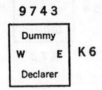

K 5

West leads the Queen. East should play the King for the same reason. However, where East can see that by unblocking he will definitely lose a trick, he must refuse to unblock.

9 7 4 3

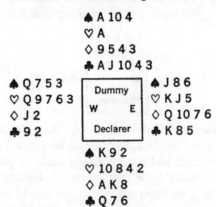

K 6

West leads the Queen. East cannot afford to unblock by playing the King, because if he does so, the 9 will subsequently become a winner. He must, therefore, reluctantly play low.

♠ A 10 4
♡ A
◇ 9 5 4 3
♣ A J 10 4 3

♠ Q 7 5 3   ♠ J 8 6
♡ Q 9 7 6 3   ♡ K J 5
◇ J 2   ◇ Q 10 7 6
♣ 9 2   ♣ K 8 5

♠ K 9 2
♡ 10 8 4 2
◇ A K 8
♣ Q 7 6

South is the declarer at a contract of 3 No Trump. West leads the 6 of Hearts, dummy plays the Ace. East should play the Jack of Hearts and not the 5. The play serves a dual purpose:

1. It signals to partner that a continuation of the suit is desired.

2. And, more important, it starts unblocking for partner, who no doubt has a five-card suit. Note the difference if East retains the Jack of Hearts. When he is in with the King of Clubs he will cash the King of Hearts and follow with the Jack, which West cannot afford to overtake, but if the 5 were retained at this point, a lead through declarer's 10 8 of Hearts would clear up the entire suit.

Holding up by third hand

It is an axiom of card playing that Aces were meant to capture Kings and Queens, and it is much better to put your Ace on the opponent's honor card than it is to wait and subsequently play it on a deuce. However, there is an exception. Where declarer has a long suit in dummy without any entries, it is frequently wise not to take your Ace until such time as declarer has no more of the suit. For example:

♣ K Q J 10 2

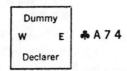

♣ A 7 4

You are East. Dummy has no other high cards. When South leads a Club you must refuse to take your Ace and wait until the third round in case South has three of the suit. If you take the Ace earlier, he will be able to enter dummy with that suit himself.

Sometimes you would take your Ace on the second round because you have found out that the declarer has only two. How you can find this out will be explained in the chapter on signals.

Returning partner's suit

When your partner leads a suit it is not always necessary for you to return it. More often than not you should, but many times the appearance of the dummy and your own hand will show you that it is advisable to lead some other suit. However, assume that you are about to return your partner's suit. The question is, Which card to select? That varies with your holding. It is not true that you always lead back the highest of your partner's suit. You lead back the highest if you originally held three cards or less, but where you originally held four or more cards of the suit it is conventional to return the fourth highest. This enables your partner to know the exact distribution of the suit around the table. It is true that sometimes your partner will be in doubt when you return a low card. He may think it is the highest and that you therefore have no more, but nine times out of ten something in the bidding or the appearance of the dummy will tell him that you cannot be short-suited, therefore you are returning your fourth best. The following hand illustrates the principle:

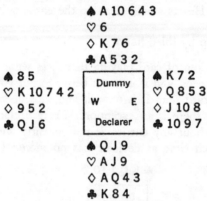

Against the contract of 3 No Trump, West leads the 4 of Hearts, East plays the Queen, and South wins with the Ace. The Spade finesse is then taken and East wins. He naturally returns Hearts. If he should lead the 8, South would play the 9 and West would win with the 10. Inasmuch as there would be absolutely no way for him to know that the Jack would fall the next time, he might fear to lead the King lest the Jack might become established in the South hand. East therefore should return the 3 instead of the 8. This will tell West that he originally had four cards of the suit, and when he knows this it will be evident that South has only one more, which must fall.

There is an exception to this principle. Where third hand holds a sequence of high cards in the suit partner has led, and there is danger that the suit may become blocked, the top of the sequence should be returned.

```
                  6
              ┌───────┐
              │   N   │
   K J 7 5 4  │ W   E │  A 10 9 3
              │   S   │
              └───────┘
                 Q 8 2
```

West opens the 5. East wins with the Ace. If he should return the 3, South will play the 8 and West will win with the Jack. The King drops the Queen, but East has left only the 10 9 and must block the run of the suit.

Third hand defensive play

When the third hand decides to lead a new suit it is important to select the proper card, especially where honors are involved. Assume that you are East:

♠ K J 10
♡ Q J 3
◊ 10 9 4 3
♣ J 9 4

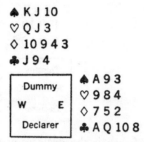

♠ A 9 3
♡ 9 8 4
◊ 7 5 2
♣ A Q 10 8

South is playing the contract at 3 No Trump. West, your partner, opens the 2 of Spades. Dummy plays the 10 and you win with the Ace. It is apparent that it will be fruitless to continue with Spades, so you decide to lead Clubs. What is the proper card? The answer is, the Queen, because you believe that South has the King. This will force him to win the trick, and when your partner regains the lead and comes back with a Club you will win all the tricks in that suit. The complete hand is as follows:

♠ K J 10
♡ Q J 3
◊ 10 9 4 3
♣ J 9 4

♠ Q 6 4 2
♡ 10 7 6 2
◊ K 6
♣ 7 5 2

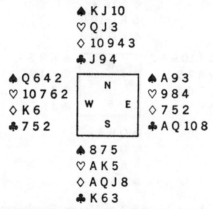

♠ A 9 3
♡ 9 8 4
◊ 7 5 2
♣ A Q 10 8

♠ 8 7 5
♡ A K 5
◊ A Q J 8
♣ K 6 3

Notice that if East had led his fourth best, South would have played low and North would win with the 9, and the King of Clubs would subsequently produce another trick. The way for East to remember the proper card to lead from this combination is as follows: When you sit over the dummy (that is, the dummy plays before you) and you surround one of dummy's honor cards (in this case your Queen and 10 of Clubs surround dummy's Jack), and you have another higher card, you should lead as though the surrounded card is in your own hand. In other words, you lead as though you held A Q J 10, from which the proper lead would be the Queen. Another illustration of this principle is the following:

♠ A 7
♡ 10 6 3
◇ K Q 10 9
♣ K Q 10 2

	♠ K 8 5
Dummy	♡ K J 9 2
W E	◇ 8
Declarer	♣ J 9 7 6 4

You are East. South is the declarer at a contract of 3 No Trump. Your partner, West, leads the Jack of Spades. Dummy plays low. You win with the King and decide the Heart suit must be attacked. The proper card to lead is the Jack. Notice that your Jack and 9 of Hearts surround the dummy's 10 and you have a higher heart—the King. Therefore you should lead as though you held K J 10 9. The complete hand is as follows:

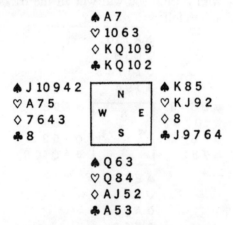

♠ A 7
♡ 10 6 3
◇ K Q 10 9
♣ K Q 10 2

♠ J 10 9 4 2
♡ A 7 5
◇ 7 6 4 3
♣ 8

♠ K 8 5
♡ K J 9 2
◇ 8
♣ J 9 7 6 4

♠ Q 6 3
♡ Q 8 4
◇ A J 5 2
♣ A 5 3

Notice that had you led the 2 of Hearts, South would have played low, West would have been forced to win with the Ace, and now the Queen would stop the suit.

There is a popular belief that when on subsequent defense you find it expedient to lead a suit in which you hold two cards, the higher of the two must be led. This is not always true. When your two cards are immaterial, the higher of the two is led.

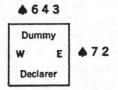

If East finds it desirable to lead Spades, the 7 is the proper card. But if, in the diagram which follows below, East desires to lead Spades, he should not lead the 10. It is too important a card. Note that if the 10 is led, West will win with the Ace but will be unable to return the suit.

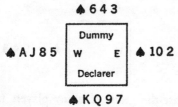

As a general proposition, the lead of a small card by a defender suggests mildly that he can "stand" the return of the suit because he has a supporting card. The lead of a high intermediate card suggests that he probably cannot stand the return.

A complete hand to illustrate this principle follows:

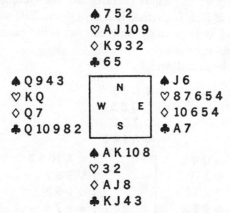

South is the declarer at a contract of 3 No Trump. West leads the 10 of Clubs, which is won with the Ace. The 7 is returned, and declarer permits this to hold the trick. At this point, naturally, East must shift, and logically the only shift is to Spades. East does not make the mistake of leading the Jack. Instead he leads the 6, in order to retain the Jack as a forcing card should West find it expedient to lead that suit later on. Declarer wins this trick and starts on the Hearts. When West is in, he is able to return a Spade. Declarer wins this trick and cashes the Hearts. It is true that South can still make the hand by guessing the adverse holding, but there is a good chance that he will not do so. Note that if East returns the Jack of Spades instead of the 6, now, when West is in with the Heart he will be unable to return Spades without giving declarer his ninth trick.

Leading up to strength

♠ K J 5

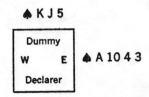

♠ A 10 4 3

It goes against the grain of many players to lead into dummy's strength. It is habitual with them to lead through strength. The above diagram represents a holding which frequently comes up in play. East has the lead and arrives at the conclusion that the defense must cash several Spade tricks to defeat the contract. Naturally this can be done only if partner holds the Queen. The proper attack, therefore, is the 3 of Spades. If declarer has the Queen, the chances are that nothing is lost. If partner has the Queen, East will now have a tenace position over dummy and can wait for partner to come through and clear up the suit.

The complete hand follows:

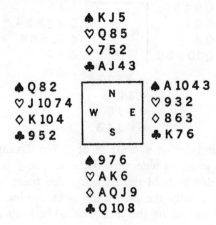

♠ K J 5
♡ Q 8 5
◇ 7 5 2
♣ A J 4 3

♠ Q 8 2
♡ J 10 7 4
◇ K 10 4
♣ 9 5 2

♠ A 10 4 3
♡ 9 3 2
◇ 8 6 3
♣ K 7 6

♠ 9 7 6
♡ A K 6
◇ A Q J 9
♣ Q 10 8

South is declarer at a contract of 3 No Trump. West leads the 4 of Hearts. East plays the 9, and declarer wins with the Ace. This is a very ineffective false card because it cannot possibly fool anyone. The Club finesse is taken, and East, knowing the declarer still holds the King of Hearts, must attack some other suit. Therefore he leads the 3 of Spades, and West's Queen forces the dummy's King. When West subsequently regains the lead on the Diamond finesse, a Spade comes through and three more tricks are cashed by the defense.

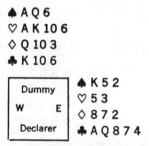

♠ A Q 6
♡ A K 10 6
◇ Q 10 3
♣ K 10 6

Dummy

W   E

Declarer

♠ K 5 2
♡ 5 3
◇ 8 7 2
♣ A Q 8 7 4

You are East defending against South's contract of 3 No Trump. West leads the 4 of Spades, dummy plays the 6, you win with the King, and declarer plays the 3. What is your proper return?

The Spade suit offers no future. If the contract is to be defeated, Clubs are the only hope. The proper return is the 7 of Clubs. This will permit declarer to win a trick cheaply, but if partner gains the lead and can return a Club, the balance of the suit will be cashed. The complete holding is as follows:

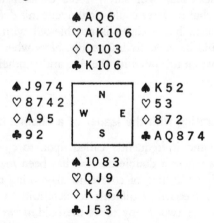

♠ A Q 6
♡ A K 10 6
◇ Q 10 3
♣ K 10 6

♠ J 9 7 4
♡ 8 7 4 2
◇ A 9 5
♣ 9 2

N

W   E

S

♠ K 5 2
♡ 5 3
◇ 8 7 2
♣ A Q 8 7 4

♠ 10 8 3
♡ Q J 9
◇ K J 6 4
♣ J 5 3

An unusual type of holdup play by third hand is illustrated in the holding depicted on the page following.

South opened with 1 No Trump, and North raised to 3 No

Trump. West led the 3 of Spades, and dummy played the 4. East's play to the first trick settles the fate of the hand. Since there is nothing in dummy to capture, it may appear that third hand should

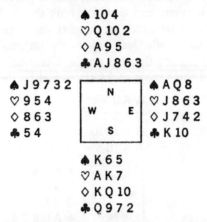

```
                    ♠ 10 4
                    ♡ Q 10 2
                    ◇ A 9 5
                    ♣ A J 8 6 3
    ♠ J 9 7 3 2      ┌─────────┐      ♠ A Q 8
    ♡ 9 5 4          │    N    │      ♡ J 8 6 3
    ◇ 8 6 3          │  W   E  │      ◇ J 7 4 2
    ♣ 5 4            │    S    │      ♣ K 10
                    └─────────┘
                    ♠ K 6 5
                    ♡ A K 7
                    ◇ K Q 10
                    ♣ Q 9 7 2
```

play high, but a moment's reflection will show that an exceptional play is called for at this point. It is quite obvious from the bidding that West can have no high cards. The lead of the 3 shows that West has either four Spades or five, if he also has the deuce, but he cannot have more than five, which means that declarer must have at least three Spades, one of which is the King. If the Ace is put up, declarer will naturally refuse to take the King until the third round and West's Spades will be shut out. East therefore should play the Queen of Spades. This will surely force declarer to win with the King. It is true that declarer could circumvent this defense by refusing to take the Queen, but declarer is not blessed with X-ray eyes and such a play would be virtually impossible. Now when the Club finesse is taken into East he follows with the Ace and another Spade to defeat the contract.

Co-operating with the leader of a doubleton

Third hand is frequently called upon to co-operate with his partner in cases where a doubleton lead has been made against a suit contract. The difficulty lies, of course, in diagnosing that the lead is a doubleton. It is frequently difficult to determine whether partner's lead is from one or two. Many times the bidding will furnish a clue. However, let us assume that you have determined that partner's lead is a doubleton. It is frequently good policy when you have the Ace of that suit to duck the first round, so that partner will retain a card

of that suit to return to you should he obtain the lead before trumps
are exhausted.

An example:

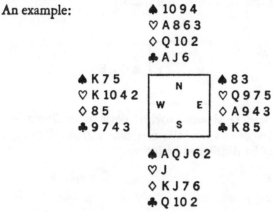

```
                        ♠ 10 9 4
                        ♡ A 8 6 3
                        ◊ Q 10 2
                        ♣ A J 6
   ♠ K 7 5          ┌─────────┐      ♠ 8 3
   ♡ K 10 4 2       │    N    │      ♡ Q 9 7 5
   ◊ 8 5            │ W     E │      ◊ A 9 4 3
   ♣ 9 7 4 3        │    S    │      ♣ K 8 5
                    └─────────┘
                        ♠ A Q J 6 2
                        ♡ J
                        ◊ K J 7 6
                        ♣ Q 10 2
```

South is declarer at a contract of 4 Spades. West leads the 8 of
Diamonds. If East should win the first trick and return a Diamond,
the trick will be won in dummy and a Spade finesse taken. West
will win with the King and will shift to a Club in an effort to reach
partner's hand for a Diamond ruff. Declarer will refuse to take the
finesse and will pull the remaining trumps, giving up in all a Club,
a Diamond, and a Spade. Note how different the play develops if
East refuses the first trick. (East should, however, signal with the
9 of Diamonds, so that partner will not be discouraged from continuing the suit.) When declarer takes the trump finesse, West still has a
Diamond to lead while he has a trump, and a ruff is obtained.

If the partner of the doubleton leader has a quick entry card, the
holdup is unnecessary. In the above hand, if East had held the Ace
of Clubs instead of the King, he could afford to win the first Diamond
trick and return the suit, West being able to enter his hand later with
the Ace of Clubs for the ruff.

Third hand frequently has the opportunity to make a neat though
very simple ducking play with the following combination of cards:

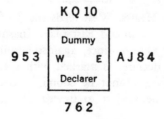

```
                    K Q 10
                ┌──────────┐
                │  Dummy   │
         9 5 3  │ W      E │  A J 8 4
                │ Declarer │
                └──────────┘
                    7 6 2
```

West leads the 9, dummy plays the Queen. East should refuse to win the trick but signal with the 8. Now when West obtains the lead, East can cash the balance of the tricks.

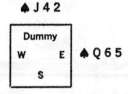

♠ J 4 2

Dummy

W E ♠ Q 6 5

S

If East has the lead he should avoid, if possible, leading a Spade. In the vast majority of cases it will cost him a trick to touch this suit. The cards may be distributed as follows:

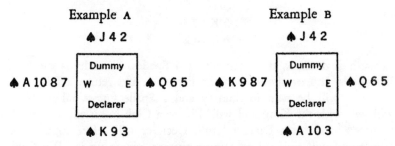

Example A

♠ J 4 2

♠ A 10 8 7 Dummy ♠ Q 6 5

W E

Declarer

♠ K 9 3

Example B

♠ J 4 2

♠ K 9 8 7 Dummy ♠ Q 6 5

W E

Declarer

♠ A 10 3

In **EXAMPLE A**, if East leads a low Spade, declarer will play low and the Ace will follow, giving the declarer one trick. If he is left to play the suit himself, he can win no tricks.

In **EXAMPLE B**, if declarer led the suit himself, he can win only the Ace, inasmuch as the Jack, if led, will be covered by the Queen. If East leads the suit, declarer will play low, forcing the King, and then a finesse is available against East's Queen, yielding the declarer two tricks.

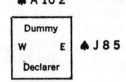

♠ A 10 2

Dummy

W E ♠ J 8 5

Declarer

The contract is 4 Hearts. West leads the 3 of Spades and dummy plays the 2. What card should East play? Inasmuch as West cannot hold the King and Queen, since, against a suit contract, he would have led the King, declarer is marked with a high honor. The play of the Jack, therefore, cannot be sound. If declarer has the King, West's Queen will be subject to finesse and three tricks taken by declarer. If declarer nas the Queen, West's King will be subject to finesse. The complete holding is as follows:

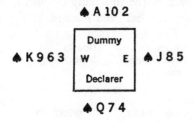

♠ A 10 2

♠ K 9 6 3

Dummy
W   E
Declarer

♠ J 8 5

♠ Q 7 4

The play of the 8 by East will go to South's Queen, but now he has no further finesse and can win only two tricks in the suit. Note if East had played the Jack, all three tricks would be taken by declarer.

THIRD HAND PLAY QUIZ

You are East in each of the following problems, defending against a No Trump contract that has been reached on this sequence of bidding:

SOUTH	NORTH
1 No Trump	3 No Trump
Pass	

1.
```
          J 5 2
         Dummy
WEST  4          K 9 6  EAST
```
West leads the 4 and dummy plays low. What card do you play?

2.
```
          A 10 4
         Dummy
WEST  3          J 8 5  EAST
```
West leads the 3 and dummy plays the 4. What card do you play?

3.
```
          K 9 6
         Dummy
WEST  4          A J 7  EAST
```
West leads the 4 and dummy plays the 6. What card do you play?

4.
```
          Q 9 5 2
         Dummy
WEST  4          K J 6  EAST
```
West leads the 4 and dummy plays the 2. What card do you play?

5.
```
          J 8
         Dummy
WEST  3          Q 9 5  EAST
```
West leads the 3 and dummy plays the 8. What card do you play?

6.
```
          7 4 2
         Dummy
WEST  K          J 5  EAST
```
West leads the King and dummy plays low. What card do you play?

7.
```
          7 6 4
         Dummy
WEST  Q          10 5  EAST
```
West leads the Queen and dummy plays low. What card do you play?

8.
```
          A 6 4
         Dummy
WEST  Q          K 7  EAST
```
West leads the Queen and dummy plays low. What card do you play?

9.
```
          Q 5
         Dummy
WEST  7          J 3  EAST
```
West leads the 7 and dummy plays the Queen. What card do you play?

10.
```
          5 4 2
         Dummy
WEST  10          K Q 9 8 7  EAST
```
West leads the 10 and dummy plays low. What card do you play?

11.
```
                NORTH
                ♠ J 9 8 3
                ♡ Q 4
                ◇ 8 4
                ♣ A Q J 8 4
WEST                        EAST
◇ 6                         ♠ A 5 4 2
                            ♡ 10 6 3 2
                            ◇ A J 3
                            ♣ K 2
```

12.
```
                NORTH
                ♠ K J 6 2
                ♡ 7 4 2
                ◇ A Q 8 5 4
                ♣ 8
WEST                        EAST
♠ 9                         ♠ A 10 8 7 4
                            ♡ 8 6
                            ◇ K 7
                            ♣ Q 4 3 2
```

The bidding:

SOUTH	NORTH
1 No Trump	2 Clubs
2 Diamonds	3 No Trump
Pass	

West leads the 6 of Diamonds and dummy plays low. What card do you play?

13.

```
            NORTH
            ♠ Q 10 4
            ♡ A J 10
            ◇ K J 10 8 3
            ♣ Q 4
WEST                    EAST
♣ J                     ♠ 8 7 3
                        ♡ 9 4 2
                        ◇ 7 2
                        ♣ A 9 8 5 3
```

The bidding:

NORTH	SOUTH
1 Diamond	1 Spade
2 Diamonds	2 No Trump
3 Spades	4 Spades
Pass	

West leads the Jack of Clubs and declarer plays low in dummy. How should East defend?

The bidding:

SOUTH	NORTH
1 Heart	2 Diamonds
2 No Trump	3 Hearts
4 Hearts	Pass

West leads the 9 of Spades and dummy plays low. What card do you play?

14.

```
            NORTH
            ♠ 8 7
            ♡ J 9 6 2
            ◇ 7 5
            ♣ A K J 8 4
WEST                    EAST
♡ K                     ♠ Q 3
                        ♡ 8 5
                        ◇ J 9 6 4 3 2
                        ♣ 10 7 3
```

The bidding:

SOUTH	NORTH
1 Spade	2 Clubs
3 Spades	4 Spades
Pass	

West wins the first two tricks with the K Q of Hearts, as East echoes. West then plays a low Heart and declarer plays the 9 from dummy. What card should East play?

ANSWERS TO THIRD HAND PLAY QUIZ

1.

The 9. The advantage of playing the 9 can be seen if you imagine declarer to hold either the A Q or A x; in either case you save a trick by not putting up the King. Admittedly, playing the 9 does not gain if declarer has the Q x or A 10, but neither does it cost: you make the same number of tricks eventually whether you play the King or the 9. It is, of course, to be assumed, in view of the bidding, that declarer has a guard in the suit.

2.

The 8. The principle of finessing against the dummy hand continues down to cards of secondary rank. If you were to play the Jack in this instance, you would present declarer with an unnecessary trick in the suit whenever he held the K x or Q x, for after winning your Jack he could finesse dummy's 10.

3.

The 7. By playing the 7 rather than the Jack you come home a winner if

South holds the Q x x. In this case, if you played the Jack, South would win and would still have a stopper in the suit with dummy's K 9. By applying the Rule of Eleven to West's opening lead of the 4, you learn that declarer has only one card that can beat the 7 and you should assume that this card is the Queen.

4.

The 6. It is surely reasonable to assume that your partner has led his fourth best, in which case the Rule of Eleven indicates that declarer holds only one card higher than the 4. In all probability that card is the Ace, and therefore you should put in the 6.

5.

The 9. Partner's lead of the 3 tells you that he has no more than five cards in the suit. It is not to be presumed that the declarer, who opened 1 No Trump, is lacking both the Ace and King, and therefore it cannot gain to play the Queen. If declarer has the Ace it will not matter whether you play the 9 or the Queen, but if he has the K 10 x, you save a trick by finessing the 9 and then leading the Queen when you get in.

6.

The Jack. In this situation you proceed on the assumption that your partner's suit is headed by the K Q 10. In this case it is essential to drop the Jack to apprise partner of the situation. If you play the 5, there is grave danger that partner will probably shift, imagining declarer to hold the A J x.

7.

The 10. The principle behind this play is similar to that in the previous example. You drop your honor card because you presume, in view of the lead, that your partner holds the card next in rank below it. If you held the 10 x x, it would be sufficient to play the middle card.

8.

The King. A defender should usually strive mightily to avoid being left with a singleton honor in a suit that his partner is trying to establish. Thus, in this instance, if you don't unblock with the King, declarer will duck a continuation of the suit, and after winning with the King you will be unable to drive out the Ace. Playing the King on the Queen is perfectly safe if your partner's suit is headed by the Q J 10, but even if it is headed by the Q J 9, the unblock is still the best play. It would also be correct to divest yourself of the King if the declarer played the Ace at the first trick.

9.

The Jack. Again you must avoid allowing yourself to be left with the singleton honor. If declarer's holding is the K 9 x, unblocking with the Jack will enable partner to cash the suit when you gain the lead and return the 3. If you didn't unblock, declarer would refuse to cover the Jack when you led it and the defense would be stymied.

10.

The 9. Partner is evidently to be congratulated on having found a brilliant lead from the 10 x, but in your enthusiasm you should not make the mistake of playing the Queen. If you did, the declarer, with A J x, would duck, and would win with the Jack when you continued the suit. Your partner would not then have another card to play when he regained the lead. By encouraging with the 9, you force declarer to play the Jack at once, and thus you keep in touch with partner.

11.

The Jack of Diamonds. It is obvious that the contract will be expunged if partner's Diamonds can be brought in. You should therefore play the Jack, for you can afford to let declarer win a free trick if he has the Q x x. Provided the play of the Jack is not preceded by great deliberation, it will appear to declarer that his best chance is to win and take the Club finesse. The complete holding was:

```
              NORTH
              ♠ J 9 8 3
              ♡ Q 4
              ◇ 8 4
              ♣ A Q J 8 4
WEST                        EAST
♠ 7 6                       ♠ A 5 4 2
♡ 9 7 5                     ♡ 10 6 3 2
◇ Q 10 7 6 2                ◇ A J 3
♣ 7 5 3                     ♣ K 2
              SOUTH
              ♠ K Q 10
              ♡ A K J 8
              ◇ K 9 5
              ♣ 10 9 6
```

If East plays the Ace of Diamonds on opening lead, declarer ducks a Diamond continuation, wins the third round, and makes the contract after establishing the Club suit.

12.

The Ace of Spades. East has to decide whether to take the Ace or duck it, playing West for a doubleton Spade and a quick entry. Declarer almost certainly has the Q x x in Spades in view of his bid of 2 No Trump. West is, therefore, marked with a singleton, and can ruff a Spade return.

13.

Win and return a Diamond. The bidding has marked declarer with the King of Clubs, so there is little point in ducking the Club lead. Since South is also marked with points in Hearts, it is not too much to hope that West may have the Ace of Diamonds and a trump entry, in which case East, if he wins and returns a Diamond, may be able to get a Diamond ruff to set the contract. The complete holding was:

```
              NORTH
              ♠ Q 10 4
              ♡ A J 10
              ◇ K J 10 8 3
              ♣ Q 4
WEST                        EAST
♠ A 5                       ♠ 8 7 3
♡ Q 7 5 3                   ♡ 9 4 2
◇ A 6 4                     ◇ 7 2
♣ J 10 7 2                  ♣ A 9 8 5 3
              SOUTH
              ♠ K J 9 6 2
              ♡ K 8 6
              ◇ Q 9 5
              ♣ K 6
```

14.

The Queen of Spades. West would have led the Ace of Hearts at the third trick if he knew South had another Heart, and East must therefore expect to be overruffed by declarer. Accordingly, he should, in effect, play 'third hand high' by ruffing with the Queen. This will promote a trump trick if West has the J x or 10 x x.

20. Defensive play by second hand

AN ADAGE from the days of Whist recommends the play of "second hand low." This is sound advice in the vast majority of cases. It is subject, of course, to the exception that when the opponents lead an honor you may desire to cover, with the hope of building up a trick for yourself or partner. It is also subject to the exception that you may play a high card second hand—as, for example, where you have both the King and Queen—in order to be sure to build up a trick in a hurry. The rule, therefore, is that if you are second hand you should play low unless you have a very definite reason for not doing so.

A simple illustration is the following:

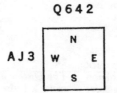

Q 6 4 2

A J 3

South, the declarer, leads a small one. You are West. What do you play? The answer is, low. If you play low, the dummy will be forced to play the Queen. Either your partner will win with the King or, if the Queen holds the trick, you now retain the Ace Jack over the declarer's King and will be able to take two tricks.

The complete holding is as follows:

Q 6 4 2

A J 3   10 8 5

K 9 7

It is quite obvious that if you had played the Ace, the declarer would have lost only one trick in the suit.

The same reasoning would apply if North held:

K 6 4 2

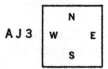

A J 3

Here again West would play low, except in the rare case where he suspects that South has a singleton and is trying to steal a trick with the King.

K J 9 4

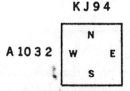

A 10 3 2

South leads a small one. West would play low, not the Ace. If partner has the Queen, he should be given a chance to make it. If the declarer has the Queen, it is useless to come up with the Ace, because the declarer will lose only one trick in the suit. The complete holding might be as follows:

K J 9 4

A 10 3 2   8 7

Q 6 5

It is a good general policy to make your Aces catch big ones. *The place for the Ace is on a King.* If you cannot catch a King, try to catch a Queen. If you cannot do that, try to win a Jack, because it is usually losing play to put your Ace on the opponent's deuces.

South, the declarer, leads the 5. West improperly plays the Jack, in order "to force the Ace." Why does he wish to force the Ace? Surely it will do him no good, but he argues, "It might do my partner

A 10 3 2

J 4

some good." This is a fallacious argument. It can do your partner some good only if he has the King or Queen, in which case he won't need your help. Either the Ace must come up or your partner will win the trick.

However, the play of the Jack might do your partner a lot of harm, because the complete holding might be as follows:

A 10 3 2

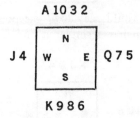

J 4

Q 7 5

K 9 8 6

South leads the 6. If West plays the Jack, declarer wins with the Ace and returns the 10, finessing against East's Queen. If West holds on to his Jack, the defense must win a trick regardless of how declarer plays.

A Q 10 4 2

Dummy

K 5 3

Declarer

South, the declarer, leads a small one. I have seen West play the King (in order to force out the Ace) because "my King is gone in any event." Why does West wish to force out the Ace? It surely will not do him any good. But he argues, "I wanted to build up my partner's Jack." The answer is, your partner's Jack needs no building up. Nature will take care of that. Suppose, for example, the complete holding were as follows:

A Q 10 4 2

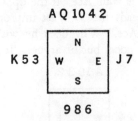

K 5 3

J 7

9 8 6

Now if the declarer plays the Queen next time, your side wins no trick. If you had played low, regardless of which card was played from dummy, either your partner would win with the Jack or you subsequently would win with the King.

To repeat: *Do not put your honor cards on deuces.*

Another frequent error is as follows:

A K 10

Q J 6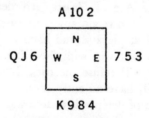

South leads a low one. If you are West, you should not play the Jack in order to force out the King, because it does you no good. Do not be afraid that the declarer will play the 10, because, first of all, he may not; second, if he does, there is nothing you could ever do about it.

Change the situation slightly:

A 10 2

Q J 6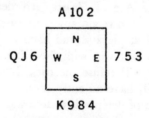

When South leads low, the play of the Jack is proper in order to force out the Ace, because now you will be sure of a trick in that suit. Whereas if the declarer inserts the 10 and wins, you may lose your trick. The complete holding may be:

A 10 2

Q J 6 7 5 3

K 9 8 4

If, however, the holding were as follows:

A 7 5 3

Q J 6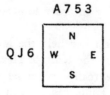

and South led the deuce, it would be improper to play the Jack in order to force out the Ace, because it is highly improbable that the declarer intends to play the 7, and if he does, your partner would no doubt have some card that could beat it. One of the dangers of playing the Jack in that case is that your partner might have the singleton King. To recapitulate: Do not split your honors unless by so doing you are sure of building up a trick.

There are cases in which second hand should play high. They will be treated presently.

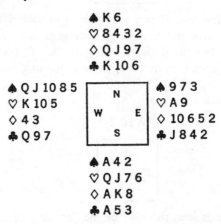

```
                        ♠ K 6
                        ♡ 8 4 3 2
                        ◇ Q J 9 7
                        ♣ K 10 6

    ♠ Q J 10 8 5                        ♠ 9 7 3
    ♡ K 10 5           N                ♡ A 9
    ◇ 4 3        W           E          ◇ 10 6 5 2
    ♣ Q 9 7             S               ♣ J 8 4 2

                        ♠ A 4 2
                        ♡ Q J 7 6
                        ◇ A K 8
                        ♣ A 5 3
```

South is the declarer at a contract of 3 No Trump. West leads the Queen of Spades, which dummy wins with the King. The 2 of Hearts is led from dummy. East should not play second hand low. He should come right up with the Ace of Hearts, in order to clear partner's Spade suit and so partner can retain any entry cards that he may hold. Note the difference if East plays second hand low. Declarer will put up the Jack, and West will win with the King. The Spade will be continued, and declarer will refuse the trick. Now when the Spades are established West will have no entry card.

The general principle of defense is as follows: When your partner has opened a long suit at No Trump, which he is obviously trying to establish, you should rush in full speed, using every possible effort to win a trick early in the play in order to clear your partner's suit while he still holds entry cards.

In the above example, if East had held the K 9 of Hearts instead of the A 9, he should still play the King of Hearts, in the hope that it will hold the trick. There is really no danger in this play, since if the declarer has the A Q, the King was doomed from the beginning.

Second hand should sometimes play high when an honor card can be captured.

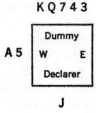

K Q 7 4 3

Declarer leads the Jack. West should win with the Ace. It is better to capture an honor with your Ace. If you duck, you will find yourself placing your Ace on the deuce next time. The complete holding is as follows:

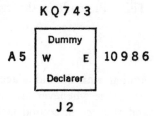

If you duck the first trick, your side is limited to one trick. If you take it, your partner still has a stopper.

Combinations

A somewhat advanced situation in which second hand should play high occurs in the following hand:

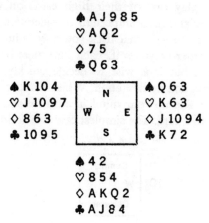

South is playing 3 No Trump. West leads the Jack of Hearts, dummy plays the Queen, and East wins and returns the suit. Declarer ducks the second round and is forced to win the third round with the Ace. He returns to his hand with a Diamond and leads the 2 of Spades. If West plays the 4, the 8 will no doubt be played from dummy and East will win with the Queen. Declarer will subsequently finesse the Jack of Spades and bring in the entire suit. West's proper play is the King of Spades. This prevents the declarer from running the suit. The play appears to be drastic but in fact is not so, inasmuch as declarer almost certainly does not have the Queen of Spades. If he does, there is really no chance to defeat the contract. There is the further chance that declarer will think you are false-carding from the K Q 4 and may permit you to hold the trick, subsequently finessing the Jack of Spades. This will result in the complete collapse of the hand.

Covering honors

We are all familiar with the old adage "Cover an honor with an honor," which means that whenever an honor card is led by the declarer or dummy and you are in second position holding a higher honor, you should cover the one played by the opponent. This would appear to contradict the other bromide, "Second hand low." As in most other departments of play, there is no such thing as *always* or *never*. If you always cover an honor with an honor you will lose a great many tricks. It is important to understand why the opponent's honor should be covered. Put briefly, it is this: If you do not cover the honor, it is apt to win a trick. If you do cover, you will force the opponents to play two of their high cards on the same trick. There is the further and more important consideration that by forcing them to play two honors on that trick you may build up a later trick for either your partner or yourself. Each case must be decided by the particular situation, but it is wise to decide quickly, so as to avoid giving away information by hesitation. When it appears that an honor will soon be led, make up your mind in advance and be ready when the declarer plays that card. The simplest case is as follows:

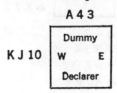

A 4 3

K J 10 | Dummy
W   E
Declarer

You are West. South, the declarer, leads the Queen. Obviously you must cover with the King, forcing the Ace and converting both your Jack and 10 into winners.

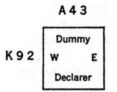

South leads the Queen. Here you cover with the King, forcing the declarer to play the Ace and Queen on the same trick. You may not profit by this procedure if the declarer has the Jack and 10 as well, but, on the other hand, you will not lose. You will build up a trick if it happens that your partner has the Jack or the 10. This time, therefore, you are covering not to promote your own cards but to promote some card that your partner might have. It will do you no good to retain the King, for you know perfectly well that the Queen will win the trick if you do not cover. The complete holding might be as follows:

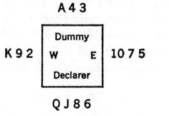

In which case you actually have gained nothing by covering the Queen, but, on the other hand, you have lost nothing. If you cover the Jack when it is played, declarer will have to give up a trick in the suit.

These examples have been relatively simple. There is one, however, which is more difficult to judge. Take the following holding:

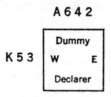

South, the declarer, leads the Queen. This is apparently the same situation as the one above, but note that this time you do not have the 9. The proper procedure in this case will depend upon the type of player who is declarer. If he is a sound player, you may depend upon it when he leads the Queen that he also has the Jack. Therefore it will do no good to cover the Queen, and you should wait for the Jack to be led. An inferior player, however, might lead the Queen when he does not have the Jack, in which case the better procedure is to cover.

The objection to covering the Queen against a good player will appear from the following diagram:

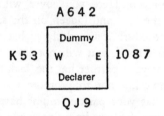

Notice that if you cover the Queen, dummy will win with the Ace and subsequently finesse the 9, losing no tricks in the suit. However, if you refuse to cover the Queen, but wait and cover the Jack, your partner's 10 will subsequently prove to be a winner.

Notice that in the combinations just under consideration the dummy has been to your left and the closed hand has led first. Let us take the other situation where the dummy is at your right, as follows:

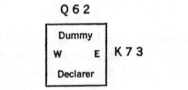

The Queen is led. The proper procedure is to cover with the King. You know that your King is lost in any event, and you hope that partner has, if not the Jack, at least the 10. The complete holding may be as follows:

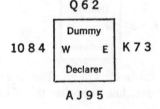

Notice that failure to cover the Queen will result in declarer's making all the tricks.

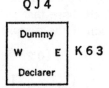

When dummy leads the Queen, you should not cover, because the the only card you can hope to promote at this time is the Jack, and that is held by the opponent. If subsequently the Jack is led, then you should cover, hoping that partner holds the 10. Which brings us to this general principle: *Never cover a sequence of honors until the lowest card of the sequence is led.* For example:

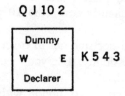

When dummy leads the Queen, do not cover. When the Jack is continued, also refuse to cover, because there is no card that you can positively develop for partner. By covering, you can lose a trick if the complete holding were as follows:

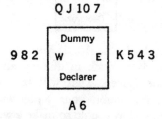

To repeat: *Never cover the first time if it is just as convenient to cover the second time or the third.*

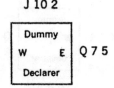

The Jack is led from dummy. Do not cover. Here the rule not to cover a sequence of honors applies. If subsequently the 10 is led, that should be covered, with the hope that partner has the 9. Notice how badly the cover will result if the complete holding were as follows:

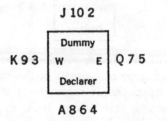

J 10 2

K 9 3   Q 7 5

A 8 6 4

If you cover the Jack with the Queen, your side will take only one trick. If you wait, your partner will win the first trick with the King and when you subsequently cover the 10 your partner will win another trick with the 9.

It is a good general doctrine not to cover an honor unless you have in your mind the possibility that your partner holds a certain card which can be promoted.

Therefore do not cover an honor without making a wish. For example:

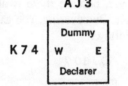

A J 3

K 7 4

South, the declarer, leads the 10. If you play low, it is probable that the declarer intends to duck in dummy and your partner will probably win with the Queen. That will be your side's last trick, because subsequently, no doubt, your King will be finessed. The proper play is to cover, and as you do so make a wish that your partner holds the Queen 9 and another card. Let us see how this will work:

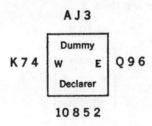

A J 3

K 7 4   Q 9 6

10 8 5 2

Notice if you fail to cover the 10, your side will win only one trick, but if the 10 is covered, declarer must win with the Ace and your partner's Queen and 9 will both be winners.

The above considerations do not apply as broadly when the suit in question is trump. Partner is then less apt to have any strength in the suit.

Where you can see that your honor cannot be captured, it will be apparent that a cover is not in order.

For example:

A 2

```
            ┌─────────┐
            │ Dummy   │
  K 6 4 3   │ W     E │
            │ Declarer│
            └─────────┘
```

Assuming the contract to be No Trump, you know that your King cannot be captured. Therefore, when South leads the Queen, you must not cover. This will, of course, give the declarer the occasional opportunity to fool you by leading the Queen when he does not really have the Jack, but the chances of the occurrence are so remote that for all practical purposes it should be disregarded.

A good general plan to remember is that you should cover when the dummy leads an honor that is not part of a sequence and you are second hand containing an honor which you know cannot win a trick in any event.

To the rule that you never cover a sequence of honors there is an exception—that is when you have just two of the suit. The reason is that the next time you may be forced to place your honor on a small card.

For example:

Q J 4 2

When the Queen is led from dummy normally we do not cover a sequence of honors, but if we duck, the declarer may lead the deuce the next time, which would force us to play the King. Therefore the cover is proper. The complete holding may be:

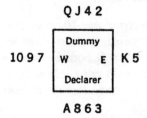

QJ42

| 1097 | Dummy | K 5 |
| W | E |
| Declarer |

A 8 6 3

In the combinations just considered for covering we had in mind principally the side suits. When the question of trumps is involved there may be other considerations, and many times where the cover might ordinarily be proper it would be otherwise if the suit led were trumps, because the bidding may have indicated to you that your partner could not possibly have a card which would be promoted by your cover. For example: Suppose the declarer had bid Spades several times, showing a long suit.

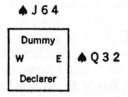

♠ J 6 4

You are East. When the Jack is led and you contemplate covering you must make a wish, and that wish would be that your partner holds the 10 and two others, but this is impossible, because that would give the declarer only a four-card suit and he would not have bid the suit several times. Therefore declarer must have at least five or six, which would give your partner either one or two. Your cover cannot gain. If your partner has the King, he will make it in any event. If he has the 10, it will fall too soon to be a winner. There is the bare possibility that your partner has the lone King. The complete holding will then have been as follows:

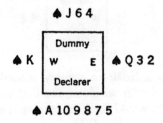

♠ J 6 4

♠ A 10 9 8 7 5

In the next hand, you are West and have opened the 10 of Spades against South's contract of 3 No Trump. Your partner plays the 8, and declarer wins with the Queen. He now leads the Jack of Diamonds. What card should you play?

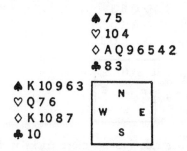

♠ 7 5
♡ 10 4
◇ A Q 9 6 5 4 2
♣ 8 3

♠ K 10 9 6 3
♡ Q 7 6
◇ K 10 8 7
♣ 10

The bidding has proceeded as shown below:

SOUTH	NORTH
1 Club	1 Diamond
1 Heart	2 Diamonds
2 No Trump	3 No Trump

The answer is, if you are playing against anyone but a most inferior player, a low Diamond. The reason is that if declarer has any knowledge of card combinations he will permit your King of Diamonds to hold if you cover, and your partner will definitely show out on this lead. Declarer, having bid No Trump enthusiastically, surely has two Diamonds. Now when East shows out, the declarer will be able to finesse the 9 on the next round and pick up the entire suit. The complete holding is as follows:

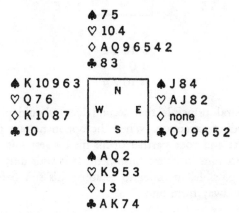

♠ 7 5
♡ 10 4
◇ A Q 9 6 5 4 2
♣ 8 3

♠ K 10 9 6 3
♡ Q 7 6
◇ K 10 8 7
♣ 10

♠ J 8 4
♡ A J 8 2
◇ none
♣ Q J 9 6 5 2

♠ A Q 2
♡ K 9 5 3
◇ J 3
♣ A K 7 4

You are West defending against South's contract of 4 Spades. The Jack of Diamonds is opened, won in dummy, and the trump Ace driven out. What is your proper lead?

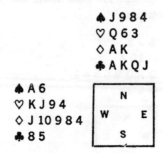

```
            ♠ J 9 8 4
            ♡ Q 6 3
            ◇ A K
            ♣ A K Q J
♠ A 6           N
♡ K J 9 4
◇ J 10 9 8 4  W   E
♣ 8 5           S
```

It is apparent that your side has no more tricks in Spades, Diamonds, or Clubs. Obviously, therefore, you must shift to a Heart, but which Heart? The proper card is the Jack. If declarer has the Ace, it makes no difference, but if your partner has the Ace and not the 10, a low Heart lead will permit declarer to win one trick in that suit.

The complete holding is as follows:

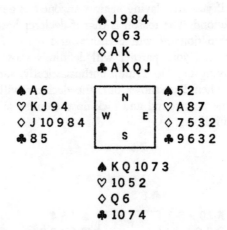

```
            ♠ J 9 8 4
            ♡ Q 6 3
            ◇ A K
            ♣ A K Q J
♠ A 6           N        ♠ 5 2
♡ K J 9 4               ♡ A 8 7
◇ J 10 9 8 4  W   E     ◇ 7 5 3 2
♣ 8 5           S        ♣ 9 6 3 2
            ♠ K Q 10 7 3
            ♡ 10 5 2
            ◇ Q 6
            ♣ 10 7 4
```

To the general principle that second hand should play low there is one outstanding exception. When the opponents are playing a No Trump contract and your partner opens his longest suit, it is essential for you to assist him in its establishment. It is your duty to win tricks as quickly as possible, in order to establish his suit before his entry cards are taken away from him.

For example:

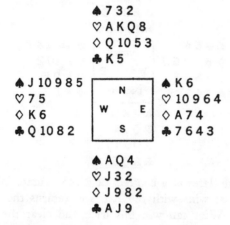

♠ 7 3 2
♡ A K Q 8
◇ Q 10 5 3
♣ K 5

♠ J 10 9 8 5   ♠ K 6
♡ 7 5   ♡ 10 9 6 4
◇ K 6   ◇ A 7 4
♣ Q 10 8 2   ♣ 7 6 4 3

♠ A Q 4
♡ J 3 2
◇ J 9 8 2
♣ A J 9

You are East. South is playing 3 No Trump. West leads the Jack of Spades, and your King falls to declarer's Ace. The dummy is entered with the Queen of Hearts and a small Diamond led. You must win this trick in a hurry, in order to clear the Spade suit for your partner. Upon a Spade return, declarer will hold up and West will clear the suit. He now has the King of Diamonds as an entry to cash the setting tricks in Spades.

Note the difference if you played second hand low. The Jack of Diamonds will force your partner's King. A Spade will be returned, and declarer will duck. Although the Spades may be cleared, your partner will have no card of entry to enable the cashing of these tricks.

Maintaining communication with partner at No Trump

Where a defender is attempting to establish a suit at No Trump, it is important for him to bear in mind that unless he has a card of entry the long suit will be worthless even when it becomes established. Partner may be able to obtain the lead but will have none of the suit to return to the opening leader. In such cases it is vital for the opening leader to play the hand in such a manner that partner will retain a card of that suit with which to communicate after the suit is established.

For example:

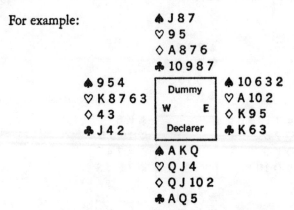

```
                    ♠ J 8 7
                    ♡ 9 5
                    ◇ A 8 7 6
                    ♣ 10 9 8 7
   ♠ 9 5 4        ┌──────────┐    ♠ 10 6 3 2
   ♡ K 8 7 6 3    │  Dummy   │    ♡ A 10 2
   ◇ 4 3          │ W      E │    ◇ K 9 5
   ♣ J 4 2        │ Declarer │    ♣ K 6 3
                  └──────────┘
                    ♠ A K Q
                    ♡ Q J 4
                    ◇ Q J 10 2
                    ♣ A Q 5
```

South is the declarer at a contract of 3 No Trump. West leads the 6 of Hearts. East wins with the Ace and returns the 10. Declarer plays the Jack. West can win this trick and clear the suit, but he would never be able to cash the two long Hearts, because he has no entry card, and, besides, partner will have no Heart left to return to him. The proper procedure is for West to permit declarer's Jack to hold the trick. One trick must be lost in any event. Now when East obtains the lead with the King of Diamonds he will have a Heart left to return to West and the setting tricks are cashed.

SECOND HAND PLAY QUIZ

What is the proper play in the defense of the following hands?

1.
          10 4
         Dummy
             A 5 EAST

Dummy leads the 10. Should East cover?

2.
        Q J 9 3
        Dummy
          K 5 4 EAST

Dummy leads the Queen. Should East cover?

3.
        J 10 7
        Dummy
        Q 6 3 EAST

Dummy leads the Jack. Should East cover?

4.
        J 10 3
        Dummy
         A Q 6 EAST

Dummy leads the Jack. Should East cover?

5.
        10 9 4
        Dummy
        K J 6 EAST

Dummy leads the 10. Should East cover?

6.
        K 10 8 7 5
        Dummy
  WEST Q 4 2

Declarer leads the Jack. Should West cover?

7.
        A 7 6 2
        Dummy
  WEST K 5 4

Declarer leads the Jack. Should West cover?

8.
        A 10 6
        Dummy
  WEST K 8 4 3

Declarer leads the Queen. Should West cover?

In the following hands you are the defender and the play has proceeded as indicated.

9.
```
              NORTH
              ♠ 7 6 2
              ♡ 5
              ◇ A Q 8 4 3
              ♣ K 10 4 3
   WEST
   ♠ K 4 3
   ♡ K J 6 2
   ◇ K J 9 6
   ♣ 8 6
```

SOUTH	NORTH
1 Spade	1 No Trump
2 Spades	3 Spades
4 Spades	Pass

West leads a low trump against 4 Spades. Declarer wins with the Jack in his own hand and plays the Queen of Hearts. Should West cover?

10.
```
              NORTH
              ♠ K 10 9
              ♡ 8
              ◇ A Q 7 6 3
              ♣ Q 10 7 2
                          EAST
                          ♠ 7 4 2
                          ♡ K 6 3
                          ◇ K J 10 5
                          ♣ 8 4 3
```

NORTH	SOUTH
1 Diamond	1 Spade
2 Spades	4 Spades
Pass	

West leads the Ace of trumps and continues with another trump. Declarer wins in dummy and leads a Heart. What should East play?

ANSWERS TO SECOND HAND PLAY QUIZ

1.

East should cover with the Ace. Otherwise he may have to play it on thin air when the next lead is made from dummy. This will cost a trick if declarer's holding is, for example, K J 8 x x or Q J 8 x x.

2.

East should duck. When dummy leads an honor from a sequence, the ground rule for the second-hand player is to cover the *last* honor of that sequence. In this instance, if East covers the first honor, the declarer, with A x x, will win and take all the tricks in the suit by finessing dummy's 9.

3.

East should duck. The disadvantage of covering can easily be appreciated by imagining that declarer has the K 8 x x or A x x x. In either case, covering the first honor costs a trick. East should wait until the 10 is led.

4.

East should cover the 10. East may cover with either the Queen or the Ace, depending on the tactical situation, but the big thing is to cover with one of them. Declarer's holding could be the K 8 x x, and if the 10 is not covered declarer will lose only one trick in the suit.

5.

East must cover the 10. Failing to cover the 10 costs a trick when declarer's holding is A Q 7 x. In this example, and the previous one, the reason for departing from the general principle of refusing to cover the first honor is that East has *two* honors in the suit led.

6.

West should cover with the Queen. When the declarer (as opposed to the dummy hand) leads an honor, it is usually correct to cover *when*

there are two honors on the defender's left. In this instance West has to accept the risk that declarer has the A J 9, because it is more important to cater for the situation where declarer has the J x.

7.

West should not cover. When there is only one honor on the defender's left, it usually does not pay to cover the declarer's first lead of an honor. In this instance declarer may have the J 10 x and East the Q 9 x, in which case covering the first lead would amount to a grave indiscretion.

8.

West should not cover. This is an exception. Although there are two honors on his left, West does not cover South's lead of the Jack because he can see that his King will command the fourth round of the suit if he ducks.

9.

West should not cover. West's opening trump lead has evidently proved an effective form of defense, for the declarer evidently wants to ruff Hearts in dummy. It is essential that the next trump lead should come from East, who is marked with the Ace of Hearts, and therefore West should duck.

10.

East should go in with the King. The reason for departing from the normal rule of Second Hand Low is that East needs an entry and needs it desperately. Declarer's play shows that he intends to ruff a Heart in dummy, and only East can stop him, for it is not to be expected that West has another trump. Therefore East must go up with the King of Hearts hoping to hold the trick and expunge dummy's ruffing potential by returning his third trump.

21.   Signals

THERE IS a tendency on the part of a great many casual players to pay no attention to the cards being played, except when they are winning tricks. By such practice they lose many opportunities to score points. Bridge is a partnership game, and during the defense of a hand the partnership angle is extremely important. You should try to make every play and every card have a special meaning. Sometimes, even with a completely useless hand, you may be of great assistance to your partner by giving him information he may need to conduct the defense. Signals have something in common with traffic lights. They may be red, which say stop. They may be green, which say go ahead, or they may be yellow, which say hesitate. In the last instance the signaler is not quite sure.

It is to be borne in mind that even when a card cannot possibly win a trick it might tell an important story to partner. There should be no meaningless play in contract. A card played by you when not attempting to win a trick should state to partner at least your desire as to whether or not the suit should be led again by your side. You may be very anxious for its continuance, in which case an unnecessarily high card is played. You may be very anxious that it be discontinued, in which case the lowest possible card is played, or you may not be sure, in which case you might play a card that is not quite your lowest.

Your desire to have the suit continued may be for one of several reasons. You may wish to trump a subsequent round of the suit. You may wish to win a trick in that suit. You may wish your partner to force the declarer by the continuance of that suit, or you may occasionally wish to force the dummy to trump that particular suit. You may even desire the continuance of that suit because you fear your partner might make a damaging shift.

However, regardless of your reason, when you have expressed it, it is not for your partner to reason why, but for him to "do or die." Otherwise bridge is not his game and he should take up 500 or gin rummy.

One of the most effective means by which the defense conveys information is the "come-on" signal. The signal is made when not attempting to win a trick. The "come-on" signal is made on the defense by playing an *unnecessarily* high card. For example, if the King and then the Ace of a suit are led by the defender and his partner follows suit first with the 7 and then with the 5, that would complete the signal and would be the "come-on" message, because the 7 was an *unnecessarily* high card, since the normal procedure would be to play the low one first and then the higher one. The departure from the normal procedure is intended as a signal. The "come-on" signal suggests to partner the continuance of that suit. Discards in the ordinary manner, such as first the 5 and then the 7, suggest that a continuance of that suit is not desired.

It is to be noted that the high-low signal is used whenever you wish partner to "come on," and you may wish him to "come on" for several reasons, as indicated above. When a defender fails to signal, there is the suggestion that he wishes some other suit led. It is not a command, but the opening leader should think twice before continuing a suit in the face of such discards by partner.

A signal may be given by a defender, not only on the lead by his partner, but also when the declarer is playing a suit. Here again the play of an unnecessarily high card suggests the desire that partner lead that suit if he gets in.

The play of the deuce or of any card which the leader can read as being the lowest assumes that partner does not wish that suit led. This may be told although partner has bid a suit.

Suppose your partner has bid Spades and you led the Ace. He follows suit with the deuce. It is quite obvious to you that he must have been able to spare some higher card when he bid the suit. Therefore it must be a violent message to you to lead some other suit even though he bid Spades.

If a defender is extremely anxious to have the suit continued, he should play the highest card he can afford for the purpose.

There is a tendency on the part of some players to say arbitrarily that a 6 or better is a come-on signal. This is unwise. You cannot help the cards that have been dealt to you. The 7 might be a discouraging card and a 4 might be an encouraging card, depending on the cards that have been dealt to you.

If partner leads the Ace and you urgently desire the suit continued, assuming that you hold the K 8 6 2, you should signal with the 8 rather than the 6, because your signal will then be more emphatic. If you signal with the 6, it might be understood by partner but there might be a doubt in his mind, whereas a signal with the 8 is more apt to impress him.

When you want a suit led and are playing with a mediocre or inattentive partner, it is better to shout rather than to whisper. That is, make your signals as violent as you reasonably can. He may not notice the mild or subtle signals. He may pay attention if you drop a 10.

Signaling at No Trump

Signaling at No Trump is slightly different from signaling at a suit declaration. The distinction must be borne in mind during this discussion. A simple illustration of an encouraging signal at No Trump is the following:

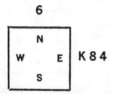

Declarer is playing No Trump. West leads the Queen. What card should East play? The answer is definitely the 8. Your partner is leading from either the Q J 10 or the Q J 9, and you must encourage him to continue the suit. If you play the 4, your partner will not know where the remaining cards are and may fail to continue the suit. The complete holding may be as follows:

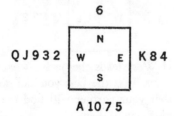

Another illustration:

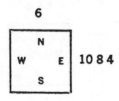

West leads the Queen. East should play the 8. Partner's lead is from the Q J 9, and as your partnership contains all the cards except the Ace and King your partner should be encouraged to continue the suit. Another example:

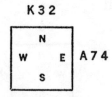

West leads the Queen. East should play the 4. He does not wish to give West any undue encouragement to continue the suit. If West's suit is solid, such as the Q J 10 9, he will not need encouragement and will go ahead anyhow.

```
         K 3 2
        ┌─────────┐
        │    N    │
        │ W     E │ A 7 4
        │    S    │
        └─────────┘
```

West leads the Jack. Dummy plays low. East should play the 7. If he plays the Ace, it permits declarer to win both the King and the Queen. The Jack forces declarer's Queen, and the Ace subsequently captures the King. However, partner must be encouraged to continue, and the 7 will provide that encouragement.

```
           6
        ┌─────────┐
        │    N    │
        │ W     E │ Q 4 3 2
        │    S    │
        └─────────┘
```

It is No Trump and West leads the Jack. What card should East play? The 4 by all means. It is the best you can do in the way of a signal, and you trust that your partner will find the 3 and 2 missing and suspect you of holding one of them.

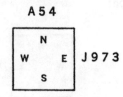

West leads the King and dummy plays low. What card should East play? The answer is the 9, violently calling for a continuance of the suit.

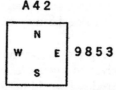

A 4 2

9 8 5 3

West plays the King. Dummy plays low. What card should you play as East? If partner has led from K Q J, you wish to encourage a continuation. If he has led from K Q 10 7, it would be dangerous for him to continue with a small card, for declarer would have J 6. Inasmuch as you are undecided, you should take no definite position. Do not signal violently for a continuation by playing the 8, nor should you shout discouragement by playing the 3. Rather, you ought to say, "Partner, I am not sure." This message you may convey by a temporizing discard of the 5. It is up to partner to decode your message. He can probably tell that the 5 is not your lowest, and should realize that you are in some doubt. He may then be resourceful enough to realize that the holding which would place you in doubt would be four small, because if you had the Jack you would surely say, "Come on." If you had three small ones, you would certainly shout, "Whoa." He should therefore lead the Queen, which will drop the Ace and Jack together. The complete holding is as follows:

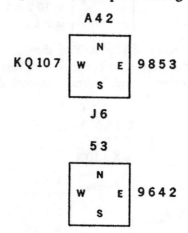

A 4 2

K Q 10 7   9 8 5 3

J 6

5 3

9 6 4 2

You are East defending against a No Trump contract. West leads the King. You are not sure whether you wish your partner to continue the suit or not. If your partner has a complete sequence, he will continue it even though your discard is discouraging. If he has a holding such as A K J 7, you certainly do not wish him to continue the suit. Therefore, with this holding, you should play the 4. When partner notices that the 2 is missing he may realize that your discard says, "I'm not quite sure."

Signals must not be given indiscriminately merely to show high cards. They must be given to suggest leads. In other words, if I should signal with the 7 of Spades, I would not merely be telling my partner that I have the Ace of Spades, let us say. I would be saying, "Partner, please lead Spades for some reason which I know best. I may not even have the winning Spade, but desire that suit to be led."

A signal may be given even on a suit that is being led by the opponents. For example, if the dummy leads a low card, you are second hand and hold A 7 3 but do not wish to put up the Ace, you should play the 7. This will serve as a signal to partner that you have something important in the suit.

Playing against a 4 Spade contract, you are East.

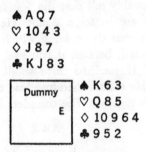

♠ A Q 7
♡ 10 4 3
◇ J 8 7
♣ K J 8 3

Dummy   ♠ K 6 3
E   ♡ Q 8 5
◇ 10 9 6 4
♣ 9 5 2

Partner leads the King of Hearts. You should signal with the 8, because you wish your partner to continue with three rounds of that suit. But, playing against a Club contract, suppose the holding were as follows:

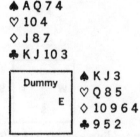

♠ A Q 7 4
♡ 10 4
◇ J 8 7
♣ K J 10 3

Dummy   ♠ K J 3
E   ♡ Q 8 5
◇ 10 9 6 4
♣ 9 5 2

Your partner leads the King of Hearts. You must not signal with the 8, because when your partner follows with the Ace you will have to play the 5 and your partner will think that you desire a third round of the suit, which is exactly what you do not wish, because the declarer may possibly be out of the suit and ruff in the dummy and discard a loser from the closed hand. Your proper play is, therefore, the 5 of Hearts. You do not signal to show the Queen. You signal because you wish a suit continued for three rounds.

Discards

Signals may be given when not following suit—that is, when discarding. Various artificial methods of signaling have from time to time been devised, such as an even-number card indicating one thing and an odd-number card another. None of these has passed the test of experience, and common-sense methods of signaling have survived.

The discard of a low card from weakness is sound. If you have some suit in which you are not interested and you have a low card, then there is no objection to discarding it.

When in discarding you play first a high card and then a low card, that is drawing your partner's attention to that suit and is calling for its lead. To illustrate: If you first discard the 3 and then the 5, that indicates you have nothing in that suit; but if you first discard the 5 and then the 3, that would draw your partner's attention to that suit and request its lead.

It is apparent that a signal by discarding will shorten your strong suit. If you do not desire to do this—as, for example, at No Trump, where you wish to retain a number of cards in your best suit—you may signal by inference. Let us suppose, for example, Spades are being run, to which you cannot follow. You wish Hearts led by your partner. You may indicate this by discarding a low Club (stating, "I do not wish Clubs") and then a low Diamond (stating, "I do not wish Diamonds"), and by this time your partner should be able to figure out that you prefer to have Hearts led.

Spades are being led by the opponents at No Trump. You have, for example:

♠ none   ♡ A K 10 8 6   ◊ 9 6 4 3   ♣ 8 7 5 2

You would like to signal for a Heart lead but you do not wish to waste one of your Hearts by playing the 8. You may signal for a Heart lead inferentially by first discarding the 2 of Clubs and then the 3 of Diamonds. If you do not wish either Clubs or Diamonds, it is probable that you desire a Heart.

However, if there is an emergency and you want to be quite sure that your partner leads Hearts, you should not signal by inference but should discard the 8 of that suit. This is especially true if you happen to be playing with a partner who is not particularly alert. In fact, if the emergency is great enough, you should discard the 10. He might not notice the 8.

An illustration of a case in which partner desires a continuance of the suit because he wants the dummy to ruff is provided by the following hand:

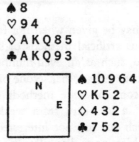

South is declarer at a contract of 6 Hearts, and West leads the King of Spades. What should East play? East knows that the King of Hearts may be captured on a finesse, but if the Spade is continued and one of dummy's trumps must be used early, declarer will not be able to come through the King of Trumps twice. He should therefore signal for a continuance of the Spades and should play the 10, a violent signal to his partner. This 10 of Spades does not mean *maybe*. It means *positively!* Note the difference if West fails to continue with a Spade.

The complete hand is as follows:

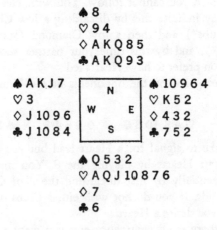

It has been shown that a signal can be made with an unnecessarily high card. The word *unnecessarily* is important, because sometimes we have actually no high card. If we have A 4 2 and wish the suit continued, we are obliged to play the 4. It is not actually a high card, but in point of fact it is an *unnecessarily* high card because we have the 2. At the time it is played partner may not recognize it, but when the 2 subsequently appears the signal will become apparent.

When, therefore, you are the defender and you win the first trick and your partner follows with a card like the 4, look around the table for the 3 and the 2. If neither one of them appears, there is the chance that your partner holds one of them and the 4 may be the beginning of a signal. Or it may be that the declarer is deliberately concealing the 3 and the 2 to give you the impression that your partner is signaling. In that case you will sometimes have to guess, but more often than not, if the 3 and 2 are missing, the chances are that your partner has begun an echo.

You are West playing against a Spade contract. You have, for example:

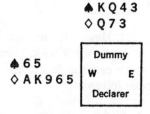

You lead the King of Diamonds, and partner follows with the 4. Declarer plays the 8. What would your next play be? Is there any danger that the Ace of Diamonds will be trumped? The answer is no. It all depends on who has the 2. If your partner has it, the 4 is the beginning of a signal. If the declarer has it, then your Ace will not be trumped.

Signaling with honors

There is a slogan that reads "Never signal with a honor." Like so many others, this is only a partial truth. A better way to state the principle is, "Never signal with a card that might later on take a trick." When, however, your honor card cannot possibly win a trick and must fall in any event, there is no objection to signaling with it. For example:

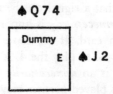

Hearts are trumps, and West leads the King of Spades. What should East play? He is anxious to ruff the third round, and his Jack cannot possibly win a trick. Therefore he should signal with it. Partner will continue with the Ace, and East will ruff the third round. If East should play the 2 on the first trick, West might lead some other suit and the Spade ruff would be lost.

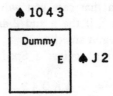

West leads the King of Spades, Hearts are trumps. East must not play the Jack, because that card might win a trick. Partner's lead may be from the King Queen, in which case the Jack could not be spared. The complete holding might be as follows:

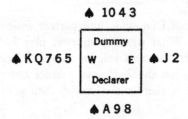

The Queen is never used as a signal. If, therefore, the defender follows suit with the Queen, it must be a singleton or that player must also have the Jack.

It is a definitely accepted convention that against a suit contract, if a player leads the King of a suit and partner follows with the Queen, the opening leader must absolutely underlead at trick two and in no case lead his Ace.

An illustration of this principle is provided in the hand which follows:

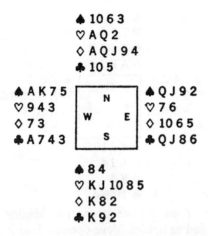

```
                  ♠ 10 6 3
                  ♡ A Q 2
                  ◊ A Q J 9 4
                  ♣ 10 5

  ♠ A K 7 5         N          ♠ Q J 9 2
  ♡ 9 4 3                      ♡ 7 6
  ◊ 7 3        W        E      ◊ 10 6 5
  ♣ A 7 4 3         S          ♣ Q J 8 6

                  ♠ 8 4
                  ♡ K J 10 8 5
                  ◊ K 8 2
                  ♣ K 9 2
```

South is the declarer at a contract of 4 Hearts. West leads the
King of Spades. East must realize that in order to defeat the contract
West will have to have the Ace of Clubs (West has bid a Spade).
Therefore East plays the Queen of Spades on the opening lead. West
is obligated to lead a low one, which East wins with the Jack, and
the Queen of Clubs comes through, defeating the contract.

As for the rule that one must not signal with honors, an exception
must be noted in the case where you are deliberately unblocking for
for your partner at No Trump. It is very vital not to let your high
cards block partner's suit

Trump echo

When a defending player follows high-low in trumps, it is
a signal to his partner which states as follows: "Partner, I have three
trumps and I can ruff something." The trump echo can also be
applied when trumps have not been led but when one of the defenders is actually ruffing. When holding only two trumps, the
defender should ruff with his lowest trump. When holding three or
more trumps, the first trick should be ruffed with a card that is not
the lowest, and the second one should be ruffed with the lowest. This
will signal your partner that you have another trump. It may be
important for your partner to know this, because he will not know
whether to give you a third ruff or not. The following hand illustrates
this principle:

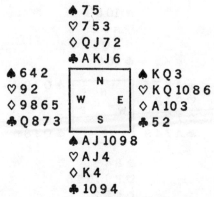

```
              ♠ 7 5
              ♡ 7 5 3
              ◊ Q J 7 2
              ♣ A K J 6
  ♠ 6 4 2                    ♠ K Q 3
  ♡ 9 2           N          ♡ K Q 10 8 6
  ◊ 9 8 6 5    W     E       ◊ A 10 3
  ♣ Q 8 7 3       S          ♣ 5 2
              ♠ A J 10 9 8
              ♡ A J 4
              ◊ K 4
              ♣ 10 9 4
```

You are West. Your partner opens the bidding with 1 Heart. South plays the hand at Spades. Your opening lead is the 9 of Hearts, which draws your partner's Queen, the trick going to declarer's Ace. Entry to dummy is gained through a Club lead to enable declarer to lead trumps toward his own hand. Your partner "splits his equals" by playing his Queen of Spades, the trick being won by declarer's Ace. The declarer next proceeds to clear his trump suit by letting your partner win with the King of Spades.

Your three-trump echo (first playing your 4, then your 2) shows East that you still hold a trump. Your play of his suit (9, then 2, when he leads out his Heart King) clearly discloses that you hold no more Hearts. Consequently your partner will lead a third round of Hearts for you to trump, giving your side a third trick; your partner's Ace of Damonds will win a fourth trick.

Unless you use the three-trump echo, your partner may lose game by laying down his Diamond Ace and leading a second round of that suit, hoping that you hold the King. In any event, your use of the echo makes your partner's proper play perfectly clear. Another example:

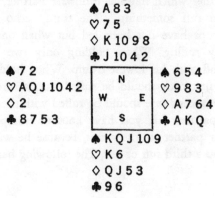

```
              ♠ A 8 3
              ♡ 7 5
              ◊ K 10 9 8
              ♣ J 10 4 2
  ♠ 7 2                       ♠ 6 5 4
  ♡ A Q J 10 4 2   N          ♡ 9 8 3
  ◊ 2           W     E       ◊ A 7 6 4
  ♣ 8 7 5 3        S          ♣ A K Q
              ♠ K Q J 10 9
              ♡ K 6
              ◊ Q J 5 3
              ♣ 9 6
```

You are West. South is playing 4 Spades doubled. You open the singleton Diamond. East wins and returns the 4 of Diamonds, which you ruff with the 2 of Spades. A Club lead is won by East's Queen and another Diamond is ruffed with the 7 of Spades. When East is back in with the King of Clubs he knows there is no use trying to give you another ruff, because your play of the trumps shows you have no more. Therefore he leads a Heart, and you take two more tricks. If you held three trumps, you would have ruffed first with the 7 and then with the 2.

Echoing with an honor

When partner opens a fourth best at No Trump and dummy plays a high card which you cannot beat, if you have some mild support in the suit you may convey the information on the first trick by the play of your second best card. If your holding includes two adjacent honors, it is customary to signal with your highest card. This serves the dual purpose of giving advice and also unblocking for future plays of the suit.

Q 4

	Dummy		
7	W	E	J 10 5

You are East. Partner opens the 7 and dummy plays the Queen. You should follow with the Jack, and partner will know that you have the 10. Furthermore, your play will prevent the possible blocking of the suit. Similarly, if you held J 9 5, your proper play would be the 9. But if you held 6 3 2, you should play the 2, which would indicate to partner that you are not interested in the suit.

Special high-low signal at No Trump

There is a specialized use of the high-low signal at No Trump which occurs under the following condition: The declarer is playing No Trump, and the dummy has the long suit with no side entries. One of the defenders holds the Ace of the dummy's long suit and he wishes to hold off until such time as the declarer has no more of the suit. How long should he hold up?

The defender wishes naturally to take his Ace at exactly the time when declarer has no more of that suit. It would be disastrous to take it too soon, leaving declarer with a card of that suit, and it might be fatal to hold up too long, for declarer might in this manner sneak away with his contract-fulfilling trick. The number of cards held by declarer may be determined by the following signals.

If the player who does not have the Ace follows suit in regular order, it shows that he has three. If the player follows suit in the reverse order—that is, high-low—it shows that he has two. Occasionally that player may have four, but that is rare. In such case he must not play his lowest. In other words, an ambiguity arises, and partner will not be sure whether it is four or two, but the bidding will usually make that clear. It will not very often be four in any event. An example follows:

```
                    ♠ 8 4
                    ♡ 8 6
                    ◊ K J 10 9 6
                    ♣ 7 5 3 2
  ♠ J 10 9 7      ┌─────────┐      ♠ 6 5 3 2
  ♡ A 10          │    N    │      ♡ 9 7 5 4 3
  ◊ 5 4 2         │ W     E │      ◊ A 8 3
  ♣ K 10 8 4      │    S    │      ♣ 9
                  └─────────┘
                    ♠ A K Q
                    ♡ K Q J 2
                    ◊ Q 7
                    ♣ A Q J 6
```

South is the declarer at 3 No Trump. He wins the opening Spade lead and leads the Queen of Diamonds. When West plays the 2, East knows that he should hold up his Ace just once but not any more, because if declarer had three Diamonds, West would have only two and would therefore have started the high-low. If West has a singleton Diamond, so that he is helpless to signal, it makes no difference, because the declarer will have four and the holdup will do no good anyhow. Notice that if East would wait until the third round to take his Ace, the declarer would have enough tricks. Taking the Ace on the second round prevents declarer from fulfilling the contract.

When declarer is running a suit at No Trump, discarding finally becomes quite embarrassing, and it is extremely undesirable for both partners to hold the same suit. Early in the play, therefore, each player should indicate which suit he really has and the other partner should let go of that suit even though he has something important in it. If East discards a high Club, he is announcing that he has something in Clubs, and West therefore should not worry about that suit.

If West discards a high Diamond, he is announcing strength in that suit, and East should not bother to protect Diamonds. This avoids the common error of both partners' keeping the same suit and both discarding what they should have kept.

Make it a point not to discard until void of a suit if it appears that the declarer may have some guessing to do as to the location of the missing honors in that suit. For example:

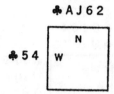

You are West. It is undesirable to let go a Club if there is some other discard to make. Declarer may require a finesse against the Queen, and your discard will "tip off" your partner's hand. Your partner might hold the Q 7 3 and declarer K 10 9 8. If you hold on doggedly to your two Clubs, he may suspect that you have the Queen. Another example:

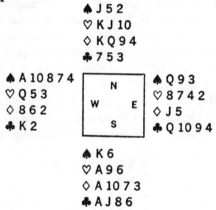

South is the declarer at a contract of 3 No Trump, having opened the bidding with 1 No Trump. West leads the 7 of Spades, and East's 9 forces declarer's King. The Diamonds are now run, and East must make two discards. He naturally must keep both Spades, and should refuse to discard a Heart but rather elect to throw two Clubs. This, on the surface, appears to be a very daring discard. Actually it is not so. The declarer surely has the Ace of Hearts and the Ace of Clubs. If he also has the King of Clubs he has nine top-card tricks. East's best chance, therefore, is that the declarer will misguess the location of the Queen of Hearts. If East elects to discard Hearts, the guess will be a cinch.

Be very careful to avoid, if possible, discarding from a suit in which you have the same length as the dummy or a suit in which you have the same length that you suspect the declarer of holding in the closed hand. Take the following:

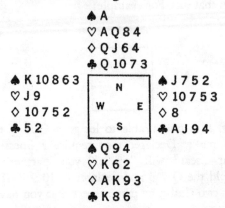

♠ A
♡ A Q 8 4
◇ Q J 6 4
♣ Q 10 7 3

♠ K 10 8 6 3   ♠ J 7 5 2
♡ J 9   ♡ 10 7 5 3
◇ 10 7 5 2   ◇ 8
♣ 5 2   ♣ A J 9 4

♠ Q 9 4
♡ K 6 2
◇ A K 9 3
♣ K 8 6

South is the declarer at a contract of 3 No Trump. West leads the 6 of Spades, and East plays the 7. As the declarer runs the Diamonds, East can afford to discard one Spade, or even two Spades, provided he lets go the Jack for unblocking purposes. His other discard must be from his good Club holding, but not from the Hearts. If the declarer has both the King and Jack of Hearts, nothing can stop 3 No Trump, but if partner has the Jack of Hearts, it is necessary for East to retain four Hearts in order to stop that suit.

A hand which illustrates the danger in discarding until void of a suit is the following:

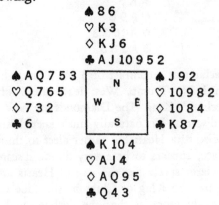

♠ 8 6
♡ K 3
◇ K J 6
♣ A J 10 9 5 2

♠ A Q 7 5 3   ♠ J 9 2
♡ Q 7 6 5   ♡ 10 9 8 2
◇ 7 3 2   ◇ 10 8 4
♣ 6   ♣ K 8 7

♠ K 10 4
♡ A J 4
◇ A Q 9 5
♣ Q 4 3

South is playing 3 No Trump, and West leads the 5 of Spades. East's Jack forces the King. The declarer has a total of eight top-card tricks, with any number of extra tricks if the Club finesse succeeds. If, however, the Club finesse fails, the contract is immediately defeated. Declarer bided his time by cashing the King of Hearts and running off the four Diamonds. On the fourth Diamond, West thoughtlessly let go the 6 of Clubs because "it was no good to him." Declarer now led the Queen of Clubs, originally intending to finesse, but when West showed out, that play was naturally abandoned. Now a Spade threw West into the lead. He was able to cash four Spades but in the end had to lead up to declarer's Ace Jack of Hearts.

West could easily have spared a Heart discard in order to keep the 6 of Clubs, and there is a fair chance that he would have defeated the contract. It is true that declarer could still have made it by first cashing the Ace of Clubs, but it is doubtful whether he would have made that play without seeing the hands exposed.

Discarding partner's suit

After having led the highest of partner's suit, it is conventional to discard from the top down. For example: if you hold the 9 6 2 in a suit your partner has bid and you lead the 9 of that suit, the 6 should be played the next time and finally the 2. At this point partner will know that you have no more of the suit. This method of discarding is usually more important at a suit contract than it is at No Trump, but even at No Trump it may be very informative.

Discarding to Ace led at No Trump

Another convention which dates back to auction days is the one calling for your play of the highest card when partner leads the Ace at No Trump. You are unconditionally required to drop your highest card, though it be the King or Queen, unless the appearance of the dummy makes it evident that your play will cost a trick.

Suit-preference signal

The purpose of the suit-preference signal in playing against suit declarations is to eliminate the guess as to which of two suits partner should return if he obtains the lead. The statement "which of two suits" may not be very clear, but in actual play there is usually no doubt which two suits are involved. When partner obtains the lead his problem as to the correct return will almost never involve a choice of three suits. For the purpose of this discussion the trump suit is immediately eliminated, and the suit that is being led when the preference signal is being made does not count, which leaves for the player's consideration a choice between the other two suits. Which to lead will frequently be a guess, and the following convention is devised in an effort to remove the doubt.

The play of an unnecessarily high card *which obviously is not a come-on signal* asks partner to return the higher-ranking of the two plain suits.

Emphasis is placed on the phrase "which obviously is not a come-on signal" because numerous abuses have been committed by players who have recently learned to employ this convention. A signal still remains a signal. If you lead an Ace of Diamonds and partner follows with a very high card, it means that he wants you to continue Diamonds, not that he wishes you to shift to Spades. An illustration of the abuse follows:

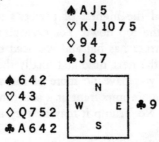

♠ A J 5
♡ K J 10 7 5
◇ 9 4
♣ J 8 7

♠ 6 4 2
♡ 4 3
◇ Q 7 5 2
♣ A 6 4 2

♣ 9

South is playing a Spade contract. West leads the Ace of Clubs, and partner plays the 9. I have heard many players say, "When you played a high Club, I thought you wanted a Heart shift through strength." This is absurd. The normal come-on signal applies here. Partner wants you to lead some more Clubs. How else can he tell you? The suit-preference convention would apply only if from the appearance of the dummy your common sense tells you that he cannot want a Club led.

Sometimes an ambiguity will arise, but not often. Bidding, combined with common sense, will usually furnish the solution to the problem.

A situation in which partner's signal cannot possibly be intended in the normal sense is the following:

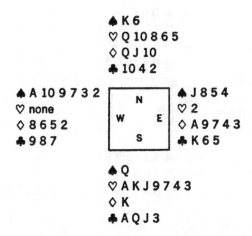

                    ♠ K 6
                    ♡ Q 10 8 6 5
                    ◇ Q J 10
                    ♣ 10 4 2

♠ A 10 9 7 3 2   ♠ J 8 5 4
♡ none   ♡ 2
◇ 8 6 5 2   ◇ A 9 7 4 3
♣ 9 8 7   ♣ K 6 5

                    ♠ Q
                    ♡ A K J 9 7 4 3
                    ◇ K
                    ♣ A Q J 3

    South is the declarer at a contract of 6 Hearts. Spades have been bid and supported. West leads the Ace of Spades. Unless the Diamond Ace is cashed at this point, declarer will win the hand. West does not know whether to shift to the Diamonds or Clubs, but it is quite apparent to everyone at the table that a shift is in order, because nothing could possibly be gained by the Spade continuance. East's discard of the Jack of Spades indicates that a diamond shift should be made—the higher-ranking suit. If Clubs were desired, the 4 would be played. Notice this principle applies only when it is quite evident that another Spade lead is not desired. The Jack of Spades is not a normal come-on signal, but a suit-preference signal.

Normal signal

    There are cases in which it might be that a Spade continuance would be logical. Then the signal would be interpreted in its normal sense. In the hand that follows South is playing 6 Spades. West leads the King of Hearts. It will be seen that another Heart lead will defeat the contract by forcing dummy to trump, and now East's King of Trumps cannot be picked up. East's discard of the 10 of Hearts should be regarded as a normal come-on signal and not as a suit-preference signal, because the appearance of the dummy does not make it clear that a shift is indicated. It is perfectly logical that East may wish dummy to trump a Heart. If dummy had a great many trumps it would be different. Then there could be no logical reason to wish dummy forced.

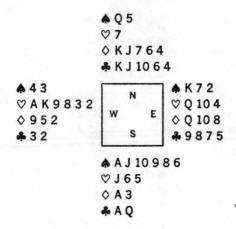

```
              ♠ Q 5
              ♡ 7
              ◊ K J 7 6 4
              ♣ K J 10 6 4
♠ 4 3                        ♠ K 7 2
♡ A K 9 8 3 2       N        ♡ Q 10 4
◊ 9 5 2          W     E     ◊ Q 10 8
♣ 3 2               S        ♣ 9 8 7 5
              ♠ A J 10 9 8 6
              ♡ J 6 5
              ◊ A 3
              ♣ A Q
```

Entry at No Trump

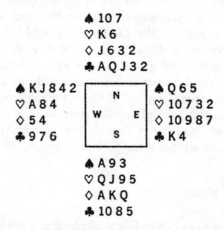

```
              ♠ 10 7
              ♡ K 6
              ◊ J 6 3 2
              ♣ A Q J 3 2
♠ K J 8 4 2                  ♠ Q 6 5
♡ A 8 4             N        ♡ 10 7 3 2
◊ 5 4           W     E      ◊ 10 9 8 7
♣ 9 7 6             S        ♣ K 4
              ♠ A 9 3
              ♡ Q J 9 5
              ◊ A K Q
              ♣ 10 8 5
```

South is playing 3 No Trump. West leads the 4 of Spades. East wins with the Queen and returns the 6. South plays the 9, and West wins with the Jack. West has the option of knocking out the Ace with either the deuce or the King. It does not really matter. Since it does not matter, the choice of the card that West selects will be a signal to his partner advising what suit to return should East obtain the lead. His proper play is to drive out the Ace of Spades with the King. This is a signal to lead back the higher-ranking suit—Hearts rather than Diamonds. Notice that when declarer wins the Spade trick he will take the Club finesse. East will win with the King, and if he should return a Diamond, the contract would be fulfilled. West's suit-preference signal of the King of Spades makes it clear to East that he should return a Heart. The suit-preference signal applies here because West had a choice of cards to lead back. If it were necessary to lead back the King in order to surely force the Ace, then, of course, the suit-preference convention would not apply. Another example:

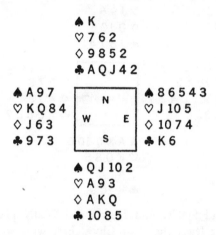

South is the declarer at a contract of 3 No Trump. West leads the 4 of Hearts. East follows with the 10 and is permitted to hold the trick. The Jack is continued, and declarer again ducks. A third round is led, and declarer wins with the Ace. West has remaining the King and Queen, and which one he drops is immaterial. Therefore he selects the one which will suggest to partner the suit in which he holds his entry. He follows with the King of Hearts. Partner knows that he has the Queen, and therefore he has made an unnatural discard. The suit-preference convention applies, and the higher-ranking suit is suggested to partner. Notice that when a Club finesse loses, the contract will be made unless East returns a Spade.

Ruffs

The most frequent application of the suit-preference convention is in obtaining ruffs. The situation is one in which you know your partner is about to trump your lead, and inasmuch as he will desire subsequent ruffs, he must know how to regain entry into your hand for the purpose of obtaining the desired ruffs. The size of the card which you lead for your partner to trump flashes the signal as to which suit he must return to you. If the card led is an unnecessarily high one, it suggests to partner a return of the higher-ranking of the two remaining side suits. If the card led to be ruffed is the lowest one, it suggests the return of the lower-ranking suit. As an example:

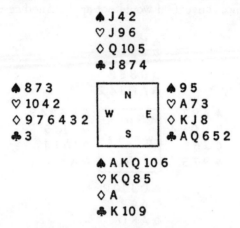

South has bid Spades and Hearts and finally plays the hand at 4 Spades. West leads the 3 of Clubs. East wins with the Ace and reads it as a singleton lead. East may return any Club he wishes, but when West ruffs the Club he will be in doubt as to the method of re-entering his partner's hand. Since Hearts have been bid, West will no doubt elect to lead a Diamond, and the contract will be easily fulfilled. East, therefore, must suggest to his partner to return a Heart, and this he does by returning the unnecessarily high Queen of Clubs. When West ruffs he knows he must lead a Heart, the higher-ranking of the two side suits. If East held the Ace of Diamonds, he would return the 2 of Clubs for his partner to ruff.

The use of the suit-preference convention may also be employed in an opening lead. In leading a suit that does not contain a complete sequence, it is customary to open with the fourth highest. If that fourth highest happens to be a deuce, the opening leader is marked with a four-card suit.

Let us suppose that your partner has opened the deuce of a suit in which you know from the bidding that he has more than four. It is apparent, therefore, that he is making an unnatural lead, and this unnatural lead must be interpreted as part of the suit-preference convention, intending to communicate to you the suggestion that he wishes the lowest-ranking suit returned. An illustration of this principle appears in the following hand:

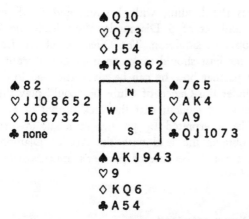

East has opened the bidding with 1 Club. South doubled, and West bid 1 Heart. South later became the declarer at 4 Spades.

West opened the 2 of Hearts, which East won with the King. He realized that his partner would not bid a four-card suit as a sign of weakness over the double. Therefore the lead of the 2 must have some other significance; namely, that a Club return was desired. East also realized that it was perfectly possible that his partner had six Hearts, in which case his Ace of Hearts would not be a. re-entry. Therefore he showed his partner that the proper return was a Diamond by playing the 3 of Clubs instead of the Queen. This was ruffed by West, and even though his partner was marked with the Ace of Hearts, West followed the suit-preference convention and returned a Diamond, thus putting East in to give West another ruff. (It might be good policy for East to win the first lead with the Ace of Hearts, in order to give partner the impression that the King is held by South.)

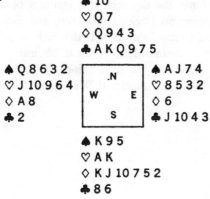

North opens the bidding with 1 Club, and South becomes the declarer at a contract of 5 Diamonds. West leads the 2 of Clubs, which is an obvious singleton. The Queen is played from dummy, and at this point East should make an unnatural discard in order to suggest to his partner how he can be given the lead in order to provide a ruff. Under the Queen of Clubs he should play the Jack. The bidding will make it evident that the Jack cannot be a singleton, so that it must be interpreted by partner as a suit-preference signal. When West obtains the lead with the Ace of Diamonds, he will know to lead a Spade, because of partner's unnecessarily high Club, rather than a Heart.

Directing a safe lead

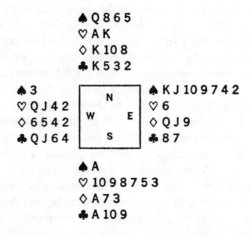

```
                ♠ Q 8 6 5
                ♡ A K
                ◇ K 10 8
                ♣ K 5 3 2
  ♠ 3                           ♠ K J 10 9 7 4 2
  ♡ Q J 4 2         N           ♡ 6
  ◇ 6 5 4 2     W       E       ◇ Q J 9
  ♣ Q J 6 4         S           ♣ 8 7
                ♠ A
                ♡ 10 9 8 7 5 3
                ◇ A 7 3
                ♣ A 10 9
```

South becomes the declarer at a contract of 4 Hearts. West leads the 3 of Spades, an obvious singleton, and East's 7 forces the Ace. On the second trump East discards the Jack of Spades. Since this would be otherwise meaningless, it must be interpreted not as a normal signal to come on, but as a suit-preference signal, meaning it is safe to lead Diamonds. Notice if West leads Clubs the hand can be made.

SIGNALS QUIZ

In each of the following problems you are defending. What card do you play in the circumstances indicated?

1.

```
            DUMMY
            ♠ A J 9
            ♡ A 9 6
            ◇ 8
            ♣ A Q 10 9 4 3
                      EAST
                      ♠ K 8 6 5 3 2
                      ♡ K 2
                      ◇ Q J 10
                      ♣ K 6
```

The bidding:

NORTH	EAST	SOUTH	WEST
1 Club	1 Spade	2 Hearts	Pass
4 Hearts	Pass	Pass	Pass

The contract is 4 Hearts and West leads the Queen of Spades. South wins in dummy and leads the Ace of Hearts and another trump, West following with the 5 and then the 3. What do you play next?

2.

```
            DUMMY
            ♠ Q 8 3 2
            ♡ Q J 7
            ◇ K 6 3
            ♣ 9 6 4
                      EAST
                      ♠ 10 7 6 5
                      ♡ 9 3 2
                      ◇ A 8 2
                      ♣ K 5 2
```

The bidding:

SOUTH	NORTH
1 No Trump	2 No Trump
Pass	

West leads a low Club, your King holds the trick, and you return the suit. West proceeds to cash the A J of Clubs, declarer following each time. West then plays the thirteenth Club. What do you discard?

3.

DUMMY
♠ Q J 10
♡ K J
◇ K 10 7 2
♣ A J 7 2

EAST
♠ 8 7 4 2
♡ A Q 10 9
◇ 9 6 3
♣ 6 5

The contract is 3 No Trump and West leads the 10 of Clubs. Declarer turns up with the K Q of Clubs and runs the suit. What do you discard?

4.

DUMMY
♠ K J
♡ K 4
◇ 10 6
♣ A J 10 8 7 5 2

WEST
♠ 10 8 7 5 4 3
♡ Q 10 3
◇ K 7
♣ 6 4

The bidding:

SOUTH	WEST	NORTH	EAST
1 Heart	Pass	2 Clubs	Pass
2 Hearts	Pass	3 Hearts	Pass
4 Hearts	Pass	Pass	Pass

You lead the 5 of Spades, dummy plays the King and East wins with the Ace. East returns the 2 of Spades, declarer plays low and dummy's Jack wins the trick. Declarer cashes dummy's King of trump, then leads the 4 of trump and finesses the Jack, losing it to your Queen. East follows with the 2 and then the 7. What do you play next?

5.

DUMMY
♠ K J 10 7
♡ K 5 3 2
◇ K Q 10 4
♣ 8

EAST
♠ A Q 6 2
♡ 6
◇ 9 7 5 3
♣ Q 10 8 3

South is playing 4 Hearts and West leads the King of Clubs. What do you play?

6.

```
        DUMMY
        ♠ K J 9 7 3
        ♡ Q
        ◇ Q J 10 4 2
        ♣ K Q
            EAST
            ♠ none
            ♡ J 10 5 2
            ◇ 8 5 3
            ♣ J 7 6 4 3 2
```

South is playing 6 Diamonds and West leads the Ace of Hearts. What do you play?

7.

```
        DUMMY
        ♠ A K J 9 7 2
        ♡ 7 2
        ◇ A J 5
        ♣ Q 10
            EAST
            ♠ 8 3
            ♡ K Q 10 9 8 6 5 3
            ◇ none
            ♣ A 8 4
```

The bidding:

EAST	SOUTH	WEST	NORTH
4 Hearts	5 Diamonds	Pass	6 Diamonds
Pass	Pass		

West leads the Ace of Hearts. What do you play?

8.

```
        DUMMY
        ♠ Q
        ♡ A 10
        ◇ A Q J 10 6 3
        ♣ Q J 8 7
    WEST
    ♠ K 9 7 5 3
    ♡ J 7 4 3
    ◇ 5 2
    ♣ 10 4
```

The bidding:

NORTH	SOUTH
1 Diamond	1 Heart
3 Diamonds	3 No Trump
Pass	

You lead the 5 of Spades, which East wins with the Ace, declarer playing the 4. East returns the 8 of Spades, which South covers with the 10. What do you play?

9.

                                    DUMMY
                                    ♠ K J
                                    ♡ 9 7 6
                                    ◇ K 10 9 8 6 3
                                    ♣ A 4
        WEST
        ♠ 10 8 7
        ♡ Q J 10 4 3
        ◇ 5 2
        ♣ Q J 8

The bidding:

NORTH	SOUTH
1 Diamond	2 Clubs
2 Diamonds	2 No Trump
3 No Trump	Pass

The contract is 3 No Trump, and you lead the Queen of Hearts, East playing the 8. Declarer wins with the Ace, plays the A Q J of Diamonds, overtaking the third one, and runs the Diamonds. What are your discards?

ANSWERS TO SIGNALS QUIZ

1.

The King and another Spade. This method of play gives you the maximum chance to defeat the contract. If you don't proceed in this fashion, declarer may draw trumps, establish the Jack of Spades and discard a losing Club on it. West's high-low in trumps is the key to the proper form of defense, for it shows that he has a third trump and can ruff the third round of Spades.

2.

The 2 of Hearts. There are times when the temptation to perform like a human semaphore should be resisted. Thus, in this situation you should not signal with the 8 of Diamonds, because the declarer may have the J 10 x and the signal would solve his problem for him. The only occasion when it may be vital for your partner to lead a Diamond at this point will be when he has the Q J x of the suit, and in this case he will doubtless lead one of his own accord.

3.

The 3 of Diamonds and the 2 of Spades. This is the equivalent of discarding a high Heart, which you cannot afford to do. You are hoping that West will obtain the lead in either Spades or Diamonds, in which case, observing your negative discards, he will be honor bound to return a Heart.

4.

The King of Diamonds. It is clear from East's failure to signal in trumps that he started with only two of them and so cannot ruff a Spade. A Diamond shift will beat the contract if East has the Ace, or if he has the Queen of Diamonds and a Club entry.

5.

The Queen of Clubs. It is highly desirable to persuade West to shift immediately to a Spade. The Queen of Clubs could hardly be a singleton and therefore West is expected to read it as a suit preference signal, calling for a shift to Spades. Reverse the holdings in Spades and Diamonds and East would drop the 3 of Clubs, asking for a Diamond.

6.

The Jack of Hearts. This is an unnecessarily high card and should be interpreted by West as a suit-preference signal calling for a shift to the higher-valued of the two remaining side suits. You can be sure that the slam will be beaten provided West shifts to a Spade.

7.

The 3. It is clear that if West plays another Heart, South will ruff and make the contract by discarding all his Clubs on the Spades. As you have so many Hearts to choose from, your lowest one should be considered as a suit preference signal, asking for the lowest-ranking suit.

8.

The 3. East, in this situation, when returning your lead, would undoubtedly lead the fourth best of his original holding if he had four or more Spades. It is clear that his eightspot isn't a fourth-best, and therefore South must have started life with the J 10 x x of Spades. If you win South's 10 with the King, the contract will be made, for you have no outside entry and will not win any more Spade tricks.

Therefore you must allow declarer's 10 of Spades to hold the trick. The contract is then automatically defeated so long as East regains the lead and returns a Spade before declarer can run nine tricks.

9.

You should discard Spades and Clubs. The contract will be icy if declarer has either the Ace of Spades, the King of Hearts or the King of Clubs among his possessions. Accordingly you assume that East has each and every one of them, and your four discards on the Diamonds should consist solely of Spades and Clubs. South will then be a deceased pigeon if your partner holds the right cards. As soon as declarer tries to establish his ninth trick, East will win and lead the King and another Heart.

If you discard one or more Hearts in order to keep the Clubs protected, declarer makes the contract by establishing a Spade trick. The situation you have to guard against is this:

```
                ♠ K J
                ♡ 9 7 6
                ◇ K 10 9 8 6 3
                ♣ A 4
  ♠ 10 8 7                      ♠ A 5 4 3 2
  ♡ Q J 10 4 3                  ♡ K 8 2
  ◇ 5 2                         ◇ 7 4
  ♣ Q J 8                       ♣ K 5 3
                ♠ Q 9 6
                ♡ A 5
                ◇ A Q J
                ♣ 10 9 7 6 2
```

Goren's New Bridge Complete **4**

advanced play

22.   Counting and discovery

COUNTING OUT the opponents' hands, i.e., their original suit distributions, is one of the declarer's first problems. It is not so complicated a procedure as the average player is led to believe. Sometimes it is really a very simple process. The point is to go about it systematically, counting one suit at a time.

There are two elements in counting a hand. One consists of the facts that are proven absolutely, such as when a player fails to follow suit. Other counts are obtained by inference. These clues are gathered from the bidding and sometimes from leads which you have no reason to believe are false.

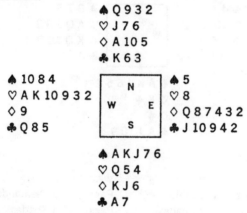

The bidding:

SOUTH	WEST	NORTH	EAST
1 Spade	2 Hearts	2 Spades	Pass
4 Spades	Pass	Pass	Pass

Declarer is playing a contract of 4 Spades. West leads the King and Ace of Hearts, upon the second of which East discards a Club. East ruffs the third round of Hearts and returns the Jack of Clubs. Declarer's problem now is to guess the location of the Queen of Diamonds. The Ace of Clubs wins the return, and three Spades are drawn. At this point the definite information for the declarer is that West held six Hearts and three Spades. This has been proven by the fall of the cards. Declarer leads a Club to the King and ruffs a Club in his own hand, for no other purpose than to find out how many Clubs West had. When West follows to the third round the count reads:

Three Spades, six Hearts, and at least three Clubs.

There is only one unknown card in his hand, which may be a Diamond or a Club. The 6 of Diamonds, therefore, is led to the Ace, and when West follows suit he does so with his last unknown card. The complete count is:

Three Spades, six Hearts, one Diamond, and three Clubs. East, therefore, must have the Queen of Diamonds.

Another example:

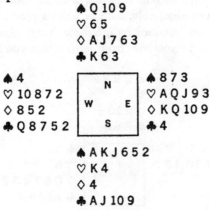

```
                    ♠ Q 10 9
                    ♡ 6 5
                    ◊ A J 7 6 3
                    ♣ K 6 3

   ♠ 4                 N            ♠ 8 7 3
   ♡ 10 8 7 2                       ♡ A Q J 9 3
   ◊ 8 5 2         W       E        ◊ K Q 10 9
   ♣ Q 8 7 5 2        S            ♣ 4

                    ♠ A K J 6 5 2
                    ♡ K 4
                    ◊ 4
                    ♣ A J 10 9
```

The bidding:

EAST	SOUTH	WEST	NORTH
1 Heart	Double	Pass	3 Diamonds
Pass	3 Spades	Pass	4 Spades
Pass	4 No Trump	Pass	5 Diamonds
Pass	6 Spades	Pass	Pass
Pass			

West leads the deuce of Hearts. East wins with the Ace and returns the King of Diamonds, which is won in dummy with the Ace. The success of the contract hinges upon declarer's ability to locate the Queen of Clubs, which may be finessed in either direction. A Diamond is led from dummy, and South wins by trumping. This play has no other purpose than to find out how many Diamonds each opponent has. A low trump is returned to dummy's 9 and another Diamond ruffed. The Jack of trumps is taken by dummy's Queen and a fourth

Diamond is ruffed out with the King of Spades. Now the Ace of Spades is cashed to draw the last trump, and at this point declarer has a perfect count on East's hand. Since West has shown just one trump, East is known to have had three. The play of the Diamonds showed that East had four. These two counts are definite. The count of the Heart suit comes by inference. West led the deuce of his partner's bid suit, which indicates that he held four. East had five Hearts (by inference), three Spades (by actual count), four Diamonds (by actual count), and, therefore, can have only one Club. The Ace of Clubs is played first, in case East's Club happened to be the Queen. When it proved to be the 4, the Jack of Clubs is led and finessed with perfect confidence.

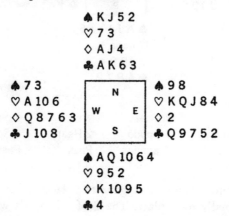

```
                    ♠ K J 5 2
                    ♡ 7 3
                    ◇ A J 4
                    ♣ A K 6 3
      ♠ 7 3           ┌─────────┐      ♠ 9 8
      ♡ A 10 6        │    N    │      ♡ K Q J 8 4
      ◇ Q 8 7 6 3     │ W     E │      ◇ 2
      ♣ J 10 8        │    S    │      ♣ Q 9 7 5 2
                      └─────────┘
                    ♠ A Q 10 6 4
                    ♡ 9 5 2
                    ◇ K 10 9 5
                    ♣ 4
```

The bidding:

NORTH	EAST	SOUTH	WEST
1 Club	1 Heart	1 Spade	Pass
3 Spades	Pass	4 Spades	Pass
Pass	Pass		

Declarer's contract of 4 Spades was not in danger. The problem centered around the Diamond play in an effort to make an overtrick. West opened the Ace of Hearts and continued the suit. East won and led a trump. Declarer drew the remaining trumps, playing the Ace and King of Clubs and ruffing one in the closed hand. The last Heart was ruffed in dummy and the remaining Club ruffed in the closed hand. On the last Club lead West showed out and East's hand was an open book. He is known to have held five Clubs (actual count), two Spades (actual count), and surely five Hearts for his vulnerable overcall, which was bad enough (inference), which would leave him with only one Diamond. The King of Diamonds, therefore, was led from the South hand and the Jack finessed from dummy with the complete assurance that it would work.

A more involved case is the following:

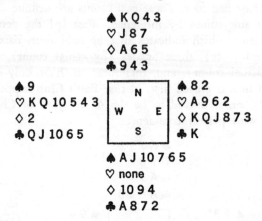

♠ K Q 4 3
♡ J 8 7
◊ A 6 5
♣ 9 4 3

♠ 9
♡ K Q 10 5 4 3
◊ 2
♣ Q J 10 6 5

♠ 8 2
♡ A 9 6 2
◊ K Q J 8 7 3
♣ K

♠ A J 10 7 6 5
♡ none
◊ 10 9 4
♣ A 8 7 2

The bidding:

EAST	SOUTH	WEST	NORTH
1 Diamond	1 Spade	2 Hearts	2 Spades
3 Hearts	4 Spades	Pass	Pass
Pass			

West, no doubt, should have gone to 5 Hearts, but the bidding is given as it actually took place. The 2 of Diamonds was opened, an obvious singleton, and the Ace took the trick. A Heart was ruffed in the closed hand and dummy entered with a trump. Another Heart was ruffed and dummy re-entered with the second high trump, and the final Heart was ruffed by South. At this point declarer stopped to count out the hand. West was known to have one Diamond and one Spade. He therefore had started with ·eleven cards in Hearts and Clubs. These were, no doubt, six Hearts and five Clubs, since with a seven-card Heart suit he would surely have bid once more (inference), and if he held a six-card Club suit he would certainly have risked a 5 Club bid over 4 Spades (by inference). East, therefore, is marked with only one Club. Declarer hit upon a means of avoiding the loss of two Club tricks. He cashed the Ace of Clubs, so that East could not return that suit, and then led the 10 of Diamonds, presenting East with the lead. He was able to cash two Diamond tricks and was then obliged to lead a red card, which permitted South to ruff, while dummy discarded one of the losing Clubs.

Discovery play

There are times when the information needed to complete the count of the hand is not immediately available. To cater for such situations, a technique has been devised for enabling the declarer to go out and get the facts. In other words, declarer plays a suit, or suits, not with the object of developing tricks in it, or establishing long cards in it, but simply with the idea of discovering how the opponents' cards are distributed. This form of play is called discovery play and its use is highly commended to the more assiduous reader. An example follows:

```
             ♠ A K 10 5
             ♡ A K 10 3
             ◊ 9
             ♣ K 9 6 4

          ┌─────────────┐
          │   Dummy      │
          │ W         E  │
          │   Declarer   │
          └─────────────┘

             ♠ 3 2
             ♡ 7 5
             ◊ K 5 4 3 2
             ♣ A Q 10 5
```

The contract is 3 No Trump and West leads the Queen of Diamonds, which East overtakes with the Ace. The 6 of Diamonds is returned and the declarer ducks. West wins and plays a third round of the suit, on which East shows out. As there is no longer any point in holding off, declarer takes the King and observes that to make the contract he needs four tricks in Clubs.

If the opponents' Clubs are 3-2, there will be no problem, and therefore the declarer should assume that they are 4-1. In this case it will be necessary to determine which defender holds the length in the suit, so that the Clubs can be played in a suitable way to enable a finesse to be taken against the Jack.

It would be easy, at this time, to assume that since East is known to be short on Diamonds he is likely to be long on Clubs, and indeed, if the declarer were forced to take a position on this supposition alone it would be proper to proceed on that basis. First, however, the declarer should endeavor to discover more about the hand before playing the Club suit. The general idea is to play out as many tricks as you safely can in the major suits without allowing West to obtain the lead.

After winning the third trick with the King of Diamonds, the recommended procedure is to lead a Spade and finesse the 10. East will probably return a Spade, which is taken in dummy. Declarer enters his hand with the Ace of Clubs and leads a Heart, again ducking the trick into East's hand.

Declarer is now ready to cash his winners in the major suits. In the course of so doing he is bound to learn a good deal about the nature of West's hand, and this will enable him to judge the Club situation. If declarer learns, for example, that West started with a doubleton in both Spades and Hearts, he will know that, contrary to expectations, West must have started with four Clubs, and he plays the Clubs accordingly.

QUIZ ON COUNTING AND DISCOVERY

1.

NORTH	SOUTH
♠ 9 8 5	♠ Q 7
♡ K 9 4 2	♡ Q J 10 8 7
◇ A 10 4	◇ K J 7
♣ A Q 9	♣ K 4 2

The bidding:

WEST	NORTH	EAST	SOUTH
1 Spade	Pass	Pass	2 Hearts
Pass	4 Hearts	Pass	Pass
Pass			

West leads the A K J of Spades and you ruff as East discards a Diamond. When trumps are led, West wins the second round as East shows out. West then exits with a trump. How do you continue?

2.

NORTH	SOUTH
♠ A 3 2	♠ J 8
♡ K 10 8	♡ A Q J
◇ K J 9 3	◇ A 10 8 7 2
♣ K Q 9	♣ A 3 2

The bidding:

SOUTH	WEST	NORTH	EAST
1 No Trump	2 Spades	6 No Trump	Pass
Pass	Pass		

West leads the King of Spades which you duck. Spades are continued and East discards a low Heart. What is your intended campaign?

3.

NORTH	SOUTH
♠ Q 4	♠ A J 10 9 8 3
♡ 10 4	♡ A Q 2
◇ A 7 6 3	◇ 8 5
♣ 8 6 4 3 2	♣ 10 5

The bidding:

WEST	NORTH	EAST	SOUTH
1 Diamond	Pass	1 Heart	1 Spade
2 Clubs	Pass	2 Diamonds	2 Spades
3 Diamonds	3 Spades	Pass	4 Spades
Pass	Pass	Pass	

West leads the K A Q of Clubs. You ruff, cross to the Ace of Diamonds, successfully finesse the Queen of Hearts, cash the Ace, and ruff a Heart, to which both defenders follow. How do you proceed?

4.

	NORTH	SOUTH
♠	A	8 3 2
♡	10 9 7 5 3	A K Q J 6
◇	K Q 4	7 2
♣	A J 6 4	K 9 5

The bidding:

WEST	NORTH	EAST	SOUTH
3 Spades	Double	Pass	5 Hearts
Pass	6 Hearts	Pass	Pass
Pass			

West leads the King of Spades. You take the A K of trump and East discards a Diamond on the second one. You lead a Diamond to the King, but East wins with the Ace and returns a Spade. You ruff, cash a Diamond, and ruff a Diamond, to which all follow. Then you ruff your last Spade, on which East shows out. How do you play the Clubs?

5.

	NORTH	SOUTH
♠	A J 6 3	Q 7 2
♡	Q 4	K 8
◇	K 6 2	A Q 10 3
♣	K 7 4 2	A J 8 3

The contract is 3 No Trump and West leads the 2 of Hearts. East wins and returns a Heart. You play a Club to the King and a Club back to the Ace, East discarding a Spade. You then lead a low Spade and finesse the Jack, which holds. How do you continue?

6.

	NORTH	SOUTH
♠	Q 10 7	K J 5
♡	A J 4	K Q 7
◇	K 7 2	A Q 9
♣	K 10 6 3	A Q 8 4

You are in 6 No Trump and West leads the 3 of Spades. East wins with the Ace and returns the 8 of Spades. How do you proceed?

ANSWERS TO QUIZ ON COUNTING AND DISCOVERY

1.

Cash the A K Q of Clubs. The contract depends on locating the Queen of Diamonds, but the correct technique is to try to obtain a count of the hand before playing Diamonds. Therefore you cash your Club winners. The full deal follows:

```
            ♠ 9 8 5
            ♡ K 9 4 2
            ◇ A 10 4
            ♣ A Q 9
♠ A K J 6 4 3        ♠ 10 2
♡ A 6 5              ♡ 3
◇ 6                  ◇ Q 9 8 5 3 2
♣ 10 7 5             ♣ J 8 6 3
            ♠ Q 7
            ♡ Q J 10 8 7
            ◇ K J 7
            ♣ K 4 2
```

When West follows to three rounds of Clubs he is known to have started with at least three Clubs, six Spades and three Hearts. Therefore he cannot have more than one Diamond, and you ensure the contract by taking dummy's Ace of Diamonds and finessing against East.

2.

You should first cash your Heart and Club winners. You have to locate the Queen of Diamonds, of course, but you do not yet have enough information to go on. If you had to take a position at this time, you might well decide to start the Diamonds by cashing the Ace and finessing the Jack into East's hand. If you did this, you would certainly avoid losing an avalanche of Spades, since East has shown out of the suit, but you would go down if East had the Queen of Diamonds.

Alternately, you might take a completely opposite tack and decide

to play East for the Queen of Diamonds on the grounds that West has become marked with seven Spades and is therefore highly likely to be short on Diamonds. In this case you would be smitten low if West had the Queen of Diamonds. The full deal was as follows:

```
            ♠ 8 3 2
            ♡ A K 8
            ◇ K J 9 3
            ♣ K Q 9
♠ K Q 10 9 6 5 4     ♠ 7
♡ 6 3                ♡ 9 7 5 4 2
◇ Q 4                ◇ 6 5
♣ 7 5                ♣ J 10 8 6 4
            ♠ A J
            ♡ Q J 10
            ◇ A 10 8 7 2
            ♣ A 3 2
```

The proper play is to cash the A K Q of Clubs and the A K Q of Hearts. You discover in this process that West has a doubleton in each suit. Since he is already marked with seven Spades, you now know that he has to have two Diamonds, and you therefore play accordingly.

3.

You must determine to play West for the singleton King of trump! You have no way of knowing whether West has the King of trump —he could still have made the bids he has made without having it— but your count of the hand informs you that you cannot make the contract if East has it.

To justify his previous bids, West has to have at least eight cards in the minor suits, probably nine.

He has followed to three rounds of Hearts, and therefore cannot have more than two Spades (probably one). Therefore, you are bound to lose the contract if you finesse in Spades, no matter who has the King.

If you finesse and West has the King, he will make it. If you finesse and West doesn't have the King, your success will be purely temporary, for you cannot repeat the finesse and East will eventually get a trick with the K x x or K x x x. The only situation you can handle is where West has the singleton King and therefore you should play him for it.

4.

You have an almost complete count of the hand. By this time you have discovered quite a lot, namely: 1. West had seven Spades. 2. West had two Hearts, since he followed twice. 3. West also had at least three Diamonds, since he followed three times.

West therefore holds one Club at most. Your chances of avoiding a Club loser are not exactly bright, but at least you have learned that it would be useless to start the Clubs by cashing the King, which in other circumstances would be the normal thing to do.

Instead, you take very good care to play the Ace of Clubs. This gives you an extra chance of making the contract, not only if West's singleton is the Queen, but also if it is the 10, for you can continue by finessing the 9.

5.

You are practically certain to make the contract. West has shown up with four Clubs and in view of the opening lead there seems no reason to doubt that he also started life with four Hearts. Therefore he cannot hold more than five cards in Spades and Diamonds combined. Now that West has also become marked with the King of Spades, you can discover the exact count of his hand and so ensure nine tricks.

You lay down the Ace of Spades. If West plays the King—having started with K x doubleton—you are home. If he plays a low Spade under the Ace, you will know that he started

with at least three Spades, and accordingly cannot have more than two Diamonds. So you simply play the A K of Diamonds and then finesse the 10, knowing it will win. The full deal was:

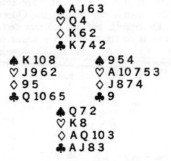

```
            ♠ A J 6 3
            ♡ Q 4
            ◇ K 6 2
            ♣ K 7 4 2
♠ K 10 8              ♠ 9 5 4
♡ J 9 6 2             ♡ A 10 7 5 3
◇ 9 5                 ◇ J 8 7 4
♣ Q 10 6 5           ♣ 9
            ♠ Q 7 2
            ♡ K 8
            ◇ A Q 10 3
            ♣ A J 8 3
```

6.

You must try to discover the Club distribution. You need four Club tricks and the normal method of tackling the suit would be to lay down the A Q. By this method of play, the only case where you would lose the contract would be where East held the J x x x. However, you may be able to cover even this possibility by first trying to gain a count of the hand. The full deal is:

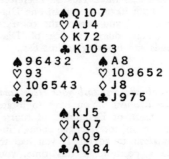

```
            ♠ Q 10 7
            ♡ A J 4
            ◇ K 7 2
            ♣ K 10 6 3
♠ 9 6 4 3 2          ♠ A 8
♡ 9 3                ♡ 10 8 6 5 2
◇ 10 6 5 4 3         ◇ J 8
♣ 2                  ♣ J 9 7 5
            ♠ K J 5
            ♡ K Q 7
            ◇ A Q 9
            ♣ A Q 8 4
```

At trick three you cash your remaining Spade winner. In the actual case East discards a Heart and you know that West started with five Spades.

Next you play three rounds of Diamonds. When East again shows out, you add to your knowledge the fact that West started with five Diamonds as well as five Spades.

You still don't know the Club distribution, but you are due to find out when you take the King of Hearts and then lead a Heart to dummy's Jack. If West showed out on the second Heart he would become marked with two Clubs and your worries would be over, inasmuch as the Clubs would be worth four tricks.

In the actual case West follows to the second Heart, and in that way becomes marked with only one Club. So you cash the King of Clubs and then expunge East's Club holding by leading twice through his J 9 x, dummy's Ace of Hearts providing the necessary reentry.

23.   Deduction and assumption

LIKE SORCERERS of old, bridge experts were, until recently, held in a considerable degree of awe. Impressionable members of the public were convinced that the bridge expert could perform almost any feat with a deck of cards, except possibly to make the Jack of Spades leap out and squirt cider in someone's ear. Even bridge players of some experience were constrained to admit that the accuracy with which a real expert could reconstruct his opponents' hands bordered on the miraculous.

Latterly, however, a feeling has arisen that the ability of the expert, if not overstated, is at least capable of being emulated. Rank and file players have realized that feats of diagnosis and card reading are the outcome of logical thought, and have begun to realize that this is a process which the majority of reasonably proficient players are capable of employing. The writer has therefore concluded that, in these enlightened times, there is a need for a chapter which might once have been out of place in a work intended for a wide public—a chapter dealing with the deductive processes by which the unseen hands may be reconstructed and a higher all-round standard of accuracy achieved.

Lest it should be apprehended that I shall thereby erase the mystique of the expert's powers, I may remind the reader that Sherlock Holmes' remarkable ability to use scientific deduction for solving unsolvable crimes was not rendered the less astonishing by his frank explanation of the unelaborate thought processes involved. I suspect that, in the same way, the bridge expert, too, will retain his position in the hierarchy of bridge no matter how I expose the simplicity of his methods.

Deductions from the opening lead

Occasionally when planning the play of a hand the declarer is forced to admit to himself that information needed to ensure a successful outcome is in short supply. It may be difficult or impossible to gain a proper count of the hand (as described in the previous chapter), or it may be that no satisfactory clue can be discovered to the location of a vital card. At this time the average player, convinced that he has done all that could reasonably be expected of him, may experience a strong urge to consult the ceiling, spin a coin, or simply plow ahead with his eyes shut. The expert, by contrast, has in reserve two techniques for filling the gaps in his knowledge: deduction—on which Mr. Holmes built his reputation—and assumption, of which more anon.

Of course, every bridge player makes use of deduction to some extent but few exploit it to the limit. They see but they do not observe. To the expert, however, every card tells a story and his chief objective is to squeeze the very last drop of information out of every card that is played and every bid that is made. The process of dissection begins, naturally enough, with the opening lead.

Some inferences are obvious. For example, if the opening lead is an 8 or 9, it is highly likely that the player who led it holds no higher card in the suit.

♡ Q 6 2

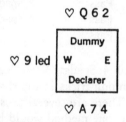

♡ 9 led

Dummy

W   E

Declarer

♡ A 7 4

Assuming that West is a squareshooter who plays the game, there is very little point in putting up the Queen when the 9 is led. The King is almost certain to be with East and therefore it will be better to play low in dummy and win with the Ace, preserving the value of the Queen for the time being.

It is well known that a low card, when led against a No Trump contract, is usually the fourth-best card from the defender's longest suit. From that it is often possible to make further deductions. Thus, if a defender leads a four-card suit against a No Trump contract, it is certainly reasonable, other things being equal, to think that he has no five-card or longer suit elsewhere in his hand; if he had, he would probably have led it. Similarly, against a suit contract a player who has a strong sequence of honors will usually lead one; if he doesn't, you may safely assume that he possesses no such sequence. All these inferences are obvious, yet they tend to be overlooked. Consider this hand:

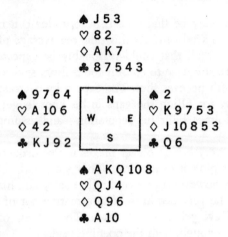

The bidding:

SOUTH	WEST	NORTH	EAST
1 Spade	Pass	2 Spades	Pass
3 No Trump	Pass	4 Spades	Pass
Pass	Pass		

Against South's contract of 4 Spades, West leads the 4 of Diamonds. Declarer has nine winning tricks in the shape of five Spades, three Diamonds and a Club. There are several possible ways of gaining a tenth trick. For example, one method would be to win the Diamond lead in dummy and lead a Heart immediately; declarer hopes that either he will succeed in establishing a Heart trick in his hand or that he will be able to ruff the third round of the suit in dummy. The drawback to this line of play is that if declarer persists in leading Hearts before drawing trumps, so as to prepare for a Heart ruff in dummy, he may suffer a Diamond ruff if one of the opponents has a singleton or doubleton in the suit.

An alternative method would be to try to establish the Club suit by conceding a Club and then ruffing one or more rounds of the suit. With this plan the declarer might make ten tricks but he might also run himself out of trumps and wind up losing control of the hand if the opponents' trumps are 4–1.

A deduction from the opening lead enables declarer to employ a far safer method. Since West has not led the King of Hearts, it is reasonable to assume that he does not have the A K of the suit, for a lead from this holding would occupy an honored place in anybody's table of recommended opening leads. Declarer capitalizes on this inference by simply winning the Diamond lead with the Queen, drawing the opponents' trumps, and leading a Heart from dummy. If the Queen is captured by the Ace or King, East will almost surely hold the other high honor and the tenth trick will be acquired without risk when a second Heart is led toward declarer's Jack.

Thus it is the practice of a sleuthlike declarer to draw deductions from what his opponents have *not* led as well as from what they *have* led. The reader may remember the Holmesian episode of the dog that didn't bark in the night. Here is another example of that type of deduction.

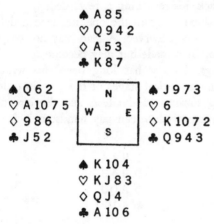

```
                    ♠ A 8 5
                    ♡ Q 9 4 2
                    ◇ A 5 3
                    ♣ K 8 7

  ♠ Q 6 2          ┌───────┐          ♠ J 9 7 3
  ♡ A 10 7 5       │   N   │          ♡ 6
  ◇ 9 8 6          │ W   E │          ◇ K 10 7 2
  ♣ J 5 2          │   S   │          ♣ Q 9 4 3
                   └───────┘
                    ♠ K 10 4
                    ♡ K J 8 3
                    ◇ Q J 4
                    ♣ A 10 6
```

The bidding (from the days of four-card majors):

SOUTH	WEST	NORTH	EAST
1 Heart	Pass	3 Hearts	Pass
3 No Trump	Pass	Pass	Pass

Declarer is playing at 3 No Trump and West leads the 9 of Diamonds, which is taken by East's King. East returns the 2 of Diamonds. Declarer is not exactly alarmed by this turn of events, for he merely needs three tricks in Hearts to ensure the success of the contract. Accordingly, he takes the Diamond return in dummy and leads a Heart to the King, which loses to West's Ace. A third Diamond is played and declarer is, in effect, in the position of having to guess which defender is more likely to have started life with four Hearts. If East started with the 10 x x x, the winning play would be to cash dummy's Queen, exposing West's shortage, and then finesse the 8 of Hearts against East's 10. However, playing the Hearts in this fashion would lead to failure in the actual case, so South should consider by what means he can ensure a successful diagnosis of the Heart situation.

From West's lead of the 9 of Diamonds and East's return of the 2 it is reasonable to suppose that West has led a short suit. It therefore becomes pertinent to inquire why West has not made a normal attacking lead in his longest suit. At this time it should occur to the declarer that it is at least possible that West's only four-card suit is Hearts, which have been bid and supported. Declarer therefore should develop the Heart suit on the assumption that West is far more likely to be lurking with four of them than East. When he wins the second heart with the Jack, his reasoning is rewarded.

In drawing deductions from the opening lead a delayed-action effect is frequently to be observed. A lead may not be particularly significant at the time it is made but may become so at some later point in the proceedings. Thus it has long been this writer's practice to pause momentarily at critical stages of the play in order to review in retrospect the significance of the lead and the circumstances which attended it. Such a procedure can pay handsomely in a case like the following.

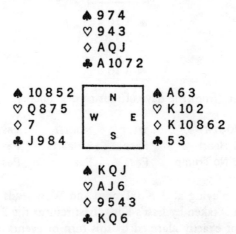

♠ 9 7 4
♡ 9 4 3
◊ A Q J
♣ A 10 7 2

♠ 10 8 5 2   N   ♠ A 6 3
♡ Q 8 7 5   W   E   ♡ K 10 2
◊ 7   S   ◊ K 10 8 6 2
♣ J 9 8 4   ♣ 5 3

♠ K Q J
♡ A J 6
◊ 9 5 4 3
♣ K Q 6

South opens 1 No Trump and is raised to 3. West leads the 2 of Spades and East wins with the Ace. The 6 of Spades is returned and declarer takes a finesse in Diamonds. East, however, is aware of the possible advantage of causing declarer to misplace the cards, and he allows the Queen to win, whereupon declarer returns to his hand and leads a second Diamond, West showing out.

'Ho, hum,' declarer should say to himself. It is evident from the opening lead of the 2 that West has only four Spades, and it certainly seems reasonable to suppose that he would not have led from a four-card suit if he held five cards in one of the other suits. Now that West has become marked with a singleton Diamond, declarer may reasonably deduce that he began with a 4–4–1–4 hand pattern. Accordingly, when declarer gets around to tackling Clubs, and the Jack does not fall on the second round, the 10 should be finessed.

The play made by the partner of the opening leader is frequently no less informative than the lead itself. Consider this situation, where West leads the Queen of Spades against 3 No Trump.

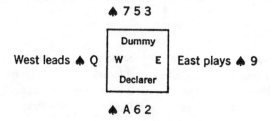

West leads ♠ Q   Dummy / W E / Declarer   East plays ♠ 9

♠ A 6 2

When East plays the 9 on his partner's Queen, the significance is not lost on a reflective declarer, who knows that he may safely assume that the opponents' Spades are 4–3. If they were 5–2, East, having the K 9, would have been obliged to play the King on the Queen to avoid blocking partner's suit. Thus the declarer, if it suits his purpose, may well decide to win the first trick with the Ace, abandoning the normal holdup lest West, with a Spade trick in the bay, should be astute enough to shift to a more dangerous suit.

The opening lead by a competent defender is more than just a lead: it is part of a long-range plan to bring about the defeat of the contract. Declarer tries to deduce what that plan is. He knows that if he can fathom what the defender is trying to do, it will be easier to reconstruct his holdings. Thus, a defender who plays passively usually has unsupported high cards that he is not anxious to lead away from. A defender who leads trumps usually does so because he has strength in the declarer's side suit. In a game of reasonable standard, it will be found that a defender who exhibits the symptoms of trying to gain a ruff is likely to have a quick entry in the trump suit: without it, the attempt to gain a ruff would be less likely to succeed. This may well determine the declarer's campaign in a hand like the following.

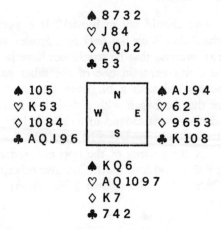

```
                    ♠ 8 7 3 2
                    ♡ J 8 4
                    ◊ A Q J 2
                    ♣ 5 3

    ♠ 10 5           ┌─────────┐        ♠ A J 9 4
    ♡ K 5 3          │    N    │        ♡ 6 2
    ◊ 10 8 4       W │         │ E      ◊ 9 6 5 3
    ♣ A Q J 9 6      │    S    │        ♣ K 10 8
                     └─────────┘

                    ♠ K Q 6
                    ♡ A Q 10 9 7
                    ◊ K 7
                    ♣ 7 4 2
```

The bidding:

SOUTH	WEST	NORTH	EAST
1 Heart	2 Clubs	2 Hearts	3 Clubs
Pass	Pass	3 Diamonds	Pass
3 Hearts	Pass	Pass	Pass

South is at 3 Hearts and West leads the 10 of Spades, which East wins with the Ace. East returns the 4 of Spades and South wins with the King.

Declarer can afford to lose a trump trick and two Clubs, and thus his main concern is to prevent a Spade ruff. However, it can hardly be said that the proper way to play the hand is cut and dried: there are several possibilities. Declarer could cross to dummy with a Diamond and take a trump finesse, or he could start by playing the Ace and another trump. Alternatively, he might decide that he would be far better off without the Queen of Spades, in which case he might proceed to try to discard it on a Diamond before touching trumps. Of course, this procedure, too, is not without risk.

Faced with this problem, South should endeavor to construct West's likely holdings, bearing in mind that Clubs have been bid and supported and that West could have selected a safe enough lead in that suit had he wished to. It is unlikely that West would have led a Spade unless his hopes were high of obtaining a ruff in the suit, and this in turn suggests not only that he has a quick entry in the shape of the King of trumps, but also that he is more likely to have the K x x than the K x. With this last holding a ruff would be less likely to benefit him.

South's proper method of play, therefore, is to take three rounds of Diamonds, divesting himself of the Queen of Spades. A Club is then led from dummy. If East wins and plays a trump, South ducks, and in the fullness of time he either ruffs his third Club in dummy or discards it on the Jack of Diamonds. Any other method of play would result in defeat, for when West got in with the King of trumps he could play the Ace and another Club and ruff his partner's Spade return.

Deductions from the bidding

The advice contained elsewhere in this book about the most effective method of playing both elementary and advanced card combinations has been coupled with several warnings as to the limitations of tables of abstract percentages. To know the mathematical odds on a suit breaking in a particular fashion is useful, but to be able to form your own opinion of the likely distribution by drawing inferences from the bidding and play is far more useful. Such inferences may not *always* be accurate, inasmuch as your opponents may not always make the same bid on a hand as you would make. Nevertheless, it will most certainly pay you to assume that if your opponent has not bid, then he hasn't got a bid, and if he has done nothing but bid Hearts for several rounds, he is unlikely to have a biddable Spade suit, and so on.

There is a tendency to assume that an opponent who has overcalled has automatically become a strong favorite to hold the missing high cards. This may be reasonable enough so far as Aces and Kings are concerned, but it should be borne in mind that most overcalls are based on winning tricks rather than high-card values, and when it comes down to a Queen or a Jack it is seldom safe to conclude that such a card necessarily forms part of the values on which the overcall was based. Suppose you are the declarer at a No Trump contract and must play this combination after West has overcalled in Spades:

◇ A K 4

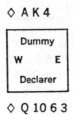

◇ Q 10 6 3

Unless West is a very exact player indeed, it hardly makes much difference to the soundness of his overcall whether he has the Jack of Diamonds. On the other hand, the mere fact that West is expected to be long in Spades raises the suspicion that he may be short of Diamonds and therefore, needing four tricks from this suit, declarer may boldly finesse the tenspot on the third round instead of following the normal procedure of playing the A K Q, which would be the usual play had there been no opposition bidding.

Similarly, suppose you have nine trumps in the combined hands, missing the Queen. In the absence of any bidding by the opponents, the normal percentage play would be to lay down the A K, but if one of your opponents has overcalled, you should assume that he is likely to be short in your trump suit. You would therefore be inclined to play the overcaller's partner to have the Q x x of the suit.

Deductions about the unseen hands are more reliable when an opponent has opened the bidding than when he has overcalled. By and large, opponents should be expected to have bid correctly. Thus a player who opens 1 Spade in first or second position and subsequently shows up with four of them should not be expected to have the same number of Clubs, for with four Clubs and four Spades he would normally open 1 Club. Deductions of this kind require greater cerebration than simply taking a peep at your opponents' hands, but they do not lead to excommunication and therefore have much to commend them. In favorable circumstances, they may enable you to reconstruct an opponent's complete hand pattern.

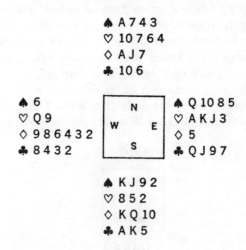

The bidding:

EAST	SOUTH	WEST	NORTH
1 Club	1 No Trump	Pass	3 No Trump
Pass	Pass	Pass	

South is the declarer at 3 No Trump, East having opened with a bid of 1 Club. The 2 of Clubs is led and covered by the 10, Jack and Ace. South observes that it will not be possible to make the contract unless he can take four tricks in Spades. The normal percentage play with this combination is to cash the Ace and finesse the Jack, but such a procedure would lead to defeat in the actual case and declarer should not proceed in that fashion without first making an attempt to construct East's hand.

The first move should be to cash the K Q of Diamonds. This is done merely to see if anything significant occurs; and sure enough, it does, for East shows up with a singleton in the suit. Declarer now has all the information he needs to complete the hand. East has opened 1 Club on what appears to be a four-card suit (since West probably would not have led the 2 from three small Clubs). East would not have opened 1 Club on a four-card suit if he held five cards in either of the major suits, and now that he has shown up with a singleton Diamond, his hand pattern must be 4–4–1–4. Therefore the normal percentage play in Spades will not work, and instead, expecting East to have four Spades, declarer should lead a Spade to the Ace and on the next Spade finesse the 9. He then crosses to the Ace of Diamonds and takes a second finesse in Spades to land 3 No Trump.

Not all deductions are so exact. Sometimes the declarer has to go by general impressions: for example, if the opponents have not entered the auction despite having a reasonable degree of strength, declarer may expect favorable breaks, while if the opponents have been active in the bidding despite being short on points, he may expect squalls. The big thing is to make sure that the line of play you adopt is not inconsistent with the opponents' bidding—or lack of it.

Deductions from the play

While the play progresses, the declarer revises his initial estimate of the situation as new or unexpected developments shed additional light on the composition of the adverse hands. It will be found that a defender, following the normal conventions of signaling and play, is usually unable to cooperate effectively with his partner without incidentally giving the declarer various clues to his holdings. If a defender echoes when a suit is being played, he usually has an even number of cards in it, and so on. Less obvious are the indications that may be gained in such situations as these:

Diagram A

A K J

Dummy

W   E

Declarer

10 5 3

Diagram B

A K 4

Dummy

W   E

Declarer

J 10 6

Suppose that in the early part of the hand West, who at this stage has no other object than merely to exit without giving away a trick, leads a low card of this suit. In DIAGRAM A, the fact that West has led the suit affords no indication of the location of the Queen. West can see the A K J in dummy and he knows that it can cost nothing to lead the suit, for declarer can take a finesse any time he likes, whether the suit is led or not.

In DIAGRAM B, however, the fact that West has led the suit suggests that he is unlikely to have the Queen. West has no way of knowing that declarer has the J 10 of the suit and is in a position to take a finesse off his own bat. It is unlikely that West would be willing to open up this combination if he had the Queen, for he would reason that leading away from it would prove a grave indiscretion if declarer happened to have the unsupported Jack and won a trick with it. Thus it will be seen that although in DIAGRAM A the fact of West's having led the suit gives no clue to the position of the Queen, in DIAGRAM B there would be some grounds for presuming the Queen to be with East.

The reader may care to see what deductions he can draw from these two situations:

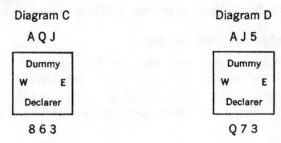

Diagram C

A Q J

Dummy

W   E

Declarer

8 6 3

Diagram D

A J 5

Dummy

W   E

Declarer

Q 7 3

This time it is assumed, in DIAGRAM C, that West, during the play of a part-score contract, leads the 2 and dummy's Queen is successfully finessed. This is most delightful, you may say to yourself, but when you think about it you realize that things are not necessarily all beer and skittles: the finesse has apparently succeeded, but you really have no guarantee about the position of the King. West may well have led away from it because he can see that to do so gives nothing away. At the same time, it is almost equally possible that East has the King and is holding it up, expecting you to repeat the finesse.

In DIAGRAM D, West again leads the 2, dummy plays low, East plays the 10 and declarer wins with the Queen. Who has the King? A careful consideration of the matter suggests that East is likely to have it, for West would be most unlikely to lead away from the King. West would reason that a lead away from the King would give declarer an extra trick if he held either the unsupported King or the unsupported 10, and therefore he would not lead away from it if he had any choice in the matter. Inklings of this kind, while not conclusive in themselves, build up the declarer's picture of the opponents' hands and help to explain why good players gain the reputation of being good guessers.

Another example:

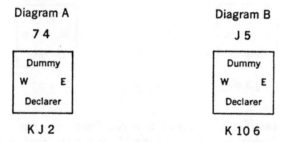

Diagram A

7 4

| Dummy |
| W   E |
| Declarer |

K J 2

Diagram B

J 5

| Dummy |
| W   E |
| Declarer |

K 10 6

In each case the declarer is playing a suit contract, with adequate trumps and entries in each hand. East is on lead and he plays a low card in this suit. Declarer's object is to avoid losing two tricks straight off, and it may appear that the chances of success and failure are the same in both cases. This, however, is not so.

In DIAGRAM A the declarer has little to go on. If East had the Ace and wanted to attack this suit, he would no doubt lead a small one, and if he held the Queen he would also lead a small one. Declarer is therefore faced with a guess.

In DIAGRAM B, however, it is more likely that East has led away from the Ace than from the Queen. The reason why this is so is that

East can see the Jack in dummy, whereas in the previous case it was not there. East does not know declarer has the 10, and can take an honest finesse in the suit whether East leads it or not. Thus, if East had the Q x x, he would be averse to leading away from it, lest the declarer, with K x x, should duck and thus hold his losses to one trick when he would have to lose two tricks if he tackled the suit himself.

By contrast it might be expected that East would willingly under-lead the Ace if he had it. In this case East would reason that declarer, with K x x, would be bound to hold himself to one loser if he is allowed to lead the suit from dummy. But he might be persuaded to lose two tricks if the suit is led from his right.

A declarer should presume that his opponents are defending intelligently, although it has to be admitted that such a presumption may be open to rebuttal in individual cases. Declarer should not proceed on the basis that the defenders have elected to play in such a manner as to present him with tricks. To illustrate:

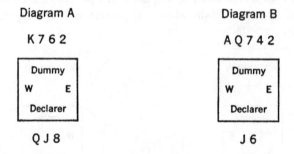

Diagram A

K 7 6 2

Dummy
W   E
Declarer

Q J 8

Diagram B

A Q 7 4 2

Dummy
W   E
Declarer

J 6

In each case South is playing at a No Trump contract and has no entries to dummy except in this suit. In DIAGRAM A, if he leads the Queen and some kind soul takes it with the Ace, declarer should not imagine that the millenium has arrived and that he is going to make three tricks in the suit. Quite clearly the adverse cards are not breaking 3–3, for if they were, the Ace would have been held up. In DIA-GRAM B, declarer leads the Jack, which holds. It is virtually certain that East has the King, for West would have covered if he could.

If a competent defender makes a play that seems wrong on general principles, the declarer should look for an explanation. In this next deal, in an attempt to promote an extra trump trick East makes the unusual play of conceding a ruff and discard, normally one of the worst things a defender can do.

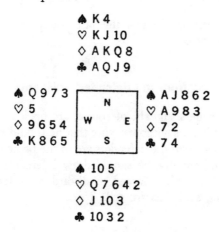

The bidding:

NORTH	EAST	SOUTH	WEST
2 Clubs	Pass	2 Diamonds	Pass
2 No Trump	Pass	3 Hearts	Pass
4 Hearts	Pass	Pass	Pass

Declarer is at 4 Hearts and West leads the 3 of Spades, the King losing to the Ace. The 6 of Spades is returned and, after winning with the Queen, West shifts to a Diamond, which is taken in dummy. The King of trumps is taken by East's Ace and a third Spade is returned.

Declarer's first reaction may be that East's lead of the third Spade is a very friendly act, to be sure. It offers declarer the chance to discard a losing Club from his hand while ruffing the trick in dummy with the 10. Provided the adverse trumps are 3–2, declarer has visions of cashing dummy's Jack of trumps, entering his own hand with a Diamond, drawing the last trump with the Queen, and then discarding his remaining Club loser on dummy's fourth Diamond. By this method of play, the risk of taking the Club finesse is avoided and the contract made—assuming the trumps are 3–2.

However, a careful player should do some serious thinking before actually putting this plan into effect. Why, declarer should ask himself, has East deliberately conceded a ruff and discard by leading a third Spade? The answer may be appreciated by looking at East's hand. If he can persuade declarer to ruff a Spade on the table, East sees that he must get a second trump trick and the contract will fail.

Accordingly, declarer should reject this Greek gift and ruff the third Spade in his own hand. He cashes the J 10 of trumps, enters his hand with a Diamond, draws the last trump and takes the Club finesse for his contract.

Deductions from the defender's discards

The defenders' signals, of course, are open to interception by the declarer and it goes without saying that he should eavesdrop on all possible occasions when the defenders are in the process of exchanging information. Additionally, he should draw inferences from the cards a defender jettisons when forced to discard on a long suit. In this type of situation, every discard tells a story:

A K 7 3

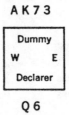

Q 6

This is a side suit at a trump contract, and while trumps are being drawn a defender discards one. You can bet on the fact that the defender has not discarded from four cards, as this would be unwise in any circumstances. Nor is it likely that the defender began with only two or three cards in the suit, for in such a case he would have been better able to afford a discard from one of the other suits. Thus the declarer may assume, without further evidence, that the defender who discarded began with five or more.

By now the reader may have begun to feel that the defenders can neither bid, play nor discard without revealing their hands in some measure and thus enabling the declarer to improve his performance at their expense. This is indeed true enough, although it will be found that drawing inferences from discards sometimes presents a test of memory. Some discards convey little at the time they are made and not until later in the hand does their real significance dawn. Thus, as he approaches the end game, the declarer should remind himself whether a defender has been reluctant to discard from a particular suit. This may provide a valuable indication when at the end of a hand it is necessary to tackle such a combination as this:

K J

```
┌─────────────────┐
│     Dummy       │
│  W          E   │
│    Declarer     │
└─────────────────┘
```

8 4 3

A low card is led and West plays low. The diagnosis should be that if West has discarded once or twice from this suit, he is more likely to hold the Ace than the Queen. If he had held this latter card, he would probably have kept it well guarded. Conversely, if East is the player who has been discarding the suit with a gay tra-la, and West has been hugging three cards until late in the hand, it is almost certain that East has the Ace and West the Queen. The same principle applies in this situation:

A 8 4 2

```
┌─────────────────┐
│     Dummy       │
│  W          E   │
│    Declarer     │
└─────────────────┘
```

Q 10 6

Declarer is playing at No Trump and East, quite early in the proceedings, discards a card in this suit. Later, declarer plays the Ace and returns the 2. East follows with a low card—his third one—and the declarer's problem is whether to play the Queen or the 10.

In effect, the question is whether to play East for an original holding of K x x x or J x x x. It is clearly much more likely that he started out with the K x x x. With that holding he would be willing to discard, whereas with the J x x x he would be reluctant to. This type of deduction is usually safe because most defenders tend to make their easiest discards first. Experts are not so accommodating, and they tend to arrange their discards in a way that will not help declarer. Against most players it is sufficient to assume that they have not discarded in such a way as to present you with tricks. For example:

K J 10 5

A 4 2

While you are running another suit, each opponent discards once from this suit. More often than not, the Queen will still be guarded: It is unlikely that one player has been so obliging as to discard from x x x and another from Q x x. The proper deduction, therefore, is that one or other of the opponents probably started out with the Q x x x, and you have to guess who it is.

Playing on an assumption

At the start of this chapter it was remarked that the expert's two principal resources when information is lacking are Deduction and Assumption. The second of these comes into operation in those relatively infrequent hands where no amount of detective work enables declarer to gain the data that he needs for a successful plan.

The use of the term 'assumption' is deserving of explanation, for the reader may object that the rules for playing on an assumption are already familiar to experienced players. It is commonplace, for example, that if the cards must lie in a certain way for you to make your contract, you should assume that they lie that way. Here is a somewhat extreme example of that principle:

♣ K Q 10 7 3 2

♣ 6 4

Declarer is playing a hand at 3 No Trump and cannot make it unless he can win several tricks in this suit. Moreover, he has no entry to dummy. It is obvious that the opponents will hold up the Ace of Clubs if they can, and therefore there is only one distribution of the cards that enables declarer to get home. He must assume that

East has the singleton Ace, and in line with this he must start the Clubs by playing a low one from each hand. If the gods are kind, and the Ace falls, a second-round finesse of the 10 will roll up the suit.

A further principle which is well understood is that a player should make no more assumptions than are absolutely necessary, inasmuch as it is far easier to have one prayer answered than two. An example of this principle is as follows:

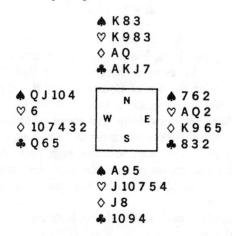

```
              ♠ K 8 3
              ♡ K 9 8 3
              ◊ A Q
              ♣ A K J 7

♠ Q J 10 4      ┌─────────┐      ♠ 7 6 2
♡ 6             │    N    │      ♡ A Q 2
◊ 10 7 4 3 2    │  W   E  │      ◊ K 9 6 5
♣ Q 6 5         │    S    │      ♣ 8 3 2
                └─────────┘
              ♠ A 9 5
              ♡ J 10 7 5 4
              ◊ J 8
              ♣ 10 9 4
```

South is the declarer at 4 Hearts and West leads the Queen of Spades. Declarer wins in his own hand, loses a trump trick to East, and wins the Spade return in dummy. The Ace of trumps is dislodged and a Spade is returned for West to win, whereupon West exits with a Diamond.

Having already lost three tricks, declarer reasons that he cannot really expect to make the contract unless West has the Queen of Clubs, and he accordingly assumes that he has it. In such a case it will be possible to discard a Diamond on dummy's fourth Club, and therefore the correct play is to win the Diamond with the Ace, refusing the finesse. Declarer has no way of knowing whether West has the Queen of Clubs or not, but he assumes that he has it, and it follows that it is unnecessary to make an assumption about the King of Diamonds.

The type of thinking that has been highly developed in recent years follows on from there, and can perhaps best be illustrated by means of an example. Declarer is playing a hand at a Spade contract and the suits which present a problem are these:

◊ 7 4
♣ J 10

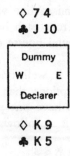

◊ K 9
♣ K 5

Let us suppose that the declarer, with adequate trumps in each hand and no entry problems, has got to hold his losses to two tricks in these suits. Straight away it becomes clear that his task will depend on East having the Ace of Diamonds, and therefore he should assume that he has it. So much is obvious—but from this it may follow that declarer can draw deductions about other high cards. For example, in the circumstances of an actual case it may happen that East has already shown up with so many high cards in Spades and Hearts that, if he also proves to have the Ace of Diamonds, he can hardly have the Ace of Clubs also. In that case declarer would play Clubs on that basis.

Here is a complete deal which shows how such a situation can arise in practical play:

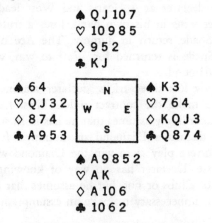

♠ Q J 10 7
♡ 10 9 8 5
◊ 9 5 2
♣ K J

♠ 6 4
♡ Q J 3 2
◊ 8 7 4
♣ A 9 5 3

♠ K 3
♡ 7 6 4
◊ K Q J 3
♣ Q 8 7 4

♠ A 9 8 5 2
♡ A K
◊ A 10 6
♣ 10 6 2

The bidding:

NORTH	EAST	SOUTH	WEST
Pass	Pass	1 Spade	Pass
3 Spades	Pass	4 Spades	Pass
Pass	Pass		

Suppose you are playing the hand at 4 Spades. The contract is an optimistic one, of course, and after the hand you intend to have a word with your partner about the values required for a double raise by a passed hand. For the time being, however, you concentrate on getting home.

West leads the 8 of Diamonds and you allow East's Jack to hold the trick. East continues with the King of Diamonds and you win with the Ace. Your first task is to try to diagnose the Club situation, as a means of entering dummy. However, you should not make your diagnosis simply on the basis of what you know about the hand; you should make it also on the basis of what you must *assume* to be so if you are to make your contract. The main assumption you must make is that East has the King of trumps, for you cannot afford a trump loser.

It is clear from the play that East has the K Q J of Diamonds. If he also held the Ace of Clubs, in addition to the King of Spades (as you are assuming), he would have opened the bidding. So you see that the Club situation, far from presenting a guess, offers only one proper method of play: you *must* play West for the Ace, for if East has it, the cards cannot possibly be distributed in such a way as to enable you to make the contract. Of course, East might have the Ace of Clubs and West a singleton King of Spades, but that is such a remote possibility it should be dismissed.

In the next deal, playing on an assumption enables declarer to take an apparently miraculous position in the Spade suit.

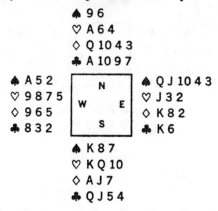

```
                    ♠ 9 6
                    ♡ A 6 4
                    ◊ Q 10 4 3
                    ♣ A 10 9 7
      ♠ A 5 2           N          ♠ Q J 10 4 3
      ♡ 9 8 7 5                     ♡ J 3 2
      ◊ 9 6 5      W        E       ◊ K 8 2
      ♣ 8 3 2          S           ♣ K 6
                    ♠ K 8 7
                    ♡ K Q 10
                    ◊ A J 7
                    ♣ Q J 5 4
```

The bidding:

EAST	SOUTH	WEST	NORTH
Pass	1 No Trump	Pass	3 No Trump
Pass	Pass	Pass	

South is declarer at 3 No Trump and West leads the 9 of Hearts. Declarer takes the losing Club finesse and East shifts to the Queen of Spades, which South ducks, West playing the 5. East now continues with the Jack of Spades and South has to decide whether to put up the King or duck again.

In the absence of any other information the correct play would be to put up the King, since it is more likely that East has the Ace than that West was dealt it with precisely two other cards. However, declarer should reflect that, whatever happens in Spades, he is unlikely to make the contract without a successful Diamond finesse. If East, who passed originally, holds the King of Diamonds as well as the cards he has already shown, he cannot hold the Ace of Spades. So declarer knows that his only chance of avoiding the loss of four Spade tricks is to duck and hope that West has no more than three cards in the suit.

The situation is not always that the declarer must assume a card to be well-placed in order to make the contract. Sometimes declarer can be sure of making the contract unless a particular card is badly placed. in such a case he should assume it is badly placed, and analyze his chances on that basis.

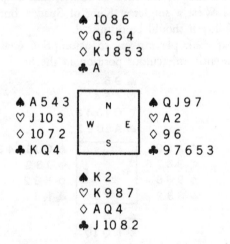

```
                    ♠ 10 8 6
                    ♡ Q 6 5 4
                    ◇ K J 8 5 3
                    ♣ A

    ♠ A 5 4 3          N         ♠ Q J 9 7
    ♡ J 10 3       W       E     ♡ A 2
    ◇ 10 7 2           S         ◇ 9 6
    ♣ K Q 4                      ♣ 9 7 6 5 3

                    ♠ K 2
                    ♡ K 9 8 7
                    ◇ A Q 4
                    ♣ J 10 8 2
```

The bidding:

WEST	NORTH	EAST	SOUTH
Pass	Pass	Pass	1 Heart
Pass	3 Hearts	Pass	4 Hearts
Pass	Pass	Pass	

South is at 4 Hearts and West leads the King of Clubs. Declarer can expect to make the contract quite easily if East happens to have the Ace of Spades, and therefore he should plan the play of the hand on the assumption that *West* has it.

In this case declarer must endeavor to restrict his trump losses to one trick, a venture that will need both good play and good luck. Declarer has to find one of the defenders with precisely the Ace doubleton of trumps, and moreover, he has to guess which defender has it. West is marked with the K Q of Clubs, and if he has the Ace of Spades also (as declarer is assuming), he is quite unlikely to have the Ace of Hearts, in view of his original pass. Declarer therefore plays East, rather than West, to have the doubleton Ace of Hearts. He leads a Heart from dummy at trick two, wins with the King if East ducks, and then plays a low Heart from each hand to bring matters to a highly satisfactory conclusion.

QUIZ ON DEDUCTION AND ASSUMPTION

In the following three hands, endeavor to plan your play by drawing deductions from the opponents' bidding.

1.

NORTH	SOUTH
♠ K 4 3	♠ A Q J 10 9
♡ J 8 5 4 3	♡ A 7
◊ 10 5 4 2	◊ A 9
♣ J	♣ A K 6 2

The bidding:

WEST	NORTH	EAST	SOUTH
3 Clubs	Pass	Pass	4 Spades
Pass			

West leads the 6 of Diamonds, dummy plays low, East plays the Jack, and you win with the Ace. How do you proceed?

2.

NORTH	SOUTH
♠ A J 8	♠ K Q 10 6 4 2
♡ 8 7 2	♡ Q 5 3
◊ A 6 4	◊ K 2
♣ A Q 10 7	♣ J 5

The bidding:

WEST	NORTH	EAST	SOUTH
Pass	1 Club	Pass	1 Spade
Pass	2 Spades	Pass	4 Spades
Pass	Pass	Pass	

West leads the King of Hearts, on which East drops the 4, and shifts to the Queen of Diamonds. Plan the play.

3.

NORTH	SOUTH
♠ Q 10 7 2	♠ K 4
♡ K 10 8 6 2	♡ A Q J 7 5 4
◊ K Q	◊ 10 7 4
♣ 8 6	♣ K 2

The bidding:

WEST	NORTH	EAST	SOUTH
1 Spade	Pass	Pass	2 Hearts
Pass	4 Hearts	Pass	Pass
Pass			

West leads a trump, to which East follows, and you return a Diamond. West takes the Ace and exits with a Diamond. How do you proceed?

In the following two deals, endeavor to plan the play by drawing deductions from the opponents' method of defense.

4.

NORTH	SOUTH
♠ A 9 7 6 4	♠ K 5 2
♡ A 7 6 3	♡ K Q J 10 8 2
◇ A 4	◇ Q 3
♣ 9 4	♣ 7 2

The contract is 4 Hearts and West leads the King of Clubs, which holds. West continues with the Queen of Clubs and East overtakes with the Ace and returns a low Diamond. Plan the play.

5.

NORTH	SOUTH
♠ J 10 4	♠ A K 9 8 6 3
♡ A K 6 2	♡ 8 5
◇ A J 7	◇ 4
♣ J 3 2	♣ 8 6 5 4

The contract is 4 Spades, East having opened with a bid of 1 Club. West leads the Queen of Clubs which holds, and continues with a low Club. East wins and cashes a third Club, on which West discards a Diamond. East then exits with a trump, which you win with the Ace as West plays low. How do you continue?

In the following two hands declarer makes his contract by making an assumption about the distribution of the defenders' cards.

6.

NORTH	SOUTH
♠ A K 6	♠ 10 4
♡ A 10	♡ K Q
◇ K 10 6 2	◇ A J 9 8 3
♣ Q 10 3 2	♣ A K 6 4

The contract is 6 Diamonds and West leads a low Heart. How do you proceed?

7.

NORTH	SOUTH
♠ Q 6 3	♠ K 8 7 5 4
♡ A J 7	♡ 8
◇ 10 8 7 3	◇ K 4
♣ Q 9 2	♣ A K J 10 4

The bidding:

WEST	NORTH	EAST	SOUTH
Pass	Pass	Pass	1 Club
Pass	1 No Trump	Pass	2 Spades
Pass	3 Clubs	Pass	3 Spades
Pass	4 Spades	Pass	Pass
Pass			

The contract is 4 Spades and West leads the King of Hearts, which you win. How do you play the trump suit?

ANSWERS TO QUIZ ON DEDUCTION AND ASSUMPTION

1.

You have nine winners and must resist the temptation to try to gain an overtrick by ruffing Clubs twice in dummy. In view of the bidding it is possible that East is void of Clubs, and if a high Club is played at trick two he will ruff, reducing you to eight tricks. You may then be unable to score two ruffs in dummy, since dummy has only one high trump. The safest form of play is to lead a *low* Club at trick two. When you regain the lead, you can ruff a Club with the King of trumps and make the contract.

2.

You seem to have three potential Heart losers and therefore cannot afford a Club loser. However, the straightforward Club finesse seems certain to fail, since West passed as dealer and is hardly likely to have the King of Clubs as well as the A K of Hearts (which he is marked with) and Q J of Diamonds, which he is also marked with. Accordingly, you would really prefer to take the Club finesse against East rather than West, and therefore you should duck West's lead of the Queen of Diamonds at trick two. You win any continuation, draw two rounds of trumps, take the King of Diamonds and cross to the Ace of Clubs. You discard the Jack of Clubs on the Ace of Diamonds and lead the Queen of Clubs from dummy. If East has the King, as expected, it will be trapped and you will make your game-going trick in Clubs.

3.

In view of the bidding you must expect the two missing Aces to be with West. Therefore, in order to have a discard for a Club, you must plan to make two tricks in Spades.

Rather than simply drive out the Ace of Spades and then finesse dummy's 10, you should enter your hand with a trump and ruff your last Diamond. Then reenter your hand with another trump and lead a low Spade.

West will be unable to afford to put up the Ace, so you will win the trick with dummy's Queen. Then you throw West in with the King of Spades, forcing him to return the same suit or concede a ruff and discard.

If West has the Jack of Spades, dummy's 10 will take a trick and the contract will be made. The advantage of this method of play is that you also get home if East happens to hold the doubleton Jack of Spades, when a straight finesse of dummy's 10 would have failed.

4.

East cannot be expected to have the King of Diamonds: if he had it, he would have left his partner on play to lead one. Therefore you should not put up the Queen of Diamonds. A better chance is to plan a partial elimination that may enable the loss of a Spade trick to be avoided.

Play low on the Diamond lead and win with dummy's Ace. Draw the opponents' trumps and cash the A K of Spades. Then exit with a Diamond.

West will win this with the King. If he has a Spade to cash, you go down, but if he has no more Spades he will have to return a Club or a Diamond, either of which you can ruff in the dummy hand, discarding a losing Spade from your own hand.

If you were to play the Queen of Diamonds at the third trick, it would almost certainly be covered by the King, and then the elimination would not work. Later, when you exited with a Diamond, the opponents would be able to win it in the hand that contained the winning Spade, and you would go down.

5.

You must ask yourself why East has not played a fourth Club in an attempt to promote a trump trick for his partner. The answer can only be that he knows that West will be unable to ruff higher than dummy. In other words, East has the Queen of Spades, and does not wish to reveal its location, as he would if he played a fourth Club and West failed to ruff with the Queen.

Therefore, rather than continue with the King of trumps, you should enter dummy with the Ace of Diamonds and take a finesse in trump to land the contract.

6.

This is an interesting problem. Declarer has to consider how to handle the trump suit, but first he should take a look at the Club situation. Clearly he is a very strong favorite not to lose a Club trick, in which case it will not matter how he plays the trumps.

Accordingly, declarer should assume that he is going to lose a Club trick: in other words, he should assume that East holds the J x x x of Clubs. In this case West, with a singleton Club, will be more likely to hold the Queen of Diamonds than East, and declarer should, therefore, play the Diamonds on that basis.

7.

You should assume East has the doubleton Ace of trump. You have

absolutely no way of knowing who has the Ace of trump, or whether it is a doubleton, but nevertheless you should assume East has the doubleton Ace. This assumption stems from the fact that you must assume West has the Ace of Diamonds.

If East has the Ace of Diamonds, you are likely to make the contract no matter how you play the trump suit (unless trumps are 4-1, in which case your cause is hopeless). Therefore you assume West has it.

The opening lead has already marked West with the K Q of Hearts, and if he has the Ace of Diamonds (as you are assuming), he cannot have the Ace of trump (since he passed originally). Therefore you assume East has it.

In line with this, you endeavor to limit your trump losses by leading a low Spade from dummy at trick two and playing the King if East plays low. If the King holds, you continue with a low trump from each hand. The full deal was:

```
              Dummy
              ♠ Q 6 3
              ♡ A J 7
              ◇ 10 8 7 3
              ♣ Q 9 2

♠ J 10 9                    ♠ A 2
♡ K Q 10 3                  ♡ 9 6 5 4 2
◇ A J 6                     ◇ Q 9 5 2
♣ 8 6 3                     ♣ 7 5

              Declarer
              ♠ K 8 7 5 4
              ♡ 8
              ◇ K 4
              ♣ A K J 10 4
```

BY THIS TIME it is to be hoped that we have mastered the general principles of the play of various card combinations. In some cases the proper procedure is clearly defined. In others a guess must be presented to a player, and where he is put to a guess the principle of percentages or probabilities should be applied in determining which guess is more apt to be successful. Occasionally, however, we are confronted with a situation in which no amount of technical correctness can save us. In other words, regardless of the adverse distribution of the cards, if the opponents play properly we are doomed to failure. In such cases the only hope is that the defense will err.

That being the case, it is our duty to make it easy for the opposition to make mistakes. The attempt to prevail by psychology is open not only to the declarer, it is available also to the defense. If you see that the declarer will surely make his contract with normal play, you should try to induce him to form a false theory about your holding. This type of strategy may take the form of a false discard or winning with a higher card when a low card would have done the work just as well. However, when you are defending, attempts at deception may prove to be a boomerang because of the fact that your partner may be fooled as readily as your opponents. Where you are the declarer you are under no such handicap, inasmuch as you have no partner to deceive. Generally speaking, therefore, a defender should practice deception only when he knows that the false-carding cannot be harmful to partner but may induce the declarer to err. False-carding by the defenders is less apt to be dangerous when done in the trump suit, because it is unlikely that partner will have such a holding that your false information will set him off stride.

Certain types of deception will be effective against experienced players but will have little or no effect against the novice, because he is probably not noticing what cards you play. It calls to mind the remark of the late Joe Penner of stage, screen, and radio fame. "You can't fool me," he once said; "I'm too ignorant."

Don't waste subtleties on an unwitting opposition.

It is important to bear in mind that when you practice deception you are really telling a lie, and in doing so you are not apt to deceive the opponents if you stutter. Speed is an essential qualification of both a liar and a false-carder. Make up your mind in advance and act promptly.

Deception may be practiced on the opening lead; as, for example, the strategy of underleading an Ace or leading a very high card from the King, in order to convey the impression to the declarer that you are leading a short suit. These have been discussed in the chapter on leads.

One of the oldest chestnuts known to bridge, but one which can still occasionally be employed with effect, is the lead of the Jack from the Queen Jack doubleton. This should be done only in the trump suit. The following diagram will illustrate the point:

A 9 8 2

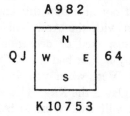

QJ | N | 64
     | W   E |
     | S |

K 10 7 5 3

The declarer holds nine trumps. If left to his own resources, he will probably play for the suit to break. If you lead the Jack, he may reach the mistaken belief that your partner has the Queen and finesse to his disaster. However, you must not get the reputation for doing this constantly, because your opponents will be less likely to fall for your deception. Occasionally, with this holding, you should "cross them up" by leading the Queen. In other words, it is well to keep the opposition guessing.

The advice has been given to use this type of strategy only in the trump suit. The reason it should not be employed in the side suit is the possibility that partner will have one of the high honors and waste the card because he believes that the declarer has the Queen. For example, the dummy may show up with a great many, including the King. Your partner may have the Ace and suspect that you are leading a singleton. He may, therefore, play his Ace, establishing dummy's King. First consider declarer's tactics.

At this point it may be appropriate to point out that there is current in certain circles the practice of leading the second best of two touching honors, such as the Queen from the King Queen, the Jack from Queen Jack, et cetera. Where partners have such an understanding, it is regarded as a private convention and should be announced to the opposition. Where, however, the partnership has no such agreement, there is no objection to the deception tactics suggested above.

In considering deception practices let us first concentrate our attention on the tactics of the declarer.

When declarer has a choice of cards with which to win a trick, the selection of the proper one, although on the surface it makes no difference, may have a vital effect on the subsequent play.

Suppose you are playing a No Trump contract. West leads the 5 of Spades. East follows with the Jack. You are South, the declarer, and hold A K Q. You are naturally anxious to have West continue when he subsequently regains the lead, but there is some other suit that you fear. If you win with the Queen, he will know that you have both the Ace and the King, else East would have played one of the higher ones. You must not give him this impression. Is it, therefore, proper for you to win with the Ace? The answer is definitely no, because you will be suspected of deception. The play of the Ace would be the truth only if East had the K Q J, which will no doubt appear improbable to West when you win the first trick without holding up. Your best play is the King. This will be an admission that you hold the Ace but will lead West to believe that his partner is following suit with the Jack, holding the Queen Jack.

When the Queen is led at No Trump and you, as declarer, hold the Ace and King, it will not be deceptive to win with the Ace. You should win with the King, which will leave the partner of the opening leader guessing. He will not know whether the opener has led from A Q J or Q J 10, but if you play the Ace he will know you have the King as soon as partner leads the Queen, because the Queen is not led from the King Queen.

In the following case you are South, playing a suit contract, and hold in a side suit:

8 7 4

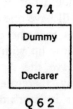

Q 6 2

West leads the King, and East follows with the 3. You know that this is East's smallest card and that he has discouraged partner from continuing the suit. Since you never can win a trick with the Queen unless West lays down his Ace, you must play in a manner which might induce him to do so. If you can make him suspect that the 3 is not his partner's lowest card, he may read it as the beginning of an echo and continue the suit. You would, therefore, follow with the 6. This might induce West to believe that his partner holds the deuce and is starting a signal. If he continues with the Ace, all is well. If not, you have lost nothing. The complete holding is as follows:

8 7 4

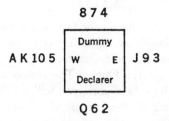

A K 10 5   J 9 3

Q 6 2

Assume that the holding was somewhat different, as follows:

Q 10 6

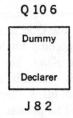

J 8 2

Against a suit contract West leads the King, and East follows with the 4. This time you are not anxious to have the suit continued. Therefore it would be suicide to false-card with the 8, because West would realize that the deuce is missing and may think that partner has it, which would indicate the start of a down-and-out signal. Your best procedure is to make the normal play of the deuce. West may be in some doubt as to who has the 3 and, feeling that declarer may have it, will read the 4 as a discouraging card and shift to some other suit. The complete holding is as follows:

Q 10 6

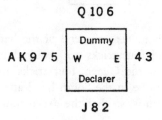

A K 9 7 5   4 3

J 8 2

You are South, the declarer, and hold the following combination:

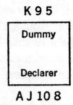

K 9 5

Dummy

Declarer

A J 10 8

You are desirous of picking up the Queen but have no clues whatsoever as to its location. You might as well guess one way as the other, but since you have no indication, on the principle of percentages you should play East for the Queen. The reason is that if East has four of the suit, including the Queen, you will still be able to pick up the suit without finessing on the first round. Whereas if it should turn out that West has four of the suit to the Queen, you would lose one trick in any event, unless you decided to take the first-round finesse, which is improbable.

Since it is desirable to postpone finesses wherever possible, it is just as well to guess East for the Queen. However, with all the cards right down to the 8, it costs nothing for South to lead the Jack, fully intending to go up with the King. The purpose of the play is to induce West to cover with the Queen if he holds it. This is apt to be very effective, inasmuch as so many players automatically cover an honor with an honor. It should be pointed out that if South has a card smaller than the 8 he could not afford to lead the Jack and overtake with the King, because an opponent's 8 spot might be developed into a winner even though the finesse succeeded.

The converse of this, a case in which it is not desired to have the opponents cover, is present in the following:

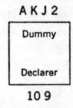

A K J 2

Dummy

Declarer

10 9

This combination is held near the end of the hand, when dummy has no more entries and four tricks are required in the suit. If the 10 is led and covered by the Queen, four tricks are not obtainable, because the 9 happens to be in the South hand and one of the opponents has at least four cards, so that the deuce cannot possibly stand up. If, however, West holds the Queen and does not cover, all four tricks are available. If the 10 is led, West will surely cover. The proper play, therefore, is the 9, which gives the declarer the best chance to capitalize on a defensive error. It is true that if West can see through your plot, the cover of the 9 by his Queen will defeat your purpose, but he is less apt to cover the 9 than he is the 10.

A somewhat ordinary card holding on which success depends upon an error by the opposition is the following:

J 10 5 4

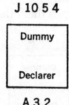

A 3 2

Assuming that you have plenty of entries and you are anxious to lose only one trick in the suit, what is your play? Technically, your only hope is that the King and the Queen are doubleton or that East has a doubleton honor, but this appears to be very unlikely, and the better chance is to hope that the honors are divided and that West can be induced to make the mistake of taking the trick early. The best play is a low card from the South hand toward dummy. If West goes up with an honor, dummy is subsequently re-entered and a finesse taken against East's remaining honor. The complete hand is as follows:

J 10 5 4

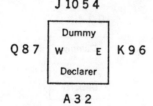

A 3 2

After a play of this kind is successful you may obtain good results with the following combination:

J 7 2

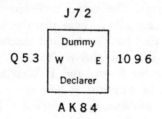

A K 8 4

South has the choice of playing out the Ace and the King, in the hope that the Queen will drop doubleton. This, however, is not very likely, and declarer decides to lead a low spot toward dummy. If West is the player who has been caught on the previous hand, he may duck, hoping that his partner has the King. If he does, you will win all four tricks. Note that your play of a low card is not apt to lose, but if West has the Queen, you will win three tricks in the suit, regardless of the distribution. If East has the Queen and one, your play will have lost, but it is worth the risk.

A somewhat kindred holding is the following:

10 2

A K Q 3

You find it necessary to win all four tricks in this suit. Unless the Jack is singleton, there is no straightforward way of doing it. The singleton Jack is such a remote possibility that it may be ignored. What is the best procedure? Obviously to play a small one toward dummy. If West holds the Jack and several others, he may not come up. In fact, he probably will not, and the 10 may win the trick. This is the only way you can accomplish your purpose.

A play that works much more often than it should is:

9 7 4 3 2

Q J 10 8 6

This is the trump suit and, as you see, two tricks must be lost unless a mix-up occurs. The proper technique is not to lead from dummy. You have practically no hope that the Ace and the King will fall together, for if East has the Ace and another one and West has the singleton King, East will surely play low. Your only hope is to lead the Queen from the South hand. If West holds the King and a small one, you will be surprised at how many times the King will come up only to be smothered by partner's Ace. I agree with you that

West should not play the King. It borders on the absurd to do so, because if declarer had the Ace and the Queen, it would be rather silly for him to lead the Queen instead of either playing out the Ace or taking the finesse. The fact remains that a great many players do not stop to analyze and are in dread fear of losing their King. It costs you nothing to try.

Another old chestnut that still keeps working is the following: You are playing a Spade contract and hold the singleton King of Diamonds. Your dummy has the J 10 6 2. All other suits are under control, but you are anxious to steal the King of Diamonds. This can be done only if second hand ducks the lead from dummy. In order to make it more sporting to duck, the Jack should be led, to create the impression that you are finessing against the Queen. This can also be effectively done with the following combination:

Q 10 2

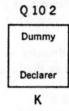

K

Assuming the rest of the hand is solid and no discards are needed, here the Queen or the 10 might be led from dummy. This gives you a much better chance that East will duck with the Ace.

As declarer you will sometimes find it necessary to steal a trick in order to win your contract. In such cases act quickly, before the opponents are organized. The following illustration, provided by Louis Watson, is a very instructive one:

♠ A 6
♡ J 6 2
◇ A Q 4
♣ K 8 5 4 3

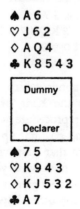

♠ 7 5
♡ K 9 4 3
◇ K J 5 3 2
♣ A 7

You are South, the declarer at a contract of 3 No Trump. West leads the 10 of Spades. You see eight tricks readily available, and it appears pointless to hold up with the Spade. It is hardly likely that West has seven of them, since they were not bid. It would be very pusillanimous to take your eight tricks and give up for down one. If East holds the Ace of Hearts, you have a fair chance to steal a trick before the defense knows that you are wide open in Spades. Your proper play is the immediate lead of the Jack of Hearts. This will make it appear to East that you are starting a finesse, and he may not come up with the Ace. If he does not, you boldly put up the King. If it holds, you are home. If not, you will be down several tricks. The question arises, does it pay to take this risk? That would depend upon how much you stand to lose if your strategy fails. If you are not vulnerable and not doubled, 50 points a trick is a cheap price to pay for the chance of fulfillment. If you are doubled, I would not like to give my out-and-out advice. That would depend somewhat on your bank balance.

Assume that you are the declarer at a contract of 4 Hearts on strong bidding, which East has doubled without hearing from his partner:

♠ A Q 2
♡ 10 8 6 4
◊ A 8 4 2
♣ Q 10

```
+----------+
| Dummy    |
|          |
|          |
| Declarer |
+----------+
```

♠ J 7
♡ K Q J 7 5 2
◊ 9 3
♣ A 6 5

West leads the 5 of Diamonds, which North wins. It is reasonable to suppose that East holds the King of Spades, and therefore the finesse will fail. The proper procedure when South obtains the lead is to play the 7 of Spades and go right up with the Ace, returning the deuce immediately. It is true that East will know that you are up to something, but he may not know what you are trying to get him to do. It may be that you have a singleton and are trying to trap him into playing the King. On the other hand, if you have the Jack, he must come up. He may guess wrong. If he does, you are home. The complete hand is as follows:

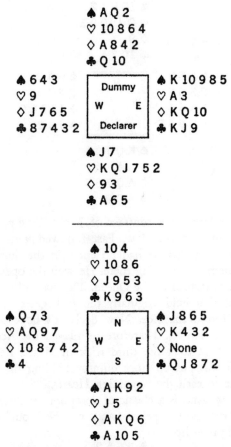

```
                    ♠ A Q 2
                    ♡ 10 8 6 4
                    ◇ A 8 4 2
                    ♣ Q 10
    ♠ 6 4 3        ┌─────────┐      ♠ K 10 9 8 5
    ♡ 9           │  Dummy  │      ♡ A 3
    ◇ J 7 6 5     │ W     E │      ◇ K Q 10
    ♣ 8 7 4 3 2   │Declarer │      ♣ K J 9
                    └─────────┘
                    ♠ J 7
                    ♡ K Q J 7 5 2
                    ◇ 9 3
                    ♣ A 6 5
```

```
                    ♠ 10 4
                    ♡ 10 8 6
                    ◇ J 9 5 3
                    ♣ K 9 6 3
    ♠ Q 7 3        ┌─────────┐      ♠ J 8 6 5
    ♡ A Q 9 7     │    N    │      ♡ K 4 3 2
    ◇ 10 8 7 4 2  │ W     E │      ◇ None
    ♣ 4           │    S    │      ♣ Q J 8 7 2
                    └─────────┘
                    ♠ A K 9 2
                    ♡ J 5
                    ◇ A K Q 6
                    ♣ A 10 5
```

South was the declarer at a contract of 3 No Trump on bidding which is not sanctioned here. West opened the 4 of Diamonds, which dummy held with the Jack, East discarding the 8 of Clubs. It is apparent that only eight tricks are available without building up a Club trick, and if the lead is surrendered, the defense will surely shift to Hearts.

It is psychologically true that the defense will usually avoid a suit that the declarer is working on. Capitalizing on this principle, the declarer immediately led the 6 of Hearts, playing the Jack from his own hand. West won with the Queen and responded to his partner's signal by leading the 4 of Clubs. The Jack forced the Ace, and the 10 of Clubs was returned, losing to East's Queen. East calling to mind that declarer had first led Hearts, decided to shift to the Spades, and declarer was home.

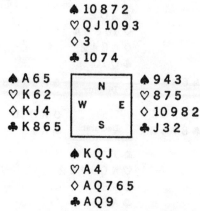

```
              ♠ 10 8 7 2
              ♡ Q J 10 9 3
              ◇ 3
              ♣ 10 7 4
♠ A 6 5                        ♠ 9 4 3
♡ K 6 2           N            ♡ 8 7 5
◇ K J 4     W          E       ◇ 10 9 8 2
♣ K 8 6 5         S            ♣ J 3 2
              ♠ K Q J
              ♡ A 4
              ◇ A Q 7 6 5
              ♣ A Q 9
```

South was declarer at a contract of 3 No Trump. West led the 5 of Clubs, dummy played low, East followed with the Jack, and declarer, recognizing that he had no entry in the dummy, hit upon an ingenious method of getting there. He won the opening trick with the Ace of Clubs instead of the Queen. This naturally gave West the impression that East held originally the Jack Queen of Clubs, since the Jack had forced the Ace. Now declarer's hope was that West held the King of Hearts. Therefore he played the Ace and another Heart. When West took the third trick in Hearts he led the 6 of Clubs. The 10 was put up from dummy holding the trick, and declarer was able to cash the remaining Hearts.

The following hand is a classic of deception. It illustrates, too, the principle that the most hopeless hands can be brought home if you maintain a stiff upper lip:

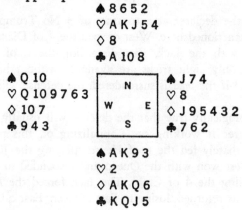

```
              ♠ 8 6 5 2
              ♡ A K J 5 4
              ◇ 8
              ♣ A 10 8
♠ Q 10                         ♠ J 7 4
♡ Q 10 9 7 6 3    N            ♡ 8
◇ 10 7      W          E       ◇ J 9 5 4 3 2
♣ 9 4 3           S            ♣ 7 6 2
              ♠ A K 9 3
              ♡ 2
              ◇ A K Q 6
              ♣ K Q J 5
```

Through a series of aggressive bids South found himself in the impossible contract of 7 Spades. West led the 10 of Diamonds. How would you play the hand?

This declarer hit upon an ingenious method. The only hope to fulfill the contract was that East had three Spades and West two, and that East could be induced to trump one of dummy's good cards. Declarer therefore led the Ace and King of Hearts immediately, and East fell into the error of trumping with the 4 of Spades. Declarer overruffed with the 9, and the Ace and King of Spades dropped the adverse trumps.

Occasionally you can get your opponents to help you make your guess. Here is a splendid bit of applied psychology:

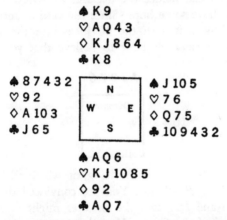

```
                    ♠ K 9
                    ♡ A Q 4 3
                    ◊ K J 8 6 4
                    ♣ K 8

    ♠ 8 7 4 3 2                      ♠ J 10 5
    ♡ 9 2           N                ♡ 7 6
    ◊ A 10 3     W     E             ◊ Q 7 5
    ♣ J 6 5           S              ♣ 10 9 4 3 2

                    ♠ A Q 6
                    ♡ K J 10 8 5
                    ◊ 9 2
                    ♣ A Q 7
```

The contract was 6 Hearts. West led a Spade, which declarer won in his own hand with the Ace, and before touching any other card led the 2 of Diamonds. West was caught flat-footed, and, fearing that declarer was trying to steal a singleton, went up with the Ace. Had declarer postponed attacking Diamonds until later, it might have become apparent to West that the hand depended upon the Diamond guess, and he would play low. Declarer, therefore, would have an even chance to play the wrong card. When the surprise attack is made at trick two, if West does not come up with the Ace it is a better gamble to play East for that card.

Deception on the defense

Deceptive tactics by the defenders must be exercised with caution. Where co-operation of partner is required on the defense, it is important not to confuse him. Occasionally these tactics may be employed without confusing partner.

Declarer plays the King. What card should East play?

AJ976

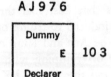

It is very likely that your partner holds the Queen and that the declarer intends to finesse the Jack—a play which you know will be successful. If you can induce the declarer to believe that the Queen might fall, you have some hope. Since the card is immaterial to you, you should follow suit with the 10 instead of the 3. It costs you nothing and may cause declarer to believe that you also have the Queen.

AJ976

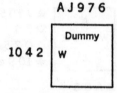

You are West. South plays the King, on which all hands play low. He follows with a small one. You are convinced that your partner has the Queen and fear that the declarer might decide to play for the drop instead of the finesse. Your best play to the second trick is the 10, since it is of no use to you and will tend to make the declarer believe that you have the Queen alone at this point or, if your partner has it, that it cannot fall. This type of false-card will almost always induce the declarer to take the finesse instead of playing for the drop.

A more advanced type of false-carding is the following:

AKJ96

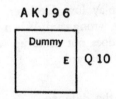

You are East. Declarer plays the Ace from dummy. If you play the 10, declarer may suspect that the Queen will fall next time and refuse the finesse. The play of the Queen instead may be very effective, if you suspect that the declarer has only two cards of the suit. He will then be certain that your partner has the 10 and will no doubt finesse the 9 on the next round. Of course there is no assurance that this type of play will succeed, because declarer might have three of the suit, but if he has only two, it is bound to work.

A type of false-carding which is frequently abused is:

A J 10 2

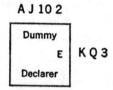

South, the declarer, plays a small one and finesses the 10. Many players false-card with the King (in order to induce declarer to believe that West has the Queen). This is usually unsound strategy, because generally you do not care what the declarer believes. He is going to have to take the finesse again in any event. If he does not, you are sure of the trick. However, if you win with the King, your partner will believe that declarer holds the Queen and may subsequently defend upon a mistaken idea of the facts.

The situation would change somewhat if the holding were:

A J 10 9 2

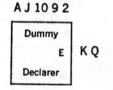

Declarer finesses the 10; you, as East, win. You fear the possibility that declarer will not finesse again but will play for the drop. Now you should try to induce South to believe that your partner has one of the honors. This you may do by winning with the King, but here again you must vary your tactics. Do not always follow the same procedure. Sometimes you should win with the King, sometimes with the Queen. It is very unprofitable to get yourself spotted as a notorious false-carder.

You are East:

K Q 10 2

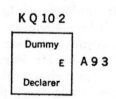

South leads the 4, West follows with the 5, and declarer plays the King. Assume that you do not fear a singleton in the declarer's hand. Your policy is to duck. If you win the trick, declarer will surely finesse against the Jack on the next round, and you know that it will succeed. If you play low, declarer may form the mistaken belief that West has the Ace and may be induced to come up with the Queen next time. But please do not go into a brown study as you make the play. Determine in advance what your action is to be. In ducking, the 9, rather than the 3, should be played.

The complete holding was:

K Q 10 2

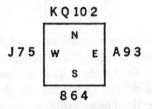

J 7 5   A 9 3

8 6 4

Another brilliant deceptive lead which is worthy of study was one made by my friend Albert H. Morehead. It has the merit of tending to deceive declarer without hurting partner:

♠ Q J 8 4
♡ J 7 5
♢ Q 5 3
♣ 9 8 3

♠ A K 7 3
♡ 10 8 6
♢ 10 9 7
♣ A Q 2

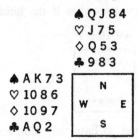

The bidding has been:

SOUTH	WEST	NORTH	EAST
1 Heart	Pass	1 No Trump	Pass
2 Diamonds	Pass	2 Hearts	Pass
4 Hearts	Pass	Pass	Pass

West led the Ace of Spades, a deliberate false-carding, because he did not wish the declarer to know that he had both the Ace and the King with the Spade bid behind him. Partner played the deuce. The bidding indicated that South might have five Hearts and five Diamonds, and the only hope from Mr. Morehead's standpoint was that one of his partner's two Diamonds was the King. If declarer were left to his own resources, he would surely play a low Diamond from

dummy and the entire suit would be picked up. In order to induce
a false theory of the Diamond distribution, he led the 9. Declarer
placed East with the King 10 and one other, and played the Queen.
This was covered by the King and the Ace, and West could not be
prevented from taking a trick with the 10. The complete hand
follows:

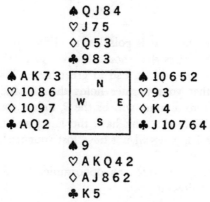

```
                    ♠ Q J 8 4
                    ♡ J 7 5
                    ◇ Q 5 3
                    ♣ 9 8 3
   ♠ A K 7 3          N          ♠ 10 6 5 2
   ♡ 10 8 6                      ♡ 9 3
   ◇ 10 9 7      W       E       ◇ K 4
   ♣ A Q 2           S          ♣ J 10 7 6 4
                    ♠ 9
                    ♡ A K Q 4 2
                    ◇ A J 8 6 2
                    ♣ K 5
```

South leads the 3. What should you play as West?

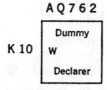

```
              A Q 7 6 2
              ┌─────────────┐
              │ Dummy       │
       K 10   │ W           │
              │ Declarer    │
              └─────────────┘
```

It is apparently immaterial, but actually it is not so. The proper
play is the King, not in order to force out the Ace, because nothing
is to be gained by doing so. You do not wish the Ace forced out
unless partner has the Jack and two others, and if partner has that
holding, no matter what card you play your side cannot be prevented
from ultimately winning a trick. The reason for your play is strategic.
Since it makes no difference to you, you wish to give the declarer the
impression that your King is alone. This may induce him to play your
partner for the 10—particularly if the complete holding were:

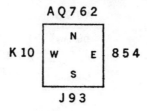

```
              A Q 7 6 2
              ┌─────────────┐
              │    N        │
       K 10   │ W       E   │  8 5 4
              │    S        │
              └─────────────┘
                   J 9 3
```

At No Trump, South leads the deuce of this suit. What should West play?

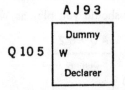

A J 9 3

K Q 5

Dummy

W

Declarer

The answer is the 5. It is pointless to climb up with the Queen to insure one trick, unless that should happen to be the setting trick or unless you should desire the lead in great haste. With this holding it is very likely that your partner holds the 10, and if so, declarer's probable play from dummy will be the 9, unless you "tip your hand" and tell him plainly that you have the King and the Queen. If the declarer has the 10, you will not have lost your trick, you will simply have postponed winning it.

Another holding in which an opportunity for the double-cross is presented is the following:

A J 9 3

Q 10 5

Dummy

W

Declarer

Declarer leads the deuce. What should West play? West knows that if declarer has the King, the finesse of the Jack will surely be taken. If partner has the King and declarer plays properly, the defenders will take only one trick, because the correct play from the dummy will be the 9, forcing out the King, and the subsequent finesse against West's Queen will take up the entire suit. West therefore should try to induce declarer to believe that he holds both the King and the Queen. This can be done by playing the Queen second hand. It is very difficult now for declarer to believe that West does not have the King, and he almost surely will play the Jack next time. The complete holding is as follows:

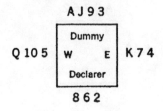

A J 9 3

Q 10 5

Dummy

W   E

Declarer

K 7 4

8 6 2

South leads the deuce. What should West play?

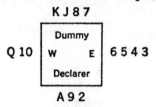

K J 8 7

Q 10 | 6 5 4 3

A 9 2

It might be profitable to play the Queen. Surely declarer intends to play the Jack from dummy and your holding will soon be apparent to him. Your play of the Queen may induce declarer to finesse the 9 on the return. Here's another:

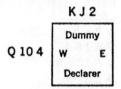

K J 2

Q 10 4

Declarer leads the 5. You are West and play the 4. Dummy's Jack holds the trick, and then the King is cashed. Notice you should drop the Queen. Declarer knows that you have it, and the 10 is the same value. If he can be induced into playing your partner for the 10, you may win a trick. The complete holding is as follows:

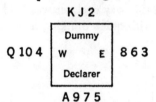

K J 2

Q 10 4 | 8 6 3

A 9 7 5

A defensive false-card which has nothing to lose and may occasionally gain a trick could be employed by West against a No Trump contract in the following situation:

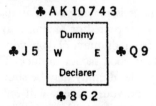

♣ A K 10 7 4 3

♣ J 5 | ♣ Q 9

♣ 8 6 2

Dummy has a sure entry card in another suit. When declarer leads the 2 of Clubs, West might obtain a good result by playing the Jack. Declarer will win and will probably return to his hand to lead another

Club. When West follows with the 5, declarer may suspect him of having originally held the Q J 5.

A slight variation of this play occurred on the following hand taken from a tournament:

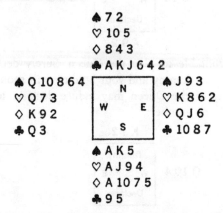

```
               ♠ 7 2
               ♡ 10 5
               ◇ 8 4 3
               ♣ A K J 6 4 2
♠ Q 10 8 6 4                    ♠ J 9 3
♡ Q 7 3           N             ♡ K 8 6 2
◇ K 9 2       W       E         ◇ Q J 6
♣ Q 3            S              ♣ 10 8 7
               ♠ A K 5
               ♡ A J 9 4
               ◇ A 10 7 5
               ♣ 9 5
```

South was playing 3 No Trump. West led the 6 of Spades. South won and played the 5 of Clubs, intending to finesse. West promptly played the Queen, and declarer paused for a moment. If the Queen were singleton, East would have 10 8 7 3 and would stop the suit. Declarer therefore was obliged to make a safety play by permitting the Queen to hold. In this way declarer was held to 3 No Trump.

Boldness combined with quick thinking may prove very effective in cases like the following:

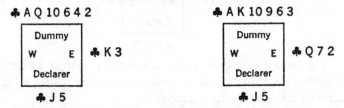

```
♣ A Q 10 6 4 2              ♣ A K 10 9 6 3
┌─────────────┐            ┌─────────────┐
│   Dummy     │            │   Dummy     │
│ W       E   │ ♣ K 3      │ W       E   │ ♣ Q 7 2
│  Declarer   │            │  Declarer   │
└─────────────┘            └─────────────┘
     ♣ J 5                      ♣ J 5
```

You are East. Declarer is playing No Trump, dummy has no entry cards. Declarer, who is suspected of having only two Clubs, leads the Jack and plays low from dummy. If you win, the declarer has the balance of the suit. It is good tactics to duck. The finesse will almost surely be repeated, and the dummy may be shut out. Of course, if you have a "lunging" partner, your strategy will fail. A "lunging" partner is one who lunges toward the trick every time declarer takes what appears to be a losing finesse. The reflex action of his forearm may prove very costly.

Here is a ruse that may work in less astute circles:

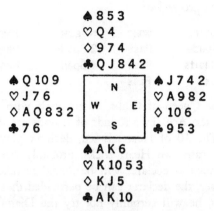

♠ 8 5 3
♥ Q 4
♦ 9 7 4
♣ Q J 8 4 2

♠ Q 10 9   ♠ J 7 4 2
♥ J 7 6   ♥ A 9 8 2
♦ A Q 8 3 2   ♦ 10 6
♣ 7 6   ♣ 9 5 3

♠ A K 6
♥ K 10 5 3
♦ K J 5
♣ A K 10

South is playing 3 No Trump. West leads the 3 of Diamonds, and South wins with the Jack. Since only eight tricks are available, declarer must build up the ninth in Hearts. The danger, however, is that East will hold the Ace and return a Diamond. If West has that card, the contract is safe, but if East has it, he may be induced to hold off once if he is given the impression that dummy has no other entries. The Ace and the King of Clubs should be played and the suit discontinued, to give the impression that declarer has no more. Then the King of Hearts is played. Naturally East should take this trick, but your play may give him the false impression that you are trying to build up the Queen as an entry and induce him to hold off one round.

Occasionally an opportunity will present itself for a defender to win a trick very cheaply, yet for purposes of deception he may decide to win with a card that on the surface would appear to cost a trick. Take the following hand as an illustration:

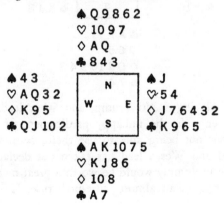

♠ Q 9 8 6 2
♥ 10 9 7
♦ A Q
♣ 8 4 3

♠ 4 3   ♠ J
♥ A Q 3 2   ♥ 5 4
♦ K 9 5   ♦ J 7 6 4 3 2
♣ Q J 10 2   ♣ K 9 6 5

♠ A K 10 7 5
♥ K J 8 6
♦ 10 8
♣ A 7

The bidding has proceeded:

SOUTH	WEST	NORTH	EAST
1 Spade	Pass	2 Spades	Pass
3 Hearts	Pass	4 Spades	Pass
Pass	Pass		

West leads the Queen of Clubs, East signals with the 9, and declarer wins with the Ace. Two rounds of trumps are drawn, winding up in dummy. The 10 of Hearts is led, declarer playing low. West sees that he can cash two Heart tricks, probably one Club, and no Diamonds, inasmuch as declarer will be forced to take the Diamond finesse. If, however, the declarer can be persuaded that East holds the Queen of Hearts, he will certainly not try the Diamond finesse but will plan to discard dummy's Queen of Diamonds on his own good Heart. So reasoned, West won the trick with the Ace instead of the Queen, cashed the Jack of Clubs, and shifted to a low Diamond. Declarer, convinced that the Heart Queen was with East, naturally refused the Diamond finesse and went up with the Ace. When the succeeding Heart finesse lost to West's Queen, the King of Diamonds was cashed for the setting trick.

A very pretty case of camouflage is the following:

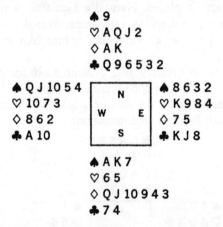

♠ 9
♡ A Q J 2
◇ A K
♣ Q 9 6 5 3 2

♠ Q J 10 5 4   ♠ 8 6 3 2
♡ 10 7 3   ♡ K 9 8 4
◇ 8 6 2   ◇ 7 5
♣ A 10   ♣ K J 8

♠ A K 7
♡ 6 5
◇ Q J 10 9 4 3
♣ 7 4

Declarer is playing 3 No Trump, and West leads the Queen of Spades. Declarer is in the unhappy predicament of having a great many tricks but not being able to use them, because the Diamond suit is blocked and West's lead has taken out declarer's only entry. Another Spade in dummy would be worth a great many points. However, South hit upon an almost "sure-fire" ruse. He quickly ducked the Queen of Spades, and West can hardly be blamed for continuing with the Jack. Now dummy's two high Diamonds were discarded on the Ace and King of Spades, which permitted the uninterrupted run of six Diamond tricks from the closed hand. It is true that if West had led no more Spades, declarer could not have made the hand, but it is a play that the defense could not have foreseen without X-ray eyes.

QUIZ ON DECEPTION

In the following cases you are defending. What is the best card to play with a view to deceiving the declarer?

1.   Q 6 5 3

WEST   2   J 9 7 4   EAST

              A K 10 8

You are East. Declarer plays the King. What card do you play?

2.   Q 2

WEST   J 10   A 7 3 EAST

              K 9 8 6 5 4

You are East. Declarer leads the 4, West plays the 10, and dummy the Queen. What card do you play?

3.   A Q 7

WEST   3   K 10 8 5   EAST

              J 9 6 4 2

You are East. Declarer leads the 2 and finesses the Queen. What card do you play?

4.   Q 7

WEST   J 10 8   4 2   EAST

              A K 9 6 5 3

You are West. Declarer leads the 3. What card do you play?

In the following cases you are West and circumstances compel you to lead this suit. What card do you play with a view to deceiving declarer?

5.   J 9 8

WEST   K Q 2   10 6 4 3   EAST

              A 7 5

6.   A 9 7

WEST   Q 8 2   J 6 4 3   EAST

              K 10 5

7.   K 5 2

WEST   Q 9 7 3   A J 6   EAST

              10 8 4

8.   A J 7 2

WEST   K 10 4   Q 5 3   EAST

              9 8 6

In the following cases you are the declarer and you are able to judge that West's lead is a singleton. Your purpose is to try to conceal this fact from East. What card do you play in the circumstances indicated?

9.   K 8 6 2

WEST   7   A Q 5 4 3   EAST

J 10 9

West leads the 7, dummy plays low and East plays the Queen.

11.   J 9 6 3

WEST   7   A K 10 5 2   EAST

Q 8 4

West leads the 7, dummy plays low and East plays the King.

10.   J 9 6 3

WEST   8   A K 10 5 2   EAST

Q 7 4

West leads the 8, dummy plays low and East plays the King.

12.   J 9 5 2

WEST   6   A Q 10 8 7   EAST

K 4 3

West leads the 6, dummy plays low and East plays the Ace.

In each of the following hands you are the declarer.

13.
- ♠ A J 6 2
- ♡ 5
- ◇ J 6 4 3
- ♣ K Q 5 4

- ♠ K 10 8 5 3
- ♡ A J 9 6 3
- ◇ K 8
- ♣ A

The contract is 6 Spades and West leads the Ace and another Diamond, East playing the 10 and Queen as dummy plays low. How do you proceed?

14.
- ♠ Q 9 3
- ♡ 8 4 3
- ◇ A J 6 4 3 2
- ♣ Q

◇ 10 led

- ♠ K J 10 8 7
- ♡ Q 9 5 2
- ◇ 5
- ♣ A K J

The contract is 4 Spades. You win the Diamond opening and decide that the best chance is to play for two Heart ruffs in dummy. How do you proceed?

15.
- ♠ J 9 8
- ♡ Q 10 9 8 2
- ◇ K 6
- ♣ J 8 4

♣ 2 led

- ♠ A K Q 10 7
- ♡ A J
- ◇ J 10 9 3
- ♣ K 5

You are declarer at 4 Spades. East wins the Club lead with the Ace and returns a Club. How do you proceed?

16.
- ♠ A J 6 3
- ♡ J 8 6
- ◇ 4 2
- ♣ Q 9 7 4

◇ 6 led   Q played

- ♠ 9 4 2
- ♡ A 5
- ◇ A K J 5 3
- ♣ K J 10

You are declarer at 3 No Trump and West leads the 6 of Diamonds, East playing the Queen. Plan the play.

ANSWERS TO QUIZ ON DECEPTION

1.

The 9. If you play the 4, declarer will continue by leading the 8 towards dummy's Queen, and when your partner shows out you will be exposed to a finesse. By playing the 9, you present declarer with the alternative possibility of playing your partner for the J 7 4 2 and you for a singleton. In this case he may lay down the Ace next, intending to lead the 10 and finesse against your partner.

2.

The 3. If you win with the Ace, declarer will compute that his only chance of avoiding a second further loser in the suit is to play West for an original holding of J 10 bare. But if you play low on the first round, declarer may assume that West has the A 10, and in this case he will continue by finessing the 9.

3.

The 8. If you take this trick with the King, it will assuredly be your last trick in the suit. (The declarer will play dummy's Ace on the next round and expose you to a finesse.) By dropping the 8 under the Queen you give the declarer much more to think about, and he may decide to reenter his hand in another suit and lead the Jack, to guard against K 10 5 3 in your partner's hand. In this case you take two tricks.

4.

The 10 or Jack. Declarer may then decide to play East to hold the 10 x x x or J x x x, and finesse the 9 on the next round. If you play the 8, this possibility is not open to declarer.

5.

The 2. Declarer may decide that the percentage play will be to put in the 8 from dummy. If you lead the King, declarer is likely to place you with the Queen.

6.

The Queen. If you lead a low card, declarer will play for the Queen and Jack to be divided, and he will manage to make three tricks in the suit. If you lead the Queen, he may win with the King and later take a finesse against your supposed Jack.

7.

The Queen. If you lead a low card, declarer will duck, allowing East's Jack to win. When you regain the lead and continue the suit, declarer will duck again, making sure of a trick with either the 10 or the King. By leading the Queen first time, you may persuade declarer that you have the Q J. In this case he will duck the Queen and will subsequently take no trick in the suit.

8.

The King. If you lead a low card, declarer will duck in dummy and East will be forced to contribute the Queen. If you lead the King, he may play you for the K Q x and lose two tricks in the suit.

9.

The 10. You hope to persuade East that West has led from the J 9 7. If you play the Jack, East will realize that West would not have led the 7 from 10 9 7. Similarly, if you play the 9, East will realize that West cannot have held the J 10 7.

10.

The Queen. From East's standpoint, the Queen could be a singleton if you play it, but the 7 or 4 could not. This is because West would not lead the 8 from the Q 8 4 or Q 8 7.

11.

The 4. At first sight the situation appears similar to the previous case, but West has led a different spot card. To play the Queen would be a mistake, for East would realize that

West would not have led the 7 from
8 7 4.

12.

The King. Your only hope is to
endeavor to impress East with the
possibility that his Queen will be
ruffed if he leads it. (It is assumed
that you can afford to play the King
because discards are available in the
other suits.)

13.

Your only real problem is to avoid
losing a trump trick. To improve
your prospects, you should adopt the
cunning stratagem of taking the Ace
of Hearts, ruffing a Heart, and then
leading the Jack of Diamonds!

East may fall into the trap by ruffing the Jack and in this case the
problem of how to play the trump
suit will be solved. The hand actually occurred in a championship
match. One declarer led the Jack of
Diamonds, had it ruffed by East, and
made the slam as a result. The other
declarer neglected the ploy of leading
the Jack of Diamonds and he went
down after taking a losing position
in the trump suit. The full deal was:

```
        ♠ A J 6 2
        ♡ 5
        ◊ J 6 4 3
        ♣ K Q 5 4
♠ Q 4                    ♠ 9 7
♡ Q 10 8                 ♡ K 7 4 2
◊ A 9 7 5 2              ◊ Q 10
♣ J 8 7                  ♣ 10 9 6 3 2
        ♠ K 10 8 5 3
        ♡ A J 9 6 3
        ◊ K 8
        ♣ A
```

14.

If you start by cashing your Club
tricks, discarding two Hearts from
the dummy, you are bound to fail,
because when you now lead a Heart
the defenders will win and play the
Ace and another trump.

The best deceptive play is to lead
a Heart from dummy at trick two!
If the Queen loses to West's Ace or
King, it is unlikely that he will return a Heart. You can win any other
return, take your discards and ruff
the Hearts without interference.

15.

Lead the Jack of Hearts! The contract is cold unless East has the Ace
and Queen of Diamonds, so you
should assume that he has them. In
this case you must plan to discard
some losing Diamonds on dummy's
Hearts. You can afford to lose a Heart
trick to East if he has the King, since
East cannot attack Diamonds effectively, but you cannot afford to lose
a Heart to West if he has the King
of Hearts.

Hence the deceptive lead of the
Jack. West may be deceived into
thinking his partner has the Ace and
may duck. You will then be able to
afford the loss of two Diamond
tricks.

16.

Duck the first Diamond! You can
tell from the card led that West has
only four Diamonds, and therefore
you can expect to make four Diamond tricks in your own hand, although you will have to lose a trick
en route. The best time to lose it is
now, for East may be expected to
return a Diamond if the Queen is
allowed to hold.

In this case you win, dislodge the
Ace of Clubs, and make the contract.
If you were to take the first Diamond,
revealing your strength in the suit,
the defenders might shift to Hearts,
when they regained the lead and you
would be defeated.

I HESITATE to use the title "Percentages," as it may frighten off some of my readers. Let me hasten to explain that no alarm need be felt; this is not to be a lesson in mathematics.

A great many players have the mistaken notion that to be a successful bridge player one must be very good in arithmetic. Nothing could be farther from the truth. Strange to say, in the select circle of bridge experts very few are mathematicians. If you are able to count thirteen and are willing to exercise ordinary common sense (not that mysterious unknown quantity frequently called card sense), you will not find this chapter difficult to wade through.

"Playing percentages" is another way of saying that where there are two ways to do a thing it is better to select that way which offers you the greater chance. If the first method offers you three chances of success and the second method offers you only one, obviously the former should be selected. But how are you to determine these chances?

I shall not burden you with the mathematics of the various situations. The mathematicians who have come before us have done all the hard work, and we must take their word for the details.

The simple way to remember their conclusions will be pointed out to you in the succeeding pages.

I should like to point out very early that the principle of percentages—or "the odds," to use a more common expression—is employed only when there are no other clues as to the distribution of the cards. The things that took place at the table during the bidding and the play are far more important than any abstract probabilities. If, for example, you are concerned with the distribution of five Spades that may be out against you, the probability is that they will be divided three in one hand and two in the other. But if the player to your left has bid a great many Hearts and a great many Diamonds, he will not have room in his hand for many Spades, and you must not be surprised if he has only one Spade, though the table of probabilities indicates that on the average he should have at least two. Remember that the man who wrote this table was not present during the bidding. When, however, you have no information from the bidding, and have nothing else to go by, the probabilities should guide you in your play.

At this point it is appropriate to say a word or two about the element of luck. It is freely conceded that luck cannot be eliminated. In a certain number of cases the correct play will lose while the improper one will succeed. This is to be expected. If you play properly, luck will be with you more often than against you. When you hear a player saying, "My finesses always fail," "My suits never break," there is a strong probability that the player is not availing himself of the proper odds. Lady Luck requires a little assistance from the persons on whom she is to shower her blessings.

It is fortunate for the game of bridge that, however scientific we may make it, the element of chance cannot be eliminated, and on a given number of hands the veriest tyro might outguess the super-expert.

While there are certain fixed principles for the management of various combinations, the play of the hand can never be reduced to an exact science. Which finesse to take or what suit to develop will many times be a sheer guess, one offering as good a prospect as the other. If, however, you find that you are guessing wrong in a majority of the cases, there is a strong suspicion that your technique has been faulty.

Bridge players at times exercise an extraordinarily peculiar sense of business. I have known men to refuse a wager on a football game at 6–5 odds when they felt the odds should be 6½–5, and yet that night they would sit down at the card table and accept a 40 per cent chance where they could have gotten 60 per cent for the same price of admission. Lady Luck usually gets the blame. Various methods are popularly employed to change the course of luck. These attempts include such well-calculated plans as sitting on a handkerchief or walking around a chair, and in some circles even more drastic acts, which cannot be discussed here.

A simple study of percentages will be more effective in changing luck than all these acts of magic.

The application of the principle is illustrated in the play of the following hand:

NORTH:	♠ 4 3	SOUTH:	♠ A 8 5
	♡ A Q 4		♡ 8 7 6 2
	◊ A K Q		◊ 10 5 4 3
	♣ A K Q 3 2		♣ 6 4

You are South, the declarer at a contract of 3 No Trump. West leads the Queen of Spades and receives an encouraging signal from

East. You duck the first round, and the Jack is continued. Now let us assume that you decide to win the second trick. You have a choice of plays. If the Clubs will break, you have ten running tricks. If they do not break, you have only eight, and the ninth might be available through a Heart finesse. But if you try one and it fails, it is too late to try the other. Which is the better chance?

If West had participated in the bidding, you would be inclined toward the belief that he held the missing King. But since there is no clue, you must fall back on the law of probability. If you try the Heart finesse, you have exactly a 50 per cent chance. In other words, West is just as apt to have the King as East, and half the time that play will succeed. Now the question is, what are the chances of the Clubs breaking 3 and 3? The answer is that the chances are distinctly against it. To put it in the form of a rule, *when there are an even number of cards out against you they will probably not break.* Therefore on the above hand the proper procedure is to take the Heart finesse.

In the next example, you are declarer at a contract of 3 No Trump. West leads the King of Spades. You have a total of eight top-card tricks, and the question arises how to develop the ninth. In Hearts you have a chance for a finesse. In Diamonds you have a chance that the suit will break 3–3, which will provide two additional tricks. In Clubs you have a chance that the suit will break 3–3, in which case the 5 of Clubs will be the ninth trick. It is obvious that the lead must not be surrendered, for in that case a sufficient number of Spades may be cashed to defeat the contract.

NORTH:	♠ 4 3	SOUTH:	♠ A 2
	♡ 7 6 5 4 3		♡ A Q 2
	◇ K 5		◇ A Q 4 3 2
	♣ 5 4 3 2		♣ A K Q

The first thing to do is to try the Clubs. If they break, your troubles are over. However, when you lead them you find that one opponent has four Clubs. Therefore you must decide to either lead out your Diamonds, in the hope that the suit will break, or enter dummy to take the Heart finesse. Which has the better chance of success? The opponents hold six Diamonds—an even number. It is probable, therefore, that they will not be divided 3–3. The percentages are against an even number of cards breaking. The Diamond suit, therefore, offers less than a 50–50 chance.

The Heart finesse is an exactly even gamble. That play, therefore, should be tried in preference to the Diamonds.

Changing the hand slightly, we have:

DUMMY:	♠ 5 4	SOUTH:	♠ A 3 2
	♡ 6 5 4 3		♡ A Q 2
	◇ K 5 4		◇ A Q 3 2
	♣ 5 4 3 2		♣ A K Q

Again you are South playing at 3 No Trump, and again West leads the King of Spades. You have eight top-card tricks. In this case you need not worry about percentages. You can discover the facts and do not need to resort to probabilities.

First you try the Clubs. They fail to break. You then try the Diamonds, making sure to win the third Diamond trick in dummy with the King. If the Diamonds have broken, your troubles are over. If they fail to break, you have only one hope left, and that is the Heart finesse.

As a corollary to the above principle it may be stated that *when there are an odd number of cards out against you they probably will break as evenly as possible.*

The principle of percentages, to repeat, means simply selecting that play which offers the greater chance of success.

Holding eight cards of a suit, missing only the Queen, the best chance to capture the Queen is by finessing rather than playing the Ace and King.

NORTH: **A K J 6**   SOUTH: **5 4 3 2**

The reason is this. The five cards out will probably be divided 3–2. The missing card, the Queen, has a greater chance of being with the 3 than with the 2. This is a fundamental principle of percentage. *The person with the greater number of cards is the one more likely to have the card you are looking for.* Since, therefore, the Queen is probably in the hand that holds three, the play of the Ace and King will not succeed in dropping it.

As we have seen above, the proper play in an attempt to capture the Queen with five missing cards is the finesse, but here you have a choice of finessing either way:

NORTH: **A J 10 2**   SOUTH: **K 9 7 4**

You must make up your mind which one of the opponents probably has the Queen. Here I might pause for a moment to point out that there is a popular superstition to the effect that the Queen lies over the Jack, and some players always finesse in that manner. This policy has about as much merit as some such doctrine as "Always finesse toward City Hall." If any of your friends would like to wager, ask them to give you odds of 11 to 10 on their belief, and you have my assurance that in very short order your friends will run out of chips.

In handling this combination you should try to ascertain which of your opponents has more Spades (let us say). There are various ways to do this. If you can find out how many of the other suits your opponents have, you will, by simple subtraction, determine the number of Spades. If you find out that one player is very long in a certain suit, there is a good chance that he will be short in Spades. Consequently his partner should be played for the Queen. If the player on your left has bid Hearts and Diamonds, there is a great likelihood that he is short in Spades. In that case the Ace should be played first (the singleton Queen may drop) and the Jack led through for the finesse, because the player on your right is more likely to have the Queen.

When you use the words "more likely" you are practicing the principle of percentages.

You are South, the declarer at a contract of 4 Spades. West leads the King of Clubs, which of course you win in dummy with the Ace. Now you have a choice of finessing either the Diamonds or the Spades. Which is the correct play?

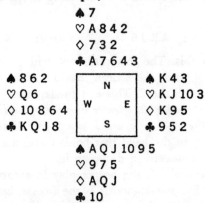

              ♠ 7
              ♡ A 8 4 2
              ◇ 7 3 2
              ♣ A 7 6 4 3

♠ 8 6 2   ♠ K 4 3
♡ Q 6   ♡ K J 10 3
◇ 10 8 6 4   ◇ K 9 5
♣ K Q J 8   ♣ 9 5 2

              ♠ A Q J 10 9 5
              ♡ 9 7 5
              ◇ A Q J
              ♣ 10

Obviously the Diamond, because it must be finessed twice, and you have another entry to do so. The Spade finesse would be improper, because even if it wins, you may not have gained anything, since the King will probably not fall anyhow. If you take the Diamond finesse, you are simply wishing for the King to be on the right. If you take the Spade finesse, you are wishing for the King to be on the right and also for it to fall on the second round. Which is more likely? The answer is obvious. One prayer is easier to have answered than two.

NORTH: ♠ A 10 6   SOUTH: ♠ Q J 9
        ♥ J 8 5   ♥ A K 6 4 2
        ♦ 9 6 4   ♦ K 7 5 3
        ♣ A K J 5   ♣ 3

You are South, the declarer at a contract of 4 Hearts. West leads the 4 of Spades. You play low from the dummy and win in your own hand. You lead the Ace and King of Hearts, and everyone follows, but the Queen does not drop. What is your proper play at this point?

Your choices appear to be:

(a) To take the Club finesse in order to discard two of South's Diamonds.

(b) To hope for the Ace of Diamonds to be with East.

Which is the better choice? Mathematically, the chances are exactly the same. There is a 50 per cent chance that the Queen of Clubs is with West, and there is also a 50 per cent chance that the Ace of Diamonds is with East. On the surface, therefore, it would appear that the choice is a mere guess.

Actually, however, this is not quite so. If you play properly, you can give yourself both chances instead of only one. If you try the Diamond and that loses, you will immediately give up three Diamonds and a Heart and fail in your contract. You have, therefore, had only one chance. But if you take the Club finesse and it loses, you still have a chance that East has the Ace of Diamonds, in which case you will lose one Club, one Diamond, and one Heart. Since two 50 per cent chances are better than one, obviously the Club finesse is the correct play.

NORTH: ♠ 7 5 4 3 2   SOUTH: ♠ none
        ♥ 9 8 5 3 2   ♥ 7
        ♦ 10   ♦ A K Q J 9 8 7
        ♣ Q 6   ♣ A K 4 3 2

South is the declarer at 6 Diamonds. West leads the King of Spades, and South ruffs. Should the declarer draw trumps?

Everything will depend on the Clubs breaking. Here percentages are not necessary. The Queen of Clubs should be cashed, then the King, and a small Club ruffed with the 10, since there is no danger of an overruff. If it is argued that the second Club might be trumped by the opponents, the answer is that if one opponent held five Clubs, the hand could never have been made even if trumps had been drawn, because two Clubs and a Heart would have been lost.

A very neat illustration of the principle of percentages is provided by the following hand:

NORTH: ♠ A 9 7 5   SOUTH: ♠ 3
♡ Q 10 9   ♡ A K J 7 4
◊ 10 8 3   ◊ J 6 4
♣ Q 7 6   ♣ A K 5 2

You are South, the declarer at a contract of 4 Hearts, and West leads the King of Spades, which of course you win in dummy. You see that the loss of three Diamonds is inevitable. Should you pull the trumps? If you do so, everything will depend upon the Clubs breaking 3–3. Since an even number of Clubs will probably not break, the chances are you will not fulfill your contract. Is there a better way to play this hand?

Yes. Since there are five trumps outstanding, an odd number, they will probably be divided 3–2, so that dummy's trumps may be used to draw those held by the adversaries and declarer's trumps may be used for ruffing Spades. The play will proceed as follows:

The Ace of Spades is won, and the 5 of Spades is ruffed with the King of Hearts. The 4 of Hearts is led to dummy's 9, and the 7 of Spades is ruffed with the Ace of Hearts. The 7 of Hearts is led to dummy's 10, and the remaining Spade is ruffed with the Jack of Hearts. Dummy is entered with the Queen of Clubs and the last trump drawn with the Queen of Hearts, declarer discarding a Diamond. The Ace and King of Clubs will be the ninth and tenth tricks, and if the Clubs happen to break, an eleventh trick is available with the 5 of Clubs. (See chapter on Dummy Reversal.) The complete hand follows:

♠ A 9 7 5
♡ Q 10 9
◊ 10 8 3
♣ Q 7 6

♠ K Q J 4   ♠ 10 8 6 2
♡ 8 3 2   ♡ 6 5
◊ K 9 5 2   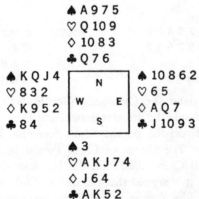   ◊ A Q 7
♣ 8 4   ♣ J 10 9 3

♠ 3
♡ A K J 7 4
◊ J 6 4
♣ A K 5 2

Let us consider the same hand with the Queen of Clubs transferred to declarer's hand.

Should trumps be drawn? Everything will depend on the Clubs breaking, since there are three losing Diamonds. This hand cannot be played in the same manner as the previous one, since dummy can-

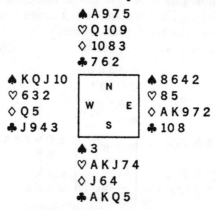

♠ A 9 7 5
♡ Q 10 9
◇ 10 8 3
♣ 7 6 2

♠ K Q J 10   ♠ 8 6 4 2
♡ 6 3 2   ♡ 8 5
◇ Q 5   ◇ A K 9 7 2
♣ J 9 4 3   ♣ 10 8

♠ 3
♡ A K J 7 4
◇ J 6 4
♣ A K Q 5

not be entered a sufficient number of times to ruff out the Spades and also to pull the trumps. The proper procedure is to play only two trumps and then A K Q of Clubs. If the Clubs have broken, the last trump is drawn. If the Clubs do not break, there is the chance that the player who was short in Clubs does not have the remaining trump, in which case the 5 of Clubs can be ruffed in dummy. If it is argued that the Queen of Clubs might be trumped, then the answer is that there was no possible way to make the hand.

♠ A J 8 6 3
♡ Q 10 4
◇ A K 8 4
♣ 4

N
W   E
S

♠ none
♡ K J 8 6 3
◇ 9 7 3 2
♣ A K Q 2

You are South, the declarer at 6 Hearts. West leads the Ace and another trump, and East follows. How do you play the hand?

Do not pull the remaining trump. Do not attempt to establish the Spades. For that play to succeed, the Spades would have to be four-

four, which is very improbable. It is better to trust that the Diamonds will be three–two, which is probable. Therefore you cash the Ace and King of Diamonds, play A K Q of Clubs, discarding two Diamonds from dummy. Lead a Diamond and ruff. Discard your Club loser on the Ace of Spades. The South hand is entered by ruffing a Spade and the last trump pulled. The complete hand:

```
                    ♠ A J 8 6 3
                    ♡ Q 10 4
                    ◇ A K 8 4
                    ♣ 4
  ♠ K 10 2          ┌─────────┐       ♠ Q 9 7 5 4
  ♡ A 5             │    N    │       ♡ 9 7 2
  ◇ Q 10 6          │ W     E │       ◇ J 5
  ♣ J 10 8 7 3      │    S    │       ♣ 9 6 5
                    └─────────┘
                    ♠ none
                    ♡ K J 8 6 3
                    ◇ 9 7 3 2
                    ♣ A K Q 2
```

Table of probabilities

YOU AND PARTNER HOLD BETWEEN YOU	THE ADVERSE CARDS WILL BE DIVIDED	% OF THE TIME
6 cards of a suit	4–3	62
	5–2	31
	6–1	7
	7–0	Less than ½
7 cards of a suit	4–2	48
	3–3	36
	5–1	15
	6–0	1
8 cards of a suit	3–2	68
	4–1	28
	5–0	4
9 cards of a suit	3–1	50
	2–2	40
	4–0	10

Table of probabilities (continued)

YOU AND PARTNER HOLD BETWEEN YOU	THE ADVERSE CARDS WILL BE DIVIDED % OF THE TIME	
10 cards of a suit	2–1	78
	3–0	22
11 cards of a suit	1–1	52
	2–0	48

Note: An even number of cards probably will not break.
An odd number of cards probably will break.

Note: If opponents hold two honors in a suit, they will be divided between the two hands 52 per cent of the time and both in the same hand 48 per cent of the time. That means 24 per cent of the time they are both in one particular hand and 24 per cent of the time they are both in the other hand.

Discussion of the percentage table

The following is a common holding which is very frequently misplayed:

A K Q 7 4

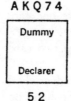

5 2

Assuming no entries in dummy, it is better to concede the first trick by playing small from both hands. Then when A K Q are played, declarer has an excellent chance of catching all the outstanding cards and thus making four tricks. Many players feel confident that such a holding will produce five tricks unless they are unlucky enough to get a bad break in the suit. Actually their reasoning is false. To take five tricks depends on a 3–3 split, which occurs just 36 times in 100. A 4–2 split, which will cause ruination if you play the A K Q, occurs about 48 times in 100, and is, therefore, to be expected.

There is a popular belief that with ten cards in a suit, missing the King, the Ace play is superior to the finesse. This is a misconception.

Unless you have some specific clue, the finesse is the proper play. The percentage table shows that the 2–1 split occurs 78 per cent of the time, but the King is much more apt to be in the larger group. The exact figures are:

The King will be singleton 26 per cent of the time—of these, 13 per cent in one hand and 13 per cent in the other. In other words, 13 times in 100, by refusing to finesse, you will pick up a singleton King behind you. When a singleton King is ahead of you, all plays succeed because the finesse becomes unnecessary.

The King will have one card with it 52 per cent of the time.

The King will have two cards with it 22 per cent of the time, which means the finesse will work 26 per cent plus 11 per cent of the time—a total of 37 per cent.

Fifty per cent of the time the play is immaterial. It will fail or work on either play. When eleven cards are held, the question is very close. There is a 2 per cent advantage in favor of the drop rather than the finesse. Two per cent is so slight that any clue at all is a better bet. Even a suspicious look in the eye of an opponent or a nervous twitch is worth more than 2 per cent.

When nine cards are held:

A particular card will be alone 12 per cent of the time (6 per cent on each side).

A particular card will have one card with it 40 per cent of the time (20 per cent on each side).

A particular card will have two cards with it 38 per cent of the time (19 per cent on each side).

If two pivotal cards are adversely held, such as the King and Queen, example, either the King or Queen will be alone 24 per cent of the time (12 per cent on each side); there will be a doubleton King Queen 14 per cent of the time (7 per cent on each side), or they will be split between the two hands 52 per cent of the time.

When eight cards are held:

A particular card will be alone 6 per cent of the time (3 per cent on each side).

A particular card will have one card with it 28 per cent of the time (14 per cent on each side).

A particular card will have two cards with it 40 per cent of the time (20 per cent on each side).

A particular card will have three cards with it 22 per cent of the time (11 per cent on each side).

If two pivotal cards are adversely held, such as the King and Queen, for example, either the King or Queen will be alone 12 per cent of the time (6 per cent on each side); there will be a doubleton King Queen 6 per cent of the time (3 per cent on each side), or they will be split 52 per cent of the time. (This is constant.)

When seven cards are held:

When a particular card is out, the chances of its being singleton are extremely remote.

The particular card will be doubleton 18 per cent of the time (9 per cent on each side).

It will have two small cards with it 54 per cent of the time (27 per cent on each side).

If two pivotal cards are out, such as the King Queen, as always they will be split 52 per cent of the time; there will be a singleton King or Queen 8 per cent of the time (4 per cent on each side); there will be a doubleton King Queen 4 per cent of the time (2 per cent on each side), or they will both appear by the third lead 50 per cent of the time.

A simplified way to figure the odds

Naturally no one but a mathematician could be expected to memorize the table of probabilities. For practical purposes only an approximate idea of the odds is required. The following will serve as a useful guide.

In order to determine the probability of a certain distribution, take the two figures involved and subtract one from the other. For example: The opponents have five cards and you wish to determine the probability of their being divided 4–1. You subtract 1 from 4, leaving 3. You divide 100 by the result, which produces about 33. The probability of the distribution 4–1 will be slightly less than 33 per cent. (The mathematical tables will show the figures to be 28 per cent.)

Let's try it again. The opponents have seven cards of a suit. You wish to determine the chances of a 5–2 division. Five minus 2 equals 3. One hundred divided by 3 equals 33. The chances are slightly less than 33 per cent. (The mathematical tables will show that the exact figure is 31 per cent.)

What are the chances of a 6–2 split of eight outstanding cards?

Six minus 2 equals 4. One hundred divided by 4 equals 25. The actual chances are slightly less than 25 per cent.

This rule obviously will not work for distributions such as 3–2, 4–3, 5–4, et cetera, where the difference is 1, because 100 divided by 1 equals 100 per cent, which naturally could not be.

Let us apply this rule practically:

NORTH:		SOUTH:	
♠	A 8 6	♠	5 4 3 2
♡	A K Q J	♡	9
◇	J 10 7	◇	A Q 9 8 6
♣	A 6 4	♣	K Q 7

Declarer is playing a contract of 5 Diamonds. The opening lead is the King of Spades, taken by dummy's Ace. The danger of the hand lies in losing the Diamond finesse while holding two losing Spades. If declarer undertakes to discard Spades on Hearts before drawing trumps, he runs the risk of a Heart ruff. The percentage player, therefore, compares the chances of a Diamond finesse with the chances of escaping a Heart ruff on discarding Spades.

Declarer needs two Spade discards. An opponent would be able to ruff Hearts only if the outstanding Hearts are divided 8–0, 7–1, or 6–2. The chances of the 8–0 or 7–1 distribution are small enough to be of no consequence. This leaves the 6–2 split to be considered. What are the chances of its occurrence? Six minus 2 equals 4. One hundred divided by 4 equals 25. It will occur about 25 per cent of the time. In other words, the two Spade discards can be safely taken 75 per cent of the time. The Diamond finesse will work only 50 per cent of the time. Therefore the better play is to take the discards immediately. There is the further consideration that if East happens to be the one who is short in Hearts, he can be overruffed by declarer and the Diamond finesse may still be tried.

NORTH:		SOUTH:	
♠	A K Q 2	♠	7 4
♡	8 6 4	♡	K Q J 10 9 7
◇	9 7	◇	K 8
♣	K Q 8 2	♣	J 10 3

The declarer is playing 4 Hearts with no adverse bidding. West leads the Jack of Spades. As declarer has three Aces to lose, he must lose no other trick.

There are two ways in which to play the hand. The first is to draw trumps and hope that East has the Ace of Diamonds or that, if West holds it, East will not lead a Diamond. The second is to lead high

Spades and take a Diamond discard at once, before giving up the lead. What line of play has a better chance of success?

The first line of play has about a 50 per cent chance of success because it is fifty-fifty on who has the Ace of Diamonds (plus the slight chance that East will not lead a Diamond). The second line of play depends for its success on the chances that three rounds of Spades will live. What Spade distribution does declarer fear? There are seven Spades out. Declarer fears that the Spades might be 5–2, so that the third round will be ruffed by the opposition.

What are the chances of a 5–2 split? Five minus 2 equals 3. One hundred divided by 3 is 33. About 33 per cent of the time the third round of Spades will be ruffed, which would apparently leave 67 per cent of the time for the play to succeed. From this must be deducted the slight possibility of a 6–1 split, which will also be detrimental to our cause. This still leaves over 60 per cent, which is better than a 50 per cent chance provided by the first line of play. Actually the second line of play has better than a 60 per cent chance of winning, because the doubleton Spade might be in the East hand, in which case declarer could overruff and still try to make the Diamond King.

Another situation in which the consideration of the odds is vital is one in which you find yourself in a very hazardous contract. Let us suppose the contract is 3 No Trump, redoubled and vulnerable. You can take eight tricks with certainty and give up for down 400, or you may try a finesse early in the play which, if it wins, will bring home the contract. If it fails, you will be down 2,800. What should you do? If there is no clue as to the location of the particular card, it is better percentage at rubber bridge to take the short loss. In other words, an attempt to make the contract would be risking the loss of 2,400 points, which is considerably more than the contract itself is worth if fulfilled.

NORTH:	♠ none	SOUTH:	♠ 9 5 4
	♡ A 9 7 4 2		♡ K 8 3
	◇ A 7 4 3		◇ K Q J 5
	♣ A Q J 8		♣ K 10 6

South is the declarer at the rather overambitious contract of 7 Diamonds. West leads the King of Spades, which is ruffed in dummy with the 3 of Diamonds. South's hand is entered with the King of Hearts, and the 5 of Spades led and ruffed with the 4 of Diamonds. Declarer returns to his own hand with the 10 of Clubs and leads the last Spade. At this point he has a decision to make. He may ruff with the 7 of Diamonds, cash the Ace of trumps, and return to his hand with the King of Clubs to draw the remaining trump, or he may trump the Spade with the Ace of Diamonds and return to his hand with a trump.

The first line of play will fail if someone has a singleton Club. The second line of play will fail if the Diamonds are 4–1. Which is the better play? It is a question of matching the probability of a 4–1 Diamond break against the probability of a 5–1 Club break. Since obviously the 5–1 Club break is less probable, declarer should ruff in dummy with the 7 of Diamonds, cash the Ace of trumps, and return with a Club. The complete hand follows:

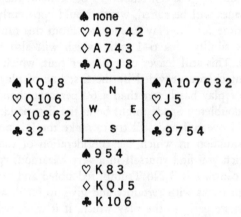

The proper play of the following very common holding is the subject of considerable discussion:

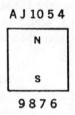

Assuming that you have plenty of entries to the South hand, the best play is to take two finesses, on the principle that the two outstanding honors will probably be split. If you have finessed the first time, by all means finesse the second time. If, however, you find yourself short of entries, so that it is inconvenient to finesse twice, the next best play is to lead the Ace first and then the Jack. This will succeed whenever the suit is split 2–2 or a singleton honor falls.

To illustrate the basis for this conclusion let us examine the possible adverse distributions and combinations:

	WEST	EAST
1.	K	Q 3 2
2.	Q	K 3 2
3.	K Q	3 2
4.	K 3 2	Q
5.	Q 3 2	K
6.	3	K Q 2
7.	2	K Q 3
8.	3 2	K Q
9.	K 3	Q 2
10.	K 2	Q 3
11.	Q 3	K 2
12.	Q 2	K 3
13.	K Q 3	2
14.	K Q 2	3
15.	K Q 3 2	Void
16.	Void	K Q 3 2

The taking of the double finesse as against playing the Ace first and then the Jack will lose only in case 8. The recommended play will gain in cases 13, 14, and 15. In all other cases both plays will attain the same degree of success or failure. In other words, taking two finesses is the correct "percentage" play. It will gain in three cases and lose in but one.

Here the lead is from the South hand, and West plays low. The problem is whether to go up with the King or play the Jack:

K J 10 4 3

7 6 5 2

A clue will very frequently be found in the bidding, but if there is no clue, the percentage guess is to play the Jack, hoping it will drive out the Ace. If West originally had the Ace and one other, the recommended play will lose, but it will gain if West had the Queen and one other. These two probabilities cancel each other. There is the further case in which West had the Ace and Queen; here the Jack will prove to be the superior play. If West has bid, he probably holds the Ace, and it is better to come up with the King.

QUIZ ON PERCENTAGES

1.

NORTH
♠ 7 5
♡ J 7 5 2
◇ 10 8 4 3 2
♣ K 10

WEST ♠ J

SOUTH
♠ A K 2
♡ A 10 4
◇ A 9
♣ A Q 7 4 2

The contract is 3 No Trump and West leads the Jack of Spades. You decide to win it and tackle the Clubs. What is the correct percentage play?

2.

NORTH	SOUTH
♠ J 8 2	♠ A 10 9 7
♡ 8 6	♡ A K Q
◇ 10 6 3	◇ A K Q J
♣ A Q 7 6 4	♣ K 8

The contract is 6 No Trump and West leads the Jack of Hearts. What is your best percentage chance?

3.

NORTH
♠ 3
♡ Q J 10 8
◇ A 7 4 2
♣ 10 8 6 3

WEST ♣ K

SOUTH
♠ A Q 8 6 4
♡ A K 9 4
◇ 9 8
♣ J 4

The contract is 4 Hearts. West cashes the King and Ace of Clubs and then shifts to a trump. How do you plan to establish the Spades?

4.

NORTH
♠ 8 5 2
♡ J 6
◇ 8 2
♣ A J 10 9 7 3

WEST ♠ 6

SOUTH
♠ A Q 3
♡ A 10 4
◇ A Q J 6 5
♣ K 4

The contract is 3 No Trump, West leads a Spade, and you win East's King with the Ace. How do you proceed?

5.

NORTH	SOUTH
♠ K 8 4	♠ A Q J
♡ A 7	♡ K 10
◇ K J 10 8 7	◇ 9 5 2
♣ K Q J	♣ 8 6 4 3 2

The contract is 3 No Trump and the 4 of Hearts is led. How do you proceed?

6.

NORTH
♠ J 9 4
♡ A 8 5
◇ 9 5 4 2
♣ 10 8 3

WEST ♡ 2

SOUTH
♠ A 8 2
♡ Q J 7 3
◇ A K J
♣ A K 6

The contract is 3 No Trump and West leads the 2 of Hearts. East wins with the King and shifts to a low Club, which you win. How do you plan to acquire your ninth trick?

7.

NORTH
♠ A K Q J
♡ A 6 2
◇ A Q J 3
♣ 5 2

WEST ♠ 4

SOUTH
♠ 10 7
♡ Q 8 7 4
◇ K 10 5
♣ A K 10 9

The contract is 6 No Trump and West leads the 4 of Spades. How do you plan to make your twelfth trick?

ANSWERS TO QUIZ ON PERCENTAGES

1.
You have to make five tricks in Clubs. There are two ways in which you might tackle the Clubs, and to select the best method it is essential for you to have prior knowledge of the fact that a 4–2 break in a suit is more likely than a 3–3 break.

It is clear that if you simply play out your high Clubs, you make five tricks in the suit when, and only when, the opponents' Clubs are 3–3. On the other hand, if you finesse the 10 of Clubs, you make five tricks when the Clubs are 3–3 and West has the Jack and also when the Clubs are 4–2 and West has the Jack. Since a 4–2 break is more likely than 3–3, it is clear that you should start the Clubs by finessing the 10.

2.

You should not rely on a 3–3 Club break. If you start by playing the K A Q of Clubs, you will be unlikely to make the contract unless the Clubs break evenly, which is against the odds. Therefore you should plan instead to take two finesses in Spades, which gives you about a 75% chance of three Spade tricks.

At trick two you lead the 8 of Clubs to the Queen, then you lead the 8 of Spades and let it ride. You win any return, overtake the King of Clubs with the Ace, and lead the Jack of Spades. This time the finesse succeeds and you make your contract. The full deal is:

```
              ♠ J 8 2
              ♡ 8 6
              ◇ 10 6 3
              ♣ A Q 7 6 4
♠ Q 6 3                    ♠ K 5 4
♡ J 10 9 3                 ♡ 7 5 4 2
◇ 9 5 4 2                  ◇ 8 7
♣ 9 5                      ♣ J 10 3 2
              ♠ A 10 9 7
              ♡ A K Q
              ◇ A K Q J
              ♣ K 8
```

3.

You lack the entries to ruff three Spades in dummy and draw the opponents' trumps. You can only really afford to ruff Spades twice, and since you cannot afford to lose a Spade trick, the choice is whether to try to drop the King in three rounds or to finesse the Queen.

Assuming that the opponents' Spades are 4–3, the King is more likely to be with the four of them

than with the three of them, so the odds are against your being able to drop it by ruffing. Therefore it is better to take the finesse. The correct sequence of play is to win West's trump lead in dummy, finesse the Queen of Spades, and ruff a Spade. You enter your hand with a trump, ruff another Spade, ruff a Club and draw the last trump. Your hand is then high except for a Diamond. The full deal is:

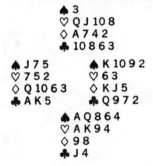

```
              ♠ 3
              ♡ Q J 10 8
              ◇ A 7 4 2
              ♣ 10 8 6 3
♠ J 7 5                    ♠ K 10 9 2
♡ 7 5 2                    ♡ 6 3
◇ Q 10 6 3                 ◇ K J 5
♣ A K 5                    ♣ Q 9 7 2
              ♠ A Q 8 6 4
              ♡ A K 9 4
              ◇ 9 8
              ♣ J 4
```

4.

You should not stake all your fortunes on the Club suit. If you were to play the King of Clubs and then finesse dummy's Jack, you would have less than a 50% chance of making the contract. You would require West to have not more than three Clubs, including the Queen, which is clearly less than an even chance. In the actual case, you would speedily be defeated, the full deal being:

```
              ♠ 8 5 2
              ♡ J 6
              ◇ 8 2
              ♣ A J 10 9 7 3
♠ J 9 7 6 4                ♠ K 10
♡ Q 8 7 5                  ♡ K 9 3 2
◇ 9 3                      ◇ K 10 7 4
♣ 8 5                      ♣ Q 6 2
              ♠ A Q 3
              ♡ A 10 4
              ◇ A Q J 6 5
              ♣ K 4
```

A much better plan is to use the Club suit as a means of entering dummy to finesse the Diamonds. At trick two you lead the 4 of Clubs and finesse the Jack. If East elected to win, you would be able to overtake the King and make five Club tricks, so we'll say East ducks. In this case you lead a Diamond and finesse the Jack: then you overtake the King of Clubs with the Ace and finesse the Diamonds again. By this means you make the contract even though the Diamonds are 4–2.

5.

You can afford to lose the lead only once. You have five winners in the major suits and therefore, to make the contract, you have to establish either four Clubs tricks or four Diamond tricks.

If you were to try to establish four Diamond tricks, you would have to find the Queen favorably placed, which is no better than a 50% chance. On the other hand, the chances of establishing four tricks in Clubs by dislodging the Ace are considerably better than 50%, since five cards can be expected to divide 3–2 about 68 times in 100. You should therefore lead a Club at trick two.

6.

The most readily apparent line of play is to enter dummy with a Heart and finesse the Jack of Diamonds. You could improve this plan slightly by first cashing the Ace of Diamonds, but you would still have very little more than a 50% chance. Therefore you should consider whether there is anything can be said for leading out the A K J of Diamonds instead of taking the finesse.

Leading out the A K J of Diamonds establishes a gamegoing trick whenever the opponents' Diamonds are 3–3, which is a 36% chance. If the Diamonds are 4–2, which is a 48% chance, you still succeed approximately one-third of the time when the Queen is a doubleton.

Already this brings you to above 50%, and you have the substantial extra chance that one of the opponents may have the doubleton 10 of Diamonds, in which case you are bound to win your ninth trick with either the 9 or the Jack. Therefore the Diamond finesse should be rejected, in favor of playing the suit down the line.

7.

You have a relatively close choice to make. You could start by leading a low Heart, hoping that East had the King. If you were disappointed in this respect, there would still be time to play East for the Q J of Clubs, taking a deep finesse in the suit.

If you proceeded in that fashion you would have a 50% chance of finding East with the King of Hearts, plus a 1 in 4 chance of finding him with the Q J of Clubs. The combined chances would amount to 62½%.

Alternatively, you could finesse the 9 of Clubs at trick two, intending, if it lost, to finesse the 10 of Clubs on the next round. This method of play fails only in one case in 4—when West has the Q J of Clubs—and amounts to a 75% chance. Therefore you should follow it.

Incidentally, you should lay down the Ace of Hearts before taking the second Club finesse. Monarchs have been known to fall!

IN CONSIDERING the use of the squeeze play, look first at this hand. You are South, the declarer at an ambitious contract of 7 Diamonds. West leads the King of Spades. Is there any way to make this hand?

♠ A J
♡ A J 4
◇ 10 9 6 4
♣ J 6 4 2

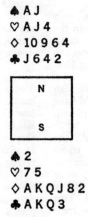

♠ 2
♡ 7 5
◇ A K Q J 8 2
♣ A K Q 3

Prospects are not bright, because a Heart loser seems to be inevitable, and it appears that you have bid one trick beyond your capacity. Suppose we show you the complete hand:

♠ A J
♡ A J 4
◇ 10 9 6 4
♣ J 6 4 2

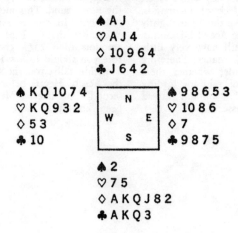

♠ K Q 10 7 4   ♠ 9 8 6 5 3
♡ K Q 9 3 2   ♡ 10 8 6
◇ 5 3   ◇ 7
♣ 10   ♣ 9 8 7 5

♠ 2
♡ 7 5
◇ A K Q J 8 2
♣ A K Q 3

Can you make it now? You naturally win with the Ace of Spades and lead out all your top cards but one, and the position becomes:

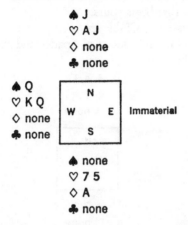

```
              ♠ J
              ♡ A J
              ◇ none
              ♣ none

    ♠ Q         ┌─────────┐
    ♡ K Q       │    N    │
    ◇ none      │ W     E │   Immaterial
    ♣ none      │    S    │
                └─────────┘
              ♠ none
              ♡ 7 5
              ◇ A
              ♣ none
```

Now lead the last trump. What can West do? The answer is, nothing. If he tosses the Queen of Spades, you will throw the Jack of Hearts and dummy becomes high. If West lets go the Queen of Hearts, you will throw the Jack of Spades and the two Hearts will be high. You have just executed a squeeze play.

By far the most fascinating of the advanced plays is the squeeze. From time immemorial the ability to execute this play seems to have been the distinguishing mark of the expert.

While the operation of this play is at times very complex, nevertheless certain of the principles which govern its execution may be reduced to simple terms, and that is my purpose in this chapter.

There are, generally speaking, three subtitles:

1. Card Placing. (That is, determining who has certain pivotal cards.)

2. Preparation.

3. Completion.

While the second and third are subject to more definite rules, the first—that is, card placing—is rather indefinite.

The position of the cards may be determined from the bidding, from the lead of the opponents, from their general behavior during the play, such as discards and signals, and by the actual fall of the cards.

It is an elementary principle of physics that two things cannot occupy the same space at the same time. It is an elementary principle of the squeeze that when a player holds three important cards he will be compelled to let one go when it is necessary for him to reduce his hand to two cards. The squeeze, therefore, is a play which will turn a low card into a winner because the opposition has been compelled to discard the card that beats yours.

In the next example, Clubs are trumps, and the opponents hold against you the King and Queen of Spades and the Queen of Hearts. Can you win all the tricks?

♠ A J
♡ J
♣ none

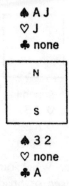

♠ 3 2
♡ none
♣ A

On the surface, no, but if West has all three cards, you will be able to do so by merely leading out the last trump.

Again Clubs are trumps. South leads the Ace. West, it will be seen, has three indispensable cards, and he is obliged to reduce his hand to two cards. He must therefore throw one of the indispensables. If he elects to throw a Heart, dummy will throw a Spade and will be good. If he elects to throw a Spade, dummy will throw a Heart and will similarly be good.

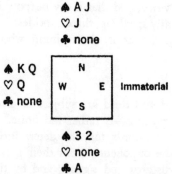

♠ A J
♡ J
♣ none

♠ K Q   N
♡ Q   W   E   Immaterial
♣ none   S

♠ 3 2
♡ none
♣ A

It will be seen that in the operation of a squeeze the essential feature is to force your adversary to select his discard before you are obliged to select yours.

The squeeze usually operates against one opponent who holds all the vital cards, but sometimes it operates against both. The procedure, then, is to knock out first one opponent and then work on the other. This will be demonstrated presently under "the three-suit squeeze" (double squeeze).

Threat cards

A losing card that may become a winner after the opponents' discard is known as a *threat card,* because it acts as a threat against a higher card that is outstanding.

In this diagram it will be seen that the dummy contains three winners, the Ace, King, and Queen:

♠ A K Q 2

♠ J 10 9 8   ♠ 7 3

♠ 6 5 4

If West sometime later in the play is obliged to discard a Spade, the 2 will become a winner. It is, therefore, a threat card against West. There must be at least two threat cards in every squeeze, so that one or the other will eventually become good, because an opponent must make a choice of discards before you make your choice. A threat card is not really a threat card unless one opponent and only one must guard it.

For example:

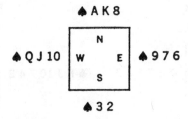

♠ A K 8

♠ Q J 10   ♠ 9 7 6

♠ 3 2

At the present time the 8 of Spades is not really a threat card, because either East or West can guard the 8 of Spades, but if East should let go the 6 of Spades, the 8 would now become a threat card against West, who is the only one who can guard Spades.

Similarly, if West should discard the 10 of Spades, then the 8 would become a threat card against East, who would have to keep all his Spades.

In the next diagram the 8 of Spades is the threat card against West, for he is the only one who can prevent it from becoming a winner:

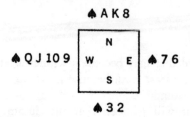

In each of the following illustrations East becomes immaterial to the play, inasmuch as he is unable to offer any protection:

In DIAGRAM A AND B the 2 of Spades is the threat against West.

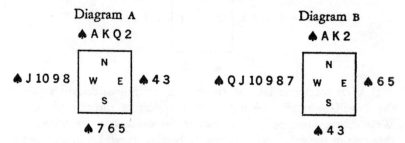

In DIAGRAM C the 10 of Spades is a threat against West, because if he should be obliged to let go a Spade, all of North's Spades will become good.

In DIAGRAM D dummy's Ace and Queen of Spades are winners, because the finesse succeeds and the 6 of Spades is a threat card against

West, who must hold at least three cards in the suit. If he is ever obliged to reduce his Spade holding to two cards, dummy's 6 will become a winner.

In order for a squeeze to operate, it has been pointed out that there must be at least two threat cards:

(a) A one-card threat.

(b) A two-or-more-card threat.

To refer back to a previous illustration:

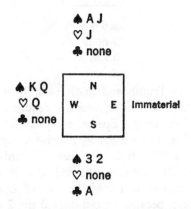

In this example the one-card threat in the North hand is the Jack of Hearts, which acts as a threat against West's Queen. The two-card threat is the Ace and Jack of Spades, which act as a threat against West's King and Queen.

An essential principle is that no squeeze can be operated unless there is a connection between the two hands. In other words, no card in the dummy can act as a threat if there is no way to get to the dummy to use it after it becomes good.

An opponent is not subject to a squeeze until such time as his hand contains only essential cards, never before this. If a defender has as little as one non-essential card in his hand, the squeeze cannot operate.

Let us suppose that West is the player to be squeezed. The declarer must ask himself the question, "How many cards must West hold?" If the answer is five essential cards, then he cannot be squeezed until the ninth trick. In other words, at that time he will hold his five essential cards and must come down to four cards. No squeeze against him is possible at the eighth trick, because he will have one surplus card at that time which he is at liberty to throw off.

Let us see what is meant by the term "five essential cards":

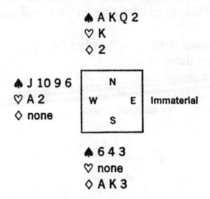

♠ A K Q 2
♡ K
◇ 2

♠ J 10 9 6
♡ A 2
◇ none

Immaterial

♠ 6 4 3
♡ none
◇ A K 3

The contract is No Trump, and South leads. West holds five essential cards. One is the Ace of Hearts, which is required to guard dummy's King. The other four are the Spades, every one of which is essential, because should West let go a Spade, North's deuce will be converted into a winner. Since West holds five essential cards, a squeeze cannot operate until the fifth trick from the end; that is, the ninth trick. At the eighth trick declarer will lead the Ace of Diamonds, and West is not in the squeeze, because he can discard the 2 of Hearts. He now comes down to his five essential cards, and on the next Diamond lead he is really squeezed and it is impossible for him to make a safe discard.

In the next example West holds three essential cards and cannot therefore be squeezed until the eleventh trick, at which trick he must come down to two cards. Since the diagram was made at the eleventh trick, the declarer is ready to operate the squeeze by leading the Ace of Diamonds:

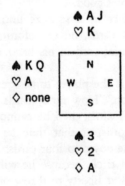

♠ A J
♡ K

♠ K Q
♡ A
◇ none

♠ 3
♡ 2
◇ A

Let us change the diagram by adding a Club to each hand:

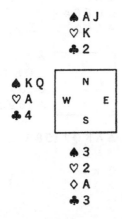

Here again West holds three essential cards, but the squeeze cannot be operated at this time, because it cannot work until the eleventh trick, and we have so far developed the hand only up to the tenth trick. If sometime during the play a Club trick had been given up, the squeeze might operate; but to repeat, when a defender has three essential cards, a squeeze cannot operate upon him at a time when he holds four cards.

We have been discussing in a general way the preparation for the squeeze. It will be seen, therefore, that in making your plans you must add up your winners—that is, the winners that are ready to be cashed —and they must come to exactly one less than the number of tricks you need to fulfill the contract.

Suppose your contract is 6 No Trump. You require twelve tricks. You must therefore immediately be able to cash eleven top-card tricks. Similarly, if your contract is 3 No Trump, you must have available to be run immediately exactly eight tricks, but that is not all. You must see to it that the opponents first take the tricks to which they are entitled. In a slam contract you will not succeed unless you first give the opponents their one trick. In a 3 No Trump contract you cannot succeed until you first permit the opposition to cash their four tricks, which brings us to this important maxim of squeezes: *Generally speaking, the squeeze will not be operative unless all inevitable losers are first conceded to the opponents. Give up your losers.*

West opens the bidding with 1 Diamond, North and East pass, and South subsequently arrives at 6 Spades. West leads the King of Diamonds.

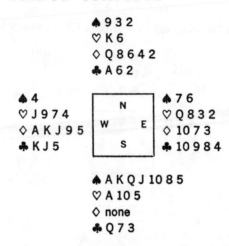

♠ 9 3 2
♡ K 6
◇ Q 8 6 4 2
♣ A 6 2

♠ 4   ♠ 7 6
♡ J 9 7 4   N   ♡ Q 8 3 2
◇ A K J 9 5 W   E   ◇ 10 7 3
♣ K J 5   S   ♣ 10 9 8 4

♠ A K Q J 10 8 5
♡ A 10 5
◇ none
♣ Q 7 3

Declarer's problem is to avoid the loss of two Club tricks, and since it is futile to hope that East has the King of Clubs, the only hope to fulfill the contract is a squeeze. The first step is card placing. The opening lead of the King of Diamonds shows that West held originally the Ace and King. The bidding corroborates this theory. The fact that East did not keep the bidding open indicates plainly that West also has the King of Clubs.

The next step is the preparation. Declarer counted his certain winners. There are seven Spade tricks, two Heart tricks, a Heart ruff in dummy, and the Ace of Clubs—a total of eleven tricks. This is one less than the twelve tricks required. However, at the present time declarer is not ready to operate the squeeze, because the opponents must be permitted to win their one trick first. At what point should the defenders be permitted to take the trick? The answer is, now. The declarer should refuse to ruff the King of Diamonds but discard the 3 of Clubs. No lead that West can make will embarrass declarer.

Let us assume that he leads a trump. The declarer draws two trumps then plays the Ace, King, and another Heart, ruffing in dummy, ruffs a Diamond and now runs down all his remaining trumps. West is obliged to keep three essential cards, one his Ace of Diamonds to guard the dummy's Queen, and the other two are the King and Jack of Clubs. The squeeze, therefore, will begin operating at such time that he must reduce his hand to two cards; namely, the eleventh trick. At the tenth trick the holding will be as follows:

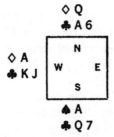

◇ Q
♣ A 6

◇ A
♣ K J

N
W   E
S

♠ A
♣ Q 7

South now leads the last trump and waits for West to discard to the eleventh trick. If West discards the Jack of Clubs, both the Ace and Queen will win. If he discards the Ace of Diamonds, the Queen becomes high.

Note the difference if South wins the opening lead. The play will proceed in the same way, and the end position will be as follows:

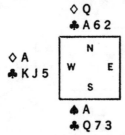

◇ Q
♣ A 6 2

◇ A
♣ K J 5

N
W   E
S

♠ A
♣ Q 7 3

South will lead his last trump, and West, having one superfluous card in his hand, the 5 of Clubs, is able safely to discard it and still retain his three essential cards. Had West been permitted to hold the trick early in the play, he would now have no superfluous card to discard. To repeat: *In almost every squeeze the inevitable losers must be given up first.*

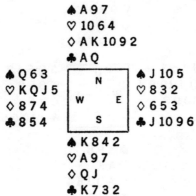

♠ A 9 7
♡ 10 6 4
◇ A K 10 9 2
♣ A Q

♠ Q 6 3
♡ K Q J 5
◇ 8 7 4
♣ 8 5 4

N
W   E
S

♠ J 10 5
♡ 8 3 2
◇ 6 5 3
♣ J 10 9 6

♠ K 8 4 2
♡ A 9 7
◇ Q J
♣ K 7 3 2

South is the declarer at a contract of 6 No Trump. West leads the King of Hearts. Declarer can count five Diamonds, three Clubs, two Spades, and one Heart—a total of eleven tricks. The only chance for a twelfth is to be found in a squeeze. What should declarer do at the first trick?

The answer is, he must allow the defenders to win their one trick before the squeeze can operate. This is the best time to concede the loser. The Queen of Hearts will be continued, which declarer wins. West is now known to hold the Jack of Hearts, so that the 10 of Hearts in dummy will be the threat card against West. The Ace and Queen of Clubs are cashed and all the Diamonds are run. The position at the eleventh trick will be as follows:

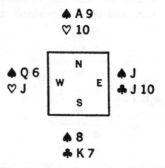

```
              ♠ A 9
              ♥ 10

                   N
  ♠ Q 6                    ♠ J
  ♥ J      W        E      ♣ J 10
                   S

              ♠ 8
              ♣ K 7
```

The lead is in the South hand, and declarer plays the King of Clubs. West will be obliged to discard the 6 of Spades, dummy discards the 10 of Hearts, and both Spades are good.

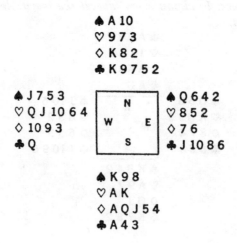

```
                    ♠ A 10
                    ♥ 9 7 3
                    ◇ K 8 2
                    ♣ K 9 7 5 2

  ♠ J 7 5 3              N          ♠ Q 6 4 2
  ♥ Q J 10 6 4                      ♥ 8 5 2
  ◇ 10 9 3       W          E       ◇ 7 6
  ♣ Q                   S           ♣ J 10 8 6

                    ♠ K 9 8
                    ♥ A K
                    ◇ A Q J 5 4
                    ♣ A 4 3
```

South is the declarer at a contract of 6 No Trump. West leads the Queen of Hearts. Declarer has eleven top tricks. If the Clubs break three–two, there will be no problem. In any event, one Club trick must be lost, so that the proper procedure is to give up the Club immediately.

West's Queen will win the trick, and the Heart will be continued. Now the Clubs are tried and they do not break. West is known to have the Hearts, East is known to have the Clubs, so that the 9 of Hearts will be the threat against West and the 9 of Clubs the threat against East, and neither one will be able to hold Spades. The end position will be as follows:

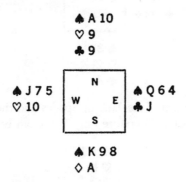

Declarer now leads the Ace of Diamonds, and West must discard the 5 of Spades. The 9 of Hearts in dummy now becomes useless and is discarded. East must retain the Jack of Clubs to guard dummy's 9 and, therefore, must discard a Spade. Declarer's three Spades now become good.

This is known as the three-suit squeeze, or, more popularly, the double squeeze, because both opponents are squeezed in turn.

Roughly speaking, the requirements for the double squeeze are as follows:

Declarer must be able to say to himself: "I am going to run suit A, which is my solid suit. I know that West must guard suit B. I know that East must guard suit C, so that no one will be able to guard suit D. Suit D must be the connecting suit between my hand and dummy (as Spades in this particular hand). Suit B must be a one-card threat (the 9 of Hearts in this particular hand), and suit C must be a one-card threat (the 9 of Clubs in this particular hand) and suit D must be a three-card threat (the K 9 8 of Spades in this case)."

Which opponent to squeeze

Where both of your threat cards are in the same hand, you can squeeze only the adversary immediately in front of your threat cards. For example:

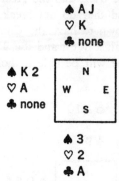

Both the threat cards (the Jack of Spades and the King of Hearts) are in the North hand. Therefore only West can be squeezed.

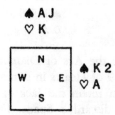

Both threat cards are in the North hand, so that only West can be squeezed. In this illustration, therefore, no squeeze is operative, because the dummy must discard before East and he waits to see what to do.

The double squeeze

South is the declarer at a contract of 4 Hearts doubled by West. West cashes the King and Queen of Spades and shifts to a Diamond. The Ace is played from dummy, and the Heart finesse loses to West's King. The Diamond is continued, and declarer ruffs. The defenders have cashed their three tricks, and the declarer has nine top tricks available, one less than his quota. The preparations for a squeeze, therefore, are completed.

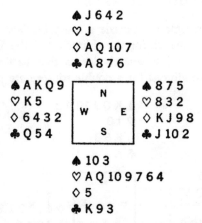

```
                    ♠ J 6 4 2
                    ♡ J
                    ◊ A Q 10 7
                    ♣ A 8 7 6
♠ A K Q 9                          ♠ 8 7 5
♡ K 5           ┌──────────┐       ♡ 8 3 2
◊ 6 4 3 2       │    N     │       ◊ K J 9 8
♣ Q 5 4         │ W      E │       ♣ J 10 2
                │    S     │
                └──────────┘
                    ♠ 10 3
                    ♡ A Q 10 9 7 6 4
                    ◊ 5
                    ♣ K 9 3
```

Now let us see if we have present the conditions for a double squeeze. Hearts is the suit declarer is to run. Let us call that suit A. West is known to hold the Ace of Spades. Let us call that suit B. It is virtually certain that East holds the King of Diamonds. Let us call that suit C. Therefore no one will be able to hold Clubs (suit D). Notice that the Jack of Spades is a one-card threat against West. The Queen of Diamonds is a one-card threat against East, and Clubs are a three-card threat against both, with a high card in each hand.

Declarer leads the last Heart, and West must hold the Ace of Spades, so he lets go a Club. Dummy's Jack of Spades is now useless and is discarded. East must hold the King of Diamonds, so he lets go a Club, and now declarer's three Clubs are good.

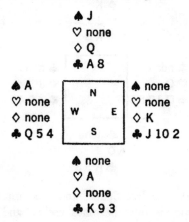

```
                    ♠ J
                    ♡ none
                    ◊ Q
                    ♣ A 8
♠ A                               ♠ none
♡ none          ┌──────────┐       ♡ none
◊ none          │    N     │       ◊ K
♣ Q 5 4         │ W      E │       ♣ J 10 2
                │    S     │
                └──────────┘
                    ♠ none
                    ♡ A
                    ◊ none
                    ♣ K 9 3
```

In the next hand, South is the declarer at a contract of 7 No Trump. West leads the King of Hearts. It need hardly be pointed out that this is no time to concede a loser. Declarer has twelve top-card tricks, with a chance for the thirteenth if the Diamonds break. He tries the suit and immediately learns that East stops Diamonds. Let us see if the conditions for a double squeeze are present.

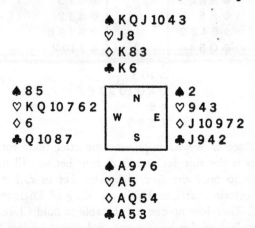

The Jack of Hearts is a definite one-card threat against West. The 5 of Diamonds is a definite one-card threat against East. The Club suit provides a three-card threat with a high card in each hand. Declarer may recite to himself, "West must hold Hearts, East must hold Diamonds, no one can hold Clubs." The end position will be as follows:

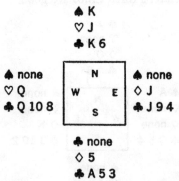

North now leads the last Spade, and East must discard a Club. South's 5 of Diamonds now becomes useless and is thrown. West is obliged to retain the Queen of Hearts to guard dummy's Jack and, therefore, lets go the 8 of Clubs. Declarer's three Clubs now are all good.

The Vienna Coup

The Vienna Coup is a preparation made for a squeeze play. The play is made by leading out a high card so that one of the opponents is deliberately given the controlling card in that suit. The declarer then proceeds to squeeze him out of that card. The Vienna Coup is really an unblocking play for the declarer:

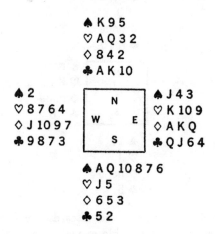

♠ K 9 5
♡ A Q 3 2
◇ 8 4 2
♣ A K 10

♠ 2
♡ 8 7 6 4
◇ J 10 9 7
♣ 9 8 7 3

♠ J 4 3
♡ K 10 9
◇ A K Q
♣ Q J 6 4

♠ A Q 10 8 7 6
♡ J 5
◇ 6 5 3
♣ 5 2

The bidding:

NORTH	EAST	SOUTH	WEST
1 No Trump	Double	Pass	2 Clubs
Pass	Pass	3 Spades	Pass
4 Spades	Pass	Pass	Pass

West leads the Jack of Diamonds, and East cashes the Ace, King, and Queen and shifts to the Queen of Clubs. Declarer can count nine top-card tricks, and the tenth apparently depends upon the Heart finesse. However, East's double indicates that he holds that card and that the finesse will fail. Since East is probably also marked with the Jack of Clubs, the conditions for a squeeze are present. The three inevitable losers have been conceded. The Jack of Hearts will be a threat card against East's King. The 10 of Clubs will be a threat card against his Jack. The connection between declarer's hand and dummy's is the Club suit. If all the high cards are led out, East will be unable to discard safely. The only difference is that dummy will have to discard first, and if in the end the Queen of Hearts is thrown, East can safely unguard his King of Hearts, because while the Jack will become good, declarer will be unable to reach it, since dummy will be blocked.

The proper play, therefore, is to cash the Ace of Hearts first. This is known as the Vienna Coup. Now all the trumps but one are led, and the position is as follows:

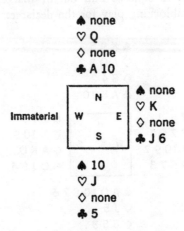

♠ none
♡ Q
◊ none
♣ A 10

Immaterial

N
W   E
S

♠ none
♡ K
◊ none
♣ J 6

♠ 10
♡ J
◊ none
♣ 5

Declarer leads the last trump and discards the Queen of Hearts from dummy. East finds it impossible to make a safe discard. Had the Ace of Hearts not been cashed, the end position would have been as follows:

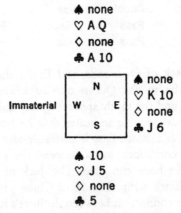

♠ none
♡ A Q
◊ none
♣ A 10

Immaterial

N
W   E
S

♠ none
♡ K 10
◊ none
♣ J 6

♠ 10
♡ J 5
◊ none
♣ 5

Now on the lead of the last trump, dummy would be obliged to discard first, and East would merely follow dummy's discard. The trouble here would be that both threat cards would be in the same hand, in which case only the person who played before that hand can be squeezed. Since East plays after dummy, and dummy has both threat cards, he could not be squeezed. The cashing of the Ace of Hearts first converts the Jack of Hearts into a threat card instead of the Queen of Hearts. Now we have a threat card in each hand and a connection (in Clubs) so that either opponent can be squeezed.

The pseudo squeeze

No description of a simple squeeze would be complete without its half brother, the pseudo squeeze or fake squeeze. The pseudo squeeze is not really a squeeze at all, but is an attempt by the declarer to make his opponents think they are being squeezed, so that they will have to guess which discards they should make. Sometimes when the opponents are thus made to guess they will fall into an error, and those are the times when the declarer will make his contract or an overtrick. The pseudo squeeze should be attempted when other means have no further chance of success.

When the contract is assured and declarer holds a number of good trumps and other established cards in his hand, it does no harm to play these out before conceding his low tricks. Frequently the opponents will not discard as well as they might and declarer will find himself presented with an entirely unexpected trick.

The squeeze coup

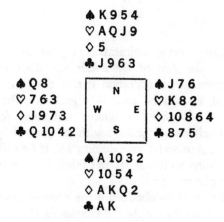

♠ K 9 5 4
♡ A Q J 9
◇ 5
♣ J 9 6 3

♠ Q 8   ♠ J 7 6
♡ 7 6 3   ♡ K 8 2
◇ J 9 7 3   ◇ 10 8 6 4
♣ Q 10 4 2   ♣ 8 7 5

♠ A 10 3 2
♡ 10 5 4
◇ A K Q 2
♣ A K

South is declarer at a contract of 6 Spades. The interesting feature is the accomplishment of the apparently impossible feat of losing no trump tricks with the above combination. This can be done by a very unusual line of play.

The 3 of Diamonds was opened, and East's 10 fell to the Queen. At the start it appears that a trump trick must be lost unless the Queen Jack are doubleton, so that apparently the success of the contract depends upon the Heart finesse. The Ace and King of Clubs were led and nothing happened. Then the deuce of Diamonds was ruffed in dummy and the 9 of Clubs ruffed in the closed hand. The 4 of Hearts was led to dummy's Queen, East winning with the King and returning a Heart. This was won with the 10, and declarer cashed the King of Diamonds, discarding the Jack of Hearts from dummy. This left the following situation:

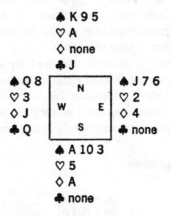

```
                    ♠ K 9 5
                    ♡ A
                    ◊ none
                    ♣ J
        ♠ Q 8   ┌─────────┐   ♠ J 7 6
        ♡ 3     │    N    │   ♡ 2
        ◊ J     │ W     E │   ◊ 4
        ♣ Q     │    S    │   ♣ none
                └─────────┘
                    ♠ A 10 3
                    ♡ 5
                    ◊ A
                    ♣ none
```

Now the declarer made a dramatic play which was not actually essential. He led the Ace of Diamonds and discarded the Ace of Hearts. The important consideration is that the Jack of Clubs must not be discarded, as will be seen in a moment. The low Heart is ruffed with the 5 of Spades in dummy and the Jack of Clubs put through. East is helpless. If he ruffs with the Jack of Spades, declarer will win with the Ace and finesse dummy's 9. If he ruffs with a small trump, declarer wins with the 10 and takes the last two tricks with the Ace and King of trumps.

The same result will be obtained if the declarer, instead of discarding the Ace of Hearts on the Ace of Diamonds, elects to ruff the Diamond in dummy and cashes the Heart before leading the Jack of Clubs.

The trump squeeze

The trump squeeze is a very rare type of squeeze. It consists of leading out all the trumps but one and forcing the adversaries to discard in such a manner that a good trick can be established by ruffing. For example:

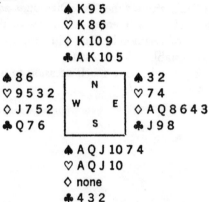

```
              ♠ K 9 5
              ♡ K 8 6
              ◊ K 10 9
              ♣ A K 10 5
♠ 8 6                        ♠ 3 2
♡ 9 5 3 2         N          ♡ 7 4
◊ J 7 5 2     W     E        ◊ A Q 8 6 4 3
♣ Q 7 6          S           ♣ J 9 8
              ♠ A Q J 10 7 4
              ♡ A Q J 10
              ◊ none
              ♣ 4 3 2
```

South is the declarer at a contract of 7 Spades, North having opened the bidding with 1 Club and East having overcalled with 1 Diamond. West leads the deuce of Diamonds, the fourth best of his partner's suit. The 10 was played from dummy, and the Queen was ruffed by declarer. Unless there is false-carding, which there is no reason to suspect in a situation of this sort, West's original holding is the Jack and three other Diamonds. Apparently declarer's only hope is for West to have both the Queen and Jack of Clubs. This appears to be asking for a little too much, and another line of play is sought. All the trumps but two are led, and then all the Hearts. The last five cards are:

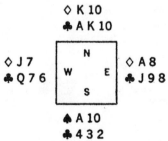

```
              ◊ K 10
              ♣ A K 10
◊ J 7            N          ◊ A 8
♣ Q 7 6       W     E       ♣ J 9 8
                 S
              ♠ A 10
              ♣ 4 3 2
```

South then leads one more trump. West must make a discard. Let us assume that he throws a Club. North throws the 10 of Clubs.

Now East must make a discard. If he should drop a Club, the Ace and King of that suit are cashed in dummy, establishing the 4 of Clubs as a winner. If East should discard the 8 of Diamonds, dummy is now entered with the King of Clubs and the 10 of Diamonds led, forcing East's Ace. Declarer ruffs and dummy is high. If West, instead of discarding a Club, throws the 7 of Diamonds and permits East to discard a Club, declarer will enter dummy with the King of Clubs and lead the King of Diamonds. This will drop the Ace and Jack on the same trick and establish dummy's 10.

I do not think you will have much occasion to use this play, but it is fun when it does occur.

QUIZ ON SQUEEZES

1.

NORTH
♠ A 7 6 5
♡ Q J 7
◇ Q 7 3 2
♣ A 7

WEST ◇ K

SOUTH
♠ K 10 2
♡ A K 10 9 3 2
◇ 8
♣ K Q 4

The contract is 6 Hearts and West leads the King of Diamonds, East playing the 4. West shifts to a Club. How do you proceed?

2.

NORTH
♠ K 7 5 4
♡ 8 7 3 2
◇ J 4
♣ A Q 7

WEST ◇ K

SOUTH
♠ A 3 2
♡ A K
◇ 8 2
♣ K J 9 6 3 2

The contract is 5 Clubs. The defenders take two rounds of Diamonds and shift to a trump. How do you proceed?

3.

NORTH
♠ A 9 5 3 2
♡ J 6 3
◇ A 7 3
♣ J 10

WEST ♡ 10

SOUTH
♠ 8
♡ A K Q
◇ Q 2
♣ K Q 9 8 7 3 2

The contract is 6 Clubs and West leads a Heart. How do you plan the play with the object of squeezing West in Spades and Diamonds?

4.

NORTH	SOUTH
♠ Q 2	♠ A K 7 4 3
♡ Q 10 4	♡ A 6
◇ K J 10 4	◇ A Q 3
♣ Q J 10 9	♣ K 9 4

The contract is 6 No Trump and West leads a Club. East wins with the Ace and returns a Spade. Assuming that the Spades do not break, what three-card ending do you aim at?

ANSWERS TO QUIZ ON SQUEEZES

1.

You have two chances to avoid losing a Spade trick. First, you may be able to make the hand without any gymnastics if you can ruff out West's Ace of Diamonds. Secondly, if the Ace of Diamonds does not fall, you may be able to squeeze West in Diamonds and Spades. For a squeeze to work, you must find West with exclusive control of Spades—any four Spades or the Q J. Suppose the full deal is something like this:

```
              ♠ A 7 6 5
              ♡ Q J 7
              ◇ Q 7 3 2
              ♣ A 7
♠ Q 9 8 3                    ♠ J 4
♡ 6 4                        ♡ 8 5
◇ A K 9 6                    ◇ J 10 5 4
♣ 10 3 2                     ♣ J 9 8 6 5
              ♠ K 10 2
              ♡ A K 10 9 3 2
              ◇ 8
              ♣ K Q 4
```

You win West's Club shift with the Ace, ruff a Diamond, enter dummy with a trump and ruff another Diamond. When the Ace does not appear, you play out your trumps and your Club winners, reaching this position:

```
              ♠ A 7 6
              ♡ —
              ◇ Q
              ♣ —
♠ Q 9 3                      ♠ J 4
♡ —                          ♡ —
◇ A                          ◇ J
♣ —                          ♣ J
              ♠ K 10 2
              ♡ 10
              ◇ —
              ♣ —
```

You play your last trump, discarding a Spade from dummy, and West is squeezed into submission.

2.

A squeeze offers the only hope of avoiding a Spade loser. You must bank on finding the same defender with four or more Hearts, and also four or more Spades, in which case he can be squeezed.

The first move is to cash the A K of Hearts, then you enter dummy with a trump and ruff a Heart. Only one defender is now left with a Heart, and if the same defender started with four or more Spades, his days are numbered. You proceed to cash out all your trumps, reaching this three-card position:

```
   NORTH         SOUTH
   ♠ K 7         ♠ A 3 2
   ♡ 8
```

If the 8 of Hearts has not yet become good, you simply play out three rounds of Spades. If the conditions that you played for exist, your low Spade is bound to take a trick, for the defender who held the Spades will have to unguard them in order to keep the master Heart.

3.

You must assume that West holds the King of Diamonds. You must also assume that somehow or other you can prevent East from guarding the Spades, so that this suit also can be made into an effective threat against West. This can be done by careful play provided East has no more than three Spades. The full deal may be this layout.

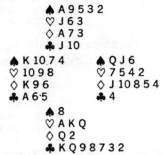

```
              ♠ A 9 5 3 2
              ♡ J 6 3
              ◇ A 7 3
              ♣ J 10
♠ K 10 7 4                   ♠ Q J 6
♡ 10 9 8                     ♡ 7 5 4 2
◇ K 9 6                      ◇ J 10 8 5 4
♣ A 6 5                      ♣ 4
              ♠ 8
              ♡ A K Q
              ◇ Q 2
              ♣ K Q 9 8 7 3 2
```

After winning the Heart opening your first play is a Spade to the Ace and a Spade ruff. Then you lead a low trump, using dummy's entry card in the suit in order to gain another Spade ruff. East's hand no longer matters and you play out the trumps to produce this ending:

NORTH
♠ 9
◇ A 7

WEST
♠ K
◇ K 9

SOUTH
◇ Q 2
♣ 9

When you now play the last trump, West has to give up the ghost. The key play in this hand was ruffing two rounds of Spades, so that only West would be able to guard the suit.

4.

If the Spades do not break the best chance will be to play for a squeeze in Spades and Hearts. You must hope

that the King of Hearts is held by the player who holds the length in Spades. Provided you cash your winners in the correct order, you do not care whether that player is East or West. You must handle matters in such a way that this becomes the end position:

NORTH
♠ 2
♡ Q 10

SOUTH
♠ A K 7

If the length in Spades was in the same hand as the King of Hearts, the defender will by now have had to unguard one suit or the other. It will be noted that to reach this end position, it was necessary to cash the Ace of Hearts, temporarily establishing a winner for the opponents (Vienna Coup). It will also be seen that declarer reaches the required position without actually testing the Spade suit: he plays the hand on the assumption that the Spades are not breaking, for if they break he is bound to make the contract.

Eliminations and end plays

END PLAYS COME in all shapes and sizes. The most common form of end play occurs at a trump contract and is called an elimination. It involves stripping an adversary of all the suits you do not wish him to lead and then throwing him in at a time when you have at least one trump in each hand. In these circumstances the unfortunate defender is obliged to lead either a suit that you want him to lead, or a suit of which you are void in both hands. In this last case you are able to ruff in one hand and discard a loser from the other, which is greatly to your advantage. A few illustrations follow:

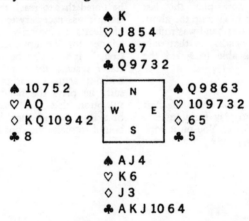

```
                  ♠ K
                  ♡ J 8 5 4
                  ◇ A 8 7
                  ♣ Q 9 7 3 2
  ♠ 10 7 5 2         N          ♠ Q 9 8 6 3
  ♡ A Q                         ♡ 10 9 7 3 2
  ◇ K Q 10 9 4 2  W     E       ◇ 6 5
  ♣ 8                 S         ♣ 5
                  ♠ A J 4
                  ♡ K 6
                  ◇ J 3
                  ♣ A K J 10 6 4
```

South is declarer at a contract of 5 Clubs. West leads the King of Diamonds, which is taken with the Ace. Declarer is faced with the danger of losing one Diamond and two Hearts unless at the proper time he can force West to lead Hearts. He must plan, therefore, to do so.

The King of Spades is cashed and the South hand entered with a trump. On the Ace of Spades a small Diamond is discarded from dummy. The Jack of Spades must be ruffed, and now the Diamond is played. The opening lead shows that West holds the Queen and must win the trick. If he continues with another Diamond, it will be trumped in dummy and a Heart discarded by declarer. If West leads a Spade, the same result is obtained. He is therefore obliged to lead the Ace of Hearts, which sets up declarer's King for the eleventh trick.

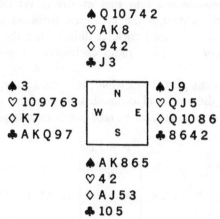

```
                    ♠ Q 10 7 4 2
                    ♡ A K 8
                    ◇ 9 4 2
                    ♣ J 3
      ♠ 3                          ♠ J 9
      ♡ 10 9 7 6 3      N          ♡ Q J 5
      ◇ K 7         W      E       ◇ Q 10 8 6
      ♣ A K Q 9 7       S          ♣ 8 6 4 2
                    ♠ A K 8 6 5
                    ♡ 4 2
                    ◇ A J 5 3
                    ♣ 10 5
```

The bidding:

SOUTH	WEST	NORTH	EAST
1 Spade	2 Clubs	3 Spades	Pass
4 Spades	Pass	Pass	Pass

West leads two rounds of Clubs and shifts to the 10 of Hearts. Declarer's problem is to lose only one Diamond trick, and his prospects do not appear bright.

The only hope is to force an advantageous lead from West. If declarer wishes to force West to make an advantageous lead, he must make it impossible for him to lead anything else. It is now impossible for West to lead Clubs safely. Two rounds of trumps will naturally make it impossible for West to lead trumps. The Ace and King of Hearts are cashed and a Heart ruffed by the closed hand. This makes it impossible for West to lead a Heart safely.

The bidding indicates the likelihood that West holds the King of Diamonds. The best chance appears to be that he holds exactly two Diamonds. Declarer, therefore, plays the Ace of Diamonds. If West plays low, another Diamond is led, which puts the opposition in a hopeless corner. Whether a Heart or a Club is returned, declarer ruffs in his own hand and discards the losing Diamond from dummy. If West drops the King of Diamonds under the Ace, dummy is entered with a trump and a low Diamond led toward the Jack.

The throw-in

The throw-in is a play that usually occurs during the latter part of the hand, although the principles involved may sometimes apply as early as the second trick. It differs from the elimination in that it may occur at a No Trump declaration as well as at a suit contract.

The nature of the play is just what the name implies. An opponent is thrown into the lead and compelled to play the suit which you desire to have led up to you. Let us take one or two simple illustrations:

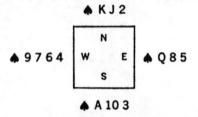

♠ K J 2

♠ 9 7 6 4   W — E   ♠ Q 8 5

♠ A 10 3

You are South, and your problem is to lose no Spade tricks. If you can guess that East has the Queen, you can, of course, successfully finesse the 10; but if you fear that you may make the wrong guess, it may be possible at the end of the hand to throw one of the opponents into the lead at a time when he has nothing left but Spades, in which case he will perforce lead a Spade to you and a guess as to the location of the Queen will be eliminated. Another illustration:

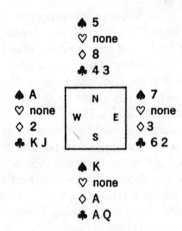

♠ 5
♡ none
◇ 8
♣ 4 3

♠ A
♡ none   W — E   ♠ 7
◇ 2   ♡ none
♣ K J   ◇ 3
                 ♣ 6 2

♠ K
♡ none
◇ A
♣ A Q

You are South playing a No Trump contract and these are your last four cards. The lead is in dummy, and you require three of the last four tricks. Apparently the Club finesse is the only hope, but you have reason to believe that West holds the King and that the finesse will fail. Your hope, therefore, is that you can force West to lead a Club to you. This can be accomplished by throwing him into the lead with a Spade. However, he will still have the deuce of Diamonds as an exit card, and you will be thrown back into the lead and be obliged to play from your Ace Queen of Clubs. Your plan, therefore, is to make it impossible for West to lead anything but Clubs. This is done by taking the Diamond out of his hand. Therefore you return to your own hand with the Ace of Diamonds and now lead the King of Spades. West is in and must lead a Club, surrendering both tricks. Let us take a complete hand:

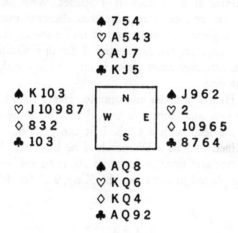

```
              ♠ 7 5 4
              ♡ A 5 4 3
              ◇ A J 7
              ♣ K J 5
 ♠ K 10 3        N       ♠ J 9 6 2
 ♡ J 10 9 8 7            ♡ 2
 ◇ 8 3 2     W       E   ◇ 10 9 6 5
 ♣ 10 3          S       ♣ 8 7 6 4
              ♠ A Q 8
              ♡ K Q 6
              ◇ K Q 4
              ♣ A Q 9 2
```

South plays 6 No Trump. West leads the Jack of Hearts. Declarer counts eleven tricks, with a chance for twelve if Hearts break three—three or the Spade finesse works. The first Heart is won with the Queen. Four Club tricks are run, and West parts with a Diamond and a Spade. Three Diamonds are run, and West lets go the 7 of Hearts. On the King of Hearts, East shows out. A Heart is led to the Ace. West is known to have three cards, one of which is the Heart 10. The other two must be Spades. Dummy plays the last Heart. West is in and must lead a Spade.

♠ Q 6 4 2
♡ A 7 5
◇ K 10 6
♣ 10 7 5

♠ 8 5
♡ K Q J 8 3
◇ Q 5 4 2
♣ Q 9

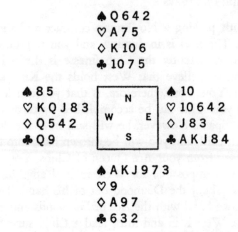

♠ 10
♡ 10 6 4 2
◇ J 8 3
♣ A K J 8 4

♠ A K J 9 7 3
♡ 9
◇ A 9 7
♣ 6 3 2

South is declarer at a contract of 4 Spades. West leads the King of Hearts. On the surface it appears that declarer must lose three Club tricks and a Diamond, since he has no finesse in that suit. However, a finessing position can be created if the opposition is forced to lead Diamonds. Declarer must make it impossible for the opposition to lead anything else.

The Ace of Hearts is taken and another Heart ruffed immediately. Trumps are drawn and dummy's last Heart ruffed by declarer. He now gives up the lead with a Club. East can cash three Club tricks but is now obliged to lead a Diamond. If he leads the Jack, declarer wins with the Ace and finesses dummy's 10. If he leads the 3, West's Queen must be played to force out the King, and South now finesses the 9.

♠ A K 4
♡ J 10 6 3
◇ A 9 4
♣ J 4 2

♠ Q J 10 9
♡ 7
◇ Q J 6
♣ K Q 10 9 7

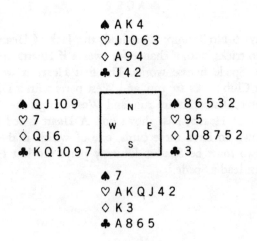

♠ 8 6 5 3 2
♡ 9 5
◇ 10 8 7 5 2
♣ 3

♠ 7
♡ A K Q J 4 2
◇ K 3
♣ A 8 6 5

The bidding:

SOUTH	WEST	NORTH	EAST
1 Heart	2 Clubs	3 Hearts	Pass
4 No Trump	Pass	5 Hearts	Pass
6 Hearts	Pass	Pass	Pass

West leads the Queen of Spades. On the surface it would appear that the declarer must lose two Clubs, but by proper manipulation he can hold his losses to one trick.

Two rounds of trumps are played, ending up in dummy. On the Ace of Spades a losing Club is discarded. The 4 of Spades is ruffed by declarer, followed by the King and Ace of Diamonds and a Diamond ruff. Declarer is now in his own hand and is confident that West holds both the King and Queen of Clubs. A low Club, therefore, is led toward the dummy, and West must win with the Queen. It is now impossible for him to make a safe lead. A Club return will permit the Jack to win. A Spade return permits declarer to ruff in one hand and discard a Club from the other.

Defense against the throw-in

In the following hand South is declarer at a contract of 4 Hearts.

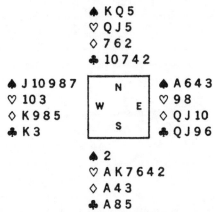

```
              ♠ K Q 5
              ♡ Q J 5
              ◇ 7 6 2
              ♣ 10 7 4 2

♠ J 10 9 8 7      N        ♠ A 6 4 3
♡ 10 3                     ♡ 9 8
◇ K 9 8 5    W       E     ◇ Q J 10
♣ K 3             S        ♣ Q J 9 6

              ♠ 2
              ♡ A K 7 6 4 2
              ◇ A 4 3
              ♣ A 8 5
```

West leads the Jack of Spades, and the Queen is taken by the Ace. The Queen of Diamonds is returned and permitted to hold. A Diamond is continued and won with the Ace. Dummy is entered with the Jack of Hearts, and on the King of Spades a Diamond is discarded. A Spade is ruffed by declarer and dummy entered with the Queen of Hearts, exhausting trumps. The remaining Diamond is ruffed by declarer, who now plays the Ace of Clubs. If West plays low, he will be obliged to win the next Club, and his lead of either a Diamond or a Spade will permit declarer to ruff in dummy and discard a losing Club from his own hand. West, therefore, must pray that his partner holds the Queen and Jack of Clubs and should toss the King under the Ace, because he cannot afford to win the lead. When the next Club is led, he plays low, and East cashes the setting trick with the two high Clubs.

QUIZ ON ELIMINATIONS AND END PLAYS

1.

	NORTH	SOUTH
♠	A J 5	K 8 2
♡	A Q 10 2	K J 9 8 4 3
◇	7 4 3	Q
♣	J 6 4	A 10 2

The bidding has gone:

WEST	NORTH	EAST	SOUTH
1 Spade	Pass	Pass	2 Hearts
Pass	4 Hearts	Pass	Pass
Pass			

West leads the King of Diamonds and continues with the Ace, which you ruff. After drawing the adverse trumps, how do you proceed?

2.

	NORTH	SOUTH
♠	K 7	A Q J 10 6 4 3
♡	A J 10 6	4
◇	A 8 5 3	K 7
♣	A Q 6	10 4 2

The contract is 6 Spades, and West leads a Diamond. Plan the play.

3.

	NORTH	SOUTH
♠	J 10 2	A 9 8 4
♡	A J 10	7 6 3
◇	A Q 8 5 3	K J 9 6 4 2
♣	K Q	none

The contract is 5 Diamonds and West leads the Ace of Clubs. Plan the play.

4.

	NORTH	SOUTH
♠	A Q	10 4
♡	K 10 8 4	A Q 9 7 3 2
◇	Q 6 2	J 7 5
♣	A K 3 2	10 5

The contract is 4 Hearts, and West leads the 2 of Spades. Plan the play.

5.

	NORTH	SOUTH
♠	7 5 2	K 10 3
♡	Q J	A 7 4
◇	A Q J 9 8	K 10 3
♣	J 9 5	A Q 10 2

The contract is 3 No Trump and West leads the 6 of Spades. East wins with the Ace and returns the 9. How do you proceed?

6.

NORTH	SOUTH
♠ A Q J 5 2	♠ K 10 9 6 4
♡ A 7 4 3	♡ K J
◇ none	◇ J 8
♣ K 8 4 2	♣ A 9 5 3

The contract is 6 Spades and West leads a Diamond, which you ruff. How do you proceed?

7.

NORTH	SOUTH
♠ J 3 2	♠ K 7 4
♡ A J	♡ none
◇ Q 10 9	◇ A K J 5 4 3 2
♣ A 10 7 3 2	♣ 8 6 4

The bidding:

SOUTH	WEST	NORTH	EAST
1 Diamond	1 Heart	2 No Trump	Pass
4 Diamonds	Pass	5 Diamonds	Pass
Pass	Pass		

Perhaps you should have supported your partner's No Trump call, but there you are at 5 Diamonds. West leads the King of Hearts. How do you proceed?

8.

NORTH	SOUTH
♠ Q 5 4 2	♠ A K J 10 3
♡ 8 4 2	♡ K 7
◇ A J 2	◇ Q 6 4
♣ A K 5	♣ 7 4 2

The bidding:

WEST	NORTH	EAST	SOUTH
1 Club	Pass	Pass	1 Spades
Pass	3 Spades	Pass	4 Spades
Pass	Pass	Pass	

The contract is 4 Spades and West leads the Queen of Clubs. Plan the play.

ANSWERS TO QUIZ ON ELIMINATIONS AND END PLAYS

1.

In view of the bidding it may seem safe to take the Spade finesse, but in fact this would represent an unnecessary hazard.

West may have opened the bidding with 10 9 x x x of Spades, and in this case, if you finessed the Jack and lost, East would return a Club.

If West had the K Q of Clubs, you would then be in trouble.

The contract is perfectly safe if you decline the Spade finesse and play for an elimination instead. After drawing trumps, you ruff dummy's last Diamond and play off the A K J of Spades. It does not matter whether the Queen falls or not, for whoever

wins the third Spade will have to
open up the Clubs or concede a ruff
and discard. For example, suppose
West has the Queen of Spades: if he
returns a Club, you lose only one
Club trick, and if he returns a Diamond or a Spade, you ruff in dummy
and discard Club from your own
hand.

The situation you have to guard
against is as follows:

```
              ♠ A J 5
              ♡ A Q 10 2
              ◇ 7 4 3
              ♣ J 6 4
  ♠ 10 9 7 4 3        ♠ Q 6
  ♡ 6                 ♡ 7 5
  ◇ A K J 6           ◇ 10 9 8 5 2
  ♣ K Q 8             ♣ 9 7 5 3
              ♠ K 8 2
              ♡ K J 9 8 4 3
              ◇ Q
              ♣ A 10 2
```

In this case, if you finesse the Jack
of Spades, East wins and returns a
Club. You duck, of course, but West
wins and exits with a Spade, after
which you eventually have to lose
another Club trick.

2.

*Elimination play virtually ensures the
contract.* The first trick is taken in
your hand, a round of trumps is
drawn and a Diamond is led to the
Ace. A Diamond is ruffed with a
high trump, dummy is reentered with
the King of trumps and the last Diamond is ruffed.

Any outstanding trumps are now
drawn and a Heart is led. If West
plays low, the 10 is finessed. If East
wins the trick, any return will give
you the contract.

If West plays an honor when the
first Heart is led, the Ace is played
and the Jack is returned. It doesn't
matter who has the outstanding
honor, for you can discard one Club
on the Jack of Hearts and another
on the 10.

3.

The play to trick one is the key. Declarer must make the sparkling play
of discarding a Heart on the Ace of
Clubs instead of ruffing it. This is
the first step in an elimination that
ensures the contract even if every
key card is badly placed. The full
deal was:

```
              ♠ J 10 2
              ♡ A J 10
              ◇ A Q 8 5 3
              ♣ K Q
  ♠ K Q 7            ♠ 6 5 3
  ♡ 9 5 2            ♡ K Q 8 4
  ◇ 10               ◇ 7
  ♣ A 9 8 7 4 2      ♣ J 10 6 5 3
              ♠ A 9 8 4
              ♡ 7 6 3
              ◇ K J 9 6 4 2
              ♣ none
```

If West shifts to a Heart, which is
the best he can do, the Ace is played,
a Heart is discarded on the King of
Clubs, and a Heart is ruffed. Dummy
is reentered with a trump and the
last Heart ruffed.

Dummy is then put in with a
trump to lead the Jack of Spades. If
West wins, any return gives you the
contract.

If you were to ruff the opening
lead, you could be defeated, for you
would be unable to prevent East from
gaining the lead some time or other
with a Heart. East would then return
a Spade, which you would have to
duck, and West would be able to win
and exit with a Heart. Eventually
you would lose another Spade trick.

4.

*Taking the finesse would be a snare
and delusion.* If you take the Spade
finesse, and it loses, you will eventually have to try to make a trick in
the Diamond suit. There is no
method known to science whereby
you can be certain of a trick with this
Diamond combination if you have
to play it yourself, and in the actual
case you would go down.

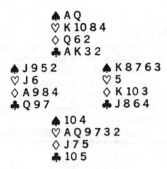

♠ A Q
♡ K 10 8 4
◇ Q 6 2
♣ A K 3 2

♠ J 9 5 2   ♠ K 8 7 6 3
♡ J 6   ♡ 5
◇ A 9 8 4   ◇ K 10 3
♣ Q 9 7   ♣ J 8 6 4

♠ 10 4
♡ A Q 9 7 3 2
◇ J 7 5
♣ 10 5

At the same time, you can make the contract against any distribution of the adverse cards provided you refuse the Spade finesse. Win with the Ace, draw the opponents' trumps and play three rounds of Clubs, ruffing the third one. Enter dummy with a trump, ruff the last Club, and exit with a Spade.

You can now show your hand and claim the contract, for whoever wins the Spade has to open up the Diamonds or concede a ruff and discard. In either case you lose only two Diamond tricks.

5.

You have only eight sure tricks and the disquieting feature of the hand is that if you take a finesse in either Hearts or Clubs, West may get in and cash enough Spades to set the contract.

There is no guaranteed method of making the contract, but you can improve your chances considerably by taking the King of Spades at trick two and cashing two rounds of Diamonds. You then exit with the 10 of Spades. You are hoping that if West held as many as five Spades originally, he may have only two Diamonds, in which case after cashing the Spades (on which you discard two Clubs) he is forced to give you your ninth trick by returning a Heart or a Club.

If, unfortunately, West is able to exit safely with a Diamond after cashing the Spades, you simply have to guess which finesse to take for your ninth trick.

6.

You are bound to make the contract if the opponents' Clubs are 3–2, and accordingly you plan to guard against a 4–1 break. In this case you might try taking the Heart finesse in order to have a parking place for a Club, but it would be better to play for an elimination.

Ruff the Diamond opening and draw the opponents' trumps. Take two rounds of Hearts, ruff a Heart, ruff a Diamond and take another Heart ruff.

With the red suits eliminated, you play a Club towards the dummy. If West plays an honor card, you intend to let him hold the trick with it, but if he plays a spot card, you intend to cover with the 8. This method of procedure ensures the contract against every possible division of the Club suit. The full deal was as follows:

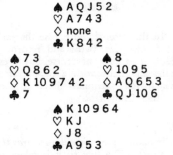

♠ A Q J 5 2
♡ A 7 4 3
◇ none
♣ K 8 4 2

♠ 7 3   ♠ 8
♡ Q 8 6 2   ♡ 10 9 5
◇ K 10 9 7 4 2   ◇ A Q 6 5 3
♣ 7   ♣ Q J 10 6

♠ K 10 9 6 4
♡ K J
◇ J 8
♣ A 9 5 3

When you lead a Club towards the dummy, West plays the 7, dummy plays the 8, and East wins with the 10. This is the last trick you lose.

If East returns a Diamond, you ruff in dummy and discard a Club from your hand. If East returns a low Club you play the 9. Finally, if East returns the Queen or Jack of Clubs, you win it in dummy and finesse the 9 of Clubs to land the slam.

7.

You must try to establish the Club suit in order to have discards for your Spades. In view of the bidding, a Spade lead from East would probably be fatal, so you must plan to keep him out.

Win the Heart opening, discarding a Club, and lead the Jack of Hearts, discarding another Club. West cannot profitably attack Spades, and provided the Clubs are 3–2, you can establish the suit by ruffing and discarding two losing Spades. The full deal was:

```
              ♠ J 3 2
              ♡ A J
              ◇ Q 10 9
              ♣ A 10 7 3 2
♠ A Q 9                      ♠ 10 8 6 5
♡ K Q 10 8 7 4 2             ♡ 9 6 5 3
◇ 7                          ◇ 8 6
♣ Q 9                        ♣ K J 5
              ♠ K 7 4
              ♡ none
              ◇ A K J 5 4 3 2
              ♣ 8 6 4
```

The key play is the discard of a Club on dummy's Jack of Hearts, technically known as a loser-on-loser play. If declarer fails to diagnose this play, he cannot establish Clubs without East gaining the lead and returning a Spade for down one.

8.

You should assume that West has the King of Diamonds. In this case the hand will be virtually icy, as you can throw him in with it after conducting a suitable elimination.

The first step is to play low from dummy on the opening lead. The Club continuation is taken and, after drawing trumps, the Jack of Diamonds is finessed.

The Ace of Diamonds and the remaining Club are cashed and West is thrown in with the King of Diamonds. He is obliged to concede a ruff and discard or lead a Heart up to your King, and in either case the contract is made.

The important point is to duck the Club opening lead, for otherwise you may be unable to eliminate the Clubs without East obtaining the lead if he has the 10 x x of Clubs. A Heart return would then lead to your undoing, for you would lose two Heart tricks and, eventually, a Diamond. The full deal was:

```
              ♠ Q 5 4 2
              ♡ 8 4 2
              ◇ A J 2
              ♣ A K 5
♠ 9 8 6                      ♠ 7
♡ A Q J                      ♡ 10 9 6 5 3
◇ K 10 7                     ◇ 9 8 5 3
♣ Q J 9 8                    ♣ 10 6 3
              ♠ A K J 10 3
              ♡ K 7
              ◇ Q 6 4
              ♣ 7 4 2
```

28.   Trump coups and grand coups

THE OPPORTUNITY for the play known as the Trump Coup occurs when declarer holds a finessing position in trumps over the right-hand player but is unable to finesse because he has no trump in dummy with which to come through. If at the proper time he can arrange to have the lead in the dummy, the same result can be obtained as though he actually had a trump.

To illustrate:

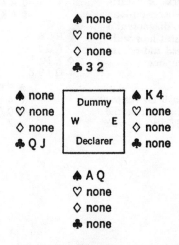

```
                ♠ none
                ♡ none
                ◇ none
                ♣ 3 2

   ♠ none   ┌─────────┐   ♠ K 4
   ♡ none   │  Dummy  │   ♡ none
   ◇ none   │ W     E │   ◇ none
   ♣ Q J    │Declarer │   ♣ none
            └─────────┘
                ♠ A Q
                ♡ none
                ◇ none
                ♣ none
```

South is declarer at a Spade contract and desires to win both Spade tricks. If at this time the lead is in dummy, the same result is obtained as though a Spade were being led, because East will be obliged to trump a Club and South will overruff.

Note that if the lead were at the present time in declarer's hand this result could not be accomplished.

Let us take this illustration with the addition of one more card:

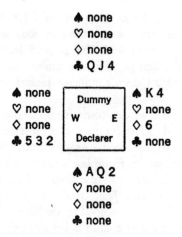

With this holding the play is not operative, because when dummy leads a Club, East will discard his Diamond and South is forced to ruff, placing the lead in his own hand.

It can be seen that the trump coup is not operative until such time as the declarer has precisely the same number of trumps as the player whom he is attempting to encircle. If early in the play the declarer had been able to use his deuce of Spades and found the lead in dummy at trick twelve, he would have succeeded. And that would be that rarest of all plays, a Grand Coup.

Let us illustrate with one or two complete hands:

Grand coup

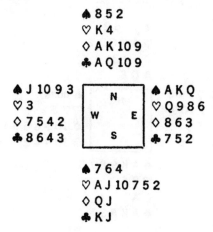

South is the declarer at a contract of 4 Hearts. West leads the Jack of Spades, three tricks are cashed in that suit, and the 6 of Hearts returned. South wins with the 10 and leads to the King of Hearts, finding out the bad news in the trump suit. On the surface it would appear that East's Queen cannot be picked up. However, there is a slight chance.

If at trick twelve the lead can come from the dummy, East's trump Queen can be trapped. In order to accomplish this result, declarer must reduce his own trumps to the exact number held by East. This can be done by unnecessarily trumping some of dummy's good cards. The Ace and King of Diamonds are cashed and another Diamond led and trumped by South. The Jack of Clubs is overtaken with the Queen and another Diamond trumped by declarer. The King of Clubs is overtaken with the Ace and a Club is led from dummy. If East ruffs with the 9, declarer will overruff. If East ruffs with the Queen, the same result is obtained.

And there you have the grand coup, which involves the ruffing of good tricks in order to reduce declarer's trumps to precisely the same number held by the adversary. An essential ingredient of the grand-coup technique is that the final lead must come through the hand that has the trump honor.

Outside trump play

South is the declarer at a contract of 6 Spades which has been doubled by West. The King of Diamonds was opened, and the first Spade lead revealed the unfortunate trump break. There is still hope for the declarer to lose only one Spade:

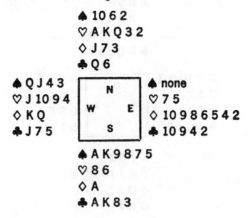

```
              ♠ 10 6 2
              ♡ A K Q 3 2
              ◊ J 7 3
              ♣ Q 6
♠ Q J 4 3        N        ♠ none
♡ J 10 9 4    W     E     ♡ 7 5
◊ K Q            S        ◊ 10 9 8 6 5 4 2
♣ J 7 5                   ♣ 10 9 4 2
              ♠ A K 9 8 7 5
              ♡ 8 6
              ◊ A
              ♣ A K 8 3
```

The technique to be employed in this hand is similar to that of the grand coup. The plan is for declarer to reduce his trumps to precisely the number held by his adversary and to relinquish the lead at trick eleven to force West to lead from his trump holding.

To trick three declarer leads a Heart; dummy wins with the Queen. A diamond is ruffed by declarer, and the fall of the Queen makes it appear that West has no more of the suit. The King and Ace of Hearts are now cashed, declarer discarding a Club. West is now known to hold another Heart, so that the fourth Heart is trumped by declarer, who now holds exactly the same number of trumps as West. The Queen, King and Ace of Clubs are cashed, and at trick eleven declarer leads a low Spade toward the 10. West is obliged to win with the Jack and is in a helpless position, since he must surrender the last two tricks.

QUIZ ON COUPS AND TRUMP COUPS

1.

	NORTH	
	♠ 7 6 4	
	♡ A 8 6 4 3	
	◇ K 5	
	♣ A 7 2	
WEST ♠ 10		EAST
	SOUTH	
	♠ K Q J	
	♡ 5	
	◇ A Q 10 8 7 3	
	♣ K Q J	

The contract is 6 Diamonds and West leads a Spade. East wins with the Ace and returns the 5. Plan the play.

2.

	NORTH	
	♠ K 9 7	
	♡ 9 4 2	
	◇ A Q 2	
	♣ A 6 4 2	
WEST ♡ 3		EAST
	SOUTH	
	♠ A Q 6 5 2	
	♡ A K 6	
	◇ K 7 4	
	♣ K 10	

The contract is 6 Spades and a Heart is led. You win it, play a trump to the King, and a trump to the Ace. East shows up with the J 10 8 x. How do you proceed?

3.

	NORTH	
	♠ 9 4 2	
	♡ A 7 5	
	◇ A 8 6 3	
	♣ A K 2	
WEST ◇ K		EAST
	SOUTH	
	♠ A 7 6	
	♡ K J 10 8 4 3	
	◇ 4	
	♣ 7 5 4	

The contract is 4 Hearts and West leads the King of Diamonds. Plan the play.

4.

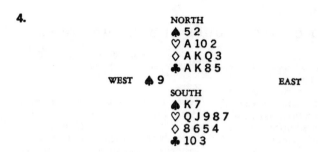

```
                    NORTH
                    ♠ 5 2
                    ♡ A 10 2
                    ◇ A K Q 3
                    ♣ A K 8 5
        WEST   ♠ 9                      EAST
                    SOUTH
                    ♠ K 7
                    ♡ Q J 9 8 7
                    ◇ 8 6 5 4
                    ♣ 10 3
```

The bidding:

EAST	SOUTH	WEST	NORTH
4 Spades	Pass	Pass	Double
Pass	5 Hearts	Pass	Pass
Pass			

The contract is 5 Hearts and a Spade is led. East wins with the Ace and returns a Spade, West following suit. You lead the Queen of trumps, which holds, and then you finesse the 10, East showing out. You take the A K of Diamonds and West shows up with four of them. How do you continue?

5.

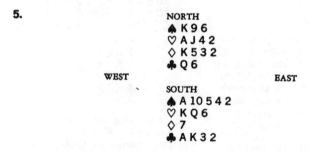

```
                    NORTH
                    ♠ K 9 6
                    ♡ A J 4 2
                    ◇ K 5 3 2
                    ♣ Q 6
        WEST                           EAST
                    SOUTH
                    ♠ A 10 5 4 2
                    ♡ K Q 6
                    ◇ 7
                    ♣ A K 3 2
```

The contract is 6 Spades. Diamonds are led and you ruff the second one. How do you proceed?

ANSWERS TO QUIZ ON COUPS AND TRUMP COUPS

1.

A far-seeing declarer will take precautions against the possibility of a 4–1 trump break. If West has four trumps, there is nothing you can do, but if East has four, you may be able to give yourself an additional chance. This is the sort of layout you have to provide for:

```
              NORTH
              ♠ 7 6 4
              ♡ A 8 6 4 3
              ◇ K 5
              ♣ A 7 2
WEST                        EAST
♠ 10 9 8 2                  ♠ A 5 3
♡ K J 7 2                   ♡ Q 10 9
◇ 4                         ◇ J 9 6 2
♣ 10 8 6 4                  ♣ 9 5 3
              SOUTH
              ♠ K Q J
              ♡ 5
              ◇ A Q 10 8 7 3
              ♣ K Q J
```

Before testing the trump suit, you should lead a Heart to the Ace and ruff a Heart. This is done purely in order to reduce your trump length. You then play the A K of Diamonds. In the actual case, where East shows up with the J 9 x x, you continue by ruffing another Heart. Your trumps are now reduced to the same length as East's, which would not have been possible unless you ruffed a Heart initially. After cashing your winners in the black suits, you arrive at this ending:

```
              NORTH
              ♡ 8 6
              ♣ A
WEST                  EAST
immaterial            ◇ J 9
                      ♣ 9
              SOUTH
              ◇ Q 10
              ♣ J
```

A Club is led to the Ace and East's Diamonds are trapped.

2.

There seems no way of avoiding a Heart loser and a trump loser, but this is not so. If you arrange matters carefully, you reach a position where East either has to let you make all your low trumps or else has to ruff your losing Heart with his master trump. As a matter of fact, this form of strategy is bound to work provided East holds a balanced hand, as in this diagram:

```
              NORTH
              ♠ K 9 7
              ♡ 9 4 2
              ◇ A Q 2
              ♣ A 6 4 2
WEST                        EAST
♠ 4                         ♠ J 10 8 3
♡ 10 8 7 3                  ♡ Q J 5
◇ 10 8 5 3                  ◇ J 9 6
♣ Q 8 7 5                   ♣ J 9 3
              SOUTH
              ♠ A Q 6 5 2
              ♡ A K 6
              ◇ K 7 4
              ♣ K 10
```

After winning the Heart opening and playing the K A of trump, you take three rounds of Clubs, ruffing. You cash your winners in the red suits, ending in dummy and leaving this position:

```
              NORTH
              ♠ 9
              ♡ 9
              ♣ 6
WEST                  EAST
immaterial            ♠ J 10
                      ♡ Q
              SOUTH
              ♠ Q 6
              ♡ 6
```

East may think he is due to take two of the last three tricks, but when you lead dummy's last Club he speedily finds that his cards are not worth their face value. If he ruffs the Club, you simply discard your losing Heart and take the last two tricks with the Q 6 of trump. Alternatively, if East sluffs a Heart when you lead the Club, you ruff with the 6 of trump. Either way, you make the slam.

3.

This hand does not depend on locating the missing Queen of trump. You are bound to lose a Club and two Spades, but if you are fortunate enough to run into a favorable distribution of the opponents' cards, you can arrange matters so that you do not lose a trump trick no matter who has the Queen. The general idea is to expend as many of your trumps as possible by ruffing, and then throw the lead to the opponents. Suppose this is the full deal:

NORTH
♠ 9 4 2
♡ A 7 5
◊ A 8 6 3
♣ A K 2

WEST
♠ Q 10 8
♡ Q 9 6
◊ K Q J 5
♣ Q 8 3

EAST
♠ K J 5 3
♡ 2
◊ 10 9 7 2
♣ J 10 9 6

SOUTH
♠ A 7 6
♡ K J 10 8 4 3
◊ 4
♣ 7 5 4

You win the Diamond opening with the Ace, ruff a Diamond, enter dummy with a Club and ruff another Diamond. Pursuing your plan, you enter dummy again with a Club and ruff the fourth Diamond. Then you cash the Ace of Spades and exit with a Spade.

At this time the defenders may cash two Spade tricks and a Club, but you no longer have to worry about the Queen of trump. Your last three cards are the K J 10 of trump and dummy has the A 7 5. The opponents have to lead, and therefore you are indifferent to the location of the Queen.

4.

A smother play is needed. You have an inescapable Diamond loser and therefore must plan to avoid losing a trump trick. The only resource open to you is to endplay East in circumstances which will enable you to smother West's King of trump. You already know everything there is to know about the opponents' hands, which are as follows:

NORTH
♠ 5 2
♡ A 10 2
◊ A K Q 3
♣ A K 8 5

WEST
♠ 6 3
♡ K 6 4 3
◊ J 10 7 2
♣ J 7 4

EAST
♠ A Q J 10 9 8 4
♡ 5
◊ 9
♣ Q 9 6 2

SOUTH
♠ K 7
♡ Q J 9 8 7
◊ 8 6 5 4
♣ 10 3

After having played the A K of Diamonds, you take three rounds of Clubs, ruffing. You cross to the Queen of Diamonds and lead dummy's last Club. Instead of ruffing it, you allow East to win the trick, shedding a Diamond from your hand.

At this time you are left with the J 9 of trump, and West is left with the K 6 of trump. Although dummy's Ace of trumps is now bare, West's King is trapped, for when East leads a Spade at trick twelve, you play one of your trump honors and wait to see what West does. If he overruffs with the King, you overruff with dummy's Ace. If he doesn't overruff with the King, you simply discard a Diamond from dummy.

5.

A rare form of trump coup is needed. You could of course hope for the Q J to be bare. The alternative is to play for the Devil's Coup, so called because of the sorcerous fashion in which the defenders' apparently sure trump trick is made to disappear. Declarer has to hope that the full deal is something like this:

```
              NORTH
              ♠ K 9 6
              ♡ A J 4 2
              ◇ K 5 3 2
              ♣ Q 6
WEST                        EAST
♠ Q 8 3                     ♠ J 7
♡ 10 8 7                    ♡ 9 5 3
◇ J 10 9 6                  ◇ A Q 8 4
♣ 10 8 4                    ♣ J 9 7 5
              SOUTH
              ♠ A 10 5 4 2
              ♡ K Q 6
              ◇ 7
              ♣ A K 3 2
```

After ruffing the second Diamond you take three rounds of Hearts, ending in dummy. Then you ruff another Diamond, take out three rounds of Clubs, discarding a Heart from dummy, and ruff dummy's last Diamond. The end position is:

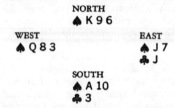

```
              NORTH
              ♠ K 9 6
WEST                        EAST
♠ Q 8 3                     ♠ J 7
                            ♣ J
              SOUTH
              ♠ A 10
              ♣ 3
```

When you now lead the 3 of Clubs from your hand, West can either ruff low or ruff with the Queen. If he ruffs low, you overruff with the 9 and take the last two tricks with the A K of trumps. If West ruffs the Club with the Queen, you overruff with the King and finesse the 10 of trump on the way back.

29.   Four-deal bridge ("Chicago")

Next time you shop for bridge scorepads, you may observe that some are printed with a big X at the top of the space for scoring each rubber. This "X" marks the spot where you can bury the problems of what to do with the fifth player and of the endless rubber that keeps you playing longer than you had expected.

The purpose of the "X" is to aid in keeping score in Four-Deal Bridge, widely called "Chicago" for the excellent reason that it was originated there for the purpose of speeding up the games played during lunch hours at clubs and also on commuter trains. Its growing popularity is due to the fact that it does much more than the job it was planned for. "Chicago" shortens the time that a player may be cut out when five or six are in the game and along comes one of those battles in which a single rubber lasts for an hour. Even in a four-hand game, it eliminates the proverbial "last rubber" that seems never to end. It may rob you of your excuse for getting home late to dinner, but it also insures that you will not lose an extra hour of sleep if you are playing at night.

In addition, Four-Deal is the widely accepted method of play in the rubber bridge tournaments that are becoming increasingly popular among players who have not tried, or find they do not enjoy duplicate bridge. At the same time, it is also a great way to learn something about the scoring methods that are used in the duplicate game; game and slam bonuses are awarded for the result of individual hands and vulnerability is arbitrarily decided by the number of the deal. Yet the great element so much missed in the duplicate game—the part score and its attendant excitement—is part of the Four-Deal game.

In Four-Deal, each player gets one chance to deal. (Passed-out hands are redealt by the same player.) When four hands have been played, the "rubber" is over and you change partners. Or you go on to another series of four deals if you are playing a set game. Thus, a fifth player, if there is one, never sits out more or less than four deals. The last rubber never lasts more than four deals. And when you cut the poorest player in the game, you know that four deals later you will escape. Meanwhile, since nothing can shorten your partnership sentence, you do your level best to achieve the maximum result on every deal.

In these four deals, however, much can happen because you can earn a game bonus and even a slam bonus on every hand. Chicago is faster; yet, although it would seem to be a swingier game, the fact is that rarely does one lose as much as one-third more points than in the usual rubber game.

The mechanics are simple. You place the number 1 in the segment of the "X" corresponding to the position of the dealer in relation to your scorepad. On that deal, neither side is vulnerable. On deals 2 and 3, the dealer's side is vulnerable. On deal 4, both sides are vulnerable. Game bid and made earns a 300 point bonus not vulnerable, 500 points when vulnerable. Slam and penalty scores, governed in the same way, are the same as at rubber bridge.

A part score made on the fourth deal earns a bonus of 100 points (unless it earns a larger bonus by converting a previous part score into a game). Otherwise, part scores get no bonus award, but are carried over to the next deal until wiped out by the scoring of a game—or until the four deals end. A hanging partial left over from an earlier deal gets no bonus when the set of four is ended; only a part score made on the final deal is rewarded in this way.

The full rules of Four-Deal Bridge are published here as promulgated by the American Contract Bridge League and with their permission. Meanwhile, let me give you a few tips on strategy, which is different from rubber bridge principally in tactics when you are fourth-hand not vulnerable against vulnerable opponents, or when you are deciding between a game and a part-score declaration on the fourth deal.

Four-deal tactics:

Obviously, since you will earn a 100-point bonus for making a partial on the last hand, the bonus for bidding and making a game is in reality only 400 points—not 500 (or 700 as it might be in rubber bridge, although never in "Chicago"). Assume that you bid four Spades and make it, you score 620. Assume that you bid three Spades and make four, you score 220. Assume that you bid four Spades and make three, you score minus 100. But if you bid and make three, you score 190. Your game bids on the fourth hand should therefore be a bit more on the conservative side. Especially as we haven't taken account of the times you run into bad breaks and are set two or more—perhaps doubled.

Suppose it is the second deal of the set and your opponents are vulnerable while you are not. If they pass the bidding around to you in fourth seat, the chances are that they can't make a game even if they can outbid you. Throw in the hand and they get a fresh deal, with a chance of dealing themselves a game-going hand. But open the bidding and even if they can outbid you, you usually risk no more than a part score. Hence, it pays to open the bidding somewhat lighter in fourth seat because you will "take them off vulnerability." In other words, if they do get that game on the next deal, it will be when they are not vulnerable and will earn only 300 points for bidding it instead of 500.

There are some other slight advantages, too, when you open fourth hand light. It is more difficult for vulnerable opponents to compete; they will be loath to risk a big penalty against a part score, which is where you intend to stop. But don't carry this strategy too far; if you open with a poor hand you may be hoist by your own petard.

Another advantage offered by Four-Deal bridge is that the value of the score on each deal is precisely limited. If you are set 500 points to save a 600 point game, you have saved 100 points and you do not wind up at a disadvantage on the next deal, when, at rubber bridge, the opponents would still need only one game to win the rubber while you need two. And, finally, if you decide later to give Duplicate Bridge a whirl, you will at least be familiar with the scoring principles.

Official Rules for Four-Deal Bridge*

*Four-Deal Bridge is a form of Rubber Bridge much
played in clubs and well suited to home play. Its effect
is to avoid long rubbers of uncertain duration; a member
never need wait longer than the time (about twenty
minutes) required to complete four deals. The game is
also called Club Bridge, and is often called Chicago for
the city in which it originated.*

A. Basic Rules

The Laws of Contract Bridge and Rules for Club Procedure are followed, except as modified by the following rules.

B. The Rubber

A rubber consists of a series of four deals that have been bid and played. If a deal is passed out, the same player deals again and the deal passed out does not count as one of the four deals.

A fifth deal is void if attention is drawn to it at any time before there has been a new cut for partners or the game has terminated; if the error is not discovered in time for correction, the score stands as recorded. A sixth or subsequent deal is unconditionally void and no score for such a deal is ever permissible.

In case fewer than four deals are played, the score shall stand for the incomplete series unless attention is drawn to the error before there has been a new cut for partners or the game has terminated.

When the players are pivoting (forming new partnerships in a fixed rotation), the fact that the players have taken their proper seats for the next rubber shall be considered a cut for partners.

C. Vulnerability

Vulnerability is not determined by previous scores but by the following schedule:

First deal: *Neither side vulnerable.*

* As prepared for the American Contract Bridge League.

Second and Third deals: *Dealer's side vulnerable, the other side not vulnerable.*

Fourth deal: *Both sides vulnerable.*

D. Premiums

For making or completing a game (100 or more trick points) a side receives a premium of 300 points if on that deal it is not vulnerable or 500 points if on that deal it is vulnerable. There is no additional premium for winning two or more games, each game premium being scored separately.

E. The Score

As a reminder of vulnerability in Four-Deal Bridge, two intersecting diagonal lines should be drawn near the top of the score pad, as shown:

The numeral "1" should be inserted in that one of the four angles thus formed that faces the first dealer. After play of the first deal is completed, "2" is inserted in the next angle in clockwise rotation, facing the dealer of the second deal. The numerals "3" and "4" are subsequently inserted at the start of the third and fourth deals respectively, each in the angle facing the current dealer.

A correctly numbered diagram is conclusive as to vulnerability. There is no redress for a bid influenced by the scorer's failure to draw the diagram or for an error or omission in inserting a numeral or numerals in the diagram. Such error or omission should, upon discovery, be immediately corrected and the deal or deals should be scored or rescored as though the diagram and the number or numbers thereon had been properly inserted.

F. Part-Scores

A part-score or -scores made previously may be combined with a part-score made in the current deal to complete a game of 100 or more trick points. The game premium is determined by the vulnerability, on that deal, of the side that completes the game. When a side makes or completes a game, no previous part-score of either side may thereafter be counted toward game.

A side that makes a part-score in the fourth deal, if the part-score is not sufficient to complete a game, receives a premium of 100 points. This premium is scored whether or not the same side or the other side has an uncompleted part-score. There is no separate premium for making a part-score in any other circumstances.

G. Deal out of Turn

When a player deals out of turn, and there is no right to a redeal, the player who should have dealt retains his right to call first, but such right is lost if it is not claimed before the actual dealer calls. If the actual dealer calls before attention is drawn to the deal out of turn, each player thereafter calls in rotation. Vulnerability and scoring values are determined by the position of the player who should have dealt, regardless of which player actually dealt or called first. Neither the rotation of the deal nor the scoring is affected by a deal out of turn. The next dealer is the player who would have dealt next if the deal had been in turn.

H. Optional Rules and Customs

The following practices, not required, have proved acceptable in some clubs and games.

(a) Since the essence of the game is speed, if a deal is passed out, the pack that has been shuffled for the next deal should be used by the same dealer.

(b) The net score of a rubber should be translated into even hundreds (according to American custom) by crediting as 100 points any fraction thereof amounting to 50 or more points: e.g., 750 points count as 800; 740 points count as 700 points.

(c) No two players may play a second consecutive rubber as partners at the same table. If two players draw each other again, the player who has drawn the highest card should play with the player who has drawn the third-highest, against the other two players.

(d) Any player may announce, prior to the auction and before he has looked at his hand, which deal it is and who is vulnerable; or may, for his own information, inquire as to these facts when it is his turn to call. There is no redress if no announcement is made or if incorrect information is given.

(e) To avoid confusion as to how many deals have been played: Each deal should be scored, even if there is no net advantage to either side (for example, when one side is entitled to 100 points for undertrick penalties and the other side is entitled to 100 points for honors). In a result that completes a game, premiums for overtricks, game, slam, or making a doubled contract should be combined with the trick score to produce one total, which is entered below the line (for example, if a side makes 2 Spades doubled and vulnerable with an overtrick, 870 should be scored below the line, not 120 below the line and 50, 500 and 200 above the line).

The International Code 1981

the laws of contract bridge

The Scope of the Laws

The Laws are designed to define correct procedure and to provide an adequate remedy whenever a player accidentally, carelessly or inadvertently disturbs the proper course of the game, or gains an unintentional but nevertheless unfair advantage. An offending player should be ready to pay a prescribed penalty graciously.

The Laws are not designed to prevent dishonorable practices and there are no penalties to cover intentional violations. In the absence of penalty, moral obligations are strongest. Ostracism is the ultimate remedy for intentional offenses.

The Object of the Proprieties

The object of the Proprieties is twofold: to familiarize players with the customs and etiquette of the game, generally accepted over a long period of years; and to enlighten those who might otherwise fail to appreciate when or how they are improperly conveying information to their partners — often a far more reprehensible offense than a violation of a law.

When these principles are appreciated, arguments are avoided and the pleasure that the game offers is materially enhanced.

Part 1   Definitions

Auction — 1. The process of determining the contract by means of successive calls. 2. The aggregate of calls made.

Auction Period — The period during which calls are made.

Bid — An undertaking to win at least a specified number of odd tricks in a specified denomination.

Call — Any bid, double, redouble or pass.

Contract — The undertaking by declarer's side to win, at the denomination named, the number of odd tricks specified in the final bid, whether undoubled, doubled or redoubled.

Convention — Any call or play that, by agreement or understanding between partners, serves to convey a special meaning that the opponents cannot reasonably be expected to understand without an explanation.

Deal — 1. The distribution of the pack to form the hands of the four players. 2. The cards so distributed as a unit, including the auction and play thereof.

Declarer — The player who, for the side that makes the final bid, first bid the denomination named in that bid. He becomes declarer when the auction is closed.

Defective Trick — A trick that contains fewer or more than four cards.

Defender — An opponent of declarer.

Denomination — The suit or notrump specified in a bid.

Double — A call over an opponent's bid increasing the scoring value of fulfilled or defeated contracts (see Law 19).

Dummy — 1. Declarer's partner. He becomes dummy when the auction is closed. 2. Declarer's partner's cards, once they are spread on the table after the opening lead.

Follow Suit — Play a card of the suit that has been led.

Game — A unit in scoring denoting 100 or more trick points scored on one deal, or accumulated over two or more deals (see Law 73).

Hand — The cards originally dealt to a player, or the remaining portion thereof.

Honor — Any Ace, King, Queen, Jack or ten.

Irregularity — A deviation from the correct procedures set forth in these Laws and Proprieties.

Lead — The first card played to a trick.

Odd Trick — Each trick won by declarer's side in excess of six.

Opening Lead — The card led to the first trick.

Opponent — A player of the other side, a member of the partnership to which one is opposed.

Overtrick — Each trick won by declarer's side in excess of the contract.

Pack — The 52 playing cards with which the game of Contract Bridge is played.

Partner — The player with whom one plays as a side against the other two players.

Partscore — 90 or fewer trick points.

Pass — A call specifying that a player does not, at that turn, elect to bid, double or redouble.

Penalty — An obligation or restriction imposed upon a side for violations of these Laws.

Penalty Card — A card prematurely exposed by a defender. It may be a major or minor penalty card (see Law 50).

Play — 1. The contribution of a card from one's hand to a trick, including the first card, which is the lead. 2. The aggregate of plays made. 3. The period during which the cards are played, starting immediately after the final pass.

Rectification — Adjustment made to permit the auction or play to proceed as normally as possible after an irregularity has occurred.

Redeal — A second or subsequent deal to replace a faulty deal.

Redouble — A call over an opponent's double increasing the scoring value of fulfilled or defeated contracts (see Law 19).

Revoke — The play of a card of another suit by a player who is able to follow suit or to comply with a lead penalty.

Rotation — The clockwise order in which the right to deal, to call or to play progresses.

Rubber — The scoring period that ends when one side has scored two games.

Side — The players who constitute a partnership against the other two players.

Slam — A contract to win twelve tricks (called Small Slam) or thirteen tricks (called Grand Slam).

Specified Suit — Any suit that a player, in exacting a penalty, requires to be led or not to be led.

Suit — One of four groups of cards in the pack, each group comprising thirteen cards and having a characteristic symbol: spades (♠), hearts (♡), diamonds (◇), clubs (♣).

Trick — The unit by which the outcome of the contract is determined, regularly consisting of four cards, one contributed by each player in rotation, beginning with the lead.

Trump — Each card of the suit, if any, named in the contract.

Turn — The correct time when a player may deal, call or play.

Undertrick — Each trick by which declarer's side falls short of fulfilling the contract (see Law 81).

Vulnerable — A side that has won a game is "Vulnerable" and is exposed to greater undertrick penalties and entitled to greater premiums.

Part 2   Preliminaries

Law 1   The players — The pack

Contract bridge is played by all four players with a pack of 52 cards of identical back design and color, consisting of 13 cards in each of four suits. Two packs should be used, of which only one is in play at any time; and each pack should be clearly distinguishable from the other in back design or color.

Law 2   Rank of cards

The suits rank downwards in order — Spades (♠), Hearts (♡), Diamonds (◊), Clubs (♣). The cards of each suit rank in descending order: Ace, King, Queen, Jack, 10, 9, 8, 7, 6, 5, 4, 3, 2.

Law 3   The draw

Before every rubber, each player draws a card from a pack shuffled and spread face down on the table. A card should not be exposed until all the players have drawn.

Unless it is otherwise agreed, the two players who draw the highest cards play as partners against the other two players. When cards of the same rank are drawn, the rank of suit determines which is higher.

The player with the highest card deals first and has the right to choose his seat and the pack with which he will deal. He may consult his partner, but having announced his decision must abide by it. His partner sits opposite him. The opponents then occupy the two remaining seats as they wish, and having made their selection must abide by it.

A player must draw again if he draws more than one card, or one of the four cards at either end of the pack, or a card adjoining one drawn by another player, or a card from the other pack.

Part 3   The Deal

Law 4   The shuffle

Before the first deal of a rubber, the player to the dealer's left should shuffle the pack thoroughly, without exposing the face of any card, in full view of the players and to their satisfaction. Thereafter, as each player deals, the dealer's partner shuffles the other pack for the next deal, and places the pack face down on his right.

A pack properly prepared should not be disturbed until the dealer picks it up for his deal; at which time he is entitled to the final shuffle.

No player other than the dealer and the player designated to prepare the pack may shuffle.

Law 5   The cut

The pack must be cut immediately before it is dealt. The dealer presents the pack to his right-hand opponent, who lifts off a portion and places it on the table toward the dealer. Each portion must contain at least four cards. The dealer completes the cut by placing what was originally the bottom portion upon the other portion.

No player other than the dealer's right-hand opponent may cut the pack.

Laws of Contract Bridge, 1981

Law 6   New cut — New shuffle

There must be a new cut if any player demands one before the first card is dealt. In this case, the dealer's right-hand opponent cuts again.

There must be a new shuffle, followed by a cut:

A.   If any player demands one before the dealer has picked up the pack for his deal. In this case, the player designated to prepare the pack shuffles again.

B.   If any player demands one after the dealer has picked up the pack but before the first card is dealt. In this case only the dealer shuffles.

C.   If a card is turned face up in shuffling. In this case the player who was shuffling shuffles again.

D.   If a card is turned face up in cutting. In this case only the dealer shuffles.

E.   If there is a redeal (see Law 10).

Law 7   Change of pack

The two packs are used alternately, unless there is a redeal.

A pack containing a card so damaged or marked so that it may be identified from its back must be replaced* if attention is drawn to the imperfection before the last card of the current deal has been dealt.

A pack originally belonging to a side must be restored on demand of any player before the last card of the current deal has been dealt.*

Law 8   The deal

The dealer distributes the cards face down, one at a time in rotation into four separate hands of thirteen cards each, the first card to the player on his left and the last card to himself. If he deals two cards simultaneously or consecutively to the same player, or fails to deal a card to a player, he may rectify the error, provided he does so immediately and to the satisfaction of the other players.

The dealer must not allow the face of any card to be seen while he is dealing. Players should not look at the face of any card until the deal is completed.†

Law 9   Rotation of the turn to deal

The turn to deal passes in rotation, unless there is a redeal. If a player deals out of turn, and attention is not drawn to the error before the last card has been dealt, the deal stands as though it had been in turn, the player who dealt the cards is the dealer, and the player who missed his turn to deal has no redress; and the rotation continues as though the deal had been in turn, unless a redeal is required under Law 10.

---

*See Footnote to Law 8.

†A player who violates this provision forfeits those rights to a change of pack (Law 7) or redeal (Law 10) marked with an asterisk (*).

Law 10   Redeal

A redeal cancels the faulty deal; the same dealer deals again, unless he was dealing out of turn; the same pack is used, unless it has been replaced as provided in Law 7; and the cards are shuffled and cut anew as provided in Laws 4 and 5.

There must be a redeal:

A.   If, before the last card has been dealt, it is discovered that

      i] a card has been turned face up in dealing or is face up in the pack or elsewhere;

      ii] the cards have not been dealt correctly;*

      iii] a player is dealing out of turn or is dealing with a pack that was not shuffled or not cut, provided any player* demands a redeal.

B.   If, before the first call has been made, it is discovered that a player has picked up another player's hand and has seen a card in it.

C.   If, before play has been completed, it is discovered that

      i] the pack did not conform in every respect to the requirements of Law 1, including any case in which a missing card cannot be found after due search;

      ii] one player has picked up too many cards, another too few;

      iii] two or more players on opposing sides have allowed any cards from their hands to be mixed together, following a claim that a redeal is in order.

Law 11   Missing card

When a player has too few cards and a redeal is not required by Law 10 (c), the deal stands as correct, and:

A.   If he has played more than once to a previous trick, Law 67 applies;

B.   If a missing card is found elsewhere, not in a previous trick, that card is deemed to have belonged continuously to the deficient hand and must be restored to that hand; it may become a penalty card, as provided in Law 23 or 49, and failure to have played it may constitute a revoke.

Law 12   Surplus card

When a player has too many cards and a redeal is not required by Law 10 (c), the deal stands as correct, and

A.   If the offender has omitted to play to a trick, Law 67 applies.

B.   If the offender has picked up a surplus card from a previous trick, or from dummy's hand, or from the other pack, or elsewhere, such surplus card shall be restored to its proper place; and

---

*See Footnote to Law 8.

i] If the surplus card is in the offender's hand when it is discovered, there is no penalty.

ii] If the surplus card had been led or played, or had been played to a previous trick, the offender must substitute for it a card of the same suit as the surplus card. The non-offending side wins that trick. When attention is drawn to the offense before the lead to the next trick, either member of the non-offending side may, without penalty, withdraw a play made subsequent to the offense, and substitute any legal play.

Part 4   General Laws Governing Irregularities

Law 13   Procedure following an irregularity

When an irregularity has occurred, any player — except dummy as restricted by Law 43 — may draw attention to it and give or obtain information as to the law applicable to it. The fact that a player draws attention to an irregularity committed by his side does not affect the rights of the opponents.

After attention has been drawn to an irregularity, no player should call or play until all questions in regard to rectification and to the assessment of a penalty have been determined. Premature correction of an irregularity on the part of the offender may subject him to a further penalty (see Law 26).

Law 14   Assessment of a penalty

A penalty may not be imposed until the nature of the irregularity to be penalized has been determined and the applicable penalty has been clearly stated; but a penalty once paid, or any decision agreed and acted upon by the players, stands and should not be corrected even though at some later time it may be judged incorrect, except by agreement of all four players.

Law 15   Waiver or forfeiture of penalty

The right to penalize an offense is forfeited if a member of the non-offending side

A.   waives the penalty;

B.   calls (Law 34) or plays (Law 60) after an irregularity committed by the opponent to his right.

Law 16   Unauthorized information

A player may be subject to penalty if he conveys information to his partner other than by a legal call or play.

Information conveyed by an illegal call, play or exposure of a card is subject to the applicable law in Part V or VI.

If a player conveys information to his partner by means of a remark or question or by an unmistakable hesitation, special emphasis, tone, gesture, movement, mannerism or any other action that suggests a call, lead or plan of play; and if attention is drawn to the offense immediately, (penalty) either member of the non-offending side (dummy excepted) may prohibit any call or play so suggested.

Part 5   The Auction

Correct Procedure

Law 17   Duration of the Auction

The auction begins when the last card of a correct deal has been placed on the table. The dealer makes the first call, and thereafter each player calls in rotation. When three passes in rotation have followed any call (but see Law 34), the auction is closed.

Law 18   Bids

Each bid must name a number of odd tricks, from one to seven, and a denomination. A bid supersedes the previous bid if it names either a greater number of odd tricks, or the same number of odd tricks in a higher denomination. A bid that fulfills these requirements is sufficient; one that does not is insufficient. The denominations rank in descending order: notrump, spades, hearts, diamonds, clubs.

Law 19   Doubles and redoubles

A player may double only the last preceding bid, and then only if it was made by an opponent and no calls other than pass have intervened.

A player may redouble only the last preceding double, and then only if it was made by an opponent and no calls other than pass have intervened.

A player should not, in doubling or redoubling, state the number of tricks or the denomination; but, if he states either or both incorrectly, he is deemed to have doubled or redoubled the bid as it was made.

All doubles and redoubles are superseded by a subsequent legal bid. If there is no subsequent bid, scoring values are increased as provided in Law 81.

Law 20   Review and explanation

A player who does not hear a call distinctly may forthwith require that it be repeated.

During the auction and at his own turn to call, a player (unless required by law to pass) may require a restatement of the auction in its entirety.

Laws of Contract Bridge, 1981

After the final pass, declarer before playing from dummy, or either defender at his first turn to play, may require a restatement of the auction in its entirety.

A request to have calls restated should be responded to only by an opponent (dummy, or a player required by law to pass, may so respond). All players should promptly correct errors in restatement.

A player may require an explanation of the partnership understanding relating to any call made by an opponent, but only at that player's own turn to call or play. A request for an explanation of a call should be responded to by the partner of the player making the call (see Proprieties 4).

Law 21   Call based on misinformation

A player has no recourse if he has made a call on the basis of his own misunderstanding.

A player may, without penalty, change any call he may have made as a result of misinformation given him by an opponent, provided his partner has not subsequently called. If he elects to correct his call, his left-hand opponent may then, in turn and without penalty, change any subsequent call he may have made.

Law 22   Procedure after the auction is closed

After the auction is closed:

A.   If no player has bid, the hands are abandoned and the turn to deal passes in rotation.

B.   If any player has bid, the final bid becomes the contract and play begins.

Irregularities

Law 23   Card exposed or led during the auction

Whenever, during the auction, a player faces a card on the table or holds a card so that it is possible for his partner to see its face, every such card must be left face up on the table until the auction closes; and (penalty) if the offender subsequently becomes a defender, declarer may treat every such card as a penalty card (Law 50).

In addition:

A.   If it is a single card below the rank of an honor and not prematurely led, there is no further penalty.

B.   If it is a single card of honor rank, or any card prematurely led, or if more than one card is so exposed, (penalty) the offender's partner must pass when next it is his turn to call.

Law 24   Immediate correction of a call

A player may substitute his intended call for an inadvertent call, but only if he does so, or attempts to do so, without pause for thought. If legal, his last call stands without penalty; if illegal, it is subject to the applicable law.

Law 25   Change of call

A call substituted for a call made previously at the same turn, when it is too late for correction as provided in Law 24, is cancelled; and:

A.   If the first call was illegal, the offender is subject to the applicable law.

B.   If the first call was a legal one, the offender must either

> *i*] allow his first call to stand and (penalty) his partner must pass when next it is his turn to call; or
>
> *ii*] make any legal call and (penalty) his partner must pass whenever it is his turn to call.

The offender's partner will also be subject to a lead penalty as provided in Law 26 if he becomes a defender.

Law 26   Change of call — lead penalties

When a player makes a call and subsequently changes it to another legal call (except as permitted under Law 24), then if he becomes a defender:

A.   if the changed call was in a suit, and the substituted call did not repeat that suit, declarer may* either require the offender's partner to lead, or prohibit him from leading, such suit when first the offender's partner has the lead (including the opening lead). A prohibition continues for as long as offender's partner retains the lead. When the irregular call artificially relates to a denomination other than the one actually named, "such suit" is the suit or suits to which the call relates.

B.   if the changed call was

> *i*] in notrump, and his final call at that turn was not, or
>
> *ii*] pass, double or redouble, other than an out-of-rotation call repeated in turn in accordance with Law 30 (a) or 32 (b)(i),

declarer may* prohibit offender's partner from leading any one specified suit when first the offender's partner has the lead (including the opening lead). This prohibition continues for as long as offender's partner retains the lead.

Law 27   Insufficient bid

An insufficient bid made in rotation must be corrected by the substitution of either a sufficient bid or a pass†, unless the irregular bid is accepted. Any insufficient bid may be accepted (treated as legal) at the option of the opponent on offender's left, and is accepted if that opponent calls.

If the call substituted is

---

*Declarer specifies the suit at the time that offender's partner first has the lead.

†The offender is entitled to select his final call at that turn after the applicable penalties have been stated, and any call he has previously attempted to substitute is cancelled, but the lead penalties of Law 26 will apply if he becomes a defender.

A.   the lowest sufficient bid in the same denomination, the auction proceeds as though the irregularity had not occurred.*

B.   any other sufficient bid, or pass, (penalty) the offender's partner must pass whenever it is his turn to call, and the lead penalties of Law 26 will apply if he becomes a defender.

If the offender attempts to substitute a double or redouble, it is cancelled; he must pass at that turn and the offense is subject to the penalty provided in subsection (b) above.

If a player makes an insufficient bid out of rotation, Law 31 applies.

Call Out of Rotation

Law 28   Calls considered to be in rotation

A call is considered to be in rotation

A.   when it is made without waiting for the right-hand opponent to pass, if that opponent is required by law to pass.

B.   when it is made by the player whose turn it was to call, before a penalty has been imposed for a call out of rotation by an opponent; it waives any penalty for the call out of rotation and the auction proceeds as though that opponent had not called at that turn.

Law 29   Procedure after a call out of rotation

After a call out of rotation, the opponent of offender's left† may either:

A.   make any legal call; if he chooses to do so, the call out of rotation stands as if it were legal (but if it is an inadmissible call, see Law 35), and the auction proceeds without penalty; or,

B.   require that the call out of rotation be cancelled. The auction reverts to the player whose turn it was to call. The offender may make any legal call in proper turn but is subject to penalty under Law 30, 31, or 32.

Law 30   Pass out of rotation

When a player has passed out of rotation

A.   before any player has bid, or when it was the turn of the opponent to his right‡ to call, (penalty) the offender must pass when next it is his turn to call.

B.   after any player has bid and when it was the turn of the offender's

---

*Offender's partner must not base any subsequent calls or plays on information gained from such a withdrawn bid.

†He alone exercises the option, although any player may draw attention to the irregularity.

‡After any player has bid, a call at offender's left-hand opponent's turn is a change of call; Law 25 applies and not this section.

partner to call, (penalty) the offender must pass whenever it is his turn to call; the offender's partner may make a sufficient bid or may pass, but may not double or redouble at that turn. The offender's partner will be subject to the lead penalties of Law 26 if he becomes a defender.

Law 31 Bid out of rotation

When a player has bid out of rotation

A. at the turn of offender's partner to call, or before any player has called when the opponent on the offender's left was the dealer, (penalty) the offender's partner must pass whenever it is his turn to call, and the lead penalties of Law 26 will apply if he becomes a defender.

B. at the turn of the opponent on the offender's right* to call,

   i] if that opponent passes, the bid out of rotation must be repeated, and there is no penalty (if the bid out of rotation was insufficient, it must be corrected as provided in Law 27);

   ii] if that opponent makes a legal† bid, double or redouble, the offender may in turn make any legal call. If such call repeats the denomination of the bid out of rotation, (penalty) the offender's partner must pass when next it is his turn to call. If the substituted call does not repeat the denomination, (penalty) the offender's partner must pass whenever it is his turn to call, and lead penalties of Law 26 will apply if he becomes a defender.

Law 32 Double or redouble out of rotation

When a player has doubled or redoubled out of rotation,‡

A. If it was the offender's partner's turn to call, (penalty) the offender's partner must pass whenever it is his turn to call; the offender may not thereafter, in turn, double or redouble the same bid he doubled or redoubled out of turn; and the lead penalties of Law 26 (b) will apply if he becomes a defender.

B. If it was the turn of the opponent on the offender's right‡ to call:

   i] If the opponent on the offender's right passes, the double or redouble out of rotation must be repeated and there is no penalty.

   ii] If the opponent on the offender's right bids, the offender may in turn make any legal call, and (penalty) the offender's partner must pass when next it is his turn to call, and the lead penalties of Law 26 (b) will apply if he becomes a defender.

---

*After any player has called, a call at offender's left-hand opponent's turn is a change of call; law 25 applies and not this section.

†An illegal call by that opponent may be penalized in the usual way, after which this subsection, (b)(ii), applies.

‡After any player has called, a call at offender's left-hand opponent's turn is a change of call; Law 25 applies and not this section.

Laws of Contract Bridge, 1981

Law 33   Simultaneous calls

A call made simultaneously with one made by the player whose turn it was to call is deemed to be a subsequent call.

Law 34   Retention of the right to call

A player may not be deprived of any turn to call by one or more passes following a pass out of rotation, when there has been no subsequent bid.* All such passes — the pass out of rotation, plus the subsequent passes that would serve to end the auction — are cancelled. The bidding reverts to the player whose turn it was to call before the pass out of rotation, and the auction continues as though there had been no irregularity.

Inadmissible Calls

Law 35   Inadmissible call condoned

When, after any inadmissible call specified below, the opponent to the offender's left makes a call before a penalty has been assessed, there is no penalty for the offense (the lead penalties of Law 26 do not apply). If the inadmissible call was

A.   a double or redouble not permitted by Law 19, that call and all subsequent calls are cancelled; the auction reverts to the player whose turn it is to call and proceeds as though there had been no irregularity;

B.   a bid, double or redouble by a player required by law to pass, that call and subsequent legal calls stand; but if the offender was required to pass for the remainder of the auction, he must still pass at subsequent turns;

C.   a bid of more than seven, that call and all subsequent calls are cancelled; the offender must substitute a pass, and the auction proceeds as though there had been no irregularity;

D.   a call after the auction is closed, that call and all subsequent calls are cancelled without penalty.

Law 36   Inadmissible double or redouble

Any double or redouble not permitted by Law 19 is cancelled, and the offender must substitute a legal call: and (penalty) the offender's partner must pass whenever it is his turn to call, and the lead penalties of Law 26 (b) will apply if he becomes a defender. Further, if the bid that was inadmissibly doubled or redoubled becomes the final contract, either member of the non-offending side may specify that the contract be played undoubled.

If the right of the non-offending side to penalize is forfeited, Law 35 applies.

---

*After a pass out of rotation that has been accepted by a pass from the player to offender's left (it thus stands as legal), three passes in rotation may follow a call; apparently, this would end this auction, as provided by Law 17. However, a player would then be deprived of an opportunity to call, and this is not permitted.

Law 37   Bid, double or redouble in violation of the obligation to pass

A bid, double or redouble by a player who is required by law to pass is cancelled, and (penalty) both members of the offending side must pass during the remainder of the auction, and the lead penalties of Law 26 will apply if they become defenders.

Law 38   Bid of more than seven

No play or score at a contract of more than seven is ever permissible. A bid of more than seven by any player is cancelled, and (penalty) both members of the offending side must pass during the remainder of the auction; and the lead penalties of Law 26 will apply if they become defenders.

Law 39   Call after the auction is closed

A call after the auction is closed is cancelled, and:

A.   If it is a pass by a defender or any call by declarer or dummy, there is no penalty.

B.   If it is a bid, double or redouble by a defender, the lead penalties of Law 26 apply, unless the call has been condoned (see Law 35 (d)).

Law 40   Conventions and psychic bids

A player may make any call or play (including an intentionally misleading call such as a 'psychic bid,' or a call or play that departs from commonly accepted or previously announced conventional practice) without prior announcement, provided that it is not based on a partnership understanding. But a player may not make use of a bidding or play convention unless,

A.   his side has disclosed its use of such a call or play beforehand, or

B.   it has been agreed beforehand that the use of partnership understandings be disclosed at the time they are used, and his partner does so disclose it. In this case, partner's disclosure must be confined to an indication that a convention has been used; he should not offer any explanation unless requested to do so.

Any group may, by agreement, restrict the use of conventions in its games.

Part 6   The Play

Correct Procedure

Law 41   Opening lead, review, questions

After the auction closes, the defender on declarer's left makes the opening lead.* After the opening lead, dummy spreads his hand in front of him on the

---

*After the final pass, either defender has the right to ask if it is his opening lead.

table, face up and grouped in suits with the trumps on his right. Declarer plays both his hand and that of dummy.

Declarer, before he plays from dummy, or either defender at his first turn to play, may require a restatement of the auction in its entirety.

After it is too late to have previous calls restated, declarer or either defender is entitled to be informed what the contract is and whether, but not by whom, it was doubled or redoubled.

Either defender may require an explanation of the partnership understanding relating to any call made by an opponent (see Proprieties 4), but only at that defender's own turn to play. Declarer may at any time require an explanation of the partnership understanding relating to any call or play made by a defender.

Law 42 Dummy's rights

Dummy is entitled to give or obtain information as to fact or law; and provided he has not forfeited his rights (see Law 43) he may also:

A.   question players regarding revokes as provided in Law 61;

B.   try to prevent any irregularity,*

C.   draw attention to any irregularity, but only after play is concluded.

Law 43 Dummy's limitations

Dummy may not participate in the play (except to play the cards of dummy's hand as directed by declarer), or make any comment on the bidding, play, or score of the current deal; and if he does so, Law 16 may apply. Dummy may not call attention to an irregularity during play except to try to prevent an irregularity before it occurs.

Dummy forfeits the rights provided in (a), (b) and (c) of Law 42 if he exchanges hands with declarer, leaves his seat to watch declarer play, or, on his own initiative, looks at the face of a card in either defender's hand; and if, thereafter,

A.   He is the first to draw attention to a defender's irregularity, declarer may not enforce any penalty for the offense.

B.   He warns declarer not to lead from the wrong hand, (penalty) either defender may choose the hand from which declarer shall lead.

C.   He is the first to ask declarer if a play from declarer's hand constitutes a revoke, declarer must substitute a correct card if his play was a revoke, and the penalty provisions of Law 64 apply.

Law 44 Sequence and procedure of play

The player who leads to a trick may play any card in his hand.† After the

---

*He may, for example, warn declarer against leading from the wrong hand.

†Unless he is subject to restriction after an irregularity committed by his side.

lead, each other player in turn plays a card, and the four cards so played constitute a trick.

In playing to a trick, each player must follow suit if possible. This obligation takes precedence over all other requirements of these Laws. If unable to follow suit, a player may play any card. *

A trick containing a trump is won by the player who has contributed to it the highest trump. A trick that does not contain a trump is won by the player who has contributed to it the highest card of the suit led. The player who has won the trick leads to the next trick.

Law 45   Card played

Each player except dummy should play a card by detaching it from his hand and placing it, face up, on the table where other players can easily reach and see it. Dummy, if instructed by declarer to do so, may play from his hand a card named or designated by declarer. †

A card must be played:

A.   If it is a defender's card held so that it is possible for his partner to see its face.

B.   If it is a card from declarer's hand that declarer holds face up, touching or nearly touching the table, or maintains in such a position as to indicate that is has been played;

C.   If it is a card in dummy deliberately touched by declarer except for the purpose of arranging dummy's cards or of reaching a card above or below the card or cards touched.

D.   If the player who holds the card names or otherwise designates it as the card he proposes to play. A player may, without penalty, change an inadvertent designation if he does so without pause for thought; but if an opponent has, in turn, played a card that was legal before the change of designation, that opponent may, without penalty, withdraw any card so played and substitute another.

E.   If it is a penalty card, subject to Law 50.

F.   If it is a card in dummy's hand that dummy has illegally suggested as a play, unless either defender forbids the play of such card, or an equal of it, or a card of the same suit, as provided in Law 16.

A card played may not be withdrawn except as provided in Law 47.

---

*Unless he is subject to restriction after an irregularity committed by his side.

†If dummy places in played position a card declarer did not name, the card must be withdrawn if attention is drawn to it before each side has played to the next trick, and a defender may withdraw (without penalty) a card played after the error but before attention was drawn to it (see Law 47).

Laws of Contract Bridge, 1981

Law 46 Partial designation of a card to be played from dummy's hand

When declarer instructs dummy to play a card from dummy's hand, as permitted by Law 45, but names only a suit or only the rank of a card, or the equivalent, without fully specifying the card to be played, declarer must comcompleted his partial designation. Dummy must not play a card before declarer has completed his partial designation, and if dummy prematurely plays a card, Law 16 applies on that trick only, unless a defender has subsequently played.

Law 47 Retraction of a card played

A card once played may be withdrawn only:

A.   to comply with a penalty, or to correct an illegal play, or to correct the simultaneous play of two or more cards (see Law 58);

B.   after a change of designation as permitted by Law 45 (d);

C.   after an opponent's change of play, to substitute a card for one played;*

D.   to correct a play* after misinformation by an opponent. A lead out of turn may be retracted without penalty if the leader was mistakenly informed by an opponent that it was his turn to lead.

Penalty Card

Law 48 Exposure of declarer's cards

Declarer is not subject to penalty for exposing a card, and no card of declarer's or dummy's ever becomes a penalty card. Declarer is not required to play any card dropped accidentally.

When declarer faces his cards after an opening lead out of turn, Law 54 applies.† When declarer faces his cards at any other time, he may be deemed to have made a claim or concession of tricks, in which case Law 68 applies.

Law 49 Exposure of a defender's cards

Whenever a defender faces a card on the table, holds a card so that it is possible for his partner to see its face, or names a card as being in his hand, before he is entitled to do so in the normal course of play or application of the law, (penalty) each such card becomes a penalty card (Law 50).‡

Law 50 Disposition of a penalty card

A card is a penalty card when prematurely exposed. It must be left face up on the table until it is played or until an alternate penalty has been selected.

A single card below the rank of an honor and exposed inadvertently (as in

---

*The offending side must not base any subsequent plays on information gained from such a withdrawn play.

†Declarer should, as a matter of propriety, refrain from spreading his hand.

‡Exposure of a card or cards by a defender who is making a claim or concession of tricks is subject to Law 70.

playing two cards to a trick, or in dropping a card accidentally) becomes a minor-penalty card. Any penalty card of honor rank, or any card exposed through deliberate play (as in leading out of turn, or in revoking and then correcting) becomes a major-penalty card; when one defender has two or more penalty cards, all such cards become major-penalty cards.

When a defender has a minor-penalty card, he may not play any other card of the same suit below the rank of an honor until he has first played the penalty card. (However, he is entitled to play an honor card instead of the minor-penalty card.) There is no further penalty, but the offender's partner must not base any subsequent play on information gained through seeing the penalty card.

When a defender has a major-penalty card, such card must be played at the first legal opportunity, whether in leading, following suit, discarding or trumping. If a defender has two or more penalty cards that can legally be played, declarer may designate which is to be played. The obligation to follow suit, or to comply with a lead or play penalty, takes precedence over the obligation to play a penalty card, but the penalty card must still be left face up on the table and played at the next legal opportunity.

When a defender has the lead while his partner has a major-penalty card, declarer may choose to impose a lead penalty at this point: he may require that defender to lead the suit of the penalty card, or may prohibit that defender from leading that suit (a prohibition continues for as long as he retains the lead). If declarer does impose a lead penalty, the penalty card is picked up at once. If declarer does not, the defender may lead any card; but the penalty card remains a penalty card. The defender may not lead until declarer has indicated his choice.

Law 51   Two or more penalty cards

When a defender has two or more penalty cards in one suit, and declarer requires the defender's partner to lead that suit, the defender may pick up every penalty card in that suit and may make any legal play to the trick.

When a defender has penalty cards in more than one suit, declarer may prohibit the defender's partner from leading every such suit; but the defender may then pick up every penalty card in every suit prohibited by declarer and may make any legal play to the trick.

Law 52   Failure to lead or play a penalty card

When a defender is required by Law 50 to play a penalty card, but instead plays another card, he must leave that illegally played card face up on the table; and

A.   declarer may accept the defender's lead or play, and declarer must accept such lead or play if he has thereafter played from his or dummy's hand, but the unplayed penalty card remains a penalty card; or

B.   declarer may require the defender to substitute the penalty card for the card illegally led or played. Every card illegally led or played by the defender in the course of committing the irregularity becomes a penalty card.

Laws of Contract Bridge, 1981

Lead Out of Turn

Law 53   Lead out of turn accepted

Any lead out of turn may be treated by an opponent as a correct lead. It becomes a correct lead if an opponent accepts it by making a statement to that effect, or if that opponent next to play plays a card to the irregular lead.*

However, the player whose proper turn it was to lead — unless he is the offender's partner — may make his proper lead subsequent to the infraction without his card being treated as played to the irregular lead. The proper lead stands, and all cards played in error to this trick may be withdrawn without penalty.

Law 54   Opening lead out of turn

When a defender makes the opening lead out of turn:

A.   Declarer may accept the irregular lead as provided in Law 53. Dummy's hand is spread in accordance with Law 41, and the second card to the trick is played from declarer's hand; but if declarer first plays to the trick from dummy's hand, dummy's card may not be withdrawn except to correct a revoke.

B.   Declarer must accept the irregular lead if he could have seen any of dummy's cards (except cards exposed during the auction, subject to Law 23). He is deemed to have accepted the irregular lead if he begins to spread his hand as though he were dummy† and in so doing exposes one or more cards; declarer must spread his entire hand, and dummy becomes declarer.‡

C.   Declarer may require the defender to retract his irregular lead (except as provided in (b) above), and then Law 56 applies.

Law 55   Declarer's lead out of turn

When declarer leads out of turn from his or dummy's hand;

A.   Either defender may accept that lead as provided in Law 53.

B.   Either defender may require declarer to retract that lead. Then,

       i] if it was a defender's turn to lead, declarer restores the card led in error to his or dummy's hand, without penalty;

      ii] if declarer has led from the wrong hand when it was his turn to lead from his or dummy's hand, he withdraws the card led in error; he must lead a card from the correct hand, and, (penalty) if able to do so, a card of the same suit. Failure to observe this obligation in playing from his own hand is a revoke (see Law 64).

---

*When such a play is made by a defender who is not next to play after the irregular lead, Law 57 applies.

†Declarer should, as a matter of propriety, refrain from spreading his hand intentionally.

‡However, if cards are so exposed from both declarer's and dummy's hands, the player who was regularly to become declarer remains declarer.

Law 56   Defender's lead out of turn

When a defender leads out of turn:

A.   Declarer may accept that lead as provided in Law 53.

B.   Declarer may require the defender to retract that lead; the card illegally led becomes a major-penalty card (see Law 50 — note that lead penalties are provided).

Irregular Leads and Plays

Law 57   Premature lead or play by a defender

When a defender leads to the next trick before his partner has played to the current trick, or plays out of turn before his partner has played, (penalty) declarer may require the offender's partner to play:

A.   his highest card of the suit led; or

B.   his lowest card of the suit led; or

C.   a legal card of another suit specified by declarer.

Declarer must select one of these options, and if the offender's partner cannot comply with the penalty selected he may play any card, as provided in Law 59.

When, as a result of the application of the penalty, the offender's partner wins the current trick, he leads to the next trick; and any card led or played out of turn by the other defender becomes a penalty card (Law 50).

A defender is not subject to penalty for playing before his partner if declarer has played from both hands; but a singleton or one of two or more equal cards in dummy is not considered automatically played unless dummy has played the card or has illegally suggested that it be played (Law 45 (f)).

Law 58   Simultaneous leads or plays

A lead or play made simultaneously with another player's legal lead or play is deemed to be subsequent to it.

If a defender leads or plays two or more cards simultaneously, and if only one such card is visible, he must play that card; if more than one card is exposed, he must designate the card he proposes to play and each other card exposed becomes a penalty card (Law 50).

If declarer leads or plays two or more cards simultaneously from either hand, he must designate the card he proposes to play and must restore any other card to the correct hand. If declarer withdraws a visible card and a defender has already played to that card, such defender may, without penalty, withdraw his card and substitute another.

If the error remains undiscovered until both sides have played to the next trick, Law 67 applies.

Law 59 *Inability to lead or play as required*

A player may play any correct card if he is unable to lead or play as required to comply with a penalty, either because he has no card of the required suit, or because he has only cards of a suit he is prohibited from leading, or because of his obligation to follow suit.

Law 60 *Play after an illegal play*

A play by a member of the non-offending side after the opponent on his right has led or played out of turn prematurely, and before a penalty has been imposed, forfeits the right to penalize the offense. The illegal play is treated as though it were legal, (except as provided in Law 53 for a play by the proper leader), unless it constitutes a revoke. If the offending side had a previous obligation to play a penalty card or to comply with a lead or play penalty, the obligation remains at future turns.

When a defender plays after declarer has been required to retract his lead out of turn from either hand, but before declarer has led from the correct hand, the defender's card becomes a penalty card (Law 50).

A play by a member of the offending side before a penalty has been imposed does not affect the rights of the opponents and may itself be subject to penalty.

The Revoke

Law 61 *Failure to follow suit — inquiries concerning a revoke*

Failure to follow suit in accordance with Law 44, or failure to lead or play, when able, a card or suit required by law or specified by an opponent in accordance with an agreed penalty, constitutes a revoke. Any player, including dummy,* may ask a player who has failed to follow suit whether he has a card of the suit led, and may demand that an opponent correct his revoke. (A claim of revoke does not warrant inspection of quitted tricks, except as permitted in Law 66.)

Law 62 *Correction of a revoke*

A player must correct his revoke if he becomes aware of the occurrence of the revoke before it becomes established. To correct a revoke, the offender withdraws the card he played in revoking and follows suit with any card. A card so withdrawn becomes a penalty card (Law 50) if it was played from a defender's unfaced hand. The card may be replaced without penalty if it was played from declarer's or dummy's hand† or if it was a defender's faced card. Each member of the non-offending side may, without penalty, withdraw any card he may have played after the revoke but before attention was drawn to it. Except as

---

*Unless he has forfeited his rights, as specified by Law 43.

†Subject to Law 43. A claim of revoke does not warrant inspection of quitted tricks except as permitted in Law 67.

provided in the next paragraph, the partner of the offender may not withdraw his card unless it too constituted a revoke.*

After the eleventh trick, a revoke, even if established, must be corrected if discovered before the cards have been mixed together. If the revoke was committed by a defender before his partner has played to the twelfth trick, and if offender's partner holds cards of more than one suit, (penalty) declarer may then require the offender's partner to play to that trick either of the two cards he could legally have played.

Law 63   Establishment of a revoke

A revoke becomes established when the offender or his partner leads or plays (whether legally or illegally) to the following trick, or names or otherwise designates a card to be so played, or makes a claim or concession of tricks orally or by facing his hand. The revoke may then no longer be corrected (except for a revoke after the eleventh trick — see Law 62), and the trick on which the revoke occurred stands as played.

Law 64   Procedure after establishment of a revoke

When a revoke has become established,

A.   if the trick on which the revoke occurred was won by the offending side, (penalty) after play ceases, the trick on which the revoke occurred plus one of any subsequent tricks won by the offending side are transferred† to the non-offending side (if no subsequent trick was won by the offending side, only the revoke trick is transferred).

B.   if the trick on which the revoke occurred was won by the non-offending side, (penalty) after play ceases, one of any subsequent tricks won by the offending side is transferred† to the non-offending side;

C.   there is no trick penalty for the established revoke if,

> i] the offending side did not win either the trick on which the revoke occurred or any subsequent trick; or if,
>
> ii] the revoke was a subsequent revoke in the same suit by the same player; or if,
>
> iii] the revoke was made in failing to play any card faced on the table or belonging to a hand faced on the table, including a card from dummy's hand; or if,
>
> iv] attention was first drawn to the revoke after all players had abandoned their hands and permitted the cards to be mixed together; or if,
>
> v] the revoke was made after the eleventh trick.

N.B. When any established revoke, including one not subject to penalty, causes damage to the non-offending side insufficiently compensated by this law,

---

*In such case, the card withdrawn becomes a penalty card if it was played from a defender's unfaced hand.

†For the scoring of transferred tricks, see Law 77.

the offending side should, under Proprieties 1, transfer additional tricks so as to restore equity.

Tricks

Law 65   *Collection and arrangement of tricks*

The cards constituting each completed trick are collected by a member of the side that won the trick and are then turned face down on the table. Each trick should be identifiable as such, and all tricks taken by a side should be arranged in sequence in front of declarer or of one defender, as the case may be, in such manner that each side can determine the number of tricks it has won and the order in which they were taken.

Law 66   *Inspection of tricks*

Declarer or either defender may, until a member of his side has led or played to the following trick, inspect a trick and inquire what card each player has played to it. Thereafter, until play ceases, quitted tricks may be inspected only to account for a missing or surplus card. After play ceases, the tricks and un-played cards may be inspected to settle a claim of a revoke, of honors, or of the number of tricks won or lost. If, after a claim has been made, a player on one side mixes the cards in such a way that the facts can no longer be ascertained, the issue must be decided in favor of the other side.

Law 67   *Trick either appropriated in error or defective*

A trick appropriated by the wrong side must, upon demand, be restored to the side that has in fact won the trick by contributing the winning card to it. The scoring value of the trick must be credited to that side.*

A trick containing more or fewer than four cards is defective. When one player is found, during play, to have fewer or more cards than all the other players, the previous tricks should be forthwith examined, face down; if a defective trick is discovered, the player with a correspondingly incorrect number of cards is held responsible. The defective trick is inspected, face up, and —

A.   Unless all four hands have played to a subsequent trick, the defective trick is rectified as follows:

> *i*] If the offender has failed to play a card to the defective trick, he adds to that trick a card he can legally play:
>
> *ii*] If the offender has played more than one card to the defective trick, he withdraws all but one card, leaving a card he can legally play;
>
> *iii*] The non-offending side may, without penalty, withdraw any cards played after the irregularity and before attention was drawn to it; but the offending side may not withdraw cards that constitute

---

*If calls have been made on a subsequent deal, see Law 78.

legal plays, and any cards they withdraw may become penalty cards (Law 50).

B.   After all four hands have played to a subsequent trick, (penalty) the defective trick, if won by the offending side, is transferred to the non-offending side; and

>   *ii*] If the offender has failed to play a card to the defective trick, he forthwith faces and adds a card to that trick, if possible one he could legally have played to it.

>   *ii*] If the offender has played more than one card to the defective trick, he withdraws all but one card, leaving the highest card he could legally have played to that trick. A withdrawn card may become a penalty card (Law 50); such a card is deemed to have belonged continuously to the offender's hand and failure to have played it to an earlier trick may constitute a revoke.

Claims and Concessions

Law 68   Declarer's claim or concession of tricks

Declarer makes a claim or a concession whenever he announces that he will win or lose one or more of the remaining tricks, or suggests that play may be curtailed, or faces his hand. Declarer should not make a claim or concession if there is any doubt as to the number of tricks to be won or lost.

Law 69   Procedure following declarer's claim or concession

When declarer has made a claim or concession, play is temporarily suspended and declarer must place and leave his hand face up on the table and forthwith make a comprehensive statement as to his proposed plan of play, including the order in which he will play the remaining cards.

Declarer's claim or concession is allowed, and the deal is scored accordingly, if both defenders agree to it. The claim or concession must be allowed if either defender has permitted any of his remaining cards to be mixed with another player's cards; otherwise, if either defender disputes declarer's claim or concession, it is not allowed. Then, play continues.

When his claim or concession is not allowed, declarer must play on, leaving his hand face up on the table. At any time, either defender may face his hand for inspection by his partner, and declarer may not impose a penalty for any irregularity committed by a defender whose hand is so faced.

The objective of subsequent play is to achieve a result as equitable as possible to both sides, but any doubtful point must be resolved in favor of the defenders. Declarer may not make any play inconsistent with the statement he may have made at the time of his claim or concession. And if he failed to make an appropriate statement at that time, his choice of plays is restricted thereby:

A.   If declarer made no relevant statement, he may not finesse* in any suit

---

*For these purposes, a finesse is a play the success of which depends on finding one defender rather than the other with or without a particular card.

unless an opponent failed to follow in that suit before the claim or concession, or would subsequently fail to follow in that suit on any conceivable sequence of plays.

B.   If declarer may have been unaware, at the time of his claim or concession, that a trump remained in a defender's hand, either defender may require him to draw, or not to draw, the outstanding trump.

C.   If declarer did not, in his statement, mention an unusual plan of play, he may adopt only a routine line of play.

If declarer attempts to make a play prohibited under this law, either defender may accept the play, or, provided neither defender has subsequently played, require declarer to withdraw the card so played and substitute another that conforms to his obligations.

Law 70   Defender's claim or concession of tricks

A defender makes a concession when he agrees to declarer's claim, or when he announces that he will lose one or more of the remaining tricks.

A defender makes a claim when he announces that he will win one or more of the remaining tricks, or when he shows any or all of his cards for this purpose. If:

A.   the claim pertains only to an uncompleted trick currently in progress, play proceeds normally; cards exposed or otherwise revealed by the defender in making his claim do not become penalty cards, but Law 16, Unauthorized Information, may apply to claimer's partner.

B.   the claim pertains to subsequent tricks, play is temporarily suspended; the claimer must place and leave his hand face up on the table and make a comprehensive statement as to his proposed plan of defense. The claim is allowed, and the deal scored accordingly, if declarer agrees to it. If declarer disputes the claim, the defenders must play on with the claimer's hand face up on the table. Those cards do not become penalty cards. However, declarer may prohibit claimer's partner, under Law 16, from making any play that could be suggested to him by seeing the faced cards.

Law 71   Concession withdrawn

A concession may be withdrawn:

A.   If a player concedes a trick his side has, in fact, won; or if declarer concedes defeat of a contract he has already fulfilled; or if a defender concedes fulfillment of a contract his side has already defeated. (If the score has been entered, see Law 78).

B.   If a trick that has been conceded cannot be lost by any probable sequence of play of the remaining cards, and if attention is drawn to that fact before the cards have been mixed together.

C.   If a defender concedes one or more tricks and his partner immediately objects, but Law 16 may apply.

Part 7   **The Score**

Law 72   Points earned

The result of each deal played is recorded in points, which fall into two classes:

1.   *Trick points.* Only declarer's side can earn trick points, and only by winning at least the number of odd tricks specified in the contract. Only the value of odd tricks named in the contract may be scored as trick points (see Law 81). Trick points mark the progression of the rubber toward its completion.

2.   *Premium Points.* Either side or both sides may earn premium points. Declarer's side earns premium points by winning one or more overtricks; by fulfilling a doubled or redoubled contract; by bidding and making a slam; by holding scorable honors in declarer's or dummy's hand; or by winning the final game of a rubber. * The defenders earn premium points by defeating the contract (undertrick penalty) or by holding scorable honors in either of their hands (see Law 81).

Each side's premium points are added to its trick points at the conclusion of the rubber.

Law 73   Partscore — game

The basic units of trick scores are partscore and game. A partscore is recorded for declarer's side whenever declarer fulfills a contract for which the trick score is less than 100 points. Game is won by that side which is the first to have scored 100 or more trick points either in a single deal or by addition of two or more partscores made separately. No partscore made by either side in the course of one game is carried forward into the next game.

Law 74   The rubber

A rubber ends when a side has won two games. At the conclusion of the rubber, the winners of two games are credited with a premium score of 500 points if the other side has won one game, or with 700 points if the other side has not won a game. The trick and premium points scored by each side in the course of the rubber are then added. The side with the larger combined total wins the rubber, and the difference between the two totals represents the margin of victory computed in points.

Law 75   Method of scoring

The score of each deal must be recorded, and it is preferable that a member of each side should keep score.

Scores are entered in two adjacent columns separated by a vertical line. Each scorer enters points earned by his side in the left-hand column, and points earned by his opponents in the right-hand column.

Each side has a trick score and a premium score, separated by a horizontal

---

*For incomplete rubber, see Law 80.

line intersecting the vertical line. All trick points are entered, as they are earned, in descending order below the horizontal line, all premium points in ascending order above that line.

Whenever a game is won, another horizontal line is drawn under all trick scores recorded for either side, in order to mark completion of the game. Subsequent trick scores are entered below that line.

Law 76   Responsibility for the score

When the play of a deal is completed, all four players are equally responsible for ascertaining that the number of tricks won by each side is correctly determined and that all scores are promptly and correctly entered.

Law 77   Transferred tricks

A trick transferred through a revoke penalty is reckoned for all scoring purposes as though it had been won in play by the side to which it had been awarded.*

Law 78   Correction of the score

When it is acknowledged by a majority of the players that a scoring error was made in recording an agreed-upon result (e.g., failure to enter honors, or incorrect computation of score), the error must be corrected if discovered before the net score of the rubber has been agreed to. However, except with the consent of all four players, an erroneous agreement as to the number of tricks won by each side may not be corrected after all players have called on the next deal.

In case of disagreement between two scores kept, the recollection of the majority of the players as to the facts governs.

Law 79   Deals played with an incorrect pack

Scores recorded for deals played with an incorrect pack are not subject to change by reason of the discovery of the imperfection after the cards have been mixed together.

Law 80   Incomplete rubber

When, for any reason, a rubber is not finished, the score is computed as follows:

If only one game has been completed, the winners of that game are credited with 300 points; if only one side has a partscore or scores in a game not completed, that side is credited with 50 points; the trick and premium points of each side are then added, and the side with the greater number of points wins the difference between the two totals.

---

*Declarer plays in 3 ♡ and makes eight tricks. A revoke by a defender is found to have been established, with the defenders having won both the trick in which the revoke occurred and a later trick. Two tricks are transferred from the defenders to declarer, who therefore has ten tricks. Since he bid only 3 ♡ , he scored 90 trick points, which count toward game, and 30 premium points for the overtrick.

Law 81   Scoring table

	Odd Tricks Bid and Won in	Undoubled	Doubled
TRICK POINTS FOR CONTRACTORS	Clubs or Diamonds, each	20	40
	Hearts or Spades, each	30	60
	No Trump {first	40	80
	{each subsequent	30	60

Redoubling doubles the doubled points for Odd Tricks.
Vulnerability does not affect points for Odd Tricks.
100 Trick Points constitute a game.

		Not Vulnerable	Vulnerable
PREMIUM POINTS FOR CONTRACTORS	*Overtricks*		
	Undoubled, each	Trick Value	Trick Value
	Doubled, each	100	200
	Making Doubled or Redoubled Contract	50	50
DEFENDERS	*Undertricks*		
	Undoubled, each	50	100
	Doubled { first	100	200
	{ each subsequent	200	300

Redoubling doubles the doubled points for Overtricks and Undertricks,
but does not affect the points for making Doubled Contracts.

PREMIUM POINTS FOR CONTRACTORS|HOLDERS	*Honors in* { 4 Trump Honors	100
	One Hand { 5 Trump Honors or 4 Aces at No-Trump	150
	Slams Bid { Small, not vulnerable 500, vulnerable	750
	and Won { Grand, " " 1000, "	1500
	Rubber { Two game	700
	Points { Three game	500

Unfinished Rubber—Winners of one game score 300 points. If but one
side has a part score in an unfinished game, it scores 50 points.
Doubling and Redoubling do not affect Honor, Slam, or Rubber points.
Vulnerability does not affect points for Honors.

Laws of Contract Bridge, 1981

Proprieties

1. General Principles

These Laws cannot cover every situation that might arise, nor can they produce equity in every situation covered. Occasionally, the players themselves must redress damage. The guiding principle: the side that commits an irregularity bears an obligation not to gain directly from the infraction itself; however, the offending side is entitled to profit after an infraction, as an indirect result, through subsequent good fortune.*

To infringe a law of propriety intentionally is a serious breach of ethics, even if there is a prescribed penalty that one is willing to pay. The offense may be the more serious when no penalty is prescribed.

There is no obligation to draw attention to an inadvertent infraction of law committed by one's own side. However, a player should not attempt to conceal such an infraction, as by committing a second revoke, concealing a card involved in a revoke or mixing the cards prematurely.

It is proper to warn partner against infringing a law of the game: for example against revoking, or against calling, leading or playing out of turn.

2. Communication Between Partners

Communication between partners during the auction and play should be effected only by means of the calls and plays themselves, not through the manner in which they are made, nor through extraneous remarks and gestures, nor through questions asked of the opponents and explanations given to them.

---

*Two examples may clarify the distinction between direct gain through an infraction and indirect gain through good luck.

(a) South, declarer at 3NT, will have nine tricks available if the diamond suit — ace-king-queen-sixth in dummy opposite declarer's singleton — divides favorably; and the six missing diamonds are in fact split evenly, three-three, between East and West. However, West, who holds jack-third, shows out on the third round of diamonds, revoking. Thus, declarer wins only three diamond tricks instead of six, for a total of six tricks instead of nine. The established revoke is later discovered, so one penalty trick is transferred after play ends. But declarer is still down two.

Here, East-West gained two tricks as a direct consequence of their infraction. The players should adjudicate this result, scoring the deal as 3 NT making three. (Note, declarer is not given a penalty trick in addition; the object is to restore equity, to restore the result likely to have occurred had the infraction not been committed.)

(b) South, declarer at 4 ♠, is entitled to require or forbid a diamond opening lead from West, because of the auction-period infraction committed by East. Declarer instructs West to lead a diamond — but West, having no diamonds, leads another suit. East, now aware that partner is void in diamonds, is able to find what would be, under normal circumstances, a most unnatural line of defense to give West two ruffs. Thereby, East-West defeat a contract that would almost certainly have been made but for the infraction.

Here, East-West profited only indirectly through their auction-period infraction; their gain was the direct consequence of declarer's decision to require a diamond lead, and of West's lucky void. So, the players should allow the result to stand. Declarer was damaged not by the infraction itself, but by bad luck afterwards — and luck is part of the game of bridge.

Calls should be made in a uniform tone without special emphasis or inflection, and without undue hesitation or haste. Plays should be made without emphasis, gesture or mannerism and so far as possible at a uniform rate.

Inadvertently to vary the tempo or manner in which a call or play is made does not in itself constitute a violation of propriety, but inferences from such variation may properly be drawn only by an opponent, and at his own risk. It is improper to attempt to mislead an opponent by means of a remark or a gesture, through the haste or hesitancy of a call or play (such as hesitation with a singleton) or by the manner in which the call or play is made.

Any player may properly attempt to deceive an opponent through a call or play (so long as the deception is not protected by concealed partnership understanding). It is entirely proper to avoid giving information to the opponents by making all calls and plays in unvarying tempo and manner.

When a player has available to him improper information from his partner's remark, question, explanation, gesture, mannerism, special emphasis, inflection, haste or hesitation, he should carefully avoid taking any advantage that might accrue to his side.

3. Conduct and Etiquette

A player should maintain at all times a courteous attitude toward his partner and opponents. He should carefully avoid any remark or action that might cause annoyance or embarrassment to another player or might interfere with the enjoyment of the game. Every player should follow uniform and correct procedure in calling and playing, since any departure from correct standards may disrupt the orderly progress of the game.

As a matter of courtesy, a player should refrain from:

(i) Paying insufficient attention to the game (as when a player obviously takes no interest in his hand, or frequently requests a review of the auction).

(ii) Making gratuitous comments during the play as to the auction or the adequacy of the contract.

(iii) Detaching a card from his hand before it is his turn to lead or play.

(iv) Arranging completed tricks in a disorderly manner, thereby making it difficult to determine the sequence of plays.

(v) Making a claim or concession of tricks if there is any doubt as to the outcome of the deal.

(vi) Prolonging play unnecessarily for the purpose of disconcerting the other players.

Furthermore, the following are considered breaches of propriety:

(a) Using different designations for the same call.

(b) Indicating approval or disapproval of a call or play.

(c) Indicating the expectation or intention of winning or losing a trick that has not been completed.

(d) Commenting or behaving during the auction or play so as to call attention to a significant occurrence, or to the state of the score or to the number of tricks still required for success.

(e) Volunteering information that should be given only in response to a question.

(f) Looking intently at any other player during the auction or play, or at another player's hand as for the purpose of seeing his cards or of observing the place from which he draws a card (but it is not improper to act on information acquired by inadvertently seeing an opponent's card).

(g) Varying the normal tempo of bidding or play for the purpose of disconcerting another player.

(h) Mixing the cards before the result of a deal has been agreed upon.

4. Partnership Agreements

It is improper to convey information by means of a call or play based on special partnership agreement, whether explicit or implicit, unless such information is fully and freely available to the opponents.

It is not improper for a player to violate an announced partnership agreement, so long as his partner is unaware of the violation (but habitual violations within a partnership may create implicit agreements, which must be disclosed). No player has the obligation to disclose to the opponents that he has violated an announced agreement; and if the opponents are subsequently damaged, as through drawing a false inference from such violation, they are not entitled to redress.

When explaining the significance of partner's call or play in reply to an opponent's inquiry, a player should disclose all special information conveyed to him through partnership agreement or partnership experience; but he need not disclose inferences drawn from his general bridge knowledge and experience. It is improper for a player whose partner has given a mistaken explanation to correct the error immediately or to indicate in any manner that a mistake has been made. (He must not take advantage of the unauthorized information so obtained).

5. Spectators

A spectator, including a member of the table not playing, must not display any reaction to bidding or play while a hand is in progress (as by shifting his attention from one player's hand to another's). He must not in any way disturb a player. During the hand, he must refrain from mannerisms or remarks of any kind (including conversation with a player). He may not call attention to any irregularity or mistake, nor speak on any question of fact or law except by request of the players.

A brief refresher on
How bridge is played

The Laws of Contract Bridge (page 653) describe in detail how the game is played but the following summary will make it possible for the beginner, or the player who wishes to refresh his memory, to understand the basic fundamentals in a very few minutes.

Contract bridge is a partnership game for four, played with a standard 52-card deck made up of four suits: Spades (♠), Hearts (♡), Diamonds (◇), and Clubs (♣). Each suit has 13 cards, ranking Ace (high), King, Queen, Jack, 10, 9, 8, 7, 6, 5, 4, 3, 2 (low).

After partnerships have been determined and partners are seated across the table from each other, the cards are shuffled, cut, and dealt out one at a time, face down, clockwise beginning at dealer's left. Dealer gets the last card. Pick up your hand and sort it into suits by rank.

The game begins with the *bidding* or *auction* and the dealer has the right to speak first. But before you bid you want to know what you are bidding *for,* so let us talk first about how the cards are played.

You win at contract bridge by scoring *points.* You score points mainly by winning *tricks.* A *trick* is a round of four cards, one from each player, placed face up on the table, clockwise in turn. The first card played to a trick is the *lead.* The *leader* may play any card in his hand. If a player has any card of the suit that is led, he must play one. (If he has more than one, he may choose which one, and he is not compelled to play a higher one if he does not wish to.)

If everyone follows suit, the trick is won by the highest card played. For example:

WEST (leader)	NORTH	EAST	SOUTH
♠ J	♠ Q	♠ K	♠ A

West was the leader. He led the Jack of Spades. North topped this card by playing the Queen of Spades, East in turn tried to win the trick by playing the King, but South played the Ace and won the trick.

Suppose that East had played a lower Spade than the King. At the time South played, if he held other Spades he could play a low one and, since North is South's partner, his side would win the trick. So North could, *if he wished,* save his Ace in order to win a later trick in Spades. In other words, the tricks won by players of the same side are counted together when the deal is over, so usually you will wish to have your side win the trick as cheaply as possible.

If you do not have a card of the suit led, you may play *any* card of *any* suit. This gives you another way to win a trick if the hand is being played at a *trump* contract. Unless the successful bidder elected to play the hand at *No Trump* (i.e., without a trump suit), he will have named one of the suits as trumps. Every card of the trump suit is higher than any card of any *other* suit and will win the trick against anything but a *higher trump*. Remember, however, that you may not trump or play a card of any *other* suit if you have in your hand a card of the suit that was led.

Suppose, for instance, that in the example shown earlier, East did not have any Spade in his hand and the declared trump suit was Diamonds. After North played the Queen of Spades, East could play any Diamond, even the 2, and win the trick unless South also did not have any Spades and was able to play a higher Diamond. In that case, South could win the trick with a higher Diamond. East has *trumped* and South has *overtrumped. A trump wins a trick against any card but a higher trump.*

However, South can play a trump only if he, too, has no Spades, the suit that was led. Otherwise he must follow suit. Of course, if he has lower Spades, he will play a low one since no matter how high a Spade he plays, East's trump will win the trick. South will therefore try to save his high Spades to win tricks later on.

A player who cannot follow suit is not compelled to trump, nor is he compelled to play a trump if some other player has already trumped the trick. Suppose, for example, that West had led the Ace of Spades. East has no Spades, but his partner's Ace is high. Instead of trumping, therefore, he may play a card of any other suit, called a *discard.*

However, with the West and North cards as shown, West leading the Jack of Spades and North playing the Queen, suppose that East trumps the trick with the 10 of Diamonds. If South is also out of

Spades, he must play a higher *Diamond* (trump) in order to win the trick. He is not compelled to do so. No matter how many Diamonds he has in his hand, he may elect to discard a card of any other suit and allow East to win the trick. But he cannot win the trick by playing a higher card of another suit—for example the Jack of Hearts. To win the trick, he must play a higher *Diamond*. The *rank* of a *discard* has no bearing on the winning of a trick.

Suppose that the trick consisted of the following cards:

WEST (leader)	NORTH	EAST	SOUTH
♠ 2	◊ 6	◊ 8	♡ J

West led the 2 of Spades. No other player had a Spade in his hand. If the contract was No Trump, or if the trump suit was Clubs, the 2 of Spades would win the trick because it is the highest card of the suit led and because no other player had trumped it.

Thus, as you have seen, there are *three* ways to win tricks: 1. By playing the highest card of the suit led. 2. By trumping or overtrumping. 3. By playing a card of a suit which no one else can follow and which no one else trumps. In reality, this is the same as (1), except that such low cards become high only after the high cards of a suit have been exhausted; when a trick is won by a low card that has become *established* as a high card it is called a *long* card.

You can see now that one of the objects of bidding is to name the final declaration that will allow the combined hands of you and your partner to win the greatest number of tricks. If you have high cards in all suits, you will wish to protect them by playing at a contract of No Trump. If you have long cards in a suit—or if your partner has named a suit in which he is long and you have a few cards in that suit and shortage in some other suit—you will be bidding to make that suit the trump suit so that you can win the most tricks by trumping.

The bidding. In order to *bid*, you name a number from one to seven and a *suit* which you would like to make trumps, or *No Trump*, which means you would like to play the hand without any trump suit.

The first six tricks the bidder wins, called the *book*, do not count toward his bid. Your lowest possible bid, 1 Club, undertakes to win seven tricks if clubs are trumps. Your highest possible bid, 7 No Trumps, proposes to take all thirteen tricks—a grand slam.

The highest bid in the auction becomes the *contract*. If you are able to fulfill your contract, your side scores points for every trick over your book. If you fail (are *set*), the opponents will collect penalty points for each trick by which you fall short. (See Scoring Table—page 656.)

The auction: The dealer speaks first. He may *bid* or *pass*.

Thereafter, each player in turn may *pass*, *bid*, *double* an opponent's bid or *redouble* an opponent's double. A pass, double or redouble is not a bid but a *call*. A player may bid or call only when it is his turn.

Each new bid must be higher than the last. In bidding, the suits rank: Clubs (low), Diamonds, Hearts, Spades. You can bid 1 Diamond over one Club; one Spade over any other suit. No trump is the highest bid, so 1 No Trump beats any bid of one in a suit. However, a bid for a greater number of tricks outranks any bid for a lesser number. Example: Four Clubs over a bid of three no trump.

A double or redouble does not raise the level of the last bid; it merely increases the points scored for each trick if that bid becomes the final contract.

After any new bid, double or redouble, each other player gets another turn. Three successive passes after any bid are like the auctioneer's "Going, going, gone!" The third pass ends the bidding. (If none of the four players wishes to bid—i.e., if there are four passes, beginning with the dealer—the hand is thrown in and a new hand is dealt by the next dealer; the player to the left of the previous dealer.)

After the auction: If your side did not make the high bid, you and your partner become the *defenders*. The opponent who first bid the suit (or No Trump) which became the final *contract* is the *declarer*. The *defender* sitting at declarer's left opens the *play* by selecting a card from his hand and placing it face up in the center of the table.

After the *opening lead*, declarer's partner places his entire hand face up in front of him. In turn thereafter the declarer will play the cards from this hand (called the *dummy*) as well as the cards from his own hand.

When each hand has played, the *trick* is complete. It is gathered up and placed face down, in a separate bundle, before one player of the side that won it. One partner keeps all the tricks for his side.

How to win points. You win a large number of points in contract bridge: when your opponents bid too high and you collect a big penalty; and when your side, as declarer, makes a *game* or a *slam* and wins a *rubber*.

To win the *rubber* and earn the bonus it carries you must win two *games* before your opponents win two. To win a game, you must score

100 points or more "below the line" that runs horizontally across the bridge score. And the only points you may enter "below the line" are those you earn for the tricks your side has *bid for and made*.

WE	THEY
	60
	60
100	

On the first deal THEY bid 2 spades and made 4. The 60 points for tricks for which they had not bid had to be scored above the line. On the next hand, WE bid and made 3 no trump.

You need not make the entire 100 points in a single deal. If you earn 60 points on one deal, you can claim the *game* by adding 40 points or more on a later deal—provided the opponents don't beat you to it by scoring 100 first. Whenever one side earns 100 or more "below," another horizontal line is drawn across the score and both sides start again at zero on the next game.

If you make more tricks than you have bid for, you get credit for them "above the line" where they do not count toward game. That is why you should bid enough to score the points you need for a game any time there is a good chance you will make it.

You will see from the Scoring Table (page 681) that, in order to make 100 points or more in a single deal, you must bid 3 No Trump, 4 Spades or Hearts, 5 Clubs or Diamonds.

Of course, if the opponents *double* your bid, you score the doubled value of your tricks under the line if you make your contract. But you also pay a much heavier penalty above the line if you are defeated; heavier still if your side has already scored a game and you are therefore *vulnerable*.

Glossary

Above the Line   The place on the Bridge Score Sheet where premiums and penalties are entered.

Ace Showing   A control-showing cue bid by opener or responder.

Advance Save   A premature sacrifice bid to make the opponents guess as to their best spot.

Asking Bid   A bid in a new suit requesting partner to show specific controls.

Assist   Raise in suit bid by partner.

Attacking Lead   A daring lead from a high-card combination; as opposed to a safer lead.

Auction   The period of bidding.

Automatic Squeeze   A simple squeeze which operates against either opponent.

Avoidance   A deliberate plan of play designed to keep the danger hand from regaining the lead.

Bad Hand   A flat hand with little or no honor strength.

Balancing   Reopening with a bid after the opposing bidding has stopped.

Barred Bid; Barred Play   A legal penalty imposed because of a breach of the Laws.

Below the Line   The place on the Bridge Score Sheet where contracted trick points are entered.

Biddable Suit   A holding which meets the minimum requirements for a bid in terms of both length and honor strength.

Blocking   Deliberate play that prevents the running of an established suit.

Blue Team   The popular name of the Italian international bridge team famed for its repeated successes in the World Team Championships (Bermuda Bowl) between 1957 and 1969, when they retired. They returned in 1972 to capture the World Team Olympiad which they had also won in 1964 and 1968.

Blue Team Club   A system played by certain members of the Blue Team.

Board   The dummy hand, the term describing an entire duplicate deal (see Duplicate Board).

Book   The number of tricks (six) a side must win before it can score toward its bid.

Break   The distribution of the outstanding cards in a suit. A "good break" implies an even distribution and so on (see Split).

Bring In   To establish and run a side suit.

Business Double   A penalty double.

Busy Card   A card which cannot be spared in the play of the hand during development of a squeeze position.

Call   Any bid, double, redouble or pass.

Card Reading   Drawing inferences about the opponent's holdings from the bidding and the fall of the cards.

Cash   To win a trick or tricks.

Chicago   A four-deal bridge game especially as played in rubber bridge clubs.

Coffee-Housing   Behaving unethically with the intention of misleading opponents.

Come-On   A signal (usually a high card) by a defender wishing the suit to be continued (see Echo).

Communication Play   A play designed to preserve entry between partnership hands.

Condoning   Waiving a penalty for an irregularity by bidding or playing before attention has been drawn to a breach of the Laws.

Cooperative Double   A double that gives partner the option of passing for penalties or bidding further.

Coup En Passant   To promote a losing trump into a winner by leading a plain-suit card through a player having a higher trump.

Cover   To play a higher card.

Crossruff   The play of a hand whereby trump tricks are made separately by both hands of the partnership.

Dealer   The player who distributes the cards at the bridge table.

Deep Finesse   A finesse of a lower card when missing two or more cards higher in rank.

Defensive Bid   A bid made by a side after the opponent has opened.

Demand Bid   A forcing bid which requires partnership to keep the bidding open.

Denial Bid   A bid showing lack of support for partner's bid, or of specified high-card strength.

Deschapelles Coup   The lead of an unsupported honor card in order to establish an entry to partner's hand.

Devil's Coup   A play by which a defender's "sure" trump winner is made to disappear.

Discard   Play of a plain suit card not of the same suit as the lead.

Discouraging Card   The play of a card (usually a low one) indicating lack of interest in that suit.

Double Dummy   Play of a hand in which a player knows the location of all the cards.

Double Jump   A bid two levels higher than necessary.

Double Jump Overcall   A preemptive jump of three levels, after an opposing opening bid.

Double Raise   A jump raise of partner's suit.

Down   A declarer who fails to make a contract is said to be "down."

Drive Out   To force out opponents' high cards.

Drury   An artificial two club response to a major suit opening used by a passed hand to demand that opener clarify his strength.

Duck To refuse to win a trick or play a higher card although able to do so.

Dummy Reversal The play of the hand whereby declarer's repeated ruffing makes dummy's the longer trump suit.

Duplicate A form of bridge in which all contestants play the same series of deals which are kept intact by use of duplicate boards.

Duplicate Board A device including four pockets to hold each player's hand intact, marked to show the dealer and vulnerability.

Duplication of Values A waste of partnership strength because of concentration of high card or distributional values in the same suit.

Echo (See Come-On and High-Low.)

Encouraging A term applied to a bid which urges partner to continue to game.

Encouraging Card A signal card indicating a desire for that suit to be led or continued.

Entry A means of gaining the lead in a particular hand.

Equals Cards in sequence or which have become sequential through the play of the cards of intervening rank.

Establish Make good a suit or a card by forcing out adverse winners.

Exit Get out of the hand by compelling another hand to win the trick.

Exposed Card One played in error or shown in an illegitimate manner and therefore subject to penalty.

Face Card Any king, queen or jack.

False Card One selected for play for the purpose of misleading the opponents.

Final Bid The last bid in the auction followed by three consecutive passes; the contract.

Fixed (colloquial) Given a bad score through no fault of one's own.

Flat Hand A hand without any distributional feature, such as 4-3-3-3. For practical purposes, 4-4-3-2 and sometimes 5-3-3-2 patterns are considered flattish.

Force Compel a player to trump if he wishes to win the trick; also a bid that partner is not expected to pass.

Forced Bid   A response to a forcing bid from partner.

Forcing Bid   A bid demanding partner to keep the bidding open.

Forcing One No Trump Response   A response to a major suit opening.

Forcing Pass   A pass which demands partner to take further action at his turn.

Forcing Raise   Double raise in a major suit demanding a game contract.

Forcing Two Club Opening   A bid which announces an undisclosed type of Strong Two-Bid.

Fourth-Best   The fourth-highest card of a suit; the principle of leading such a card.

Fragment Bid   A double jump rebid in a new suit on the second round of bidding, showing a shortage in the unbid suit and a fit in partner's suit.

Freak   A hand of abnormally unbalanced distribution.

Free Bid   A bid made by a player who is not obliged to do so in order to keep the bidding open.

Free Double   (Primarily used in rubber bridge.) The double of an adverse contract which is sufficient for game if undoubled.

Free Finesse   A finesse which can be taken without costing a trick (as when declarer is void and can ruff if the finesse loses).

Free Raise   A single raise of partner's suit after an intervening call by an opponent.

Gadget   A highly artificial bidding device.

Gambit   Deliberate sacrifice of one trick in order to gain additional tricks.

Good Cards   Established winners; also, in general, preponderance of strength.

Goulash   A deal in which the cards of a passed out hand are not shuffled and are dealt in two rounds of *five* and one round of *three*.

Grand Coup   A trump-reduction play involving ruffing a winner or winners.

Grand Slam   The winning of all thirteen tricks by one side; a bid to do so.

Grand Slam Force   A bid of five no trump, not preceded by four no trump, asking responder to bid a grand slam if he holds two of the top three trump honors.

Guard   An honor holding in a suit which protects another card, or which prevents the opponent running a suit.

Guard Squeeze   A squeeze in three suits against an opponent who controls two suits and whose holding in the third suit prevents declarer from taking a winning finesse.

Hand   1. The cards held by one player. 2. Position at the table, as third-hand. 3. (colloquial) A deal.

Hexagon Squeeze   A double guard squeeze in which each of the three suits is protected by both opponents.

High-Low   A signal play of a high card followed by a low one; an Echo or Come-on.

Hold Up   To delay the winning of a trick; the play which does so (see Duck).

Huddle   A protracted pause to consider one's action.

IMP   An abbreviation for International Match Point.

Inference   Any conclusion drawn from bidding or play of the cards.

Informatory Double   A take-out double.

Initial Bid   The opening bid.

Insufficient Bid   A bid which is lower in rank than a bid previously made in the same auction.

Interference Bid   A defensive action employed to deprive the opponents of bidding space.

Intervening Bid   An overcall.

Inverted Minors   A convention whereby single minor suit raises are forcing and double minor suit raises are preemptive.

Irregularity   Any departure from correct procedures set forth in the "Laws and Proprieties."

Jacoby Transfer   A convention used in responding at the 2-level to one no trump opening by partner.

Jettison   Discard; more specifically the deliberate discard of a high honor to effect an unblock, to create an entry, or to avert a ruff.

Journalist Leads   A specialized method of opening leads, usually involving the lead of third- or fifth-best rather than fourth-best.

Jump Overcall   A suit overcall at a level one higher than necessary; may be played as strong or weak.

Jump Shift   A new suit response at a level one higher than necessary, usually forcing to game.

Kibitzer   A non-playing spectator.

LHO   Left-hand opponent.

Lead-Directing Double   The conventional double of a voluntarily bid contract by a player not on lead.

Leg   One of the two games required to win a rubber.

Length Signals   A play by which a defender indicates to his partner the length held in a particular suit.

Life Master   The highest player rank conferred by the American Contract Bridge League.

Lift   Raise.

Lightner Double   A lead-directing double of a slam contract.

Limit Bid   Any bid which limits a player's strength; not forcing.

Limit Raise   A (non-forcing) raise with closely defined limits of strength.

Long Cards   Those left after all other cards of that suit have been played.

Long Suit   The suit in which a player has most cards; any suit of six cards or more.

Loser   A card that must lose a trick to the opponents.

Major Tenace   A holding of the highest and third highest cards remaining in a suit.

Make   1. To shuffle the deck. 2. To succeed in a contract. 3. To score a winning card. 4. In auction bridge, the contract.

Master Card   The highest unplayed card of a suit.

McKenney   A suit preference signal named after William McKenney (see Suit-Preference).

Menace   A threat card which may be a potential winner if a squeeze develops.

Merrimac Coup   The deliberate sacrifice of a high card to knock out a vital entry from an opponent's hand.

Minor Tenace   A holding of the second and fourth highest cards remaining in a suit.

Misdeal   Any departure from the laws of correct procedure in dealing.

Misfit   A deal in which partners' hands are short in each other's suits.

Monster   A hand of great trick-taking potential; also a freak distribution.

Morton's Fork   A coup by which declarer presents a defender with a choice of taking a trick cheaply or ducking, either action costing the defense a trick.

MUD   Acronym for *M*iddle, *U*p, *D*own; the conventional lead of the middle card from three small, usually followed in play by the higher one and then the lower one.

Negative Double   Take-out double of an overcall of partner's bid.

Nuisance Bid   A bid made to hinder the opponents' exchange of information.

Obligatory Finesse   The play of a small card on the second lead of a suit, hoping that next player's master card is unguarded.

Odd-Even   Method of signaling in the play which assigns different meanings to odd-numbered and even-numbered spot cards.

Optional Double (See Cooperative Double.)

Overboard   Being too high in a given auction.

Overruff   To trump higher than the right-hand opponent after a plain suit lead.

Overtake   To play a higher card than the one played by partner, usually in order to gain the lead.

Penalty Double   A double for the purpose of increasing the points won against the opponent's overbid.

Penalty Pass   A pass by a player after a take-out double from his partner and a pass by the right-hand opponent.

Phantom Save   A sacrifice bid against a contract which would have been defeated.

Pick Up   To drop an outstanding high card.

Pin   Play that picks up an unguarded middle card while finessing higher card from the other opponent.

Plain Suit   A suit other than the trump suit.

Playing Tricks   Tricks that a hand may be expected to produce if the holder buys the contract.

Post-Mortem   Discussion of bridge hands after the conclusion of the play.

Precision Club   An artificial forcing one club opening system developed by C. C. Wei.

Preemptive Bid   An unnecessarily high bid or overcall in a long suit, usually with a hand of limited high card strength.

Progressive Squeeze   A squeeze which results in an ensuing squeeze to gain a second trick.

Protect   1. To guard an honor with a small card. 2. To re-open or balance.

Psychic Bid   Any bid made without the required length and strength, made primarily to mislead the opponents.

Pull   To draw trumps; to take out partner's penalty double.

Push   A raise in partner's suit aimed at inducing opponents to contract one level higher; also, in tournament play, a tie score on a deal.

Quick Trick   A high card holding which, because of the rank of the cards, would usually win a trick.

RHO   Right-hand opponent.

Redeal   A new deal by the same dealer.

Redouble   A call that further increases the scoring value of tricks and penalties after an opposing double; sometimes also used as a request for partner to rescue (S.O.S. redouble).

Renege   Revoke.

Rescue   To take out to a new suit after partner has been doubled for penalties.

Respond   Make a bid other than pass in answer to a bid by partner.

Responsive Double   A take-out double when there has been a raise immediately over partner's take-out double.

Revaluation   The reassessment of a hand resulting from the previous bidding.

Reverse   A rebid at the level of two or more in a higher-ranking suit.

Revoke   Failure to follow suit when able, the act of so doing.

Rhythm   Bidding and play at a uniform tempo.

Ripstra   A conventional overcall in a minor suit over an opening one no trump guarantees a three-suited hand and shortness in the other minor.

Roman Two Diamonds   A bid showing a strong three-suited hand.

Roth-Stone   A system of bidding developed by Alvin Roth and Tobias Stone.

Ruff and Discard (Sluff)   The lead of a plain suit at a trump contract when both declarer and dummy are void, allowing declarer to trump in either hand while discarding from the other.

Ruffing Finesse   A play by which a missing honor lying behind a finesse holding can be ruffed if it is covered, otherwise permitting the discard of a loser.

Rule of Eleven   Mathematical rule which states that when a player leads the fourth-best card of a suit, the difference between its pip value and 11 is the combined number of cards in the other three hands that are higher than that led.

Rusinow Leads   A specialized method of opening leads, usually the lead of the second highest from touching honors.

Save   A sacrifice bid.

Safety Play   The play of a suit so as to protect against abnormal breaks.

Schenken Club   An artificial and forcing one club system devised by Howard Schenken.

Scissors Coup   A play which cuts opponents' communications, usually in order to prevent a ruff; also called "the coup without a name".

Set   To defeat the contract.

Set Up   To establish one or more cards in a suit.

Shaded   A bid made on less than minimum requirements.

Short Club   A "prepared" club opening bid (non-forcing) made on a three-card suit in order to facilitate a sound rebid.

Short Suit   A holding of less than four cards in a suit.

Shorten   To punch; to shorten trumps by forcing to ruff.

Show Out   To fail to follow suit.

Signal   A play by which information is conveyed (see High-Low, Odd-Even, Suit-Preference).

Sign-Off   To make a minimum bid or rebid in order to close the auction.

Simple Squeeze   A squeeze which acts against one opponent in two suits.

Singleton   An original holding of one card in a suit.

Skip Bid   A jump bid.

Slow Pass   A pass at a slow tempo in an auction.

Small Slam   The winning of twelve tricks; a bid to do so.

Splinter Bid   An unusual jump bid which guarantees a fit for partner's suit and shows a singleton or void in the suit in which the jump is made.

Split   (See Break.)

Spot Card   Any card below the ten, from the nine to the two.

Squeeze   A play which compels an opponent to discard a winner or unguard a suit.

Stacked   Cards are said to be stacked when a single opponent holds nearly all of the outstanding cards in a crucial suit.

Stiff   A singleton honor.

Strip Play   A method of play wherein an opponent is stripped of his cards in a certain suit so as later to throw him on lead for an advantageous return.

Suit-Preference   A signal in defensive play whereby the play of a high card calls for a lead in the higher-ranking suit, the play of a low card calling for a lead in the lower-ranking suit.

Take-Out   A bid at a denomination other than one bid by partner.

Take-Out Double   A convention wherein a low-level double requests partner to bid an unbid suit.

Tenace   A holding of two cards in a suit lacking one or more of intervening rank.

Throw In   1. Pass out a deal. 2. An endplay compelling an opponent to lead to his disadvantage.

Trial Bid   A new suit bid after a major suit has been agreed upon.

Triple Squeeze   A squeeze in three suits.

Trump Signal   A play by a defender to indicate length of his trump holding.

Two-Suiter   A hand containing five or more cards in one suit and four or more in another.

Unblock   Cash or discard high cards in a suit, usually to promote partner's cards.

Unusual No Trump   A method of showing two-suited hands in competitive situations.

Uppercut   A ruff with a high trump aimed at promoting a trump trick for partner.

Vanderbilt Club   The first artificial and forcing 1 Club system, devised by Harold S. Vanderbilt

Void   Blank suit; an original holding of no cards in a suit.

Vulnerable   Said of a side that has won a game towards rubber.

Winner   A card that may reasonably be expected to win a trick.

Yarborough   A hand containing no card higher than a nine.

Index